J. Dassow / G. Păun

Regulated Rewriting in Formal Language Theory

Mathematische Lehrbücher und Monographien
Herausgegeben von der Akademie der Wissenschaften der DDR
Karl-Weierstraß-Institut für Mathematik

II. Abteilung
Mathematische Monographien
Band 74

Regulated Rewriting in Formal Language Theory

von J. Dassow und G. Păun

Regulated Rewriting in Formal Language Theory

by Jürgen Dassow and Gheorghe Păun

with 15 figures and 4 tables

Akademie-Verlag Berlin
1989

Verfasser:

Prof. Dr. sc. nat. Jürgen Dassow
Technische Hochschule Magdeburg
Sektion Mathematik und Physik

Dr. Gheorghe Păun
Universität Bukarest
Mathematische Fakultät

ISBN 3-05-500408-6
ISSN 0076-5430

Erschienen im Akademie-Verlag Berlin, Leipziger Str. 3–4, Berlin, DDR-1086

Lizenznummer: 202 · 100/402/88
Printed in the German Democratic Republic
Gesamtherstellung: VEB Druckhaus „Maxim Gorki", Altenburg, DDR-7400
Lektor: Dipl.-Math. Gesine Reiher
LSV 1025
Bestellnummer: 763 752 7 (9075)
07500

Preface

To our families

The formal language theory was born in the middle of our century as a tool for modelling and investigating the syntax of natural languages, and it has been developed mainly in connection with programming language handling. Of course, one cannot deny the impulses from neuronal net investigations, from logic, as well as the mathematical motivation of the early researches. The theory has rapidly become a mature one, with specific problems, techniques and results and with an internal self-motivated life. Abstract enough to deal with the essence of modelled phenomena, formal language theory has been applied during the last years to many further non-linguistical fields, sometimes surprisingly far from the previous areas of applications; such fields are developmental biology, economic modelling, semiotics of folklore, dramatic and musical works, cryptography, sociology, psychology, and so on.

All these applications as well as the traditional ones to natural and programming languages revealed a rather common conclusion: very frequently, context-free grammars, the most developed and the most "tractable" type of Chomsky grammars, are not sufficient. "The world is non-context-free" (and we shall "prove" this statement in Section 0.4). On the other hand, the context-sensitive grammars are too powerful and definitely "intractable" (many problems are undecidable or are still open; there is no semantic interpretation of the nonterminals and so on).

This is the reason to look for intermediate generative devices, conjoining the simplicity and the beauty of context-free grammars with the power of context-sensitive ones. Therefore, grammars with restrictions in derivations have been introduced, i.e. grammars with context-free core rules used in a non-context-free manner. The first type of such grammars were the matrix grammars defined by Abraham in 1965. Their rules are grouped in sequences ("matrices"), and a step of a derivation consists in using, one by one, all rules of a matrix. About twenty five further different restrictions have been defined in the meantime (some with many variants). We quote the most well known of them: programmed, random context, indexed, scattered context, and parallel grammars. A powerful branch of formal language theory has been appeared in this way, a branch which so far has no summarizing monographs.

The present book aims to fill this gap.

Its purpose is to present — in a unified and systematic manner — the state-of-the-art of regulated rewriting. Of course, it cannot be exhaustive. The domain literature is too rich to be covered by a book of about 300 pages. We have tried to include as much material as possible; besides the "main" results presented in the chapters, the reader can find further results in the concluding remarks, in exercises and sometimes in the bibliographic notes. Moreover, the bibliography contains all titles in this field known to the authors, although some of them are not referred to in the text.

Naturally, the selection of the material is sometimes subjective. For instance, choosing the matrix, programmed, and random context restrictions as prototypes might be disputable. We hope that the reader has not too different (perhaps also subjective) preferences. Anyway, her or his comments, suggestions, solutions to open problems are cordially welcomed.

The book was possible thanks to some meetings of the two authors, meetings supported by the Technological University Otto von Guericke Magdeburg and by the Roumanian Academy of Sciences. Deep gratitude is expressed to both these institutions.

We also acknowledge the help in writing this monograph (suggestions, comments on parts of the first version of the text, bibliographical support, etc.) given to us by many researchers in the field, friends, and colleagues. We quote gratefully here H. Bordihn, M. Gheorghe, A. Kelemanova, J. Kelemen, H. C. M. Kleijn, S. Marcus, B. Reichel, G. Rozenberg, A. Salomaa and D. Vaida.

We are also indebted to Akademie-Verlag Berlin and Springer-Verlag, especially to G. Reiher and R. Höppner and G. M. Hayes, for the pleasant and highly professional collaboration during the preparation of this monograph.

August 1986

Jürgen Dassow
Gheorghe Păun

Contents

0. Introduction

The aim of this introductory chapter is two fold. First, we introduce the basic terminology, notation, and results concerning the Chomsky hierarchy and L languages in order to give the reader the necessary prerequisites for the understanding of the theory of regulated rewriting. However, we omit all details and proofs since we assume that the reader has already some basic knowledge of formal languages. For further information the reader is referred to Ginsburg (1966), Hopcroft and Ullman (1979), Salomaa (1973-a), Ginsburg (1975), Rozenberg and Salomaa (1980).

Second, we give here some motivation for introducing of regulating mechanisms for language generating devices.

0.1. Languages and Language Families

Throughout the book we consider a fixed countable set Σ of abstract symbols. Its finite and non-empty subsets are referred to as *alphabets* and its elements as *letters*. Let $V = \{a_1, a_2, \ldots, a_n\}$ be an alphabet. A *word* over V is a finite string consisting of zero or more letters of V. By λ we denote the *empty* word of zero letters. The set of all (non-empty) words over V is denoted by V^* (V^+).

For two words w_1 and w_2 we define the *product* (or *concatenation*, or *catenation*) as the juxtaposition w_1w_2. With respect to this operation λ is the identity. Thus, algebraically spoken, V^* (V^+) is the free monoid (free semigroup) generated by V. As usual we write the n-fold product of some string w as w^n.

We say that $y \in V^+$ is a *subword* of $w \in V^*$ iff w can be represented as $w = xyz$ with $x, z \in V^*$. It is called a *proper subword* iff $w \neq y$ and $y \neq \lambda$. If $w = uv$, then we say that u is a *prefix* and v is a *suffix* of w. These are termed proper prefix and proper suffix if they are proper subwords.

We denote by Sub (w), Pref (w), Suf (w) the sets of subwords, prefixes, and suffixes, respectively, of the word w.

For a string $w = a_1a_2 \ldots a_n$, $a_i \in V$, $1 \leq i \leq n$, we denote by Mi (w) the *mirror image* of w, that is the string Mi $(w) = a_n \ldots a_2a_1$.

The length of the word $w \in V^*$, written as $|w|$, is the number of letters in w (each letter is counted as many times as it occurs in w). Obviously, $|\lambda| = 0$. For a subset V' of V we denote the number of occurrences of letters of V' in $w \in V^*$ by $|w|_{V'}$. If $V' = \{a\}$, then we simplywrite $|w|_a$. (In general, in notations we identify the letter a and the set $\{a\}$.) To a word $w \in V^*$ we associate its *Parikh vector* $\mathrm{p}_V(w)$ defined by

$$\mathrm{p}_V(w) = (|w|_{a_1}, |w|_{a_2}, \ldots, |w|_{a_n}) ;$$

p_V is also called the *Parikh mapping associated to* V (if the alphabet V can be understood from the context, we omit the index).

For $w \in V^*$, let $\min(w) = \{a \in V : |w|_a > 0\}$.

Subsets of V^* are referred to as *languages* over V. Since we regard languages as sets, we can define their finiteness and the Boolean operations union, difference, and intersection as in the set theory. By $\mathcal{L}(\mathrm{FIN})$ we denote the family of all finite languages, i.e. $\mathcal{L}(\mathrm{FIN}) = \{L : L \text{ is a finite subset of } V^* \text{ for some alphabet } V\}$.
A language $L \subseteq V^*$ is termed *λ-free* if $\lambda \notin L$.

A set of vectors is called *semilinear* if it can be represented as a union of a finite number of sets of the form

$$\left\{v_0 + \sum_{i=1}^{m} \alpha_i v_i : \alpha_i \in \mathbb{N} \quad \text{for} \quad 1 \leqq i \leqq m\right\}$$

where $v_i \in \mathbb{N}^n$ for $0 \leqq i \leqq m$. A language L is termed *semilinear* if the set

$$\mathrm{p}_V(L) = \{\mathrm{p}_V(w) : w \in L\}$$

is a semilinear set. Two languages L, L' over V are called *letter-equivalent* iff $\mathrm{p}_V(L) = \mathrm{p}_V(L')$.

Let $L, L_1, L_2 \subseteq V^*$ (this can be assumed without loss of generality because, for $L_1 \subseteq V_1^*$ and $L_2 \subseteq V_2^*$, we can choose a new vocabulary $V \supseteq V_1 \cup V_2$). We define

$$L_1 \cdot L_2 = \{w_1 w_2 : w_1 \in L_1, w_2 \in L_2\} \quad \text{(concatenation or product of languages)},$$

$$L^0 = \{\lambda\},\ L^{i+1} = L^i L \quad \text{for} \quad i \geqq 0,$$

$$L^* = \bigcup_{i \geqq 0} L^i \quad (\textit{Kleene-closure, *-operator}),$$

$$L^+ = \bigcup_{i \geqq 1} L^i \quad (\textit{λ-free Kleene-closure, +-operator}).$$

Algebraically, L^+ (L^*) is the smallest semigroup (monoid) which contains L.

A language L over V is called *regular* if it can be constructed by a finite number of applications of the operations union, product, and Kleene-closure from subsets of $V \cup \{\lambda\}$. By $\mathcal{L}(\mathrm{REG})$ we denote the family of all regular languages.

Let U be a further (not necessarily different) alphabet. Let s be a mapping from V into 2^{U^*}, i.e. $s(a) \subseteq U^*$ for all $a \in V$. We extend this mapping s to V^* by

$$s(\lambda) = \{\lambda\},\ s(w_1 w_2) = s(w_1)\, s(w_2) \quad \text{for} \quad w_1, w_2 \in V^*.$$

For languages $L \subseteq V^*$, we define

$$s(L) = \bigcup_{w \in L} s(w).$$

We call s a *substitution* from V into U. If $s(a)$ is a finite language for all $a \in V$, it is a *finite substitution*. We say that s is *λ-free* if $\lambda \notin s(a)$ for all $a \in V$. A substitution is called a *homomorphism* if $s(a)$ consists of exactly one word for all $a \in V$ (and again we write $s(a) = w$ instead of $s(a) = \{w\}$). A homomorphism is termed a *coding* if $|s(a)| = 1$ for all $a \in V$. Further, for a language $L \subseteq U^*$ and a homomorphism h from V into U, we define the mapping $h^{-1}: U^* \to 2^{V^*}$ (and we call it *inverse homomorphism*) by

$$h^{-1}(w) = \{v \in V^* : h(v) = w\}.$$

Some particular classes of homomorphisms will be useful in the next chapters: a homomorphism h for which there is a constant k such that $|x| \leqq k|h(x)|$ for all strings x in some given language L is said to be a *k-linear erasing* homomorphism with respect to L. If $L \subseteq (V\{\lambda, c, c^2, \ldots, c^{k-1}\})^*$ for some $c \notin V$ and some constant k and if h is a homomorphism defined by $h(a) = a$ for $a \in V$ and $h(c) = \lambda$, then we say that h is *k-restricted* on L. Clearly, each k-restricted homomorphism is k-erasing.

Let τ be a k-ary operation on languages and let $\mathcal{L}$ be a family of languages. We say that $\mathcal{L}$ is closed under the operation τ if, for all languages $L_1, L_2, \ldots, L_k \in \mathcal{L}$, $\tau(L_1, L_2, \ldots, L_k)$ is also an element of $\mathcal{L}$. A language family is called an *abstract family of languages* (abbreviated AFL) iff it is closed under union, product, $+$-operator, λ-free homomorphisms, inverse homomorphisms and intersections with regular languages. An AFL is called *full* if it is closed with respect to arbitrary homomorphisms. A family of languages closed under all AFL operations except concatenation and $+$-operator is termed a *semi-AFL*; a semi-AFL is full if it is closed under arbitrary homomorphisms.

In order to prove that a given family of languages is an AFL it is not necessary to check the closure under all the above operations. The next theorems will be useful in this respect.

Theorem 0.1.1. *If $\mathcal{L}$ is a family of λ-free languages which is closed under concatenation, λ-free homomorphisms, inverse homomorphisms and the $+$-operator, then $\mathcal{L}$ is an AFL.*

Theorem 0.1.2. *If $\mathcal{L}$ is a family of languages closed under intersections with regular sets, union with regular sets, substitution by λ-free regular sets and restricted homomorphisms, then $\mathcal{L}$ is closed under inverse homomorphisms.*

A *generalized sequential machine* (gsm, for short) is a 6-tuple $A = (K, V_1, V_2, s_0, f, F)$ where K, V_1, V_2 are finite non-empty sets, F is a subset of K, s_0 is an element of K, and f is a mapping from $K \times V_1$ into $2^{(V_2^* \times K)}$ (K is the set of states, V_1 is the input alphabet, V_2 is the output alphabet, s_0 is the initial state, F is the set of final states, and f is the move mapping or transition function). We define the *gsm mapping* g induced by A in the following way. Let $w = a_{i_1}a_{i_2} \ldots a_{i_m}$, $a_{i_j} \in V$ for $1 \leqq j \leqq m$. Then

$$g(w) = \{y_1 y_2 \ldots y_m : (y_j, s_j) \in f(s_{j-1}, a_{i_j}) \quad \text{for} \quad 1 \leqq j \leqq m, s_m \in F\}.$$

Again, we extend g to languages by

$$g(L) = \{y : y \in g(w) \quad \text{for some} \quad w \in L\}.$$

Any full AFL is also closed under gsm mappings; any AFL is closed with respect to λ-free gsm mappings.

In fact, a gsm can be regarded as a *finite automaton* with outputs, where a finite automaton is a system $A = (K, V, s_0, f, F)$ where K, s_0, F are as above, V is an alphabet and $f: K \times V \to 2^K$. Such an automaton recognizes a string $w \in V^*$, $w = a_{i_1}a_{i_2} \ldots a_{i_m}$, $a_{i_j} \in V$ for $1 \leqq j \leqq m$, iff there are $s_{i_1}, s_{i_2}, \ldots, s_{i_m}$ in K such that

$$s_{i_1} \in f(s_0, a_{i_1}), s_{i_{j+1}} \in f(s_{i_j}, a_{i_{j+1}}) \quad \text{for} \quad 1 \leqq j \leqq m-1, s_{i_m} \in F.$$

The set of all strings recognized by A is denoted by $L(A)$.

For two languages L_1 and L_2, we define the left and right *quotients* of L_2 by L_1 by

$$d^l_{L_1}(L_2) = \{x : wx \in L_2 \quad \text{for some} \quad w \in L_1\},$$

$$d^r_{L_1}(L_2) = \{x : xw \in L_2 \quad \text{for some} \quad w \in L_1\}.$$

The quotient by a singleton language, $L_1 = \{x\}$, written as $d^l_x(L_2)$ and $d^r_x(L_2)$, respectively, is called the *derivative* with respect to the word x. Each semi-AFL is closed under right and left derivatives, and each full semi-AFL is closed under right and left quotients by regular sets.

Let us introduce two further operations. For $w \in V^*$ let

$$\text{Perm}\,(w) = \{x \in V^* : p_V(x) = p_V(w)\}$$

(the set of all permutations of w). For two languages $L_1, L_2 \subseteq V^*$, we define

$$\text{Shuf}\,(L_1, L_2) = \{x_1y_1x_2y_2 \dots x_ny_n : n \geqq 1,\ x_1x_2 \dots x_n \in L_1,$$
$$y_1y_2 \dots y_n \in L_2,\ x_i, y_i \in V^* \quad \text{for} \quad 1 \leqq i \leqq n\}$$

and, for $L \subseteq V^*$,

$$\text{Shuf}^1\,(L) = L,$$

$$\text{Shuf}^i\,(L) = \text{Shuf}\,\big(\text{Shuf}^{i-1}\,(L), L\big) \quad \text{for} \quad i \geqq 2,$$

$$\text{Shuf}^*\,(L) = \bigcup_{i \geqq 1} \text{Shuf}^i\,(L).$$

Finally in this section we introduce a convention: Two languages L_1 and L_2 are called *equal* if $L_1 \setminus \{\lambda\} = L_2 \setminus \{\lambda\}$, i.e. if they differ at most in the empty string. Analogously, two language families $\mathcal{L}_1$ and $\mathcal{L}_2$ are called equal if, for each language $L_1 \in \mathcal{L}_1$, there is a language $L_2 \in \mathcal{L}_2$ which is equal to L_1 and vice versa.

0.2. Language Generating Devices

First we define the sequential grammars of the Chomsky hierarchy. A *phrase structure grammar* is a quadruple $G = (V_N, V_T, P, S)$ where V_N and V_T are two disjoint alphabets, the alphabets of *nonterminals* and *terminals*, respectively, $S \in V_N$, and P is a finite set of pairs (w, v) where w and v are words over $V_N \cup V_T$ and $|w|_{V_N} \geqq 1$. S is called the *axiom* (the start symbol) and the elements of P are referred to as *production rules* or simply *rules* or *productions*. For $(w, v) \in P$ we usually write $w \to v$. Further we set $V_G = V_N \cup V_T$.

If not specified otherwise, we shall denote the axiom by S, the nonterminals by capital letters and the terminals by lower case letters. Thus the specification of the production rules precisely identifies the grammar.

We say that $x \in V_G^*$ *directly derives* $y \in V_G^*$ in G, written as $x \underset{G}{\Longrightarrow} y$, iff $x = w_1ww_2$, $y = w_1vw_2$ for some $w \to v \in P$, $w_1, w_2 \in V_G^*$. (If G can be seen from the context we write only $\Rightarrow$.) Let $\overset{*}{\Rightarrow}$ be the transitive and reflexive closure of the yield relation $\Rightarrow$. The language generated by G is defined by

$$L(G) = \{w : w \in V_T^*, S \overset{*}{\Rightarrow} w\}.$$

A word over V_G is called a *sentential form* of G iff $S \overset{*}{\Rightarrow} w$. Thus, the language generated by G consists of all sentential forms contained in V_T^*.

By restrictions on the set P we now define special types of grammars. We say that

i) G is *monotone* (or *length-increasing*) iff $|w| \leqq |v|$ for all $w \to v \in P$, with the possible exception of $S \to \lambda$ which occurrence requires that S does not appear in the right-hand side of any rule,

ii) G is *context-sensitive* iff all productions are of the form $w_1Aw_2 \to w_1ww_2$ where $A \in V_N$, $w \in V_G^+$, $w_1, w_2 \in V_G^*$, with the same exception as in i),

iii) G is *context-free* iff all productions are of the form $A \to w$ with $A \in V_N$, $w \in V_G^*$,

iv) G is *linear* iff each production has the form $A \to w_1Bw_2$ or $A \to w$ where $A, B \in V_N$, $w_1, w_2, w \in V_T^*$,

v) G is *metalinear* iff all productions have the form given in iv) with the possible exception of rules of the form $S \to w_1A_1w_2A_2 \ldots w_mA_mw_{m+1}$ with $A_i \in V_N$, $w_i \in V_T^*$ whose occurrence implies that S does not occur on the right-hand side of any rule,

vi) G is *regular* iff each production has one of the following forms: $A \to wB$ or $A \to w$ where $A, B \in V_N$, $w \in V_T^*$,

vii) G is *λ-free* iff the right-hand side of any production is non-empty.

Generally, in the literature the grammars of type vi) are called *right linear*, the grammars with rules of the form $A \to Bw$ or $A \to w$, $A, B \in V_N$, $w \in V_T^*$ are called *left linear*, and the right linear grammars with rules $A \to wB$, $A \to w$ with $w \in V_T$ are termed *simply regular*. All these three types of grammars have the same generative capacity, i.e. they generate the same family of languages. For regulated rewriting reasons specific to we shall work only with regular grammars in the sense of above type vi).

Languages generated by arbitrary phrase structure grammars are called *recursively enumerable*, and the family of these languages is denoted by $\mathcal{L}(\mathrm{RE})$. If G is context sensitive (context-free, linear, metalinear, regular), then we also call the generated language $L(G)$ context-sensitive (context-free, linear, metalinear, regular, respectively) and we denote the associated families of languages by $\mathcal{L}(\mathrm{CS})$ ($\mathcal{L}(\mathrm{CF})$, $\mathcal{L}(\mathrm{LIN})$, $\mathcal{L}(\mathrm{MLIN})$, $\mathcal{L}(\mathrm{REG})$, respectively). As usual in formal language theory, we shall refer to the phrase structure, the length-increasing, the context-free and the regular grammars as *grammars of type* 0, 1, 2, 3, respectively. Similarly, the corresponding languages are said to be of type i, $i \in \{0, 1, 2, 3\}$.

Concerning the regular languages the justification of the above notation may be seen from the following theorem.

Theorem 0.2.1. *Each regular language can be generated by a regular grammar, and conversely, each regular grammar generates a regular language. Moreover, the family* $\mathcal{L}(\mathrm{REG})$ *is exactly the family of languages recognizable by finite automata.*

Theorem 0.2.2. i) *Any length-increasing grammar generates a context-sensitive language.*

ii) *For each context-sensitive language L there is a grammar G whose productions are of the following forms*

$$A \to BC, \quad AB \to CD, \quad A \to a \quad (\textit{and possibly } S \to \lambda)$$

where $A, B, C, D \in V_N$, $a \in V_T$ such that $L(G) = L$ (Kuroda normal form).

Thus monotone and context-sensitive grammars have the same generative power.

Also for a context-free (linear, metalinear, regular) grammar G we can construct a grammar G' of the same type such that the right-hand member of each production of G' is non-empty with the possible exception of $S \to \lambda$, whose occurrence requires that S does not occur on the right-hand side of any production, and such that $L(G) = L(G')$. Hence λ-free context-sensitive (context-free, etc.) languages can be generated by λ-free context-sensitive (context-free, etc.) grammars.

Theorem 0.2.3. $\mathcal{L}(\mathrm{REG}) \subset \mathcal{L}(\mathrm{LIN}) \subset \mathcal{L}(\mathrm{MLIN}) \subset \mathcal{L}(\mathrm{CF}) \subset \mathcal{L}(\mathrm{CS}) \subset \mathcal{L}(\mathrm{RE})$.

Here are some languages which prove the strictness of these inclusions (excepting the last one):

$$L_1 = \{a^n b^n : n \geqq 1\} \in \mathcal{L}(\mathrm{LIN}) \setminus \mathcal{L}(\mathrm{REG}),$$

$$L_1 \cdot L_1 \in \mathcal{L}(\mathrm{MLIN}) \setminus \mathcal{L}(\mathrm{LIN}),$$

$$L_1^+ \in \mathcal{L}(\mathrm{CF}) \setminus \mathcal{L}(\mathrm{MLIN}),$$

$$\{a^n b^n c^n : n \geqq 1\} \in \mathcal{L}(\mathrm{CS}) \setminus \mathcal{L}(\mathrm{CF}),$$

$$\{a^{2^n} : n \geqq 1\} \in \mathcal{L}(\mathrm{CS}) \setminus \mathcal{L}(\mathrm{CF}).$$

The two latter relations can be proved by means of the following results.

Theorem 0.2.4. (Parikh's theorem) *Each context-free language is semilinear.*

Theorem 0.2.5. (Ogden's lemma) *For each language $L \in \mathcal{L}(\mathrm{CF})$ there exists an integer k such that any word $z \in L$ which has at least k marked letters has a factorization $z = uvwxy$ such that*

— *either each of u, v, w or each of w, x, y contains a marked letter,*
— *vwx contains at most k marked letters,*
— *$uv^iwx^iy \in L$ for all $i \geqq 0$.*

Theorem 0.2.6 (Bar-Hillel's lemma, pumping lemma). *For each $L \in \mathcal{L}(\mathrm{CF})$ there exist two integers $p \geqq 0$, $q \geqq 0$ such that each word $z \in L$ with $|z| > p$ has a factorization $z = uvwxy$ such that $|vx| > 0$, $|vwx| \leqq q$, and $uv^iwx^iy \in L$ for all $i \geqq 0$.*

The closure properties of the above introduced families are summarized in the following theorem.

Theorem 0.2.7. i) $\mathcal{L}(\mathrm{REG})$ *and* $\mathcal{L}(\mathrm{RE})$ *are full AFLs, and they are closed under intersection.*

ii) $\mathcal{L}(\mathrm{CF})$ *is a full AFL, and it is not closed under intersection.*

iii) $\mathcal{L}(\mathrm{CS})$ *is an intersection closed AFL. It is not closed under arbitrary homomorphisms.*

Theorem 0.2.8. *For each language $L \in \mathcal{L}(\mathrm{RE})$ there are a homomorphism h and two context-free languages L_1 and L_2 such that $L = h(L_1 \cap L_2)$.*

The *Dyck language* D_n over $V_n = \{a_1, a_1', a_2, a_2', \ldots, a_n, a_n'\}$ is generated by the grammar

$$(\{S\}, V_n, \{S \to SS, S \to \lambda, S \to a_1 S a_1', \ldots, S \to a_n S a_n'\}, S).$$

Intuitively, it consists of all correct expressions over n pairs of brackets.

Theorem 0.2.9. *For any language $L \in \mathcal{L}(\mathrm{CF})$ there are a Dyck language D_n, a regular set R and a homomorphism h such that $L = h(D_n \cap R)$.*

A result with many applications in the sequel is the following. Let $G = (V_N, V_T, P, S)$ be a type-0 grammar. For a derivation

$$D : S = w_0 \Rightarrow w_1 \Rightarrow \cdots \Rightarrow w_n = x \in V_T^*$$

we set

$$WS(x, D) = \max \{|w_i| : 0 \leqq i \leqq n\}.$$

Then let

$$WS(x, G) = \min \{WS(x, D) : D \text{ is a derivation of } x \text{ in } G\}$$

($WS(x, G)$ is called the *workspace* needed to produce x in the grammar G). If there is a constant k such that, for all $x \in L(G) \setminus \{\lambda\}$, we have

$$WS(x, G) \leqq k|x|,$$

then we say that G has *bounded workspace*.

Theorem 0.2.10. *If a type-0 grammar G has bounded workspace, then $L(G)$ is a context-sensitive language.*

The languages considered hitherto are obtained by a *sequential* derivation process since only a part of a word (mostly only one letter) is rewritten in a direct derivation step. Now we define language generating devices whose derivation process is characterized by a *parallel* rewriting of all letters of the sentential forms.

An *ETOL system* is a quadruple $G = (V, V', \mathfrak{P}, w)$ where V' is a non-empty subset of the alphabet V, $w \in V^+$, and $\mathfrak{P}$ is a finite set of tables (systems of productions), $\mathfrak{P} = \{P_1, P_2, \ldots, P_r\}$ where each P_i, $1 \leqq i \leqq r$, is a finite subset of $V \times V^*$ which satisfies the condition that, for each $a \in V$, there is a word $w_a \in V^*$ such that $(a, w_a) \in P_i$ (the elements of the tables are written as $a \to w_a$, again).

The yield relation $\Rightarrow$ is defined for ETOL systems in the following way: $x \Rightarrow y$ holds in G (if necessary, then we write $x \underset{G}{\Rightarrow} y$) iff the following conditions are satisfied:

a) $x = a_{i_1} a_{i_2} \ldots a_{i_m}$, $a_{i_j} \in V$ for $1 \leqq j \leqq m$,

b) $y = y_1 y_2 \ldots y_m$,

c) there is a table $P \in \mathfrak{P}$ such that $a_{i_j} \to y_j \in P$ for $1 \leqq j \leqq m$.

The language $L(G)$ generated by G is given by

$$L(G) = \{x : x \in V'^*, w \overset{*}{\Rightarrow} x\}$$

where, again, $\overset{*}{\Rightarrow}$ is the reflexive and transitive closure of $\Rightarrow$.

The tables can be considered as finite substitutions. Therefore the language $L(G)$ consists of all words over V' which are obtained by an iterative application of a finite set of finite substitutions to the axiom.

Besides the parallelism, another difference between these systems and phrase structure grammars appears. The ETOL systems make no distinction between terminals and nonterminals, all letters have to be rewritten. By definition, there is also a difference concerning the axiom (a nonterminal versus a word), however, this point has no effect on to the generative power.

An ETOL system is called *deterministic* (EDTOL *system*) iff each table $P \in \mathfrak{P}$ satisfies the condition: if $a \to w \in P$ and $a \to w' \in P$, then $w = w'$. If $V = V'$, we refer to these as *TOL* and *DTOL systems*, respectively. If no table $P \in \mathfrak{P}$ contains the production $a \to \lambda$, then we call the system *propagating* or λ-free, and in this case we add the letter P to the notation of the system. (The abbreviation ETOL has the following sources: L stands for A. Lindenmayer, the originator of this type of derivation by biological motivations; 0 (zero) stands for no context conditions. T is for tables, and E is taken from extended since the original systems were TOL systems. We call these devices systems in order to distinguish them from the sequential grammars.)

We denote by $\mathcal{L}$(ETOL), $\mathcal{L}$(TOL), $\mathcal{L}$(EDTOL), $\mathcal{L}$(DTOL) the families of languages generated by ETOL, TOL, EDTOL, DTOL systems, respectively. We omit the letter T if the set $\mathfrak{P}$ consists of exactly one table P.

We mention only the following results for these families.

Theorem 0.2.11. i)

$$\mathcal{L}(\mathrm{DTOL}) \begin{array}{c} \subset \mathcal{L}(\mathrm{TOL}) \subset \\ \subset \mathcal{L}(\mathrm{EDTOL}) \subset \end{array} \mathcal{L}(\mathrm{ETOL}) \subset \mathcal{L}(\mathrm{CS}),$$

and $\mathcal{L}$(TOL) *and* $\mathcal{L}$(EDTOL) *are incomparable.*

ii) $\mathcal{L}(\mathrm{CF}) \subset \mathcal{L}(\mathrm{ETOL})$, *and* $\mathcal{L}$(CF) *is incomparable with* $\mathcal{L}$(EDTOL), $\mathcal{L}$(TOL), *and* $\mathcal{L}$(DTOL).

iii) *For any* ETOL (EDTOL) *system G there is a propagating* ETOL (EDTOL) *system G′ such that* $L(G) = L(G')$.

As examples we note:

$$\{a^n b^n : n \geqq 1\} \in \mathcal{L}(\mathrm{CF}) \setminus \mathcal{L}(\mathrm{TOL}),$$

$$\{a^{2^n} : n \geqq 1\} \in \mathcal{L}(\mathrm{DTOL}) \setminus \mathcal{L}(\mathrm{CF}),$$

$$\{w : w \in \{a, b\}^*, |w|_a = 2^n \quad \text{for some} \quad n \geqq 0\} \in \mathcal{L}(\mathrm{ETOL}) \setminus \mathcal{L}(\mathrm{EDTOL}),$$

$$\{(ab^n)^m : m \geqq n \geqq 1\} \in \mathcal{L}(\mathrm{CS}) \setminus \mathcal{L}(\mathrm{ETOL}),$$

$$D_i \in \mathcal{L}(\mathrm{CF}) \setminus \mathcal{L}(\mathrm{EDTOL}) \quad \text{for all} \quad i \geqq 2.$$

Theorem 0.2.12. $\mathcal{L}$(ETOL) *is a full AFL.* $\mathcal{L}$(EDTOL) *is not closed under inverse homomorphisms, and it is closed under the remaining five AFL operations.* $\mathcal{L}$(TOL) *and* $\mathcal{L}$(DTOL) *are both closed under none of the AFL operations.*

Two language generating devices G_1 and G_2 (grammars or systems) are called *equivalent* iff $L(G_1) = L(G_2)$ holds.

0.3. Algorithms and Decidability

In this book we shall sometimes consider decision problems and algorithms to solve them. In order to define the concepts of algorithm and decidability in a mathematically exact way we have to develop a theory of its own. This can be done by means of Turing machines, partially recursive functions, Markov normal algorithms, or (formalized) flow diagrams. We shall not give such exact definitions and refer to Kleene (1967), Trach-

TENBROT (1977), or HERMES (1961). For our purposes an intuitive notion of an algorithm will be sufficient.

By an *algorithm* we mean a finite set of rules or instructions such that the following holds:

- There is a uniquely determined instruction which has to be applied first.
- If we have applied an instruction, then we have a uniquely determined instruction which either has to be applied at the next step or we know that the work of the algorithm is finished.
- The applicability of an instruction can be done "without" intelligence, for instance by a machine.

By the application of an algorithm the input data can be transformed into output data (if the algorithm stops after a finite number of steps), and thus any algorithm induces a (possibly partial) function.

Let M and M' be two sets and $M \subseteq M'$. Then we define the characteristic function of M (with respect to M') by

$$f_M(w) = \begin{cases} a & \text{if} \quad w \in M, \\ b & \text{if} \quad w \in M' \setminus M, \end{cases}$$

where $a \neq b$. We say that M is decidable (with respect to M') iff the characteristic function of M is induced by some algorithm, i.e. there is an algorithmic procedure to decide whether or not the relation $w \in M$ holds. Since (binary) relations can be considered as subsets of a Cartesian product, we can define the decidability of a relation in the same way.

By a *(decision) problem* we mean an expression containing one or more variables, and that becomes "true" or "false" if elements of the basic sets are substituted for the variables. In general, we formulate the problem as a question, and then, for special elements, we obtain the answer "yes" or "no". We say that a (decision) problem is *decidable* iff the set of all tuples of elements for which the expression becomes "true" is decidable, i.e. there is an algorithm which, for a given tuple, decides whether or not the expression becomes "true" (or the answer to the question is "yes").

By these definitions, in order to prove the decidability of a problem it is sufficient to give a deciding algorithm (in the above intuitive sense). We note that we shall emphasize the existence of an algorithm only in connection with decision problems, however, algorithms will also appear in other chapters of this book, e.g. the normal forms can be constructed by an algorithm, and the reader should take into consideration the algorithmic (and therefore effective) character of the proof and/or the statement.

On the other hand, the proof of the undecidability of a problem usually is given by reduction to another problem which is known to be undecidable. In this book we shall use the reduction to the *Post Correspondence Problem.*

Let $P = \{(u_1, v_1), (u_2, v_2), \ldots, (u_m, v_m)\}$ be a finite set of pairs in $V^+ \times V^+$. We say that a sequence $i_1, i_2, \ldots, i_r$ of integers is a solution for P iff

$$u_{i_1} u_{i_2} \ldots u_{i_r} = v_{i_1} v_{i_2} \ldots v_{i_r}.$$

Now the Post Correspondence Problem is the following question: Does there exist a solution for a given P?

Theorem 0.3.1. *For a vocabulary V with* card $(V) \geqq 2$, *the Post Correspondence Problem is undecidable.*

We now formulate some decision problems which are important in formal language theory and which will be considered in this book. Let $\mathcal{G}$ be a family of grammars (e.g. the family of context-free grammars) or systems.

Membership Problem: Given $w \in V^*$ and $G \in \mathcal{G}$, does $w \in L(G)$ *hold?*

Equivalence Problem: Are given grammars $G_1 \in \mathcal{G}$ and $G_2 \in \mathcal{G}$ equivalent?

Inclusion Problem: Given grammars $G_1 \in \mathcal{G}$ and $G_2 \in \mathcal{G}$, does $L(G_1) \subseteq L(G_2)$ hold?

Emptiness Problem: Is the language generated by a grammar $G \in \mathcal{G}$ emty?

Finiteness Problem: Is the language generated by a grammar $G \in \mathcal{G}$ finite?

The undecidability of the equivalence problem implies the undecidability of the inclusion problem (since the decidability of "$L(G_1) \subseteq L(G_2)$" and "$L(G_2) \subseteq L(G_1)$" directly gives the decidability of "$L(G_1) \Rightarrow L(G_2)$").

In the following Table 0.3.1 we summarize the results for the decidability of these problems for the grammar families introduced above. (We write "+" or "−" if the problem is decidable or undecidable, respectively, and in the notation for the classes of grammars or systems we use the same abbreviations as for the corresponding language families.)

Table 0.3.1

	REG	CF	CS	RE	DTOL	ETOL
Membership	+	+	+	−	+	+
Equivalence	+	−	−	−	−	−
Inclusion	+	−	−	−	−	−
Emptiness	+	+	−	−	+	+
Finiteness	+	+	−	−	+	+

Since for two families of grammars or systems $\mathcal{G}_1 \subseteq \mathcal{G}_2$, the undecidability of a problem for $\mathcal{G}_1$ (the decidability for $\mathcal{G}_2$) implies the undecidability for $\mathcal{G}_2$ (the decidability for $\mathcal{G}_1$), the table implicitly contains the corresponding results for TOL and EDTOL systems.

0.4. Seven Circumstances Where Context-Free Grammars Are Not Enough

The theory of context-free grammars is the most developed part of formal language theory due to the wide applicability and to the mathematical appeal of these grammars. However, "the world is not context-free": there is a lot of circumstances where naturally non-context-free languages appear. (This is similar to linearity versus non-linearity in mathematics: linear mathematics is more developed, but "the world is not linear".) This calls for more powerful grammars. As the context-sensitive grammars are "too powerful", we need intermediate grammars which are stronger than the context-free grammars and have similar properties. This is the ("practical") motivation of introducing grammar with restrictions in derivations. They aim — and sometimes succeed — to cover the above requirements.

Here we now discuss only a few circumstances where non-context-free languages appear. Of course, one can discover many more.

On the other hand, this does not mean that the context-free grammars are not useful. They are quite important, but — simply — they are not sufficient.

(i) *Natural languages.* These have been the very motivation of Chomsky grammars, but it was early discovered that English is neither a regular nor a context-free language. The same assertion is true for most (probably all) natural languages.

For, consider the following phrases presented by BAR-HILLEL and SHAMIR (1960) (we use the quotation of MARCUS (1964)):

John, Mary, David ... are a widower, a widow, a widower, ..., respectively.

Such a phrase is correct if and only if the list of names has the same length as the list of words "a widower", "a widow", and if the ith name in the first list has the same gender as the ith adjective in the second list. From the point of view of the English grammar, the set L of such phrases is infinite (of course, no English speaker will use a phrase of this type with more than, let us say, six names, but this is not relevant for us). This set of phrases is not a context-free language. Indeed, let g be the mapping induced by a gsm which replaces each masculine name by the symbol a, each feminine name by b, erases each comma and the final period, erases the words "are" and "respectively", and replaces each occurrence of "a widower" by a and each occurrence of "a widow" by b. We obtain

$$g(L) = \{xx : x \in \{a, b\}^*, |x| \geqq 2\}$$

(before "are" we need at least two names). This language is not context-free (one can use the Bar-Hillel lemma in order to prove this).

This is a fragment of English. What about the whole language: is it context-free? Let us consider the regular grammar

$$G = (\{S, X, Y\}, V_T, P, S)$$

where

$$V_T = \{a\ widower,\ a\ widow,\ are,\ respectively,\ period,\ comma\} \cup N,$$

with N being a list of names, and the set P contains the following rules:

$$\begin{array}{ll} S \to Name\ comma\ X, & Name \in N, \\ X \to Name\ comma\ X, & Name \in N, \\ X \to Name\ are\ Y, & Name \in N, \\ Y \to a\ widow\ comma\ Y, & \\ Y \to a\ widower\ comma\ Y, & \\ Y \to respectively\ period & \end{array}$$

(we use *comma* and *period* instead of "," and "." in order to avoid confusion between these symbols and the metalanguage periods and commas). Of course, if we intersect E, the whole set of correct English phrases, with $L(G)$, we obtain exactly the above non-context-free language L. It follows that the English language itself is not context-free. Clearly, a similar argument can be used in order to prove that many other natural languages are not context-free.

(ii) *Programming languages.* The Chomsky grammars are motivated by natural language modelling, but the formal language theory (especially the theory of context-free languages) has been developed by computer science motivation. Indeed, in 1962 GINSBURG and RICE proved that the ALGOL-like languages defined by Backus-Naur formalism are identical to the context-free languages. However, in the same year FLOYD pointed out that ALGOL is not context-free due to the semantic conditions involved in the definition of correct ALGOL programs. For instance, such a "non-context-free condition" is one which requires that each identifier has to be declared. If we have a one-block program, then the declarations has to be made at the head of this block. For example, the programs of the form

```
begin  integer x;
       y := 1;
end
```

are correct if and only if $x = y$. Let us denote by R the set of all programs as above with arbitrary x, y over $\{a, b\}$, and let ALGOL be the set of all correct ALGOL programs. If g is the gsm which erases all symbols different from those in x and y, then we obtain

$$\begin{aligned} g(\text{ALGOL} \cap R) &= g\left(\left\{\textsf{begin integer } x;\ x := 1;\ \textsf{end} : x \in \{a, b\}^+\right\}\right) \\ &= \left\{xx : x \in \{a, b\}^+\right\} \end{aligned}$$

which is not a context-free language. Hence ALGOL is not context-free.

As FLOYD (1962) said, "it seems likely that similar considerations would apply to any other reasonable language in which all variables must be declared". It follows that any reasonable programming language is not context-free, either.

(iii) *The language of logic.* Let us consider the propositional calculus with four connectives: *and* ($\wedge$), *or* ($\vee$), *not* ($\sim$), *implies* ($\rightarrow$), and as atomic propositions we take letters in an enumerable set $W = \{p_1, p_2, \ldots\}$. Let us look for the language of theorems (tautologies) in this calculus. In order to have a formal language, the infinite set W must be codified over a finite alphabet, that is, we need a one-to-one mapping $\varphi : W \rightarrow V^*$ for some given finite V. As W is infinite, $\varphi(W)$ is infinite, and hence it contains strings of arbitrary length. Let us denote by LT the set of theorems in the above propositional calculus with atomic propositions in $\varphi(W)$, and let us consider the regular language

$$R = \{(x \vee y) \rightarrow z : x, y, z \in V^*\}.$$

Then we obtain

$$LT \cap R = \{(x \vee x) \rightarrow x : x \in \varphi(W)\}.$$

As $\varphi(W)$ is an infinite set, this language is not context-free (apply the Bar-Hillel lemma again). Hence LT is not context-free.

Of course, the above argument essentially depends on the assumption that we code the elements of W by strings over V. If W is finite, then this coding is not necessary. We do not know whether $LT(W_n)$, the set of theorems over n letters, $W_n = \{p_1, p_2, \ldots, p_n\}$, is context-free or not. Anyway, LT is a context-sensitive language (PĂUN (1981-a)).

(iv) *The mapping graphs.* Given a partially defined mapping $f : \mathbb{N}^k \rightarrow \mathbb{N}$ one can imagine many "natural" ways to define an associated language. An often used, simple and fruitful idea (see van Leeuwen (1972), Păun and Tătarăm (1985), etc.) is to codify the graph of f as a language over the vocabulary $\{a_1, a_2, \ldots, a_k, a_{k+1}\}$ as follows:

$$L_f = \{a_1^{n_1}a_2^{n_2} \ldots a_k^{n_k}a_{k+1}^{f(n_1,\ldots,n_k)} : n_i \in \mathbb{N}, 1 \leqq i \leqq k, (n_1, n_2, \ldots, n_k) \in \operatorname{dom} f\}.$$

Many significant questions about the mapping f (injectivity, surjectivity, finiteness, equivalence, etc.) can be expressed (and sometimes solved) at the level of the language L_f (and of its grammars). However, for very "simple" mappings, the language L_f is non-context-free. Such examples are

$$f_1 : \mathbb{N}^2 \to \mathbb{N},\ f_1(x, y) = \begin{cases} x & \text{if } x = y, \\ 0 & \text{otherwise}, \end{cases}$$

$$f_2 : \mathbb{N} \to \mathbb{N},\ f_2(x) = x^2 \quad \text{for} \quad x \in \mathbb{N},$$

$$f_3 : \mathbb{N}^2 \to \mathbb{N},\ f_3(x, y) = xy \quad \text{for} \quad x, y \in \mathbb{N},$$

where the associated languages are

$$L_{f_1} = \{a_1^n a_2^n a_3^n : n \geqq 0\} \cup \{a_1^n a_2^m : n \neq m,\ n \in \mathbb{N},\ m \in \mathbb{N}\},$$

$$L_{f_2} = \{a_1^n a_2^{n^2} : n \geqq 0\},$$

$$L_{f_3} = \{a_1^n a_2^m a_3^{nm} : n, m \geqq 0\}.$$

None of these languages is context-free (the latter two are not semilinear).

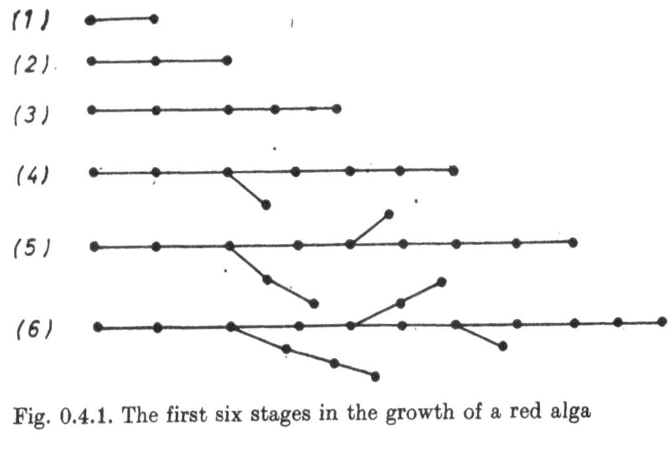

Fig. 0.4.1. The first six stages in the growth of a red alga

(v) *Developmental biology.* Let us recall from Chapter 1 of Herman and Rozenberg (1975) the following example concerning the growth of a red alga. The first six stages are represented in Fig. 0.4.1. "From stage 6 onwards we may divide the organism into two parts. The first six cells (from the left) of the main branch form a basal part while the rest of the cells forms an apical part. Every second cell in the basal part carries a non-branching filament. These filaments develop linearly in time, they repeat at each stage their own previous structure with the addition of one new cell. At stage 6 the lengths of these filaments are 3, 2, 1, respectively, the longer ones being nearer the base. The apical part at stage 6 consists of four cells without any branches. After this, the apical part at each stage is a repeat of the apical part of the previous stage, together with two new cells at the base end of the apical part. The second of these new cells carries a branch which is identical to the whole organism six stages previously."

The structure of the organism at different stages can be codified by using names for cells of various types and parentheses for identifying the current branches. The verbal rules of development considered above can be codified by the following rewriting rules (involving ten types of cells: 0, 1, ..., 9):

$$
\begin{array}{ll}
0 \to 10, & 1 \to 32, \\
2 \to 3(4), & 3 \to 3, \\
4 \to 56, & 5 \to 37, \\
6 \to 58, & 7 \to 3(9), \\
8 \to 50, & 9 \to 39
\end{array}
$$

(Herman and Rozenberg (1975), p. 51). Starting from a single cell of type 4 we can derive the following strings describing exactly the stages in Fig. 0.4.1 (at each step all cells are "rewritten", this is also the motivation for introducing L systems):

(1) 4

(2) 56

(3) 3758

(4) 33(9) 3750

(5) 33(39) 33(9) 3710

(6) 33(339) 33(39) 33(9) 3210

From this stage on the organism develops very uniformly:

(7) 33(3339) 33(339) 33(39) 33(4) 3210

(8) 33(33339) 33(3339) 33(339) 33(56) 33(4) 3210

and so on. Inductively, one can see that x_n, the string describing the nth stage, $n \geqq 7$, is

$$x_n = 33(3^{n-4}9)\ 33(3^{n-5}9)\ 33(3^{n-6}9)\ 33(x_{n-6})\ 33(x_{n-7})\ 33 \ldots 33(x_2)\ 33(x_1)\ 3210 .$$

This implies

$$|x_{i+1}| - |x_i| = |x_{i-5}| + 5 \quad \text{for} \quad i \geqq 6,$$

and therefore, for all $i \geqq 2$,

$$|x_{i+1}| - |x_i| > |x_i| - |x_{i-1}| .$$

In conclusion, the language $L = \{x_i : i \geqq 1\}$ is not context-free (the length set of an infinite context-free language must contain an infinite arithmetical progression, a consequence of the Bar-Hillel lemma, and this does not hold for the language L).

Similar non-context-free languages describing various biological phenomena can be found in many papers by A. Lindenmayer.

(vi) *Economic modelling*. In Păun (1980-a) the Chomsky grammars were used for modelling various economic processes. Many of them lead to non-context-free languages. We discuss here only two examples.

The courier problem. Let $\Gamma = (X, U)$ be a directed graph. A courier must circulate in Γ picking up letters from certain points and delivering them to others. Many variants of this problem can be imagined. For instance, let us consider only one restriction about the courier's activity: each letter must be delivered (without care about the courier "capacity", the time between picking up a letter and delivering it, etc.).

If $X = \{x_1, x_2, \ldots, x_n\}$, then the courier activity can be described by strings over the vocabulary $\{a_1, b_1, a_2, b_2, \ldots, a_n, b_n\}$, a_i denoting the action of picking up a letter from point x_i and b_i denoting the action of delivering a letter to point x_i.

Let us consider the simple case where

$$\Gamma = \big(\{x_1, x_2\}, \{(x_1, x_2), (x_2, x_1)\}\big)$$

and each point sends letters to the other. Let L be the set of all strings describing intervals of correct courier activity (starting with no letter in his bag, the courier also ends the interval with no letter in his bag), and let us consider the regular language

$$R = \{a_1^i a_2^j b_2^k b_1^p : i, j, k, p \geqq 1\}.$$

Then we have

$$L \cap R = \{a_1^i a_2^j b_2^i b_1^j : i, j \geqq 1\},$$

and this language is not context-free. Hence L also is not context-free. The courier activity cannot be simulated (controlled) by a push-down automaton.

A scheduling problem. Let us consider a section of an enterprise which contains only two machines, m_1, m_2, with the help of which one manufactures an arbitrary number of pieces of two types, p_1 and p_2. We ignore the time a piece p_i must be processed on the machine m_j. Both types of pieces are first processed on m_1 and then on m_2, spending exactly one unit of time on each machine. Let us denote by d the action "do nothing". The state of the enterprise section in a given time unit could be described by a couple (α, β), $\alpha, \beta \in \{p_1, p_2, d\}$, α indicating the state of m_1 (working on p_1, on p_2, or not working) and β indicating the state of m_2. We consider the language L of all strings (over the above vocabulary) describing correct manufacturing processes. Further let R be the regular language

$$R = \{(p_1, d)^i (p_2, d)^j (d, p_1)^k (d, p_2)^r : i, j, k, r \geqq 1\}.$$

Clearly, we have

$$L \cap R = \{(p_1, d)^i (p_2, d)^j (d, p_1)^i (d, p_2)^j : i, j \geqq 1\},$$

and again, we have obtained a non-context-free language. This implies that L also is not context-free.

(vii) *The semiotics of fairy-tales, music and visual arts.* In a series of papers by S. Marcus and his collaborators (see, for instance, the collective volumes Marcus (1978), Marcus (1982)) a rather common program is used for associating infinite languages to various artistical objects. The main steps are the following: segment the artistical work into "epical" unitary parts, associate a semantic mark to these segments, look for recurrences and dependencies between these semantic marks, and infinitely prolong the work according to the personal reading of it. In this way an infinite language of strings is obtained (a linearization is involved in the case of visual arts), which describe the "reader" attitude when faced with the work regularities, a possible work co-authored by the "reader" and the actual author. Such languages can say something about the artistic work in discussion, about its complexity, various works can be compared by comparing the classes of languages which can be associated to them, and so on.

The natural prolongation procedure used in this frame is the following: if, for instance, a given fairy-tale is described by the string of semantic marks

$$\alpha\beta\gamma\alpha'\beta'\gamma'\alpha'\beta'\gamma'\alpha\beta\gamma$$

with α, β, γ related in a precise manner to α', β', γ' (successful and unsuccessful trials which the heroes have to face, for instance) the action can be prolonged to

$$(\alpha\beta\gamma)^n (\alpha'\beta'\gamma')^{2n} (\alpha\beta\gamma)^n$$

or to

$$\alpha_1\alpha_2 \ldots \alpha_n\alpha_1'\alpha_2' \ldots \alpha_n'\alpha_1'\alpha_2' \ldots \alpha_n'\alpha_1\alpha_2 \ldots \alpha_n$$

with arbitrarily large n. Both these prolongations lead to non-context-free languages.

This procedure is more adequate to folklore works polished over long periods of time.

In approaching visual arts with languages one can reach rapidly non-context-free levels. For instance, if we describe an $n \times n$ square by its n^2 units we obtain easily non-semilinear languages.

Indeed, the world seems to be non-context-free ...

Chapter 1. Three Types of Regulation: Matrix, Programmed, and Random Context Grammars

In a usual Chomsky grammar, at some given step in a derivation one can use any applicable rule in any desired place (to rewrite any occurrence of its left-hand side). It is quite natural to restrict this "nondeterminism" looking to for regulating devices which can select only certain derivations as correct in such a way that the obtained language has certain useful properties. For instance, such a restriction (as "natural" and as simple as possible) which allows a regular or a context-free grammar to generate non-regular or non-context-free languages, respectively, could be of a definite interest (recall the discussion in the previous section).

There are many possibilities to restrict the use of rules in a Chomsky grammar, and a lot of them have been investigated in formal language theory. In this chapter we deal with only three of them, taken as representatives of three classes or regulating mechanisms. Indeed, the following ideas are very natural in restricting the derivation process: prescribing the sequence of rules in a derivation, determining the next rule by the previous one(s), and choosing the rule in dependence on the current sentential form of the derivation. We take as prototypes of these the matrix grammars, the programmed grammars, and the random context grammars, respectively. Many related grammars will be discussed later. (Of course, there are also regulating devices which cannot be included in these classes. The parallel restriction is an example. Also such "isolated" restrictions will be discussed later.)

These three main restrictions are taken as pilot mechanisms and are investigated in some details because they will be the frame of reference for all subsequent restrictions. And, as we shall see, they are also very interesting per se.

1.1. Definitions and Examples

Definition 1.1.1. A *matrix grammar* is a quadruple $G = (V_N, V_T, M, S)$ where V_N, V_T, and S are exactly as in a Chomsky grammar (the nonterminal vocabulary, the terminal alphabet, and the axiom), whereas M is a finite set of sequences of the form

$$m : (r_1, r_2, \ldots, r_n), \quad n \geqq 1,$$

with the usual rewriting rules $r_i : \alpha_i \to \beta_i$ over $V_G = V_N \cup V_T$, that is $\alpha_i \in V_G^* V_N V_G^*$, $\beta_i \in V_G^*$, $1 \leqq i \leqq n$. Such a sequence m is called a matrix of rules.

We denote the set of all rules in M by $P(M)$, and we say that G is a matrix grammar of type i, $i \in \{0, 1, 2, 3\}$, iff the grammar $G' = (V_N, V_T, P(M), S)$ is of type i. Similarly, G is λ-free iff G' is λ-free.

Definition 1.1.2. Let $G = (V_N, V_T, M, S)$ be a matrix grammar as above. For two strings x, y in V_G^* we write $x \Rightarrow y$ (or $x \underset{G}{\Rightarrow} y$ when there is a danger of confusion) iff there are strings $x_0, x_1, \ldots, x_n$ in V_G^* and a matrix $(r_1, r_2, \ldots, r_n) \in M$, $r_i : \alpha_i \to \beta_i$, $1 \leqq i \leqq n$, such that $x_0 = x$, $x_n = y$, and

$$x_{i-1} = x'_{i-1}\alpha_i x''_{i-1},\ x_i = x'_{i-1}\beta_i x''_{i-1} \quad \text{for some} \quad x'_{i-1}, x''_{i-1} \in V_G^*$$

for all $0 \leqq i \leqq n - 1$.

In other words, a direct derivation in the matrix grammar G corresponds to an n-step derivation in the Chomsky grammar $G' = \big(V_N, V_T, P(M), S\big)$, namely, using one by one all the rules of a matrix in M.

Denoting by $\overset{*}{\Rightarrow}$ the reflexive and transitive closure of $\Rightarrow$, the language generated by the grammar G is given as

$$L(G) = \{x : x \in V_T^*, S \overset{*}{\Rightarrow} x\}.$$

Clearly, if G, G' are as given above, then we have $L(G) \subseteq L(G')$.

Example 1.1.1. Let G_1 be the grammar with the matrices

$$m_1\colon (S \to ABC),$$

$$m_2\colon (A \to aA, B \to bB, C \to cC),$$

$$m_3\colon (A \to a, B \to b, C \to c)$$

(the other components of a matrix grammar can be seen from these matrices). It is easy to see that

$$L(G_1) = \{a^n b^n c^n : n \geqq 1\}.$$

(Each string $a^n b^n c^n$, $n \geqq 1$, can be generated by using the matrix m_1, then the matrix m_2 for $n - 1$ times and finally the matrix m_3; conversely, all terminal derivations in the grammar G_1 lead to strings of the form $a^n b^n c^n$, $n \geqq 1$, since the matrices have to be used as above.)

All the rules of G_1 are context-free (in fact, only m_1 contains a non-regular rule), but the language $L(G_1)$ is not context-free.

Also the non-context-free languages

$$L_1 = \{a^n b^m a^n b^m : n, m \geqq 1\},$$

$$L_2 = \big\{xx : x \in \{a, b\}^*\big\}$$

which occurred in Section 0.4. can be generated by (λ-free) context-free matrix grammars. We leave the task to construct such grammars to the reader.

Example 1.1.2. We now give a grammar for the non-semilinear language

$$L_3 = \{a^n b^m : n \geqq 1, 1 \leqq m \leqq 2^n\}.$$

Let us consider the matrices

m_1: $(S \to AE)$, m_6: $(A \to C)$,

m_2: $(A \to A, E \to DD)$, m_7: $(B \to C)$,

m_3: $(A \to aB)$, m_8: $(C \to a)$,

m_4: $(B \to B, D \to EE)$, m_9: $(C \to C, E \to b)$,

m_5: $(B \to aA)$, m_{10}: $(C \to C, D \to b)$,

m_{11}: $(S \to ab)$.

Except for the derivation $S \Rightarrow ab$, all derivations in this grammar begin by using the matrix m_1 and contain two main phases: one which uses the matrices m_8, m_9, m_{10} (in the presence of C) and one which uses the matrices $m_2, \ldots, m_5$. These phases are separated by a derivation step which uses either m_6 or m_7. In the first phase the matrices m_2 and m_4 can double the number of occurrences of the symbols D and E; this is possible only in the presence of symbols A, B, respectively. The change from A to B and vice versa introduces an occurrence of the terminal a. Since it is not necessary to double all occurrences by m_2 or m_4 the number of occurrences of D and E is smaller than 2^n or equal to 2^n if n is the number of occurrences of a. The second phase of the derivation simply replaces each D and E by b. Hence the terminal string obtained in this way belongs to L_3.

Conversely, each string in L_3 can be generated by the above grammar using suitably the matrices m_2, m_3, m_4, m_5.

In a matrix grammar as above, when using a matrix, all its rules have to be effectively used. The following is a powerful generalization.

Definition 1.1.3. Let $G = (V_N, V_T, M, S)$ be a matrix grammar, and let F be a set of occurrences of rules in M. On the set V_G^* we define the relation $\underset{\text{ac}}{\Longrightarrow}$ in the following way: for given $x, y \in V_G^*$, $x \underset{\text{ac}}{\Longrightarrow} y$ if and only if there are $x_0, x_1, \ldots, x_n \in V_G^*$ and a matrix $(r_1, r_2, \ldots, r_n) \in M$, $r_i\colon \alpha_i \to \beta_i$, $1 \leq i \leq n$, such that for each i, $1 \leq i \leq n$, either

$$x_{i-1} = x'_{i-1}\alpha_i x''_{i-1},\ x_i = x'_{i-1}\beta_i x''_{i-1},$$

or the rule $\alpha_i \to \beta_i$ is not applicable to x_{i-1} (i. e. α_i is not a subword of x_{i-1}), this occurrence of $\alpha_i \to \beta_i$ is contained in F, and $x_i = x_{i-1}$.

In other words, the rules whose occurrences are in F can be passed over if they cannot be applied, whereas the other rules have to be effectively used; also the rules in F must be effectively used if this is possible. One says that the rules in F are used in the *appearance checking mode*. The language generated in this way is

$$L(G, F) = \left\{x : S \overset{*}{\underset{\text{ac}}{\Longrightarrow}} x \in V_T^*\right\}$$

where $\overset{*}{\underset{\text{ac}}{\Longrightarrow}}$ is the reflexive and transitive closure of $\underset{\text{ac}}{\Longrightarrow}$.

In the sequel we shall incorporate the set F into G, thus writing $G = (V_N, V_T, M, S, F)$ instead of (G, F), $G = (V_N, V_T, M, S)$. Then we shall also write $L(G)$ for the generated language.

Clearly, each usual matrix grammar (as in Definitions 1.1.1. and 1.1.2.) can be interpreted as a matrix grammar with appearance checking taking $F = \emptyset$. However, it seems that the appearance checking feature can do more than the usual mode of derivation.

Example 1.1.3. Let us consider the grammar G with the matrices

$$\begin{array}{ll} m_1: (S \to a), & m_6: (A' \to A', C \to B), \\ m_2: (S \to aa), & m_7: (A' \to A, C \to X), \\ m_3: (S \to AB), & m_8: (A' \to A'', C \to X), \\ m_4: (A \to A, B \to CC), & m_9: (A'' \to A'', B \to a), \\ m_5: (A \to A'C, B \to X), & m_{10}: (A'' \to a), \end{array}$$

and let the set F contain all occurrences of the rules $B \to X$ and $C \to X$ in matrices. Let us observe that X is a trap symbol, therefore if the rules in F are effectively used, then the derivation cannot terminate.

Let us examine a derivation according to the grammar G. Except for the one-step derivations $S \Rightarrow a$ and $S \Rightarrow aa$, such a derivation starts with m_3. A string AB^i can be rewritten only by m_4, and m_4 must be used to replace all occurrences of B by CC. We obtain the string AC^{2i}. The only continuation is by m_5 yielding $A'C^{2i+1}$; using m_6, m_7 we obtain the string AB^{2i+1}. The length of the string was doubled $\big(|AB^i| = i + 1$, $|AB^{2i+1}| = 2(i + 1)\big)$, and the procedure can be reiterated. Eventually, a string AB^j can be replaced by the terminal string a^{j+1} by using m_8, m_9, m_{10}. Consequently, we obtain

$$L(G) = \{a^{2^n} : n \geqq 0\}.$$

It is not known whether this language can be generated by a context-free matrix grammar without appearance checking.

Definition 1.1.4. A *programmed* grammar is a system $G = (V_N, V_T, P, S)$ where V_N, V_T, S are as in a usual Chomsky grammar and P is a finite set of triples

$$\big(r : \alpha \to \beta, \sigma(r), \varphi(r)\big)$$

where $r : \alpha \to \beta$ is a rewriting rule over V_G labelled by r and $\sigma(r)$ and $\varphi(r)$ are two sets of labels of such core rules in P.

We can interpret P as being constructed from a set R of usual rewriting rules $\alpha \to \beta$ over V_G, a set Lab(R) of labels associated to rules in R in a one-to-one manner and two mappings σ, φ from Lab(R) to $2^{\mathrm{Lab}(R)}$.

Sometimes we use the notation

$$\mathrm{Lab}(P) = \big\{r : \big(r : \alpha \to \beta, \sigma(r), \varphi(r)\big) \in P\big\}.$$

The grammar G is said to be of type i or λ-free if the rules appearing in P are all of type i, $i \in \{0, 1, 2, 3\}$, or λ-free, respectively.

Definition 1.1.5. For (x, r_1), (y, r_2) in $V_G^* \times \mathrm{Lab}(P)$ we write $(x, r_1) \Rightarrow (y, r_2)$ iff either

a) $x = x_1\alpha x_2$, $y = x_1\beta x_2$, $x_1, x_2 \in V_G^*$, $\big(r_1 : \alpha \to \beta, \sigma(r_1), \varphi(r_1)\big) \in P$, and $r_2 \in \sigma(r_1)$

or

b) $x = y$, the rule $r_1 : \alpha \to \beta$ for some $\big(r_1 : \alpha \to \beta, \sigma(r_1), \varphi(r_1)\big)$ in P is not applicable to x and $r_2 \in \varphi(r_1)$.

As in a matrix grammar with appearance checking, either the rule $r_1 : \alpha \to \beta$ is effectively used and then we use a rule with a label in $\sigma(r_1)$ in the next step, or $r_1 : \alpha \to \beta$

cannot be applied and we pass on to a rule with a label in $\varphi(r_1)$ for the next step. The set $\sigma(r)$ is called the *success field* associated to r, and $\varphi(r)$ the *failure field* of r.

The language generated by the grammar G is

$$L(G) = \{x : x \in V_T^* \quad \text{and} \quad (S, r_1) \overset{*}{\Rightarrow} (x, r_2) \quad \text{for some} \quad r_1, r_2 \in \text{Lab}(P)\}$$

where $\overset{*}{\Rightarrow}$ is the reflexive and transitive closure of $\Rightarrow$.

Example 1.1.4. Let us consider a programmed grammar with the following rules (the other components of the grammar are identified, too, in this way):

$$(r_1: S \to ABC, \{r_2, r_5\}, \emptyset),$$
$$(r_2: A \to aA, \{r_3\}, \emptyset),$$
$$(r_3: B \to bB, \{r_4\}, \emptyset),$$
$$(r_4: C \to cC, \{r_2, r_5\}, \emptyset),$$
$$(r_5: A \to a, \{r_6\}, \emptyset),$$
$$(r_6: B \to b, \{r_7\}, \emptyset),$$
$$(r_7: C \to c, \{r_7\}, \emptyset).$$

It is easy to see that this grammar (with only one non-regular rule) generates the non-context-free language $\{a^n b^n c^n : n \geqq 1\}$. Note that the failure fields of all rules in this grammar are empty, and remark that $\sigma(r_7) = \{r_7\}$ only for convenience with Definition 1.1.5, where also the last step of a derivation must lead to a couple (w, r). In fact, no rule with a label in $\sigma(r_7)$ is used. Sometimes in such situations we shall write $\sigma(r_7) = \emptyset$.

Example 1.1.5. Consider the programmed grammar $G = (\{S, A\}, \{a\}, P, S)$ where P consists of the rules

$$(r_1: S \to AA, \{r_1\}, \{r_2, r_3\}),$$
$$(r_2: A \to S, \{r_2\}, \{r_1\}),$$
$$(r_3: A \to a, \{r_3\}, \emptyset).$$

Because $\sigma(r_i) = \{r_i\}$ for $i = 1, 2, 3$, the rules $S \to AA$, $A \to S$, and $A \to a$ must be used as many times as possible. Therefore, starting from S^n for some $n \geqq 1$, we must pass to A^{2n} and then, using the rule r_2, to S^{2n}, or using the rule r_3, to a^{2n}. Each such cycle consisting of the use of r_1 and r_2 doubles the number of symbols. In conclusion, we obtain

$$L(G) = \{a^{2^n} : n \geqq 1\}.$$

Example 1.1.6. The language $\{a^n : n \text{ is a prime number}\}$ can also be generated by a context-free programmed grammar. Indeed, let us consider the grammar with the rules

$$(r_1: S \to SC, \{r_1, r_2\}, \emptyset),$$
$$(r_2: S \to AA, \{r_3\}, \emptyset),$$
$$(r_3: A \to B, \{r_4\}, \{r_5\}),$$
$$(r_4: C \to D, \{r_3\}, \{r_7\}),$$
$$(r_5: C \to C, \{r_6\}, \emptyset),$$

$(r_6: B \to A, \{r_6\}, \{r_3\}),$

$(r_7: B \to A, \{r_7\}, \{r_8\}),$

$(r_8: D \to A, \{r_9\}, \{r_{10}\}),$

$(r_9: D \to C, \{r_9\}, \{r_3\}),$

$(r_{10}: A \to a, \{r_{10}\}, \emptyset).$

Each derivation starts by using n times, $n \geqq 0$, the rule r_1, then the rule r_2, thus producing the string A^2C^n. Starting from a string A^pC^m the rules r_3 to r_7 check whether m can be divided by p. In the affirmative case the derivation is blocked by rule r_5. If m is not divisible by p then, at some step, r_4 cannot be used and one reaches r_8 which increases the number of As. Thus one obtains the string $A^{p+1}C^{m-1}$, and again one checks whether $m - 1$ is divisible by $p + 1$. When we obtain a string A^{p+m}, this implies that $p + m$ is a prime number, and the rule r_{10} can lead to a^{p+m}. This finishes the derivation.

Definition 1.1.6. A *random context grammar* is a system $G = (V_N, V_T, P, S)$ where V_N, V_T, S are as in a usual Chomsky grammar, and P is a finite set of random context rules, that is triples of the form

$$(\alpha \to \beta, Q, R),$$

where $\alpha \to \beta$ is a rewriting rule over V_G and Q and R are subsets of V_N. For $x, y \in V_G^*$, we write $x \Rightarrow y$ iff $x = x'\alpha x''$, $y = x'\beta x''$ for some $x', x'' \in V_G^*$, $(\alpha \to \beta, Q, R)$ is a triple in P, all symbols of Q appear in $x'x''$, and no symbol of R appears in $x'x''$. (Q is called the *permitting* context of $\alpha \to \beta$ and R is the *forbidding context* of this rule.)

The language generated by this grammar G is defined as

$$L(G) = \{x : x \in V_T^* \quad \text{and} \quad S \overset{*}{\Rightarrow} x\}$$

where, again, $\overset{*}{\Rightarrow}$ is the reflexive and transitive closure of $\Rightarrow$.

The grammar is of type i (λ-free) iff the rules $\alpha \to \beta$ in P are of type i (λ-free), $i \in \{0, 1, 2, 3\}$, respectively.

Example 1.1.7. We consider again the languages

$$L_1 = \{a^nb^nc^n : n \geqq 1\},$$

$$L_2 = \{a^nb^m : n \geqq 1, 1 \leqq m \leqq 2^n\},$$

$$L_3 = \{a^{2^n} : n \geqq 1\}.$$

They can be generated by the random context grammars with the following rules:

$$P_1 = \{(S \to ABC, \emptyset, \emptyset), (A \to aA', \{B\}, \emptyset), (B \to bB', \{C\}, \emptyset),$$
$$(C \to cC', \{A'\}, \emptyset), (A' \to A, \{B'\}, \emptyset), (B' \to B, \{C'\}, \emptyset),$$
$$(A \to a, \{B\}, \emptyset), (B \to b, \{C\}, \emptyset), (C \to c, \emptyset, \emptyset)\},$$

$$P_2 = \{(S \to AE, \emptyset, \emptyset), (E \to DD, \{A\}, \emptyset), (A \to aB, \emptyset, \emptyset),$$
$$(D \to EE, \{B\}, \emptyset), (B \to aA, \emptyset, \emptyset), (A \to C, \emptyset, \emptyset),$$
$$(B \to C, \emptyset, \emptyset), (C \to a, \emptyset, \emptyset),$$
$$(E \to b, \{C\}, \emptyset), (D \to b, \{C\}, \emptyset), (S \to ab, \emptyset, \emptyset)\},$$

$$P_3 = \{(S \to AA, \emptyset, \{B, D\}), (A \to B, \emptyset, \{S, D\}), (B \to S, \emptyset, \{A, D\}),$$
$$(A \to D, \emptyset, \{S, B\}), (D \to a, \emptyset, \{S, A, B\})\},$$

respectively.

We shall show this only for L_3 and P_3. Let us consider a word of the form S^i, $i \geqq 1$. Then we have to apply the rule $S \to AA$ as long as S is present in the current string, since S is in the forbidding context of $A \to B$ and $A \to D$. Thus we obtain A^{2i}. If we apply $A \to B$, then we have to do this until no A is present and this yields B^{2i}; now, using $B \to S$, we generate S^{2i}. If we apply $A \to D$ to A^{2i}, then we obtain D^{2i} and then a^{2i}. Therefore it is clear that we generate the language L_3.

Note that in P_1 and P_2 all forbidding contextes are empty, whereas in P_3 all permitting contexts are empty.

Certain variants of matrix, programmed, and random context grammars will be discussed later. We are now going into studying the properties of these grammars; some of them are fundamental in the theory of regulated rewriting.

Open problem

1.1.1. Can the languages $\{a^{2^n} : n \geqq 1\}$, $\{a^{n^2} : n \geqq 1\}$, $\{a^n : n \text{ prime}\}$ be generated by matrix grammars without appearance checking and with context-free rules?

Exercises

1.1.1. Construct context-free matrix grammars for the languages

$$L_1 = \{a^n b^m c^p d^q : 1 \leqq n \leqq m \leqq p \leqq q\},$$

$$L_2 = \{x : x \in \{a, b, c\}^* \quad \text{and} \quad |x|_a = |x|_b = |x|_c\}.$$

1.1.2. Construct context-free matrix grammars with appearance checking for the languages

$$L_3 = \{a^{n^2} : n \geqq 1\},$$

$$L_4 = \{a^n : n \quad \text{is a non-prime number}\}.$$

(Hint: for L_3 use the equality $n^2 = 1 + 3 + \cdots + (2n - 1)$.)

1.1.3. Construct programmed grammars for the languages in the above exercises (with empty failure fields for L_1, L_2).

1.1.4. Construct random context grammars for the languages in Exercises 1.1.1 and 1.1.2.

1.2. The Generative Capacity

We shall denote the families of languages generated by the previous three types of regulated grammars as follows: $\mathscr{L}(\text{M}, X, \text{ac})$, $X \in \{\text{RE}, \text{CS}, \text{CF}, \text{CF} - \lambda, \text{REG}\}$, is the family of languages generated by matrix grammars of type X with appearance checking.

If programmed or random context grammars are used, then we replace M by P or RC, respectively; thus we obtain the families $\mathscr{L}(\mathrm{P}, X, \mathrm{ac})$, $\mathscr{L}(\mathrm{RC}, X, \mathrm{ac})$. When no appearance checking features are involved, that is $F = \emptyset$ in the matrix case, $\varphi(r) = \emptyset$ for each rule r in programmed grammars, and $R = \emptyset$ for each rule $(\alpha \to \beta, Q, R)$ in random context grammars, then we erase the letters ac and we obtain the families $\mathscr{L}(\mathrm{M}, X)$, $\mathscr{L}(\mathrm{P}, X)$, $\mathscr{L}(\mathrm{RC}, X)$, respectively.

Lemma 1.2.1. i) *For* $X \in \{\mathrm{RE}, \mathrm{CS}, \mathrm{CF}, \mathrm{CF} - \lambda, \mathrm{REG}\}$, $Y \in \{\mathrm{M}, \mathrm{P}, \mathrm{RC}\}$, *we have*

$$\mathscr{L}(X) \subseteq \mathscr{L}(Y, X) \subseteq \mathscr{L}(Y, X, \mathrm{ac}).$$

ii) *For* $Y \in \{\mathrm{M}, \mathrm{P}, \mathrm{RC}\}$, *we have*

$$\mathscr{L}(Y, \mathrm{REG}) \subseteq \mathscr{L}(Y, \mathrm{CF} - \lambda) \subseteq \mathscr{L}(Y, \mathrm{CS}) \subseteq \mathscr{L}(Y, \mathrm{RE}) \subseteq \mathscr{L}(\mathrm{RE})$$

and

$$\mathscr{L}(Y, \mathrm{REG}, \mathrm{ac}) \subseteq \mathscr{L}(Y, \mathrm{CF} - \lambda, \mathrm{ac}) \subseteq \mathscr{L}(Y, \mathrm{CS}, \mathrm{ac}) \subseteq \mathscr{L}(Y, \mathrm{RE}, \mathrm{ac})$$
$$\subseteq \mathscr{L}(\mathrm{RE}).$$

iii) *For* $Y \in \{\mathrm{M}, \mathrm{P}, \mathrm{RC}\}$, *we have*

$$\mathscr{L}(Y, \mathrm{CF} - \lambda) \subseteq \mathscr{L}(Y, \mathrm{CF}) \subseteq \mathscr{L}(\mathrm{RE})$$

and

$$\mathscr{L}(Y, \mathrm{CF} - \lambda, \mathrm{ac}) \subseteq \mathscr{L}(Y, \mathrm{CF}, \mathrm{ac}) \subseteq \mathscr{L}(\mathrm{RE}).$$

Proof. Each Chomsky grammar $G = (V_N, V_T, P, S)$ can be considered as a matrix grammar (with each rule $r \in P$ constituting a matrix (r)), as a programmed grammar (with $\sigma(r) = \varphi(r) = \mathrm{Lab}(P)$ for all $r \in \mathrm{Lab}(P)$), and as a random context grammar (with rules of the form $(\alpha \to \beta, \emptyset, \emptyset)$ for each $\alpha \to \beta \in P$). We obtain in this way the inclusions $\mathscr{L}(X) \subseteq \mathscr{L}(Y, X)$. As a matrix, programmed, or random context grammar without appearance checking is a particular case of matrix, programmed, or random context grammars, point i) follows. Points ii) and iii) are obvious (the inclusions in $\mathscr{L}(\mathrm{RE})$ follow from the Church thesis, or can be proved directly, see Lemma 1.2.4.).

Lemma 1.2.2. $\mathscr{L}(\mathrm{M}, \mathrm{REG}, \mathrm{ac}) \subseteq \mathscr{L}(\mathrm{REG})$.

Proof. Let $G = (V_N, V_T, M, S, F)$ be a regular matrix grammar. For each matrix $m : (r_1, r_2, \ldots, r_n)$ in M, $r_i : A_i \to x_i$, $x_i \in V_T^*(V_N \cup \{\lambda\})$, $1 \leqq i \leqq n$, which induces the derivation $A_1 \Rightarrow w$ with respect to G by its use, we consider the rule $A_1 \to w$. Clearly, this is a regular rule. Let P be the set of all these rules, and let $G' = (V_N, V_T, P, S)$. Then G' is a regular grammars and the equality $L(G) = L(G')$ is obvious. Hence $L(G)$ is regular.

Remark. Note that the above argument also proves that the matrix restriction does not increase the generative capacity of linear grammars.

The following normal form for matrix grammars will simplify some of the next proofs.

Definition 1.2.1. A matrix grammar $G = (V_N, V_T, M, S, F)$ is said to be in the (preliminary) 2-*normal form* iff

$$V_N = \{S\} \cup V_N^{(1)} \cup V_N^{(2)} \quad \text{with} \quad V_N^{(1)} \cap V_N^{(2)} = \emptyset,\ S \notin V_N^{(1)} \cup V_N^{(2)}$$

and M contains only matrices of the following forms:

(i) $(S \to AX)$, $A \in V_N^{(1)}$, $X \in V_N^{(2)}$,

(ii) $(\alpha \to \beta, X \to Y)$, $\alpha, \beta \in (V_N^{(1)} \cup V_T)^*$, $X, Y \in V_N^{(2)}$,

(iii) $(\alpha \to \beta, X \to \lambda)$, $\alpha, \beta \in (V_N^{(1)} \cup V_T)^*$, $X \in V_N^{(2)}$.

Moreover, the set F contains only rules of the form $\alpha \to \beta$ in matrices of types (ii) and (iii).

We say that such a grammar is of type X, $X \in \{\text{RE, CS, CF, CF} - \lambda, \text{REG}\}$, if the rules $\alpha \to \beta$ in matrices of types (ii) and (iii) are of type X.

Lemma 1.2.3. *For each matrix grammar G one can construct an equivalent matrix grammar G' in the (preliminary) 2-normal form. Moreover, G' is of the same type as G.*

Proof. Let $G = (V_N, V_T, M, S, F)$ be a matrix grammar with

$$M = \{m_1, m_2, \ldots, m_p\},\ m_i : (r_{i1}, r_{i2}, \ldots, r_{ik_i}),\ 1 \leqq i \leqq p.$$

We construct the 2-normal grammar $G' = (V_N', V_T, M', S', F')$ with

$$V_N' = V_N^{(1)} \cup V_N^{(2)} \cup \{S'\}$$

where

$$V_N^{(1)} = V_N,\ V_N^{(2)} = \{(i, j) : 1 \leqq i \leqq p,\ 1 \leqq j \leqq k_i\},$$

S' is a new symbol, and M' contains the following groups of matrices:

1) $\big(S' \to S(i, 1)\big)$, $1 \leqq i \leqq p$,

2) $\big(\alpha \to \beta, (i, j) \to (i, j + 1)\big)$, $1 \leqq i \leqq p$, $1 \leqq j \leqq k_i - 1$, $r_{ij} : \alpha \to \beta$,

3) $\big(\alpha \to \beta, (i, k_i) \to (i', 1)\big)$, $1 \leqq i \leqq p$, $1 \leqq i' \leqq p$, $r_{ik_i} : \alpha \to \beta$,

4) $\big(\alpha \to \beta, (i, k_i) \to \lambda\big)$, $1 \leqq i \leqq p$, $r_{ik_i} : \alpha \to \beta$,

and the set F' contains all rules $\alpha \to \beta$ corresponding to the rules which occur in F.

It is easy to see that the nonterminals (i, j) control the derivation in such a way that the rules at the first position in the matrices in the groups 2), 3), 4) are correctly used (in the same order as in matrices in M). The equality $L(G) = L(G')$ is therefore obvious and, clearly, the grammar G' is of the same type as G (in the sense of Definition 1.2.1).

Lemma 1.2.4. *For $X \in \{\text{RE, CS}\}$, $\mathcal{L}(M, X, \text{ac}) \subseteq \mathcal{L}(X)$.*

Proof. Let $G = (V_N, V_T, M, S, F)$ be a type-0 matrix grammar. Assume that G is in the above 2-normal form and let $V_N^{(1)}$ and $V_N^{(2)}$ be as in Definition 1.2.1. We construct a type-0 grammar $G' = (V_N', V_T, P, S)$ which is equivalent to G as follows.

For each matrix $m \in M$ of type (ii) or (iii) in Definition 1.2.1 we introduce three new symbols A_m, B_m, and C_m. Then we set

$$V_N' = V_N \cup \{C, D\} \cup \bigcup_{m \in M} \{A_m, B_m, C_m\}$$

where C and D are new symbols. For each matrix $(S \to AX)$ in M we introduce in P a rule

$$S \to CAXD.$$

Let m: $(\alpha \to \beta, X \to U)$, $U \in V_N^{(2)} \cup \{\lambda\}$, be a matrix of type (ii) or (iii). Then we introduce in P the rules

$$X \to A_m,$$

$$\gamma A_m \to \gamma' A_m z,\ \gamma, \gamma' \in (V_N^{(1)} \cup V_T)^*,\ z \in V_N^{(1)} \cup V_T,\ |\gamma| = |\alpha|,\ \alpha \neq \gamma = \gamma' z,$$

$$\alpha A_m \to \alpha B_m,$$

$$z B_m \to B_m z,\ z \in V_N^{(1)} \cup V_T,$$

$$\alpha B_m \to \beta C_m,$$

$$C_m z \to z C_m,\ z \in V_N^{(1)} \cup V_T,$$

$$C_m D \to UD.$$

If the rule $\alpha \to \beta$ in this matrix appears in F, then we also introduce the rules

$$C\gamma A_m \to C\gamma C_m,\ \gamma \in (V_N^{(1)} \cup V_T)^*,\ |\gamma| \leqq |\alpha| - 1.$$

Further, the set P also contains the rules $C \to \lambda$ and $D \to \lambda$.

The nonterminal A_m checks whether the first rule of the matrix m is applicable. In the affirmative case it introduces B_m which can be eliminated only by simulating the rule $\alpha \to \beta$ and introducing C_m which moves to the right and derives U. The removal of A_m is also possible if the rule $\alpha \to \beta$ is in F and α does not appear in the current string. Then A_m introduces C_m and thus U. Since the strings contain at most one letter A_m, B_m, or C_m, the equality $L(G) = L(G')$ is obvious. For the type-0 case the lemma is proved.

If G is a length-increasing grammar, then one can see that for each $x \in L(G')$ we have

$$WS(x, G') \leqq |x| + 3.$$

From the workspace theorem (Theorem 0.2.10) we obtain $L(G') \in \mathcal{L}(\mathrm{CS})$. Hence $L(G) \in \mathcal{L}(\mathrm{CS})$, and the proof is complete.

By Lemmas 1.2.1, 1.2.2, and 1.2.4 we obtain

Theorem 1.2.1. *For* $X \in \{\mathrm{RE}, \mathrm{CS}, \mathrm{REG}\}$, *we have*

$$\mathcal{L}(\mathrm{M}, X) = \mathcal{L}(\mathrm{M}, X, \mathrm{ac}) = \mathcal{L}(X).$$

A similar result can be obtained for programmed and random context grammars combining this theorem with the next ones.

Theorem 1.2.2. *For* $X \in \{\mathrm{RE}, \mathrm{CS}, \mathrm{CF}, \mathrm{CF} - \lambda, \mathrm{REG}\}$, *we have*

$$\mathcal{L}(\mathrm{M}, X) = \mathcal{L}(\mathrm{P}, X) \quad \text{and} \quad \mathcal{L}(\mathrm{M}, X, \mathrm{ac}) = \mathcal{L}(\mathrm{P}, X, \mathrm{ac}).$$

Proof. i) $\mathcal{L}(\mathrm{M}, X) \subseteq \mathcal{L}(\mathrm{P}, X)$, $\mathcal{L}(\mathrm{M}, X, \mathrm{ac}) \subseteq \mathcal{L}(\mathrm{P}, X, \mathrm{ac})$. Let $G = (V_N, V_T, M, S, F)$ be a matrix grammar (with appearance checking), $V_N = \{A_1, A_2, \ldots, A_t\}$, $M = \{m_1, m_2, \ldots, m_r\}$, $m_i : (r_{i1}, r_{i2}, \ldots, r_{ik_i})$, $r_{ij} : \alpha_{ij} \neq \beta_{ij}$, $1 \leqq i \leqq r$, $1 \leqq j \leqq k_i$. We set

$$V_N' = \{A' : A \in V_N\},$$

and we define the homomorphism h by

$$h(a) = a \quad \text{for} \quad a \in V_T, \quad h(A) = A' \quad \text{for} \quad A \in V_N.$$

With r_{ij} we associate the following programmed rules (we set $\delta = \emptyset$ if $r_{ij} \notin F$ and δ is equal to the success field if $r_{ij} \in F$):

$$([i, j]: \alpha_{ij} \to \beta_{ij}, \{[i, j+1]\}, \delta) \quad \text{if} \quad |\beta_{ij}|_{V_N} > 0, \ 1 \leqq j < k_i$$

(we simulate the rule r_{ij} and the next rule has to be $r_{i,j+1}$), or

$$([i, j]: \alpha_{ij} \to h(\alpha_{ij}), \{[i, j, 1], [i, j, 2], \ldots, [i, j, t]\}, \{[i, j]'\}),$$
$$([i, j, k]: A_k \to A_k, \{[i, j]'\}, \emptyset), \ 1 \leqq k \leqq t,$$
$$([i, j]': h(\alpha_{ij}) \to \beta_{ij}, \{[i, j+1]\}, \delta),$$

for $|\beta_{ij}|_{V_N} = 0$, $1 \leqq j \leqq k_i$ (since it is forbidden to stop a derivation inside a matrix, we check before simulating the application of r_{ij} whether or not the obtained string will be a terminal string),

$$([i, k_i]: \alpha_{ik_i} \to \beta_{ik_i}, \{[1, 1], [2, 1], \ldots, [r, 1]\}, \delta)$$

(we simulate r_{ik_i} and continue with the first rule of a matrix). Let P consist of all rules constructed in this way and the starting rule

$$(*, S'' \to S, \{[1, 1], [2, 1], \ldots, [r, 1]\}, \emptyset).$$

Now it is easy to see that the programmed grammar

$$G' = (V_N \cup V_N' \cup \{S''\}, V_T, P, S'')$$

also generates $L(G)$. Hence $L(G) \in \mathscr{L}(\mathrm{P}, X, \mathrm{ac})$, and hence $\mathscr{L}(\mathrm{M}, X, \mathrm{ac}) \subseteq \mathscr{L}(\mathrm{P}, X, \mathrm{ac})$.

In the case when no appearance checking features are present we can use the same construction where we take only empty failure fields instead of those in the above construction.

ii) $\mathscr{L}(\mathrm{P}, X) \subseteq \mathscr{L}(\mathrm{M}, X)$, $\mathscr{L}(\mathrm{P}, X, \mathrm{ac}) \subseteq \mathscr{L}(\mathrm{M}, X, \mathrm{ac})$. Let $G = (V_N, V_T, P, S)$ be a programmed grammar. We construct the matrix grammar $G' = (V_N', V_T, M, S', F)$ with

$$V_N' = V_N \cup \big(V_N \times \mathrm{Lab}\,(P)\big) \cup \{S', Z\},$$

and M containig the following matrices:

$$\big(S' \to (S, b)\big), \ b \in \mathrm{Lab}\,(P)$$

(we shall simulate a derivation $S = w_1 \Rightarrow w_2 \Rightarrow w_3 \Rightarrow \cdots \Rightarrow w_t$ in G by a derivation $S' \Rightarrow v_1 \Rightarrow v_2 \Rightarrow \cdots \Rightarrow v_t$ such that v_i is obtained from w_i by substituting one occurrence of a nonterminal X by (X, b) for $1 \leqq i < t$, and the same holds for v_t or $v_t = w_t$; matrices can only be applied if a letter (X, b) occurs in the current string),

$$\big((A, b) \to A, \alpha \to \beta, B \to (B, c)\big) \quad \text{for} \quad \big(b: \alpha \to \beta, \sigma(b), \varphi(b)\big) \in P,$$
$$c \in \sigma(b), \ A, B \in V_N$$

(this matrix simulates an effective application of the rule labelled by b),

$$\big((A, b) \to A, \alpha \to \beta\big) \quad \text{for} \quad \big(b: \alpha \to \beta, \sigma(b), \varphi(b)\big) \in P, \ A \in V_N$$

(this matrix simulates an effective application of the rule labelled by b, and then the derivation stops since no letter of the form (X, r) is present),

$$\big((A, b) \to A, \alpha \to Z^{|\alpha|}, B \to (B, c)\big) \quad \text{for} \quad \big(b; \alpha \to \beta, \sigma(b), \varphi(b)\big) \ \text{in} \ P,$$
$$c \in \varphi(b), \ A, B \in V_N,$$

and let F be the set of all occurrences of rules of the form $\alpha \to Z^{|\alpha|}$ (the latter matrix simulates the passing over of $\alpha \to \beta$ and continuing with a rule whose label is in the failure field, since an effective application of $\alpha \to Z^{|\alpha|}$ introduces the trap symbol Z which cannot be rewritten; clearly, F is empty if all sets $\varphi(b)$ are empty). By this explanation, it is obvious that $L(G) = L(G')$. Hence $L(G) \in \mathcal{L}(\mathrm{M}, X, \mathrm{ac})$ or $L(G) \in \mathcal{L}(\mathrm{M}, X)$, respectively.

Corollary. *For* $X \in \{\mathrm{RE}, \mathrm{CS}, \mathrm{REG}\}$, *we have*

$$\mathcal{L}(\mathrm{P}, X) = \mathcal{L}(\mathrm{P}, X, \mathrm{ac}) = \mathcal{L}(X).$$

Proof. This is a direct consequence of Theorems 1.2.1 and 1.2.2.

Theorem 1.2.3. i) *For* $X \in \{\mathrm{RE}, \mathrm{CS}, \mathrm{REG}\}$, *we have*

$$\mathcal{L}(\mathrm{M}, X) = \mathcal{L}(\mathrm{RC}, X).$$

ii) *For* $X \in \{\mathrm{CF}, \mathrm{CF} - \lambda\}$, *we have*

$$\mathcal{L}(\mathrm{RC}, X) \subseteq \mathcal{L}(M, X).$$

iii) *For* $X \in \{\mathrm{RE}, \mathrm{CS}, \mathrm{CF}, \mathrm{CF} - \lambda, \mathrm{REG}\}$, *we have*

$$\mathcal{L}(\mathrm{M}, X, \mathrm{ac}) = \mathcal{L}(\mathrm{RC}, X, \mathrm{ac}).$$

Proof. Let $G = (V_N, V_T, P, S)$ be a random context grammar. For each symbol $x \in V_G$, let x' be a new symbol and denote by α' the primed version of the string $\alpha \in V_G^*$, i.e. if $\alpha = a_1a_2 \dots a_n$ then $\alpha' = a_1'a_2' \dots a_n'$. We construct the matrix grammar

$$G' = (V_N', V_T, M, S, F)$$

with

$$V_N' = V_N \cup \{x' : x \in V_G\} \cup \{Z\} \quad \text{where } Z \text{ is a new symbol,}$$

$$M = \big\{(\alpha \to \alpha', A_1 \to A_1, A_2 \to A_2, \dots, A_n \to A_n, B_1 \to Z, B_2 \to Z, \dots, B_m \to Z, \alpha' \to \beta) : (\alpha \to \beta, \{A_1A_2, \dots, A_n\}, \{B_1, B_2, \dots, B_m\}) \in P\big\},$$

and we take F as consisting of all rules of the form $B \to Z$ occurring in M.

After marking an occurrence of the left-hand member of the rule $\alpha \to \beta$, the matrices in M check whether the symbols of the permitting context appear in the current string and whether or not the forbidding context symbols do not occur (note that Z is a trap symbol) and only after that α' is replaced by β. Consequently, $L(G) = L(G')$. As $F = \emptyset$ if the forbidding context of all rules in P is empty and as G' is of the same type as G, we obtain the inclusions $\mathcal{L}(\mathrm{RC}, X) \subseteq \mathcal{L}(\mathrm{M}, X)$ and $\mathcal{L}(\mathrm{RC}, X, \mathrm{ac}) \subseteq \mathcal{L}(\mathrm{M}, X, \mathrm{ac})$ for all values of X.

Since $\mathcal{L}(\mathrm{M}, X) = \mathcal{L}(\mathrm{M}, X, \mathrm{ac}) = \mathcal{L}(X) \subseteq \mathcal{L}(\mathrm{RC}, X) \subseteq \mathcal{L}(\mathrm{RC}, X, \mathrm{ac})$ for $X \in \{\mathrm{RE}, \mathrm{CS}, \mathrm{REG}\}$, in order to complete the proof we have only to show that $\mathcal{L}(\mathrm{M}, X, \mathrm{ac}) \subseteq \mathcal{L}(\mathrm{RC}, X, \mathrm{ac})$ for $X \in \{\mathrm{CF}, \mathrm{CF} - \lambda\}$.

Let $G = (V_N, V_T, M, S, F)$ be a matrix grammar with context-free rules and with appearance checking. Without loss of generality we assume that G is in the 2-normal form (with $V_N = V_N^{(1)} \cup V_N^{(2)} \cup \{S\}$). We construct the following random context grammar

$$G' = (V_N', V_T \cup \{c\}, P, S)$$

where

$$V'_N = V_N \cup \{(A, m) : A \in V_N^{(1)} \cup V_N^{(2)}, m\colon (A \to x, X \to z) \in M \quad \text{or}$$
$$m\colon (B \to x, A \to z) \in M\},$$

c is a new symbol, and P contains the following random context rules:

(1) $(S \to AX, \emptyset, \emptyset)$ for $(S \to AX) \in M$,

(2) $\big(A \to (A, m), \{X\}, \{(B, m') : B \in V_N^{(1)} \cup V_N^{(2)}, m' : (B \to y, U \to z) \in M\}\big)$,

$\big(X \to (X, m), \{(A, m)\}, \emptyset\big)$,

$\big((A, m) \to x, \{(X, m)\}, \emptyset\big)$,

$\big((X, m) \to Y, \emptyset, \{(A, m)\}\big)$

for each matrix $m\colon (A \to x, X \to Y) \in M$; for each matrix $m\colon (A \to x, X \to \lambda) \in M$ we also introduce the first three rules of group (2) together with the rule

$$\big((X, m) \to \lambda, \emptyset, \{(A, m)\}\big)$$

if G is an arbitrary context-free grammar, or with the rule

$$\big((X, m) \to c, \emptyset, \{(A, m)\}\big)$$

if G is λ-free.

The above group (2) of rules simulates the application of the corresponding matrix. Therefore we get $L(G') = L(G)$ in the arbitrary context-free case and $L(G') = L(G)\,\{c\}$ in the λ-free case. In order to finish the proof we can use the following assertion.

Assertion. *Let $L \subseteq V^*$ be a language such that $L\{c\} \in \mathcal{L}(\mathrm{RC}, \mathrm{CF} - \lambda, \mathrm{ac})$ for some c not in V. Then the language L belongs to $\mathcal{L}(\mathrm{RC}, \mathrm{CF} - \lambda, \mathrm{ac})$, too.*

Proof of the assertion. Let $G = (V_N, V_T, P, S)$ be a λ-free context-free random context grammar generating $L\{c\}$, and let $V_T = V \cup \{c\}$. We construct the random context grammar

$$G' = (V'_N, V, P', S')$$

where

$$V'_N = V_N \cup V_G \times V_G \cup \{(\mathfrak{b}, z) : z \in V_G\} \qquad (\mathfrak{b} \text{ stands for "blank"}),$$
$$S' = (\mathfrak{b}, S),$$

and P is constructed as follows. For a set $W \subseteq V_N$, $W = \{B_1, B_2, \ldots, B_n\}$, we define the sets

$$f(W) = W \cup W \times V_G \cup (V_G \cup \{\mathfrak{b}\}) \times W,$$

$$p_{i,x}(W) = \{B_1, B_2, \ldots, B_{i-1}, (B_i, x), B_{i+1}, \ldots, B_n\},$$

$$q_{i,y}(W) = \{B_1, B_2, \ldots, B_{i-1}, (y, B_i), B_{i+1}, \ldots, B_n\},$$

where $1 \leqq i \leqq n$, $x \in V_G$, $y \in V_G \cup \{\mathfrak{b}\}$. In the sequel by $p(W)$ we denote one of the sets $p_{i,x}(W)$, $q_{i,y}(W)$, or W. For each rule $(A \to x, Q, R)$, $|x| = 1$, $Q, R \subseteq V_N$, we introduce in P' the rules

$$\big(A \to x, p(Q), f(R)\big),$$

$$\big((\mathfrak{b}, A) \to (\mathfrak{b}, x), Q, R\big),$$
$$\big((z, A) \to (z, x), Q \setminus \{z\}, R\big) \quad \text{for} \quad z \in V_G, z \notin R,$$
$$\big((A, z) \to (x, z), Q \setminus \{z\}, R\big) \quad \text{for} \quad z \in V_G, z \notin R,$$

and for each rule $(A \to x, Q, R) \in P$, $|x| \geqq 2$, $Q, R \leqq V_N$, we introduce in P the rules

$$\big(A \to x, p(Q), f(R)\big),$$
$$\big((\mathfrak{b}, A) \to x'(z_1, z_2), Q, R\big) \qquad \text{for} \quad x = x'z_1z_2, z_1, z_2 \in V_G, x' \in V_G^*,$$
$$\big((z, A) \to zx'(z_1, z_2), Q \setminus \{z\}, E\big) \quad \text{for} \quad x = x'z_1z_2, z, z_1, z_2 \in V_G, x' \in V_G^*, z \notin R,$$
$$\big((A, z) \to x'(z_1, z), Q \setminus \{z\}, R\big) \quad \text{for} \quad x = x'z_1, z, z_1 \in V_G, x' \in V_G^*, z \notin R,$$

and we also introduce the terminating rules

$$\big((a, c) \to a, \emptyset, \emptyset\big) \quad \text{for each} \quad a \in V.$$

It is easy to see that in the above construction we simply combine the last two symbols of each string (with a blank symbol if the word has the length 1; in particular c is combined with its left neighbour). Therefore we get $L(G') = L$. Since the grammar G' is λ-free, the assertion is proved.

Corollary. *For* $X \in \{\text{RE}, \text{CS}, \text{REG}\}$, *we have*

$$\mathscr{L}(\text{RC}, X) = \mathscr{L}(\text{RC}, X, \text{ac}) = \mathscr{L}(X).$$

Proof. The statement follows from Theorems 1.2.1 and 1.2.3.

By the above results the study of the families $\mathscr{L}(Y, X)$ and $\mathscr{L}(Y, X, \text{ac})$, $Y \in \{\text{M, P, RC}\}$, $X \in \{\text{RE, CS, REG}\}$ is not necessary; therefore in what follows we shall ignore them, and we shall study only families of context-free regulated languages. The next theorem summarizes the results obtained so far for these families and presents some further relationships.

Theorem 1.2.4. i) $\mathscr{L}(\text{RC}, \text{CF}) \subseteq \mathscr{L}(\text{M}, \text{CF}) = \mathscr{L}(\text{P}, \text{CF})$,

$$\mathscr{L}(\text{RC}, \text{CF} - \lambda) \subseteq \mathscr{L}(\text{M}, \text{CF} - \lambda) = \mathscr{L}(\text{P}, \text{CF} - \lambda),$$

ii) $$\mathscr{L}(\text{M}, \text{CF}, \text{ac}) = \mathscr{L}(\text{P}, \text{CF}, \text{ac}) = \mathscr{L}(\text{RC}, \text{CF}, \text{ac}),$$

$$\mathscr{L}(\text{M}, \text{CF} - \lambda, \text{ac}) = \mathscr{L}(\text{P}, \text{CF} - \lambda, \text{ac}) = \mathscr{L}(\text{RC}, \text{CF} - \lambda, \text{ac}).$$

iii) $\mathscr{L}(\text{CF})$ *is strictly contained in* $\mathscr{L}(\text{RC}, \text{CF} - \lambda)$.

iv) *For* $X \in \{\text{M, P, RC}\}$ *we have*

$$\mathscr{L}(X, \text{CF} - \lambda) \subsetneq \mathscr{L}(X, \text{CF}) \subseteq \mathscr{L}(X, \text{CF}, \text{ac}) \subseteq \mathscr{L}(\text{RE}),$$

$$\mathscr{L}(X, \text{CF} - \lambda) \subseteq \mathscr{L}(X, \text{CF} - \lambda, \text{ac}) \subseteq \mathscr{L}(X, \text{CF}, \text{ac}) \subseteq \mathscr{L}(\text{RE}).$$

v) *For* $X \in \{\text{M, P, RC}\}$, *the family* $\mathscr{L}(X, \text{CF} - \lambda, \text{ac})$ *is strictly included in* $\mathscr{L}(\text{CS})$.

Proof. Points i), ii), and iv) have been proved already, and iii) follows from the examples considered in Section 1.1.; here we omit the proof of point v) and refer to the proof of Theorem 1.4.5 which is a stronger result by Lemma 1.4.8 and Theorems 1.2.6 and 1.2.8.

From the above relations it follows that the families $\mathscr{L}(X, \text{CF} - \lambda)$ and $\mathscr{L}(X, \text{CF} - \lambda, \text{ac})$ for $X \in \{\text{M, P, RC}\}$ are strictly intermediate between the families of context-free and context sensitive languages. Note also that the families $\mathcal{L}(X, \mathrm{CF} - \lambda)$ for $X \in \{\mathrm{M}, \mathrm{P}, \mathrm{RC}\}$ contain non-semilinear languages (remember that $\{a^n b^m : n \geqq 1, 1 \leqq m \leqq 2^n\}$ belongs to $\mathcal{L}(\mathrm{RC}, \mathrm{CF} - \lambda)$) and that the families $\mathcal{L}(X, \mathrm{CF} - \lambda, \mathrm{ac})$, $X \in \{\mathrm{M}, \mathrm{P}, \mathrm{RC}\}$, contain non-regular languages over one-letter alphabets (see examples in Section 1.1.).

Now what about the generative capacity of regulated grammars with λ-rules? As we shall point out at the end of this section, a lot of problems remains open in this area. Here we present a fundamental result due to ROSENKRANTZ (1969): if both λ-rules and appearance checking are used, then the matrix, programmed, and random context grammars are as powerful as the type-0 Chomsky grammars.

Theorem 1.2.5. *For* $X \in \{\mathrm{M}, \mathrm{P}, \mathrm{RC}\}$, *we have* $\mathcal{L}(X, \mathrm{CF}, \mathrm{ac}) = \mathcal{L}(\mathrm{RE})$.

Proof. Clearly, it is enough to prove the inclusion $\mathcal{L}(\mathrm{RE}) \subseteq \mathcal{L}(\mathrm{M}, \mathrm{CF}, \mathrm{ac})$. Let $G = (V_N, V_T, P, S)$ be a type-0 grammar in Kuroda normal form (thus containing only rules of the form $A \to CD$, $AB \to CD$, $A \to a$, $A \to \lambda$). We construct the type-0 grammar

$$G' = (V_N \cup \{S', E\}, V_T, P', S')$$

where S' and E are new symbols and

$$P' = \{S' \to ES, E \to EE, E \to \lambda\} \cup \{AE \to EA : A \in V_N\}$$
$$\cup \{EA \to AE : A \in V_N\} \cup \{AE \to CD : A \to CD \in P\} \cup P_0,$$

where P_0 is the set of all rules of P of the form $AB \to CD$, $A \to a$, $A \to \lambda$. Clearly, $L(G) = L(G')$, and each string $w \in L(G')$ can be generated by a derivation of the form

$$S' \overset{*}{\Rightarrow} w_1 \overset{*}{\Rightarrow} w_2 \overset{*}{\Rightarrow} w$$

where the subderivation $S' \overset{*}{\Rightarrow} w_1$ uses only the rules $S' \to ES$, $E \to EE$ (we call this the preliminary phase of the derivation), the subderivation $w_1 \overset{*}{\Rightarrow} w_2$ (called the basic phase) uses only rules of the form $XY \to ZU$, and the subderivation $w_2 \overset{*}{\Rightarrow} w$ (the final phase) uses only context-free rules with a terminal word on the right-hand side. We call such a derivation a standard derivation.

The next codification of the strings over some given alphabet $V = \{a_1, a_2, \ldots, a_n\}$ is the basic idea of the proof. Let $h_i \colon V^* \to \{0, 1\}^*$ be the homomorphism defined by

$$h_i(a_i) = 1, h_i(a_j) = 0 \quad \text{for} \quad i \neq j,$$

$1 \leqq i \leqq n$. Let $\mathrm{val}\,(h_i(x))$, $x \in V^+$, be the binary value of the string $h_i(x)$ and denote by $Q(x)$ the set of all strings in V^* which are letter-equivalent to

$$a_1^{m_1} a_2^{m_2} \ldots a_n^{m_n}, \; m_i = \mathrm{val}\,(h_i(x)), \; 1 \leqq i \leqq n.$$

Each string in $Q(x)$ contains exactly $\mathrm{val}\,(h_i(x))$ occurrences of the symbol a_i and the number of these occurrences precisely identifies the occurrences of a_i in the string x. Therefore, each string in $Q(x)$ uniquely identifies the string x.

The plan of the proof is the following: take a standard derivation $S' \overset{*}{\Rightarrow} w_1 \overset{*}{\Rightarrow} w_2 \overset{*}{\Rightarrow} w$ in the previous grammar G', replace the preliminary phase $S' \overset{*}{\Rightarrow} w_1$ by a derivation of a string in $Q(w_1)$, then simulate the basic phase by a derivation from some $z \in Q(w_1)$ to some $y \in Q(w_2)$, and finally pass from y to w simulating also the final phase. These operations are easy to do in terms of matrix grammars (with appearance checking and with λ-rules). Here are the details of this construction.

Let us consider the matrix grammar $G'' = (V'_N, V_T, M, S', F)$ where

$$V'_N = V_N \cup \{E, S', X, X', Y, Y', Z\} \cup \{A_i : 1 \leqq i \leqq 11\}$$
$$\cup \{A' : A \in V_N \cup \{E\}\} \cup \{A'' : A \in V_N \cup \{E\}\}$$
$$\cup \{[r] : r : AB \to CD \in P'\},$$

X, X', Y, Y', Z, and A_i, $1 \leqq i \leqq 11$, being new symbols, Z a trap-symbol which will appear only in rules of the form $C \to Z$, $C \in V'_N \setminus \{Z\}$, and the set F will consist exactly of these rules, and the set M contains the following matrices:

$$(S' \to ES'),$$
$$(S' \to ESA_1). \tag{1}$$

(we generate a string E^nSA_1, $n \geqq 1$; if there is no string E^kS such that $E^nS \in Q(E^kS)$, that is there is no k such that $n = 2^{k+1} - 2$, then the derivation cannot be terminated: the rules in group 9 below cannot introduce the symbol A_{11} because the current string will not be in $Q(w)$ for some $w \in (V_N \cup \{E\})^*$),

$$(A_1 \to A_1X). \tag{2}$$

For each rule r: $AB \to CD$ in P' we introduce the following rules:

$$(A_1 \to A_2[r]\,X) \tag{3}$$

(starting from wA_1, $w \in Q(x)$ for some $x \in (V_N \cup \{E\})^*$, we produce a string $wA_2[r]\,X^k$, and we try to apply the rule $AB \to CD$ for rewriting the symbols occuring in the positions k, $k + 1$ of the string x, counting these positions from right to left),

$$(A_2 \to A_2, [r] \to [r], B \to B'', B \to B') \tag{4}$$

(in the presence of A_2 and $[r]$ we divide by 2 the number of occurrences of B),

$$(A_2 \to A_3, [r] \to [r], B \to Z, X \to X')$$

(there is no remainder),

$$(A_2 \to A_3, [r] \to [r], B \to B'', B \to Z, X \to X')$$

(there is a remainder),

$$(A_3 \to A_3, [r] \to [r], B' \to B),$$
$$(A_3 \to A_2, [r] \to [r], B' \to Z)$$

(the operation is re-iterated),

$$(A_2 \to A_4, [r] \to [r], B \to B', B \to Z, X \to X', X \to Z)$$

(we check whether the string x contains a symbol B in the position k; if the answer is negative, then the derivation is blocked),

$$(A_4 \to A_4, [r] \to [r], A \to A'', A \to A'),$$
$$(A_4 \to A_5, [r] \to [r], A \to Z, X' \to X), \tag{5}$$
$$(A_4 \to A_5, [r] \to [r], A \to A'', A \to Z, X' \to X),$$

$$(A_5 \to A_5, [r] \to [r], A' \to A),$$
$$(A_5 \to A_4, [r] \to [r], A' \to Z), \quad (5)'$$
$$(A_4 \to A_6, [r] \to [r], A \to A'', A \to Z, X' \to Z)$$

(we check whether the string x contains the symbol A in the position $k+1$; in the affirmative case we pass to a string $w'A_6[r]\,X^k$, $w' \in (V_N \cup \{E, A', A'', B', B''\})^*$),

$$(A_6 \to A_6, H' \to H) \quad \text{for} \quad H \in V_N \cup \{E\},$$
$$(A_6 \to A_6, H'' \to H) \quad \text{for} \quad H \in V_N \cup \{E\}, \quad (6)$$
$$(A_6 \to A_7Y, H_1' \to Z, H_1'' \to Z, \ldots, H_s' \to Z, H_s'' \to Z, X \to \lambda), \quad \text{where}$$
$$V_N \cup \{E\} = \{H_1, H_2, \ldots, H_s\}$$

(we return to a string $wA_7Y[r]\,X^{k-1}$, $w \in (V_N \cup \{E\})^*$),

$$(A_7 \to A_7, Y \to Y'Y'),$$
$$(A_7 \to A_8, Y \to Z, X \to \lambda),$$
$$(A_8 \to A_8, Y' \to Y), \quad (7)$$
$$(A_8 \to A_7, Y' \to Z),$$
$$(A_8 \to A_9, Y' \to Z, X \to Z),$$
$$(A_7 \to A_9, Y' \to Z, Y \to Y', Y \to Z, X \to Z, Y' \to Y)$$

(we pass from $wA_7Y[r]\,X^{k-1}$ to a string $wA_9Y^{2^{k-1}}[r]$),

$$(A_9 \to CCDA_9, Y \to \lambda, A \to \lambda, A \to \lambda, B \to \lambda, [r] \to [r]), \quad (8)$$
$$(A_9 \to A_1, Y \to Z, [r] \to \lambda)$$

(we simulate the use of the rule $r: AB \to CD$ by erasing 2^{k-1} occurrences of the symbol B and 2^k occurrences of the letter A and by introducing 2^{k-1} occurrences of the symbol D and 2^k occurrences of the letter C; the process can be iterated in the presence of A_1).

We consider also the following rules:

$$(A_9 \to A_{10}, \alpha, A \to \lambda) \quad \text{for} \quad A \to \alpha \in P', \alpha \in V_T \cup \{\lambda\},$$
$$(A_{10} \to A_{10}, H \to \lambda, H \to H') \quad \text{for} \quad H \in V_N \cup \{E\},$$
$$(A_{10} \to A_{11}, H_1 \to Z, H_2 \to Z, \ldots, H_s \to Z),$$
$$(A_{11} \to A_{11}, H' \to H) \quad \text{for} \quad H \in V_N \cup \{E\}, \quad (9)$$
$$(A_{11} \to A_9, H_1' \to Z, H_2' \to Z, \ldots, H_s' \to Z),$$
$$(A_9 \to \alpha, A \to \lambda, H_1 \to Z, H_2 \to Z, \ldots, H_s \to Z) \quad \text{for}$$
$$A \to \alpha \in P', \alpha \in V_T \cup \{\lambda\},$$

where $\{H_1, H_2, \ldots, H_s\} = V_N \cup \{E\}$ (we pass from a string $w \in Q(x)$, $x \in (V_N \cup \{E\})^*$ to a string x' obtained from x by replacing each $A \in V_N \cup \{E\}$ by $\alpha \in V_T \cup \{\lambda\}$ in the same way as in the final phase of the standard derivation according to the grammar G'; note that after using the rules $A_9 \to A_{10}\alpha$ and $A \to \lambda$ one checks whether the number of remaining symbols is a multiple of 2, that is A has indeed appeared in the rightmost position of the string x, and only in the affirmative case one can continue, and this ensures the correctness of the derivation). From these explanations it is easy to see that $L(G') = L(G'')$, and the proof is complete.

Corollary. i) *$\mathscr{L}$(M, CF $-$ λ, ac) is strictly included in $\mathscr{L}$(M, CF, ac).* ii) *Each language $L \in \mathscr{L}$(RE) is the homomorphic image of a language in $\mathscr{L}$(M, CF $-$ λ, ac).*

Proof. i) The assertion follows from the strict inclusions $\mathscr{L}$(M, CF $-$ λ, ac) $\subset \mathscr{L}$(CS) $\subset \mathscr{L}$(RE).

ii) Let $G = (V_N, V_T, M, S, F)$ be a matrix grammar with appearance checking and λ-rules such that $L(G) = L$ for some given language $L \in \mathscr{L}$(RE). We consider the new symbol c and replace each rule $X \to \lambda$ in G by $X \to c$. Thus we obtain the λ-free grammar $G' = (V_N, V_T \cup \{c\}, M', S, F')$ with the set M' of all matrices obtained by the above replacement and the set F' consisting of all occurrences of rules which correspond to the rule occurrences in F. Further we define the homomorphism h by

$$h(a) = a \quad \text{for} \quad a \in V_T \quad \text{and} \quad h(c) = \lambda.$$

Clearly, $h(L(G')) = L$, and the proof is finished.

So far we have examined the power of regulated rewriting compared with that of Chomsky grammars of various types. A further problem is the comparison of regulated grammars and L systems, particularly with ETOL systems. For the sake of completeness, we mention here the following result whose proof is omitted since we prove a stronger result in Theorem 1.5.11.

Theorem 1.2.6. *For $X \in$ {M, P, RC}, $\mathscr{L}$(ETOL) is strictly included in $\mathscr{L}(X$, CF $-$ λ, ac).*

Open problems

1.2.1. Which relation holds between $\mathscr{L}$(M, CF) and each of the families $\mathscr{L}$(M, CF $-$ λ, ac), $\mathscr{L}$(CS) and $\mathscr{L}$(RE)? Clearly, $\mathscr{L}$(M, CF) $\subseteq \mathscr{L}$(RE), but it is not known whether this inclusion is proper. On the other hand, if — as is expected — $\mathscr{L}$(RE) $\setminus \mathscr{L}$(M, CF) $\neq \emptyset$, then $\mathscr{L}$(M, CF $-$ λ, ac) $\setminus \mathscr{L}$(M, CF) $\neq \emptyset$ (hence also $\mathscr{L}$(CS) $\setminus \mathscr{L}$(M, CF) $\neq \emptyset$), since the family $\mathscr{L}$(M, CF) is closed under arbitrary homomorphisms and each language in $\mathscr{L}$(RE) is the homomorphic image of a language in $\mathscr{L}$(M, CF $-$ λ, ac) which would imply $\mathscr{L}$(RE) $\subseteq \mathscr{L}$(M, CF) if $\mathscr{L}$(M, CF $-$ λ, ac) $\subseteq \mathscr{L}$(M, CF).

1.2.2. Which of the following inclusions are proper: $\mathscr{L}$(RC, X) $\subseteq \mathscr{L}$(M, X) for $X \in$ {CF, CF $-$ λ}, $\mathscr{L}$(M, CF $-$ λ) $\subseteq \mathscr{L}$(M, CF), $\mathscr{L}$(M, CF $-$ λ) $\subseteq \mathscr{L}$(M, CF $-$ λ, ac)?

1.2.3. Find "concrete" languages in $\mathscr{L}$(CS) $\setminus \mathscr{L}$(M, CF $-$ λ, ac) or in $\mathscr{L}$(CS) $\setminus \mathscr{L}$(M, CF $-$ λ). Probably, all languages over one-letter alphabets in $\mathscr{L}$(M, CF) are regular; if confirmed, this conjecture would solve many of the previous open problems. Another possible canditate for a language in $\mathscr{L}$(CS) $\setminus \mathscr{L}$(M, CF) or even $\mathscr{L}$(CS) $\setminus \mathscr{L}$(M, CF $-$ λ, ac) is:

$$L = \{xcx : x \in D_1\}$$

where D_1 is the Dyck language over the alphabet $\{a, b\}$. The difficulty to ensure the equality of the two "halfs" of the strings in L makes this conjecture plausible.

1.2.4. Investigate the relations between $\mathcal{L}$(ETOL) and $\mathcal{L}$(M, CF) and $\mathcal{L}$(M, CF $-\lambda$), respectively. An incomparability result is expected in both cases (remember that $\{a^{2^n} : n \geqq 1\}$ is a DTOL language). In fact, the pairs $(\mathcal{F}, \mathcal{F}')$, $\mathcal{F} \in \{\mathcal{L}(\text{M, CF}), \mathcal{L}(\text{M, CF} - \lambda)\}$, $\mathcal{F}' \in \{\mathcal{L}(\text{EDTOL}), \mathcal{L}(\text{TOL}), \mathcal{L}(\text{DTOL})\}$ are also probably incomparable (each $\mathcal{F}'$ is incomparable with $\mathcal{L}$(CF)).

Exercises

1.2.1. Prove directly the equalities $\mathcal{L}(\text{P, CF, ac}) = \mathcal{L}(\text{RC, CF, ac})$ and $\mathcal{L}(\text{P, CF} - \lambda, \text{ac}) = \mathcal{L}(\text{RC, CF} - \lambda, \text{ac})$.

1.2.2. Prove directly the inclusion of $\mathcal{L}$(ETOL) in $\mathcal{L}$(M, CF $-\lambda$, ac).

1.2.3. Define a nonterminal-matrix grammar as a couple (G, M) where G is a context-free grammar and M is a finite set of sequences of the form $(A_1, A_2, \ldots, A_k)$, $k \geqq 1$, $A_i \in V_N$, $1 \leqq i \leqq k$ ("matrices" of nonterminals) and define the relation $\Rightarrow$ as follows: $x \Rightarrow y$ if there is a context-free derivation $x = x_0 \Rightarrow x_1 \Rightarrow \cdots \Rightarrow x_k = y$ in the grammar G and there is a matrix $(A_1, A_2, \ldots, A_k) \in M$ such that $x_i \Rightarrow x_{i+1}$ is obtained by an application of a rule with the left side A_{i+1}, $0 \leqq i \leqq k - 1$. Define also the appearance checking in the natural way. Prove that such grammars have the same generative power as the corresponding matrix grammars (see PĂUN (1976)).

1.2.4. Define a compound matrix grammar as a couple (G_1, G_2), $G_i = (V_N^{(i)}, V_T^{(i)}, M^{(i)}, S^{(i)}, F^{(i)})$, $i = 1, 2$, where G_1 is a usual matrix grammar, $V_T^{(1)} \subseteq V_N^{(2)} \cup V_T^{(2)}$, and $S^{(2)} = L(G_1)$. The language generated by (G_1, G_2) is defined as

$$L(G_1, G_2) = \{x \in (V_T^{(2)})^*\colon \text{there is a derivation } \alpha \overset{*}{\Rightarrow} x \text{ in } G_2,\ \alpha \in S^{(2)}\}.$$

Prove that this composition does not increase the generative capacity of CF, CF $-\lambda$, CS matrix grammars, but that it increases the power of regular and linear matrix grammars. (*Hint*: the language $\{a^n b^n c^n : n \geqq 1\}$ can be generated by a regular compound matrix grammar.)

1.3. Fundamental Properties

In this section we investigate the closure properties of the families of regulated languages (which do not equal families in the Chomsky hierarchy), as well as the decision problems for the associated grammars. As a prototype, we shall again take the matrix grammars.

First we present some auxiliary results.

In the previous 2-normal form we restricted the number of rules in a matrix. A similar restriction can be imposed on the form of the rules.

Definition 1.3.1. A context-free matrix grammar is said to be in the *binary form if* all rules $A \to \alpha$ in its matrices satisfy $|\alpha| \leqq 2$.

Lemma 1.3.1. *For each language in* $\mathcal{L}(\text{M}, X, \text{ac})$, $X \in \{\text{CF, CF} - \lambda\}$, *there is a matrix grammar in the binary form generating it.*

Proof. Let $G = (V_N, V_T, M, S, F)$ be a matrix grammar, and let X be a new symbol. For each rule $A \to \alpha$ which appears in F we consider the rule $A \to X$, and for each matrix m in M we consider all matrices m' obtained by replacing each rule $A \to \alpha$ which appears in F by a rule in the set $\{A \to \alpha, A \to X\}$. We denote the set of these matrices by M', and by F' the set of rules $A \to X$ appearing in M'. The grammar $G' = (V_N \cup \{X\}, V_T, M', S, F')$ is clearly equivalent to G.

Consider now a rule $A \to \alpha$, $\alpha = z_1 z_2 \ldots z_k$, $k \geqq 3$, $z_i \in V_G$, $1 \leqq i \leqq k$, which appears in a matrix of G'. We replace this rule by the sequence

$$A \to z_1 B,\ B \to z_2 B,\ \ldots,\ B \to z_{k-2} B,\ B \to z_{k-1} z_k$$

of rules, where B is a new symbol. By M'' we denote the set of matrices obtained by this procedure. Clearly,

$$G'' = (V_N \cup \{X, B\}, V_T, M'', S, F')$$

is equivalent to G' and hence to G, and it has the desired form.

Of course, if $F = \emptyset$ then $F' = \emptyset$, and therefore the above result holds also for matrix grammars without appearance checking.

Lemma 1.3.2. *Each of the families $\mathscr{L}(\mathrm{M}, \mathrm{CF} - \lambda)$, $\mathscr{L}(\mathrm{M}, \mathrm{CF} - \lambda, \mathrm{ac})$ is closed under restricted homomorphisms.*

Proof. Let $G = (V_N, V_T, M, S, F)$ be a λ-free matrix grammar (possibly with empty set F). Consider also the homomorphism $h : V_T^* \to U^*$ which is k-restricted with respect to $L(G)$. Note that $h(x) \neq \lambda$ for $x \in V_T^*$, $|x| \geqq k$.

Without loss of generality we assume that the grammar G is in the binary form. We construct the matrix grammar

$$G' = (V_N', U, M', S', F')$$

in the following way. We set

$$V_N' = \{[\alpha] : \alpha \in V_G^+, |\alpha| \leqq 2k\} \cup \{S'\},$$

$$N_1 = \{[\alpha] : \alpha \in V_G^+, k \leqq |\alpha| \leqq 2k - 1\},$$

$$N_2 = \{[\alpha] : \alpha \in V_G^+, k \leqq |\alpha| \leqq 2k\}.$$

Then we consider the following groups of rules:

1) $S' \to h(\alpha)$ for $\alpha \in L(G)$, $|\alpha| \leqq k$,

2) $S' \to [\alpha]$ for $[c] \in N_2$ and $S \overset{*}{\Rightarrow} \alpha$,

3) $[\alpha X \beta] \to [\alpha u \beta]$ for $[\alpha X \beta] \in N_1$ and $X \to u \in P(M)$,

4) $[\alpha] \to [\beta][\gamma]$ for $[\alpha] \in N_2$, $[\beta], [\gamma] \in N_1$ and $\alpha = \beta\gamma$,

5) $[\alpha] \to h(\alpha)$, $\alpha \in V_T^+$, $k \leqq |\alpha| \leqq 2k - 1$.

Let M_1 be the set of all one-rule matrices (r) with r in the above groups 1), 2), or 5), and let M_2 be the set of all matrices of the form

$$(r_1', r_1'', r_2', r_2'', \ldots, r_n', r_n'')$$

where $r_1', r_2', \ldots, r_n'$ are rules $[\alpha_i X_i \beta_i] \to [\alpha_i u_i \beta_i]$ of type 3) associated to rules $r_1, r_2, \ldots, r_n$ such that $(r_1, r_2, \ldots, r_n)$ is a matrix in M, $r_i : X_i \to u_i$, $1 \leqq i \leqq n$, and r_i'' is either a rule in group 4) or is omitted. Then we set

$$M' = M_1 \cup M_2 .$$

The set F' consists of all rules of type 3) obtained from a rule in F.

Then $L(G') = h(L(G))$ holds. Indeed, it is easy to see that for each derivation $S \stackrel{*}{\Rightarrow} x$ according to G the matrices containing rules of types 1) to 4) can construct a derivation $S \stackrel{*}{\Rightarrow} \alpha$ for some $\alpha = [\alpha_1][\alpha_2] \ldots [\alpha_p]$ such that $x = \alpha_1 \alpha_2 \ldots \alpha_p$, $k \leqq |\alpha_i| \leqq 2k - 1$, $1 \leqq i \leqq p$. If x is a terminal string, then the rules of type 5) will rewrite α into $h(x)$. Conversely, each derivation in G' corresponds to a derivation according to G, the only difference being the occurrence of the brackets [,]. Clearly, G' is λ-free. In conclusion $h(L(G)) \in \mathcal{L}(M, \mathrm{CF} - \lambda, \mathrm{ac})$. If $F = \emptyset$, then also $F' = \emptyset$. This completes the proof.

A similar proof can show that also the family $\mathcal{L}(\mathrm{RC}, \mathrm{CF} - \lambda)$ is closed under restricted homomorphisms, the only point being a suitable definition of the permitting contexts (the idea used to prove the assertion in the proof of Theorem 1.2.3 can be used). Therefore we state

Lemma 1.3.3. *The family $\mathcal{L}(\mathrm{RC}, \mathrm{CF} - \lambda)$ is closed under restricted homomorphisms.*

Lemma 1.3.4. *Each of the families $\mathcal{L}(\mathrm{M}, X)$, $\mathcal{L}(\mathrm{RC}, X)$, $X \in \{\mathrm{CF}, \mathrm{CF} - \lambda\}$, and $\mathcal{L}(\mathrm{M}, \mathrm{CF} - \lambda, \mathrm{ac})$ is closed under union, concatenation, mirror image, and substitution by λ-free context-free languages. The families $\mathcal{L}(\mathrm{M}, \mathrm{CF})$ and $\mathcal{L}(\mathrm{RC}, \mathrm{CF})$ are closed under substitution by arbitrary context-free languages, whereas $\mathcal{L}(\mathrm{M}, \mathrm{CF} - \lambda, \mathrm{ac})$ is not closed with respect to arbitrary homomorphisms.*

Proof. Let $G_i = (V_N^{(i)}, V_T^{(i)}, M^{(i)}, S^{(i)}, F^{(i)})$, $i = 1, 2$, be two matrix grammar. We assume $V_N^{(1)} \cap V_N^{(2)} = \emptyset$ and construct the matrix grammars

$$G_3 = (V_N^{(1)} \cup V_N^{(2)} \cup \{S\}, V_T^{(1)} \cup V_T^{(2)},$$
$$M^{(1)} \cup M^{(2)} \cup \{(S \to S^{(1)}), (S \to S^{(2)})\}, S, F^{(1)} \cup F^{(2)}),$$

$$G_4 = (V_N^{(1)} \cup V_N^{(2)} \cup \{S\}, V_T^{(1)} \cup V_T^{(2)}, M^{(1)} \cup M^{(2)} \cup \{(S \to S^{(1)}S^{(2)})\},$$
$$S, F^{(1)} \cup F^{(2)}).$$

Clearly, we obtain

$$L(G_3) = L(G_1) \cup L(G_2) \quad \text{and} \quad L(G_4) = L(G_1)\, L(G_2).$$

Also by a standard proof we obtain the closure of $\mathcal{L}(\mathrm{RC}, \mathrm{CF})$ and $\mathcal{L}(\mathrm{RC}, \mathrm{CF} - \lambda)$ under union and concatenation and the closure of all families in the lemma with respect to mirror image.

Now let us consider a grammar $G = (V_N, V_T, M, S, F)$ and a substitution $s : V_T^* \to 2^{U^*}$ with $s(a) \in \mathcal{L}(\mathrm{CF})$ for each $a \in V_T$. Let $G_a = (V_N^a, V_T^a, P^a, S^a)$ be a context-free grammar for $s(a)$, $a \in V_T$. We assume (without loss of generality) that these grammars are λ-free and have pairwise disjoint nonterminal alphabets which are also disjoint with V_N.

Let M_S be the set of matrices obtained by replacing each occurrence of each $a \in V_T$ by S_a in M, and let F_S be the set of occurrences of rules in M_S which correspond to rules in

F. Then we construct the matrix grammar

$$G' = \left(V_N \cup \bigcup_{a \in V_T} V_N^a, U, M_S \cup \bigcup_{a \in V_T} M_a, S, F_S\right)$$

where

$$M_a = \{(A \to x) : A \to x \in P^a\}.$$

Clearly, we get $L(G') = L(G)$.

A similar construction proves the closure of $\mathscr{L}(\mathrm{RC}, \mathrm{CF})$, $\mathscr{L}(\mathrm{RC}, \mathrm{CF} - \lambda)$ under substitutions with context-free languages. (Of course, for families $\mathscr{L}(X, \mathrm{CF} - \lambda)$ we take λ-free context-free languages.) The family $\mathscr{L}(\mathrm{M}, \mathrm{CF} - \lambda, \mathrm{ac})$ is not closed under arbitrary homomorphisms since otherwise we get $\mathscr{L}(\mathrm{RE}) = \mathscr{L}(\mathrm{M}, \mathrm{CF} - \lambda, \mathrm{ac})$ by the Corollary of Theorem 1.2.5 and this contradicts Theorem 1.2.4 v).

Lemma 1.3.5. *The families* $\mathscr{L}(\mathrm{M}, X)$, $\mathscr{L}(\mathrm{RC}, X)$, $X \in \{\mathrm{CF}, \mathrm{CF} - \lambda\}$, *and* $\mathscr{L}(\mathrm{M}, \mathrm{CF} - \lambda, \mathrm{ac})$ *are closed under intersections by regular sets.*

Proof. Again, we shall prove the assertion only for $\mathscr{L}(\mathrm{M}, \mathrm{CF} - \lambda, \mathrm{ac})$, the modifications needed for the other families are straightforward.

Let $G = (V_N, V_T, M, S, F)$ be a λ-free matrix grammar in binary form. (According to the proof of Lemma 1.3.2, we can assume that the rules in F are of the form $C \to X$ where X is a trap symbol.) Let L be a regular language recognized by the (deterministic) finite automaton $A = (K, V_T, s_0, f, H)$.

Then we set

$$V_N' = \{(s, z, s') : s, s' \in K, z \in V_G\}.$$

For each rule r in M we construct the set $A(r)$ in the following way:

1) If $r: X \to z_1z_2$ with $z_1, z_2 \in V_G$, then

$$A(r) = \{(s, X, s') \to (s, z_1 s'')(s'', z_2, s') : s, s', s'' \in K\}.$$

2) If $r: X \to z$ with $z \in V_G$, then

$$A(r) = \{(s, X, s') \to (s, z, s') : s, s' \in K\}.$$

Let M_1 be the set of all matrices obtained from the matrices in M by replacing each rule r which does not occur in F by some rule of $A(r)$ and by replacing each rule r which appears in F by the sequence of all rules of $A(r)$. Further we set

$$M_2 = \left\{\left((s, a, s') \to a\right) : s' = f(s, a), s, s' \in K, a \in V_T\right\}.$$

Now, for $s \in H$, we define the matrix grammar

$$G_s = \left(V_N', V_T, M_1 \cup M_2, (s_0, S, s), F'\right)$$

where

$$F' = \{(s_1, C, s_2) \to (s_1, D, s_2) : C \to D \text{ appears in } F, s_1, s_2 \in K\}.$$

It is easy to see that

$$L(G) \cap L = \bigcup_{s \in H} L(G_s).$$

(The rules in the sets $A(r)$ associated to rules in F cannot be effectively used because the nonterminal on the right-hand side of r is a trap symbol.) As the family $\mathscr{L}(\mathrm{M}, \mathrm{CF} - \lambda, \mathrm{ac})$ is closed under union, it follows that this family is closed under intersections by regular languages.

Theorem 1.3.1. *The families* $\mathscr{L}(\mathrm{M}, \mathrm{CF})$ *and* $\mathscr{L}(\mathrm{RC}, \mathrm{CF})$ *are full semi-AFLs, and* $\mathscr{L}(\mathrm{M}, \mathrm{CF} - \lambda)$ *and* $\mathscr{L}(\mathrm{RC}, \mathrm{CF} - \lambda)$ *are semi-AFLs.*

Proof. From the previous lemmas if follows that all these families are closed under union, intersections with regular sets, substitutions by λ-free regular sets and restricted homomorphisms. According to Theorem 0.1.2, they are also closed under inverse homomorphisms, they are therefore semi-AFLs. As $\mathscr{L}(\mathrm{M}, \mathrm{CF})$ and $\mathscr{L}(\mathrm{RC}, \mathrm{CF})$ are closed under arbitrary homomorphisms, these families are full semi-AFLs.

Corollary. *The above families are closed under λ-free gsm mappings, inverse gsm mappings,* and *right and left derivatives. The families* $\mathscr{L}(\mathrm{M}, \mathrm{CF})$ *and* $\mathscr{L}(\mathrm{RC}, \mathrm{CF})$ *are also closed with respect to arbitrary gsm mappings and right and left quotients by regular sets.*

Lemma 1.3.6. *The family* $\mathscr{L}(\mathrm{M}, \mathrm{CF} - \lambda, \mathrm{ac})$ *is closed under λ-free substitutions.*

Proof. Let $G = (V_N, V_T, M, S, F)$ be a λ-free context-free matrix grammar, and let $s: V_T^* \to 2^{U^*}$ be a substitution such that $s(a) \in \mathscr{L}(\mathrm{M}, \mathrm{CF} - \lambda, \mathrm{ac})$ for each $a \in V_T$. Further let $G_a = (V_N^a, V_T^a, M^a, S^a, F^a)$ be a grammar such that $s(a) = L(G_a)$, $a \in V_T$. Again we assume that $V_N^a \cap V_N^b = \emptyset$ for $a, b \in V_T$, $a \neq b$ and that $V_N \cap V_N^a = \emptyset$ for $a \in V_T$. Then we set

$$V_N' = V_N \cup \bigcup_{a \in V_T} V_N^a, \quad V_T' = \{a' : a \in V_T\},$$

and let Z be a new symbol. We consider the matrix grammar

$$G' = \left(V_N' \cup V_T' \cup \{Z\}, U, M' \cup M'' \cup \bigcup_{a \in V_T} M^a, S, F'\right)$$

where M' is obtained from M by replacing each symbol $a \in V_T$ by a' and

$$M'' = \{(X_1 \to Z, X_2 \to Z, \ldots, X_r \to Z, a' \to S^a) : \{X_1, X_2, \ldots, X_r\} = V_N^a,$$
$$a \in V_T\},$$

and the set F' contains all occurrences of rules in M' corresponding to rules in M which appear in F, all rules in F^a for all $a \in V_T$, and all occurrences of rules of the form $X \to Z$, $X \in V_N'$. The equality $L(G') = s(L(G))$ is easy to prove. Indeed, the matrices of M' simulate the derivations in the grammar G (with appearance checking), at some stage of this derivation, a symbol a' can be replaced by S_a and a derivation in G_a can be performed. If this derivation is not finished, then no further a' can be replaced by S_a. Therefore the derivations cannot be "shuffled".

Theorem 1.3.2. *The family* $\mathscr{L}(\mathrm{M}, \mathrm{CF} - \lambda, \mathrm{ac})$ *is a substitution closed (non-full) AFL.*

Proof. The proof of Theorem 1.3.1 remains valid for $\mathscr{L}(\mathrm{M}, \mathrm{CF} - \lambda, \mathrm{ac})$. Therefore this family is a semi-AFL closed under substitution. We have only to prove the closure under the $+$-operator.

Let $L \subseteq V^*$ be a language in $\mathscr{L}(\mathrm{M}, \mathrm{CF} - \lambda, \mathrm{ac})$. Then we consider

$$L_0 = \{a^n : n \geqq 1\}$$

which is in $\mathscr{L}(\mathrm{M}, \mathrm{CF} - \lambda, \mathrm{ac})$, and we use the λ-free substitution $s\colon \{a\}^* \to 2^{V^*}$ defined by $s(a) = L \setminus \{\lambda\}$. Clearly,

$$s(L_0) \cup (\{\lambda\} \cap L) = L^+ .$$

Therefore the family $\mathscr{L}(\mathrm{M}, \mathrm{CF} - \lambda, \mathrm{ac})$ is also closed under the $+$-operator.

The nonclosure under arbitrary homomorphisms has been already pointed out (Lemma 1.3.4).

Corollary. *The family* $\mathscr{L}(\mathrm{M}, \mathrm{CF} - \lambda, \mathrm{ac})$ *is closed under λ-free gsm mappings, inverse gsm mappings, right and left derivatives.*

Table 1.3.1.

Operation ↓ \ Family →	$\mathscr{L}(\mathrm{RC}, \mathrm{CF} - \lambda)$	$\mathscr{L}(\mathrm{RC}, \mathrm{CF})$	$\mathscr{L}(\mathrm{M}, \mathrm{CF} - \lambda)$	$\mathscr{L}(\mathrm{M}, \mathrm{CF})$	$\mathscr{L}(\mathrm{M}, \mathrm{CF} - \lambda, \mathrm{ac})$
Union	+	+	+	+	+
Concatenation	+	+	+	+	+
+, *	?	?	?	?	+
Intersection	?	?	?	?	?
Complementation	?	?	?	?	?
Intersection by regular sets	+	+	+	+	+
Mirror image	+	+	+	+	+
Substitution	?	?	?	?	—
λ-free substitution	?	?	?	?	+
Substitution by λ-free context-free sets	+	+	+	+	+
Substitution by context-free languages	?	+	?	+	+
Homomorphisms	?	+	?	+	—
λ-free homomorphisms	+	+	+	+	+
Restricted homomorphisms	+	+	+	+	+
gsm mappings	?	+	?	+	—
λ-free gsm mappings	+	+	+	+	+
Inverse gsm mappings	+	+	+	+	+
Right/left quotient by regular sets	?	+	?	+	?
Right/left derivative	+	+	+	+	+
Permutation	?	?	+	+	+
Quasiintersection	?	?	+	+	+

The closure properties of matrix families obtained above are summarized in Table 1.3.1 (including the closure under permutation and quasiintersection, for which the reader is referred to Exercises 1.3.3 and 1.3.4), where + stands for closure, — for nonclosure, and ? for an open problem. We also add (without proof) the closure properties of the families $\mathscr{L}(\mathrm{RC}, \mathrm{CF} - \lambda)$ and $\mathscr{L}(\mathrm{RC}, \mathrm{CF})$.

The closure properties can be used in order to obtain a more accurate and stronger normal form for context-free matrix grammars than those in Definitions 1.2.1 and 1.3.1.

Definition 1.3.2. A matrix grammar $G = (V_N, V_T, M, S, F)$ is said to be in *accurate normal form* if

i) $V_N = V_N^{(1)} \cup V_N^{(2)} \cup \{S, Z\}$, $V_N^{(1)} \cap V_N^{(2)} = \emptyset$, $S, Z \notin V_N^{(1)} \cup V_N^{(2)}$,

ii) M contains matrices of the following forms:

a) $(S \to \alpha)$, $\alpha \in L(G)$, $\alpha \in V_T \cup \{\lambda\}$,

b) $(S \to AX)$, $A \in V_N^{(1)}$, $X \in V_N^{(2)}$,

c) $(A \to x, X \to Y)$, $A \in V_N^{(1)}$, $x \in (V_N^{(1)} \cup V_T)^* \cup \{Z\}$, $|x| \leqq 2$, $X, Y \in V_N^{(2)}$,

d) $(A \to x, X \to a)$, $A \in V_N^{(1)}$, $x \in V_T^*$, $|x| \leqq 2$, $X \in V_N^{(2)}$, $a \in V_T$,

iii) F consists of occurrences of all rules of the form $A \to Z$ in matrices of type c).

Lemmma 1.3.7. *For each language $L \in \mathcal{L}(\mathrm{M, CF} - \lambda, \mathrm{ac})$ there is a λ-free matrix grammar in the accurate normal form generating L.*

Proof. Let $L_a = d_a^r(L)$ for $a \in V_T$. Then $L_a \in \mathcal{L}(\mathrm{M, CF} - \lambda, \mathrm{ac})$ holds and we have

$$L = \bigcup_{a \in V_T} L_a\{a\} \cup (\{\lambda\} \cap L).$$

For each language $L_a \setminus \{\lambda\}$ let $G_a = (V_N^a, V_T^a, M^a, S^a, F^a)$ be a matrix grammar in the binary form (obtained as in the proof of Lemma 1.3.1 and therefore with the rules used in the appearance checking mode of the form $A \to Z$ where Z is a trap symbol) generating it. We assume that the alphabets $V_N^a \setminus \{Z\}$ are pairwise disjoint and that Z belongs to all V_N^a, and we follow the proof of Lemma 1.2.3 in order to obtain 2-normal matrices starting from matrices in the set

$$M = \bigcup_{a \in V_T} M^a$$

the only difference being that we also consider matrices $(S \to \alpha)$ for each $\alpha \in L(G)$, $|\alpha| \leqq 1$, and that the final matrices (of type 4) in the proof of Lemma 1.2.3) are replaced by

$$\left(A \to x, (i, k_i) \to a\right)'$$

where $A \to x$ is a terminal rule appearing on the position k_i in the ith matrix of M (i.e., $A \to x$ is the last rule of this matrix).

The rigorous writing down of this construction is left to the reader.

Of course, a similar accurate normal form and a result similar to the above lemma can be formulated for matrix grammars without appearance checking (for languages in $\mathcal{L}(\mathrm{M, CF})$ the rules $A \to x$ in matrices of type c) in Definition 1.3.2 can have $x = \lambda$).

We shall consider now the decision questions for grammars corresponding to the families $\mathcal{L}(\mathrm{M}, X)$, $X \in \{\mathrm{CF}, \mathrm{CF} - \lambda\}$, and $\mathcal{L}(\mathrm{M, CF} - \lambda, \mathrm{ac})$ (for the other classes of grammars, as the equivalence with grammars in the Chomsky hierarchy is effective, the answers are identical to those for the corresponding Chomsky grammars).

Clearly, all the decision questions which have negative answers for context-free grammars also have negative answers for matrix grammars. However, there are certain problems which can be algorithmically decided for context-free grammars, but which are undecidable for matrix grammars.

Theorem 1.3.3. *The emptiness and the finiteness problems are undecidable for λ-free context-free matrix grammars with appearance checking.*

Proof. Let G be an arbitrary type-0 grammar, and let $G' = (V_N, V_T, M, S, F)$ be a context-free matrix grammar such that $L(G) = L(G')$ (Theorem 1.2.5). Replace each rule $A \to \lambda$ in G' by $A \to c$ where c is a new symbol, and let $G'' = (V_N, V_T \cup \{c\}, M', S, F')$ be the obtained grammar. Then $L(G'') \in \mathcal{L}(\mathrm{M}, \mathrm{CF} - \lambda, \mathrm{ac})$, and this language is non-empty if and only if the language $L(G') = L(G)$ is non-empty. The passing from G to G' is algorithmic. As the emptiness problem for type-0 grammars is undecidable, the problem is also undecidable for (λ-free) matrix grammars with appearance checking.

Now we add to G'' two matrices

$$(S' \to aS'),\ (S' \to S)$$

for some $a \in V_T$. Let M'' be the new set of matrices and consider the matrix grammar

$$G''' = (V_N \cup \{S'\}, V_T \cup \{c\}, M'', S', F').$$

Clearly, $L(G''') = \{a^n : n \geqq 0\}\ L(G'')$. Therefore $L(G''')$ is infinite if and only if $L(G'')$ is non-empty. The undecidability of the emptiness problem now implies the undecidability of the finiteness problem.

If the appearance checking feature is removed, the answer to the emptiness problem is again similar to that for context-free grammars: decidability. To prove that, we need the notion of a vector addition system and a powerful result of Kosaraju (1982).

Definition 1.3.3. An n-dimensional *vector addition system* is a couple (x_0, V) where $x_0 \in \mathbb{N}^n$ (the initial point) and V is a finite subset of $\mathbb{Z}^n$ ($\mathbb{Z}$ is the set of integers). A point $y \in \mathbb{N}^n$ is reachable within this vector addition system iff there are vectors $v_1, v_2, \ldots, v_t$, $t \geqq 1$, in V such that

a) $$x_0 + \sum_{i=1}^{j} v_i \in \mathbb{N}^n \quad \text{for} \quad 1 \leqq j \leqq t,$$

b) $$x_0 + \sum_{i=1}^{t} v_i = y.$$

Kosaraju (1982) proved that the reachability problem in vector addition systems is decidable. (There is an algorithm which decides whether an arbitrary point $y \in \mathbb{N}^n$ is reachable in an arbitrarily given vector addition system (x_0, V).)

Theorem 1.3.4. *The emptiness problem is decidable for arbitrary context-free matrix grammars without appearance checking.*

Proof. Let $G = (V_N, V_T, M, S)$ be a matrix grammar in the accurate normal form, hence with matrices with one or two rules, the rules of matrices $(A \to x, X \to y)$ having nonterminals A and X in disjoint alphabets ($A \in V_N^{(1)}, X \in V_N^{(2)}, V_N = V_N^{(1)} \cup V_N^{(2)} \cup \{S\}$). Let

$$V_N = \{A_1, A_2, \ldots, A_n\}.$$

For a matrix m: $(S \to x)$ in M, we set

$$v(m) = (|x|_{A_1} - |S|_{A_1}, |x|_{A_2} - |S|_{A_2}, \ldots, |x|_{A_n} - |S|_{A_n}),$$

and for a matrix m: $(A \to x, X \to y)$, we define the vector

$$v(m) = (|xy|_{A_1} - |AX|_{A_1}, |xy|_{A_2} - |AX|_{A_2}, \ldots, |xy|_{A_n} - |AX|_{A_n}).$$

Further we set

$$x_0 = (|S|_{A_1}, |S|_{A_2}, \ldots, |S|_{A_n}).$$

Then the language $L(G)$ is non-empty if and only if the vector $y = (0, 0, \ldots, 0)$ is reachable in the vector addition system (x_0, V) where

$$V = \{v(m) : m \in M\}.$$

Using the result of KOSARAJU (1982) our theorem follows.

Remark. Note that this theorem does not entail that $\mathcal{L}$(M, CF) being strictly included in $\mathcal{L}$(RE) because we can have the equality of both families without an effective (algorithmic) passing from a type-0 grammar to a matrix grammar. Thus the above theorem does not contradict the undecidability of the emptiness problem for type-0 grammars.

Clearly, the membership problem is decidable for λ-free context-free matrix grammars with appearance checking since the proof of the inclusion $\mathcal{L}(\text{M, CF} - \lambda, \text{ac}) \subseteq \mathcal{L}(\text{CS})$ is constructive. Moreover, we can say something on the complexity of this membership problem. In order to do this it is necessary to introduce some notions of complexity theory. We give here only the intuitive informal concepts and refer to GAREY and JOHNSON (1979) for the mathematically exact notions. Our intuitive concept of an algorithm given in Section 0.3 is a deterministic one since the next instruction is uniquely determined. If it is taken from a set of next instructions we get nondeterministic algorithms. Let P and NP be the sets of problems which can be solved in polynomial time by a deterministic and nondeterministic algorithm, respectively. A problem is called *NP-complete* if it is in NP and its being in P implies $P = NP$.

Theorem 1.3.5. *The membership problem for λ-free context-free matrix grammars with appearance checking is NP-complete.*

We omit the proof since it requires more knowledge on complexity.

On matrix grammars one can raise one specific problem, that of context free-ness.

Theorem 1.3.6. *It is undecidable whether a λ-free matrix grammar without appearance checking generates a context-free language.*

Proof. Let $L_1 \subseteq V_1^*$ be an arbitrary language in $\mathcal{L}$(CF), and let $L_2 \subseteq V_2^*$ be a given language in $\mathcal{L}(\text{M, CF} - \lambda) \setminus \mathcal{L}(\text{CF})$, and let $V_1 \cap V_2 = \emptyset$. Then we consider the language

$$L_3 = L_1 V_2^* \cup V_1^* L_2.$$

This language is in $\mathcal{L}(\text{M, CF} - \lambda)$ because this family is closed under concatenation and union. If $L_1 = V_1^*$, then $L_3 = V_1^* V_2^*$, and this is a regular language. Now suppose that $L_1 \neq V_1^*$ and let w be a string in $V_1^* \setminus L_1$. Then $L_3 \cap \{w\} V_2^* = \{w\} L_2$. This language is not context-free, and therefore also L_3 is not context-free. In conclusion, L_3 is context-free if and only if $L_1 = V_1^*$. This problem is undecidable for arbitrary context-free grammars. Hence the context-freeness for matrix grammars is also undecidable. (Note that the proofs of the closure properties of $\mathcal{L}(\text{M, CF} - \lambda)$ are constructive.)

The decision results pointed out in this section are summarized in Table 1.3.2 (again

Table 1.3.2.

Question ↓ / Family →	$\mathscr{L}$(RC, CF — λ)	$\mathscr{L}$(RC, CF)	$\mathscr{L}$(M, CF — λ)	$\mathscr{L}$(M, CF)	$\mathscr{L}$(M, CF — λ, ac)
Membership	+	?	+	?	+
Equivalence	—	—	—	—	—
Inclusion	—	—	—	—	—
Emptiness	+	+	+	+	—
Finiteness	?	?	?	?	—
Is $L(G)$ regular?	—	—	—	—	—
Is $L(G)$ context-free?	—	—	—	—	—
Is $L(G_1) \cap L(G_2)$ empty?	—	—	—	—	—
Is $L(G_1) \cap L(G_2)$ finite?	—	—	—	—	—
Is $L(G_1) \cap L(G_2)$ regular?	—	—	—	—	—
Is $L(G_1) \cap L(G_2)$ context-free?	—	—	—	—	—
Is $V^* \setminus L(G)$ empty?	—	—	—	—	—
Is $V^* \setminus L(G)$ finite?	—	—	—	—	—
Is $V^* \setminus L(G)$ regular?	—	—	—	—	—
Is $V^* \setminus L(G)$ context-free?	—	—	—	—	—

+ indicates a decidable question for the grammars associated to the family in the head of the corresponding column, — indicates an undecidable problem, and ? shows an open problem).

Open problems

1.3.1. Are the semi-AFLs $\mathscr{L}(\mathrm{M}, \mathrm{CF} - \lambda)$, $\mathscr{L}(\mathrm{RC}, \mathrm{CF} - \lambda)$ full? (Are they closed under arbitrary homomorphisms?) What about the closure of the families $\mathscr{L}(X, Y)$, $X \in \{\mathrm{M}, \mathrm{RC}\}$, $Y \in \{\mathrm{CF}, \mathrm{CF} - \lambda\}$, under intersection, complementation, Kleene-+, and (λ-free) substitutions?

Clearly, if $\mathscr{L}(\mathrm{M}, \mathrm{CF})$ were closed under intersection, then $\mathscr{L}(\mathrm{M}, \mathrm{CF}) = \mathscr{L}(\mathrm{RE})$, because $\mathscr{L}(\mathrm{CF}) \subseteq \mathscr{L}(\mathrm{M}, \mathrm{CF})$ and each language in $\mathscr{L}(\mathrm{RE})$ is the homomorphic image of the intersection of two context-free languages. As $\mathscr{L}(\mathrm{M}, \mathrm{CF})$ is probably strictly included in $\mathscr{L}(\mathrm{RE})$ (Theorem 1.3.4 supports such a conjecture), it is plausible that $\mathscr{L}(\mathrm{M}, \mathrm{CF})$ is not closed under intersection, moreover, that there are context-free languages L_1, L_2 such that $L_1 \cap L_2 \notin \mathscr{L}(\mathrm{M}, \mathrm{CF})$.

On the other hand, the closure under (λ-free) substitution implies the closure under Kleene-+, but the standard proofs for the closure of $\mathscr{L}(\mathrm{CF})$ under substitution and + do not work in the matrix (or the random context) case, because the matrices (and the context conditions) can be illegally shuffled.

1.3.2. Are the families $\mathscr{L}(\mathrm{RC}, X)$, $X \in \{\mathrm{CF}, \mathrm{CF} - \lambda\}$, closed under permutation? We feel that the answer is negative. If this conjecture were to be confirmed, then the inclusion $\mathscr{L}(\mathrm{RC}, X) \subseteq \mathscr{L}(\mathrm{M}, X)$, $X \in \{\mathrm{CF}, \mathrm{CF} - \lambda\}$, were to be proved to be proper, because $\mathscr{L}(\mathrm{M}, X)$ is closed under permutation (Exercise 1.3.3).

1.3.3. What about the membership problem for arbitrary context-free matrix grammars without appearance checking and what about the finiteness problem for context-free (with or without λ-rules) matrix grammars without appearance checking?

Exercises

1.3.1. Prove that for each random context language $L \in \mathcal{L}(\text{RC}, \text{CF} - \lambda, \text{ac})$ there is a random context grammar $G = (V_N, V_T, P, S)$ such that the rules in P have the form $(A \to x, Q, R)$, $|x| \leqq 2$, card $(Q) \leqq 1$, card $(\text{R}) \leqq 1$.

1.3.2. Prove that there are linear languages which cannot be generated by context-free programmed grammars containing only rules $(r: A \to x, \sigma(r), \varphi(r))$ with card $(\sigma(r)) \leqq 1$, card $(\varphi(r)) \leqq 1$. (*Hint:* take the language $\{a^n b^m a^n : n, m \geqq 1\}$.) Prove that each language in $\mathcal{L}(\text{P}, \text{CF} - \lambda, \text{ac})$ can be generated by a programmed grammar with rules $(r: A \to x, \sigma(r), \varphi(r))$ with card $(\sigma(r)) \leqq 2$, card $(\varphi(r)) \leqq 2$.

1.3.3. Prove that all families $\mathcal{L}(\text{M}, \text{CF} - \lambda, \text{ac})$, $\mathcal{L}(\text{M}, X)$ for $X \in \{\text{CF}, \text{CF} - \lambda\}$ are closed under the operation Perm.

1.3.4. For two languages L_1 and L_2 define the operation

$$\text{Qi}(L_1, L_2) = L_1 \cap \text{Perm}\,(L_2)$$

(quasiintersection). Prove that the families $\mathcal{L}(\text{M}, X)$, $X \in \{\text{CF}, \text{CF} - \lambda\}$, $\mathcal{L}(\text{M}, \text{CF} - \lambda, \text{ac})$ are closed under this operation.

1.3.5. Prove that the family $\mathcal{L}_1(\text{M}, \text{CF} - \lambda, \text{ac})$ of languages $L \subseteq \{a\}^*$ in $\mathcal{L}(\text{M}, \text{CF} - \lambda, \text{ac})$ is closed under intersection.

1.3.6. Prove that there are languages in $\mathcal{L}(\text{M}, \text{CF} - \lambda)$ which cannot be represented as a finite intersection of context-free languages. (Otherwise it would follow that each one-letter language in $\mathcal{L}(\text{M}, \text{CF} - \lambda)$ is regular. *Hint*: take the language

$$L = \{xcx : x \in \{a, b\}^*\},$$

which is in $\mathcal{L}(\text{M}, \text{CF} - \lambda)$, and suppose that it can be written as the intersection of k context-free languages. Then translate this language by suitable operations to

$$L' = \{a_1^{i_1} a_2^{i_2} \dots a_{k+1}^{i_{k+1}} a_1^{i_1} a_2^{i_2} \dots a_{k+1}^{i_{k+1}} : i_j \geqq 0,\ 1 \leqq j \leqq k + 1\}$$

for which Liu and Weiner (1973) proved that it cannot be represented as the intersection of k context-free languages.

1.3.7. Define the circular closure of a language L by $c(L) = \{w_2 w_1 : w_1 w_2 \in L\}$. Prove that the family $L(\text{M}, \text{CF} - \lambda, \text{ac})$ is closed under this operation.

1.4. Leftmost Derivations

In the previous matrix, programmed, and random context grammars, there is no restriction on which a nonterminal rule has to be applied; any nonterminal which can be rewritten may be rewritten. A natural idea is to reduce this nondeterminism and a simple restriction is to rewrite extreme nonterminals, thus obtaining leftmost or rightmost derivations. As it makes no difference in what concerns the generative capacity (and thus other properties), we shall discuss here only leftmost derivations. Moreover, we shall take into consideration only context-free grammars.

Roughly speaking, three types of leftmost derivations can be considered:

I) at each step of a derivation the leftmost occurrence of a nonterminal has to be rewritten,

II) at each step of a derivation the leftmost occurrence of a nonterminal which can be rewritten (note that in regulated grammars only certain nonterminal occurrences can be rewritten in a given stage of a derivation) has to be rewritten,

III) to use each rule in a leftmost manner, i.e. the leftmost appearance of its left-hand member is rewritten.

Let us consider rigorously these three possibilities.

Definition 1.4.1. Let G be a matrix, programmed, or random context grammar (with context-free rules). A derivation in G is called *leftmost of type* 1 if each rule used in this derivation either rewrites the leftmost nonterminal occurrence in the current string, or (this is important in the matrix and programmed case for appearance checking mode of derivation) it cannot be applied to this leftmost nonterminal occurrence and then we say that the rule is not applicable to the whole current string.

By $L_{\text{left-1}}(G)$ we denote the language generated by G in this way, and we denote the families of languages generated in this way by $\mathscr{L}(X, Y, \text{left-1})$, $\mathscr{L}(X, Y, \text{ac}, \text{left-1})$ where $X \in \{\text{M}, \text{P}, \text{RC}\}$, $Y \in \{\text{CF}, \text{CF} - \lambda\}$.

In order to investigate these families we need the following result by Matthews (1964) concerning leftmost type-0 grammars. We omit its proof which can be found in Matthews (1964) and Baker (1974).

Lemma 1.4.1. *Let* $G = (V_N, V_T, P, S)$ *be a type-0 grammar such that the rules in* P *have the form* $\alpha \to \beta$, $\alpha \in V_N^+$. *Then the language generated by* G *in a leftmost manner* (i.e. a string x_1Ax_2, $x_1 \in V_T^*$, $A \in V_N$, $x_2 \in V_G^*$, can be rewritten only by rules $\alpha \to \beta$ with $\alpha \in \text{Pref}\,(Ax_2)$) *is context-free.*

Similar results are true also for regulated rewriting grammars with leftmost derivation of type 1.

Lemma 1.4.2. $\mathscr{L}(\text{M}, \text{CF}, \text{ac}, \text{left-1}) \subseteq \mathscr{L}(\text{CF})$.

Proof. Let $G = (V_N, V_T, M, S, F)$ be a matrix grammar with leftmost derivation of type 1. Let

$$M = \{m_1, m_2, \ldots, m_n\},$$

$$m_i\colon (r_{i,1}, r_{i,2}, \ldots, r_{i,k_i}),\ 1 \leqq i \leqq n,$$

$$r_{i,j}\colon A_{i,j} \to x_{i,j},\ 1 \leqq i \leqq n,\ 1 \leqq j \leqq k_i.$$

We construct a Chomsky grammar $G' = (V_N', V_T, P, S_0)$ with

$$V_N' = V_N \cup \{a' : a \in V_T\} \cup \{S_0, C\} \cup \{X_{i,j} : 1 \leqq i \leqq n,\ 1 \leqq j \leqq k_i\}$$

and with P containing the following rules:

1) $S_0 \to X_{i,1}SC,\ 1 \leqq i \leqq n,$

2) $X_{i,j}A_{i,j} \to X_{i,j+1}x'_{i,j}$, $1 \leqq i \leqq n$, $1 \leqq j \leqq k_i - 1$, and $x'_{i,j}$ is obtained by replacing each $a \in V_T$ in $x_{i,j}$ by a',

$X_{i,j}B \to X_{i,j+1}B$, $B \neq A_{i,j}$, $B \in V_N$, $1 \leqq i \leqq n$, $1 \leqq j \leqq k_i - 1$, $r_{i,j}$ is a rule in F,

$X_{i,j}a' \to aX_{i,j}$, $1 \leqq i \leqq n$, $1 \leqq j \leqq k_i$, $a \in V_T$,

$X_{i,k_i}A_{i,k_i} \to X_{j,1}x'_{i,k_i}$, $1 \leqq i \leqq n$, $1 \leqq j \leqq n$, x'_{i,k_i} is obtained by replacing each $a \in V_T$ in x_{i,k_i} by a',

$X_{i,k_i}B \to X_{j,1}B$, $B \neq A_{i,k_i}$, $B \in V_N$, $1 \leqq i \leqq n$, $1 \leqq j \leqq n$, r_{i,k_i} is a rule in F,

3) $X_{i,1}C \to \lambda$, $1 \leqq i \leqq n$.

It is easy to see that the nonterminals $X_{i,j}$ control the derivation in such a way that the leftmost derivations in G are simulated by leftmost derivations in G'. Therefore $L_{\text{left}}(G') = L_{\text{left-1}}(G)$. As G' fulfils the conditions in Lemma 1.4.1 (all rules have nonterminal left-hand members), it follows that $L_{\text{left}}(G') \in \mathscr{L}(\text{CF})$. Therefore $L_{\text{left-1}}(G)$ also is context-free. This proves the statement.

Lemma 1.4.3. $\mathscr{L}(\text{P, CF, ac, left-1}) \subseteq \mathscr{L}(\text{CF})$.

Proof. Let $G = (V_N, V_T, P, S)$ be a programmed grammar. We construct the type-0 grammar $G' = (V'_N, V_T, P', S_0)$ with

$$V'_N = V_N \cup \{a' : a \in V_T\} \cup \{S_0, C\} \cup \{[r] : r \in \text{Lab}(P)\}$$

and with P' consisting of the following rules:

1) $S_0 \to [r]\,SC$, $r \in \text{Lab}(P)$,

2) $[r]\,a' \to a[r]$, $r \in \text{Lab}(P)$, $a \in V_T$,

3) $[r]\,A \to [r']\,x'$, $(r: A \to x, \sigma(r), \varphi(r)) \in P$, $r' \in \sigma(r)$, x' is obtained by replacing each $a \in V_T$ in x by a',

4) $[r]\,B \to [r']\,B$, $(r: A \to x, \sigma(r), \varphi(r)) \in P$, $r' \in \varphi(r)$, $B \neq A$, $B \in V_N$,

5) $[r]\,C \to \lambda$.

We obtain $L_{\text{left}}(G') = L_{\text{left-1}}(G)$ and $L_{\text{left}}(G') \in \mathscr{L}(\text{CF})$ (use Lemma 1.4.1 again). Therefore $L_{\text{left-1}}(G)$ also is a context-free language.

Lemma 1.4.4. $\mathscr{L}(\text{RC, CF, ac, left-1}) \subseteq \mathscr{L}(\text{CF})$.

Proof. Let $G = (V_N, V_T, P, S)$ be a random context grammar. We consider the context-free grammar $G' = (V'_N, V_T, P', S')$ with

$$V'_N = \{S'\} \cup \{(A, U) : A \in V_N, U \subseteq V_N\}$$

and with P' containing the following rules:

1) $S' \to (S, \emptyset)$,

2) $(A, U) \to x_1(B_1, U \cup \{B_2, \ldots, B_k\})\, x_2(B_2, U \cup \{B_3, \ldots, B_k\})\, x_3 \ldots x_k(B_k, U)\, x_{k+1}$
where i) $(A \to x_1B_1x_2B_2 \ldots x_kB_kx_{k+1}, Q, R) \in P$,
$x_i \in V_T^*$, $1 \leqq i \leqq k+1$, $B_i \in V_N$, $1 \leqq i \leqq k$,
ii) $U \subseteq V_N$ such that $Q \subseteq U$, $R \cap U = \emptyset$.

As the derivation is leftmost, the random contexts Q, R in the rules of G need be checked only to the right of the leftmost symbol of the current string. The component U in the symbols (A, U) of V_N' memorizes the nonterminals occurring to the right of A in the current string. Therefore, the rules of the grammar G' simulate — by leftmost derivations — the leftmost derivations in G. In conclusion, $L_{\text{left}}(G') = L_{\text{left-1}}(G)$, and the lemma is proved.

Theorem 1.4.1. *For* $X \in \{\text{M}, \text{P}, \text{RC}\}$,

$$\mathcal{L}(X, \text{CF}, \text{left-1}) = \mathcal{L}(X, \text{CF}, \text{ac}, \text{left-1}) = \mathcal{L}(X, \text{CF} - \lambda, \text{left-1})$$
$$= \mathcal{L}(X, \text{CF} - \lambda, \text{ac}, \text{left-1}) = \mathcal{L}(\text{CF}).$$

Proof. The inclusions

$$\mathcal{L}(\text{CF}) \subseteq \mathcal{L}(X, \text{CF} - \lambda, \text{left-1}) \subseteq \mathcal{L}(X, \text{CF} - \lambda, \text{ac}, \text{left-1})$$
$$\subseteq \mathcal{L}(X, \text{CF}, \text{ac}, \text{left-1})$$

and

$$\mathcal{L}(\text{CF}) \subseteq \mathcal{L}(X, \text{CF}, \text{left-1}) \subseteq \mathcal{L}(X, \text{CF}, \text{ac}, \text{left-1})$$

are obvious. The above lemmas also prove the opposite inclusions

$$\mathcal{L}(X, \text{CF}, \text{ac}, \text{left-1}) \subseteq \mathcal{L}(\text{CF}).$$

Consequently, this leftmost restriction decreases the generative capacity of matrix, programmed, and random context grammars.

The second type of leftmost derivation must be specifically defined for each class of grammars.

Definition 1.4.2. i) Let $G = (V_N, V_T, M, S)$ be a matrix grammar (without appearance checking) and let $x \Rightarrow y$ be a direct derivation with respect to G. We say that this derivation *holds with specification* (m, z_1) if $m\colon (A_1 \to \alpha_1, A_2 \to \alpha_2, \ldots, A_k \to \alpha_k)$ is the matrix used in it (i.e. $x = x_0 \Rightarrow x_1 \Rightarrow \cdots \Rightarrow x_k = y$, the step $x_i \Rightarrow x_{i+1}$ is realized by the rule $A_{i+1} \to \alpha_{i+1}$) and $x_0 = z_1A_1z_2$, $x_1 = z_1\alpha_1z_2$. For two strings $x, y \in V_G^*$ we write $x \underset{\text{left-2}}{\Longrightarrow} y$ if $x \Rightarrow y$ holds with specification (m, z_1), $m \in M$, $z_1 \in V_G^*$, and there is no $y' \in V_G^*$ such that $x \Rightarrow y'$ holds with a specification (m', z_1'), $m' \in M$, $z_1' \in V_G^*$, with $|z_1'| < |z_1|$. (In words, one considers the occurrences of the left-hand member of the first rules of matrices in M, and one uses that matrix which rewrites the leftmost of these occurrences without care about the subsequent rules of that matrix.)

ii) Let $G = (V_N, V_T, P, S)$ be a programmed grammar. We say that a derivation according to G is *leftmost of type* 2 if it develops as follows:

a) Start with S and apply any rule $S \to x$ in P.

b) If the current string y has been obtained from some string x by an effective use of some rule r, then at the next step we use a rule $r' \in \sigma(r)$ such that $y = y_1Ay_2$, $r'\colon A \to \alpha$ and there is no rule $r''\colon B \to \beta$ in $\sigma(r)$ such that $y = y_1'By_2'$, $|y_1'| < |y_1|$, and the string obtained in this way is $z = y_1 \alpha y_2$ (we say that y is rewritten in the leftmost manner by the rules of the set $\sigma(r)$), or if no rule $r' \in \sigma(r)$ can be used for rewriting y, then we choose an arbitrary rule $r' \in \sigma(r)$ and we pass to rewrite y in the leftmost manner by the rules of $\varphi(r')$.

c) Continue in this way until a terminal string is obtained.

iii) Let $G = (V_N, V_T, P, S)$ be a random context grammar. A derivation $x \Rightarrow y$, $x = x_1 A x_2$, $y = x_1 \alpha x_2$ realized by a rule $(A \to \alpha, Q, R)$ is called *leftmost of type* 2 if there is no rule $(B \to \beta, Q', R') \in P$ such that $x = x_1' B x_2'$, $|x_1'| < |x_1|$, and $x_1' x_2'$ contains all symbols of Q' and no symbol of R'.

By $L_{\text{left-2}}(G)$ we denote in all cases the language generated in this way. The families of languages obtained in this way are denoted by $\mathcal{L}(X, Y, \text{left-2})$, $X \in \{\text{M, P, RC}\}$, $\mathcal{L}(X, Y, \text{ac, left-2})$, $X \in \{\text{P, RC}\}$, $Y \in \{\text{CF, CF} - \lambda\}$.

The following relations are straightforward.

Lemma 1.4.5. *For all possible values of X (for X = M the component* ac *is missing),*

i) $\mathcal{L}(X, \text{CF} - \lambda, \text{left-2}) \subseteq \mathcal{L}(X, \text{CF}, \text{left-2}) \subseteq \mathcal{L}(X, \text{CF}, \text{ac, left-2}) \subseteq \mathcal{L}(\text{RE})$,

ii) $\mathcal{L}(X, \text{CF} - \lambda, \text{left-2}) \subseteq \mathcal{L}(X, \text{CF} - \lambda, \text{ac, left-2}) \subseteq \mathcal{L}(\text{CS})$.

The next result is also obvious.

Lemma 1.4.6. *All families in the previous lemma are closed under union.*

Theorem 1.4.2. $\mathcal{L}(\text{M, CF} - \lambda, \text{left-2}) = \mathcal{L}(\text{CS})$, $\quad \mathcal{L}(M, \text{CF}, \text{left-2}) = \mathcal{L}(\text{RE})$.

Proof. In view of Lemma 1.4.5, it is sufficient to prove that

$$\mathcal{L}(\text{CS}) \subseteq \mathcal{L}(\text{M, CF} - \lambda, \text{left-2}) \quad \text{and} \quad \mathcal{L}(\text{RE}) \subseteq \mathcal{L}(\text{M, CF, left-2}).$$

Let us consider a language $L \subseteq V^*$. Then

$$L = \bigcup_{a \in V} d_a^r(L)\,\{a\} \cup (L \cap \{\lambda\}).$$

Therefore, in view of Lemma 1.4.6, it is sufficient to prove that, for each language $L' \in \mathcal{L}(\text{CS})$ and for some symbol b,

$$L'\{b\} \in \mathcal{L}(\text{M, CF} - \lambda, \text{left-2}),$$

and similarly for $L' \in \mathcal{L}(\text{RE})$.

Let us consider a length increasing grammar $G = (V_N, V_T, P, S)$ in Kuroda normal form, i.e. containing only rules of the forms

(i) $X \to YZ$,

(ii) $XU \to YZ$,

(iii) $X \to a$, $X, Y, Z, U \in V_N$, $a \in V_T$,

and possibly also a rule

(iv) $S \to \lambda$

if S does not appear in the right-hand member of any rule in P. Further we consider a one-to-one assignment of labels to rules of type (ii), and we set

$$V_N' = \{X' : X \in V_N\},\ V_N'' = \{X'' : X \in V_N\},$$

$$V_1 = \{A_0, A_1, A_2, A_3, A_4\} \cup \{A_f : f \text{ is a label of a rule of type (ii) in } P\}.$$

Let $b \in V_T$ be a given symbol. Then we construct the matrix grammar

$$G' = (V_N \cup V_N' \cup V_N'' \cup V_1, V_T, M, A_0)$$

where M contains the following matrices:

$$(A_0 \to SA_1),$$
$$(Y \to Y', A_1 \to A_1),\ Y \in V_N$$

(in the presence of A_1, from the left to the right of the current string, one replaces some nonterminals Y by Y'),

$$(X \to Y'Z'', A_1 \to A_2) \quad \text{for rules} \quad X \to YZ \quad \text{of type (i) in } P$$

(after simulating rules in P one introduces the indicator A_2),

$$\left.\begin{array}{l}(X \to Y', A_1 \to A_f),\\ (U \to Z'', A_f \to A_2),\\ (B \to A_4, A_f \to A_4),\ B \in V_N \setminus \{U\}\end{array}\right\} \begin{array}{l}\text{for rules } f\colon XU \to YZ\\ \text{of type (ii) in } P\end{array}$$

(one simulates a rule of type (ii); the symbol A_f can be removed only if the symbol to the right of Y' is U, otherwise one introduces the trap symbol A_4 which blocks the derivation),

$$\left.\begin{array}{l}(Y' \to Y, A_2 \to A_2)\\ (Y'' \to Y, A_2 \to A_1)\end{array}\right\} Y \in V_N$$

(each primed symbol Y' is replaced by Y in the presence of A_2; if the doubly primed symbol Y'' is replaced by Y one replaces A_2 by A_1, and one can start to simulate another rule in P),

$$\left.\begin{array}{l}(X \to a, A_1 \to A_3),\\ (X \to a, A_3 \to A_3),\\ (X \to a, A_3 \to b),\\ (X \to a, A_1 \to b)\end{array}\right\} \begin{array}{l}\text{for rules } X \to a\\ \text{of type (iii) in } P\end{array}$$

(the derivation ends in the presence of A_3 by passing to a terminal string),

$$(A_0 \to b) \quad \text{if} \quad S \to \lambda \in P.$$

From the above explanations it is easy to see that we have

$$L_{\text{left-2}}(G') = L(G)\,\{b\}.$$

Hence $L(G)\,\{b\} \in \mathcal{L}(\text{M, CF} - \lambda, \text{left-2})$.

If we start from a type-0 grammar we follow the same construction, but we add to M the following matrices for each rule of the form $X \to \lambda$ in P:

$$(X \to X'', A_1 \to A_5),$$
$$(Y' \to Y, A_5 \to A_5),\ Y \in V_N,$$
$$(X'' \to \lambda, A_5 \to A_1),$$
$$(X \to \lambda, A_1 \to b).$$

Of course, the symbol A_5 is added to the nonterminal alphabet of G'. Again we obtain $L_{\text{left-2}}(G') = L(G)\{b\}$, and the theorem is proved.

A similarly strong result (also without using appearance checking features) can be obtained for programmed and random context grammars.

Theorem 1.4.3. i) $\mathscr{L}(\text{P}, \text{CF} - \lambda, \text{left-2}) = \mathscr{L}(\text{CS})$,

ii) $\mathscr{L}(\text{P}, \text{CF}, \text{left-2}) = \mathscr{L}(\text{RE})$.

Proof. Again it is enough to prove that for each language $L \in \mathscr{L}(\text{CS})$ $(L \in \mathscr{L}(\text{RE}))$ and symbol b, the language $L\{b\}$ is in $\mathscr{L}(\text{P}, \text{CF} - \lambda, \text{left-2})$ (in $\mathscr{L}(\text{P}, \text{CF}, \text{left-2})$, respectively).

Let $G = (V_N, V_T, P, S)$, $V_N = \{X_1, X_2, \ldots, X_n\}$, be a length increasing grammar in Kuroda normal form. We consider the programmed grammar $G' = (V'_N, V_T, P', S_0)$ with

$$V' = V_N \cup \{X' : X \in V_N\} \cup \{S_0, E, B_1, B_2\},$$

and using the following notations

$$\begin{aligned}
F_1 &= \{r : r : X \to YZ \in P\},\\
F_2 &= \{(X_1), (X_2), \ldots, (X_n)\},\\
F_3 &= \{(X'_1), (X'_2), \ldots, (X'_n)\},\\
F_4 &= \{r : r : XU \to YZ \in P\},\\
F_5 &= \{r : r : X \to a \in P, a \in V_T\},\\
F_6 &= \{[X_1], [X_2], \ldots, [X_n]\}.
\end{aligned}$$

P' contains the following rules:

$$\begin{aligned}
&(r_0 : S_0 \to SB_1, F_1 \cup F_2 \cup \{r_3\}, \emptyset),\\
&\big((X_i) : X_i \to X'_i, F_1 \cup F_2 \cup F_4 \cup \{r_1\}, \emptyset\big), 1 \leqq i \leqq n,\\
&(r : X \to Y'Z', F_1 \cup F_2 \cup F_4 \cup \{r_1\}, \emptyset) \quad \text{for} \quad r : X \to YZ \in P,\\
&(r_1 : B_1 \to B_2, F_3, \emptyset),\\
&\big((X'_i) : X'_i \to X_i, F_3 \cup \{r_2\}, \emptyset\big), 1 \leqq i \leqq n,\\
&(r_2 : B_2 \to B_1, F_1 \cup F_2 \cup F_4 \cup \{r_1, r_3\}, \emptyset),\\
&\left.\begin{array}{l}(r : X \to Y', \{r'\} \cup (F_6 \setminus \{[U]\}), \emptyset)\\ (r' : U \to Z', F_1 \cup F_2 \cup F_4 \cup \{r_1\}, \emptyset)\end{array}\right\} \text{for} \quad r : XU \to YZ \in P,\\
&([X_i] : X_i \to E, \emptyset, \emptyset), 1 \leqq i \leqq n,\\
&(r_3 : B_1 \to b, F_5, \emptyset),\\
&(r : X \to a, F_5, \emptyset) \quad \text{for} \quad r : X \to a \in P,\\
&(r_4 : S_0 \to b, \emptyset, \emptyset) \quad \text{if} \quad \lambda \in L(G).
\end{aligned}$$

The equality $L_{\text{left-2}}(G') = L(G)\{b\}$ is easily checked (E is a trap symbol which together with the leftmost derivation of type 2 ensures the correct simulation of the rules $r : XU \to YZ \in P$).

For the recursively enumerable case, we add the labels of the rules $r: X \to \lambda$ to F_1 and the rules

$$(r: X \to \lambda, F_1 \cup F_2 \cup F_4 \cup \{r_1\}, \emptyset)$$

to the production set of G'. The obtained grammar generates the language $L(G)\{b\}$. This completes the proof.

Theorem 1.4.4. i) $\mathscr{L}(\mathrm{RC}, \mathrm{CF} - \lambda, \text{left-2}) = \mathscr{L}(\mathrm{CS})$,

ii) $\mathscr{L}(\mathrm{RC}, \mathrm{CF}, \text{left-2}) = \mathscr{L}(\mathrm{RE})$.

Proof. We use again the trick in the beginning of the proofs of the previous theorems (the families $\mathscr{L}(\mathrm{RC}, X, \text{left-2})$, $X \in \{\mathrm{CF}, \mathrm{CF} - \lambda\}$, are closed under union — Lemma 1.4.6), hence it suffices to prove that, for each $L \in \mathscr{L}(\mathrm{CS})$ $\big(L \in \mathscr{L}(\mathrm{RE})\big)$ and given symbols a, b, $\{a\} L\{b\} \in \mathscr{L}(\mathrm{RC}, \mathrm{CF} - \lambda, \text{left-2})$ ($\{a\} L\{b\} \in L(\mathrm{RC}, \mathrm{CF}, \text{left-2})$, respectively).

For a length increasing grammar $G = (V_N, V_T, P, S)$ in Kuroda normal form we construct the random context grammar $G' = (V'_N, V_T, P', S_0)$ with

$$V'_N = V_N \cup \{X' : X \in V_N\} \cup \{S_0, E, A_1, A_2, A_3, B_1, B_2, B_3, B_4\} \cup \bigcup_{r: XU \to YZ \in P} \{X_r, A_r, Z_{re}\}$$

and the set P' consisting of the following rules:

$$(S_0 \to A_1SB_1, \emptyset, \emptyset)$$

(the current string will be of the form A_ixB_j for suitable i, j),

$$(X \to X', \{A_1\}, \emptyset),\ X \in V_N,$$
$$(B_1 \to B_2, \{A_1\}, \emptyset),$$
$$(A_1 \to A_2, \{B_2\}, \emptyset),$$
$$(X' \to X, \{A_2\}, \emptyset),\ X \in V_N,$$
$$(B_2 \to B_1, \{A_2\}, \emptyset),$$
$$(A_2 \to A_1, \{B_1\}, \emptyset),$$
$$(B_1 \to B_3, \{A_1\}, \emptyset),$$
$$(A_1 \to A_3, \{B_3\}, \emptyset),$$
$$(B_3 \to B_4, \{A_3\}, \emptyset),$$
$$(B_4 \to b, \emptyset, \emptyset)$$

(these are auxiliary rules which make possible the simulation of rules in P by leftmost derivations in the grammar G'),

$$(X \to Y'Z', \{A_1\}, \emptyset) \quad \text{for each rule} \quad X \to YZ \in P,$$

$$\left.\begin{array}{l}
(X \to X_r, \{A_1\}, \emptyset)\\
(A_1 \to A_r, \{X_r\}, \emptyset)\\
(X_r \to Y', \{A_r\}, \emptyset)\\
(U \to Z_{re}, \{A_r\}, \emptyset)\\
(T \to E, \{A_r\}, \emptyset),\ T \in V_N \setminus \{U\}\\
(A_r \to A_1, \{Z_{re}\}, \emptyset)\\
(Z_{re} \to Z', \{A_1\}, \emptyset)
\end{array}\right\} \text{for each rule} \quad r: XU \to YZ \in P$$

(note that E is a trap symbol; after replacing X by X_r and then by Y' the only possibility to remove A_r is in the presence of Z_{re} and this supposes that no rule $(T \to E, \{A_1\}, \emptyset)$ can be used, therefore U is the symbol to the right of Y', i.e. the rule $XU \to YZ$ is correctly simulated),

$$(X \to c, \{A_3\}, \emptyset) \quad \text{for each rule} \quad X \to c \in P, c \in V_T.$$

The equality $L_{\text{left-2}}(G') = \{a\}\, L(G)\, \{b\}$ is obvious, and hence we obtain the inclusion $\mathscr{L}(\text{CS}) \subseteq \mathscr{L}(\text{RC}, \text{CF} - \lambda, \text{left-2})$.

For the case of type-0 grammars we add to P' of G' a rule

$$(X \to \lambda, \{A_1\}, \emptyset) \quad \text{for each rule} \quad X \to \lambda \in P.$$

Again the three types of regulated grammars are equivalent under this type of leftmost derivation, and their generative capacity is considerable. The third type of leftmost restriction has an intermediate effect.

Definition 1.4.3. Let G be a matrix, programmed, or random context grammar. A derivation according to G is called *leftmost of type* 3 if each rule used in it replaces the leftmost occurrence of its left-hand member (if no occurrence of this symbol exists, then the rule is not applicable; it can possibly be "applied" in the appearance checking mode in matrix and programmed grammars).

By $L_{\text{left-3}}(G)$ we denote the language generated by G in this way, and for $X \in \{\text{M, P, RC}\}$, $Y \in \{\text{CF}, \text{CF} - \lambda\}$, the families of languages obtained in this way are denoted by $\mathscr{L}(X, Y, \text{left-3})$ and $\mathscr{L}(X, Y, \text{ac}, \text{left-3})$.

A natural generalization is to apply in this leftmost manner certain distinguished rules and to use the others freely. By $\mathscr{L}(X, Y, \text{left-}g)$, $\mathscr{L}(X, Y, \text{ac}, \text{left-}g)$, $X \in \{\text{M, P, RC}\}$, $Y \in \{\text{CF}, \text{CF} - \lambda\}$, we denote the corresponding families of languages.

The following relations are obvious.

Lemma 1.4.7. i) *For* $X \in \{\text{M, P, RC}\}$, $m \in \{3, g\}$, $\mathscr{L}(X, \text{CF} - \lambda, \text{left-}m) \subseteq \mathscr{L}(X, \text{CF}, \text{left-}m) \subseteq \mathscr{L}(X, \text{CF}, \text{ac}, \text{left-}m) \subseteq \mathscr{L}(\text{RE})$.

ii) *For* $X \in \{\text{M, P, RC}\}$,

$$\mathscr{L}(X, \text{CF} - \lambda, \text{ac}, \text{left-3}) \subseteq \mathscr{L}(\text{CS}).$$

iii) *For* $X \in \{\text{M, P, RC}\}$, $Y \in \{\text{CF}, \text{CF} - \lambda\}$,

$$\mathscr{L}(X, Y, \text{left-3}) \subseteq \mathscr{L}(X, Y, \text{left-}g),$$

$$\mathscr{L}(X, Y, \text{ac}, \text{left-3}) \subseteq \mathscr{L}(X, Y, \text{ac}, \text{left-}g).$$

Lemma 1.4.8. $\mathscr{L}(\text{CF}) \subset \mathscr{L}(\text{P}, \text{CF} - \lambda) \subseteq \mathscr{L}(\text{P}, \text{CF} - \lambda, \text{left-3}) \subseteq \mathscr{L}(\text{P}, \text{CF} - \lambda, \text{ac}, \text{left-3}) \subseteq \mathscr{L}(\text{CS})$ *where the first inclusion is proper, and moreover, for* $Y \in \{\text{CF}, \text{CF} - \lambda\}$,

$$\mathscr{L}(\text{P}, Y, \text{ac}) \subseteq \mathscr{L}(\text{P}, Y, \text{ac}, \text{left-3}).$$

Proof. The first inclusion is already discussed in Section 1.2. The inclusions $\mathscr{L}(\text{P}, \text{CF} - \lambda, \text{left-3}) \subseteq \mathscr{L}(\text{P}, \text{CF} - \lambda, \text{ac}, \text{left-3}) \subseteq \mathscr{L}(\text{CS})$ are obvious. In order to prove the inclusion $\mathscr{L}(\text{P}, \text{CF} - \lambda, \text{ac}) \subseteq \mathscr{L}(\text{P}, \text{CF} - \lambda, \text{ac}, \text{left-3})$, we consider a programmed grammar $G = (V_N, V_T, P, S)$, and with each rule

$$\big(r\colon A \to x, \sigma(r), \varphi(r)\big) \in \text{P}$$

we associate the rules

$$\big(r\colon A \to A, \{(r, A), r'\}, \varphi(r)\big),$$
$$\big((r, A)\colon A \to A', \{(r, A), r'\}, \emptyset\big),$$
$$\big(r'\colon A \to x, \{(r, A')\}, \emptyset\big),$$
$$\big((r, A')\colon A' \to A, \{(r, A')\}, \sigma(r)\big).$$

Then we construct the programmed grammar $G' = (V_N', V_T, P', S)$ by introducing all the new symbols in V_N' together with V_N and by replacing each rule $r \in P$ by the above corresponding group of rules in order to obtain P'. Thus by leftmost derivations in G' we can simulate free derivations in G because before using a rule $A \to x$ we can replace an arbitrary number of leftmost occurrences of the symbol $A \in V_N$ by A'. Hence we get $\mathcal{L}(\mathrm{P}, \mathrm{CF} - \lambda, \mathrm{ac}) \subseteq \mathcal{L}(\mathrm{P}, \mathrm{CF} - \lambda, \mathrm{ac}, \text{left-3})$.

If $\varphi(r) = \emptyset$ for all rules in G, then, for a rule

$$\big(r\colon A \to x, \sigma(r), \emptyset\big) \in P$$

we consider the group

$$\big((r, A)\colon A \to A', \{(r, A), r\}, \emptyset\big),$$
$$\big(r\colon A \to x, \{(r, A')\} \cup \sigma(r) \cup \{(r', B) : r' \in \sigma(r), r'\colon B \to y\}, \emptyset\big),$$
$$\big((r, A')\colon A' \to A, \{(r, A')\} \cup \sigma(r) \cup \{(r', B) : r' \in \sigma(r), r'\colon B \to y\}, \emptyset\big)$$

of rules. The grammar G' constructed as above satisfies $L(G) = L_{\text{left-3}}(G')$ and the failure fields are empty for all rules in G'.

As $\mathcal{L}(\mathrm{P}, \mathrm{CF}, \mathrm{ac}) = \mathcal{L}(\mathrm{RE})$, in view of the above lemma, we have $\mathcal{L}(\mathrm{P}, \mathrm{CF}, \mathrm{ac}, \text{left-3}) = \mathcal{L}(\mathrm{RE})$. Hence this family needs no further study.

Theorem 1.4.5. *The inclusion* $\mathcal{L}(\mathrm{P}, \mathrm{CF} - \lambda, \mathrm{ac}, \text{left-3}) \subset \mathcal{L}(\mathrm{CS})$ *is proper.*

Sketch of a proof. We omit a complete formal proof of this important result since it contains some lengthy technical constructions and it uses some knowledge of complexity theory (which cannot be given here with proofs for reason of space).

Let L be a language over V and let c, d be new letters. Then we say that K is L with tail if

i) each word in K is of the form wdc^m with $w \in L$, $m \geqq 0$,
ii) for each $w \in L$, there is an m such that $wdc^m \in K$.

For $x \in L$, let

$$m(x) = \min \{m : xdc^m \in K\}.$$

Further let f be a computable function from $\mathbb{N}$ into $\mathbb{N}$. We say that K has an *f-bounded tail* if, for all $x \in L$, $m(x) \leqq f(|x|)$.

We need the following claim.

Claim. *Let $L \in \mathcal{L}(\mathrm{RE})$, and let G be a context-free programmed grammar without λ-rules and with leftmost derivation of type 3 such that $L_{\text{left-3}}(G)$ is L with tail and $L_{\text{left-3}}(G)$ has an f-bounded tail. Then there is a context-sensitive grammar G' such that $L(G')$ is L with tail and $L(G')$ has a $q(\log f + 1)$-bounded tail, where q is the number of nonterminals in G.*

Sketch of the proof of the claim. The idea is the following. If $u_1u_2 \overset{*}{\Rightarrow} wdc^m$ in G and u_2 generates a string c^k, then u_1u_3 with $|u_2|_A = |u_3|_A$ for all nonterminals A of G also generates wdc^m. Therefore it is sufficient to use the vector $(|u_2|_{A_1}, |u_2|_{A_2}, \ldots, |u_2|_{A_q})$ instead of u_2, where G has the nonterminals $A_1, A_2, \ldots, A_q$. Since $|u_2| < m$, the vector can be stored by at most $q(\log m + 1)$ letters ($|u_2|_{A_i}$ is represented as a binary number and the adding of 1 is needed for separators). Now G' is constructed following the next informal instructions:

1. G' simulates G (this can be done by a combination of the constructions in (part ii) of the proof) of Theorem 1.2.2 and Lemma 1.2.4 taking into consideration the leftmost application of rules).

2. After simulating a derivation step in G, G' can put a marker at the right-hand end of the current string and to the right of this marker the coded vector $(0, 0, \ldots, 0)$ is written.

3. If now a production $A \to w$ is simulated, then the grammar G' first searches the leftmost A in the string and we distinguish three cases:

a) The leftmost A is to the left of the marker. Then the production is simulated by a replacement of A by w, the marker moves $|w| - 1$ letters to the left, cancelling the terminals of G or increasing the number $|z|_B$ in the vector by one. (The cancellation of the terminals increases the workspace by a fixed amount and by the Workspace Theorem 0.2.10 this does not destroy the context-sensitivity.) Thus again the same number of letters is to the left of the marker, and it is followed only by the coded vector.

b) There is no A to the left of the marker, but in the vector $|z|_A$ is positive. Then the components of the vector are changed to

$$|z|_B - |A|_B + |w|_B$$

for a nonterminal B of G. The changing of the vector is performed such that if the length of the binary representation is decreased we use a leading 0, thus we avoid erasing rules.

In both cases we continue in the success field.

c) There is no A to the left of the marker and $|z|_A = 0$. Then we pass directly to the failure field of $A \to w$.

4. After such a simulation of an application of $A \to w$ we check whether wd stands to the left of the marker with the terminal word w and whether the vector is $(0, 0, \ldots, 0)$. If the answer is negative, we continue the simulation; in the affirmative case we replace the marker and all symbols to the right of the marker by c and then the derivation stops with wdc^m.

Thus $L(G')$ is L with tail. Further, if $wdc^m \in L_{\text{left-3}}(G)$, then there is wdc^r in $L(G')$ with $r < q(\log m + 1)$. Since $m \leqq f(|x|)$ we get $r < q\big(\log f(|x|) + 1\big)$. This shows that $L(G')$ has a $q(\log f + 1)$-bounded tail.

Now we recall informally some notions and results of complexity theory. In this part of the proof the reader is assumed to be familiar with Turing machines.

Let M be a Turing machine. By $\text{Space}_M(x)$ we denote the number of different cells which are entered by the head of M if it computes the value of the input word x. We say that a language L is in Space (f) for some function $f: \mathbb{N} \to \mathbb{N}$ if there is a deterministic off-line Turing machine which, for any input word x, determines whether or not it is in L and this computation can be performed such that $\text{Space}_M(x) \leqq f(|x|)$. We need the following facts:

Fact 1. *For each computable function* $f\colon \mathbb{N} \to \mathbb{N}$ *there is a recursive language* L *in* Space (f) *such that, for each function* g *with* $\lim\limits_{n\to\infty} \dfrac{g(n)}{f(n)} = 0$, $L \notin$ Space (g).

Fact 2. *For each context-sensitive language* L *there is a constant* k *such that* $L \in$ Space(g) *with* $g(n) = k^n$.

We are now in a position to prove the existence of a language L in $\mathcal{L}(\text{CS}) \setminus \mathcal{L}(\text{P}, \text{CF} - \lambda, \text{ac}, \text{left-3})$. Assume the contrary, i.e. each context-sensitive language can be generated by a λ-free context-free programmed grammar with appearance checking and with leftmost derivation of type 3.

Let $f(n) = 2^{2^n}$, and let L be an associated language whose existence is stated in Fact 1. Now we construct the following sequence of languages.

Step 1. Let $G = (V_N, V_T, P, S)$ be a type-0 Chomsky grammar generating L. We substitute each rule $A \to \lambda$ by $A \to A'$, $A'x \to xA'$ for $x \in V_N$, $A'c \to cc$ and add the new rule $S'' \to Sc$. Then the context-sensitive grammar

$$G' = (V_N \cup V_N' \cup \{S''\}, V_T \cup \{c\}, P', S'')$$

generates a language L_1 which is L with tail (A' moves to the right, and it is replaced by c). Further, L_1 has an f-bounded tail.

Step 2. By the assumption, $L_1 \in \mathcal{L}(\text{P}, \text{CF} - \lambda, \text{ac}, \text{left-3})$. By the above claim there is a language $L_2 \in \mathcal{L}(\text{CS})$ such that L_2 is L with tail, and L_2 has a $q\,(\log f + 1)$-bounded tail, where q is a constant depending on L only. Clearly, then L_2 has a $2q\,(\log f)$-bounded tail.

Step 3. We repeat the construction of step 2, and we obtain a language L_3 which is L with tail and which has an $r(\log(2q \cdot \log f) + 1)$-bounded tail. Clearly, there is a constant r' such that L_3 has an $r' \log(\log f)$-bounded tail.

Now, for each word $x \in L$, there is a word xdc^m of length strictly smaller than $|x| + 1 + r' \cdot \log\log f(|x|)$ in L_3. Since L_3 is context-sensitive, there is a constant k such that xdc^m can be accepted/rejected by a Turing machine entering only $k^{|x|+1+r'\log\log f(|x|)}$ cells (Fact 2). Since

$$k^{|x|+r'\log\log f(|x|)} = \left(\log f(|x|)\right)^p \quad \text{with} \quad p = \log k^{r'+1}$$

it follows that $L_3 \in \text{Space}\left(k(\log f)^p\right)$. It is clear that the Turing machine recognizing L_3 can also be used for the recognition of L (instead of $x \in L$ we check $xdc^m \in L_3$ for $m < r' \log\log f(|x|)$). However this contradicts Fact 1, because

$$\lim_{n\to\infty} \frac{k\left(\log f(n)\right)^p}{f(n)} = 0,$$

and thus it contradicts the choice of L as well. Therefore our assumption does not hold, and this proves the statement of the theorem.

Lemma 1.4.9. *For* $Y \in \{\text{CF}, \text{CF} - \lambda\}$,

$$\mathcal{L}(\text{M}, Y, \text{ac}, \text{left-}g) \subseteq \mathcal{L}(\text{P}, Y, \text{ac}, \text{left-3}).$$

Proof. Let $G = (V_N, V_T, M, S, F)$ be a matrix grammar. Assume

$$M = \{m_1, m_2, \ldots, m_n\},$$

$$m_i\colon (r_{i,1}, r_{i,2}, \ldots, r_{i,k_i}),\ r_{i,j}\colon A_{i,j} \to x_{i,j},\ 1 \leqq i \leqq n,\ 1 \leqq j \leqq k_i.$$

We construct the programmed grammar $G' = (V'_N, V_T \cup \{b\}, P, S_0)$ with

$$V'_N = V_N \cup \{A' : A \in V_N\} \cup \{S_0, B\}$$

and P containing the following rules:

$$(r_0\colon S_0 \to SB, \{r_{i,1}\}, \emptyset),\ 1 \leqq i \leqq n,$$

$$(r_{i,j}\colon A_{i,j} \to x_{i,j}, \{r_{i,j+1}\}, \emptyset),\ 1 \leqq i \leqq n,\ 1 \leqq j \leqq k_i - 1,$$

$r_{i,j}$ is a leftmost rule and not in F,

$$(r_{i,j}\colon A_{i,j} \to x_{ij}, \{r_{i,j+1}\}, \{r_{i,j+1}\}),\ 1 \leqq i \leqq n,\ 1 \leqq j \leqq k_i - 1,$$

$r_{i,j}$ is a leftmost rule in F,

$$(r_{i,k_i}\colon A_{i,k_i} \to x_{i,k_i}, \{r_{j,1}, f\}, \emptyset),\ 1 \leqq i \leqq n,\ 1 \leqq j \leqq n,$$

r_{i,k_i} is a leftmost rule and not in F,

$$(r_{i,k_i}\colon A_{i,k_i} \to x_{i,k_i}, \{r_{j,1}, f\}, \{r_{j,1}, f\}),\ 1 \leqq i \leqq n,\ 1 \leqq j \leqq n,$$

r_{i,k_i} is a leftmost rule in F,

$$\left.\begin{array}{l}
(f\colon B \to b, \emptyset, \emptyset),\\
\left.\begin{array}{l}
(r_{i,j}\colon A_{i,j} \to A_{i,j}, \{r'_{i,j}, r''_{i,j}\}, \emptyset)\\
(r'_{i,j}\colon A_{i,j} \to A'_{i,j}, \{r'_{i,j}, r''_{i,j}\}, \emptyset)\\
(r''_{i,j}\colon A_{i,j} \to x_{i,j}, \{r''_{i,j}\}, \emptyset)
\end{array}\right\} \begin{array}{l} 1 \leqq i \leqq n \\ 1 \leqq j \leqq k_i \end{array}\\
(r'''_{i,j}\colon A'_{i,j} \to A_{i,j}, \{r'''_{i,j}\}, \{r_{i,j+1}\}),\ 1 \leqq i \leqq n,\ 1 \leqq j < k_i\\
(r'''_{i,k_i}\colon A'_{i,k_i} \to A_{i,k_i}, \{\{r'''_{i,k_i}\}, r_{j,1}, f\}),\ 1 \leqq i \leqq n,\ 1 \leqq j \leqq n
\end{array}\right\} \begin{array}{l} r_{i,j}, r_{i,k_i} \\ \text{respectively, is not} \\ \text{leftmost and} \\ \text{is not in } F \end{array}$$

$$\left.\begin{array}{l}
(r_{i,j}\colon A_{i,j} \to A_{i,j}, \{r'_{i,j}, r''_{i,j+1}\}, \{r_{i,j+1}\}),\ 1 \leqq i \leqq n,\ 1 \leqq j < k_i\\
(r_{i,k_i}\colon A_{i,k_i} \to A_{i,k_i}, \{r'_{i,k_i}, r''_{i,k_i}\}, \{r_{j,1}, f\}),\ 1 \leqq i \leqq n,\ 1 \leqq j \leqq n\\
(r'_{i,j}\colon A_{i,j} \to A'_{i,j}, \{r'_{i,j}, r''_{i,j}\}, \emptyset),\ 1 \leqq i \leqq n,\ 1 \leqq j \leqq k_i\\
(r''_{i,j}\colon A_{i,j} \to x_{i,j}, \{r'''_{i,j}\}, \emptyset),\ 1 \leqq i \leqq n,\ 1 \leqq j \leqq k_i\\
(r'''_{i,j}\colon A'_{i,j} \to A_{i,j}, \{r'''_{i,j}\}, \{r_{i,j+1}\}),\ 1 \leqq i \leqq n,\ 1 \leqq j \leqq k_i - 1\\
(r'''_{i,k_i}\colon A'_{i,k_i} \to A_{i,k_i}, \{r'''_{i,k_i}\}, \{r_{j,1}, f\}),\ 1 \leqq i \leqq n,\ 1 \leqq j \leqq n
\end{array}\right\} \begin{array}{l} r_{i,j}, r_{i,k_i}, \\ \text{respectively, is} \\ \text{in } F \text{ but is not} \\ \text{leftmost} \end{array}$$

The labels of the rules in P control the derivation as M does, whereas the presence of the symbol B ensures the complete simulation of matrices in M. It is easy to see that the leftmost derivations in G' correspond to the leftmost derivations in G. Therefore $L_{\text{left-3}}(G') = L_{\text{left-}g}(G)\,\{b\}$. As the family $\mathcal{L}(\text{P}, \text{CF} - \lambda, \text{ac}, \text{left-3})$ is closed under restricted homomorphisms (for a proof see ROSENKRANTZ (1969)), the lemma is proved.

Lemma 1.4.10. *For* $Y \in \{\text{CF}, \text{CF} - \lambda\}$,

i) $\mathcal{L}(\text{P}, Y, \text{ac}, \text{left-3}) \subseteq \mathcal{L}(\text{M}, Y, \text{ac}, \text{left-3})$,

ii) $\mathcal{L}(\text{P}, Y, \text{ac}, \text{left-}g) \subseteq \mathcal{L}(\text{M}, Y, \text{ac}, \text{left-}g)$.

Proof. We give the proof only for i). The necessary modifications for ii) are left to the reader.

As $\mathcal{L}(\text{P}, Y, \text{ac}, \text{left-3})$, $Y \in \{\text{CF}, \text{CF} - \lambda\}$, are closed under right derivative and $\mathcal{L}(\text{M}, Y, \text{ac}, \text{left-3})$ are closed under union, it suffices to prove that, for each $L \in \mathcal{L}(\text{P}, Y, \text{ac}, \text{left-3})$ and a symbol b, the language $L\{b\}$ is in $\mathcal{L}(\text{M}, Y, \text{ac}, \text{left-3})$.

Let $G = (V_N, V_T, P, S)$ be a programmed grammar. We construct the matrix grammar $G' = (V_N', V_T \cup \{b\}, M, S', F)$ with

$$V_N' = V_N \cup \{S', X\} \cup \{[r] : r \in \text{Lab}(P)\} \cup \{[r'] : r \in \text{Lab}(P)\},$$

$$\begin{aligned} M = {} & \{(S' \to S[r]) : r \in \text{Lab}(P)\} \\ & \cup \{(A \to x, [r_1] \to [r_2]) : (r_1 : A \to x, \sigma(r_1), \varphi(r_1)) \in P, r_2 \in \sigma(r_1)\} \\ & \cup \{(A \to x, [r_1] \to [r_2']) : (r_1 : A \to x, \sigma(r_1), \varphi(r_1)) \in P, r_2 \in \sigma(r_1)\} \\ & \cup \{(A \to X, [r_1'] \to [r_2]) : (r_1 : A \to x, \sigma(r_1), \varphi(r_1)) \in P, r_2 \in \varphi(r_1)\} \\ & \cup \{(A \to X, [r_1'] \to [r_2']) : (r_1 : A \to x, \sigma(r_1), \varphi(r_2)) \in P, r_2 \in \varphi(r_1)\} \\ & \cup \{(A \to x, [r] \to b) : (r : A \to x, \sigma(r), \varphi(r)) \in P\}, \end{aligned}$$

$$F = \{A \to X : A \in V_N\}.$$

We obtain the equality $L_{\text{left-3}}(G') = L_{\text{left-3}}(G)\,\{b\}$, and the proof is complete.

Remark. This proof is the standard passing from programmed grammars to matrix grammars. We considered it here in order to point out that we can take as leftmost only the first rule of each matrix and, moreover, that a binary normal form is obtained in this way for matrix grammars with leftmost derivations of type 3.

Theorem 1.4.5. *For* $Y \in \{\text{CF}, \text{CF} - \lambda\}$,

i) $\mathcal{L}(\text{M}, Y, \text{ac}, \text{left-3}) = \mathcal{L}(\text{P}, Y, \text{ac}, \text{left-3}) = \mathcal{L}(\text{RC}, Y, \text{ac}, \text{left-3})$,

ii) $\mathcal{L}(\text{M}, Y, \text{ac}, \text{left-}g) = \mathcal{L}(\text{P}, Y, \text{ac}, \text{left-}g) = \mathcal{L}(\text{RC}, Y, \text{ac}, \text{left-}g)$.

Proof. The above lemmas prove the relations for the programmed and matrix grammars.

The inclusion $\mathcal{L}(\text{RC}, Y, \text{ac}, \text{left-3}) \subseteq \mathcal{L}(\text{M}, Y, \text{ac}, \text{left-3})$ are straightforward (each random context rule $(A \to x, Q, R)$ can be simulated by a matrix

$$(A \to A', B_1 \to B_1, \ldots, B_k \to B_k, C_1 \to Z, \ldots, C_p \to Z, A' \to x)$$

where $Q = \{B_1, \ldots, B_k\}$, $R = \{C_1, \ldots, C_p\}$, Z a trap symbol), whereas the binary normal form obtained above for matrix grammars can be used for obtaining $\mathcal{L}(M, Y, \text{ac}, \text{left-3}) \subseteq \mathcal{L}(\text{RC}, Y, \text{ac}, \text{left-3})$ (take a matrix $m : (A \to x, X \to Y)$ and simulate it by the random context rules

$$(A \to (A, m), \{X\}, \{(B, m') : B \in V_N, m' \in M\}),$$

$$(X \to (X, m), \{(A, m)\}, \emptyset),$$

$$((A, m) \to x, \{(X, m)\}, \emptyset),$$
$$((X, m) \to Y, \emptyset, \{(A, m)\}).$$

Modified constructions can be used for the left-g derivations.

Corollary. *For* $Y \in \{\mathrm{CF}, \mathrm{CF} - \lambda\}$,

$$\mathcal{L}(\mathrm{RC}, Y, \text{left-3}) \subseteq \mathcal{L}(\mathrm{RC}, Y, \text{left-}g) \subseteq \mathcal{L}(\mathrm{M}, Y, \text{left-3})$$
$$= \mathcal{L}(\mathrm{P}, Y, \text{left-3}) = \mathcal{L}(\mathrm{M}, Y, \text{left-}g) = \mathcal{L}(\mathrm{P}, Y, \text{left-}g).$$

A simple examination of the above constructions proves these relations.

Consequently, if the three types of grammars — matrix, programmed, and random context — work in the same leftmost manner, then their generative capacity is the same, a result which is expected and fits with the situation met if free derivations are used.

Open problems

1.4.1. Which of the following inclusions are proper:

$$\mathcal{L}(\mathrm{P}, \mathrm{CF} - \lambda) \subseteq \mathcal{L}(\mathrm{P}, \mathrm{CF} - \lambda, \text{left-3}) \subseteq \mathcal{L}(\mathrm{P}, \mathrm{CF} - \lambda, \text{ac}, \text{left-3}),$$
$$\mathcal{L}(\mathrm{P}, \mathrm{CF} - \lambda, \text{left-3}) \subseteq \mathcal{L}(\mathrm{P}, \mathrm{CF}, \text{left-3}) \subseteq \mathcal{L}(\mathrm{RE}),$$
$$\mathcal{L}(\mathrm{RC}, Y, \text{left-3}) \subseteq \mathcal{L}(\mathrm{P}, Y, \text{left-3}) \quad \text{for} \quad Y \in \{\mathrm{CF}, \mathrm{CF} - \lambda\}?$$

What about the relations between $\mathcal{L}(\mathrm{P}, \mathrm{CF}, \text{left-3})$ and $\mathcal{L}(\mathrm{CS})$ or $\mathcal{L}(\mathrm{P}, \mathrm{CF} - \lambda, \text{ac}, \text{left-3})$, respectively.

Exercises

1.4.1. Define the above leftmost restrictions also for non-context-free grammars and prove that $\mathcal{L}(\mathrm{M}, Y, \text{left-}i) = \mathcal{L}(Y)$, $i \in \{2, 3\}$, $Y \in \{\mathrm{REG}, \mathrm{CS}, \mathrm{RE}\}$ (the only difficult point is the inclusion $\mathcal{L}(\mathrm{M}, \mathrm{CS}, \text{left-}i) \subseteq \mathcal{L}(\mathrm{CS})$ which requires a long construction).

1.4.2. Construct matrix, programmed, and random context grammars with leftmost derivation of type 2 (without appearance checking) which generate the languages

$$L_1 = \{a^{2^n} : n \geqq 1\},$$
$$L_2 = \{a^{n^2} : n \geqq 1\}.$$

1.4.3. Prove that $\mathcal{L}(\mathrm{P}, \mathrm{CF} - \lambda, \text{ac}, \text{left-3})$ has the same closure properties as $\mathcal{L}(\mathrm{P}, \mathrm{CF} - \lambda, \text{ac})$ (i.e. that it is a non-full AFL closed under λ-free substitution).

1.4.4. Prove Lemma 1.4.6.

1.5. Special Cases

The matrix, programmed, and random context grammars have some interesting variants. The main idea behind their definition is to impose further restrictions on the form of rules/matrices/derivations in order to obtain certain subfamilies of matrix, programmed, and random context languages with more properties.

Some of such special cases will be presented here: simple matrix grammars, programmed grammars with unconditional transfer, string random context grammars etc. Sometimes, their properties will be given without proof.

Definition 1.5.1. A *simple matrix grammar* of degree n, $n \geqq 1$, is an $(n+3)$-tuple

$$G = (V_1, V_2, \ldots, V_n, V_T, M, S)$$

where

(1) $V_1, V_2, \ldots, V_n, V_T$ are pairwise disjoint alphabets (the V_i are the nonterminal and V_T is the terminal vocabulary),

(2) $S \notin V_T \cup V_N$, $V_N = \bigcup_{i=1}^{n} V_i$ (the start symbol),

(3) M is a finite set of matrices of the following form:

(a) $(S \to x)$, $x \in V_T^*$,

(b) $(S \to A_1A_2 \ldots A_n)$, $A_i \in V_i$, $1 \leqq i \leqq n$,

(c) $(A_1 \to x_1, A_2 \to x_2, \ldots, A_n \to x_n)$, $A_i \in V_i$, $x_i \in (V_T \cup V_i)^*$,

and $|x_i|_{V_i} = |x_j|_{V_j}$ for all $1 \leqq i, j \leqq n$.

The grammar G is called *linear*, *regular*, or λ-free if all rules in matrices of type (c) are linear, regular, or λ-free, respectively.

Let $V_G = V_N \cup V_T \cup \{S\}$. For $x, y \in V_G^*$ we write $x \Rightarrow y$ iff either

(i) $x = S$ and $(S \to y) \in M$

or

(ii) $x = y_1A_1z_1y_2A_2z_2 \ldots y_nA_nz_n$, $y = y_1w_1z_1y_2w_2z_2 \ldots y_nw_nz_n$,

$y_i \in V_T^*$, $A_i \in V_i$, $z_i, w_i \in (V_i \cup V_T)^*$ for $1 \leqq i \leqq n$, and

$(A_1 \to w_1, A_2 \to w_2, \ldots, A_n \to w_n) \in M$.

In words, the derivation is leftmost on each of the n substrings in $(V_i \cup V_T)^*$ of the current string. As usual, we define

$$L(G) = \{x \in V_T^* : S \overset{*}{\Rightarrow} x\},$$

$\overset{*}{\Rightarrow}$ being the reflexive and transitive closure of the relation $\Rightarrow$.

Let $X \in \{\mathrm{CF}, \mathrm{CF} - \lambda, \mathrm{LIN}, \mathrm{LIN} - \lambda, \mathrm{REG}, \mathrm{REG} - \lambda\}$. By $\mathcal{L}(\mathrm{SM}, X, n)$ we shall denote the family of languages generated by simple matrix grammars of degree n, $n \geqq 1$, of type X and by $\mathcal{L}(\mathrm{SM}, X)$ the family

$$\mathcal{L}(\mathrm{SM}, X) = \bigcup_{n \geqq 1} \mathcal{L}(\mathrm{SM}, X, n).$$

Examples. Let us consider the grammars

$$G_i = (\{A, B\}, \{a, b\}, M_i, S),$$

$i = 1, 2$, with

$$M_1 = \{(S \to AB), (A \to aAb, B \to aBb), (A \to ab, B \to ab)\},$$

$$M_2 = \{(S \to AB), (A \to aA, B \to aB), (A \to bA, B \to bB), (A \to a, B \to a), (A \to b, B \to b)\}.$$

The following equalities hold:

$$L(G_1) = \{a^n b^n a^n b^n : n \geqq 1\},$$

$$L(G_2) = \{xx : x \in \{a, b\}^*\}.$$

The former language belongs to $\mathscr{L}(\mathrm{SM}, \mathrm{LIN} - \lambda, 2)$ and the latter to $\mathscr{L}(\mathrm{SM}, \mathrm{REG} - \lambda, 2)$; both these languages are not context-free.

Lemma 1.5.1. i) *Let* $X \in \{\mathrm{REG}, \mathrm{LIN}, \mathrm{CF}\}$. *Then*

$$\mathscr{L}(X) = \mathscr{L}(\mathrm{SM}, X - \lambda, 1),$$

$$\mathscr{L}(\mathrm{SM}, X - \lambda, n) \subseteq \mathscr{L}(\mathrm{SM}, X, n) \quad \textit{for} \quad n \geqq 1,$$

$$\mathscr{L}(\mathrm{SM}, X - \lambda) \subseteq \mathscr{L}(\mathrm{SM}, X).$$

ii) $\mathscr{L}(\mathrm{SM}, \mathrm{REG}, n) \subseteq \mathscr{L}(\mathrm{SM}, \mathrm{LIN}, n) \subseteq \mathscr{L}(\mathrm{SM}, \mathrm{CF}, n) \quad \textit{for} \quad n \geqq 1,$

$$\mathscr{L}(\mathrm{SM}, \mathrm{REG}) \subseteq \mathscr{L}(\mathrm{SM}, \mathrm{LIN}) \subseteq \mathscr{L}(\mathrm{SM}, \mathrm{CF}) \subseteq \mathscr{L}(\mathrm{RE}),$$

and the analogous inclusions hold for λ-free grammars (with $\mathscr{L}(\mathrm{RE})$ replaced by $\mathscr{L}(\mathrm{CS})$).

Proof. The only nontrivial relation is $\mathscr{L}(\mathrm{CF}) = \mathscr{L}(\mathrm{SM}, \mathrm{CF} - \lambda, 1)$. It follows from the known result that the leftmost derivation does not modify the generative capacity of context-free grammars.

We now present some auxiliary lemmas useful in the investigation of the power of simple matrix grammars of various types.

Let V be an alphabet and n a natural number. Further let

$$[V, n] = V \times \{1, 2, \ldots, n\}.$$

We define the mapping $\tau_n : [V, n]^* \to (V^*)^n$ by

1) $\tau_n(\lambda) = (\lambda, \lambda, \ldots, \lambda)$,

2) $\tau_n((a, i)\, x) = (x_1, \ldots, x_{i-1}, ax_i, x_{i+1}, \ldots, x_n)$ where $a \in V$, $1 \leqq i \leqq n$, $x \in [V, n]^*$, $\tau_n(x) = (x_1, x_2, \ldots, x_n)$.

The mapping $f : (V^*)^n \to V^*$ is defined by $f(x_1, x_2, \ldots, x_n) = x_1 x_2 \ldots x_n$.

Lemma 1.5.2. *A language* $L \subseteq V^*$ *is in* $\mathscr{L}(\mathrm{SM}, X, n)$, $X \in \{\mathrm{CF}, \mathrm{LIN}, \mathrm{REG}\}$, $n \geqq 1$, *if and only if there is a language* $L' \in \mathscr{L}(X)$ *such that* $L' \subseteq [V, n]^*$ *and* $L = f(\tau_n(L'))$.

Proof. Let $G = (V_1, V_2, \ldots, V_n, V_T, M, S)$ be a simple matrix grammar of degree n. We define the context-free grammar

$$G' = (V'_N, [V_T, n], P, S)$$

with

$$V'_N = \{S\} \cup V_1 \cup V_2 \cup \ldots \cup V_n$$

and P containing the following rules:

$$S \to \alpha,\ \alpha \in \tau_n^{-1}(\lambda, \lambda, \ldots, \lambda, w) \quad \text{for each} \quad (S \to w) \in M,\ w \in V_T^*,$$

$$S \to (A_1, A_2, \ldots, A_n) \quad \text{for matrices} \quad (S \to A_1A_2 \ldots A_n) \in M,\ A_i \in V_i,$$
$$1 \leqq i \leqq n,$$

$$(A_1, A_2, \ldots, A_n) \to \alpha,\ \alpha \in \tau_n^{-1}(w_1, w_2, \ldots, w_n) \quad \text{for each matrix}$$
$$(A_1 \to w_1, A_2 \to w_2, \ldots, A_n \to w_n) \in M \quad \text{with} \quad A_i \in V_i,\ w_i \in V_T^*,\ 1 \leqq i \leqq n,$$

$$(A_1, A_2, \ldots, A_n) \to \alpha_1(A_{11}, A_{21}, \ldots, A_{n1})\, \alpha_2(A_{12}, A_{22}, \ldots, A_{n2}) \ldots$$
$$\ldots \alpha_k(A_{1k}, A_{2k}, \ldots, A_{nk})\, \alpha_{k+1},$$
$$\alpha_j \in \tau_n^{-1}(x_{1j}, \ldots, x_{nj}) \quad \text{for} \quad 1 \leqq j \leqq k, \quad \alpha_{k+1} \in \tau_n^{-1}(y_1, \ldots, y_n)$$
$$\text{for} \quad (A_1 \to x_{11}A_{11}x_{12}A_{12} \ldots x_{1k}A_{1k}y_1, \ldots, A_n \to x_{n1}A_{n1}x_{n2}A_{n2} \ldots x_{nk}A_{nk}y_n)$$
$$\text{in } M \text{ with} \quad y_i \in V_T^*,\ x_{ij} \in V_T^*,\ A_{ij} \in V_i,\ 1 \leqq i \leqq n,\ 1 \leqq j \leqq k,\ k \geqq 1.$$

The equality $L(G) = f(\tau_n(L(G')))$ is easily checked. Moreover, the grammar G' is context-free, linear, regular if G was context-free, linear, regular, respectively.

Conversely, let us consider a context-free grammar $G = (V_N, [V_T, n], P, S)$ in Chomsky normal form (i.e. the rules are of the form $A \to BC$, $A \to a$, $A \to \lambda$ with $A, B, C \in V_N$, a terminal a, i.e. essentially these are the context-free rules of the Kuroda normal form). We define the simple matrix grammar

$$G' = (V_1, V_2, \ldots, V_n, V_T, M, S')$$

where

$$V_i = \{(A, i) : A \in V_N, 1 \leqq i \leqq n\},$$

S' is a new symbol,

$$M = \{(S' \to (S, 1)\,(S, 2) \ldots (S, n))\}$$
$$\cup \{((A, 1) \to (B, 1)\,(C, 1), \ldots, (A, n) \to (B, n)\,(C, n)) : A \to BC \in P,$$
$$A, B, C \in V_N\}$$
$$\cup \{((A, 1) \to p_1(\tau_n(x)), \ldots, (A, n) \to p_n(\tau_n(x))) : A \to x \in P,$$
$$A \in V_N,\ x \in [V_T, n]^*, \text{ and } p_i\colon (V_T^*)^n \to V_T^* \text{ is the } i^{\text{th}} \text{ projection},$$
$$p_i(x_1, \ldots, x_n) = x_i,\ 1 \leqq i \leqq n\}.$$

The equality $L(G') = f(\tau_n(L(G)))$ is again easily checked. Further, the construction can be modified without difficulty in order to cover the case of linear and regular simple matrix grammars.

This lemma has a series of important consequences.

Corollary 1. *For each language $L \in \mathcal{L}(\mathrm{SM}, \mathrm{CF})$ there is a simple matrix grammar G_0 which generates L and which does not contain λ-matrices, i.e. matrices of the form $(A_1 \to \lambda, A_2 \to \lambda, \ldots, A_n \to \lambda)$.*

This follows from the second part of the above proof: the context-free grammar G in Chomsky-normal form contains terminal rules of the form $A \to (a, i)$, and therefore the terminal matrices in G' are of the form $\big((A, 1) \to \lambda, \ldots, (A, i-1) \to \lambda, (A, i) \to a, (A, i+1) \to \lambda, \ldots, (A, n) \to \lambda\big)$ Thus, for each language $L \in \mathscr{L}(\mathrm{SM}, \mathrm{CF})$ we can find a simple matrix grammar G_0 whose terminal matrices contain at least a λ-free rule.

Corollary 2. *Each language in* $\mathscr{L}(\mathrm{SM}, \mathrm{CF})$ *is semilinear (hence the one-letter languages in* $\mathscr{L}(\mathrm{SM}, \mathrm{CF})$ *are regular).*

These properties hold for context-free languages, and the mappings f and τ_n rearrange only the symbols in the strings (n-tuples), i.e. they preserve semilinearity.

Corollary 3. *The emptiness and the finiteness problems are decidable for context-free simple matrix grammars.*

It is easy to see that the language $L(G)$ in the first part of the proof of Lemma 1.5.2 is empty, finite, or infinite if and only if the language $L(G')$ is empty, finite, or infinite, respectively. Hence the problems are again reduced to the corresponding decision questions for context-free grammars.

Corollary 4. *Let* $L \subseteq V^*$ *be an infinite language in* $\mathscr{L}(\mathrm{SM}, \mathrm{CF}, n)$ *for some* $n \geqq 1$. *Then there exist integers* p *and* q *such that each* $z \in L$ *with* $|z| > p$ *can be written as*

$$z = u_1 v_1 w_1 x_1 u_2 v_2 w_2 x_2 \ldots u_n v_n w_n x_n u_{n+1}$$

where $|v_1 x_1 v_2 x_2 \ldots v_n x_n| > 0$, $|v_1 w_1 x_1 v_2 w_2 x_2 \ldots v_n w_n x_n| \leqq q$, *and* $u_1 v_1^k w_1 x_1^k u_2 v_2^k w_2 x_2^k \ldots u_n v_n^k w_n x_n^k u_{n+1} \in L$ *for all* $k \geqq 0$.

This generalization of the Bar-Hillel lemma can be obtained by "translating" the Bar-Hillel lemma from (infinite) context-free languages to simple matrix languages by using the mappings τ_n and f:

$$\begin{aligned} \tau_n(uv^k wx^k y) &= \tau_n(u) \big(\tau_n(v)\big)^k \tau_n(w) \big(\tau_n(x)\big)^k \tau_n(y) \\ &= (u_1, \ldots, u_n)(v_1, \ldots, v_n)^k (w_1, \ldots, w_n)(x_1, \ldots, x_n)^k (y_1, \ldots, y_n) \\ &= (u_1 v_1^k w_1 x_1^k y_1, \ldots, u_n v_n^k w_n x_n^k y_n) \end{aligned}$$

and so on.

In the same way one can prove that, for each language $L \in \mathscr{L}(\mathrm{SM}, \mathrm{REG}, n)$, there is a constant p such that each $z \in L$, $|z| > p$, can be written as $z = u_1 x_1 u_2 x_2 \ldots u_n x_n u_{n+1}$ such that $|x_1 x_2 \ldots x_n| > 0$ and $u_1 x_1^k u_2 x_2^k \ldots u_n x_n^k u_{n+1} \in L$ for each $k \geqq 0$.

Theorem 1.5.1. *There is a strict inclusion* $\mathscr{L}(\mathrm{SM}, \mathrm{CF}) \subset \mathscr{L}(\mathrm{CS})$.

Proof. As $\mathscr{L}(\mathrm{CS})$ contains non-semilinear languages (even over one-letter alphabets) we get $\mathscr{L}(\mathrm{CS}) \setminus \mathscr{L}(\mathrm{SM}, \mathrm{CF}) \neq \emptyset$ by Corollary 2.

Consider now a simple matrix grammar of degree n, $G = (V_1, V_2, \ldots, V_n, V_T, M, S)$. We construct a type-0 grammar G' which simulates the matrices in M, as for usual matrix grammars (see the proof of Lemma 1.2.4), taking care to obtain only leftmost derivations in the sense of Definition 1.5.1. We get $L(G') = L(G)$. By Corollary 1, each terminal matrix in G can be assumed to introduce at least one terminal symbol. Therefore the grammar G' has a bounded workspace, which implies that $L(G') \in \mathscr{L}(\mathrm{CS})$ by Theorem 0.2.10. Hence $\mathscr{L}(\mathrm{SM}, \mathrm{CF}) \subseteq \mathscr{L}(\mathrm{CS})$, and the theorem follows.

Definition 1.5.2. Let $G = (V_1, V_2, \ldots, V_n, V_T, M, S)$ be a simple matrix grammar of degree n. For $x_i \in (V_i \cup V_T)^*$, $1 \leq i \leq n$, with $|x_i|_{V_i} = |x_j|_{V_j}$, $1 \leq i, j \leq n$, by $\text{poz}_k\ (x_1, x_2, \ldots, x_n)$ we denote the vector of the kth nonterminals occurring in strings $x_1, x_2, \ldots, x_n$, $1 \leq k \leq |x_1|_{V_1}$. We say that the grammar G is *reduced* if and only if, for each $(x_1, x_2, \ldots, x_n)$ such that $S \overset{*}{\Rightarrow} x_1x_2 \ldots x_n$, $x_i \in (V_i \cup V_T)^*$, and for each matrix $(A_1 \to w_1, A_2 \to w_2, \ldots, A_n \to w_n) \in M$, we have either $\text{poz}_1\ (x_1, x_2, \ldots, x_n) = (A_1, A_2, \ldots, A_n)$ or $\text{poz}_1\ (x_1, x_2, \ldots, x_n) = (B_1, B_2, \ldots, B_n)$ and $A_i \neq B_i$ for $1 \leq i \leq n$.

Lemma 1.5.3. *For each simple matrix grammar there is an equivalent reduced simple matrix grammar.*

Proof. Let $G = (V_1, V_2, \ldots, V_n, V_T, M, S)$ be a simple matrix grammar. Clearly, we can eliminate from M all matrices $(A_1 \to x_1, A_2 \to x_2, \ldots, A_n \to x_n)$ for which $(A_1, A_2, \ldots, A_n) \neq \text{poz}_j\ (w_1, w_2, \ldots, w_n)$ for all possible j and for all $(S \to w_1w_2 \ldots w_n)$ or $(B_1 \to w_1, B_2 \to w_2, \ldots, B_n \to w_n)$ in M, $w_i \in (V_i \cup V_T)^*$, $1 \leq i \leq n$.

Now take a matrix $(A_1 \to x_1, A_2 \to x_2, \ldots, A_n \to x_n) \in M$ and consider nonterminals $C_1, C_2, \ldots, C_n$ such that there is a matrix $(B_1 \to w_1, B_2 \to w_2, \ldots, B_n \to w_n) \in M$ and there is an integer j, $1 \leq j \leq |x_1|_{V_1}$, such that $\text{poz}_j\ (w_1, w_2, \ldots, w_n) = (C_1, C_2, \ldots, C_n)$, $A_i = C_i$ for certain values of i, but $(C_1, C_2, \ldots, C_n) \neq (A_1, A_2, \ldots, A_n)$. For each such matrix $(B_1 \to w_1, B_2 \to w_2, \ldots, B_n \to w_n)$ and for each such j, we replace $C_1, C_2, \ldots, C_n$ by new symbols $D_1, D_2, \ldots, D_n$, respectively, and introduce in M a matrix $(D_1 \to y_1, D_2 \to y_2, \ldots, D_n \to y_n)$ for each matrix $(C_1 \to y_1, C_2 \to y_2, \ldots, C_n \to y_n) \in M$.

This procedure is also applied to each matrix $(S \to C_1C_2 \ldots C_n)$ for which $(C_1, C_2, \ldots, C_n) \neq (A_1, A_2, \ldots, A_n)$ and there is an integer k such that $C_k = A_k$.

In this way, for the matrix $(A_1 \to x_1, A_2 \to x_2, \ldots, A_n \to x_n)$ and each $w_1, w_2, \ldots, w_n$ such that $S \overset{*}{\Rightarrow} w_1w_2 \ldots w_n$ we have either $\text{poz}_j\ (w_1, w_2, \ldots, w_n) = (A_1, A_2, \ldots, A_n)$ or $\text{poz}_j\ (w_1, w_2, \ldots, w_n) = (B_1, B_2, \ldots, B_n)$ with $B_i \neq A_i$ for all $1 \leq i \leq n$.

We apply this procedure in some given order to all n-tuples $(A_1, A_2, \ldots, A_n)$ for which the initial set M of matrices contains a matrix $(A_1 \to x_1, A_2, \to x_2, \ldots, A_n \to x_n)$. The procedure is finite, and we obtain a grammar G' which is reduced and equivalent to G.

As the above proof does not change the form of the rules, this lemma holds for all types of simple matrix grammars.

Lemma 1.5.4. *For each language* $L \in \mathcal{L}(\text{SM}, X, n)$, $X \in \{\text{CF, LIN, REG}\}$, *there are n languages $L_1, L_2, \ldots, L_n$ in $L(X)$ such that*

1) $L \subseteq L_1L_2 \ldots L_n$,

2) *for each i, $1 \leq i \leq n$,* and *for each $x_i \in L_i$, there are $x_j \in L_j$, $1 \leq j \leq n$, $i \neq j$, such that $x_1x_2 \ldots x_n \in L$.*

Proof. Let $G = (V_1, V_2, \ldots, V_n, V_T, M, S)$ be a reduced simple matrix grammar and construct the context-free grammars

$$G_i = (V_i, V_T, P_i, S),\ 1 \leq i \leq n, \text{ with}$$

$$P_i = \{S \to A_i : (S \to A_1A_2 \ldots A_n) \in M\}$$
$$\cup \{A_i \to x_i : (A_1 \to x_1, A_2 \to x_2, \ldots, A_n \to x_n) \in M\}.$$

If M contains matrices $(S \to w)$, $w \in V_T^*$, then we introduce a rule $S \to \lambda$ in each set P_i, $1 \leq i \leq n - 1$, and the rules $S \to w$ are added to P_n.

The inclusion $L \subseteq L(G_1)\, L(G_2) \ldots L(G_n)$ is obvious. Moreover, as the grammar G is reduced, all derivations in the grammars G_i, $1 \leqq i \leqq n$, correspond to some derivations in G, such that the second condition of the lemma is satisfied.

Clearly, the grammars G_i, $1 \leqq i \leqq n$, are linear or regular if G is linear or regular, respectively.

A similar proof leads to the following result.

Lemma 1.5.5. *If* $L \in \mathcal{L}(\text{SM, LIN}, n)$, then *there are* $2n$ *regular languages* $L_1, L_2, \ldots, L_{2n}$ *such that*

1) $L \subseteq L_1 L_2 \ldots L_{2n}$,
2) *for each* i, $1 \leqq i \leqq 2n$, *and for each* $x_i \in L_i$, *there are* $x_j \in L_j$, $1 \leqq j \leqq 2n$, $i \neq j$, *such that* $x_1 x_2 \ldots x_{2n} \in L$.

The above necessary conditions can be used in order to prove that certain useful languages are not simple matrix languages of some type.

Lemma 1.5.6. i) $H_1 = \{a^n b^n c^n : n \geqq 1\}^* \notin \mathcal{L}(\text{SM, CF})$,

ii) $K_n = \{a_1^k a_2^k \ldots a_{2n+1}^k : k \geqq 1\} \notin \mathcal{L}(\text{SM, CF}, n)$ *for* $n \geqq 1$,

iii) $H_2 = \{a^n b^n : n \geqq 1\}^* \notin \mathcal{L}(\text{SM, LIN})$,

iv) $K'_n = \{a_1^k a_2^k \ldots a_{n+1}^k : k \geqq 1\} \notin \mathcal{L}(\text{SM, REG}, n)$ *for* $n \geqq 1$.

Proof. If $H_1 \in \mathcal{L}(\text{SM, CF}, n)$ for some $n \geqq 1$, then, according to Lemma 1.5.4, there are n context-free languages $L_1, L_2, \ldots, L_n$ which satisfy the two properties in that lemma. Let us consider the sets

$$I(L_i) = \{j : a^j b^j c^j \text{ is a subword of } L_i\},\ 1 \leqq i \leqq n.$$

Since each L_i is context-free, each set $I(L_i)$ must be finite (otherwise using Ogden's lemma, one can see that L_i is not context-free). We set

$$m = \max \{j : j \text{ is in some } I(L_i),\ 1 \leqq i \leqq n\}$$

and consider strings in H_1 of the form $w = (a^p b^p c^p)^r$, $p > m$, $r \geqq 4n + 1$. The strings in L_i can be written in the form

$$z = z_1 a^{i_1} b^{i_1} c^{i_1} a^{i_2} b^{i_2} c^{i_2} \ldots a^{i_k} b^{i_k} c^{i_k} z_2 \tag{*}$$

with $k \geqq 0$, $1 \leqq i_j \leqq m$, z_1 and z_2 containing no substrings of the form $a^t b^t c^t$. For a string w as above there are $x_1, x_2, \ldots, x_n$, $x_i \in L_i$, $1 \leqq i \leqq n$, such that $w = x_1 x_2 \ldots x_n$. By $p > m$, it follows that for all x_i, $1 \leqq i \leqq n$, if they are written in the form (*), we have $k = 0$, that is $x_i = z_{i,1} z_{i,2}$ with $z_{i,1}, z_{i,2}$ containing no substrings $a^t b^t c^t$ with $t \geqq 1$, and $w = z_{1,1} z_{1,2} z_{2,1} z_{2,2} \ldots z_{n,1} z_{n,2}$.

Now, for an arbitrary string $x = a_1 a_2 \ldots a_m$ over some alphabet V, $a_i \in V$, $1 \leqq i \leqq m$, we set

$$\text{ch}(x) = \text{card}\, \{i : a_i \neq a_{i+1}\}.$$

Clearly, each $z_{i,j}$ as above satisfies $\text{ch}(z_{i,j}) \leqq 5$. It follows that

$$\text{ch}(w) = \text{ch}(z_{1,1} z_{1,2} \ldots z_{n,1} z_{n,2}) \leqq 5 \cdot 2n + 2n - 1 = 12n - 1.$$

On the other hand,

$$\mathrm{ch}\big((a^pb^pc^p)^r\big) = 2r + r - 1 = 3r - 1.$$

For $r \geqq 4n + 1$ we get

$$\mathrm{ch}\,\big((a^pb^pc^p)^r\big) \geqq 3(4n + 1) - 1 = 12n + 2$$

which contradicts $(a^pb^pc^p)^r = z_{1,1}z_{1,2} \dots z_{n,1}z_{n,2}$. Therefore $H_1 \notin \mathscr{L}(\mathrm{SM}, \mathrm{CF}, n)$.

By a similar argument one can prove that $H_2 \notin \mathscr{L}(\mathrm{SM}, \mathrm{LIN})$ (use Lemma 1.5.5 and the fact that a language $L \subseteq H_2$ for which the set $I(L) = \{i : a^ib^i \in \mathrm{Sub}\,(L)\}$ is infinite is not regular).

For the languages K_n and K_n' it is easy to prove that $K_n \notin \mathscr{L}(\mathrm{SM}, \mathrm{CF}, n)$, $K_n' \notin \mathscr{L}(\mathrm{SM}, \mathrm{REG}, n)$ using the generalization of the Bar-Hillel lemma (Corollary 4 of Lemma 1.5.2). In a context-free simple matrix grammar of degree n one can iterate at most $2n$ positions, whereas K_n contains $2n + 1$ simultaneously pumped positions; in a regular simple matrix grammar of degree n one can iterate at most n positions and K_n' contains $n + 1$ pumped positions.

Theorem 1.5.2. *All the following inclusions are proper:*

$$\mathscr{L}(\mathrm{SM}, \mathrm{REG}, n) \subset \mathscr{L}(\mathrm{SM}, \mathrm{LIN}, n) \subset \mathscr{L}(\mathrm{SM}, \mathrm{CF}, n) \quad \text{for} \quad n \geqq 1,$$

$$\mathscr{L}(\mathrm{SM}, \mathrm{REG}) \subset \mathscr{L}(\mathrm{SM}, \mathrm{LIN}) \subset \mathscr{L}(\mathrm{SM}, \mathrm{CF}),$$

and analogous relations hold for the corresponding λ-free families.

Proof. We consider the linear simple matrix grammar

$$G = (\{A_1\}, \{A_2\}, \dots, \{A_n\}, \{a_1, a_2, \dots, a_{n+1}\}, M, S),$$

$$M = \{(S \to A_1A_2 \dots A_n),$$

$$(A_1 \to a_1A_1, A_2 \to a_2A_2, \dots, A_{n-1} \to a_{n-1}A_{n-1}, A_n \to a_nA_na_{n+1})$$

$$(A_1 \to a_1, A_2 \to a_2, \dots, A_{n-1} \to a_{n-1}, A_n \to a_na_{n+1})\}.$$

Clearly, $L(G) = K_n'$. Therefore $K_n' \in \mathscr{L}(\mathrm{SM}, \mathrm{LIN} - \lambda, n) \setminus \mathscr{L}(\mathrm{SM}, \mathrm{REG}, n)$.

As H_2 is a context-free language and $L(\mathrm{CF}) = \mathscr{L}(\mathrm{SM}, \mathrm{CF} - \lambda, 1)$, the only inclusions which remain to be proved to be proper are $\mathscr{L}(\mathrm{SM}, \mathrm{REG}) \subset \mathscr{L}(\mathrm{SM}, \mathrm{LIN})$ and $\mathscr{L}(\mathrm{SM}, \mathrm{REG} - \lambda) \subset \mathscr{L}(\mathrm{SM}, \mathrm{LIN} - \lambda)$. They follow from the fact that there are linear languages which are not in $\mathscr{L}(\mathrm{SM}, \mathrm{REG})$.

Such a language is

$$L = \big\{wcMi(w) : w \in \{a, b\}^*\big\}.$$

Let us suppose that $L \in \mathscr{L}(\mathrm{SM}, \mathrm{REG}, n)$ for some n, and let $G = (V_1, V_2, \dots, V_n, \{a, b, c\}, M, S)$ be a regular simple matrix grammar generating L. We consider all strings of L of the form

$$z = a^{i_1}ba^{i_2}b \dots a^{i_{n+1}}ca^{i_{n+1}}b \dots ba^{i_2}ba^{i_1},$$

$i_j \geqq 1$, $1 \leqq i \leqq n$. As i_j can be arbitrarily large and G is of degree n and regular, there is a derivation of the form

$$D: S \Rightarrow A_1A_2 \dots A_n \overset{*}{\Rightarrow} x_1B_1x_2B_2 \dots x_nB_n \overset{*}{\Rightarrow} x_1y_1B_1x_2y_2B_2 \dots x_ny_nB_n$$

with $x_1y_1 \in \{a\}^*$, $y_1 \neq \lambda$, x_1, y_1 being subwords of the prefix a^{i_1} of z. From the form of the strings in L it follows that there is a k_1 such that $y_{k_1} \in \{a\}^+$ is a subword of the suffix a^{i_1} of z (otherwise we can iterate the matrices which contribute to the subderivation $x_1B_1x_2B_2 \ldots x_nB_n \stackrel{*}{\Rightarrow} x_1y_1B_1x_2y_2B_2 \ldots x_ny_nB_n$ in such a way to obtain strings in $L(G)$ of the form

$$a^{i_1}ba^{i_2}b \ldots a^{i_n}ca^{i_n}b \ldots ba^{j_1}$$

with $i_1 \neq j_1$). Clearly, all symbols $B_{k_1}, B_{k_1+1}, \ldots, B_n$ will generate only symbols a in the suffix a^{i_1} of z (and there is at least one such symbol B_{k_1+t}, $t \geqq 0$). Now we continue the derivation D by

$$x_1y_1B_1x_2y_2B_2 \ldots x_ny_nB_n \stackrel{*}{\Rightarrow} x_1y_1z_1bu_1C_1x_2y_2z_2bu_2C_2 \ldots x_ny_nz_nbu_nC_n$$

$$\stackrel{*}{\Rightarrow} x_1y_1z_1bu_1v_1C_1x_2y_2z_2bu_2v_2C_2 \ldots x_ny_nz_nbu_nv_nC_n$$

such that $v_1 \neq \lambda$, $v_1 \in \{a\}^+$, contributes to the left substring a^{i_2} of z (there is such a derivation because i_2 is arbitrarily large). Again some k_2 has to exist such that $v_{k_2} \in \{a\}^+$ is a substring of the right-hand subword a^{i_2} of z. Clearly, the corresponding C_{k_2} cannot be in the same alphabet V_{k_1} as the above B_{k_1} (the symbol C_{k_2} is not derived from B_{k_1} because B_{k_1} generates only terminals in the suffix of a^{i_1}).

Continuing in this way, for each position $j = 1, 2, \ldots, n + 1$ in the second half of the string, we can find a different vocabulary V_j which contains some symbols D_j which appear in a derivation of the form

$$\alpha_1E_1\alpha_2E_2 \ldots \alpha_nE_n \stackrel{*}{\Rightarrow} \alpha_1\beta_1E_1\alpha_2\beta_2E_2 \ldots \alpha_n\beta_nE_n$$

where at least one E_k is equal to some D_j, $1 \leqq j \leqq n + 1$, and $\beta_k \neq \lambda$ contributes to the right subword a^{i_j}, $1 \leqq k \leqq n$.

However, the grammar G contains exactly n non-terminal alphabets. By this contradiction the grammar G cannot exist.

Corollary. $\mathcal{L}(\text{LIN}) \setminus \mathcal{L}(\text{SM}, \text{REG}) \neq \emptyset$,

$$\mathcal{L}(\text{CF}) \setminus \mathcal{L}(\text{SM}, \text{LIN}) \neq \emptyset,$$

and

$$\mathcal{L}(\text{M}, \text{CF} - \lambda) \setminus \mathcal{L}(\text{SM}, \text{CF}) \neq \emptyset.$$

These relations are proved by the languages $\{wcMi(w) : w \in \{a, b\}^*\}$, $\{a^nb^n : n \geqq 1\}^*$ and $\{a^nb^nc^n 0\ n \geqq 1\}^*$, respectively.

We shall now prove that λ-rules do not increase the generative capacity of linear and regular simple matrix grammars of degree n, $n \geqq 1$. The following technical result is used for this purpose.

Lemma 1.5.7. *For each language $L \in \mathcal{L}(\text{SM}, \text{LIN}, n)$ $(L \in \mathcal{L}(\text{SM}, \text{REG}, n))$ there is a linear (regular) simple matrix grammar $G = (V_1, V_2, \ldots, V_n, V_T, M, S)$ generating L such that in each derivation of the form*

$$S \Rightarrow A_1A_2 \ldots A_n \stackrel{*}{\Rightarrow} w_1w_2 \ldots w_n,$$

w_i being derived from A_i, $1 \leqq i \leqq n$, we have $w_i \neq \lambda$ *for* $1 \leqq i \leqq n$.

Proof. Let $G = (V_1, V_2, \ldots, V_n, V_T, M, S)$ be a linear simple matrix grammar of degree n. We construct the equivalent linear simple matrix grammar $G' = (V_1', V_2', \ldots, V_n', V_T, M', S)$ in the following way.

We consider the pairs (a^+, j), (a^-, j), (a, j), $a \in V_T$, $1 \leqq j \leqq n$, meaning that a symbol a will be borrowed from position j, a symbol a will be lent to position j, and that a symbol a will be introduced at the current position j, respectively. Then we set

$$V_i' = V_i \cup \{[A; c_{j_1}, c_{j_2}, \ldots, c_{j_k}]: 1 \leqq k \leqq n+1, 1 \leqq j_i \leqq n, 1 \leqq i \leqq k,$$

c_{j_t} are pairs (a^+, j_t), (a^-, j_t), (a, j_t) and at most one of is of the form $(a, j_t)\}$.

The set M' contains the following matrices:

1) $(S \to w)$ for $(S \to w) \in M$, $w \in V_T^*$ or $w \in L(G)$, $|w| \leqq n$.

2) $(S \to [A_1; c_{j_{1,1}}, \ldots, c_{j_{1,k_1}}] \ldots [A_n; c_{j_{n,1}}, \ldots, c_{j_{n,k_n}}])$

for each $(S \to A_1 A_2 \ldots A_n) \in M$ where the pairs $c_{j_{u,v}}$ are chosen in such a way that each nonterminal $[A_i; \ldots]$ contains a pair (a, i) and the symbols $a \in V_T$, the superscripts $+$, $-$, and the integers j in the pairs (a^+, j), (a^-, j) are arranged in such a way that if we ignore pairs (a, i) and concatenate in increasing order of the integers j all symbols a^+ and all symbols a^-, then we obtain the same string modulo the superscripts $+$ and $-$. In other words, the pairs (a^+, j), (a^-, j) describe a correct translation of symbols from some position of the derivation to another, correct in the sense that the "senders" and the "receivers" of symbols correspond to each other. (An example could be enlightened: consider a derivation

$$S \Rightarrow A_1 A_2 \ldots A_7 \overset{*}{\Rightarrow} (abc)\,(d)\,(e)\,(\lambda)\,(\lambda)\,(\lambda)\,(fg);$$

then we introduce the matrix

$$\begin{aligned}(S \to {} & [A_1; (a, 1), (b^-, 2), (c^-, 3)]\,[A_2; (b^+, 1), (d^-, 4), (b, 2)] \\ & [A_3; (c^+, 1), (e^-, 5), (c, 3)]\,[A_4; (d^+, 2), (d, 4)] \\ & [A_5; (e^+, 3), (e, 5)]\,[A_6; (f^+, 7), (f, 6)]\,[A_7; (f^-, 6), (g, 7)])\end{aligned}$$

and obtain $w^+ = b^+c^+d^+e^+f^+$, $w^- = b^-c^-d^-e^-f^-$.)

3) $$([A_1; c_{j_{1,1}}, \ldots, c_{j_{1,k_1}}] \to x_1'[B_1; c_{r_{1,1}}, \ldots, c_{r_{1,u_1}}]\,y_1', \ldots$$
$$\ldots [A_n; c_{j_{n,1}}, \ldots, c_{j_{n,k_n}}] \to x_n'[B_n; c_{r_{n,1}}, \ldots, c_{r_{n,u_n}}]\,y_n')$$

for each matrix $(A_1 \to x_1 B_1 y_1, \ldots, A_n \to x_n B_n y_n) \in M$ where the pairs $c_{j_{t,v}}$, $c_{r_{t,v}}$ are chosen in such a way that

a) $k_t, u_t \geqq 0$; if $k_t = 0$ or $u_t = 0$, then $[A_t; \ldots]$ is in fact A_t,

b) either $x_i' = x_i = \lambda = y_i' = y_i$ and then $c_{j_{i,t}} = c_{r_{i,t}}$ for all $1 \leqq t \leqq k_i = u_i$, or

c) $x_i = a x_i'$, $a \in V_T$, and there is $c_{j_{i,t}} = (a^-, p)$, $p < i$, and $[B_i; \ldots]$ does not contain (a^-, p), or

d) $x_i = \lambda$, $x_i' = a$, $a \in V_T$, and there is $c_{j_{i,t}} = (a^+, p)$, $p < i$, and $[B_i; \ldots]$ does not contain (a^+, p) and (a, i), and

e) $y_i = y'_i a$, $a \in V_T$, and there is $c_{j_{i,t}} = (a^-, p)$, $p > i$, and $[B_i; \ldots]$ does not contain (a^-, p), or

f) $y_i = \lambda$, $y'_i = a$, $a \in V_T$, and there is $c_{j_{i,t}} = (a^+, p)$, $p > i$, and $[B_i; \ldots]$ does not contain (a^+, p) and (a, i), or

g) $x_i = x'_i$, $y_i = y'_i$, $x_i y_i$ contains the symbol $a \in V_T$ and (a, i) appears in $[A_i; \ldots]$ but not in $[B_i; \ldots]$, or

h) $k_i = u_i = 0$ and $x'_i = x_i$, $y'_i = y_i$.

(The translation of symbols is memorized by couples (a^+, j), (a^-, j), (a, j).)

4) $$([A_1; c_{j_{1,1}}, \ldots, c_{j_{1,k_1}}] \to x'_1, \ldots, [A_n; c_{j_{n,1}}, \ldots, c_{j_{n,k_n}}] \to x'_n)$$

for each matrix $(A_1 \to x_1, \ldots, A_n \to x_n) \in M$ with

a) either $x'_i = x_i$ and then $k_i = 0$, or

b) $x_i = \lambda$, $x'_i = a$, and there are (a, i), (a^+, p) in $[A_i; \ldots]$ for some p ($p < i$ or $p > i$), or

c) $x_i = a x'_i$ ($x_i = x'_i a$), $a \in V_T$, and there is (a^-, p) in $[A_i; \ldots]$ for some $p < i$ ($p > i$, respectively).

From the above (cumbersome) construction one can see that all non-initial matrices in M are also in M'. From the given explanation one can check that $L(G) = L(G')$ and that each alphabet V'_i in each derivation according to G' introduces at least a terminal symbol (the pairs c_j are eliminated only in such circumstances).

One can verify that the above construction can be performed in a similar way also for regular simple matrix grammars.

Theorem 1.5.3. *Let* $X \in \{\text{LIN}, \text{REG}\}$. *Then*

$$\mathcal{L}(\text{SM}, X) = \mathcal{L}(\text{SM}, X - \lambda) \quad \textit{and} \quad \mathcal{L}(\text{SM}, X, n) = \mathcal{L}(\text{SM}, X - \lambda, n)$$

for $n \geqq 1$.

Proof. Let $G = (V_1, V_2, \ldots, V_n, V_T, M, S)$ be a linear (regular) simple matrix grammar having the property of Lemma 1.5.7 and take a matrix

$$(A_1 \to x_1, \ldots, A_{i-1} \to x_{i-1}, A_i \to \lambda, A_{i+1} \to x_{i+1}, A_n \to x_n)$$

of M containing the rule $A_i \to \lambda$ and with $x_j \in V_T^*$ for $1 \leqq j \leqq n$. With it we associate the matrices

$$(A_1 \to x_1, \ldots, A_{i-1} \to x_{i-1}, (a, A_i) \to a, A_{i+1} \to x_{i+1}, \ldots, A_n \to x_n)$$

where $a \in V_T$. Further, with each matrix of M of the form

$$(B_1 \to y_1 C_1 z_1, \ldots, B_i \to y_i C_i z_i, \ldots, B_n \to y_n C_n z_n)$$

with either $y_i = y'_i a$ or $z_i = a z'_i$, $a \in V_T$, $y_i, z_i \in V_T^*$, $1 \leqq i \leqq n$, we associate the matrices

$$(B_1 \to y_1 C_1 z_1, \ldots, B_{i-1} \to y_{i-1} C_{i-1} z_{i-1}, B_i \to y''_i (a, C_i) z''_i,$$
$$B_{i+1} \to y_{i+1} C_{i+1} z_{i+1}, \ldots, B_n \to y_n C_n z_n)$$

with either $y_i'' = y_i'$ and $z_i'' = z_i$ or $y_i'' = y_i$ and $z_i'' = z_i'$. With a matrix of the form

$$(B_1 \to y_1C_1z_1, \ldots, B_i \to C_i, \ldots, B_n \to y_nC_nz_n),$$

$y_i, z_i \in V_T^*$, we associate the matrices

$$(B_1 \to y_1C_1z_1, \ldots, (a, B_i) \to (a, C_i), \ldots, B_n \to y_nC_nz_n)$$

where $a \in V_T$. Then we consider the grammar

$$G'' = (V_1, V_2, \ldots, V_{i-1}, V_i \cup V_T \times V_i, V_{i+1}, \ldots, V_n, V_T, M'', S)$$

where M'' is the set obtained by adding to M all the above constructed matrices and removing the matrix $(A_1 \to x_1, \ldots, A_i \to \lambda, \ldots, A_n \to x_n)$. Obviously, we have $L(G'') = L(G)$ and G'' has fewer λ-rules than G. By repeating the above procedure for each λ-rule in G we obtain a λ-free linear (regular) simple matrix grammar equivalent to G.

We can now prove the next basic result.

Theorem 1.5.4. *The inclusions* $\mathcal{L}(\text{SM}, X, n) \subset \mathcal{L}(\text{SM}, X, n+1)$ *are proper for all* $n \geqq 1$ *and* $X \in \{\text{REG, LIN, CF}\}$ *(the hierarchies* $\mathcal{L}(\text{SM}, X, n), n \geqq 1$, *are infinite for* $X \in \{\text{REG, LIN, CF}\}$*).*

Proof. Let $G = (V_1, V_2, \ldots, V_n, V_T, M, S)$ be a simple matrix grammar of degree n and construct the simple matrix grammar

$$G' = (V_1, V_2, \ldots, V_n, \{T\}, V_T, M', S) \quad \text{of degree } n+1 \text{ where}$$

$$M' = \{(S \to A_1A_2 \ldots A_nT) : (S \to A_1A_2 \ldots A_n) \in M\}$$

$$\cup \{(S \to w) : w \in V_T^*, (S \to w) \in M\}$$

$$\cup \{(A_1 \to x_1, \ldots, A_n \to x_n, T \to T^u) : (A_1 \to x_1, \ldots, A_n \to x_n) \in M,$$

$$u = |x_1|_{V_1}\}.$$

The equality $L(G) = L(G')$ is obvious, G' is of the same type as G (but not λ-free). Therefore $L(G) \in \mathcal{L}(\text{SM}, X, n+1)$, and hence $\mathcal{L}(\text{SM}, X, n) \subset \mathcal{L}(\text{SM}, X, n+1)$ for each X as in the theorem.

Consider now the languages K_n, K_n' of Lemma 1.5.6. The linear simple matrix grammar

$$G_n = (\{A_1\}, \{A_2\}, \ldots, \{A_{n+1}\}, \{a_1, a_2, \ldots, a_{2n+1}\}, M, S)$$

with

$$M = \{(S \to A_1A_2 \ldots A_{n+1}),$$
$$(A_1 \to a_1A_1a_2, A_2 \to a_3A_2a_4, \ldots, A_n \to a_{2n-1}A_na_{2n}, A_{n+1} \to a_{2n+1}A_{n+1})$$
$$(A_1 \to a_1a_2, A_2 \to a_3a_4, \ldots, A_n \to a_{2n-1}a_{2n}, A_{n+1} \to a_{2n+1})\}$$

has degree $n+1$ and generates K_n. Thus $K_n \in \mathcal{L}(\text{SM, LIN}, n+1) \setminus \mathcal{L}(\text{SM, CF}, n)$. Moreover, the regular simple matrix grammar

$$G_n' = (\{A_1\}, \{A_2\}, \ldots, \{A_{n+1}\}, \{a_1, a_2, \ldots, a_{n+1}\}, M', S)$$

with

$$M' = \{(S \to A_1A_2 \ldots A_{n+1}), (A_1 \to a_1A_1, A_2 \to a_2A_2, \ldots, A_{n+1} \to a_{n+1}A_{n+1}),$$
$$(A_1 \to a_1, A_2 \to a_2, \ldots, A_{n+1} \to a_{n+1})\}$$

has degree $n + 1$ and generates K'_n. Hence $K'_n \in \mathcal{L}(\text{SM, REG}, n + 1) \setminus \mathcal{L}(\text{SM, REG}, n)$. This completes the proof.

Remark In the above theorem we have considered only families $\mathcal{L}(\text{SM, LIN}, n)$ and $\mathcal{L}(\text{SM, REG}, n)$ but, in view of Theorem 1.5.3, the assertion holds also for λ-free linear and regular grammars. However, the above proof cannot be used for proving also that $\mathcal{L}(\text{SM, CF} - \lambda, n) \subseteq \mathcal{L}(\text{SM, CF} - \lambda, n + 1)$. On the other hand, we have $K_n \in \mathcal{L}(\text{SM, CF} - \lambda, n + 1) \setminus \mathcal{L}(\text{SM, CF} - \lambda, n)$.

Theorem 1.5.5. *The inclusions* $\mathcal{L}(\text{SM, CF} - \lambda, n) \subset \mathcal{L}(\text{SM, CF}, n)$ *for* $m \geqq 2$ *and* $\mathcal{L}(\text{SM, CF} - \lambda) \subset \mathcal{L}(\text{SM, CF})$ *are proper.*

Proof. It is enough to find a language $L \in \mathcal{L}(\text{SM, CF}, 2) \setminus \mathcal{L}(\text{SM, CF} - \lambda)$ since the inclusions have already been pointed out. We consider the language

$$L = \{a^n b^n c^{k_1} d^{k_1} c^{k_2} d^{k_2} \dots c^{k_m} d^{k_m} e^n f^n : n, m \geqq 1, k_i \geqq 1, 1 \leqq i \leqq m\}.$$

The context-free simple matrix grammar

$$G_0 = (\{A, B, C, D\}, \{E, F, T\}, \{a, b, c, d, e, f\}, M, S)$$

with

$$\begin{aligned} M = \{&(S \to AE), (A \to BC, E \to FT), (B \to aBb, F \to eFf), \\ &(B \to ab, F \to ef), (C \to DC, T \to TT), (C \to D, T \to T), \\ &(D \to cDd, T \to T), (D \to cd, T \to \lambda)\} \end{aligned}$$

has degree 2 and generates L. Therefore $L \in \mathcal{L}(\text{SM, CF}, 2)$.

Let us suppose that there is a λ-free simple matrix grammar of degree n, $n \geqq 1$, say $G = (V_1, V_2, \dots, V_n, V_T, M, S)$, $V_T = \{a, b, c, d, e, f\}$, which generates L. We must have $n \geqq 2$ since L is not a context-free language. We construct the context-free grammars $G_i = (V_i, V_T, P_i, S)$, $1 \leqq i \leqq n$, as in the proof of Lemma 1.5.4. Then there is at least one language $L(G_i)$ which contains arbitrarily many strings of the form

$$xc^{k_1}d^{k_1}c^{k_2}d^{k_2} \dots c^{k_r}d^{k_r}y,$$

$x, y \in V_T^*$. As k_i can be arbitrarily large, it follows that we have to use a terminal rule for each $c^{k_j}d^{k_j}$ if we generate such a string. Such a rule belongs to a terminal matrix in M.

Let us suppose that $1 < i < n$. Using a terminal rule at position i we also use a terminal rule at positions 1 and n (in grammars G_1 and G_n). The language $L(G_1)$ contains only strings of the form $a^t u$, whereas $L(G_n)$ contains only strings of the form vf^s. If the terminal rules used in G_1 simultaneously with the terminal rules used in G_i introduce symbols a and/or b, then the terminal rules in G_n introduce symbols e and/or f (we cannot increase arbitrarily the number of symbols a/b (or e/f) without also increasing the number of e/f (and a/b, respectively)). The language L contains strings with m substrings $c^k d^k$ and p symbols a with an arbitrarily large difference $m - p$. This implies that there are terminal rules in G_1 which introduce symbols c and/or d simultaneously with using terminal rules in G_i. However, this implies that the derivation of the prefix $a^p b^p$ is terminated, which, in turn, implies that the derivation of the suffix $e^p f^p$ is almost terminated, in the sense that at most a well-defined number of symbols e, f will be introduced in the next steps of the derivation. But also at position n we must use terminal rules when we use terminal rules at positions 1 and i, and this implies that further arbitrarily many symbols e, f are to be introduced. This is a contradiction.

Now let $i = 1$, that is the language $L(G_1)$ contains strings $a^pb^pc^{k_1}d^{k_1}c^{k_2}d^{k_2} \dots c^{k_r}d^{k_r}y$ with arbitrarily large r and k_i. The use of a terminal rule which introduces symbols c, d is possible only after finishing the generation of the string a^pb^p, but simultaneously with some terminals rules which introduce symbols e, f. Again the correspondence between a^pb^p and e^pf^p is violated.

Finally, suppose that $i = n$. Now if we use a terminal rule $A_n \to x_n$, x_n containing c and/or d, the derivation of e^pf^p is not started, but we have to use a rule $A_1 \to x_1$ in G_1. If this rule introduces symbols c and/or d, then the derivation of the prefix a^pb^p is already terminated, hence the correspondence between a^pb^p and e^pf^p cannot be observed. If the terminal rules $A_1 \to x_1$ satisfy $x_1 \in \{a, b\}^*$, then we can introduce arbitrarily many occurrences of symbols a, b before starting the derivation of e^pf^p, and again we obtain strings not in L.

Since all cases lead to a contradiction, the grammar G cannot exist, and hence L is not in $\mathcal{L}(\mathrm{SM}, \mathrm{CF} - \lambda)$.

Corollary. *The families $\mathcal{L}(\mathrm{SM}, \mathrm{CF} - \lambda, n)$ for $n \geqq 2$ and $\mathcal{L}(\mathrm{SM}, \mathrm{CF} - \lambda)$ are not closed under arbitrary homomorphisms.*

In what follows we shall specify some closure properties of the families $\mathcal{L}(\mathrm{SM}, X, n)$, $n \geqq 1$, and $\mathcal{L}(\mathrm{SM}, X)$, $X \in \{\mathrm{REG}, \mathrm{LIN}, \mathrm{CF}\}$. The proofs of the positive results follow standard constructions or can be obtained by using the known results for families $\mathcal{L}(X)$, $X \in \{\mathrm{REG}, \mathrm{LIN}, \mathrm{CF}\}$, and the constructions in the proof of Lemma 1.5.2. The negative results can be proved using the languages in Lemma 1.5.6 or other similar languages and the necessary conditions considered above.

Theorem 1.5.6. i) *Each of the families $\mathcal{L}(\mathrm{SM}, \mathrm{CF}, n)$, $n \geqq 1$, and $\mathcal{L}(\mathrm{SM}, \mathrm{CF})$ is closed under union, substitution by context-free languages, intersection with regular languages, concatenation with context-free languages, arbitrary gsm mappings (and homomorphisms), inverse gsm mappings, right and left quotients by regular sets.*

ii) *Each of the families $\mathcal{L}(\mathrm{SM}, \mathrm{REG}, n)$, $\mathcal{L}(\mathrm{SM}, \mathrm{LIN}, n)$, $n \geqq 1$, $\mathcal{L}(\mathrm{SM}, \mathrm{REG})$, and $\mathcal{L}(\mathrm{SM/LN})$ is closed under union, substitutions, intersection and concatenation with regular languages, under arbitrary gsm mappings (and homomorphisms), inverse gsm mappings, right and left quotients by regular sets.*

iii) *Let $X \in \{\mathrm{REG}, \mathrm{LIN}, \mathrm{CF}\}$. Then the families $\mathcal{L}(\mathrm{SM}, X, n)$, $n \geqq 2$, are not closed under concatenation, but each family $\mathcal{L}(\mathrm{SM}, X)$ is closed under concatenation. No family $\mathcal{L}(\mathrm{SM}, X, n)$, $n \geqq 2$, and $\mathcal{L}(\mathrm{SM}, X)$ is closed under intersection, complementation, substitution and Kleene $+$.*

The only point which does not follow simply from the previous considerations is the non-closure under intersection. Therefore we consider the languages

$$L_1 = \{a^nb^nc^m : n, m \geqq 1\}^*,$$

$$L_2 = \{a^nb^mc^m : n, m \geqq 1\}^*.$$

As $L_1, L_2 \in \mathcal{L}(\mathrm{CF})$ and $L_1 \cap L_2 = \{a^nb^nc^n : n \geqq 1\}^*$, it follows that $\mathcal{L}(\mathrm{SM}, \mathrm{CF}, n)$, $n \geqq 1$, and $\mathcal{L}(\mathrm{SM}, \mathrm{CF})$ are not closed under intersection.

Now we consider the languages

$$L_3 = \{xch(x) : x \in \{a, b\}^*\}$$

with h defined by $h(a) = d$, $h(b) = e$, and

$$L_4 = \{a^{i_1}b^{j_1}a^{i_2}b^{j_2} \dots a^{i_k}b^{j_k}cd^{r_1}e^{i_1}d^{r_2}e^{i_1} \dots d^{r_k}e^{i_k} : k \geqq 1,$$
$$i_s, j_s, r_s \geqq 1 \quad \text{for} \quad 1 \leqq s \leqq k\} \cup \{c\}.$$

$L_4 \in \mathscr{L}(\text{SM, REG}, 2)$ holds since the grammar

$$G_4 = (\{A_1, A_2, A_3, A_4\}, \{B_1, B_2, B_3, B_4\}, \{a, b, c, d, e\}, M, S),$$
$$M = \{(S \to c), (S \to A_1B_1), (A_1 \to A_2, B_1 \to dB_2), (A_2 \to A_2, B_2 \to dB_2),$$
$$(A_2 \to aA_3, B_2 \to eB_3), (A_3 \to aA_3, B_3 \to eB_3),$$
$$(A_3 \to bA_4, B_3 \to B_4), (A_4 \to bA_4, B_4 \to B_4), (A_4 \to c, B_4 \to \lambda),$$
$$(A_4 \to A_2, B_4 \to dB_2)\}$$

generates the language L_4. But we have

$$L_3 \cap L_4 = \{a^{i_1}b^{i_1} \dots a^{i_k}b^{i_k}cd^{i_1}e^{i_1} \dots d^{i_k}e^{i_k} : k \geqq 1, i_j \geqq 1, 1 \leqq j \leqq k\} \cup \{c\},$$

and this language is not in $\mathscr{L}(\text{SM, LIN})$ because by erasing the symbols c, d, and e by a homomorphism h we obtain

$$h(L_3 \cap L_4) = \{a^n b^n : n \geqq 1\}^*$$

which is not in $\mathscr{L}(\text{SM, LIN})$.

We have pointed out that the emptiness and the finiteness problems are decidable for arbitrary context-free simple matrix grammars. From Theorem 1.5.1 it follows that the membership problem also is decidable. However, many other problems are undecidable for simple matrix grammars of various types.

Theorem 1.5.7. *The following decision problems are undecidable for arbitrary regular simple matrix grammars G_1, G_2:*

i) *Is $L(G_1)$ regular?*

ii) *Is $L(G_1)$ equal to V^*?*

iii) *Is $L(G_1) \cap L(G_2)$ empty, finite, regular, or in the family $\mathscr{L}(\text{SM, REG})$?*

iv) *Is $L(G_1) \subseteq L(G_2)$ or $L(G_1) = L(G_2)$?*

The following problems are also undecidable:

v) *Is $L(G)$ in $\mathscr{L}(\text{SM, LIN})$ for an arbitrary context-free grammar G?*

vi) *Is $L(G)$ in $\mathscr{L}(\text{SM}, X, k)$, $X \in \{\text{REG, LIM, CF}\}$, for an arbitrary simple matrix grammar G of degree n, $n > k$, of type X?*

Proof. i), ii), iv) Let $x = (x_1, x_2, \dots, x_n)$ be an n-tuple of nonempty strings over $\{a, b\}$. We consider the language

$$L'(x) = \{ba^{i_1}ba^{i_2} \dots ba^{i_k}cx_{i_1}x_{i_2} \dots x_{i_k} : k \geqq 1, 1 \leqq i_j \leqq n, 1 \leqq j \leqq k\}.$$

One can prove that the language $\{a, b, c\}^* \setminus L'(x)$ belongs to the family $\mathscr{L}(\text{SM, REG}, 2)$.

Now let $V = \{a, b, c\}$, and let x, y be two n-tuples of non-empty strings over $\{a, b\}$. We consider the language

$$L_1 = (V^* \setminus L'(x)) \cup (V^* \setminus L'(y)).$$

Clearly, if $L_1 = V^*$, then $V^* \setminus L_1 = L'(x) \cap L'(y) = \emptyset$ and conversely. According to the Post correspondence theorem, the problem whether or not $L_1 = V^*$ is undecidable. In this way i), ii), and iv) are obtained.

iii) The considerations above prove the undecidability of the emptiness and finiteness of $L'(x) \cap L'(y)$. Now let $L_1, L_2 \subseteq \{d, e\}^*$ be two languages in $\mathcal{L}(\text{SM, REG})$ whose intersection is not in $\mathcal{L}(\text{SM, REG})$. The languages $L_1L'(x)$ and $L_2L'(y)$ are in $\mathcal{L}(\text{SM, REG})$ because this family is closed under concatenation. Now let

$$L_3 = L_1L'(x) \cap L_2L'(y).$$

If $L'(x) \cap L'(y) = \emptyset$, then $L_3 = \emptyset$. Now assume that $L'(x) \cap L'(y) \neq \emptyset$ and let h be the homomorphism which erases the symbols a, b, c. Then we get $h(L_3) = L_1 \cap L_2$. In conclusion, $L_3 \in \mathcal{L}(\text{SM, REG})$ if and only if $L'(x) \cap L'(y) = \emptyset$, which is undecidable. This completes the proof of point iii).

vi) Let now V_1, V_2 be two disjoint alphabets, and let $L_2 \subseteq V_2^*$, $L_2 \in \mathcal{L}(\text{SM}, X, n) \setminus \mathcal{L}(\text{SM}, X, k)$ for given $X \in \{\text{REG, LIN, CF}\}$, and $n > k$. Further let $L_1 \subseteq V_1^*$, $L_1 \in \mathcal{L}(\text{SM, REG}, 2)$, and consider the language $L_4 = L_1L_2^* \cup V_1^*L_2$. Clearly, $L_4 \in \mathcal{L}(\text{SM}, X, n)$ (this family is closed under union and under concatenation with regular languages). If $L_1 = V_1^*$, then $L_4 = V_1^*V_2^*$ and hence $L_4 \in \mathcal{L}(\text{REG})$. If $L_1 \neq V_1^*$, then $L_4 \notin \mathcal{L}(\text{SM}, X, k)$. Indeed, let $w \in V_1^* \to L_1$. Then we get $L_4 \cap \{w\}\, V_2^* = \{w\}\, L_2$. Since $\mathcal{L}(\text{SM}, X, k)$ is closed under homomorphisms it follows that $L_2 \in \mathcal{L}(\text{SM}, X, k)$ if L_4 is in this family. This contradicts the choice of L_2. Therefore $L_4 \in \mathcal{L}(\text{SM}, X, k)$ if and only if $L_1 = V_1^*$ which is undecidable.

v) follows in the same way taking $L_1 \in \mathcal{L}(\text{CF})$ and $L_2 \in \mathcal{L}(\text{CF}) \setminus \mathcal{L}(\text{SM, LIN})$.

We consider here without proof some representation and characterization theorems for simple matrix languages of various types.

Theorem 1.5.8. *Each language $L \in \mathcal{L}(\text{SM, CF})$ can be written in the form*

$$L = h(D_n \cap R)$$

where h is a homomorphism, D_n is a Dyck context-free language, and R is a language in $\mathcal{L}(\text{SM, REG})$.

Theorem 1.5.9. *Let V be an alphabet and c a symbol not in V and*

$$V(n, c) = \{(wc)^n : w \in V^*\}$$

for some natural number n. A language L is in $\mathcal{L}(\text{SM, REG})$ if and only if there are V, n, and c as above and a gsm mapping g such that $L = g(V(n, c))$.

Let us now pass on to programmed grammars and consider the following natural variant of them.

Definition 1.5.3. A programmed grammar G is said to be with *unconditional transfer* if $\varphi(r) = \sigma(r)$ for each rule in G.

The next rule is selected from the same set, irrespectively of applying or not applying effectively the current rule.

Example. We consider the grammar

$$G = (\{S, A, B, A', B'\}, \{a, b, c\}, P, S)$$

where P consists of the rules

$$(r_0: S \to abc, \emptyset, \emptyset),$$
$$(r_1: S \to AB, \{r_2\}, \{r_2\}),$$
$$(r_2: A \to aA'b, \{r_3\}, \{r_3\}),$$
$$(r_3: B \to cB', \{r_4\}, \{r_4\}),$$
$$(r_4: A' \to A, \{r_5\}, \{r_5\}),$$
$$(r_5: B' \to B, \{r_2, r_6\}, \{r_2, r_6\}),$$
$$(r_6: A \to ab, \{r_7\}, \{r_7\}),$$
$$(r_7: B \to c, \{r_7\}, \{r_7\}).$$

The equality

$$L(G) = \{a^n b^n c^n : n \geqq 1\}$$

is obvious.

Clearly, each context-free grammar can be regarded as an unconditional transfer programmed grammar with $\sigma(r) = \varphi(r) = \mathrm{Lab}\,(P)$.

The family of unconditional transfer programmed languages is strictly included in $\mathcal{L}(\mathrm{P, CF} - \lambda, \mathrm{ac})$. In order to prove this assertion we use the following lemma, formulated and proved in Rosenkrantz (1969) for leftmost derivation, but also true for free derivations.

Lemma 1.5.8. *The prefix property is decidable for unconditional transfer λ-free context-free programmed grammars, i.e. there is an algorithm which decides for an arbitrary grammar G and an arbitrary string x whether or not $xy \in L(G)$ for some y.*

Theorem 1.5.10. *The family of languages generated by λ-free context-free unconditional transfer programmed is strictly included in $\mathcal{L}(\mathrm{P, CF} - \lambda, \mathrm{ac})$.*

Proof. Let $L \in \mathcal{L}(\mathrm{RE})$ be a nonrecursive language over some alphabet V. According to Theorem 1.2.5, there is a matrix grammar with appearance checking and λ-rules which generates L. In fact, we can modify the proof of Theorem 1.2.5 in the following way: replace the initial matrices

$$(S' \to ES'), (S' \to ESA_1)$$

by

$$(S' \to S'E), (S' \to A_1ES)$$

and replace all rules of the form $X \to \lambda$ in other matrices by $X \to c$ for some new symbol c. The matrix grammar G' obtained in this way generates a language containing strings of the form xc^n, $x \in L$, $n \geqq 1$, such that $L = \{x : xc^n \in L(G')\}$ for some n.

Clearly, the language $L(G')$ is in $\mathcal{L}(\mathrm{P, CF} - \lambda, \mathrm{ac})$. Assume that this is an unconditional transfer programmed language and let G'' be such a grammar for $L(G')$. Obviously, xc is a prefix of $L(G')$ if and only if $x \in L$. According to Lemma 1.5.8, we can decide whether $xc \in \mathrm{Pref}\,(L(G''))$ which implies that we can decide whether or not $x \in L$. This contradicts the fact that L is not recursive. Therefore $L(G')$ cannot be generated by an unconditional transfer programmed grammar.

The above Lemma 1.5.8 also has further consequences whose proofs are left to the reader (the ideas used in the proof of Theorem 1.5.7 can be used).

Theorem 1.5.11. *The emptiness problem is decidable for unconditional transfer programmed grammars, but the context-freeness and the question whether a programmed grammar generates a unconditional transfer language are undecidable.*

Remark. A sort of dual of unconditional transfer programmed grammars could be defined, namely the disjoint programmed grammars, that is grammars with rules $(r: A \to x, \sigma(r), \varphi(r))$ having $\sigma(r) \cap \varphi(r) = \emptyset$ for all rules. However, for each programmed grammar G one can construct an equivalent disjoint programmed grammar by replacing each rule $(r: A \to x, \sigma(r), \varphi(r))$ by

$$(r_1: A \to x, \{t_1 : t \in \sigma(r)\} \cup \{t_2 : t \in \sigma(r)\}, \emptyset),$$

$$(r_2: A \to Z, \emptyset, \{t_1 : t \in \varphi(r)\} \cup \{t_2 : t \in \varphi(r)\})$$

where Z is a trap symbol. Therefore such grammars are not of further interest.

Finally let us discuss some variants of random context grammars. So far, we considered such grammars with the rules $(A \to x, Q, R)$ where Q and R are arbitrary, or $R = \emptyset$ for all rules. A natural possibility is to consider also random context grammars with only forbidding contexts, i.e. with $Q = \emptyset$ for all rules as above. By $\mathscr{L}(\text{fRC}, X)$ we denote the family of languages generated by random context grammars of type X with only forbidding contexts.

A stronger result than that in Theorem 1.2.6 can be obtained for these grammars.

Theorem 1.5.12. $\mathscr{L}(\text{ETOL}) \subset \mathscr{L}(\text{fRC}, \text{CF} - \lambda)$.

Proof. Let $L \in \mathscr{L}(\text{ETOL})$, $L = L(G)$ for some ETOL system $G = (V, V_1, P, w)$, $P = \{P_1, P_2, \ldots, P_r\}$. Without loss of generality we can assume that G is λ-free (Theorem 0.2.11). Now we introduce the alphabets

$$V^{(i)} = \{a^{(i)} : a \in V\},\ 1 \leqq i \leqq r,$$

$$V' = \{a' : a \in V\},\ V'' = \{a'' : a \in V\},\ \{\overline{V} = \bar{a} : a \in V_1\}$$

(as usually, for $w \in V^*$, by $w^{(i)}$, w', w'', $\overline{w}$ we denote the words obtained from w by replacing each occurrence of a symbol $a \in V$ by $a^{(i)}$, a', a'', $\bar{a}$, respectively). Let P be the set of all random context rules of the following types:

(1) $(a' \to a'', \emptyset, \overline{V} \cup V^{(1)} \cup V^{(2)} \cup \cdots \cup V^{(r)})$ for $a \in V$,

(2) $(a'' \to a^{(i)}, \emptyset, \overline{V} \cup V' \cup V^{(1)} \cup \cdots \cup V^{(i-1)} \cup V^{(i+1)} \cup \ldots \cup V^{(r)})$
for $a \in V, 1 \leqq i \leqq r$,

(3) $(a^{(i)} \to u', \emptyset, V'' \cup \overline{V})$ for $a \to u \in P_i$,

(4) $(a' \to \bar{a}, \emptyset, V'' \cup V^{(1)} \cup V^{(2)} \cup \cdots \cup V^{(r)})$ for $a \in V_1$,

(5) $(\bar{a} \to a, \emptyset, V' \cup V'' \cup V^{(1)} \cup V^{(2)} \cup \cdots \cup V^{(r)})$ for $a \in V_1$,

(6) $(S \to w', \emptyset, \emptyset)$.

We consider the random context grammar

$$G' = (\{S\} \cup V' \cup V'' \cup \overline{V} \cup V^{(1)} \cup V^{(2)} \cup \cdots \cup V^{(r)}, V_1, P, S)$$

which has only forbidding contexts.

Let x' be a string over V'. To x' we can apply only rules whose left side is in V'.

Case 1. We use $a' \to a''$ for some $a' \in V'$. Now the obtained sentential form contains letters of V' and V''. Hence we can use only rules of type (1). Continuing in this way we get $x' \Rightarrow x''$. By analogous arguments we now have to rewrite all letters of x'' by rules of type (2) with the same "index" i. Thus we obtain $x^{(i)}$. Now to each letter $a^{(i)}$ of $x^{(i)}$ we apply a rule $a^{(i)} \to u'$ where $a \to u \in P_i$. Since again all letters of $x^{(i)}$ have to be replaced before starting with rules of another type we simulate a derivation step in G and get z' where $x \Rightarrow z$ in G. Therefore starting with a rule type (1) we simulate a derivation step in G, and conversely, each derivation step in G can be simulated in this way.

Case 2. We apply to x' a rule $a' \to \bar{a}$. Then each letter a' of V_1' occurring in x' has to be substituted by $\bar{a}$ and then by a using rules of type (5). Therefore we obtain a terminal word only if $x' \in (V_1')^*$.

By these considerations the terminating derivations in G' are of the form

$$S \Rightarrow w' \Rightarrow w'' \Rightarrow w^{(i_0)} \Rightarrow z_1' \Rightarrow z_1'' \Rightarrow z_1^{(i_1)} \Rightarrow \cdots \Rightarrow z_n' \Rightarrow z_n'' \Rightarrow z_n^{(i_n)} \Rightarrow z_{n+1}'$$

$$\Rightarrow \bar{z}_{n+1} \Rightarrow z_{n+1}$$

and such a derivation exists if and only if

$$w \Rightarrow z_1 \Rightarrow z_2 \Rightarrow \cdots \Rightarrow z_n \Rightarrow z_{n+1}$$

is a derivation in G. In conclusion, $L(G) = L(G')$.

In order to finish the proof it suffices to find a language which is not in $\mathcal{L}$(ETOL) and which can be generated by a forbidding random context grammar. Such a language is

$$L = \{b(ba^m)^n : m \geqq n \geqq 0\}$$

which can be generated by the grammar

$$G = (\{S, A, A', B, B', B'', C, D, E\}, \{a, b\}, P, S)$$

with P consisting of the following rules:

$$(S \to SA, \emptyset, \emptyset),$$

$$(S \to C, \emptyset, \emptyset),$$

$$(C \to D, \emptyset, \{S, A', B', B'', D, E\}),$$

$$(B \to B'a, \emptyset, \{S, C, E\}),$$

$$(A \to B''a, \emptyset, \{S, C, E, B''\}),$$

$$(A \to A'a, \emptyset, \{S, C, E\}),$$

$$(D \to C, \emptyset, \{A, B\}),$$

$$(B' \to B, \emptyset, \{D\}),$$

$$(B'' \to B, \emptyset, \{D\}),$$

$$(A' \to A, \emptyset, \{D\}),$$

$$(D \to E, \emptyset, \{S, A, A', B', B'', C, E\}),$$

$$(B \to b, \emptyset, \{S, A, A', B', B'', C, D\}),$$

$$(E \to b, \emptyset, \{S, A, A', B, B', B'', C, D\})$$

(first we have the derivation

$$S \Rightarrow SA^n \Rightarrow CA^n \Rightarrow DA^n$$

and then we have to replace all occurrences of A; if we want to replace an A by a terminal word in some steps it is necessary to use $A \to B''a$, however, this can be done at most once in a phase which replaces all A; therefore $m \geqq n$).

Another natural modification of the random context grammars is obtained by considering strings as random contexts instead of symbols.

Definition 1.5.4. A *string random context grammar of degree* (i, j), $i, j \geqq 0$, is a quadruple $G = (V_N, V_T, P, S)$ where V_N, V_T, S are as in a usual grammar and P is a finite set of production rules of the form $(A \to x, \alpha, \beta)$ where

i) $A \to x$ is a context-free rule over V_G,

ii) $i = 0$ and $\alpha = \emptyset$, or $i > 0$ and $\alpha \in V_G^*$, $|\alpha| \leqq i$, or $\alpha = \emptyset$,

iii) $j = 0$ and $\beta = \emptyset$, or $j > 0$ and $\beta \in V_G^*$, $|\beta| \leqq j$, or $\beta = \emptyset$.

Such a rule can be applied to a string w if and only if the string α (if $\alpha \neq \emptyset$) is a substring of w and the string β (if $\beta \neq \emptyset$) is not a substring of w. (Clearly, if $\alpha = \emptyset$, $\beta = \emptyset$, then the rule can be applied without restrictions.)

By $\mathscr{L}(\mathrm{SRC}, X, (i, j))$, $X \in \{\mathrm{CF}, \mathrm{CF} - \lambda\}$, we denote the family of languages generated by string random context grammars of degree (i, j), $i, j \geqq 0$.

Lemma 1.5.9. i) $\mathscr{L}(\mathrm{CF}) = \mathscr{L}(\mathrm{SRC}, \mathrm{CF} - \lambda, (0, 0))$,

ii) $\mathscr{L}(\mathrm{SRC}, X, (i, j)) \subseteq \mathscr{L}(\mathrm{SRC}, X, (i', j')$ *for* $X \in \{\mathrm{CF}, \mathrm{CF} - \lambda)$, *and* $i \leqq i'$, $j \leqq j'$,

iii) $\mathscr{L}(\mathrm{SRC}, \mathrm{CF} - \lambda, (i, j)) \subseteq \mathscr{L}(\mathrm{SRC}, \mathrm{CF}, (i, j))$ *for* $i \geqq 0, j \geqq 0$,

iv) $\mathscr{L}(\mathrm{SRC}, \mathrm{CF} - \lambda, (i, j)) \subseteq \mathscr{L}(\mathrm{CS})$ and $\mathscr{L}(\mathrm{SRC}, \mathrm{CF}, (i, j)) \subseteq \mathscr{L}(\mathrm{RE})$ *for* $i \geqq 0, j \geqq 0$.

Proof. Obvious.

In Exercises 1.5.6 and 1.5.7 we shall point out that both families $\mathscr{L}(\mathrm{SRC}, \mathrm{CF} - \lambda, (1, 0))$ and $\mathscr{L}(\mathrm{SRC}, \mathrm{CF} - \lambda, (0, 1))$ strictly include $\mathscr{L}(\mathrm{CF})$ and that $\mathscr{L}(\mathrm{SRC}, \mathrm{CF} - \lambda, (1, 1))$ is strictly included in $\mathscr{L}(\mathrm{CS})$ as being included in $\mathscr{L}(\mathrm{RC}, \mathrm{CF} - \lambda, \mathrm{ac})$. However, if string contexts of length 2 are considered, the generative capacity is considerably increased.

Theorem 1.5.13. i) $\mathscr{L}(\mathrm{SRC}, \mathrm{CF} - \lambda, (1, 2)) = \mathscr{L}(\mathrm{SRC}, \mathrm{CF} - \lambda, (2, 1)) = \mathscr{L}(\mathrm{CS})$,

ii) $\mathscr{L}(\mathrm{SRC}, \mathrm{CF}, (1, 2)) = \mathscr{L}(\mathrm{SRC}, \mathrm{CF}, (2, 1)) = \mathscr{L}(\mathrm{RE})$.

Proof. We have to prove only the inclusions of $\mathscr{L}(\mathrm{CS})$ and $\mathscr{L}(\mathrm{RE})$ in the corresponding families of string random context languages. For, let us consider a context-sensitive language $L \subseteq V^*$. We can write

$$L = \bigcup_{c \in V} d_c^r(L)\{c\} \cup (L \cap \{\lambda\}).$$

As, clearly, the families of string random context languages are closed under union and contain the finite languages, it is enough to prove that, for each language $M \in \mathscr{L}(\mathrm{CS})$ and each symbol c, $M\{c\} \in \mathscr{L}(\mathrm{SRC}, \mathrm{CF} - \lambda, (2, 1))$ and $M\{c\} \in \mathscr{L}(\mathrm{SRC}, \mathrm{CF} - \lambda, (1, 2))$, respectively.

Let us consider a context-sensitive grammar $G = (V_N, V_T, P, S)$ in Kuroda normal form. We construct the following string random context grammar $G' = (V'_N, V_T \cup \{c\}, P', S')$ of degree (2,1) with

$$V'_N = V_N \cup \{(A, r), [A, r], (X, r), [U, r] : r: XU \to YZ \in P\} \cup \{S', A\}$$

and P' containing the rules:

1.1. $(S' \to SA, \emptyset, \emptyset)$,

1.2. $(X \to x, A, \emptyset)$ for a context-free rule $X \to x \in P$, $x \neq \lambda$.

(The context-free rules of P are simulated in the presence of A only.)

$$\left.\begin{array}{ll} 2.1. & (A \to (A, r), \emptyset, \emptyset),\\ 2.2. & (X \to (X, r), (A, r), (X, r)),\\ 2.3. & (U \to [U, r], (X, r), [U, r]),\\ 2.4. & ((X, r) \to Y, (X, r)[U, r], A),\\ 2.5. & ([U, r] \to Z, (A, r), (X, r)),\\ 2.6. & ((A, r) \to [A, r], \emptyset, (X, r)),\\ 2.7. & ([A, r] \to A, \emptyset, [U, r]) \end{array}\right\} \begin{array}{l}\text{for each rule}\\ r: XU \to YZ \in P\end{array}$$

(At each moment, the right marker A can be replaced by some (A, r) and the rule $r: XU \to YZ$ can then be simulated. After using rule 2.2 all rules 2.3 to 2.7 must be used in this order. Any sentential form can contain at most one symbol (X, r) and at most one symbol $[U, r]$ for a given rule r. The removing of (X, r) is only possible by rule 2.4 which checks whether X and U are adjacent. After using this rule the current string does not contain (X, r); hence rule 2.2 can be applied again. However, in the presence of (X, r) we cannot eliminate $[U, r]$; and in order to remove first (X, r) we need the subword $(X, r)[U, r]$. This means that $Y = X$ for the rule r under discussion, hence the string was not modified by using two — or more — times rules 2.2, 2.4 for only one use of rule 2.5. As (A, r) can be replaced by A only if no (X, r), $[U, r]$ are present, it follows also that no rule in group 1.2 can be intercalated when the rule r is simulated.)

3.1. $(A \to c, \emptyset, \emptyset)$,

3.2 $(S' \to c, \emptyset, \emptyset)$ if $S \to \lambda \in P$.

From the above explanations it is easy to see that $L(G') = L(G)\{c\}$ and the inclusion $\mathscr{L}(\mathrm{CS}) \subseteq \mathscr{L}(\mathrm{SRC}, \mathrm{CF} - \lambda, (2, 1))$ follows.

Consider now the inclusion $\mathcal{L}(\mathrm{CS}) \subseteq \mathcal{L}(\mathrm{SRC}, \mathrm{CF} - \lambda, (1, 2))$. Again let $G = (V_N, V_T, P, S)$ be a Kuroda normal form grammar. We construct the string random context grammar $G'' = (V''_N, V_T \cup \{c\}, P'', S'')$ of degree (1, 2) with

$$V''_N = V_N \cup \{S'', A\} \cup \bigcup_{r: XU \to YZ \in P} \{(A, r), [A, r], (X, r), [U, r], [\![Y, r]\!]\}$$

$$\cup \{(X, r, D_j) : r : XU \to YZ \in P, D_j \in W_r\}$$

where

$$W_r = \{D_1, D_2, \ldots, D_p\} = V_N \cup V_T \cup \bigcup_{r: XU \to YZ \in P} \{(X, r), (A, r)\}$$

and with P'' containing the rules

$(X \to x, A, \emptyset)$ for a context-free rule $X \to x \in P, x \neq \lambda$,

$(S'' \to SA, \emptyset, \emptyset)$ (initial rule),

$(A \to c, \emptyset, \emptyset)$ (final rule),

$(S'' \to c, \emptyset, \emptyset)$ if $S \to \lambda \in P$

and the following rules for each $r: XU \to YZ \in P$:

$\big(X \to (X, r), A, (X, r)\big)$,
$\big(A \to (A, r), (X, r), \emptyset\big)$,
$(U \to [U, r], (A, r), [U, r])$,
$\big((X, r) \to (X, r, D_1), [U, r], (X, r)\, D_1\big)$,
$\big((X, r, D_j) \to (X, r, D_{j+1}), (A, r), (X, r, D_j)\, D_{j+1}\big)$, $1 \leqq j \leqq p - 1$,
$\big((X, r, D_p) \to [\![Y, r]\!], (A, r), \emptyset\big)$,
$\big((A, r) \to [A, r], [\![Y, r]\!], \emptyset\big)$,
$\big([U, r] \to Z, [A, r], [\![Y, r]\!]\big)$,
$([\![Y, r]\!] \to Y, [A, r], \emptyset)$,
$([A, r] \to A, \emptyset, [U, r])$.

One checks whether the two symbols X, U replaced by (X, r), $[U, r]$ are adjacent. In the affirmative case one introduces the symbol $[\![Y, r]\!]$ which allows the introduction of $[A, r]$, which, in turn, can be replaced by A only after introducing Y, Z for the rewritten occurrences of X, U.

It is easy to see that the equality $L(G'') = L(G)\, \{c\}$ holds. Hence the inclusion $\mathcal{L}(\mathrm{CS}) \subseteq \mathcal{L}(\mathrm{SRC}, \mathrm{CF} - \lambda, (1, 2))$ is true.

For $\mathcal{L}(\mathrm{RE})$ we take a grammar G as above, but containing also λ-rules and these rules are introduced in G', G'' together with all context-free rules of G.

As we have seen in Section 1.4., the leftmost derivation (of type 2) increases the power of the usual random context grammars. Let us consider leftmost derivations of type 2 for string random context grammars (a rule $(A \to x, w_1, w_2)$ is applied to x_1Ax_2 for rewriting of this occurrence of A only if no rule can be used in order to rewrite a symbol in x_1). By $\mathscr{L}(\text{SRC}, X, (i, j), \text{left})$, $X \in \{\text{CF}, \text{CF} - \lambda\}$, $i, j \geqq 0$, we denote the families of languages generated in this way.

Let us note that the random context grammar G' constructed in the proof of Theorem 1.4.4. in order to simulate a context-sensitive grammar has only rules $(A \to x, \emptyset, \emptyset)$ or $(A \to x, \{B\}, \emptyset)$ with $B \neq A$. Therefore it is a string random context grammar of degree (1, 0). Consequently, we obtain

Theorem 1.5.14. $\mathscr{L}(\text{CS}) = \mathscr{L}(\text{SRC}, \text{CF} - \lambda, (1, 0), \text{left})$,

$$\mathscr{L}(\text{RE}) = \mathscr{L}(\text{SRC}, \text{CF}, (1, 0), \text{left}).$$

A similar result can also be obtained for (0, 2) string random context grammars.

Theorem 1.5.15. $\mathscr{L}(\text{CS}) = \mathscr{L}(\text{SRC}, \text{CF} - \lambda, (0, 2), \text{left})$,

$$\mathscr{L}(\text{RE}) = \mathscr{L}(\text{SRC}, \text{CF}, (0, 2), \text{left}).$$

Proof. Let $L \subseteq V^*$ be a context-sensitive language. We have

$$L = \bigcup_{\substack{a_i \in V \\ i \leq 1 \leq 4}} \{a_1\}\, d^l_{a_1}\big(d^r_{a_2a_3a_4}(L)\big)\, \{a_2a_3a_4\} \cup \{x \in L : |x| \leq 3\}.$$

As $\mathscr{L}(\text{CS})$ is closed under right and left derivative and, clearly, the family $\mathscr{L}(\text{SRC}, \text{CF} - \lambda, (0, 2), \text{left})$ is closed under union and contains all finite languages, it is sufficient to prove that for each language $L \in \mathscr{L}(\text{CS})$ and given symbols $\{a_1, a_2, a_3, a_4\}$ the language $\{a_1\}L\{a_2a_3a_4\}$ is in $\mathscr{L}(\text{SRC}, \text{CF} - \lambda, (0, 2), \text{left})$.

Let us consider a length increasing grammmar $G = (V_N, V_T, P, S)$ in Kuroda normal form, and let us assume that it contains k non-context-free rules $r_i\colon X_iU_i \to YZ_i$, $1 \leqq i \leqq k$. We construct the string random context grammar

$$G' = (V'_N, V_T \cup \{a_1, a_2, a_3, a_4\}, P', S_0)$$

of degree (0, 2) with

$$V'_N = V_N \cup \{X' : X \in V_N\} \cup \{S_0, B, C, B', T\}$$
$$\cup \bigcup_{1 \leq i \leq k} \{(X_i, r_i), [U_i, r_i], [\![Y_i, r_i]\!], \lfloor Z_i, r_i \rfloor\} \cup \bigcup_{\substack{1 \leq i \leq k \\ 1 \leq j \leq k}} \{(X_i, r_i, r_j)\}$$
$$\cup \bigcup_{\substack{1 \leq i \leq k \\ D_t \in W}} \{(X_i, r_i, D_t), [U_i, r_i, D_t]\}$$

where

$$W = V_N \cup \{X' : X \in V_N\} \cup \{B, a_1\} \cup \{[\![Y_i, r_i]\!] : 1 \leqq i \leqq k\}$$

and with P' containing the following rules:

1) $(S_0 \to a_1SBC, \emptyset, \emptyset)$,

2) $(X - X', \emptyset, B')$ for $X \in V_N$,

$(X \to Y'Z', \emptyset, B')$ for $X \to YZ \in P$

(when B' is not present, from the left to the right, we can replace arbitrarily many symbols $X \in V_N$ by X', and we can simulate some rules $X \to YZ$ of P),

3) $(X_i \to (X_i, r_i), \emptyset, B')$ for $1 \leqq i \leqq k$

(we start the simulation of the rule r_i: $X_iU_i \to Y_iZ_i$),

4) $((X_i, r_i) \to (X_i, r_i, r_1), \emptyset, [\![Y_1, r_1]\!])$ for $1 \leqq i \leqq k$,

$((X_i, r_i, r_j) \to (X_i, r_i, r_{j+1}), \emptyset, [\![Y_{j+1}, r_{j+1}]\!])$, $1 \leqq i \leqq k$, $1 \leqq j \leqq k-1$

(we check whether another rule r_j was simulated when the current string was passed through before simulating the rule r_i),

5) $((X_i, r_i) \to T, \emptyset, \emptyset)$, $1 \leqq i \leqq k$,

$((X_i, r_i, r_j) \to T, \emptyset, \emptyset)$, $1 \leqq i \leqq k$, $1 \leqq j \leqq k$

(if another rule simulation was started before, then the derivation is blocked by the trap symbol T),

6) $((X_i, r_i, r_k) \to (X_i, r_i, D_1), \emptyset, (X_i, r_i, r_k)\, D_1)$, and

$((X_i, r_i, D_j) \to (X_i, r_i, D_{j+1}), \emptyset, (X_i, r_i, D_j)\, D_{j+1})$

where $1 \leqq i \leqq k$, $1 \leqq j \leqq p-1$ and $\{D_1, D_2, \ldots, D_p\} = (V_N \cup \{B\}) \setminus \{U_i\}$,

$((X_i, r_i, D_p) \to [\![Y_i, r_i]\!], \emptyset, \emptyset)$, $1 \leqq i \leqq k$

(we check whether U_i appears on the right-hand side of X_i, and only if the answer is affirmative we can introduce the symbol $[\![Y_i, r_i]\!]$),

7) $((X_i, r_i, D_j) \to T, \emptyset, \emptyset)$, $1 \leqq i \leqq k$, $1 \leqq j \leqq p-1$, D_j as in group 6)

(the derivation if blocked is a symbol different from U_i appears in the right-hand side of X_i),

8) $(U_i \to [U_i, r_i], \emptyset, B')$,

$([U_i, r_i] \to [U_i, r_i, D_1], \emptyset, D_1[U_i, r_i])$,

$([U_i, r_i, D_j] \to [U_i, r_i, D_{j+1}], \emptyset, D_{j+1}[U_i, r_i, D_j])$,

$([U_i, r_i] \to T, \emptyset, \emptyset)$,

$([U_i, r_i, D_j] \to T, \emptyset, \emptyset)$,

$([U_i, r_i, D_p] \to \lfloor Z_i, r_i \rfloor, \emptyset, \emptyset)$

where $1 \leqq i \leqq k$, $1 \leqq j \leqq p-1$, and

$$\{D_1, D_2, \ldots, D_p\} = \{a_1\} \cup \{X' : X \in V_N\} \cup \{[\![Y_j, r_j]\!] : 1 \leqq j \leqq k, j \neq i\}$$

(we replace U_i by $\lfloor Z_i, r_i \rfloor$, but this is performed only in the presence of $[\![Y_i, r_i]\!]$ on the left-hand side of U_i; if $[\![Y_i, r_i]\!]$ is not present, then the trap symbol T is introduced and the derivation is blocked; using the rules in groups 2—8 we can pass from a string a_1wBC, $w \in V_N^*$, to a string $a_1w_1\, [\![Y_t, r_t]\!]\, \lfloor Z_t, r_t \rfloor\, w_2BC$ with w_1w_2 containing only primed symbols and $1 \leqq t \leqq k$),

9) $(B \to B', \emptyset, B')$

(in the presence of B' only the next rules can be applied, again, from the left to the right of the current string),

10) $(X' \to X, \emptyset, B)$, $X \in V_N$,

$$\left.\begin{array}{l}([\![Y_i, r_i]\!] \to Y_i, \emptyset, B) \\ (\lfloor Z_i, r_i \rfloor \to Z_i, \emptyset, B)\end{array}\right\} 1 \leq i \leq k,$$

$(B' \to B, \emptyset, \emptyset)$

(using these rules we reobtain a string of the form $a_1 w' BC$, $w' \in V_N^*$, hence the passing through the rules in groups 2 to 10 can be reiterated),

11) $(B' \to BB', \emptyset, BB')$

(this rule determines the termination of the derivation, because in the presence of both B and B' the rules of groups 2, 3, 8, 9, 10 cannot be applied, hence the rules in groups 4, 5, 6, 7 cannot be applied, too; we can now use the following rule because C is the leftmost replaceable symbol in the current string),

12) $(C \to a_4, \emptyset, \emptyset)$,

$(X \to a, \emptyset, C)$, $X \to a \in P$,

$(B \to a_2, \emptyset, C)$,

$(B' \to a_3, \emptyset, C)$

(the only possibility is to replace each nonterminal by a terminal symbol according to the rules in P; note that these rules cannot be used before eliminating C and that the rule 11 can be used only once),

13) $(S_0 \to \lambda, \emptyset, \emptyset)$ if $\lambda \in L(G)$.

From the above explanations it is easy to see that $L_{\text{left}}(G') = \{a_1\} L(G) \{a_2 a_3 a_4\}$, and thus the inclusion $\mathscr{L}(\text{CS}) \subseteq \mathscr{L}(\text{SRC}, \text{CF} - \lambda, (0, 2), \text{left})$ is obtained.

The converse inclusion is straightforward.

If G is a type-0 grammar in Kuroda normal form, then we introduce in group 2 the rule

$$(X \to \lambda, \emptyset, B')$$

and in group 12 the rule

$$(X \to \lambda, \emptyset, C)$$

for each $X \to \lambda$ in P. In this way we obtain the inclusion $\mathscr{L}(\text{RE}) \subseteq \mathscr{L}(\text{SRC}, \text{CF}, (0, 2), \text{left})$, too.

Open problems

1.5.1. What is the relation between $\mathscr{L}(\text{SM}, \text{CF})$, $\mathscr{L}(\text{SM}, \text{CF} - \lambda)$ and $\mathscr{L}(\text{M}, \text{CF})$, $\mathscr{L}(\text{M}, \text{CF} - \lambda)$, $\mathscr{L}(\text{M}, \text{CF} - \lambda, \text{ac})$? We have pointed out that each family of matrix languages contains languages which are not simple matrix languages, but no further relation is known. In open problem 1.2.3 we conjectured that $L = \{xcx : x \in D_{ab}\}$ is not in $\mathcal{L}(\mathrm{M}, \mathrm{CF} - \lambda, \mathrm{ac})$. This language belongs to $\mathcal{L}(\mathrm{SM}, \mathrm{CF} - \lambda, 2)$ as being generated by the grammar

$$G = (\{A_1, A_2\}, \{B_1, B_2\}, \{a, b, c\}, M, S)$$

with

$$M = \{(S \to A_1B_1), (A_1 \to A_2c, B_1 \to B_2), (A_2 \to A_2A_2, B_2 \to B_2B_2),$$
$$(A_2 \to aA_2b, B_2 \to aB_2b), (A_2 \to ab, B_2 \to ab)\}.$$

Therefore an incomparability result is expected as an answer to open problem 1.5.1.

1.5.2. Prove or disprove the inclusions

$$\mathcal{L}(\mathrm{SM}, \mathrm{CF} - \lambda, n) \subseteq \mathcal{L}(\mathrm{SM}, \mathrm{CF} - \lambda, n + 1), n \geqq 1.$$

(Remember the remark after Theorem 1.5.4 as well as Theorem 1.5.5.) *Conjecture:* the Dyck language over $\{a, b\}$ belongs to $\mathcal{L}(\mathrm{SM}, \mathrm{CF} - \lambda, 1) \setminus \mathcal{L}(\mathrm{SM}, \mathrm{CF} - \lambda, 2)$, and therefore $\mathcal{L}(\mathrm{SM}, \mathrm{CF} - \lambda, 1) = \mathcal{L}(\mathrm{CF})$ and $\mathcal{L}(\mathrm{SM}, \mathrm{CF} - \lambda, 2)$ are incomparable.

1.5.3. Is the family $\mathcal{L}(\mathrm{CS})$ included in $\mathcal{L}\big(\mathrm{SRC}, \mathrm{CF} - \lambda, (i, 0)\big)$ or in $\mathcal{L}\big(\mathrm{SRC}, \mathrm{CF} - \lambda, (0, i)\big)$ for some value of i? Is $\mathcal{L}(\mathrm{CS})$ included in $\mathcal{L}\big(\mathrm{SRC}, \mathrm{CF} - \lambda, (0, 1), \mathrm{left}\big)$?

Exercises

1.5.1. In the definition of a simple matrix grammar $G = (V_1, V_2, \ldots, V_n, V_T, M, S)$ four conditions appear which make a simple matrix grammar different from a usual matrix grammar, namely:

(1) S does not belong to V_N,

(2) for each matrix $(A_1 \to w_1, A_2 \to w_2, \ldots, A_n \to w_n)$ in M, A_i and the nonterminals in w_i are in V_i, $1 \leqq i \leqq n$,

(3) for each such matrix, all w_i contain the same number of nonterminals (possibly none),

(4) the derivation is leftmost in the sense of Definition 1.5.1.

Prove that all these conditions are essential, that is, if we remove one of them one can generate languages not contained in $\mathcal{L}(\mathrm{SM}, \mathrm{CF})$.

1.5.2. Prove that in a context-free or regular simple matrix grammar $G = (V_1, V_2, \ldots, V_n, V_T, M, S)$ we can take initial matrices of the form

$$(S \to x_1x_2 \ldots x_n)$$

with arbitrary $x_i \in (V_i \cup V_T)^*$, $1 \leqq i \leqq n$, such that $|x_i|_{V_i} = |x_j|_{V_j}$, $1 \leqq i, j \leqq n$ (and not only $(S \to A_1A_2 \ldots A_n)$ as in Definition 1.5.1) without changing the generative capacity.

1.5.3. Prove that the converse of the assertion in Theorem 1.5.8 is not true. (***Hint:*** take the Dyck language D over pairs of parentheses (a, b), (c, d), (e, f), (g, h) and the regular simple matrix language

$$R = \{ea^{i_1}b^{j_1}c^{n_1}d^{m_1}fea^{i_2}b^{j_2}c^{n_2}d^{m_2}f \ldots ea^{i_k}b^{j_k}c^{n_k}d^{m_k}fghea^{j_1}b^{n_1}fea^{j_2}b^{n_2}f \ldots ea^{j_k}b^{n_k}f : k \geqq 1,$$
$$i_r, j_r, n_r, m_r \geqq 1, 1 \leqq r \leqq k\}$$

and translate $D \cap R$ by a gsm into $\{a^nb^nc^n : n \geqq 1\}^*$, which is not in $\mathcal{L}(\mathrm{SM}, \mathrm{CF})$.)

1.5.4. Let $w_1, w_2, \ldots, w_k$ be strings over some alphabet V. Prove that $L \subseteq w_1^* w_2^* \ldots w_k^*$ is in $\mathscr{L}(\mathrm{SM}, \mathrm{REG})$ if and only if the set $\{(i_1, i_2, \ldots, i_k) : w^{i_1} w^{i_2} \ldots w^{i_k} \in L\}$ is semilinear.

1.5.5. Call a production $(A \to u, \emptyset, R)$ in a forbidding random context grammar nonrecurrent if R contains a nonterminal symbol of u. Prove that the language generated by a forbidding random context grammar which does not contain nonrecurrent productions is in $\mathscr{L}(\mathrm{ETOL})$.

1.5.6. Prove that both families $\mathscr{L}(\mathrm{SRC}, \mathrm{CF} - \lambda, (1, 0))$ and $\mathscr{L}(\mathrm{SRC}, \mathrm{CF} - \lambda, (0, 1))$ contain non-semilinear languages. (*Hint:* consider $\{a^n b^m c : m \geqq 1, 1 \leqq n \leqq 2^{m+1}\}$ or similar languages.)

1.5.7. Prove that $\mathscr{L}(\mathrm{SRC}, \mathrm{CF} - \lambda, (1, 1))$ is included in $\mathscr{L}(\mathrm{RC}, \mathrm{CF} - \lambda, \mathrm{ac})$.

Bibliographical and historical notes

The matrix grammars were first introduced by ABRAHAM (1965), the programmed grammars by ROSENKRANTZ (1969), and the random context grammars by VAN DER WALT (1970). The simple matrix grammars were first independently introduced by IBARRA (1970) and KUICH and MAURER (1970). The leftmost derivation of type-2 for matrix grammars was proposed in SALOMAA (1972) (where Theorem 1.4.2 is proved). For random context grammars this restriction has been defined in CREMERS, MAURER and MAYER (1973) (where Theorem 1.4.4 appears). ROSENKRANTZ considered programmed grammars with leftmost derivation of type 3, but many of the obtained results also hold for free derivations. Motivated by considerations in Artificial Intelligence the string KELEMEN (1984-a), (1984-b) proposed random context grammars in a special form that the forbidden context is empty (they are called conditional there). Further results on these grammars can be found in KELEMEN (1985), KELEMENOVA and KELEMEN (1985) and PĂUN (1985-c).

The equivalence of programmed and matrix grammars has been established by SALOMAA (1970-b), whereas the equivalence of matrix and random context grammars (with appearance checking) has been proved by MAYER (1972). The present proof of Theorem 1.2.5 appears in PĂUN (1984-a); initially, the result was obtained in ROSENKRANTZ (1969). It appears also in SALOMAA (1973-a), VAN LEEUWEN (1972), and it is derived as a simple consequence of a powerful lemma in VAN LEEUWEN (1979).

Closure properties of matrix and programmed language families can be found in or adapted from ROSENKRANTZ (1969), SALOMAA (1969-a), SALOMAA (1970-b), and FRIANT (1968). The notion of quasiintersection has been introduced (c. f. SALOMAA (1970-b)) by STOTSKIJ (1968). The circular closure of languages (Exercise 1.3.4) has been investigated by DASSOW (1979-b) (among others for programmed and random context languages).

In ROSENKRANTZ (1969) one can also find most of the decision results specified here for programmed and for unconditional transfer programmed grammars. Theorem 1.3.5 was first proved in SHAMIR and BEERI (1974) and a stronger form was given in VAN LEEUWEN (1975).

In IBARRA (1970) one can find many further results on simple matrix languages (for instance, results on bounded languages) as well as complete proofs for those given here. Exercise 1.5.1 is discussed in IBARRA (1970) and in PASCU and PĂUN (1976). The linear simple matrix grammars have been investigated in PĂUN (1978-b). A variant of leftmost derivation in simple matrix grammars is introduced in MAURER (1973) and a characterization of context-sensitive (recursively enumerable, if λ-rules are allowed) languages has been obtained in this way. The elimination of λ-rules in simple matrix grammars has been discussed in PĂUN (1981-e). Representation and characterization theorems for simple matrix languages of various types and for related "tuple-languages" (including Theorem 1.5.9) can be found in a series of papers by WOOD (1975), (1977) and ROSEBRUGH and WOOD (1973), (1974), (1975). Theorem 1.5.8 is taken from PASCU and PĂUN (1977). The regular simple matrix grammars have been considered (under the name "equal matrix grammars") also by SIROMONEY (1969-a), (1969-b). Theorem 1.5.12 has been proved by PENTTONEN (1975) and VON SOLMS (1975-c) in the stronger form suggested by Exercise 1.5.5. The more precise placing of ETOL languages in the family of programmed languages has been investigated in ROZENBERG and VERMEIR (1978-c) where variants of programmed grammars were introduced for this purpose. Many variants of random context grammars (the permitting/forbidding symbols to appear/not to appear on the left/right-hand side of the rewritten symbol etc.) have been considered in a series of papers by M. LOMKOVSKAJA.

The nonterminal matrix (and programmed) grammars (Exercise 1.2.3) have been considered in PĂUN (1976); compound (matrix) grammars (Exercise 1.2.4) have been proposed by ABRAHAM (1972).

Results and references on matrix and programmed grammars (as well as on other grammars with regulated rewriting) can be found in Chapter V of SALOMAA (1973-a). The monograph PĂUN (1981-f) is entirely devoted to matrix grammars and variants of them and presents most of the known results by the middle of 1980 in the field (as well as many open problems some of which are solved in the meantime and some of which are reformulated also in this book).

Chapter 2. Other Grammars with Regulation

The aim of this chapter is to introduce some further grammars with regulated rewriting. Clearly, for reasons of space, it is impossible to cover all types of grammars known from the literature. We restrict ourselves here to (some) grammars which — in a certain sense — are context-free grammars and the application of those context-free core productions is regulated by a certain mechanism. Thus we do not include such important grammars as two-level grammars (where we can have an infinite set of "nonterminals" and "productions") or IO-grammars (where terms are rewritten).

Further we present a test classification of the regulation mechanisms. In particular we shall see that there is a lot of grammars whose regulation mechanism belongs to one of the following types:

— prescribed sequences of productions,
— dependence of the rule on the history of the derivation,
— certain context conditions.

Therefore the three mechanisms introduced and studied in the preceding chapter can be considered as representatives of typical kinds of regulation.

In this chapter, for each type of regulation we shall give only the definition, one or two examples (especially the generation of well-known non-context-free languages), and one or two basic properties of this grammar type (especially results oriented on hierarchies).

2.1. Prescribed Sequences

Definition 2.1.1. A *periodically time variant grammar* is a quintuple $G = (V_N, V_T, P, S, \varphi)$ where P is a finite set of context-free productions $A \to w$ with $A \in V_N$, $w \in V_G^*$, and φ is a mapping from $\mathbb{N}$ into $2^P \setminus \{\emptyset\}$ satisfying the following condition: there is an integer k such that $\varphi(n) = \varphi(n + k)$ for all $n \in \mathbb{N}$. A word $w \in V_T^*$ belongs to the language $L(G)$ generated by G if there is a context-free derivation

$$S \underset{p_1}{\Longrightarrow} w_1 \underset{p_2}{\Longrightarrow} \cdots \underset{p_n}{\Longrightarrow} w_n = w$$

such that $p_i \in \varphi(i)$ for $1 \leq i \leq n$.

Example 2.1.1. Let $V_N = \{S, A, B, C\}$, $V_T = \{a, b, c\}$, $P = \{p_i : 1 \leqq i \leqq 6\}$ where

$$p_1: S \to AB, \quad p_2: A \to aAb, \quad p_3: A \to ab,$$

$$p_4: B \to Bc, \quad p_5: B \to C, \quad p_6: C \to c,$$

$$\varphi(2n) = \{p_2, p_3, p_6\}, \quad \varphi(2n-1) = \{p_1, p_4, p_5\} \quad \text{for} \quad n \in \mathbb{N}.$$

Then the periodically time-variant grammar $G = (V_N, V_T, P, S, \varphi)$ generates the language $L = \{a^n b^n c^n : n \geqq 1\}$.

This can be seen as follows. The derivation starts with $S \Rightarrow AB$. Now we prove that after $2n-1$ steps, $n \geqq 1$, the sentential forms are of the type $a^n A b^n B c^n$ or $a^n b^n C c^{n-1}$. In the former case we can apply $p_2 \in \varphi(2n)$ or $p_3 \in \varphi(2n)$ and we obtain $w_1 = a^{n+1} A b^{n+1} B c^n$ or $v_1 = a^{n+1} b^{n+1} B c^n$. If we apply p_5 to w_1 we get $w_2 = a^{n+1} A b^{n+1} C c^n$. Independently of the rule of $\varphi(2n+2)$ which we apply to w_2, we generate a word containing the nonterminals A and/or C and we cannot apply any rule of $\varphi(2n+3)$, i.e. the derivation is blocked. Thus we have to apply p_4 to w_1 and we obtain $a^{n+1} A b^{n+1} B c^{n+1}$. Now let us consider v_1. If we apply $p_4 \in \varphi(2n+1)$ to v_1 we get $a^{n+1} b^{n+1} B c^{n+1}$ and the derivation is blocked. Thus we can obtain only $a^{n+1} b^{n+1} C c^n$ by application of p_5. Hence the derivation only terminates if we apply p_6 to $a^{n+1} b^{n+1} C c^n$, and thus the statement is proved.

Note that we have defined above the simplest type of periodically time-variant grammars. Introducing a set F of occurrences of productions as a sixth component in the definition and allowing rules in F to be passed over if they are not applicable, we can add appearance checking. Further, it is clear that we can use context-sensitive, linear, etc. core productions.

We denote by $L(TV, X)$ the family of languages generated by periodically time-variant grammars with core productions of type X (context-free, linear, etc.), and $L(TV, X, ac)$ denotes the corresponding family of languages generated with appearance checking.

Example 2.1.1. proves that $\mathcal{L}(\text{CF}) \subset \mathcal{L}(\text{TV}, \text{CF} - \lambda)$ (for a context-free grammar G we can take $\varphi(n) = P$ and the periodically time-variant grammar generates the language $L(G)$). The following lemma improves this relation.

Lemma 2.1.1. *For* $X \in \{\text{CF}, \text{CF} - \lambda\}$, *we have*

$$\mathcal{L}(\text{M}, X) \subseteq \mathcal{L}(\text{TV}, X).$$

Proof. Let $G = (V_N, V_T, M, S)$ be a matrix grammar (without appearance checking). By Lemma 1.3.7 we can assume that M contains only matrices of the form $(A_i \to w_i, B_i \to v_i)$ (the matrix $(S \to AB)$ can be replaced by $(S \to S', S' \to AB)$), $1 \leqq i \leqq n$. Let Y_i, Z_i, $1 \leqq i \leqq n$, be new letters. We define the function φ (where P is the set of all productions occurring in the definition of φ) as follows:

$$\varphi(1) = \{A_1 \to w_1 Y_1, A_2 \to w_2 Y_2, \ldots, A_n \to w_n Y_n\},$$

$$\varphi(2) = \{B_1 \to v_1 Z_1, B_2 \to v_2 Z_2, \ldots, B_n \to v_n Z_n\},$$

$$\varphi(2j+1) = \{Y_1 \to Y_1, \ldots, Y_{j-1}, \to Y_{j-1}\ Y_{j+1} \to Y_{j+1}, \ldots, Y_n \to Y_n, Z_j \to Z_j\},$$
$$1 \leqq j \leqq n,$$

$$\varphi(2j+2) = \{Z_1 \to Z_1, \ldots, Z_{j-1} \to Z_{j-1}, Z_{j+1} \to Z_{j+1}, \ldots, Z_n \to Z_n, Y_j \to Y_j\},$$
$$1 \leqq j \leqq n,$$

$$\varphi(2n+3) = \{Y_1 \to \lambda, Y_2 \to \lambda, \ldots, Y_n \to \lambda\},$$
$$\varphi(2n+4) = \{Z_1 \to \lambda, Z_2 \to \lambda, \ldots, Z_n \to \lambda\},$$
$$\varphi(r+2n+4) = \varphi(r) \quad \text{for} \quad r \in \mathbb{N}.$$

Let w be a sentential form obtained after $t(2n+4)$ steps. Then we have to apply a rule of $\varphi(1)$ and then one of $\varphi(2)$. Assume we use $A_i \to w_i Y_i$ and $B_k \to v_k Z_k$.

Case 1. $i \neq k$. Without loss of generality, let $1 \leqq i < k \leqq n$. Then there is no rule in $\varphi(2i+1)$ which can be applied since we have introduced only Y_i and Z_k. Thus the derivation is blocked.

Case 2. $i = k$. Then, for $j \neq i$, $\varphi(2j+1)$ and $\varphi(2j+2)$ contain the applicable rule $Y_i \to Y_i$ and $Z_i \to Z_i$, respectively. Further, $\varphi(2i+1)$ contains $Z_i \to Z_i$, and $Y_i \to Y_i$ is in $\varphi(2i+2)$. Hence we can continue the derivation. From $\varphi(2n+3)$ and $\varphi(2n+4)$ we have to use $Y_i \to \lambda$ and $Z_i \to \lambda$, respectively. Thus we have simulated the application of the matrix $(A_i \to w_i, B_i \to v_i)$.

Now $L(G) = L(G')$ follows easily.

In the λ-free case, instead of $A_i \to w_i Y_i$, $Y_i \to \lambda$ we use $A_i \to w_i' Y_i$ and $Y_i \to a_i$ where $w_i = w_i' a_i$. Accordingly we also change the part concerning the introduction and erasing of Z_i.

Definition 2.1.2. Let $G' = (V_N, V_T, P, S)$ be a context-free grammar, and let R be a regular language over P. Then $G = (V_N, V_T, P, S, R)$ is called a (context-free) *grammar with regular control*. Its generated language consists of all words w which have a derivation

$$S \underset{p_1}{\Longrightarrow} w_1 \underset{p_2}{\Longrightarrow} w_2 \underset{p_3}{\Longrightarrow} \cdots \underset{p_n}{\Longrightarrow} w_n = w \in V_T^*$$

in G' satisfying $p_1 p_2 \ldots p_n \in R$.

Again, we have defined the "simplest" type. We can add appearance checking by giving a set $F \subseteq P$ of rules which can be passed over if not applicable. By $\mathcal{L}(\mathrm{rC}, X, \beta)$ we denote the set of languages generated by grammars with regular control and core productions of type X, with appearance checking if $\beta = \mathrm{ac}$, and without appearance checking if β is empty (omitted).

Example 2.1.2. Let $V_N = \{S, A, B\}$, $V_T = \{a, b, c\}$,

$P = \{p_1, p_2, \ldots, p_5\}$ where

$$p_1\colon S \to AB, \quad p_2\colon A \to aAb, \quad p_3\colon B \to Bc,$$
$$p_4\colon A \to ab, \quad p_5\colon B \to c,$$
$$R = \{p_1\}\,\{p_2 p_3\}^*\,\{p_4 p_5\}$$

and consider $G = (V_N, V_T, P, S, R)$.

Then each derivation has the following form: first we apply p_1, then we apply p_2 and p_3 iteratively, let us say n times, $n \geqq 0$, and finally we use p_4 and p_5. This gives

$$S \underset{p_1}{\Longrightarrow} AB \underset{p_2}{\Longrightarrow} aAbB \underset{p_3}{\Longrightarrow} aAbBc \underset{p_2}{\Longrightarrow} a^2Ab^2Bc \underset{p_3}{\Longrightarrow} a^2Ab^2Bc^2$$
$$\cdots \underset{p_2}{\Longrightarrow} a^nAb^nBc^{n-1} \underset{p_3}{\Longrightarrow} a^nAb^nBc^n \underset{p_4}{\Longrightarrow} a^{n+1}b^{n+1}Bc^n \underset{p_5}{\Longrightarrow} a^{n+1}b^{n+1}c^{n+1}.$$

Therefore $L(G) = \{a^nb^nc^n : n \geqq 1\}$.

Example 2.1.3. Let $G = (V_N, V_T, P, S, R, F)$ be a grammar with regular control and appearance checking where

$$V_N = \{S, A, N\}, \quad V_T = \{a\}, \quad P = \{p_1, p_2, \ldots, p_5\},$$

$$p_1\colon S \to AA, \quad p_2\colon S \to N, \quad p_3\colon A \to S, \quad p_4\colon A \to N, \quad p_5\colon S \to a,$$

$$R = (p_1^* p_2 p_3^* p_4)^* \, p_5^* \cup \{p_5\},$$

$$F = \{p_2, p_4\}.$$

Then $L(G) = \{a^{2^n} : n \geqq 0\}$.

This can be seen as follows. The derivation starts with p_5 yielding a or with p_1 deriving AA. In the latter case we continue with p_2 which has to be passed over (appearance checking) and then with p_3, i.e. we generate without loss of generality SA, or with p_4 which gives NA. In the latter case we cannot terminate since N cannot be rewritten by the rules of P. In the former case we have to rewrite also the remaining A which yields S^2. This cycle can be iterated, and thus the only possibility where we do not introduce N is the derivation

$$S \Rightarrow S^2 \stackrel{*}{\Rightarrow} S^4 \stackrel{*}{\Rightarrow} S^8 \stackrel{*}{\Rightarrow} \ldots \stackrel{*}{\Rightarrow} S^{2^n}$$

since by iterated application of p_1 we double the number of S. Now we can only terminate by 2^n applications of p_5. This gives a^{2^n}.

Lemma 2.1.2. *For $X \in \{\mathrm{CF}, \mathrm{CF} - \lambda\}$, we have*

$$\mathcal{L}(\mathrm{TV}, X) \subseteq \mathcal{L}(\mathrm{rC}, X).$$

Proof. If $G = (V_N, V_T, P, S, \varphi)$ is a periodically time-variant grammar and $\varphi(n) = \varphi(n + k)$ for some fixed $k \geqq 1$ and all $n \geqq 1$, then we define

$$R = \big(\varphi(1)\,\varphi(2) \ldots \varphi(k)\big)^* \, \big(\varphi(1) \cup \varphi(1)\,\varphi(2) \cup \cdots \cup \varphi(1)\,\varphi(2) \ldots \varphi(k)\big).$$

Obviously, R is regular and $G' = (V_N, V_T, P, S, R)$ permits exactly the same set of terminating derivations. Hence $L(G) = L(G')$.

Lemma 2.1.3. *For $X \in \{\mathrm{CF}, \mathrm{CF} - \lambda\}$, we have*

$$\mathcal{L}(\mathrm{rC}, X) \subseteq \mathcal{L}(\mathrm{P}, X).$$

Proof. Let $G = (V_N, V_T, P, S, R)$ be a grammar with regular control. Further let $G^{(1)} = (V_N^{(1)}, P, P^{(1)}, S^{(1)})$ be a regular grammar which generates R. We can assume that each production in $P^{(1)}$ has the form $A^{(1)} \to p$ or $A^{(1)} \to pB^{(1)}$ where $A^{(1)}, B^{(1)} \in V_N^{(1)}$, $p \in P$ (we can split a production $A^{(1)} \to p_1 p_2 \ldots p_k$ into $A^{(1)} \to p_1 A_1$, $A_1 \to p_2 A_2, \ldots$, $A_{k-2} \to p_{k-1} A_{k-1}$, $A_{k-1} \to p_k$ etc.). Now we construct a programmed grammar $G' = (V_N'',$ $V_T, P', S)$ in the following way. We set

$$V_N'' = V_N' \cup V_T' \cup \{\bar{S}\}$$

where V_N' and V_T' are primed copies of V_N and V_T, respectively, and $\bar{S}$ is a new letter. With each rule $p\colon A \to w$, we associate the following programmed productions (we omit the failure fields which are empty in all cases):

$$([A^{(1)}, p]: A' \to w', \{[B^{(1)}, q]: A^{(1)} \to pB^{(1)} \in P^{(1)}, q \in P\}),$$

$$\text{if} \quad A^{(1)} \to p \notin P^{(1)},$$

$$([A^{(1)}, p]: A' \to w', \{[B^{(1)}, q]: A^{(1)} \to pB^{(1)} \in P^{(1)}, q \in P\} \cup \{[a]: a \in V_T\}),$$

$$\text{if} \quad A^{(1)} \to p \in P^{(1)}$$

and we add the productions

$$([b]: b' \to b, \{[a]: a \in V_T\}) \quad \text{for} \quad b \in V_T,$$

$$(x: \bar{S} \to S', \{[S^{(1)}, p]: p \in P\}).$$

P' is the set of all productions of this form. It is easy to see that each terminating derivation in G' has the following form:

$$\bar{S} \underset{*}{\Longrightarrow} S' \underset{[S^{(1)},p_1]}{\Longrightarrow} w_1 \underset{[A_1^{(1)},p_2]}{\Longrightarrow} w_2 \underset{[A_2^{(1)},p_3]}{\Longrightarrow} \cdots \underset{[A_{r-1}^{(1)},p_r]}{\Longrightarrow} w_r \underset{[a_1]}{\Longrightarrow} w_{r+1}$$

$$\underset{[a_2]}{\Longrightarrow} w_{r+2} \underset{[a_3]}{\Longrightarrow} \cdots \underset{[a_s]}{\Longrightarrow} w_{r+s} \tag{2.1.1}$$

where

$$S^{(1)} \Rightarrow p_1 A_1^{(1)} \Rightarrow p_1 p_2 A_2^{(1)} \Rightarrow \cdots \Rightarrow p_1 p_2 \ldots p_{r-1} A_{r-1}^{(1)} \Rightarrow p_1 p_2 \ldots p_{r-1} p_r \tag{2.1.2}$$

is a derivation in $G^{(1)}$ and $w_r = w'_{r+s}$, $w_r \in (V'_T)^*$. By the definition of G' it is clear that

$$S \underset{p_1}{\Longrightarrow} v_1 \underset{p_2}{\Longrightarrow} v_2 \underset{p_3}{\Longrightarrow} \cdots \underset{p_r}{\Longrightarrow} v_r \tag{2.1.3}$$

with $v'_i = w_i$ for $1 \leqq i \leqq r$ is a terminating derivation in G. This proves the relation $L(G') = L(G)$.

On the other hand, for each $p_1 p_2 \ldots p_r \in P^*$, there is a derivation of the form (2.1.2) in $G^{(1)}$, and it is not difficult to prove the existence of a derivation of the form (2.1.1) which corresponds to (2.1.3). Hence $L(G) = L(G')$, too.

Summarizing the above lemmas we obtain

Theorem 2.1.1. *For* $X \in \{\text{CF}, \text{CF} - \lambda\}$, *we have*

$$\mathcal{L}(\text{M}, X) = \mathcal{L}(\text{TV}, X) = \mathcal{L}(\text{rC}, X).$$

Without proof we mention the following more general form of this result.

Theorem 2.1.1'. *For* $X \in \{\text{REG}, \text{CF}, \text{CF} - \lambda, \text{CS}\}$, *we have*

$$\mathcal{L}(\text{M}, X) = \mathcal{L}(\text{TV}, X) = \mathcal{L}(\text{rC}, X)$$

and

$$\mathcal{L}(\text{M}, X, \text{ac}) = \mathcal{L}(\text{TV}, X, \text{ac}) = \mathcal{L}(\text{rC}, X, \text{ac}).$$

Now we consider some modifications of the matrix concept. Let $G = (V_N, V_T, M, S)$ be a matrix grammar. Then the application of a matrix $m: (p_1, p_2, \ldots, p_s)$ to x, i.e. $x \underset{m}{\Longrightarrow} y$, is defined as

$$x = w_0 \underset{p_1}{\Longrightarrow} w_1 \underset{p_2}{\Longrightarrow} w_2 \underset{p_3}{\Longrightarrow} \cdots \underset{p_s}{\Longrightarrow} w_s = y.$$

i.e. we have to apply the rules of m in the order given by m. This is changed in the unordered matrix grammars.

Definition 2.1.3. An *unordered matrix grammar* is a construct $G = (V_N, V_T, M, S)$ whose components are defined as for matrix grammars. The application of a matrix m: $(p_1, p_2, \ldots, p_s)$ to some $x \in V_G^*$ yielding $y \in V_G^*$ is defined as follows: there are words $w_0, w_1, \ldots, w_s$ and a permutation π of $\{1, 2, \ldots, s\}$ such that

$$x = w_0 \underset{p_{\pi(1)}}{\Longrightarrow} w_1 \underset{p_{\pi(2)}}{\Longrightarrow} w_2 \underset{p_{\pi(3)}}{\Longrightarrow} \cdots \underset{p_{\pi(s)}}{\Longrightarrow} w_s = y .$$

The language $L(G)$ generated by G is defined as the set of all words over V_T which can be generated by iterated applications of (entire) matrices of M.

Considering matrices as strings of rules, the difference between ordered and unordered matrix grammars can be stated as follows. If G is a matrix grammar and $w \in L(G)$, then there is a derivation

$$S \underset{p_1}{\Longrightarrow} w_1 \underset{p_2}{\Longrightarrow} w_2 \underset{p_3}{\Longrightarrow} \cdots \underset{p_r}{\Longrightarrow} w_r = w$$

with $p_1p_2 \ldots p_r \in M^*$. If G is an unordered matrix grammar, then $p_1p_2 \ldots p_r \in (\mathrm{Perm}\,(M))^*$.

Example 2.1.4. We consider the grammar G with $V_N = \{A, B, C, S\}$, $V_T = \{a, b, c\}$, the axiom S, and the matrices

$$m_1\colon (S \to ABC),$$

$$m_2\colon (A \to aA, B \to bB, C \to cC),$$

$$m_3\colon (A \to a, B \to b, C \to c).$$

If we consider G as a matrix grammar, then

$$L(G) = \{a^nb^nc^n : n \geqq 1\},$$

and the same statement holds also if G is considered as an unordered matrix grammar since in both cases the application of a matrix consists in the rewriting of A, B, and C (besides the first step) and only the order of these rewritings can be different. E.g. the word $a^2b^2c^2$ can be generated by the (usual) matrix grammar only by the derivation

$$S \Rightarrow ABC \Rightarrow aABC \Rightarrow aAbBC \Rightarrow aAbBcC \Rightarrow a^2bBcC \Rightarrow a^2b^2cC \Rightarrow a^2b^2c^2,$$

however, in the unordered matrix grammar G we have among others the following possible derivations:

$$S \Rightarrow ABC \Rightarrow AbBC \Rightarrow aAbBC \Rightarrow aAbBcC \Rightarrow a^2bBcC \Rightarrow a^2bBc^2 \Rightarrow a^2b^2c^2,$$

$$S \Rightarrow ABC \Rightarrow aABC \Rightarrow aABcC \Rightarrow aAbBcC \Rightarrow aAbBc^2 \Rightarrow aAb^2c^2 \Rightarrow a^2b^2c^2,$$

and also the above given one. In the unordered matrix grammar G there are 36 different derivations of $a^2b^2c^2$.

By $\mathscr{L}(\mathrm{uM}, X)$ we denote the family of languages generated by unordered matrix grammars with core productions of type X.

Lemma 2.1.4. *For* $X \in \{\mathrm{CF}, \mathrm{CF} - \lambda\}$, *we have*

$$\mathscr{L}(\mathrm{uM}, X) \subseteq \mathscr{L}(\mathrm{M}, X).$$

Proof. With each matrix $m\colon (p_1p_2, \ldots, p_r) \in M$ of the unordered matrix grammar $G = (V_N, V_T, M, S)$ and each permutation π of $\{1, 2, \ldots, r\}$ we associate the matrices

$$m_\pi : (p_{\pi(1)}, p_{\pi(2)}, \ldots, p_{\pi(r)})$$

and define the matrix grammar $G' = (V_N, V_T, M', S)$ where M' is the set of all matrices introduced above. By definition, $L(G) = L(G')$.

Lemma 2.1.5. *For* $X \in \{\text{CF}, \text{CF} - \lambda\}$, *we have*

$$\mathcal{L}(\text{M}, X) \subseteq \mathcal{L}(\text{uM}, X).$$

Proof. The assertion is a direct consequence of Lemma 1.3.7 since in accurate normal form matrix grammars each matrix $(A_1 \to x_1, A_2 \to x_2)$ contains rules involving nonterminals in disjoint alphabets. The unordered use of such a matrix is, in fact, equivalent to the ordered use and conversely.

Both the above variants of matrix grammars have the following in common: if one starts with the application of the rules of a matrix, a second matrix can be started only after finishing the application of the first one. This feature is omitted in the definition of a vector grammar.

Definition 2.1.4. i) A *vector grammar* is a quadruple $G = (V_N, V_T, M, S)$ whose components are defined as for matrix grammars. The language $L(G)$ generated by G consists of all words $w \in V_T^*$ which have a derivation

$$S \underset{p_1}{\Longrightarrow} w_1 \underset{p_2}{\Longrightarrow} w_2 \underset{p_3}{\Longrightarrow} \cdots \underset{p_{r-1}}{\Longrightarrow} w_{r-1} \underset{p_r}{\Longrightarrow} w_r = w \tag{2.1.4}$$

where $p_1p_2 \ldots p_{r-1}p_r \in \text{Shuf}^*(M)$.

ii) An *unordered vector grammar* is defined as a vector grammar, and its language $L(G)$ consists of all words $w \in V_T^*$ with a derivation (2.1.4) such that $p_1p_2 \ldots p_{r-1}p_r \in \text{Perm}(M^*)$.

Example 2.1.4. (continued) If we consider G as a vector grammar then we have, among others, the following derivations of $a^2b^2c^2$:

$$S \Rightarrow ABC \Rightarrow aABC \Rightarrow aAbBC \Rightarrow a^2bBC \Rightarrow a^2bBcC \Rightarrow a^2b^2cC \Rightarrow a^2b^2c^2,$$

$$S \Rightarrow ABC \Rightarrow aABC \Rightarrow a^2BC \Rightarrow a^2bBC \Rightarrow a^2bBcC \Rightarrow a^2b^2cC \Rightarrow a^2b^2c^2,$$

and $a^2b^2c^2$ has five different derivations in the vector grammar G.

If we consider G as an unordered vector grammar, $a^2b^2c^2$ also has the derivation

$$S \Rightarrow ABC \Rightarrow AbBC \Rightarrow AbBcC \Rightarrow AbBc^2 \Rightarrow Ab^2c^2 \Rightarrow aAb^2c^2 \Rightarrow a^2b^2c^2$$

and all the derivations given in this example, too. In the unordered vector grammar G, $a^2b^2c^2$ has more than 72 derivations.

By $\mathcal{L}(\text{V}, X)$ and $\mathcal{L}(\text{uV}, X)$ we denote the families of languages generated by vector and unordered vector grammars with core productions of type X.

Lemma 2.1.6. *For* $X \in \{\text{CF}, \text{CF} - \lambda\}$, *we have*

$$\mathcal{L}(\text{uV}, X) \subseteq \mathcal{L}(\text{V}, X).$$

Proof. We can repeat the arguments of the proof of Lemma 2.1.4.

Lemma 2.1.7. $\mathcal{L}(\mathrm{V}, \mathrm{CF}) \subseteq \mathcal{L}(\mathrm{M}, \mathrm{CF})$.

Proof. Let $G = (V_N, V_T, M, S)$ be a vector grammar, $M = \{m_1, m_2, \ldots, m_n\}$ and

$$m_i: (A_{i,1} \to w_{i,1}, A_{i,2}, \to w_{i,2}, \ldots, A_{i,r_i} \to w_{i,r_i}), \quad 1 \leqq i \leqq n.$$

We set

$$V'_N = V_N \cup \{\bar{S}, D\} \cup \{D_{i,j} : 1 \leqq i \leqq n, 1 \leqq j \leqq r_i\}$$

where $\bar{S}$, D, $D_{i,j}$, $1 \leqq i \leqq n$, $1 \leqq j \leqq r_i$, are new symbols. We associate with m_i, $1 \leqq i \leqq n$, the matrices

$$(A_{i,1} \to w_{i,1}, D \to DD_{i,1}),$$

$$(A_{i,j} \to w_{i,j}, D_{i,j-1} \to D_{i,j}), 2 \leqq j \leqq r_i,$$

$$(D_{i,r_i} \to \lambda).$$

Further we add the starting matrix

$$(\bar{S} \to SD)$$

and the erasing rule

$$(D \to \lambda),$$

and we consider the matrix grammar $G' = (V'_N, V_T, M, \bar{S})$ where M' is the set of all matrices constructed above. By the definition of the matrices we can apply the matrix $(A_{i,j} \to w_{i,j}, D_{i,j-1} \to D_{i,j})$, $1 \leqq i \leqq n$, $2 \leqq j \leqq r_i$, only if we have applied the matrices $(A_{i,1} \to w_{i,1}, D \to DD_{i,1})$ and $(A_{i,k} \to w_{i,k}, D_{i,k-1} \to D_{i,k})$ for $2 \leqq k \leqq j$, i.e. each matrix of G has to be applied entirely and in the given order. Moreover, we can start a matrix of G at any moment as long as D is present. Hence $L(G') = L(G)$.

Lemma 2.1.8. *For* $X \in \{\mathrm{CF}, \mathrm{CF} - \lambda\}$, *we have*

$$\mathcal{L}(\mathrm{M}, X) \subseteq \mathcal{L}(\mathrm{V}, X).$$

Proof. We consider only the case $X = \mathrm{CF}$. Let $G = (V_N, V_T, M, S)$ be a matrix grammar, and by Lemma 1.3.7, we can assume that

$$M = \{m_1, m_2, \ldots, m_n\},$$

$$m_i: (A_i \to w_i) \quad \text{for} \quad 1 \leqq i \leqq s,$$

$$m_j: (A_{j,1} \to w_{j,1}, A_{j,2} \to w_{j,2}) \quad \text{for} \quad s < j \leqq n.$$

We define the vector grammar G' by

$$G' = (V_N \cup \{\bar{S}, D\} \cup \{D_i : 1 \leqq i \leqq n\}, V_T, M', \bar{S}),$$

$$M' = \{(\bar{S} \to SD), (D \to \lambda)\}$$
$$\cup \{(D \to D_i, A_i \to w_i, D_i \to D) : 1 \leqq i \leqq s\}$$
$$\cup \{(D \to D_j, A_{j,1} \to w_{j,1}, A_{j,2} \to w_{j,2}, D_j \to D) : s + 1 \leqq j \leqq n\}.$$

Obviously, any derivation starts with $\bar{S} \Rightarrow SD$, and now we can start a matrix of G', i.e. $SD \Rightarrow SD_i$. Since each matrix of G' (except $(\bar{S} \to SD)$) starts with a rewriting of D, it cannot start until we have finished the started matrix by application of $D_i \to D$. Now it is easy to see that $L(G) = L(G')$.

Summarizing Lemmas 2.1.4 to 2.1.8 we obtain

Theorem 2.1.2. $\mathcal{L}(\mathrm{M}, \mathrm{CF} - \lambda) = \mathcal{L}(\mathrm{uM}, \mathrm{CF} - \lambda) \subseteq \mathcal{L}(\mathrm{V}, \mathrm{CF} - \lambda)$,

$$\mathcal{L}(\mathrm{M}, \mathrm{CF}) = \mathcal{L}(\mathrm{uM}, \mathrm{CF}) = \mathcal{L}(\mathrm{V}, \mathrm{CF}).$$

Now we want to prove that unordered vector grammars have a smaller generative power. This will follow from the following lemma.

Lemma 2.1.9. *Each language in* $\mathcal{L}(\mathrm{uV}, \mathrm{CF})$ *is semilinear.*

Proof. Let $L = L(G)$ for some unordered vector grammar $G = (V_N, V_T, M, S)$. Let us consider the context-free grammar $G' = \left(V_N, V_T, P(M), S\right)$. We regard the language U over $P(M)$ consisting of all words $p_1 p_2 \ldots p_n$ such that

$$S \underset{p_1}{\Longrightarrow} w_1 \underset{p_2}{\Longrightarrow} w_2 \underset{p_3}{\Longrightarrow} \cdots \underset{p_n}{\Longrightarrow} w_n \in V_T^*$$

is a derivation in G' and the language V over $P(M)$ consisting of such words for which the corresponding derivations are correct with respect to G. Clearly,

$$V = U \cap \mathrm{Perm}\,(M^*)$$

by the definition of an unordered vector grammar.

We show that $p_{P(M)}(V)$ is a semilinear set. By well-known set-theoretic properties,

$$\begin{aligned} p_{P(M)}(V) &= p_{P(M)}\left(U \cap \mathrm{Perm}\,(M^*)\right) \\ &= p_{P(M)}\left(U \cap p_{P(M)}^{-1}\left(p_{P(M)}(M^*)\right)\right) \\ &= p_{P(M)}(U) \cap p_{P(M)}(M^*). \end{aligned}$$

Clearly, since the intersection of semilinear sets is again a semilinear set and since $p_{P(M)}(M^*)$ is a semilinear set, it is sufficient to prove that $p_{P(M)}(U)$ is a semilinear set. In order to do this we construct the context-free grammar $G'' = (V_N, V_T, P(M) \cup P', S)$ from G' in the following way: with each production $p: A \to w \in P(M)$ we associate the production $p': A \to wp$, and P' is the set of all these productions. Obviously, $S \underset{p_1 p_2 \ldots p_n}{\Longrightarrow} z$ is a terminating derivation in G' if and only if $S \underset{p_1' p_2' \ldots p_n'}{\Longrightarrow} z'$ is a terminating derivation in G''. Moreover, $z' = u_1 p_{i_1} u_2 p_{i_2} \ldots u_n p_{i_n}$ with $z = u_1 u_2 \ldots u_n$, $\{i_1, i_2, \ldots, i_n\} = \{1, 2, \ldots, n\}$. Further,

$$p_{V_T \cup P(M)}(z p_1 p_2 \ldots p_n) = p_{V_T \cup P(M)}(z').$$

Now let h be the homomorphism given by

$$h(a) = \lambda \quad \text{for} \quad a \in V_T, \qquad h(p) = p \quad \text{for} \quad p \in P(M).$$

Then

$$p_{P(M)}\left(h(L(G''))\right) = p_{P(M)}(U).$$

By Theorem 0.2.4, $p_{P(M)}\left(h(L(G''))\right)$ is a semilinear set and hence $p_{P(M)}(U)$ is a semilinear set, too.

Now we define the homomorphisms $g: V_G^* \to V_T^*$ and $f: P(M)^* \to V_T^*$ by

$$g(A) = \lambda \quad \text{for} \quad A \in V_N, \quad g(a) = a \quad \text{for} \quad a \in V_T, \; f(A \to w) = g(w).$$

Clearly,

$$p_{V_T}(f(V)) = p_{V_T}(L).$$

Since $f(V)$ is semilinear for a semilinear set V, it is proved that L is semilinear.

Theorem 2.1.3. *For $X \in \{\mathrm{CF}, \mathrm{CF} - \lambda\}$, we have the strict inclusion*

$$\mathscr{L}(\mathrm{uV}, X) \subset \mathscr{L}(\mathrm{V}, X)$$

Proof. The inclusion follows from Lemma 2.1.6. It is proper since $\mathscr{L}(\mathrm{uV}, X)$ contains only semilinear languages by Lemma 2.1.9 and, on the other hand, by Theorem 2.1.2 and the examples of Section 1.1, $\mathscr{L}(\mathrm{V}, X)$ contains non-semilinear languages.

Now we introduce the valence grammars.

Definition 2.1.5. An *additive valence grammar* is a quintuple $G = (V_N, V_T, P, S, v)$ where V_N, V_T, P, S are defined as for phrase structure grammars and v is a mapping from P into the set Z of integers. The language $L(G)$ generated by G consists of all words $w \in V_T^*$ such that there is a derivation

$$S \underset{p_1}{\Longrightarrow} w_1 \underset{p_2}{\Longrightarrow} w_2 \underset{p_3}{\Longrightarrow} \cdots \underset{p_n}{\Longrightarrow} w_n = w$$

such that $v(p_1) + v(p_2) + \cdots + v(p_n) = 0$.

The notation "valence" comes from the following example.

Example 2.1.5. Let $G = (V_N, V_T, P, S)$ be a context-free grammar such that S does not occur on the right-hand side of any production. (This can be assumed without loss of generality.) Then we define

$$v(S \to w) = |w|_{V_N},$$

$$v(A \to w) = |w|_{V_N} - 1 \quad \text{for} \quad A \in V_N, A \neq S.$$

Then let $S \underset{p_1}{\Longrightarrow} w_1 \underset{p_2}{\Longrightarrow} \cdots \underset{p_n}{\Longrightarrow} w_n$ be a derivation in G. We obtain

$$v(p_1) + v(p_2) + \cdots + v(p_n) = |w_n|_{V_N}.$$

Since $|w_n|_{V_N}$ gives the number of places in w_n where the derivation can be continued, in analogy to chemistry and graph theory, this value can be called the valence of the sentential form. Clearly, $w \in L(G)$ if and only if there is a derivation of w using the rules $p_1, p_2, \ldots, p_k$ with $v(p_1) + v(p_2) + \cdots + v(p_k) = 0$. Hence any context-free language can be generated by an additive valence grammar.

Example 2.1.6. Let $G = (\{S, A, B\}, \{a, b, c\}, \{p_1, p_2, \ldots, p_5\}, S, v)$ with

$$p_1 \colon S \to AB, \quad p_2 \colon A \to aA, \quad p_3 \colon B \to bBc,$$

$$p_4 \colon A \to a, \quad p_5 \colon B \to bc,$$

$$v(p_1) = v(p_4) = v(p_5) = 0, \quad v(p_2) = 1, \quad v(p_3) = -1.$$

Then

$$L(G) = \{a^n b^n c^n : n \geqq 1\}.$$

This can be seen as follows. Each sentential form contains at most one A and at most one B. Further the starting production $S \to AB$ and both terminating productions can be used only once. The application of these productions gives $v(p_1) + v(p_4) + v(p_5) = 0$. If we use p_2 r times and if p_3 is applied s times, then we obtain for this derivation the valence $r - s$. By the definition of the generated language $r - s = 0$ has to hold, and thus both rules are applied r times. Since the order in which these productions are used can be changed we get

$$S \Rightarrow AB \xRightarrow[r \text{ times } p_2]{*} a^r AB \xRightarrow[r \text{ times } p_3]{*} a^r Ab^r Bc^r \Rightarrow a^{r+1}b^r Bc^r \Rightarrow a^{r+1}b^{r+1}c^{r+1}$$

as the only possible type of terminating derivations.

Example 2.1.7. We show that $L = \{a^n b^n c^n : n \geqq 1\}^2$ cannot be generated by an additive valence grammar. Suppose the contrary. Then there is an additive valence grammar $G = (V_N, \{a, b, c\}, P, S, v)$ with $L(G) = L$. For any string $x = a^n b^n c^n a^m b^m c^m \in L$ we call $a^n b^n c^n$ the left part and $a^m b^m c^m$ the right part of x; moreover, we call each subword of the form α^i, $\alpha \in \{a, b, c\}$ "position" in x. If n and m are large enough, the derivation $S \overset{*}{\Rightarrow} x$ contains (without loss of generality since we can change the order of the application of the rules) a subderivation

$$D : T \underset{p_1}{\Longrightarrow} w_1 \underset{p_2}{\Longrightarrow} \cdots \underset{p_r}{\Longrightarrow} w_r = xTy$$

with $T \in V_N$, $x, y \in V_T^+$. Let

$$v(D) = v(p_1) + v(p_2) + \cdots + v(p_r).$$

Assume $v(D) = 0$. Then we can iterate the application of D, i.e. we obtain the derivation

$$S \overset{*}{\Rightarrow} uTv \overset{*}{\Rightarrow} uxTyv \overset{*}{\Rightarrow} ux^2Ty^2v \overset{*}{\Rightarrow} \cdots \overset{*}{\Rightarrow} ux^nTy^nv \overset{*}{\Rightarrow} z \in L.$$

Therefore x^n and y^n are subwords of words in L for each $n \in \mathbb{N}$. Hence x and y are powers of letters in $\{a, b, c\}$. However, then the iteration leads to a word not contained in L since it increases only the power of at most two letters. Thus $v(D) \neq 0$.

Since L is infinite, there are strings involving arbitrarily many times such a derivation D. As we can change the order in which D is used and iterate D without intercalating other subderivations, we again get that x, y has to be of the form α^i, $\alpha \in \{a, b, c\}$. Such a subderivation can contribute to at most two positions of strings in L. Therefore at least three derivations $D_i: T_i \overset{*}{\Rightarrow} x_iT_iy_i$, $i = 1, 2, 3$, are necessary, all with $v(D_i) \neq 0$, each contributing to at least a position different from the positions increased by the others. Suppose without loss of generality that $v(D_1) > 0$, $v(D_3) > 0$. Again, by the infinity of L there is a word $z \in L$ such that its derivation contains the application of D_1 k times, where $k > v(D_3)$ (or the application of D_3 $k > v(D_1)$ times) and the application of D_3 (or D_1) at least once. Because

$$kv(D_1) + jv(D_3) = \big(k - v(D_3)\big)\, v(D_1) + \big(j + v(D_1)\big)\, v(D_3)$$

there is another terminating derivation D which uses D_1 only $k - v(D_3)$ times and which applies D_3 $\big(j + v(D_1)\big)$ times. Obviously, D produces a word which is not in L. This contradicts our assumption $L = L(G)$.

Next we prove a normal form result.

Lemma 2.1.10. *For each additive valence grammar G there is an additive valence grammar $G' = (V_N, V_T, P, S, v)$ such that $v(p) \in \{1, 0, -1\}$ for each $p \in P$ and $L(G) = L(G')$.*

Proof. Let $G = (V_N, V_T, P, S, v)$ be an additive valence grammar. If there exists a rule $p: A \to w$, in P with $v(p) \notin \{1, 0, -1\}$, then we proceed as follows: Let $v(p) = r > 1$. With p we associate the new nonterminals $A_{p,1}, A_{p,2}, \ldots, A_{p,r-1}$ and the productions

$$p_1: A \to A_{p,1},$$

$$p_{i+1}: A_{p,i} \to A_{p,i+1}, \quad 1 \leqq i \leqq r-2,$$

$$p_r: A_{p,r-1} \to w,$$

and we define the mapping v' by $v'(p_i) = 1$, $1 \leqq i \leqq r$. If $v(p) < -1$, then we introduce new nonterminals and rules in the same way and define $v'(p_i) = -1$. Now we set $G' = (V'_N, V_T, P', S, v')$ where V'_N is the union of V_N and all the above introduced nonterminals $A_{p,i}$ for p with $v(p) \notin \{1, 0, -1\}$, P' consists of all rules $q \in P$ with $v(q) \in \{1, 0, -1\}$ and all productions constructed above, and v' is defined as in the construction for the new rules with $v'(q) = v(q)$ for those $q \in P$ with $v(q) \in \{1, 0, -1\}$. By the construction, G' has the desired form.

Now we prove that $L(G) = L(G')$. This follows by the fact that the application of p_1 requires the application of $p_2, p_3, \ldots, p_r$ in this order in order to terminate the derivation, i.e. the application of the rule $p: A \to w$ is simulated and

$$v(p_1) + v(p_2) + \cdots + v(p_{r-1}) + v(p_r) = v(p) = r,$$

and conversely, each p can be simulated by $p_1, p_2, \ldots, p_r$. Therefore there is a derivation $D: S \overset{*}{\Rightarrow} v \in V_T^*$ with $v(D) = 0$ in G iff there is a derivation $D': S \overset{*}{\Rightarrow} v$ with $v'(D') = 0$ in G'.

By $\mathcal{L}(\text{aV}, X)$ we denote the family of all languages generated by additive valence grammars with productions of type X.

Lemma 2.1.11. *For $X \in \{\text{CF}, \text{CF} - \lambda\}$, we have*

$$\mathcal{L}(\text{aV}, X) \subseteq \mathcal{L}(\text{uV}, X).$$

Proof. Let $L \in \mathcal{L}(\text{aV}, \text{CF})$. By Lemma 2.1.10 we can assume that L is generated by an additive valence grammar $G = (V_N, V_T, P, S, v)$ such that $v(p) \in \{1, 0, -1\}$ for each $p \in P$. We define the unordered vector grammar G' by $G' = (V_N, V_T, M, S)$ with

$$M = \{(A_1 \to w_1, A_2 \to w_2) : v(A_1 \to w_1) = -v(A_2 \to w_2) \neq 0\}$$
$$\cup \{(A \to w) : v(A \to w) = 0\}.$$

Then the equality $L(G) = L(G')$ follows since in both cases the number of applications of rules p with $v(p) = 1$ is the same as that of applications of rules q with $v(q) = -1$ in a derivation.

Example 2.1.6 shows that additive valence grammars are able to ensure that both productions of one pair of rules are applied the same number of times, and by Example 2.1.7 it seems that this does not hold for any number of couples of productions. In order to have this ability too, we can conceive of valence grammars with multiplication (of positive rational numbers), because then we can use the prime numbers and their inverses for counting. Formally this leads to the following definition.

Definition 2.1.6. A *multiplicative valence grammar* is a quintuple $G = (V_N, V_T, P, S, v)$ where V_N, V_T, P, S are defined as for phrase structure grammars and v is a mapping from P into the set Q of positive rational numbers. The language $L(G)$ generated by G consists of all words $w \in V_T^*$ such that there is a derivation

$$S \underset{p_1}{\Longrightarrow} w_1 \underset{p_2}{\Longrightarrow} w_2 \underset{p_3}{\Longrightarrow} \cdots \underset{p_{n-1}}{\Longrightarrow} w_{n-1} \underset{p_n}{\Longrightarrow} w_n = w$$

with

$$v(p_1)\, v(p_2) \ldots v(p_n) = 1 .$$

Example 2.1.8. Let $G = (V_N, V_T, P, S, v_1)$ where V_N, V_T, P, S are as in Example 2.1.6 and v_1 is given by

$$v_1(p_1) = v_1(p_4) = v_1(p_5) = 1, \quad v_1(p_2) = 2, \quad v_1(p_3) = \frac{1}{2}.$$

As in Example 2.1.6 we can prove that $\{a^nb^nc^n : n \geqq 1\} = L(G)$.

The following example will show a difference between additive and multiplicative valence grammars.

Example 2.1.9. Let

$$G = (\{S, A, B, T, A_1, B_1\}, \{a, b, c\}, \{p_i : 0 \leqq i \leqq 9\}, S, v)$$

with

$$p_0: S \to ABT,\ v(p_0) = 1, \qquad p_1: T \to A_1B_1,\ v(p_1) = 1,$$

$$p_2: A \to aA,\ v(p_2) = 2, \qquad p_3: B \to bBc,\ v(p_3) = \frac{1}{2},$$

$$p_4: A \to a,\ v(p_4) = 1, \qquad p_5: B \to bc,\ v(p_5) = 1,$$

$$p_6: A_1 \to aA_1,\ v(p_6) = 3, \qquad p_7: B_1 \to bB_1c,\ v(p_7) = \frac{1}{3},$$

$$p_8: A_1 \to a,\ v(p_8) = 1, \qquad p_9: B_1 \to bc,\ v(p_9) = 1.$$

Then, by definition, any rule p with $v(p) = 1$ can be applied any number of times and the rules p_2 and p_3 (p_6 and p_7, respectively) have to be used as often as the other. Therefore (besides the order) each derivation in G has the form

$$S \Rightarrow ABT \overset{*}{\Rightarrow} a^nABT \Rightarrow a^{n+1}BT \overset{*}{\Rightarrow} a^{n+1}b^nBc^nT \Rightarrow a^{n+1}b^{n+1}c^{n+1}T$$

$$\Rightarrow a^{n+1}b^{n+1}c^{n+1}A_1B_1 \overset{*}{\Rightarrow} a^{n+1}b^{n+1}c^{n+1}a^mA_1B_1 \Rightarrow a^{n+1}b^{n+1}c^{n+1}a^{m+1}B_1$$

$$\overset{*}{\Rightarrow} a^{n+1}b^{n+1}c^{n+1}a^{m+1}b^mB_1c^m \Rightarrow a^{n+1}b^{n+1}c^{n+1}a^{m+1}b^{m+1}c^{m+1}.$$

Therefore $L(G) = \{a^nb^nc^n : n \geqq 1\}^2$, which is not in $\mathcal{L}(\text{aV, CF})$ by Example 2.1.7.

By $\mathcal{L}(\text{mV}, X)$ we denote the family of all languages generated by multiplicative valence grammars with core productions of type X.

Lemma 2.1.12. *For each $L \in \mathcal{L}(\text{mV, CF})$ there is a multiplicative valence grammar $G = (V_N, V_T, P, S, v)$ such that for each production $r \in P$ there is a prime number p such that $v(r) = p$ or $v(r) = \frac{1}{p}$.*

Proof. Let G be a multiplicative valence grammar generating L, and let $r\colon A \to w$ be a production of it. Then $v(r) = \frac{z}{z'}$ for two positive integers z and z'. There exist prime numbers $p_1, p_2, \ldots, p_s, q_1, q_2, \ldots, q_t$ such that

$$v(r) = \frac{p_1 p_2 \cdots p_s}{q_1 q_2 \cdots q_t} = p_1 p_2 \cdots p_s \frac{1}{q_1} \frac{1}{q_2} \cdots \frac{1}{q_t}.$$

Now we proceed as in the proof of Lemma 2.1.10.

Lemma 2.1.13. *For* $X \in \{\mathrm{CF}, \mathrm{CF} - \lambda\}$, we *have*

$$\mathcal{L}(\mathrm{mV}, X) \subseteq \mathcal{L}(\mathrm{uV}, X).$$

Proof. Using the normal form result of Lemma 2.1.12 and matrices which consist of pairs (r_1, r_2) with $v(r_1) = \frac{1}{v(r_2)} = p$ for some prime number, we can repeat the proof of Lemma 2.1.11.

We now prove the opposite inclusion.

Lemma 2.1.14. *For* $X \in \{\mathrm{CF}, \mathrm{CF} - \lambda\}$, *we have*

$$\mathcal{L}(\mathrm{uV}, X) \subseteq \mathcal{L}(\mathrm{mV}, X).$$

Proof. Let $G = (V_N, V_T, M, S)$ be an unordered vector grammar,

$$M = \{m_1, m_2, \ldots, m_t\},$$

$$m_i : (A_{i,1} \to w_{i,1}, A_{i,2} \to w_{i,2}, \ldots, A_{i,r_i} \to w_{i,r_i}), \quad 1 \leqq i \leqq t.$$

Then we define the unordered vector grammar G' by $G' = (V'_N, V_T, M', S)$,

$$V'_N = V_N \cup \{B_{i,j} : 1 \leqq i \leqq t, 1 \leqq j \leqq r_i\},$$

$$M' = \{n_1, n_2, \ldots, n_t\},$$

$$n_i : (A_{i,1} \to B_{i,1}, B_{i,1} \to w_{i,1}, A_{i,2}, \to B_{i,2}, B_{i,2} \to w_{i,2}, \ldots,$$
$$A_{i,r_i} \to B_{i,r_i}, B_{i,r_i} \to w_{i,r_i}), 1 \leqq i \leqq t.$$

Obviously, $L(G) = L(G')$. The grammar G' has the property that no production $A \to w$ occurs twice in the matrices. For simplicity, let us use the notation

$$n_i\colon (q_{i,1}, q_{i,2}, \ldots, q_{i,s_i}),\ s_i = 2r_i.$$

Let $s = s_1 + s_2 + \cdots + s_t - t$, and let $p_1, p_2, \ldots, p_s$ be the first s prime numbers. Now we define the following multiplicative valence grammar $G'' = (V'_N, V_T, P', S, v)$ where P' is the set of all rules occurring in M' and v' is defined as follows.

Let $u = s_1 + s_2 + \cdots + s_{i-1} - (i - 1)$. Then we set

$$v(q_{i,j}) = p_{u+j} \quad \text{for} \quad 1 \leqq j < s_i$$

and

$$v(q_{i,s_i}) = \frac{1}{p_{u+1} p_{u+2} \cdots p_{u+s_i-1}}.$$

Clearly, if we use a rule $q_{i,j}$ then it is necessary also to apply the productions $q_{i,1}, \ldots, q_{i,j-1}, q_{i,j+1}, \ldots, q_{i,s_i}$ in order to get 1 for the product of the valences associated with the used productions. Hence we simulate the application of a matrix. By these facts it is easy to see that $L(G') = L(G'')$. This proves that $L(G)$ can be generated by a multiplicative valence grammar.

Theorem 2.1.4. *For* $X \in \{\mathrm{CF}, \mathrm{CF} - \lambda\}$, *we have*

$$\mathscr{L}(\mathrm{aV}, X) \subset \mathscr{L}(\mathrm{mV}, X) = \mathscr{L}(\mathrm{uV}, X).$$

Proof. The equalities $\mathscr{L}(\mathrm{mV}, X) = \mathscr{L}(\mathrm{uV}, X)$ follow from Lemmas 2.1.13 and 2.1.14. The first inclusion is given by Lemma 2.1.11, and its strictness is a consequence of Examples 2.1.7 and 1.2.9.

Again we have the analogous results for the other types of productions. Without proof we summarize them in

Theorem 2.1.4'. *Let* $X \in \{\mathrm{REG}, \mathrm{CF}, \mathrm{CF} - \lambda, \mathrm{CS}\}$. Then

$$\mathscr{L}(\mathrm{aV}, X) \subset \mathscr{L}(\mathrm{mV}, X) = \mathscr{L}(\mathrm{uV}, X).$$

In the final part of this section we consider iterated grammars. Although they work in a purely sequential way, they have the same generative capacity as the ETOL systems which use a purely parallel derivation process. Intuitively, an iterated grammar consists of a "sequence" of context-free grammars where the set of terminals of a grammar coincides with the set of nonterminals of its succeeding grammar, and if a derivation in a grammar terminates, we start with the derivation in the next grammar.

Definition 2.1.7. An *iterated grammar* is an $(m + n + 3)$-tuple $G = (V, W_1, W_2, \ldots, W_m, R_1, R_2, \ldots, R_n, S, f)$ where

i) $V, W_1, W_2, \ldots, W_m$ are finite non-empty, pairwise disjoint sets,

ii) $S \in W_1$,

iii) f is a mapping from $\{1, 2, \ldots, n\}$ into $\{V, W_1, W_2, \ldots, W_m\} \times \{V, W_1, W_2, \ldots, W_m\}$,

iv) if $f(i) = (W_{i_1}, W_{i_2})$ then R_i is a finite subset of $W_{i_1} \times (W_{i_1} \cup W_{i_2})^*$.

For given $R \subseteq W \times (W \cup W')^*$, a direct derivation (a direct R-derivation) $x \underset{R}{\Longrightarrow} y$ is defined by $x = x_1Ax_2$, $y = x_1wx_2$, $A \to w \in R$. An R-derivation $x \overset{*}{\underset{R}{\Longrightarrow}} y$ is defined by

a) $x \in W^+, y \in (W')^*$,

b) there exist an integer $n \geqq 1$ and words $w_0, w_1, \ldots, w_n$ such that $x = w_0$, $w_i \underset{R}{\Longrightarrow} w_{i+1}$ is a direct R-derivation for $0 \leqq i \leqq n - 1$, $y = w_n$.

Let $\varrho = i_1i_2 \ldots i_s$. We call $x \overset{\varrho}{\Longrightarrow} y$ a *ϱ-derivation* iff there exist the words $w_0, w_1, \ldots, w_s$ such that $w_0 = x$, $w_s = y$, and $w_{j-1} \underset{R_{i_j}}{\Longrightarrow} w_j$ for $1 \leqq j \leqq s$. The language $L(G)$ generated by the iterated grammar G is defined as

$$L(G) = \{w : w \in V^*, S \overset{\varrho}{\Longrightarrow} w \quad \text{for some} \quad \varrho \in \{1, 2, \ldots, n\}^+\}.$$

In the following we interpret f as a graph: the sets $V, W_1, \ldots, W_m$ are the vertices, and there is a directed edge (arc) from W_{i_1} to W_{i_2} labelled by R_i iff $f(i) = (W_{i_1}, W_{i_2})$.

Example 2.1.10. Let $G = (V, W_1, W_2, R_1, R_2, R_3, S, f)$ where

$$V = \{a, b, c\},\ W_1 = \{S, A, B, a'', b'', c''\},\ W_2 = \{A', B', a', b', c'\},$$

$$R_1 = \{S \to AB,\ A \to a'A',\ B \to b'B'c',\ a'' \to a',\ b'' \to b',\ c'' \to c'\},$$

$$R_2 = \{A' \to A,\ B' \to B,\ a' \to a'',\ b' \to b'',\ c' \to c''\},$$

$$R_3 = \{S \to abc,\ A \to a,\ B \to bc,\ a'' \to a,\ b'' \to b,\ c'' \to c\},$$

and f is given by the graph in Fig. 2.1.1.

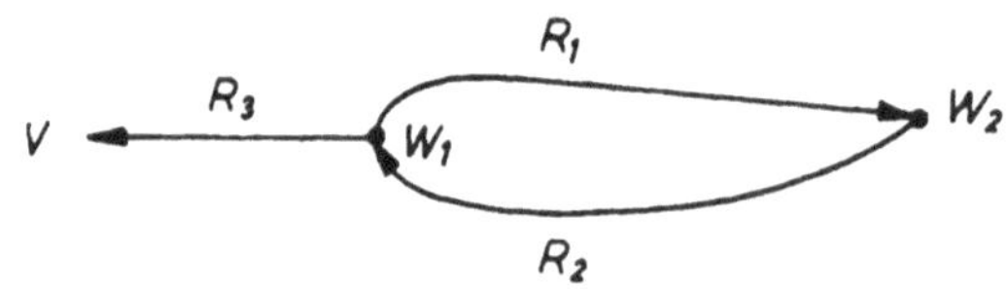

Fig. 2.1.1

If we start with R_3, then we have the only derivation $S \underset{R_3}{\Longrightarrow} abc$. If we start with R_1 we obtain

$$S \underset{R_1}{\Longrightarrow} AB \underset{R_1}{\Longrightarrow} a'A'B \underset{R_1}{\Longrightarrow} aA'b'B'c'$$

(where without loss of generality we have used the rules in the order given in R_1). Then we have to apply rules of R_2 for as long as possible. This gives $a'A'b'B'c' \overset{*}{\underset{R_2}{\Longrightarrow}} a''Ab''Bc''$. If we continue with R_3 we derive $a''Ab''Bc'' \overset{*}{\underset{R_3}{\Longrightarrow}} a^2b^2c^2$. Otherwise we have to apply rules of R_1 and then those of R_2 again, and we obtain

$$a''Ab''Bc'' \underset{R_1}{\Longrightarrow} a'^2A'b'^2B'c'^2 \underset{R_2}{\Longrightarrow} a''^2Ab''^2Bc''^2.$$

Continuing in this way it is easy to see that

$$L(G) = \{a^nb^nc^n : n \geqq 1\}.$$

Example 2.1.11. The language $\{a^{2^n} : n \geqq 0\}$ is generated by the iterated grammar

$$G = (\{a\}, \{S\}, \{S'\}, \{S \to S'S'\}, \{S' \to SS\}, \{S \to a\}, S, f)$$

where f is the same as in Example 2.1.10.

By $\mathscr{L}(Z)$ we denote the set of all languages generated by (context-free) iterated grammars.

Theorem 2.1.5. $\mathscr{L}(\mathrm{Z}) = \mathscr{L}(\mathrm{ETOL})$.

Proof. $\mathscr{L}(\mathrm{ETOL}) \subseteq \mathscr{L}(\mathrm{Z})$. Let $L \in \mathscr{L}(\mathrm{ETOL})$ be generated by the ETOL system $G = (V, V_T, \{P_1, P_2, \ldots, P_r\}, w)$. Then we consider the iterated grammar G' defined by

$$G' = (V_T, W_1, W_2, W_3, R_0, R_{1,1}, R_{1,2}, \ldots, R_{1,r}, R_2, R_3, U, f)$$

where

$$W_1 = \{U\}, \quad W_2 = \{x' : x \in V\}, \quad W_3 = \{x'' : x \in V\},$$

$$R_0 = \{U \to x_1'x_2' \dots x_n'\} \quad \text{if} \quad w = x_1x_2 \dots x_n,\ x_i \in V,\ 1 \leqq i \leqq n,$$

$$R_{1,i} = \{x' \to x_1''x_2'' \dots x_s'' : x \to x_1x_2 \dots x_s \in P_i\},\ 1 \leqq i \leqq r,$$

$$R_2 = \{x'' \to x' : x \in V\},$$

$$R_3 = \left\{x' \to x''' : x \in V, \quad x''' = \begin{Bmatrix} x & \text{for} \quad x \in V_T \\ x' & \text{otherwise} \end{Bmatrix}\right\},$$

and f is given by the graph in Fig. 2.1.2.

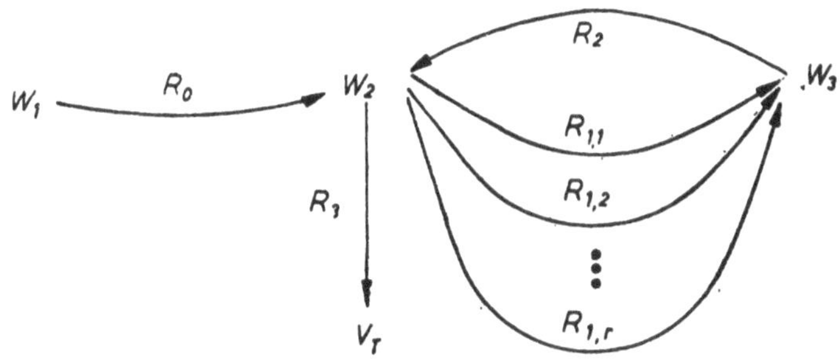

Fig. 2.1.2

It is easy to see that

$$U \Rightarrow x_1'x_2' \dots x_n' \xRightarrow[R_{1,i_1}]{*} y_{1,1}''y_{1,2}'' \cdots y_{1,r_1}'' \xRightarrow[R_2]{*} y_{1,1}'y_{1,2}' \cdots y_{1,r_1}' \xRightarrow[R_{1,i_2}]{*} y_{2,1}''y_{2,2}'' \cdots y_{2,r_2}''$$

$$\xRightarrow[R_2]{*} y_{2,1}'y_{2,2}' \cdots y_{2,r_2}' \xRightarrow[R_{1,i_3}]{*} \cdots \xRightarrow[R_2]{*} y_{n,1}'y_{n,2}' \cdots y_{n,r_n}' \xRightarrow[R_3]{} y_{n,1}y_{n,2} \cdots y_{n,r_n}$$

terminates in G' if and only if

$$w \xRightarrow[P_{i_1}]{} y_{1,1}y_{1,2} \cdots y_{1,r_1} \xRightarrow[P_{i_2}]{} y_{2,1}y_{2,2} \cdots y_{2,r_2} \xRightarrow[P_{i_3}]{} \cdots \xRightarrow[P_{i_n}]{} y_{n,1}y_{n,2} \cdots y_{n,r_n} \in V_T^*$$

holds in G. Thus $L(G) = L(G')$ and $L \in \mathcal{L}(\mathrm{Z})$.

$\mathcal{L}(\mathrm{Z}) \subseteq \mathcal{L}(\mathrm{ETOL})$. Now let $G_1 = (V_T, W_1, W_2, \dots, W_m, R_1, R_2, \dots, R_n, S', f)$ be an iterated grammar. With each i, $f(i) = (W_{i_1}, W_{i_2})$, we associate the new alphabets

$$W_{i_1}^{(i)} = \{x^{(i)} : x \in W_{i_1}\} \quad \text{and} \quad \overline{W}_{i_2}^{(i)} = \{\overline{x}^{(i)} : x \in W_{i_2}\}$$

and the tables

$$P_{i,1} = \{x \to x^{(i)} : x \in W_{i_1}\} \cup \{A \to F : A \in W \setminus W_{i_1}\},$$

$$P_{i,2} = \left\{x^{(i)} \to x_1'x_2' \dots x_r' : x \to x_1x_2 \dots x_r \in R_i,\ x \in W_{i_1},\ x_j' = \begin{Bmatrix} x_j^{(i)} & \text{if} \quad x_j \in W_{i_1} \\ \overline{x}_j^{(i)} & \text{if} \quad x_j \in W_{i_2} \end{Bmatrix}\right.$$

$$\cup \{\overline{x}^{(i)} \to \overline{x}^{(i)} : x \in W_{i_2}\} \cup \{A \to F : A \in W \setminus (W_{i_1}^{(i)} \cup \overline{W}_{i_2}^{(i)})\},$$

$$P_{i,3} = \{\overline{x}^{(i)} \to x : x \in W_{i_2}\} \cup \{A \to F : A \in W \setminus \overline{W}_{i_2}^{(i)}\}$$

where

$$W = V_T \cup W_1 \cup W_2 \cup \cdots \cup W_m \cup \{F\} \cup \bigcup_{f(i)=(W_{i_1},W_{i_2})} (W_{i_1}^{(i)} \cup \overline{W}_{i_2}^{(i)}),$$

and we define the ETOL system G_2 by

$$G_2 = (W, V_T, \{P_{1,1}, P_{1,2}, P_{1,3}, P_{2,1}, P_{2,2}, P_{2,3}, \ldots, P_{n,1}, P_{n,2}, P_{n,3}\}, S).$$

Now let $z \in W_j$ for some j. By the definition of the tables we can apply to z only a table $P_{i,1}$ where i satisfies $f(i) = (W_j, W_{i_2})$ since we introduce the trap-symbol F otherwise and then we cannot terminate the derivation. Thus we obtain $z = x_1x_2 \ldots x_s \Rightarrow x_1^{(i)}x_2^{(i)} \ldots x_s^{(i)}$. Now we can continue only by the use of $P_{i,2}$ and as long as the generated sentential form contains a letter of $W_j^{(i)}$ we have to iterate the application of $P_{i,2}$. Therefore we get $z \Rightarrow \bar{y}_1^{(i)}\bar{y}_2^{(i)} \ldots \bar{y}_t^{(i)} = z'$ with $\bar{y}_k^{(i)} \in \overline{W}_{i_2}^{(i)}$ for $1 \leqq k \leqq t$. Further applications of $P_{i,2}$ do not change the sentential form and since besides $P_{i,2}$ only $P_{i,3}$ is applicable to z' without introducing F we obtain $z \Rightarrow z' \Rightarrow y_1y_2 \ldots y_t \in W_{i_2}^*$. Thus this derivation simulates an R_i-derivation in G_1. On the other hand, each R_i-derivation can be simulated by G_2. This proves $L(G_1) = L(G_2)$, and hence $L(G_1) \in \mathcal{L}(\mathrm{ETOL})$.

By the proof of Theorem 2.1.5 we see that each iterated language can be generated already by an iterated grammar, the interpretation of whose mapping f is a planar graph. However, if we consider only chains we obtain a proper restriction. Without proof (see Păun (1977-a)) we mention

Theorem 2.1.6. *Let $G = (V, W_1, W_2, \ldots, W_m, R_1, R_2, \ldots, R_n, S, f)$ be an iterated grammar such that the interpretation of f is a chain, i.e. a graph of the form*

$$W_1 \to W_2 \to W_3 \to \cdots \to W_m \to V.$$

Then $L(G)$ is context-free. And conversely, each context-free language can be, obviously, generated by such an iterated grammar.

Open problems

2.1.1. Investigate the size of families $\mathcal{L}(\mathrm{V}, X)$ for $X \in \{\mathrm{REG}, \mathrm{REG} - \lambda, \mathrm{LIN}, \mathrm{LIN} - \lambda\}$. (It is easy to see that $\mathcal{L}(\mathrm{V}, \mathrm{REG} - \lambda) \setminus \mathcal{L}(\mathrm{CF}) \neq \emptyset$, therefore for such grammars the inclusions $\mathcal{L}(V, X) \subseteq \mathcal{L}(M, X)$ corresponding to those in Lemma 2.1.7 do not hold.)

2.1.2. Investigate valence grammars $G = (V_N, V_T, S, P, v)$ with $v : P \to T$ where T is a given group (other then $\mathbb{Z}$ and $\mathbb{Q}_+$ considered above). For instance, take $T = Z^n$ (with componentwise addition and the null element $(0, 0, \ldots, 0)$) and denote the corresponding families of languages by $\mathcal{L}_n(V, X)$, $X \in \{\mathrm{CF}, \mathrm{CF} - \lambda\}$. Then we have $\mathcal{L}(\mathrm{aV}, X) = \mathcal{L}_1(\mathrm{V}, X) \subseteq \mathcal{L}_2(\mathrm{V}, X) \subseteq \cdots \subseteq \mathcal{L}_n(\mathrm{V}, X) \subseteq \cdots \subseteq \mathcal{L}(\mathrm{mV}, X)$. Is this hierarchy infinite?

2.1.3. Consider length-increasing grammars with control languages of various types. It is an open problem whether such grammars with context-free control languages generate only context-sensitive languages. (In Păun (1978-b) it is proved that length-increasing grammars with linear simple matrix control languages generate only context-sensitive languages.)

2.1.4. As there are very few regulating mechanisms which increase the power of regular (linear) grammars, it is of interest to find further such mechanisms and to investigate the corresponding families of languages.

Exercises

2.1.1. Give a periodically time-variant grammar with appearance checking and without λ-rules which generates the language $\{a^{2^n} : n \geqq 1\}$.

2.1.2. Let us require in the definition of a periodically time-variant grammar only that the mapping φ be ultimately periodic, i.e. there are integers j and k such that $\varphi(n + k) = \varphi(n)$ for $n \geqq j$. Prove that this weakening of the definition does not change the generative power.

2.1.3. Prove that the finiteness problem is decidable for unordered vector grammars.

2.1.4. Prove that $\{a^n b^n c^n : n \geqq 0\}^k$ is in $\mathscr{L}(\mathrm{mV}, \mathrm{REG})$ and that $\{a^n b^n c^n : n \geqq 1\}^*$ is not in $\mathscr{L}(\mathrm{mV}, \mathrm{CF})$.

2.1.5. Complete the proof of Lemma 2.1.12.

2.1.6. Extend the valence restriction to gsms in the natural way. Prove that the languages in $\mathscr{L}(\mathrm{aV}, X)$, $\mathscr{L}(\mathrm{mV}, X)$, $X \in \{\mathrm{CF}, \mathrm{CF} - \lambda\}$, can be characterized as the images of context-free languages by (λ-free for $X = \mathrm{CF} - \lambda$) additive or multiplicative gsm mappings, respectively.

2.1.7. i) Prove that $\mathscr{L}(\mathrm{aV}, \mathrm{CF})$ is closed under union, intersection with regular sets, homomorphisms, and that it is not closed under concatenation and Kleene closure.
ii) Prove that $\mathscr{L}(\mathrm{mV}, \mathrm{CF})$ is closed under union, concatenation, intersection with regular sets and homomorphisms, but it is not closed under Kleene closure.

2.1.8. Prove Theorem 2.1.6.

2.2. Dependence on Previous Productions

As we have mentioned, the programmed grammars are typical for such types of rewriting where the next production is calculated from the previous ones. We study here some related mechanisms.

Definition 2.2.1. A *nonterminal-programmed grammar* is a quadruple $G = (V_N, V_T, P, S)$ where the productions of P are of the type $p\colon (A \to w, E_p)$ where E_p is a subset of V_N, $A \in V_N$, $w \in V_G^*$. The language $L(G)$ generated by G consists of all words $w \in V_T^*$ such that there is a derivation

$$S \underset{p_1}{\Longrightarrow} w_1 \underset{p_2}{\Longrightarrow} w_2 \underset{p_3}{\Longrightarrow} \cdots \underset{p_n}{\Longrightarrow} w_n = w$$

such that, for $1 \leqq i \leqq n$, the left-hand side A_{i+1} of the core production p_{i+1} is contained in E_{p_i}.

Example 2.2.1. *Let* $G = (\{S, A, B\}, \{a, b, c\}, \{p_1, p_2, p_3, p_4, p_5\}, S)$ where

$p_1\colon (S \to AB, \{A\})$, $p_2\colon (A \to aA, \{B\})$, $p_3\colon (B \to bBc, \{A\})$,

$p_4\colon (A \to a, \{B\})$, $p_5\colon (B \to bc, \emptyset)$.

Each derivation begins with an application of p_1 and yields AB, and then we have to apply p_2 or p_4. We prove that a word of the form $z = a^nAb^nBc^n$ (if $n = 0$ we get AB), to which only p_2 and p_4 can be applied, derives $a^{n+1}b^{n+1}c^{n+1}$ or again a word of this form $z' = a^{n+1}Ab^{n+1}Bc^{n+1}$ to which again only p_2 and p_4 are applicable. This follows from the following consideration. If we apply p_2 to z we obtain $a^{n+1}Ab^{n+}Bc^n$ and we have to use p_3 or p_5. In the former case z' is derived and we have to continue with p_2 or p_4; in the latter case the derivation stops with $a^{n+1}Ab^{n+1}c^{n+1} \notin V_T^*$. If we apply p_4 we obtain $a^{n+1}b^nBc^n$ from z and we have to use a rule whose left-hand side of the core production is B. If we apply p_3 we get $a^{n+1}b^{n+1}Bc^{n+1}$ and the derivation stops since the rules which we have to use are now of the form $A \to w$. Therefore we can derive only $a^{n+1}b^{n+1}c^{n+1}$ by application of p_5 without blocking the derivation.

Therefore $L(G) = \{a^nb^nc^n : n \geqq 1\}$.

By $\mathcal{L}(\text{nP, CF})$ we denote the family of languages generated by nonterminal-programmed grammars (with context-free core productions). If only non-erasing rules are allowed we denote the corresponding family by $\mathcal{L}(\text{nP, CF} - \lambda)$.

Theorem 2.2.1. *For* $X \in \{\text{CF, CF} - \lambda\}$, *we have*

$$\mathcal{L}(\text{nP}, X) = \mathcal{L}(\text{P}, X).$$

Proof. We consider only the case $X = \text{CF}$; the λ-free case can be settled by the same construction.

$\mathcal{L}(\text{nP, CF}) \subseteq \mathcal{L}(\text{P, CF})$. Let $L \in \mathcal{L}(\text{nP, CF})$ be generated by the nonterminal-programmed grammar $G = (V_N, V_T, P, S)$. With each rule p: $(A_p \to w_p, E_p)$ of P we associate the rule

$$(p' : A_p \to w_p, \{q' : q\colon (B_q \to v_q, E_q) \in P, B_q \in E_p\}),$$

and we construct the programmed grammar $G' = (V_N, V_T, P', S)$ (with empty and therefore omitted failure where P' consists of all rules constructed above. By the definition of G', if we apply p' in G', then we have to continue with a rule whose left-hand side of the core production is in E_p. On the other hand, if we apply p in G we have to use a rule with left-hand side in E_p in the next step. From this it follows easily that $L(G) = L(G')$.

Before proving the opposite inclusion we transform a programmed grammar into an equivalent one of special form. Let $G_1 = (V_N, V_T, P_1, S)$ be a programmed grammar. By $t(A)$ we denote the number of labels r such that A is in the left hand side of the core production of the rule labelled by r. We define the finite substitution τ by

$$\tau(a) = \{a\} \quad \text{for} \quad a \in V_T, \quad \tau(A) = \{A_1, A_2, \ldots, A_{t(A)}\} \quad \text{for} \quad A \in V_N.$$

Let $(r\colon A \to w, E)$ be the ith rule with the core production with the left-hand side A, $1 \leqq i \leqq t(A)$. Then we associate with this rule the production

$$([r, i, j]\colon A_i \to w_j, E')$$

where w_j is the j-th word in $\tau(w)$ and

$$E' = \{[p, k, l] : (p\colon B \to v, \bar{E}) \in P_1, p \in E, 1 \leqq k \leqq t(B), 1 \leqq l \leqq \operatorname{card}(\tau(v))\}.$$

Let $G_1' = (V_N', V_T, P_1', S_1')$ where V_N' is the union of the sets $\tau(A)$ taken over all $A \in V_N$ and S_1', P_1' consists of all rules constructed above and the rules $([*, i]\colon S_1' \to S_{1,i}, U)$ where $1 \leqq i \leqq t(S_1)$ and U is the set of all labels introduced above.

Now $L(G_1) = L(G'_1)$ can be seen as follows. Let $S \overset{*}{\Rightarrow} w \in V_T^*$ be a terminating derivation in G_1. If we replace each occurrence of a nonterminal A by A_i if the ith rule with the left-hand side A is applied to this occurrence of A, then we obtain a derivation in G'_1. Hence $L(G_1) \subseteq L(G'_1)$.

On the other hand, if we replace each nonterminal A_i in a terminating derivation in G'_1 by A we get a terminating derivation in G_1. Thus $L(G'_1) = L(G_1)$.

$\mathcal{L}(\text{P, CF}) \subseteq \mathcal{L}(\text{nP, CF})$. The above constructed grammar G'_1 has the property that two productions which have the same left-hand side in the core productions of G_1 have different left-hand sides in G'_1. Therefore, the rules of G_1 can be determined by their left-hand sides in G'_1. Thus it is now easy to construct a nonterminal-programmed grammar which generates $L(G_1)$.

With each programmed grammar we can associate a graph whose nodes are the productions of the grammar, and there is a directed edge from $(r_1: A_1 \to w_1, E_1, \emptyset)$ to $(r_2: A_2 \to w_2, E_2, \emptyset)$ if $r_2 \in E_1$. If we consider grammars with appearance checking we have to use two different types of edges. This idea is generalized by the following type of regulated rewriting.

Definition 2.2.2. A *grammar controlled by a bicoloured digraph* is a 7-tuple $G = (V_N, V_T, P, S, \Gamma, \Sigma, h)$ where

i) V_N, V_T, P, S are defined as in a phrase structure grammar,

ii) Γ is a bicoloured digraph, i.e. $\Gamma = (U, E)$ where U is a finite set of nodes and $E \subseteq U \times \{g, r\} \times U$ is a finite set of (directed) edges labelled (coloured) by g or r (the abbreviations g and r stand for green and red in analogy to the light of a traffic light,

iii) Σ is a subset of the set U of nodes (initial nodes),

iv) h is a mapping from U into $2^P \setminus \{\emptyset\}$.

We now define two types of derivation.

Definition 2.2.3. Let G be a grammar controlled by a bicoloured digraph (with the notation of Definition 2.2.2.).

i) We say that $(x, u) \Rightarrow (y, v)$ holds in G, $(x, u) \in V_G^+ \times U$, $(y, v) \in V_G^* \times U$, if either $x = x_1wx_2$, $y = x_1zx_2$, $w \to z \in h(u)$, $(u, g, v) \in E$ or no rule of $h(u)$ is applicable to x, $y = x$, $(u, r, v) \in E$.

ii) We say that $(x, u) \overset{c}{\Longrightarrow} (y, v)$ holds in G if either $x = x_1wx_2$, $y = x_1zx_2$, $w \to z \in h(u)$, $(u, g, v) \in E$ or one rule of $h(u)$ is not applicable to x, $y = x$, $(u, r, v) \in E$.

We denote the reflexive and transitive closure of $\Rightarrow$ and $\overset{c}{\Longrightarrow}$ by $\overset{*}{\Rightarrow}$ and $\overset{*c}{\Longrightarrow}$, respectively. Then we define the corresponding languages generated by G by

$$L(G) = \{x : x \in V_T^*, (S, u) \overset{*}{\Rightarrow} (x, v) \quad \text{for some} \quad u \in \Sigma, v \in U\},$$

$$L_c(G) = \{x : x \in V_T^*, (S, u) \overset{*c}{\Longrightarrow} (x, v) \quad \text{for some} \quad u \in \Sigma, v \in U\},$$

Let us illustrate the concepts and the differences between them by the following example.

Example 2.2.2. Let g be given by the following components:

$V_N = \{S, A, B\}, \quad V_T = \{a, b, c, d\},$

$P = \{S \to ABC, A \to Sa^2, A \to Aa, A \to a, B \to bBc, B \to bc, C \to d\},$

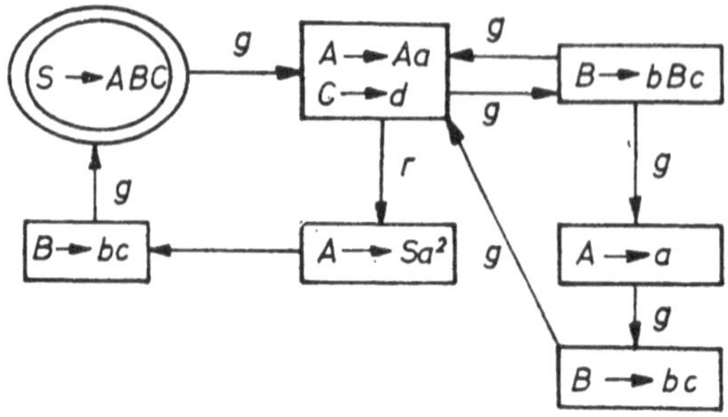

Fig. 2.2.1

and the graph Γ is given in Fig. 2.2.1 where the nodes of Σ are circled twice, and $h(u)$ is added as a label of u.

First let us consider the relation $\Rightarrow$. After applying $S \to ABC$ we use the pair $A \to Aa$, $B \to bBc$ a certain number of times, say n times, or this pair a certain number of times and $C \to d$ once and again $B \to bBc$ once. In both cases we continue with $A \to a$ and $B \to bc$. Thus we obtain the derivation $S \overset{*}{\Rightarrow} a^{n+1}b^{n+1}c^{n+1}C$ or $S \overset{*}{\Rightarrow} a^n b^{n+1} c^{n+1} d$. In the latter case the derivation terminates, in the former case we have to use $C \to d$ yielding $a^{n+1}b^{n+1}c^{n+1}d$ and thus this derivation also terminates. Hence

$$L(G) = \{a^n b^n c^n d : n \geqq 2\} \cup \{a^n b^{n+1} c^{n+1} d : n \geqq 1\}.$$

Now we consider the relation $\overset{c}{\Longrightarrow}$. For instance, then we have the derivation

$$S \overset{c}{\Longrightarrow} ABC \overset{c}{\Longrightarrow} ABd \overset{c}{\Longrightarrow} AbBcd \overset{c}{\Longrightarrow} Sa^2bBcd \overset{c}{\Longrightarrow} Sa^2b^2c^2d \overset{c}{\Longrightarrow} a^2b^2c^2da^2b^2c^2d$$

since in the fourth step $C \to d$ is not applicable, and hence we can pass over this node and proceed with $A \to Sa^2$, and moreover,

$$L_c(G) = \left\{(\{a^n b^n c^n d : n \geqq 2\} \cup \{a^n b^{n+1} c^{n+1} d : n \geqq 1\})\ \{a^n b^n c^n d : n \geqq 2\}\right\}.$$

We call a grammar $G = (V_N, V_T, P, S, \Gamma, \Sigma, h)$ controlled by a bicoloured digraph Γ in *canonical form* if $h(u)$ is a singleton for each $u \in U$, i.e. with each node of Γ exactly one production is associated. Obviously, if a grammar G controlled by a bicoloured digraph is into canonical form, then $L(G) = L_c(G)$.

We now show that each grammar controlled by a bicoloured digraph can be transformed in another grammar of this type which generates the same language and which is in canonical form.

Lemma 2.2.1. *For each grammar G controlled by a bicoloured digraph there exists a grammar G' controlled by a bicoloured digraph such that G' is in canonical form and $L_c(G) = L_c(G')$.*

Proof. Let $G = (V_N, V_T, P, S, \Gamma, \Sigma, h)$ with $\Gamma = (U, E)$ be a grammar controlled by the bicoloured digraph Γ. We construct the grammar $G' = (V_N, V_T, P, S, \Gamma', \Sigma', h')$ by setting

$$\Gamma' = (U', E'),$$

$$U' = \{[u, w \to z] : w \to z \in h(u),\ u \in U\},$$

$$E' = \{([u, w \to z], \alpha, [v, x \to y]) : (u, \alpha, v) \in E\},$$

$$\Sigma' = \{[u, S \to x] : u \in \Sigma\},$$

$$h'([u, w \to z]) = \{w \to z\}.$$

By construction, G' is in canonical form. We now prove that $L_c(G) = L_c(G')$.

Let $(S, u') \overset{*c}{\Longrightarrow} (y, v)$ be an arbitrary derivation in G'. Then there is a sequence (x_0, u_0'), (x_1, u_1'), ..., (x_n, u_n') such that $x_0 = S$, $u_0' = u'$, $x_n = y$, $u_n' = v$, and $(x_i, u_i') \overset{c}{\Longrightarrow} (x_{i+1}, u_{i+1}')$ is a direct derivation step in G' for $1 \leqq i \leqq n$. Let $u_i' = [u_i, w_i \to z_i]$. Then $h(u_i') = \{w_i \to z_i\}$ and further $w_i \to z_i \in h(u_i)$. By the definition of the derivation in G' we obtain $x_{i+1} = q_1 z_i q_2$ if $x_i = q_1 w_i q_2$ for some $q_1, q_2 \in V_G^*$ or we get $x_{i+1} = x_i$ if w_i is not a subword of x_i. In both cases we have $(x_i, u_i) \overset{c}{\Longrightarrow} (x_{i+1}, u_{i+1})$ in G, too. Hence $(S, u) \overset{*c}{\Longrightarrow} (y, v)$ is a correct derivation in G and this implies $L_c(G') \subseteq L_c(G)$.

In analogy to these considerations we can prove that for each derivation $(S, u) \overset{*c}{\Longrightarrow} (y, v)$ in G we have a derivation $(S, u') \overset{*c}{\Longrightarrow} (y, v')$ in G'. Thus $L_c(G) \subseteq L_c(G')$.

Lemma 2.2.2. *For each grammar G controlled by a bicoloured digraph, there exists a grammar G' controlled by a bicoloured digraph such that G' is in canonical form and $L(G) = L(G')$.*

Proof. Let $G = (V_N, V_T, P, S, \Gamma, \Sigma, h)$ be a grammar controlled by the digraph $\Gamma = (U, E)$. For $u \in U$, let $k(u) = \operatorname{card}\big(h(u)\big)$ and

$$h(u) = \{w_{u,1} \to z_{u,1}, w_{u,2} \to z_{u,2}, \ldots, w_{u,k(u)} \to z_{u,k(u)}\}.$$

We define the grammar $G' = (V_N, V_T, P, S, \Gamma', \Sigma', h')$ by

$$\Gamma' = (U', E'),$$

$$U' = \{[u, w \to z] : w \to z \in h(u), u \in U\} \cup \{[\overline{u}, w \to z] : w \to z \in h(u), u \in U\},$$

$$\begin{aligned} E' = \{&([u, w \to z], g, [v, x \to y]) : (u, g, v) \in E \\ &\cup \{([u, w \to z], r, [\overline{u}, w_{u,1} \to z_{u,1}]) : u \in U\} \\ &\cup \{([\overline{u}, w_{u,i} \to z_{u,i}], r, [\overline{u}, w_{u,i+1} \to z_{u,i+1}]) : 1 \leqq i \leqq k(u) - 1\} \\ &\cup \{([\overline{u}, w_{u,k(u)} \to z_{u,k(u)}], r, [v, x \to y]) : (u, r, v) \in E\}, \end{aligned}$$

$$\Sigma' = \{[u, S \to x] : u \in \Sigma\},$$

$$h'([u, w \to z]) = \{w \to z\}.$$

Intuitively, the subgraph in Fig. 2.2.2. is substituted by the subgraph in Fig. 2.2.3. Again, G' is in canonical form.

Now let $(x, u) \Rightarrow (y, v)$ be a derivation in G along an edge (u, g, v) by application of $w \to z \in h(u)$. Then $(x, [u, w \to z])$ derives $(y, [v, s \to t])$ in G' for all $s \to t \in h(v)$. If $(x, u) \Rightarrow (x, v)$ is a derivation in G along an edge $(u, r, v) \in E$, then no rule of $h(u)$ is applicable to x. Then for all rules $w \to z \in h(u)$, $s \to t \in h(v)$, there exists the correct derivation

$$\begin{aligned} &(x, [u, w \to z]) \Rightarrow (x, [\overline{u}, w_{u,1} \to z_{u,1}]) \Rightarrow (x, [\overline{u}, w_{u,2} \to z_{u,2}]) \cdots \\ &\Rightarrow (x, [\overline{u}, w_{u,k(u)} \to z_{u,k(u)}]) \Rightarrow (x, [v, s \to t]) \end{aligned}$$

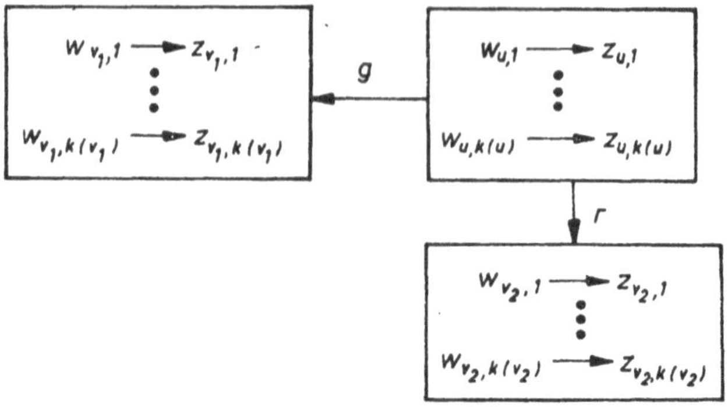

Fig. 2.2.2

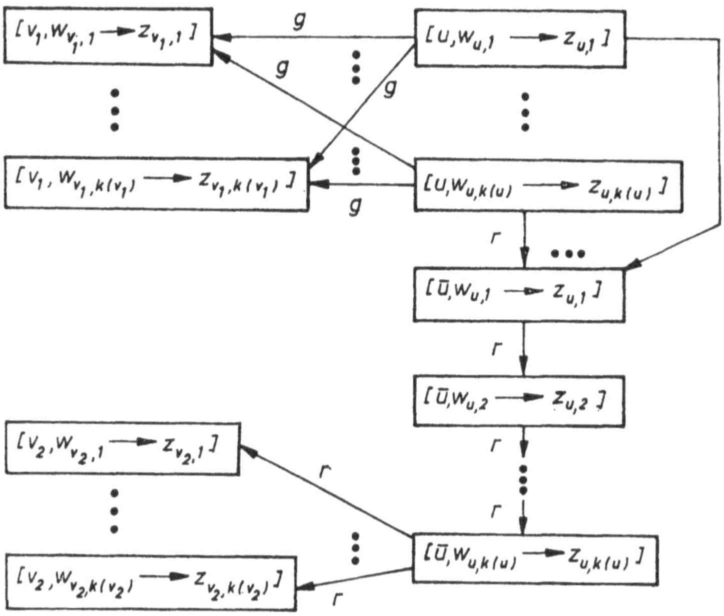

Fig. 2.2.3

in G' (in all cases we go along "red" edges). Hence $(x, [u, w \to z]) \Rightarrow (x, [v, s \to t])$ holds in G'. Therefore for each derivation $(S, u) \overset{*}{\Rightarrow} (y, v)$, $u \in \Sigma$, in G, we find a derivation $(S, [u, S \to x]) \overset{*}{\Rightarrow} (y, [v, s \to t])$ in G' (for some $s \to t \in h(v)$ and where x is derived from the axiom in the first step of the derivation in G). Thus $L(G) \subseteq L(G')$.

In order to prove the converse inclusion we use induction on the length of a derivation. For derivations consisting of one step, obviously, $(S, [u_1, S \to x]) \overset{*}{\Rightarrow} (x, [v_1, s \to t])$ holds in G' and $(S, u) \overset{*}{\Rightarrow} (x, v)$ holds in G. Now let $(S, [u_1, r_1 \to r_1']) \Rightarrow (x, [u, w \to z])$ be a derivation in G' and assume that $(S, u_1) \overset{*}{\Rightarrow} (x, u)$ holds in G. Now let $(x, [u, w \to z]) \Rightarrow (y, [v, s \to t])$ be a direct derivation in G' along a "green" edge. Then $(x, u) \Rightarrow (y, v)$ holds in G and thus $(S, u_1) \overset{*}{\Rightarrow} (y, v)$ holds in G.

If $(x, [u, w \to z]) \Rightarrow (x, [v, s \to t])$ is a derivation in G' along a "red" edge, then $v = \overline{u}$ and $s \to t = w_{u,1} \to z_{u,1}$ hold and we obtain the derivation

$$(x, [u, w \to z]) \Rightarrow (x, [\overline{u}, w_{u,1} \to z_{u,1}]) \Rightarrow \cdots$$

$$\Rightarrow (x, [\overline{u}, w_{u,k(u)} \to z_{u,k(u)}]) \Rightarrow (x, [q, r \to r'])$$

using only "red" edges and $(x, u) \Rightarrow (x, q)$ holds in G, or we can apply $w_{u,i} \to z_{u,i}$ effectively for some i, $1 \leqq i \leqq k(u)$, and we get a word $z' = z_1 z_{u,i} z_2$ and the derivation stops, i.e. this is only of interest if $z' \in V_T^*$. Then there is also a derivation $(S, [u_1, r_1 \to r_1']) \stackrel{*}{\Rightarrow} (x, [u, w_{u,i} \to z_{u,i}])$ in G' and the application of $w_{u,i} \to z_{u,i}$ to this situation along a "green" edge also gives z'. By the above considerations, on "green" edges we have $(S, u_1) \stackrel{*}{\Rightarrow} (z', u')$, $z' \in V_T^*$, in G. (If the derivation step along a "red" edge starts with $(x, [\overline{u}, w \to z])$, then by looking forward and backward we obtain the above situation.) Hence $L(G') = L(G)$.

Let

$\mathcal{L}(\mathrm{B}, X) = \{L : L = L(G)$ for some grammar G controlled by a bicoloured digraph and with productions of type $X\}$,

$\mathcal{L}(\mathrm{B_c}, X) = \{L : L = L_c(G)$ for some grammar G controlled by a bicoloured digraph and with productions of type $X\}$.

Theorem 2.2.2. *Let* $X \in \{\mathrm{REG}, \mathrm{CF}, \mathrm{CF} - \lambda, \mathrm{CS}\}$. *Then*

$$\mathcal{L}(\mathrm{B}, X) = \mathcal{L}(\mathrm{B_c}, X) = \mathcal{L}(\mathrm{P}, X, \mathrm{ac}).$$

Proof. Let $L \in \mathcal{L}(\mathrm{B}, X)$, $L = L(G)$ for some grammar G controlled by a bicoloured digraph. By Lemma 2.2.3 there is a grammar G' of this type in canonical form such that $L(G) = L(G')$, and since G' is in canonical form $L(G') = L_c(G')$ also holds. Hence $L(G) = L_c(G')$. This implies $\mathcal{L}(\mathrm{B}, X) \subseteq \mathcal{L}(\mathrm{B_c}, X)$.

Using Lemma 2.2.2 the opposite inclusion can be proved. Thus the first equality holds.

Now let $G_1 = (V_N, V_T, P, S)$ be a programmed grammar (with appearance checking). We construct the grammar $G_1' = (V_N, V_T, P', S, \Gamma, \Sigma, h)$ controlled by the bicoloured digraph $\Gamma = (U, E)$ as follows:

$$P' = \{w \to z : (b : w \to z, \sigma(b), \varphi(b)) \in P\},$$

$$U = P,$$

$$E = \{((b : w \to z, \sigma(b), \varphi(b)), g, (c : s \to t, \sigma(c), \varphi(c))) : c \in \sigma(b)\}$$
$$\cup \{((b : w \to z, \sigma(b), \varphi(b)), r, (c : s \to t, \sigma(c), \varphi(c))) : c \in \varphi(b)\},$$

$$\Sigma = \{(b : w \to z, \sigma(b), \varphi(b)) : w = S\},$$

$$h((b : w \to z, \sigma(b), \varphi(b))) = \{w \to z\}.$$

By construction, $(x, (b : w \to z, \sigma(b), \varphi(b))) \Rightarrow (y, (c : s \to t, \sigma(c), \varphi(c)))$ holds in G along a "green" ("red") edge iff $(x, b) \Rightarrow (y, c)$ holds in G_1 and $c \in \sigma(b)$ ($c \in \varphi(b)$, respectively). Thus $L(G_1) = L(G_1')$, and therefore $\mathcal{L}(\mathrm{P}, X, \mathrm{ac}) \subseteq \mathcal{L}(\mathrm{B}, X)$.

Conversely, let $L \in \mathcal{L}(\mathrm{B}, X)$. Then $L = L(G_2)$ for some grammar G_2 controlled by a bicoloured digraph which is in canonical form. Then we associate with a node u the programmed production

$$\left(u : h(u), \{v_1 : (u, g, v_1) \in E\}, \{v_2 : (u, r, v_2) \in E\}\right).$$

Let P' be the set of all these productions, and let

$$G_2' = \left(V_N \cup \{\bar{S}\}, V_T, P' \cup \{(* : \bar{S} \to S, \Sigma, \emptyset)\}, \bar{S}\right).$$

The production added to P' ensures that after the application of $\bar{S} \to S$ we have to proceed with a production which can be used in the first step of a derivation in G_2. It is easy to see that $L(G_2) = L(G_2')$. Therefore $\mathcal{L}(\mathrm{B}, X) \subseteq \mathcal{L}(\mathrm{P}, X, \mathrm{ac})$.

The proof of Theorem 2.2.2 shows that — in a certain sense — programmed grammars can be considered as a normal form of grammars controlled by a bicoloured digraph with respect to the mapping h. Now we show that with respect to the digraph Γ we can also derive a normal form, more precisely, we prove that we can construct an equivalent grammar whose digraph is planar.

Lemma 2.2.3. *For each $L \in \mathcal{L}(\mathrm{B}, X)$ there is a grammar $G = (V_N, V_T, P, S, \Gamma, \Sigma, h)$ controlled by a bicoloured digraph such that G is in canonical form, Γ is a planar graph and $L = L(G)$.*

Proof. Let $L \in \mathcal{L}(\mathrm{B}, X)$. Then $L \in \mathcal{L}(\mathrm{M}, X, \mathrm{ac})$ by Theorem 1.2.2 and Theorem 2.2.2. Let $L = L(G)$ for some matrix grammar $G = (V_N, V_T, M, S, F)$, $M = \{m_1, m_2, \ldots, m_s\}$, $m_i : (r_{i,1}, r_{i,2}, \ldots, r_{i,s_i})$, $1 \leq i \leq s$. Then we construct the grammar $G' = (V_N, V_T, P, S, \Gamma, \Sigma, h)$ by

$$P = \{w \to z : w \to z \quad \text{occurs in some matrix of } M\}$$

and describe Γ, Σ, h by the digraph in Fig. 2.2.4, where a directed edge labelled by r from $r_{i,j}$ to $r_{i,j+1}$ or to $S \to S$ (if $j = s_i$) exists if $r_{i,j} \in F$. It is easy to prove that $L(G) = L(G')$.

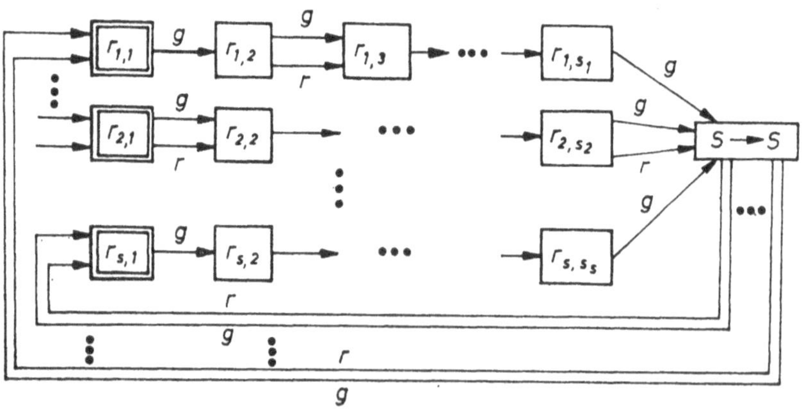

Fig. 2.2.4

Finally we define state grammars.

Definition 2.2.4. A *state grammar* is a construct $G = (K, V_N, V_T, P, p_0, S)$ where K is a finite set, $p_0 \in K$, V_N, V_T, and S are defined as in a phrase structure grammar, and the rules of P are of the form $(p, w) \to (q, z)$ where $p, q \in K$, $w \in V_G^+$, $z \in V_G^*$. We say that $(p, u) \in K \times V_G^*$ directly derives $(q, v) \in K \times V_G^*$ iff $u = u_1wu_2$, $v = u_1zu_2$, and $(p, w) \to (q, z) \in P$ for some $u_1, u_2 \in V_G^*$. Then we write $(p, u) \Rightarrow (q, v)$.

We denote the reflexive and transitive closure of $\Rightarrow$ by $\stackrel{*}{\Rightarrow}$, and we define the language generated by G by

$$L(G) = \{y : y \in V_T^*, (p_0, S) \stackrel{*}{\Rightarrow} (q, y) \quad \text{for some} \quad q \in K\}.$$

Let $\mathcal{L}(\mathrm{S}, X)$ be the family of languages generated by state grammars of type X. Without proof we mention

Theorem 2.2.3. *For* $X \in \{\mathrm{CF}, \mathrm{CF} - \lambda\}$, *we have*

$$\mathcal{L}(\mathrm{S}, X) = \mathcal{L}(\mathrm{M}, X).$$

Exercises

2.2.1. Construct a grammar controlled by a bicoloured digraph generating the language $\{a^{2^n} : n \geqq 0\}$.

2.2.2. i) Prove that in addition we can require in Lemma 2.2.3 that G be controlled by an Eulerian (and planar) digraph.

ii) Prove that in Lemma 2.2.3 the planarity can be substituted by Hamiltonicity.

2.2.3. Prove Theorem 2.2.3.

2.3. Context Conditions

The third group of regulating devices, which will be considered now, is characterized by some global context conditions in contrast to the local ones of the context-sensitive grammars. The conditions have to be satisfied by a sentential form for a production to be applied to it. Clearly, since the sentential form is a result of a derivation, one can consider this type of regulation as a special case of the type studied in Section 2.2 (dependence of the next rule on the history).

Let us regard a random context grammar G, and let p: $(A \to w, Q, R)$ be a rule of G. Then it is applicable to the word $x \in V_G^+$ iff all symbols in Q occur in x and no symbol of R occurs in x, i.e. the sentential form x has to be an element of the language

$$\bigcap_{B \in Q} V_G^* B V_G^* \setminus \bigcup_{C \in R} V_G^* C V_G^*.$$

This idea is generalized by the following definition.

Definition 2.3.1. A *conditional grammar* is a construct $G = (V_N, V_T, P, S)$ where the rules of P are of the form $(w \to z, Q)$ where Q is a regular language over V_G. The rule $(w \to z, Q)$ is applicable to $x = x_1wx_2$ yielding $y = x_1zx_2$ iff $x \in Q$. We then write $x \Rightarrow y$ and define $\stackrel{*}{\Rightarrow}$ as the reflexive and transitive closure of $\Rightarrow$ and

$$L(G) = \{x : x \in V_T^*, S \stackrel{*}{\Rightarrow} x\}.$$

Example 2.3.1. The language $\{a^{2^n} : n \geqq 0\}$ is generated by the conditional grammar $G = (\{S, A, B\}, \{a\}, P, S)$ with the rules

$$p_1: (S \to A^2, \{S, A\}^*), \qquad p_2: (S \to a, \{S, a\}^*),$$
$$p_3: (A \to B, \{A, B\}^*), \qquad p_4: (B \to S, \{B, S\}^*).$$

In order to see this we consider a word S^n. If we apply p_1 to one occurrence of S we derive $S^{k_1}A^2S^{k_2}$ with $k_1 + k_2 = n - 1$. Now we have to apply p_1 again yielding $S^{k_3}A^2S^{k_4}A^2S^{k_5}$ and so on until we obtain A^{2n}. The only applicable rule is p_3, and then we have to continue by $(2n - 1)$ applications of p_3. This gives B^{2n}. Now we have to use the rule p_4 $2n$ times, and we obtain S^{2n}, and thus we have doubled the number of S. However, if we apply p_2 to S^n, then we have to do this n times, and we obtain a^n. Therefore the terminating derivations are of the form

$$S \Rightarrow S^2 \Rightarrow S^4 \Rightarrow \cdots \Rightarrow S^{2^n} \Rightarrow a^{2^n}.$$

By $\mathcal{L}(\mathrm{K}, X)$ we denote the set of languages generated by conditional grammars with core productions of type X.

The above remark about random context grammars also holds for string random context grammars. Therefore $\mathcal{L}(\mathrm{SRC}, X, (i, j)) \subseteq \mathcal{L}(\mathrm{K}, X)$ for all (i, j). By Theorem 1.5.12 we obtain $\mathcal{L}(\mathrm{CS}) \subseteq \mathcal{L}(\mathrm{K}, \mathrm{CF} - \lambda)$. We now prove the converse inclusion; moreover, we show that $\mathcal{L}(\mathrm{K}, \mathrm{CS}) \subseteq \mathcal{L}(\mathrm{CS})$. In order to do this let $G = (V_N, V_T, P, S)$ be a conditional grammar with the productions $p_i: (w_i \to z_i, Q_i)$, $1 \leqq i \leqq n$. Moreover, let Q_i be generated by the grammar $G_i = (V_N^{(i)}, V_G, P_i, S_i)$ whose rules are — without loss of generality — of the form $A_i \to aB_i$ or $A_i \to a$ with $A_i, B_i \in V_N^{(i)}$, $a \in V_G$, and let us assume that the sets $V_N^{(i)}$ are pairwise disjoint. We define the monotone grammar $G' = (V'_N, V'_T, P', S')$ by

$$V'_N = \{S', X, X_1, X_2, \ldots, X_n\} \cup V_N \cup \bigcup_{i=1}^{n} V_N^{(i)},$$
$$V'_T = V_T \cup \{a_1, a_2\},$$

with P' consisting of all rules of the following forms:

$$S' \to a_1S_iSa_2, \quad 1 \leqq i \leqq n$$

(initial rules introducing the markers a_1, a_2 and the axiom of one of the grammars G_i),

$$A_ix_1x_2 \to x_1B_ix_2 \quad \text{for} \quad x_2 \in V_G, A_i \to x_1B_i \in P_i, 1 \leqq i \leqq n,$$
$$A_ix_1a_2 \to X_ix_1a_2 \quad \text{for} \quad A_i \to x_1 \in P_i, 1 \leqq i \leqq n$$

(by these rules we simulate a derivation in G_i, and hence we enter X_i if the letters of V_G between a_1 and a_2 form a word of Q_i),

$$xX_i \to X_ix, 1 \leqq i \leqq n, x \in V_G,$$
$$X_iw_i \to Xz_i, 1 \leqq i \leqq n, p_i: w_i \to z_i \in P$$

(the symbol X_i moves to the left and the rule p_i is applied to an occurrence of w_i),

$$xX \to Xx, x \in V_G,$$
$$a_1X \to a_1S_i, 1 \leqq i \leqq n$$

(the symbol X — which indicates that we have already applied a rule of P — moves to the left and it is replaced by S_i if it is the neighbour of the marker a_1),

$$a_1S_j \to a_1a_1,\ 1 \leqq j \leqq n$$

(terminating rules).

It is easy to see that a non-blocking derivation of a string $u = a_1S_iu'a_2$, $u' \in V_G^*$ is only possible if $p_i: (w_i \to z_i, Q_i)$ is applicable to u', and it consists of applications of the rules of P' in the order given above yielding $v = a_1S_kv'a_2$ iff $u' \Rightarrow v'$ holds in G. Hence $S' \Rightarrow a_1S_iSa_2 \overset{*}{\Rightarrow} a_1a_1wa_2$ holds in G' iff $S \overset{*}{\Rightarrow} w$ holds in G. This proves that $a_1a_1L(G)a_2 = L(G') \in \mathscr{L}(\mathrm{CS})$. Since $\mathscr{L}(\mathrm{CS})$ is closed under left and right derivatives we obtain $L(G) \in \mathscr{L}(\mathrm{CS})$.

Theorem 2.3.1. i) $\mathscr{L}(\mathrm{K}, \mathrm{CF} - \lambda) = \mathscr{L}(\mathrm{K}, \mathrm{CS}) = \mathscr{L}(\mathrm{CS})$,

ii) $\mathscr{L}(K, \mathrm{CF}) = \mathscr{L}(\mathrm{RE})$.

Proof. Point i) follows from the above considerations and ii) can be proved analogously.

In random context grammars, conditional grammars, and their variations, the context conditions have to be satisfied by the intermediate steps of a derivation, by the sentential forms. However, with each derivation in a context-free grammar $G = (V_N, V_T, P, S)$ a further concept is associated, the so-called derivation tree, defined as follows. This is a tree with root in the graph-theoretical sense whose nodes are labelled in the following way. The root is labelled by the axiom. If a node is labelled by a nonterminal A and it is connected with the nodes labelled by $a_1, a_2, \ldots, a_r$, respectively (read from left to right), then $A \to a_1a_2 \ldots a_r$ is a rule of P. Then the leaves are labelled by terminals, and if we read them from left to right they form a word w of $L(G)$. We say that a node is at level i if there is a path from the root to it consisting of i edges. If we read all labels of the nodes of a level from left to right, then we obtain the word of this level.

We now introduce a type of regulation where the derivation tree is used for the squeezing out of derivations.

Definition 2.3.2. A *tree-controlled grammar* is a construct $G = (V_N, V_T, P, S, R)$ where $G' = (V_N, V_T, P, S)$ is a context-free grammar and R is a regular set. The language $L(G)$ consists of all words w generated by the underlying grammar G' such that there is a derivation tree of w whose words of all levels (except the last one) are in R.

Example 2.3.2. Let $G_1 = (\{S\}, \{a\}, \{S \to a, S \to SS\}, S, S^*)$. Let $w \in L(G)$. Then each level of one of its derivation trees contains only nodes labelled by S. By the productions of G, in order to obtain the nodes of level i from the nodes of level $i - 1$ we have used the rule $S \to S^2$ in all cases. Moreover, w is the word at the last level and therefore we have applied $S \to a$ to all "nodes" of the level before. Hence the derivation tree has the form given in Fig. 2.3.1. Thus $L(G) = \{a^{2^n} : n \geqq 0\}$.

Example 2.3.3. Let

$$G_1 = (\{S, A_1, B_1, C_1\}, \{a, b, c\}, P_1, S, R_1)$$

with

$$P_1 = \{S \to A_1B_1, A_1 \to aA_1, A_1 \to a, B_1 \to bB_1c, B_1 \to bC_1c, C_1 \to cC_1, C_1 \to c\},$$

$$R_1 = \{S\} \cup \{a\}^* \{A_1\} \{b\}^* \{B_1\} \{c\}^* \cup \{a\}^* \{b\}^* \{C_1\} \{c\}^*.$$

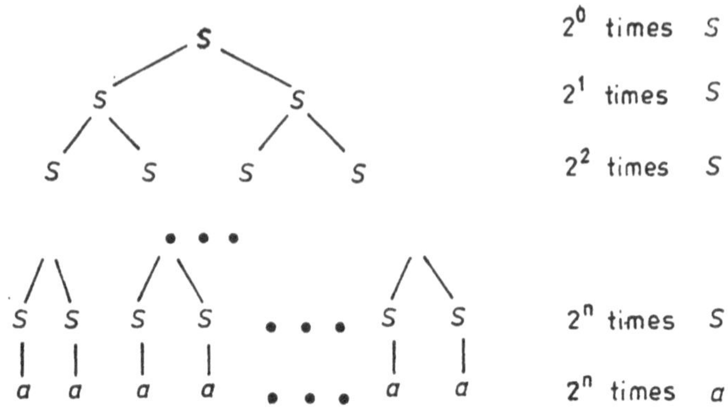

Fig. 2.3.1

Then the existence of A_1 and B_1 together at a level requires that the productions $A_1 \to aA_1$ and $B_1 \to bB_1c$ have to be applied the same number of times, and if A_1 is erased by using $A_1 \to a$, then we have also to apply $B_1 \to bC_1c$. Further, each derivation beginning with C_1 gives c^m for some $m \geqq 1$. Therefore

$$L(G_1) = \{a^n b^n c^{n+m} : n \geqq 1, m \geqq 1\}.$$

Let $G_2 = (\{S, A_2, B_2, C_2\}, \{a, b, c\}, P_2, S, R_2)$ with

$$P_2 = \{S \to A_2B_2, A_2 \to aA_2, A_2 \to a, B_2 \to bB_2c, B_2 \to bC_2c, C_2 \to bC_2, C_2 \to b\},$$

$$R_2 = \{S\} \cup \{a\}^* \{A_2\} \{b\}^* \{B_2\} \{c\}^* \cup \{a\}^* \{A_2\} \{b_0\}^* \{C_2\} \{c\}^*.$$

Then, since $A_2 \to aA_2$ and $B_2 \to bB_2c$, $A_2 \to aA_2$ and $C_2 \to bC_2$ have to be used the same number of times, respectively, and the pairs $A_2 \to aA_2$ and $B_2 \to bC_2c$, $A_2 \to a$ and $C_2 \to b$ have to be used at the same level we obtain

$$L(G_2) = \{a^{n+m} b^{n+m} c^n : n \geqq 1, m \geqq 1\}.$$

Let $G_3 = (\{S, A_3, B_3\}, \{a, b, c\}, P_3, S, V_{G_3}^*)$ with

$$P_3 = \{S \to A_3B_3, A_3 \to aA_3, A_3 \to a, B_3 \to bB_3c, B_3 \to bc\}.$$

We obtain

$$L(G_3) = \{a^m b^n c^n : n \geqq 1, m \geqq 1\}.$$

Now we consider

$$G = (\{S, A_1, B_1, C_1, A_2, B_2, C_2, A_3, B_3\}, \{a, b, c\}, P_1 \cup P_2 \cup P_3, S, R_1 \cup R_2 \cup V_{G_3}^*).$$

It is easy to prove that

$$L(G) = L(G_1) \cup L(G_2) \cup L(G_3) = \{a^m b^n c^n : n \geqq 1, m \geqq 1\} \cup \{a^n b^n c^m : m \geqq 1, n \geqq 1\}.$$

Before studying the generative power of tree-controlled grammars let us say some words why they can be of interest. We consider the membership problem, i.e. the question "$x \in L(G)$?", and its complexity, i.e. the number of steps which is necessary if we solve the problem with an algorithm (since we do not go into detail we omit the necessary explanations of what a step is etc.). Let us summarize some (optimal) known results (for the proofs we refer to Aho and Ullman (1972)):

— If G is a regular grammar, then the membership problem can be decided in $O(|x|)$ steps.

— If G is an unambiguous context-free grammar, i.e. for each $x \in L(G)$ there is a unique derivation tree of x in G, then it is decidable in $O(|x|^2)$ steps whether or not $x \in L(G)$, and moreover, the derivation tree can be determined in this time.

— The best-known algorithm for the decision of the membership problem for general context-free grammars needs $O(|x|^{2.73})$ steps.

We recall that there exist inherently ambiguous context-free languages, i.e. languages L such that each context-free grammar G with $L = L(G)$ is ambiguous. Therefore the decision whether $x \in L$ for these languages requires $O(|x|^{2.73})$ steps if we use algorithms analysing context-free grammars. An example of such a languaee is $\{a^n b^n c^m : n \geqq 1, m \geqq 1\} \cup \{a^n b^m c^m : n \geqq 1, m \geqq 1\}$. This language is generated in Example 2.3.3 by a tree-controlled grammar, but the underlying context-free grammar is unambiguous, i.e. the regu-lation mechanism squeezes out an inherently ambiguous languages from an unambiguously generated set of words. The following theorem shows that under these conditions the membership problem of L can be decided in $O(|x|^2)$ steps, too.

Theorem 2.3.2. *Let $G = (V_N, V_T, P, S, R)$ be a tree-controlled grammar such that the context-free grammar $G' = (V_N, V_T, P, S)$ is unambiguous. Then there is an algorithm deciding whether $x \in L(G)$ for $x \in V_T^*$ in $O(|x|^2)$ steps.*

Proof. The following algorithm is used.

1) Decide whether $x \in L(G')$. If $x \notin L(G')$, then $x \notin L(G)$, and we have finished.
2) Determine the unique derivation tree T of x in G'.
3) Check whether or not the words of all levels of T belong to R (except the last level). If they belong to R, then $x \in L(G)$; otherwise $x \notin L(G)$.

By the above mentioned facts, 1) and 2) can be performed in $O(|x|^2)$ steps. Further T has at most $k|x|$ levels (where k is a constant depending on G' only), and the word of each level is not longer than x. Therefore each level can be checked in $O(|x|)$ steps, and thus 3) can be done in $O(|x|^2)$ steps.

We denote the family of all languages generated by tree-controlled grammars whose productions are of type X by $\mathcal{L}(\mathrm{TC}, X)$.

Lemma 2.3.1. $\mathcal{L}(\mathrm{TC}, \mathrm{CF} - \lambda) \subseteq \mathcal{L}(\mathrm{CS})$.

Proof. Let $G = (V_N, V_T, P, S, R)$ be a tree-controlled grammar. If the word of level i of a derivation tree is $x_1 A_1 x_2 A_2 \ldots x_n A_n x_{n+1}$, where $x_i \in V_T^*$ and $A_i \in V_N$, and if we apply the rules $A_i \to w_i$ according to the derivation tree, then the word of level $i + 1$ is $w_1 w_2 \ldots w_n$. Now the context-sensitive grammar works as follows. We introduce end markers a_1, a_2 as in the construction which proves Theorem 2.3.1 and start with $a_1 X S a_2$, i.e. besides the checking symbols and barred letters we scan the word of level s between a_1 and a_2. We check whether it is in R (see the proof above mentioned). If not, then the derivation is block. If it is in R, then we move from right to left replacing the nonterminals according to rules in P and the terminals x by the barred version of x. Then besides the checking and barred symbols the word of the next level is between a_1 and a_2.

Lemma 2.3.2. $\mathscr{L}(\mathrm{CS}) \subseteq \mathscr{L}(\mathrm{TC}, \mathrm{CF} - \lambda)$.

Proof. Let $L \in \mathscr{L}(\mathrm{CS})$ be generated by the monotone grammar $G = (V_N, V_T, P, S)$ in Kuroda normal form. Let us denote by P_1 the set of rules $X \to YZ \in P$, and by P_2 the set of rules $X \to a \in P$. Further let $r_1, r_2, \ldots, r_k$ be labels for the rules of the form r_i: $X_iU_i \to Y_iZ_i$. We construct the following λ-free context-free grammar $G' = (V'_N, V_T, P', S)$ where

$$V'_N = V_N \cup \overline{V}_N \cup V_N \times \{r_1, r_2, \ldots, r_k\} \times \{1, 2\}$$

with $\overline{V}_N = \{\overline{X} : X \in V_N\}$ and

$$P' = P_1 \cup P_2 \cup P_3 \cup P_4 \cup P_5$$

where

$$P_3 = \bigcup_{i=1}^{k} \{X_i \to (X_i, r_i, 1),\ U_i \to (U_i, r_i, 2)\} \cup \{X \to \overline{X} : X \in V_N\},$$

$$P_4 = \bigcup_{i=1}^{k} \{(X_i, r_i, 1) \to Y_i,\ (U_i, r_i, 2) \to Z_i\} \cup \{\overline{X} \to X : X \in V_N\},$$

$$P_5 = \{X \to X : X \in V_N\},$$

and we consider the following regular language

$$M = V_N^* \cup M'$$

with

$$M' = \overline{V}_N^*\{(X_i, r_i, 1)\,(U_i, r_i, 2) : 1 \leqq i \leqq k\}\,\overline{V}_N^*.$$

Clearly, for any derivation in G there is an equivalent derivation which can be divided into two phases: one in which only non-terminal rules are used and one in which only rules of P_2 are used. Such a derivation can be simulated by a derivation in the tree-controlled grammar $G'' = (V'_N, V_T, P', S, N)$ in the following way. When a rule of P_1 is used, we apply a rule of P_5 for all other nonterminals in the sentential form. Thus we pass to another level of the derivation tree. The use of a rule $X_iU_i \to Y_iZ_i$ can be simulated by a successive use of the rules in P_3 and P_4 to rewrite all the nonterminals in the sentential form. Thus we pass from a string in V_N^* to one in M', then to one in V_N^*. Therefore $L(G) \subseteq L(G'')$.

Conversely, let us consider a derivation tree in the grammar G' such that each level belongs to M. Then each level word of this tree is either in V_N^* or in M'. A word in V_N^* can be rewritten using rules of $P_1 \cup P_5$ to obtain another string in V_N^* and this is a derivation in G, or using rules in P_3. But if a rule of P_3 is applied then we have to derive a level word in M'. This implies that we rewrite some X_iU_i by $(X_i, r_i, 1)\,(U_i, r_i, 2)$ for some rule r_i of P and all other nonterminals X are replaced by $\overline{X}$. On the other hand, from a string in M' we can derive in only one way: we replace $(X_i, r_i, 1)$ by Y_i, $(U_i, r_i, 2)$ by Z_i, and each $\overline{X}$ by X. Thus we obtain a word in V_N^* which represents the word which is derived by the application of $X_iU_i \to Y_iZ_i$ in G. Hence $L(G'') \subseteq L(G)$.

Theorem 2.3.3. $\mathscr{L}(\mathrm{CS}) = \mathscr{L}(\mathrm{TC}, \mathrm{CF} - \lambda)$.

Proof. Combine Lemmas 2.3.1 and 2.3.2.
Now we introduce ordered grammars.

Definition 2.3.3. An *ordered grammar* is a quintuple $G = (V_N, V_T, P, S <)$ where V_N, V_T, P, S are defined as in a phrase structure grammar, and $<$ is a partial order on P. A production $w \to z$ is applicable to a string x if $x = x_1 w x_2$ for some $x_1, x_2 \in V_G^*$ and x contains no subword w' such that $w' \to z' \in P$ for some z' and $w' \to z' > w \to z$; the application of $w \to z$ to x yields $y = x_1 z x_2$.

Again, we write $x \Rightarrow y$ and by $\overset{*}{\Rightarrow}$ we denote the reflexive and transitive closure of $\Rightarrow$. We define the language generated by G as

$$L(G) = \{x : x \in V_T^*, S \overset{*}{\Rightarrow} x\}.$$

Intuitively, the direct derivation $x \Rightarrow y$ is performed by the application of a rule which is maximal in the set of applicable rules.

Example 2.3.4. Let $G = (\{S, A, B, A', B', A'', N\}, \{a, b, c\}, P, S, <)$ where P and the order $<$ are given in Fig. 2.3.2 ($X \to x < Y \to y$ is denoted by $(X \to x) \to (Y \to y)$).

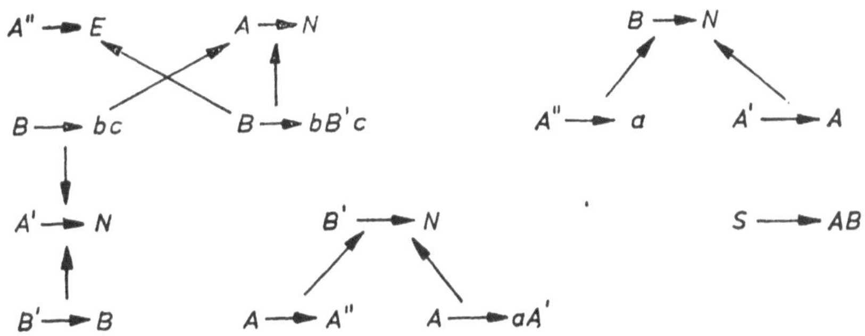

Fig. 2.3.2

We prove that $L(G) = \{a^n b^n c^n : n \geqq 1\}$. In order to do this let $w = a^r A b^r B c^r$. By definition of the order we can apply the rules $A \to N$, $B \to N$, $A \to A''$, $A \to aA'$ (the other rules with left-hand side B are not applicable). In the first two cases we introduce the trap-symbol N which cannot be rewritten and hence the derivation is blocked. Therefore let us assume that we apply $A \to A''$ which yields $a^r A'' b^r B c^r$. A'' cannot be replaced since B is present. Further $B \to bB'c$ cannot be used since $A'' \to N$ is greater. Therefore the only derivation which does not introduce N is $a^r A'' b^r B c^r \Rightarrow a^r A'' b^{r+1} c^{r+1}$ by application of $B \to bc$. Now we have to rewrite A'' and obtain $a^{r+1} b^{r+1} c^{r+1}$. Let us now discuss the fourth case, the application of $A \to aA'$ to w. This yields the following unique derivation

$$w \Rightarrow a^{r+1} A' b^r B c^r \Rightarrow a^{r+1} A' b^{r+1} B' c^{r+1} \Rightarrow a^{r+1} A b^{r+1} B' c^{r+1} \Rightarrow a^{r+1} A b^{r+1} B c^{r+1}$$

if we do not introduce the trap-symbol N.

In conclusion, the above statement holds.

Clearly, by the definition, the derivation process in an ordered grammar is regulated by a context condition concerning the sentential forms, since the left-hand sides of greater rules must not exist in this form. This relates the ordered grammars to random context grammars with forbidding context. More precisely, the following theorem holds for the family $\mathcal{L}(\mathrm{O}, X)$ of languages generated by ordered grammars with productions of type X.

Theorem 2.3.4. *For* $X \in \{\mathrm{CF}, \mathrm{CF} - \lambda\}$, *we have*

$$\mathcal{L}(\mathrm{fRC}, X) = \mathcal{L}(\mathrm{O}, X),$$

and moreover,

$$\mathcal{L}(\mathrm{O}, \mathrm{REG}) = \mathcal{L}(\mathrm{fRC}, \mathrm{REG}) = \mathcal{L}(\mathrm{REG}).$$

Proof. We consider only the case $X = \mathrm{CF}$, proof for $X = CF - \lambda$ is left to the reader.

Let $L \in \mathcal{L}(\mathrm{O}, \mathrm{CF})$. Then $L = L(G)$ for some ordered grammar $G = (V_N, V_T, P, S, <)$. With each rule $A \to w \in P$ we associate the production $(A \to w, \emptyset, R)$ with

$$R = \{B : B \to x > A \to w, B \to x \in P\}.$$

Let $G' = (V_N, V_T, P', S)$ be the random context grammar where P' is the set of all rules constructed above. Clearly, G' is a grammar with forbidding contexts. By the definition of the derivation in an ordered grammar and in a random context grammar, we have that $A \to w$ is applicable to x in G iff $(A \to w, \emptyset, R)$ is applicable to x in G', and in both cases the application derives the same sentential form. Therefore $L(G) = L(G')$, i.e. $L \in \mathcal{L}(\mathrm{fRC}, \mathrm{CF})$ and $\mathcal{L}(\mathrm{O}, \mathrm{CF}) \subseteq \mathcal{L}(\mathrm{fRC}, \mathrm{CF})$.

Conversely, let $G_1 = (V_N, V_T, P, S)$ be a random context grammar whose productions are of the form $(A \to w, \emptyset, R)$. We define the ordered grammar $G_1' = (V_N', V_T, P', S, <)$ by

$$V_N' = V_N \cup \{Z\} \quad \text{where } Z \text{ is a new symbol (trap symbol)},$$

$$P' = \{A \to Z : A \in V_N\} \cup \{A \to w : (A \to w, \emptyset, R) \in P\},$$

and $<$ is given as follows:

$$A \to w < B \to Z \quad \text{if} \quad (A \to w, \emptyset, R) \in P \quad \text{and} \quad B \in R.$$

By the definition of $<$, $A \to w$ is again applicable to x in G_1' iff $(A \to w, \emptyset, R)$ is applicable to x in G_1 yielding the same word. Thus $L(G_1) = L(G_1')$ and $\mathcal{L}(\mathrm{fRC}, \mathrm{CF}) \subseteq \mathcal{L}(\mathrm{O}, \mathrm{CF})$.

Combining this result with Theorem 1.5.12 we obtain

Corollary. $\mathcal{L}(\mathrm{ETOL})$ *is strictly included in* $\mathcal{L}(\mathrm{O}, \mathrm{CF} - \lambda)$.

Exercises

2.3.1. Construct a conditional metalinear grammar G such that

$$L(G) = \{a^n b^n c^n : n \geqq 1\}.$$

2.3.2. Give a complete proof of Lemma 2.3.1.

2.3.3. Prove $\mathcal{L}(\mathrm{K}, \mathrm{REG}) = \mathcal{L}(\mathrm{REG})$ (see PĂUN (1979-c)).

2.3.4. A directed conditional grammar is a construct $G = (V_N, V_T, P, S)$ where P contains rules of the form $(w \to z, Q_1, Q_2)$, where Q_1 and Q_2 are regular languages. Such a rule is applicable to $x = x_1wx_2$ iff $x_1 \in Q_1$ and $x_2 \in Q_2$, and its application derives x_1zx_2. Prove that directed conditional grammars have the same generative capacity as conditional grammars (the core productions being of the same type) (see PĂUN (1979-c)).

2.3.5. A conditional grammar is called *weak* if the regular language associated with the rules is the same for all rules. Prove that each conditional language can be generated by a weakly conditional grammar (see KRAL (1970), PĂUN (1979-c)).

2.3.6. Construct a tree-controlled context-free grammar generating $\{a^nb^nc^n : n \geqq 1\}$.

2.3.7. Prove that $\mathscr{L}(\mathrm{TC}, \mathrm{REG}) = \mathscr{L}(\mathrm{REG})$ (see PĂUN 1979-f)).

2.3.8. Prove that L is i) regular, ii) linear, iii) context-free, iv) an EOL language (the generating ETOL system has exactly one table), v) an ETOL language iff there is a tree-controlled grammar $G = (V_N, V_T, P, S, R)$ generating L with i) $R = V_T^*V_N$, ii) $R = V_T^*V_NV_T^*$, iii) $R = V_G^*$, iv) $R = V_N^*$, and v) $R = V_1^* \cup V_2^* \cup \cdots \cup V_k^*$ where $V_N = V_1 \cup V_2 \cup \cdots \cup V_k$, $V_i \cap V_j = \emptyset$ for $i \neq j$, respectively (see CULIK and MAURER (1977)).

2.4. Further Regulated Devices

The grammars considered in the previous three sections have the following in common: if the core productions are context-free, then they are applied in a context-free manner, i.e. they are applied to one (arbitrary) occurrence of the left-hand side in the current string. In this section we study grammars whose productions are context-free, i.e. they are of the form $A \to w$, $A \in V_N$, $w \in V_G^*$, however, their application is not a simple replacing of one occurrence of its left-hand side by the right-hand side.

First we consider some types of parallelism in the derivation process.

Definition 2.4.1. An *Indian parallel grammar* is a construct $G = (V_N, V_T, P, S)$ where the components are defined as in a context-free grammar. We say that $x \overset{i}{\Longrightarrow} y$ holds in G, $x \in V_G^+$, $y \in V_G^*$, iff the following conditions are satisfied:

$$x = x_1Ax_2A \ldots x_nAx_{n+1},\ A \in V_N,\ x_i \in (V_G \setminus \{A\})^* \quad \text{for} \quad 1 \leqq i \leqq n+1,$$

$$y = x_1wx_2w \ldots x_nwx_{n+1},$$

$$A \to w \in P.$$

Again, the language $L(G)$ consists of all words $y \in V_T^*$ with $S \overset{i*}{\Longrightarrow} y$ where $\overset{i*}{\Longrightarrow}$ is the reflexive and transitive closure of the relation $\overset{i}{\Longrightarrow}$.

Note that this type of parallelism lies between the sequential context-free derivations and the purely parallel derivations in L systems. In a context-free derivation one occurrence of one letter is replaced, in an L system all occurrences of all letters are rewritten (and different rules for the same letter can be used), whereas in an Indian parallel grammar all occurrences of one letter are replaced (according to one production).

Example 2.4.1. We consider the Indian parallel grammar

$$G = (\{S\}, \{a\}, \{S \to SS, S \to a\}, S).$$

Let $w = S^n$. If we apply the first rule we obtain $S^n \overset{i}{\Longrightarrow} S^{2n}$, and the rewriting of S^n by $S \to a$ yields a^n. Therefore the terminating derivations have the form

$$S \overset{i}{\Longrightarrow} S^2 \overset{i}{\Longrightarrow} S^4 \overset{i}{\Longrightarrow} \cdots \overset{i}{\Longrightarrow} S^{2^n} \overset{i}{\Longrightarrow} a^{2^n}.$$

Hence $L(G) = \{a^{2^n} : n \geqq 0\}$.

Example 2.4.2. The Dyck language over two letters cannot be generated by an Indian parallel grammar.

We omit the proof and refer to Skyum (1974).

Lemma 2.4.1. *For each Indian parallel grammar G there is a λ-free Indian parallel grammar such that $L(G') = L(G)$.*

Proof. This can be given by obvious modifications of the standard method for the elimination of λ-rules from a context-free grammar (see, e.g. Aho and Ullman (1972)).

We denote the family of languages generated by Indian parallel grammars by $\mathcal{L}(\text{iCF})$ (i stands for Indian and CF for the type of productions). Note that, by Lemma 2.4.1, it is not necessary to introduce $\mathcal{L}(\text{iCF} - \lambda)$ since $\mathcal{L}(\text{iCF}) = \mathcal{L}(\text{iCF} - \lambda)$. We restrict ourselves to context-free productions since overlapping of the contexts and their parallel substitution leads to problems in the definition (whereas for linear grammars the parallelism makes no difference).

We now define a grammar (and its derivation process) which combines the context-free and the Indian parallel feature.

Definition 2.4.2. A *Russian parallel grammar* is a quadruple $G = (V_N, V_T, P, S)$ whose components are defined as in a context-free grammar and the set P is divided into two disjoint parts, i.e. $P = P_1 \cup P_2$. The yield relation $x \overset{r}{\Longrightarrow} y$ is defined as follows: either

$$x = x_1 A x_2,\ y = x_1 w x_2 \quad \text{for some} \quad x_1, x_2 \in V_G^*, \quad \text{and} \quad A \to w \in P_1$$

or

$$x = x_1 A x_2 A \ldots x_n A x_{n+1},\ y = x_1 w x_2 w \ldots x_n w x_{n+1} \quad \text{for some} \quad x_i \in (V_G \setminus \{A\})^*,$$
$$1 \leqq i \leqq n + 1, \quad \text{and} \quad A \to w \in P_2.$$

The language $L(G)$ is defined by

$$L(G) = \left\{x : x \in V_T^*,\ S \overset{r*}{\Longrightarrow} x\right\}$$

(where $\overset{r*}{\Longrightarrow}$ is the reflexive and transitive closure of $\overset{r}{\Longrightarrow}$).

If in a Russian grammar as above we choose $P_1 = \emptyset$ or $P_2 = \emptyset$, we obtain an Indian parallel or a context-free grammar, respectively. Thus each context-free and each Indian parallel language is a Russian parallel language, too.

Example 2.4.3. $\{a^n b^n c^n : n \geqq 1\}$ cannot be generated by a Russian parallel grammar.

Assume the contrary, i.e. $L = \{a^n b^n c^n : n \geqq 1\} = L(G)$ for some Russian parallel grammar $G = (V_N, V_T, P, S)$, $P = P_1 \cup P_2$. Clearly, $P_2 \neq \emptyset$ since otherwise we generate a context-free language. Now let p: $A \to w \in P_2$. If there is no derivation of the form $S \overset{r*}{\Longrightarrow} v \underset{p}{\overset{r}{\Longrightarrow}} y \overset{r*}{\Longrightarrow} z \in V_T^*$ where v contains at least two occurrences of A, then it is also clear that p is applicable only in the context-free manner, i.e. the removing of $A \to w$ from P_2 and adding it to P_1 do not change the generated language. Therefore there are productions $p_i\colon A_i \to w_i \in P_2$, $1 \leqq i \leqq m$ for some $m \geqq 1$, such that there is a derivation

$$S \overset{r*}{\Longrightarrow} v_i \underset{p_i}{\overset{r}{\Longrightarrow}} y_i \overset{r*}{\Longrightarrow} r_i \in V_T^*$$

where v_i contains at least two occurrences of A_i. If there is a unique $u_i \in V_T^*$ with $A_i \overset{r*}{\Longrightarrow} u_i$ in G then we cancel all rules with left-hand side A_i and substitute them by $A_i \to u_i$ which is added to P_1 without changing the generated language. Hence there is a letter A_i, $1 \leqq i \leqq m$, such that there are two different words $y_1, y_2 \in V_T^*$ with $A_i \overset{r*}{\Longrightarrow} y_1$ and $A \overset{r*}{\Longrightarrow} y_2$. Then there exist the following two derivations in G:

$$S \overset{r*}{\Longrightarrow} v_i = v_1' A_i v_2' A_i \ldots v_r' A_i v_{r+1}' \overset{r*}{\Longrightarrow} v_1' y_1 v_2' y_1 \ldots v_r' y_1 y_{r+1}' = z_1 \in V_T^*,$$

$$S \overset{r*}{\Longrightarrow} v_i = v_1' A_i v_2' A_i \ldots v_r' A_i v_{r+1}' \overset{r*}{\Longrightarrow} v_1' y_2 v_2' y_2 \ldots v_r' y_2 v_{r+1}' = z_2 \in V_T^*.$$

Clearly, $z_1 = a^{s_1} b^{s_1} c^{s_1}$ and $z_2 = a^{s_2} b^{s_2} c^{s_2}$. If y_1 contains two different symbols of $\{a, b, c\}$, say $y_1 = y_1' a b y_1''$ without loss of generality, then

$$z_1 = v_1' y_1' a b y_1'' v_2' y_1' a b y_1'' \ldots v_r' y_1' a b y_1'' v_{r+1}'$$

and hence $z_1 \notin L$. Thus $y_1 = a^s$ or $y_1 = b^s$ or $y_1 = c^s$ for some s. In the sequel we consider the case $y_1 = a^s$ (in the other cases we conclude analogously). Then

$$v_1' = a^{r_1} \quad \text{for some} \quad r_i, 1 \leqq i \leqq r,$$

$$v_{r+1}' = a^k b^{s_1} c^{s_1} \quad \text{for some } k.$$

Further,

$$z_2 = v_1' y_2 v_2' y_2 \ldots v_r' y_2 a^k b^{s_1} c^{s_1} = a^{s_2} b^{s_2} c^{s_2}.$$

This implies $s_1 = s_2$ and therefore $z_1 = z_2$ and $y_1 = y_2$ in contrast to our choice.

By $\mathscr{L}(\mathrm{r}X)$, $X \in \{\mathrm{CF}, \mathrm{CF} - \lambda\}$, we denote the families of languages generated by Russian parallel grammars with rules of type X.

Theorem 2.4.1. i) $\mathscr{L}(\mathrm{iCF})$ *and* $\mathscr{L}(\mathrm{CF})$ *are incomparable.*

ii) $\mathscr{L}(\mathrm{CF})$ *is strictly included in* $\mathscr{L}(\mathrm{rCF} - \lambda)$.
iii) $\mathscr{L}(\mathrm{iCF})$ *is strictly included in* $\mathscr{L}(\mathrm{rCF} - \lambda)$.
iv) $\mathscr{L}(\mathrm{rCF})$ *is strictly included in* $\mathscr{L}(\mathrm{ETOL})$.

Proof. i) follows from Example 2.4.1 and 2.4.2.

ii) and iii). As mentioned above, the inclusions are obvious. Their strictness follows from i).

iv) It is sufficient to prove the inclusion since its properness follows from Example 2.4.3 because $\{a^n b^n c^n : n \geqq 1\} \in \mathscr{L}(\mathrm{EDTOL})$ can be easily proved.

Let $G = (V_N, V_T, P, S)$ be a Russian parallel grammar and $P = P_1 \cup P_2$. We define the ETOL system $G' = (V_N \cup V_T, V_T, \mathfrak{P}, S)$ by the following construction of $\mathfrak{P}$: With each rule $A \to w \in P_1$ we associate the table with the productions

$$A \to w, A \to A, B \to B \quad \text{for} \quad B \in V_N \setminus \{A\}, a \to a \quad \text{for} \quad a \in V_T.$$

With $A \to w \in P_2$ we associate the table with the productions

$$A \to w, B \to B \quad \text{for} \quad B \in V_N \setminus \{A\}, \quad \mathrm{a} \to \mathrm{a} \quad \text{for} \quad \mathrm{a} \in V_T.$$

Let $x \Rightarrow y$ by the application of $A \to w$ to x in G. If $A \to w$ is in P_1, then the application of the table associated with $A \to w$ allows the rewriting of exactly one A by w and the replacing of all other A by A again. Therefore $x \Rightarrow y$ holds in G', too. If $A \to w$ is a rule in P_2, then the application of the table which corresponds to $A \to w$ also gives $x \Rightarrow y$ in G'. Therefore each derivation in G can be simulated in G'. Hence $L(G) \subseteq L(G')$.

Now assume that $x \Rightarrow y$, $x \neq y$, holds in G' by application of a table. If the table is associated with $A \to w \in P_1$, then some occurrences of A in x are replaced by w and the other occurrences of A remain unchanged. If r occurrences are rewritten, then this can be simulated by r applications of $A \to w \in P_1$ in a context-free manner to these occurrences. If the table is associated with $A \to w$ of P_2, then all occurrences of A are replaced by w and all other symbols are not rewritten. The same effect is given by the application of $A \to w \in P_2$ in the Indian parallel manner. Therefore $L(G') \subseteq L(G)$.

Thus we obtain $L(G') = L(G)$.

The Indian parallelism allows the parallel substitution of an arbitrary number of symbols in one derivation step, however, only the occurrences of one symbol can be rewritten. Now we regard another type of parallelism where only a fixed number of symbols can be replaced in a step but the symbols can be different.

Definition 2.4.3. A *scattered context grammar* is a construct $G = (V_N, V_T, P, S)$ where P is a finite set of finite sequences of context-free productions, $P = \{p_1, p_2, \ldots, p_n\}$,

$$p_i\colon (A_{i,1}, A_{i,2}, \ldots, A_{i,r_i}) \to (w_{i,1}, w_{i,2}, \ldots, w_{i,r_i}),\ 1 \leqq i \leqq n,$$

and V_N, V_T, S are defined as in a context-free grammar. For $x \in V_G^*$, $y \in V_G^*$, we say that x directly derives y in G, written as $x \Rightarrow y$, iff, for some $i \in \{1, 2, \ldots, n\}$,

$$x = x_1 A_{i,1} x_2 A_{i,2} \ldots x_{r_i} A_{i,r_i} x_{r_i+1},\ x_j \in V_G^* \quad \text{for} \quad 1 \leqq j \leqq r_i + 1,$$

$$y = x_1 w_{i,1} x_2 w_{i,2} \ldots x_{r_i} w_{i,r_i} x_{r_i+1}.$$

Let $\overset{*}{\Rightarrow}$ be the reflexive and transitive closure of $\Rightarrow$. We define

$$L(G) = \{x : x \in V_T^*, S \overset{*}{\Rightarrow} x\}.$$

Example 2.4.4. Let $G = (\{S, A\}, \{a, b, c\}, \{p_1, p_2, p_3\}, S)$ with

$$p_1\colon (S) \to (AAA),\ p_2\colon (A, A, A) \to (aA, bA, cA),$$

$$p_3\colon (A, A, A) \to (a, b, c).$$

Clearly, each terminating derivation has the following form:

$$S \Rightarrow AAA \Rightarrow aAbAcA \Rightarrow a^2Ab^2Ac^2A \Rightarrow \cdots \Rightarrow a^{n-1}Ab^{n-1}Ac^{n-1}A \Rightarrow a^nb^nc^n,$$

and therefore $L(G) = \{a^nb^nc^n : n \geqq 1\}$.

Example 2.4.5. The language $\{ww : w \in \{a, b\}^*\}$ is generated by

$$G = \big(\{S, A\}, \{a, b\}, \{(S) \to (\lambda), (S) \to (AA), (A, A) \to (aA, aA),$$
$$(A, A) \to (bA, bA), (A, A) \to (a, a), (A, A) \to (b, b)\}, S\big).$$

The differences between matrix and scattered context grammars are the following:

— In a matrix grammar the rules are used sequentially, i.e. the second rule $A_2 \to w_2$

of a matrix can also be applied to an occurrence of A_2 introduced by the application of the first rule $A_1 \to w_1$ of this matrix etc.; scattered context rules are applied in a parallel fashion.

- The productions of a matrix can be applied to each occurrence of its left-hand side (independently of its position), in a scattered context grammar the order of the positions of the replaced symbols is important.

Let $\mathscr{L}(\mathrm{SC})$ $\big(\mathscr{L}(\mathrm{SC} - \lambda)\big)$ denote the family of languages generated by scattered context grammars (without erasing rules).

Lemma 2.4.2. i) $\mathscr{L}(\mathrm{SC} - \lambda) \subseteq \mathscr{L}(\mathrm{CS})$,

ii) $\mathscr{L}(\mathrm{SC}) \subseteq \mathscr{L}(\mathrm{RE})$.

Proof. We prove only i). Let $L \in \mathscr{L}(\mathrm{SC} - \lambda)$. Then $L = L(G)$ for some scattered context grammar $G = (V_N, V_T, P, S)$, $P = \{p_1, p_2, \ldots, p_n\}$, $p_i\colon (A_{i,1}, A_{i,2}, \ldots, A_{i,r_i}) \to (w_{i,1}, w_{i,2}, \ldots, w_{i,r_i})$, $1 \leqq i \leqq n$. We now construct the monotone grammar $G' = (V'_N, V'_T, P', S')$ as follows. We set

$$V'_N = V_N \cup \{[i, j] : 1 \leqq i \leqq n, 1 \leqq j \leqq r_i\} \cup \{Z, S'\},$$

$$V'_T = V_T \cup \{a_1, a_2\}.$$

The set P' of productions is constructed as the set of all rules of the following forms:

$$S' \to a_1[i, 1]\, S a_2,\ 1 \leqq i \leqq n$$

(the initial rules introduce the markers a_1, a_2 and the checking symbol $[i, 1]$),

$$[i, j]\, x \to x[i, j],\ x \in V_G,\ 1 \leqq i \leqq n,\ 1 \leqq j \leqq r_i,$$

$$[i, j]\, A_{i,j} \to w_{i,j}[i, j + 1],\ 1 \leqq j \leqq r_i,\ 1 \leqq i \leqq n,$$

$$[i, r_i]\, A_{i,r_i} \to Zw_{i,r_i},\ 1 \leqq i \leqq n$$

(the checking symbol $[i, j]$ moves from left to right and then it replaces an occurrence of $A_{i,j}$ by $w_{i,j}$ and introduces $[i, j + 1]$; thus the application of $(A_{i,1}, \ldots, A_{i,r_i}) \to (w_{i,1}, \ldots, w_{i,r_i})$ is simulated; the letter Z indicates that the simulation is finished),

$$xZ \to Zx,\ x \in V_G,$$

$$a_1Z \to a_1[i, 1],\ 1 \leqq i \leqq n,$$

$$a_1Z \to a_1a_1$$

(the symbol Z moves from the right to the left, and if it is in its leftmost position it starts the simulation of another rule or it terminates the derivation).

By these explanations it is easy to show that $L(G') = a_1a_1L(G)\, a_2$. By the closure of $\mathscr{L}(\mathrm{CS})$ under derivatives we get $L(G) \in \mathscr{L}(\mathrm{CS})$. Thus the assertion is proved.

We now slightly modify the derivation in a scattered context grammar by adding the appearance checking.

Definition 2.4.4. A *scattered context grammar with appearance checking* is a construct $G = (V_N, V_T, P, S, F)$ where V_N, V_T, P, S are defined as in a scattered context grammar, and F is a set of occurrences of context-free rules $A_{i,j} \to w_{i,j}$ in P. We say that $x \Rightarrow y$

holds in G if

$$x = x_1 A_{i_1} x_2 A_{i_2} \dots x_n A_{i_n} x_{n+1},\ x_i \in V_G^* \quad \text{for} \quad 1 \leqq i \leqq n+1,$$

$$y = x_1 w_{i_1} x_2 w_{i_2} \dots x_n w_{i_n} x_{n+1},$$

$$(A_1, A_2, \dots, A_m) \to (w_1, w_2, \dots, w_m) \in P,$$

$$A_j \to w_j \in F \quad \text{for} \quad j \neq i_k,\ 1 \leqq k \leqq n,$$

and

$$x_t \ \text{ does not contain the letters } \ A_{i_{t-1}+1}, \dots, A_{i_t-1} \quad \text{for} \quad 1 \leqq t \leqq n+1.$$

Again, $L(G) = \{x : x \in V_T^*,\ S \stackrel{*}{\Rightarrow} x\}$.

Intuitively, a rule can be passed over if its left-hand side does not occur in a position with respect to the other nonterminals as it is required in the production.

By $\mathcal{L}(\mathrm{SC, ac})$ $\big(\mathcal{L}(\mathrm{SC} - \lambda, \mathrm{ac})\big)$ we denote the family of languages generated by scattered context grammars with appearance checking (without λ-rules).

Lemma 2.4.3. i) $\mathcal{L}(\mathrm{SC} - \lambda, \mathrm{ac}) = \mathcal{L}(\mathrm{CS})$,

ii) $\mathcal{L}(\mathrm{SC, ac}) = \mathcal{L}(\mathrm{RE})$.

Proof. Again we prove only i). The inclusion $\mathcal{L}(\mathrm{SC} - \lambda, \mathrm{ac}) \subseteq \mathcal{L}(\mathrm{CS})$ can be shown as in Lemma 2.4.2, the necessary modifications being left to the reader.

Consider now a language $L \in \mathcal{L}(\mathrm{CS})$ and a monotone grammar $G = (V_N, V_T, P, S)$ in Kuroda normal form generating L. Thus P contains only productions of the forms $A \to BC$, $AB \to CD$, $A \to a$ where $A, B, C, D \in V_N$, $a \in V_T$. Let N be an additional letter, $N \notin V_G$ (it will be used as a trap-symbol), and let $V_N = \{A_1, A_2, \dots, A_n\}$. With $A \to BC$ we associate the scattered context rule $(A) \to (BC)$. For $AB \to CD$ we introduce the productions

$$(A, A_1, A_2, \dots, A_n, B) \to (C, N, N, \dots, N, D),$$

and we associate with $A \to a$ the rules

$$(A_1, A_2, \dots, A_n, A) \to (N, N, \dots, N, a).$$

Let P' be the set of all scattered context productions constructed in this way. Moreover we set

$$F = \{A \to N : A \in V_N\}$$

and

$$G' = (V_N \cup \{N\}, V_T, P', S, F).$$

We prove that $L(G') = L(G)$. This follows easily by the following facts. Since the trap-symbol N cannot be replaced, any terminating derivation cannot contain a sentential form in which N occurs. Therefore the rules corresponding to $A \to a$ can be applied only if A is the leftmost nonterminal in the sentential form and it is rewritten by a. This implies that between two nonterminals only nonterminals can occur. However, then $(A, A_1, \dots, A_n, B) \to (C, N, \dots, N, D)$ is only applicable if no letter exists between A and B, i.e. the application of $AB \to CD$ is simulated.

In Section 2.1. we considered unordered versions of matrix grammars. Therefore it is natural also to study unordered scattered context grammars (with appearance checking, too).

Definition 2.4.5. An *unordered scattered context grammar* is a quadruple $G = (V_N, V_T, P, S)$ whose components are defined as in a scattered context grammar. The application of a rule $(A_1, A_2, \ldots, A_n) \to (w_1, w_2, \ldots, w_n) \in P$ to some $x \in V_G^+$ yields $y \in V_G^*$ (written as $x \Rightarrow y$) if the following condition is satisfied: there is a permutation π of $\{1, 2, \ldots, n\}$ such that

$$x = x_1 A_{\pi(1)} x_2 A_{\pi(2)} \ldots x_n A_{\pi(n)} x_{n+1},\ y = x_1 w_{\pi(1)} x_2 w_{\pi(2)} \ldots x_n w_{\pi(n)} x_{n+1}$$

The generated language is

$$L(G) = \{x : x \in V_T^*, S \stackrel{*}{\Rightarrow} x\}$$

where $\stackrel{*}{\Rightarrow}$ is the reflexive and transitive closure of $\Rightarrow$.

Example 2.4.6. Let G be defined as in Example 2.4.4 (but now considered as an unordered scattered context grammar). Then

$$L(G) = \Big\{w : w = x_1 x_2 \ldots x_{3n} \quad \text{for some} \quad n \geqq 1,\ x_i \in V_T,\ 1 \leqq i \leqq 3n,$$
$$\{x_j, x_{n+j}, x_{2n+j}\} = \{a, b, c\} \quad \text{for} \quad 1 \leqq j \leqq n\Big\}.$$

Compare this with Example 2.4.4.

By $\mathscr{L}(\text{uSC})$ $(\mathscr{L}(\text{uSC} - \lambda))$ we denote the family of all languages generated by unordered scattered context grammars (without λ-rules).

Lemma 2.4.4. $\mathscr{L}(\text{uSC}) \subseteq \mathscr{L}(\text{SC})$ and $\mathscr{L}(\text{uSC} - \lambda) \subseteq \mathscr{L}(\text{SC} - \lambda)$.

Proof. Trivial (see also the proof of Lemma 2.1.5 combined with Exercise 2.4.3).

Lemma 2.4.5. i) $\mathscr{L}(\text{uSC} - \lambda) \subseteq \mathscr{L}(\text{P, CF} - \lambda)$,

ii) $\mathscr{L}(\text{uSC}) \subseteq \mathscr{L}(\text{P, CF})$.

Proof. We prove i) only.

Let G be an unordered scattered context grammar, $G = (V_N, V_T, P, S)$. Let $V'_N = \{A' : A \in V_N\}$, and let h be the homomorphism from V_G^* into $(V'_N \cup V_T)^*$ defined by

$$h(a) = a \quad \text{for} \quad a \in V_T \quad \text{and} \quad h(A) = A' \quad \text{for} \quad A \in V_N.$$

Let p: $(A_1, A_2, \ldots, A_n) \to (w_1, w_2, \ldots, w_n)$ be a rule of P, and let $h(w_1 w_2 \ldots w_n) = z_1 B'_1 z_2 B'_2 \ldots z_m B'_m z_{m+1}$ where $z_i \in V_T^*$ for $1 \leqq i \leqq m + 1$. We define the programmed grammar $G' = (V''_N, V_T, P', \bar{S})$ by

$$V''_N = V_N \cup V'_N \cup \{\bar{S}\}$$

and the following construction of P':

$$(* : \bar{S} \to S, \{[p, 1, 0] : p \in P\}, \emptyset)$$

is the starting rule and with each rule $p \in P$ we consider the rules

$$([p, i, 0] : A_i \to h(w_i), \{[p, i + 1, 0]\}, \emptyset),\ 1 \leqq i \leqq n,$$
$$([p, n, 0] : A_n \to h(w_n), \{[p, 1, 1]\}, \emptyset),$$
$$([p, i, 1] : B'_i \to B_i, \{[p, i + 1, 1]\}, \emptyset),\ 1 \leqq i \leqq m,$$
$$([p, m, 1] : B'_m \to B_m, \{[q, 1, 0] : q \in P\}, \emptyset);$$

Clearly, the programmed rules associated with $p \in P$ have to be applied in a fixed order and they simulate an application of $p \in P$ (the primed letters are necessary in order to ensure that the productions can be applied only to the sentential form which is rewritten in G). Now it is easy to show that, for $x, y \in V_G^*$, $x \Rightarrow y$ holds in G iff $x \Rightarrow y$ holds in G'. Hence $L(G) = L(G')$, and the statement is proved.

Lemma 2.4.6. i) $\mathscr{L}(\mathrm{P}, \mathrm{CF} - \lambda) \subseteq \mathscr{L}(\mathrm{uSC} - \mathscr{S})$,

ii) $\mathscr{L}(P, \mathrm{CF}) \subseteq \mathscr{L}(\mathrm{uSC})$.

Proof. Again we consider only i).

Let $G = (V_N, V_T, P, S)$ be a programmed grammar. We set

$$V'_N = V_N \cup \{[x, b] : x \in V_G, b \in \mathrm{Lab}\,(P)\} \cup \{\bar{S}\}.$$

For each rule $(b: A \to xw, \sigma(b), \emptyset)$ in P, $x \in V_G$, $w \in V_G^*$, we consider the following scattered context rules:

(1) $([A, b]) \to ([x, t]\, w)$ for $t \in \sigma(b)$,

(2) $([y, b], A) \to ([y, t], xw)$ for $t \in \sigma(b), y \in V_G$

(the second component in $[A, b]$ or $[y, b]$ indicates the rule which is simulated), and we add the terminating rules

(3) $([y, b]) \to (y)$ for $y \in V_T, b \in \mathrm{Lab}\,(P)$

and the initial rules

(4) $(\bar{S}) \to ([S, t])$ where $t \in \mathrm{Lab}\,(\mathrm{P})$.

Let P' be the set of all rules constructed in this way. We consider the unordered scattered context grammar $G' = (V'_N, V_T, P', \bar{S})$.

Assume that v is a sentential form of G' and $v \neq \bar{S}$. By the definition of the productions the number of terminals of the form $[x, b]$ in v is 1 or 0. In the latter case v is in V_T^*, i.e. the derivation is terminated, or it contains a nonterminal and then the derivation is blocked since each rule (besides the initial ones) requires the presence of a nonterminal $[x, b]$.

We now discuss the following cases:

Case 1. $v = v_1[A, b]\, v_2$, $v_1, v_2 \in (V_{G'} \setminus \{A\})^*$. Then we can apply only a rule of type (1) yielding $z = v_1[x, t]\, wv_2$ with $t \in \sigma(b)$. This corresponds to the application of $(b: A \to xw, \sigma(b), \emptyset)$ to $v' = v_1Av_2$ which derives $z' = v_1xwz_2$.

Case 2. $v = v_1[y, b]\, v_2Av_3$.

Case 2.1. We apply a rule of type (2) and obtain $z = v_1[y, t]\, v_2xwv_3$, $t \in \sigma(b)$. Again, in G we then have $v' = v_1yv_2Av_3 \Rightarrow z' = v_1yv_2xwv_3$.

Case 2.2. We apply a rule of type (1). Then $y = A$ and we can conclude as in Case 1.

Case 3. $v = v_1Av_2[y, b]\, v_3$. We can use analogous arguments as in Case 2.

Thus in all cases, if $v \Rightarrow z$ in G' then $v' \Rightarrow z'$ in G, where v' and z' are obtained by replacing $[y, t]$ by y for some $y \in V_G$ and some label t, and, furthermore, both these derivations can be continued only by a production with a label in $\sigma(b)$ or associated to a label in $\sigma(b)$, respectively.

Case 4. $v = v_1[y, b]\, v_2$, $y \in V_T$, $v_1, v_2 \in V_T^*$. We can apply only a terminating rule and obtain $z = v_1 y v_2$.

This implies that terminating derivations in G' are of the form

$$\bar{S} \Rightarrow [S, t_1] \underset{p_1'}{\Longrightarrow} w_1 \underset{p_2'}{\Longrightarrow} w_2 \Rightarrow \cdots \underset{p_n'}{\Longrightarrow} w_n \underset{q}{\Longrightarrow} w_n'$$

where p_i' is associated with $p_i = \big(t_i\colon A_i \to r_i, \sigma(t_i), \emptyset\big)$ for $1 \leqq i \leqq n$, $t_{i+1} \in \sigma(t_i)$ for $1 \leqq i \leqq n-1$, and q is a terminating production. Such a derivation implies a derivation

$$S \underset{p_1}{\Longrightarrow} w_1' \underset{p_2}{\Longrightarrow} w_2' \cdots \underset{p_n}{\Longrightarrow} w_n'$$

in G. Therefore $L(G') \subseteq L(G)$.

The opposite inclusion holds since each derivation in G can be simulated by a derivation in G' which can be shown by analogous considerations.

Again, we can add the appearance checking to unordered scattered grammars. This consists of an overpassing of those productions of a distinguished set F whose left-hand side does not occur in the current string. Let $\mathscr{L}(\text{uSC}, \text{ac})$ and $\mathscr{L}(\text{uSC} - \lambda, \text{ac})$ be the corresponding families of languages. One can prove results analogously to Lemmas 2.4.5 and 2.4.6 for the appearance checking mode.

The following theorem summarizes the hierarchy statements proved above and the corresponding statements for the appearance checking case.

Theorem 2.4.2. $\mathscr{L}(\text{uSC} - \lambda) = \mathscr{L}(\text{P}, \text{CF} - \lambda) \subseteq \mathscr{L}(\text{SC} - \lambda) \subseteq \mathscr{L}(\text{CS})$,

$$\mathscr{L}(\text{uSC}) = \mathscr{L}(\text{P}, \text{CF}) \subseteq \mathscr{L}(\text{SC}),$$

$$\mathscr{L}(\text{SC} - \lambda) \subseteq \mathscr{L}(\text{SC}) \subseteq \mathscr{L}(\text{RE}),$$

$$\mathscr{L}(\text{uSC} - \lambda) \subseteq \mathscr{L}(\text{uSC} - \lambda, \text{ac}) = \mathscr{L}(\text{P}, \text{CF} - \lambda, \text{ac}) \subset \mathscr{L}(\text{CS}) = \mathscr{L}(\text{SC} - \lambda, \text{ac})$$

$$\subset \mathscr{L}(\text{RE}) = \mathscr{L}(\text{uSC}, \text{ac}) = \mathscr{L}(\text{SC}, \text{ac}).$$

Next we introduce the so-called indexed grammars.

Definition 2.4.6. An *indexed grammar* is a quintuple $G = (V_N, V_T, I, P, S)$ where V_N, V_T, S are defined as in a context-free grammar, $I = \{i_1, i_2, \ldots, i_r\}$ where, for $1 \leqq j \leqq r$, i_j is a finite set of productions of the form $A \to w$ with $A \in V_N$, $w \in V_G^*$, and P is a finite set of productions of the form $A \to \alpha$ with $A \in V_N$, $\alpha \in (V_N I^* \cup V_T)^*$.

Let $x, y \in (V_N I^* \cup V_T)^*$. We say that x directly derives y in G, written as $x \Rightarrow y$, if either

$$x = x_1 A \beta x_2 \quad \text{for some} \quad x_1, x_2 \in (V_N I^* \cup V_T)^*, A \in V_N, \beta \in I^*,$$

$$A \to X_1 \beta_1 X_2 \beta_2 \ldots X_k \beta_k \in P,$$

$$y = x_1 X_1 \gamma_1 X_2 \gamma_2 \ldots X_k \gamma_k x_2 \quad \text{with} \quad \gamma_j = \beta_j \beta \quad \text{for} \quad X_j \in V_N \quad \text{and}$$

$$\gamma_j = \lambda \quad \text{for} \quad X_j \in V_T, 1 \leqq j \leqq k,$$

or

$$x = x_1 A i \beta x_2 \quad \text{for some} \quad x_1, x_2 \in (V_N I^* \cup V_T)^*, A \in V_N, i \in I, \beta \in I^*,$$

$$A \to X_1 X_2 \ldots X_k \in i,$$

$$y = x_1 X_1 \gamma_1 X_2 \gamma_2 \ldots X_k \gamma_k x_2 \quad \text{with} \quad \gamma_j = \beta \quad \text{for} \quad X_j \in V_N \quad \text{and}$$

$$\gamma_j = \lambda \quad \text{for} \quad X_j \in V_T, 1 \leqq j \leqq k.$$

We denote the reflexive and transitive closure of $\Rightarrow$ by $\overset{*}{\Rightarrow}$, and we define

$$L(G) = \{w : w \in V_T^*, S \overset{*}{\Rightarrow} w\}.$$

The regulation is done by means of the elements of I, the so-called indexes. The application of rules of P gives sentential forms where the nonterminals are followed by a sequence of indexes (in a certain sense this sequence describes the history of the nonterminal), and the indexes can be erased only by productions contained in these indexes but erasing of the indexes is done in reverse order of their appearance.

Example 2.4.7. Let

$$G = (\{S, A, B\}, \{a, b, c\}, \{f, g\}, P, S)$$

where

$$f = \{B \to b\}, g = \{B \to bB\},$$

$$P = \{S \to aAfc, A \to aAgc, A \to B\}.$$

We show that G generates our standard language $\{a^n b^n c^n : n \geqq 1\}$. The productions of the indexes f and g can be used only if B occurs in the sentential form, and its application does not derive occurrences of S and A. On the other hand, there is no rule with left-hand side B in P. Therefore each derivation in G can be divided into two phases, the first one uses only productions of P, the second consists of applications of rules in the indexes. The possibilities for the first part are given in Fig. 2.4.1 where in the horizontal line we use $A \to aAgc$ (besides the first step), and $A \to B$ is applied in vertical direction.

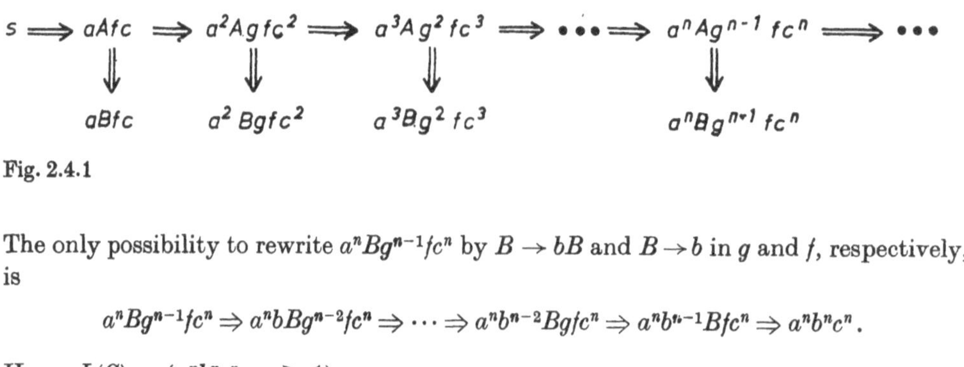

Fig. 2.4.1

The only possibility to rewrite $a^n B g^{n-1} f c^n$ by $B \to bB$ and $B \to b$ in g and f, respectively, is

$$a^n B g^{n-1} f c^n \Rightarrow a^n b B g^{n-2} f c^n \Rightarrow \cdots \Rightarrow a^n b^{n-2} B g f c^n \Rightarrow a^n b^{n-1} B f c^n \Rightarrow a^n b^n c^n.$$

Hence $L(G) = \{a^n b^n c^n : n \geqq 1\}$.

Clearly, if in an indexed grammar we choose $I = \emptyset$, then we obtain a context-free grammar.

As an example of a result concerning indexed grammars we give a generalization of the well-known Chomsky normal form for context-free grammars.

Definition 2.4.7. Let G be an indexed grammar as in Definition 2.4.6. Then we say that G is in *normal form* iff

i) for all $i \in I$, each production in i has the form $A \to B$ with $A, B \in V_N$,
ii) each production of P has one of the following forms:

$$A \to BC, A \to Bi, A \to a, A \to \lambda \quad \text{where} \quad A, B, C \in V_N, i \in I, a \in V_T.$$

Theorem 2.4.3. *For each indexed grammar G there is an indexed grammar G' in normal form such that $L(G) = L(G')$.*

Proof. Let $G = (V_N, V_T, I, P, S)$ be an indexed grammar. We define the indexed grammar $G' = (V'_N, V_T, I', P', S)$ in normal form by constructing its indexes and its productions (the set of nonterminals can be seen from this construction, and S will be the axiom, again). For each $i \in I$ we define $i' \in I'$ as follows: If $A \to B \in i$, then $A \to B \in i'$, too. If $A \to w \in i$, $|w| \geqq 2$, then let $A \to C \in i'$ and add the rule $C \to w$ to P where C is a new symbol. Since $C \to w$ is the only rule with left-hand side C the application of $A \to C$ has to be followed (perhaps some steps later) by a use of $C \to w$ and together this gives $A \Rightarrow w$.

Now we construct P' from P and the rules $C \to w$ added to P. With a production $A \to X_1\alpha_1X_2\alpha_2 \ldots X_k\alpha_k$, $k \geqq 2$, we associate the rules

$$\left.\begin{array}{l} A \to B_1B_2 \quad \text{if} \quad k = 2, \\ A \to B_1C_1, \\ C_i \to B_{i+1}C_{i+1},\ 1 \leqq i \leqq k-2, \\ C_{k-1} \to B_{k-1}B_k \end{array}\right\} \text{for} \quad k \geqq 2,$$

where B_i and C_i for $1 \leqq i \leqq k$ are new nonterminals (the application of $A \to B_1C_1$ requires a unique continuation in the sequel and gives $A \Rightarrow B_1B_2 \ldots B_k$),

$$\left.\begin{array}{l} B_i \to X_i \quad \text{if} \quad \alpha_i = \lambda, \\ B_i \to X_ij \quad \text{if} \quad \alpha_i = j, \\ \left.\begin{array}{l} B_i \to D_{i,r}j_r \\ D_{i,l} \to D_{i,l-1}j_{l-1},\ 3 \leqq l \leqq r \\ D_{i,2} \to X_ij_1 \end{array}\right\} \text{if} \quad \alpha_i = j_1j_2 \ldots j_r \end{array}\right\} 1 \leqq i \leqq k,$$

where $D_{i,l}$, $2 \leqq l \leqq r$, $1 \leqq i \leqq k$, are new symbols, again (by these rules we ensure the only possible derivations $B_i \overset{*}{\Rightarrow} X_ij_1j_2 \ldots j_r$ or $B_i \Rightarrow X_i$ and thus $A \Rightarrow B_1B_2 \ldots B_k \Rightarrow X_1\alpha_1X_2\alpha_2 \ldots X_k\alpha_k$). With a production $A \to Bj_1j_2 \ldots j_r$ we associate the productions

$$A \to D_rj_r,\ D_i \to D_{i-1}j_{i-1},\ 3 \leqq i \leqq r,\ D_2 \to Bj_1$$

with new nonterminals $D_2, D_3, \ldots, D_r$.

By this construction we obtain an indexed grammar which also generates $L(G)$ as can be seen from the explanations given in parenthesis, but it is not necessarily in normal form since it can contain in P some rules of the form $A' \to B'$, $A', B' \in V_N$. Using these rules we obtain some derivations $A \overset{*}{\Rightarrow} B \in V_N$. Now we delete all productions of type $A' \to B'$ and if there is a derivation $A \overset{*}{\Rightarrow} B$, then we add all rules of the form $A \to CD$, $A \to Cf$, $A \to a$, or $A \to \lambda$ if $B \to CD$, $B \to Cf$, $B \to a$, or $B \to \lambda$, respectively, are in P' by the above construction (then a derivation $A \to B \Rightarrow w$ can be simulated by $A \Rightarrow w$).

Clearly, the grammar G' constructed in this way is in normal form and $L(G') = L(G)$ holds.

Without proof we mention results on the generative power of indexed grammars (we refer to Aho (1968)). By $\mathscr{L}(\mathrm{I})$ we denote the family of languages generated by indexed grammars.

Theorem 2.4.4. $\mathscr{L}(\mathrm{ETOL}) \subseteq \mathscr{L}(\mathrm{I}) \subset \mathscr{L}(\mathrm{CS})$.

We now consider grammars based on graphs where intuitively the topological structure of graphs will be used in order to model context conditions.

Let $\Gamma = (U, E)$ be a finite directed graph, and let $E = \{e_1, e_2, \ldots, e_r\}$. With each $v \in U$ we associate its star $S(v)$ of edges starting and/or ending in v. We describe $S(v)$ as a tuple $(i_1^{\alpha_1}, i_2^{\alpha_2}, \ldots, i_s^{\alpha_s})$ where $1 \leqq i_j \leqq r$ and $\alpha_j \in \{+, -\}$ for $1 \leqq j \leqq s$, and i_j^+ is in $S(v)$ iff e_{i_j} starts in v and i_j^- is in $S(v)$ iff e_{i_j} ends in v. Without loss of generality we assume that $i_k < i_j$ for $k < j$ and that i_j^+ is the predecessor of i_j^- if both occur in $S(v)$; s is called the *length* of $S(v)$ and it is denoted by $s(v)$.

A Γ-word w over an alphabet Z is a labelling of the edges of Γ by words over Z such that the direction of the edge corresponds to a reading of the word from left to right. If the label of e_i is $w(i)$, then we write $w = w(1)w(2) \ldots w(r)$.

Definition 2.4.8. A *grammar based on the directed graph* $\Gamma = (U, E)$ is a construct $G = (V_N, V_T, \Gamma, P, \sigma)$ where V_N, V_T have the usual meaning, σ is a Γ-word, and $P = \bigcup_{v \in U} P_v$ where, for $v \in U$, P_v is a finite set of productions of the form

$$(p_1, p_2, \ldots, p_{s(v)}) \to (q_1, q_2, \ldots, q_{s(v)})$$

with $p_i, q_i \in V_G^*$ for $1 \leqq i \leqq s(v)$.

We say that the Γ-word $w = w(1)\, w(2) \ldots w(r) \in V_G^*$ *directly derives* the Γ-word $z = z(1)z(2) \ldots z(r)$, written as $w \Rightarrow z$, if there is a node $v \in U$ and a production $(p_1, p_2, \ldots, p_{s(v)})$ $(q_1, q_2, \ldots, q_{s(v)}) \in P_v$ such that:

- $w(i) = z(i)$ if i^+ and i^- do not occur in $S(v)$.
- If i^+ (and not i^-) occurs in $S(v)$ in position j (that is $i^+ = i_j^+$), then $w(i) = p_j x$ and $z(i) = q_j x$ for some $x \in V_G^*$.
- If i^- (and not i^+) occurs in $S(v)$ in position j, then $w(i) = x p_j$ and $z(i) = x q_j$ for some $x \in V_G^*$.
- If i^+ and i^- occur in $S(v)$ in positions j and $j+1$, then $w(i) = p_j x p_{j+1}$ and $z(i) = q_j x q_{j+1}$ for some $x \in V_G^*$.

Let $\stackrel{*}{\Rightarrow}$ be the reflexive and transitive closure of $\Rightarrow$. Then we define

$$L(G) = \{w(1) : \sigma \stackrel{*}{\Rightarrow} w(1)\, w(2) \ldots w(r) \text{ and } w(j) = \lambda \text{ for } 2 \leqq j \leqq r \text{ and } w(1) \in V_T^*\}.$$

Note that the restriction to the first edge in the definition of the language can be made without loss of generality (change the numbering if another edge is of interest).

In the sequel we describe a rule $(p_1, p_2, \ldots, p_n) \to (q_1, q_2, \ldots, q_n)$ by

and we add the orientation of the edge if it is necessary.

Example 2.4.8. Let

$$G = (\{S, A, B\}, \{a, b, c\}, \Gamma, P, \sigma)$$

where Γ is given by

$\sigma = \lambda S$ (interpreted as

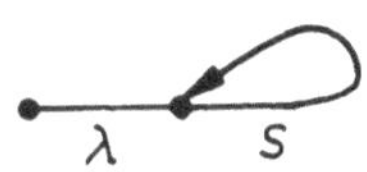

and P contains only rules for the node v_2 given by

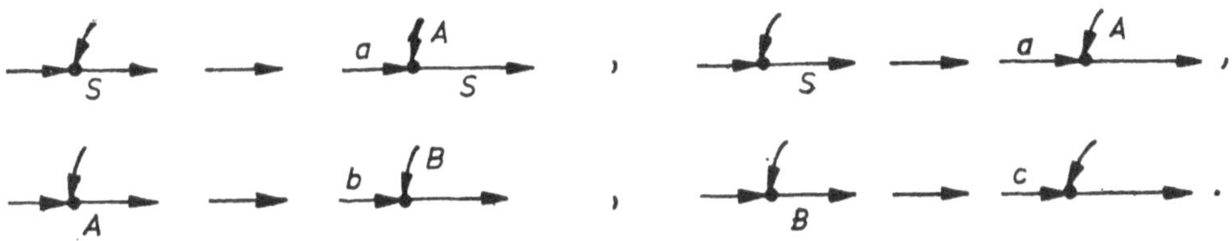

Then a terminating derivation in G has the form (instead of the Γ-words we give the associated labelled version of Γ):

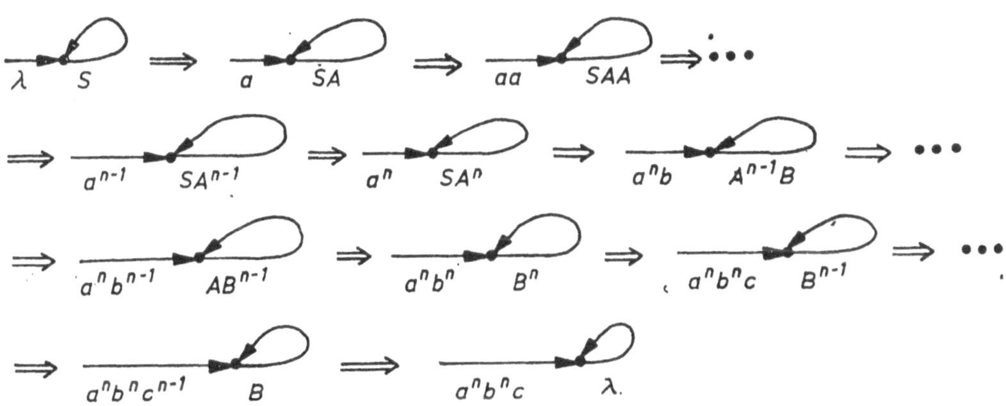

Thus $L(G) = \{a^nb^nc^n : n \geqq 1\}$.

G is called a *context-free grammar based on a graph* iff, for all nodes v, the productions are of the form

$$(\lambda, \lambda, \ldots, \lambda, A, \lambda, \ldots, \lambda) \to (q_1, q_2, \ldots, q_n)$$

with $A \in V_N$, $|q_1q_2 \ldots q_n| \geqq 1$, i.e. with the exception of one word all p_i are empty.

For a given graph Γ by $\mathcal{L}(\Gamma\mathrm{CF})$ we denote the family of languages generated by grammars based on Γ with context-free productions.

Lemma 2.4.7. *For all connected graphs Γ with at least two edges,*

$$\mathscr{L}(\mathrm{CF}) \subseteq \mathscr{L}(\Gamma\mathrm{CF}).$$

Proof. We give the proof only for the special case where Γ is given by

(if Γ has more edges, then we label the remaining ones by λ, and if the orientation of the edges differs from the given orientation we use the reversed words as their labels). Let $G = (V_N, V_T, P, S)$ be a context-free grammar (without λ-rules). Then we set

$$V'_N = V_N \cup \overline{V}_T \quad \text{where} \quad \overline{V}_T = \{\bar{a} : a \in V_T\},$$

and we define the homomorphism h by

$$h(A) = A \quad \text{for} \quad A \in V_N \quad \text{and} \quad h(a) = \bar{a} \quad \text{for} \quad a \in V_T.$$

Further let σ be the word given by

With the production $A \to \alpha B\beta \in P$, $\alpha \in V_T^*$, $\beta \in V_G^*$, $B \in V_N$, we associate the rule

and with $A \to \alpha \in P$, $\alpha \in V_T^*$, we associate

and add the rules

Let P' be the set of all productions constructed in this way. We consider the grammar $G' = (V'_N, V, \Gamma, P', \sigma)$ based on Γ.

It is easy to see that the derivations in G' simulate the leftmost derivations in G. Therefore $L(G') = L(G)$.

Lemma 2.4.8. *For all graphs Γ, $\mathscr{L}(\Gamma\,\mathrm{CF}) \subseteq \mathscr{L}(\mathrm{CS})$.*

Proof. Let $G = (V_N, V_T, \Gamma, P, \sigma)$ be a context-free grammar based on $\Gamma = (U, E)$, $E = \{e_1, e_2, \ldots, e_r\}$. Let $P = \{p_1, p_2, \ldots, p_s\}$, and let v_j be a node of U such that $p_j \in P_{v_j}$. Then we set

$$V'_N = V_N \cup \{[i, j] : 1 \leqq i \leqq s, 1 \leqq j \leqq s(v_i) + 1\}$$
$$\cup \{A_1, A_2, \ldots, A_r, B_1, B_2, \ldots, B_r, Z, Z', S\}.$$

A Γ-word $w = w(1)\, w(2) \ldots w(r)$ will be described now by

$$A_1 w(1)\, B_1 A_2 w(2)\, B_2 \ldots A_r w(r)\, B_r.$$

We define P' as the set of the following productions:

$$S \to [i, 1]\, A_1\, \sigma(1)\, B_1 A_2 \sigma(2)\, B_2 \ldots A_r \sigma(r)\, B_r,\ 1 \leqq i \leqq s$$

(the description of the axiom σ of G is introduced and the symbol $[i, 1]$ indicating the start of the simulation of the production p_i),

$$[i, j]\, x \to x[i, j] \quad \text{for} \quad 1 \leqq i \leqq s, 1 \leqq j \leqq s(v_i) \quad \text{and}$$
$$x \neq A_{i'} \quad \text{if} \quad \alpha_j = +, x \neq B_{i_j} \quad \text{if} \quad \alpha_j = -$$
$$\text{where} \quad S(v_i) = (i_1^{\alpha_1}, i_2^{\alpha_2}, \ldots, i_{s(v_i)}^{\alpha_{s(v_i)}})$$

($[i, j]$ indicates the application of p_i on edge i_j, and it moves from left to right until it reaches A_{i_j} or B_{i_j}),

$$[i, j]\, A_{i_j} p_{i_j} \to A_{i_j} q_{i_j}\, [i, j+1] \quad \text{for} \quad 1 \leqq j \leqq s(v_i), \alpha_{i_j} = +,$$
$$[i, j]\, p_{i_j} B_{i_j} \to q_{i_j} B_{i_j} [i, j+1] \quad \text{for} \quad 1 \leqq j \leqq s(v_i), \alpha_{i_j} = -$$

(this simulates the application of $p_i = (p_{i_1}, \ldots, p_{i_n}) \to (q_{i_1}, \ldots, q_{i_n})$, $n = s(v_i)$ by rewriting of p_{i_j} by q_{i_j} on edge e_{i_j}),

$$x[i, s(v_i) + 1] \to [i, s(v_i) + 1]\, x \quad \text{for} \quad x \neq A_1, 1 \leqq i \leqq s,$$
$$A_1[i, s(v_i) + 1] \to [k, 1]\, A_1 \quad \text{for} \quad 1 \leqq i \leqq s, 1 \leqq k \leqq s$$

($[i, s(v_i) + 1]$ indicates that a rule has been completely simulated, it moves to the left and enforces the simulation of a further production),

$$A_1[i, s(v_i) + 1] \to Z,\ 1 \leqq i \leqq s,$$
$$Zx \to xZ,\ x \in V_T,$$
$$ZB_1 \to Z',$$
$$Z'A_i \to Z',\ 2 \leqq i \leqq r,$$
$$Z'B_i \to Z',\ 2 \leqq i \leqq r - 1,$$
$$Z'B_r \to \lambda$$

(after a complete simulation of a production Z and Z' are introduced, they cancel all symbols A_i, B_i and Z' checks whether the label words on the edges $e_2, e_3, \ldots, e_r$ are empty).

From the explanations given above it follows that $L(G) = L(G')$ for the phrase structure grammar $G' = (V'_N, V_T, P', S)$. Since the rules are length-increasing, except the rules in the last group, which erase $2r + 2$ symbols in each derivation, it follows by the workspace theorem (Theorem 0.2.10) that $L(G') \in \mathcal{L}(\text{CS})$, and the proof is complete.

Finally, we shall say some words on walk grammars. Let us start with a context-free grammar $G = (V_N, V_T, P, S)$. If in some string $w = x_1 A x_2 B x_3$ we first rewrite the mentioned occurrence of A and then the occurrence of B, we can say that the "write head" of the grammar has moved from A to B. We can thus think in terms of automata even when dealing with grammars. We shall formalize this in the following way.

Definition 2.4.9. Let $G = (V_N, V_T, P, S)$ be a context-free grammar, and let D be a derivation according to G,

$$D: S = w_0 \Rightarrow w_1 \Rightarrow \cdots w \Rightarrow w_n \in V_T^*.$$

The "grammar scanner" is initially positioned on S, and for w_j, $1 \leqq j \leqq n$, it is positioned according to the following rules (conventions):

1. If $w_i \Rightarrow w_{i+1}$, $w_i = x_1Ax_2$, $w_{i+1} = x_1yzx_2$, $x_1, x_2, y \in V_G^*$, $z \in V_G$, and the scanner is positioned on A in w_i, then the scanner is positioned on z in w_{i+1}.

2. If $w_i \Rightarrow w_{i+1}$, w_i as above, the used rule is $A \to \lambda$, and the scanner is positioned on A in w_i, then in w_{i+1} the scanner is positioned on the first letter of x_2 if $x_2 \neq \lambda$ or on the last letter of x_1 if $x_2 = \lambda$, $x_1 \neq \lambda$, and the scanner is "lost" if $w_{i+1} = \lambda$.

3. In order to be positioned on the letter which has to be rewritten the scanner can move to the right or to the left.

The walk of the grammar scanner can be coded as follows. If according to the above definition the scanner is positioned on z in $w_i = y_1zy_2Ay_3$, and this occurrence of A is rewritten in $w_i \Rightarrow w_{i+1}$, then we say that the scanner moved k steps to the right, $k = |y_2A|$. If $w_i = x_1Ay_1zy_2$, we say that the scanner moved k steps to the left, $k = |Ay_1|$.

Let us denote the action of rewriting (using a rule) by 0, the scanner moving for one step to the right by 1, and the scanner moving for one step to the left by 2. According to the above cases we write

$$\text{walk } (w_i, D) = 1^k \quad \text{or} \quad \text{walk } (w_i, D) = 2^k,$$

respectively. Thus the scanner walk (including rewriting) in the derivation D will be described by the string

$$\text{walk } (D) = 0 \text{ walk } (w_1, D)\, 0 \text{ walk } (w_2, D) \ldots 0 \text{ walk } (w_{n-1}, D)\, 0\,.$$

In this way a language

$$\text{walk } (G) = \{\text{walk } (D) : D \text{ is a derivation in } G\}$$

can be associated with the grammar G.

Example 2.4.9. Clearly, if G is a linear grammar, then walk (G) is a regular sublanguage of $\{0, 2\}^*$.

Let us now consider the metalinear grammar G with the rules

$$S \to AB,\ A \to Aa,\ B \to bB,\ A \to a,\ B \to b\,.$$

We obtain

$$\text{walk } (G) \cap 0(2^+01^+0)^* = \{020102^301^30 \ldots 2^{2k+1}01^{2k+1}0 : k \geqq 1\}\,.$$

Therefore the language walk (G) is not context-free.

The language walk (G) can be investigated as a goal per se. We shall not insist on this direction here, but we shall define a regulating mechanisms on this basis (in a way analogous to the grammars with control).

Definition 2.4.10. A *regular walk grammar* is a system $G = (V_N, V_T, P, S, C)$ where $G' = (V_N, V_T, P, S)$ is a usual context-free grammar and C is a regular language over $\{0, 1, 2\}$. The language $L(G)$ is defined as

$$L(G) = \{x : x \in V_T^* \text{ and there is a derivation } D : S \overset{*}{\Rightarrow} x \text{ in } G' \text{ such that } \text{walk } (D) \in C\}\,.$$

Let $\mathscr{L}(\text{RW}, X)$, $X \in \{\text{CF}, \text{CF} - \lambda\}$, be the family of languages generated by regular walk grammars. The inclusions

$$\mathscr{L}(\text{RW}, \text{CF} - \lambda) \subseteq \mathscr{L}(\text{CS}) \quad \text{and} \quad \mathscr{L}(\text{RW}, \text{CF}) \subseteq \mathscr{L}(\text{RE})$$

can be proved by a standard construction. The following example will show that the inclusion

$$\mathscr{L}(\text{CF}) \subset \mathscr{L}(\text{RW}, \text{CF} - \lambda)$$

is proper.

Example 2.4.10. We consider the grammar

$$G = (\{S, A, B\}, \{a, b, c\}, P, S, C)$$

with

$$P = \{S \to AB, A \to aAb, B \to cB, A \to ab, B \to c\},$$
$$C = 02(01^+ 02^+)^*.$$

It is easy to see that all correctly terminating derivations have the form

$$S \Rightarrow AB \Rightarrow aAbB \Rightarrow aAbcB \Rightarrow a^2Ab^2cB \Rightarrow a^2Ab^2c^2B \Rightarrow \cdots \Rightarrow a^nAb^nc^nB$$
$$\Rightarrow a^{n+1}b^{n+1}c^nB \Rightarrow a^{n+1}b^{n+1}c^{n+1}.$$

Hence

$$L(G) = \{a^nb^nc^n : n \geqq 1\}.$$

Some variants of the walk restricted grammars might be of interest. For instance, instead of 0 in the walk control language we can consider a nonterminal; the rewriting specified by 0 must now be a rewriting of the corresponding nonterminal. Another possibility is to replace 0 by a production rule label and to use this rule at the corresponding step of a derivation.

Such grammars can be used to characterize context-sensitive languages. For example, let G be a grammar in Kuroda normal form, and let $r: AB \to CD$ be a (non-context-free) rewriting rule in G. Then we can construct a context-free regular walk grammar G' by introducing the associated rules

$$A \to A_r, A_r \to C, B \to B_r, B_r \to D$$

and considering the string AA_r1BB_r (instead of 00100) as a substring of the associated walk control language. Clearly, in this way we can simulate the application of the rule r in G'. Hence we obtain $L(G') = L(G)$.

A similar result is true for the case if we replace 0 by rule labels.

Open problems

2.4.1. Determine $\mathscr{L}(\text{CF}) \cap \mathscr{L}(\text{iCF})$.

2.4.2. Prove or disprove the equality $\mathscr{L}(\text{rCF}) = \mathscr{L}(\text{rCF} - \lambda)$.

2.4.3. Which of the inclusions in Theorem 2.4.2 are proper? In particular, prove or disprove $\mathscr{L}(\text{SC} - \lambda) = \mathscr{L}(\text{CS})$.

2.4.4. Investigate further the generative capacity of grammars based on graphs and regular walk grammars. Is the inclusion $\mathscr{L}(\text{RW}, \text{CF} - \lambda) \subseteq \mathscr{L}(\text{CS})$ proper?

Exercises

2.4.1. Prove that $\mathscr{L}$(rCF) is not closed under intersection with regular languages (see Stotskij (1972-b)).

2.4.2. Prove that $\mathscr{L}$(I) is an AFL (see Aho (1968)).

2.4.3. Prove that $\mathscr{L}(\mathrm{SC} - \lambda)$ is an AFL (see Greibach and Hopcroft (1969)).

2.4.4. A scattered context grammar is called 2-*bounded* if its rules are of the form $(A_1, A_2) \to (w_1, w_2)$ with $|w_1| \leqq 2$, $|w_2| \leqq 2$ and $w_1, w_2 \in (V_G \setminus \{S\})^*$ or $(S) \to (w)$.

Prove that each scattered context language can be generated by a 2-bounded scattered context grammar (see Greibach and Hopcroft (1969)).

2.5. Conclusions

In this section we summarize the hierarchy results given in the previous sections. In order to obtain a not too complicated picture we restrict ourselves to the context-free case. Further we give without proof closure properties and decidability results in Table 2.5.1.

Fig. 2.5.1 contains the hierarchy results. We give only the inclusions. In all cases, if two families are connected, then the upper family contains the lower one, and the containment is proper if the families are connected by an arrow. (In contrast to some other diagrams in this monograph, it is not necessary that two families be incomparable if

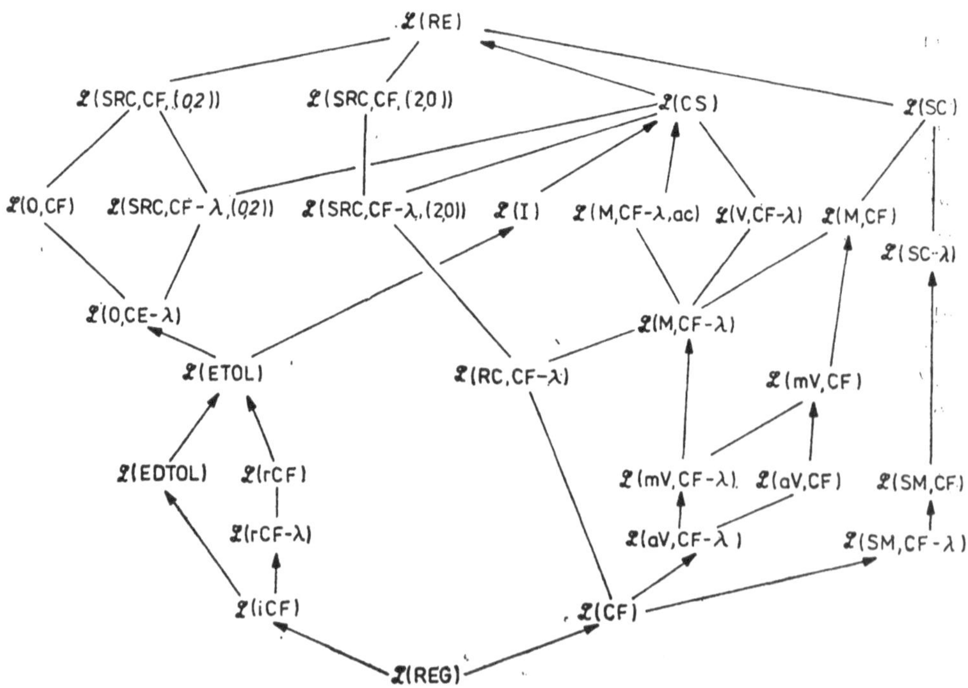

Fig. 2.5.1

Table 2.5.1.

Family ↓ / Operation →	Union	Concatenation	Kleene closure	λ-free homomorphisms	Homomorphisms	Inverse homomorphisms	Intersection with regular languages	Intersection	Membership	Emptiness	Finiteness	Equivalence
$\mathscr{L}$(SC)	+	+	+	+	+	+	+	+	?	−	−	−
$\mathscr{L}$(SC-λ)	+	+	+	+	?	+	+	+	+	−	−	−
$\mathscr{L}$(I)	+	+	+	+	+	+	+	−	+	+	+	−
$\mathscr{L}$(O, CF)	+	+	+	+	+	?	+	?	?	?	?	−
$\mathscr{L}$(O, CF-λ)	+	+	+	+	?	?	+	?	+	?	?	−
$\mathscr{L}$(rCF)	+	+	?	+	+	?	−	−	+	+	?	−
$\mathscr{L}$(rCF-λ)	+	+	?	+	?	?	−	−	+	+	?	−
$\mathscr{L}$(iCF)	+	+	?	+	+	?	?	−	+	+	?	−
$\mathscr{L}$(mV, CF)	+	+	−	+	+	?	+	−	+	+	+	−
$\mathscr{L}$(mV, CF-λ)	+	+	−	+	?	?	+	−	+	+	+	−
$\mathscr{L}$(aV, CF)	+	−	−	+	+	?	+	−	+	+	+	−
$\mathscr{L}$(aV, CF-λ)	+	−	−	+	?	?	+	−	+	+	+	−

they are not connected.) In the diagram we give only one family if there is a number of families which coincide, and below we add the equalities:

$$\begin{aligned}\mathscr{L}(\mathrm{RE}) &= \mathscr{L}(\mathrm{M}, \mathrm{CF}, \mathrm{ac}) = \mathscr{L}(\mathrm{P}, \mathrm{CF}, \mathrm{ac}) = \mathscr{L}(\mathrm{RC}, \mathrm{CF}, \mathrm{ac})\\ &= \mathscr{L}(\mathrm{TV}, \mathrm{CF}, \mathrm{ac}) = \mathscr{L}(\mathrm{rC}, \mathrm{CF}, \mathrm{ac}) = \mathscr{L}(\mathrm{TC}, \mathrm{CF}) = \mathscr{L}(\mathrm{K}, \mathrm{CF})\\ &= \mathscr{L}(\mathrm{B}, \mathrm{CF}) = \mathscr{L}(\mathrm{B_c}, \mathrm{CF}) = \mathscr{L}(\mathrm{SC}, \mathrm{ac}),\end{aligned}$$

$$\mathscr{L}(\mathrm{CS}) = \mathscr{L}(\mathrm{TC}, \mathrm{CF} - \lambda) = \mathscr{L}(\mathrm{K}, \mathrm{CF} - \lambda) = \mathscr{L}(\mathrm{SC} - \lambda, \mathrm{ac}),$$

$$\begin{aligned}\mathscr{L}(\mathrm{M}, \mathrm{CF} - \lambda, \mathrm{ac}) &= \mathscr{L}(\mathrm{P}, \mathrm{CF} - \lambda, \mathrm{ac}) = \mathscr{L}(\mathrm{RC}, \mathrm{CF} - \lambda, \mathrm{ac})\\ &= \mathscr{L}(\mathrm{B}, \mathrm{CF} - \lambda) = \mathscr{L}(\mathrm{B_c}, \mathrm{CF} - \lambda) = \mathscr{L}(\mathrm{TV}, \mathrm{CF} - \lambda, \mathrm{ac})\\ &= \mathscr{L}(\mathrm{rC}, \mathrm{CF} - \lambda, \mathrm{ac}),\end{aligned}$$

$$\begin{aligned}\mathscr{L}(\mathrm{M}, \mathrm{CF}) &= \mathscr{L}(\mathrm{P}, \mathrm{CF}) = \mathscr{L}(\mathrm{TV}, \mathrm{CF}) = \mathscr{L}(\mathrm{rC}, \mathrm{CF}) = \mathscr{L}(\mathrm{uM}, \mathrm{CF})\\ &= \mathscr{L}(\mathrm{V}, \mathrm{CF}) = \mathscr{L}(\mathrm{uSC}) = \mathscr{L}(\mathrm{S}, \mathrm{CF}) = \mathscr{L}(\mathrm{nP}, \mathrm{CF}),\end{aligned}$$

$$\begin{aligned}\mathscr{L}(\mathrm{M}, \mathrm{CF} - \lambda) &= \mathscr{L}(\mathrm{P}, \mathrm{CF} - \lambda) = \mathscr{L}(\mathrm{TV}, \mathrm{CF} - \lambda) = \mathscr{L}(\mathrm{rC}, \mathrm{CF} - \lambda)\\ &= \mathscr{L}(\mathrm{uM}, \mathrm{CF} - \lambda) = \mathscr{L}(\mathrm{uSC} - \lambda) = \mathscr{L}(\mathrm{S}, \mathrm{CF} - \lambda)\\ &= \mathscr{L}(\mathrm{nP}, \mathrm{CF} - \lambda),\end{aligned}$$

$$\mathscr{L}(\mathrm{O}, \mathrm{CF}) = \mathscr{L}(\mathrm{fRC}, \mathrm{CF}),$$

$$\mathscr{L}(\mathrm{O}, \mathrm{CF} - \lambda) = \mathscr{L}(\mathrm{fRC}, \mathrm{CF} - \lambda),$$

$$\mathscr{L}(\mathrm{ETOL}) = \mathscr{L}(\mathrm{Z}, \mathrm{CF})$$

$$\mathscr{L}(\mathrm{mV}, \mathrm{CF}) = \mathscr{L}(\mathrm{uV}, \mathrm{CF}),$$

$$\mathscr{L}(\mathrm{mV}, \mathrm{CF} - \lambda) = \mathscr{L}(\mathrm{uV}, \mathrm{CF} - \lambda).$$

Bibliographical and historical notes

Periodically time variant grammars were first introduced in SALOMAA (1970-a) where their equivalence to matrix grammars was also proved. In some papers the restriction of time variance is considered in connection with (finite) automata, e.g. in BAER and SPANIER (1969), AGASANDJAN (1967), SALOMAA (1968), TEIXEIRA (1974), MASALAGIU (1981).

The regulation by a regular control language (over the production set) was introduced in GINSBURG and SPANIER (1968), but there is a restriction to leftmost derivations. The theory of languages with (regular) control was developed by FRIANT (1968), STOTSKIJ (1968), (1971-b), (1971-c), SALOMAA (1969-a), (1970—a), (1970-b).

Unordered matrix grammars and both types of vector grammars were first introduced in CREMERS and MAYER (1973) where further modifications of the vector grammars can be found (precisely we considered generalized vector grammars in the sense of CREMERS and MAYER (1973)). Their generative power is studied in CREMERS and MAYER (1973). Theorem 2.1.3. with its consequences also first appeared in CREMERS and MAYER (1973); our proof follows the ideas by JANTZEN (1979).

Valence grammars have been defined in PĂUN (1980-b), and there all our results on them can be found.

First the special case of iterative grammars where the graph is a chain was introduced in ABRAHAM (1972) and their equivalence to their associated family in the Chomsky hierarchy was shown in PĂUN (1977-a). The general case has been defined and investigated in GALJUKSHOV (1978). The equivalence to ETOL systems has been proved in DASSOW (1979-a).

The nonterminal-programmed grammars have been defined in PĂUN (1976) where nonterminal versions for matrix and regularly controlled grammars were also studied (see Exercise 1.2.2) and it was shown that all these grammars generate the same family as do the usual ones (with the same type of regulation).

Grammars controlled by a bicolored digraph have been introduced in WOOD (1973-a). The results given in Section 2.2 are taken from PĂUN (1979-d) and from PASCU and PĂUN (1979), partially with new proofs. Also WOOD (1973-b) concerns these grammars.

State grammars have been defined in KASAI (1970). Theorem 2.2.6 is proved in SALOMAA (1970-b) and MORIYA (1973-b) where some modifications are also discussed.

Conditional grammars were introduced in FRIS (1968). SALOMAA (1973-a) proved Theorem 2.3.1. Further results can be found in PĂUN (1979-c) and URBANEK (1983). Modifications of the concept of a conditional grammar (see Exercises 2.3.4, 2.3.5) have been considered by KRAL (1973), NAVRATIL (1970), PĂUN (1979-c).

Tree-controlled grammars have been defined in CULIK and MAURER (1977) with the motivation mentioned in connection with Theorem 2.3.2. The generative power of tree-controlled grammars has been studied in PĂUN (1979-f).

Ordered grammars were introduced in FRIS (1968) where the power with regular and context-sensitive core productions has been determined. Theorem 2.3.4 is taken from MAYER (1972).

The Indian parallelism and Russian parallelism were defined by SIROMONEY and KRITHIVASAN (1974) from India and by LEVITINA (1972) from Russia. The generative power and some further properties are studied in SKYUM (1974), (1976), SALOMAA (1974), CIOBOTARU and PĂUN (1975), KLEIJN and ROZENBERG (1980).

Greibach and Hopcroft (1969) introduced the scattered context grammars and proved that their language family is contained in $\mathscr{L}$(CS), forms an AFL, some normal forms and decidability properties. The comparison of their generative capacity with that of simple matrix grammars is given in Păun (1982-a). The unordered version was studied in Milgram and Rosenfeld (1971) and Mayer (1972).

Aho (1968) defined the indexed grammars and gave already their fundamental properties. Further results can be found in Hayashi (1973), Duske et al. (1979-a), Duske and Parchmann (1984), and Parchmann (1984).

The material on grammars based on graphs is taken from Wechsung (1984) and that on regular walk grammars from Păun (1986).

Theorems of the Bar-Hillel-lemma type for languages generated by regulated rewriting have been presented in Mayer (1972) (for finite index languages, however), Hayashi (1973), Kleijn and Rozenberg (1980). Algorithmic questions and the complexity of the corresponding algorithms have been investigated e.g. in Sudborough (1977), Albert (1982), van Leeuwen (1975). Von Solms (1975-a) gave descriptions of some families in summaterms of special automata.

The monographs by Salomaa (1973-a), Păun (1981-f), Maurer (1969) contain some rizing material on regulated rewriting.

As we already mentioned at the beginning of this chapter we were not able to give explicitly all regulated devices. Finally we give some references to further types of regulations:

Controlled position grammars (Mückstein-Wotschke et al. (1977)) use prescribed sequences of rules given by a regular language and the productions have to be applied to the leftmost symbol of a partition block (partition of the nonterminal set). They generate $\mathscr{L}$(CS). Mückstein-Wotschke et al. (1977) contains results on the size and index of the partition necessary to generate some families.

In *cooperating grammar systems* (Meersman et al. (1978)) the next rule which has to be applied is calculated by the preceding one and the current string. Some modifications have been considered; in most cases their generative power is that of programmed grammars.

In a *functional grammar* (Bachmann (1979)) a sequence of environments is associated with each derivation where the next environment is determined by the applied rule and the preceding environment and the applicability of a rule depends on the current environment. The families of the Chomsky hierarchy can be described in terms of these grammars with leftmost derivations depending on the used environments, functions, and underlying grammars.

1S grammars (Ehrenfeucht et al. (1985)) are grammars with a global forbidden context (which is directed), i.e. all rules have the same forbidden context. They generate $\mathscr{L}$(CF).

In Rozenberg and von Solms (1976) the definition of a random context grammar is changed slightly by requiring that a symbol has to occur at least/at most a certain number of times in the sentential form. This additional counting mechanism does not increase the generative power.

Von Solms (1979), (1982) considered random context grammars where the symbols have to occur or are forbidden in a certain neighbourhood of the letter to be rewritten. These extensions lead to $\mathscr{L}$(CS).

Absolutely parallel grammars (Rajlich (1972)) differ from scattered context grammars in the requirement that all nonterminals of the sentential form have to be rewritten in one derivation step. Therefore these grammars are of finite index (see Chapter 3). Their language family coincides with the family of languages accepted by two-way deterministic finite state transducers.

Further we note that material on indexed grammars and languages can be also found in the papers on *macro grammars*. They are characterized by rewriting of subterms by terms modelling the "call by value" and "call by name" constructs of programming languages; however, their generative power coincides with that of indexed grammars. We mention the following basic papers in this area: Fischer (1968), Engelfriet and Schmidt (1977/78), Mehlhorn (1979), Asveld (1981), Vogler (1986).

Further references to such types of regulated grammars (which mostly do not meet our restrictions mentioned at the beginning of this chapter) which are mainly introduced in order to take into consideration features of programming languages are: Knuth (1968), van Wijngaarden (1969), Koster (1972), Barth (1977), (1978-a), and (1978-b), Dembiński and Małuszyński (1978), Riedewald (1975) and (1978).

Chapter 3. Grammars of Finite Index

Informally speaking, the index of a grammar is the maximal number of nonterminals simultaneously appearing in its terminal derivations (considering the most economical derivations for each string). The finiteness of the index is a natural and a very strong condition with a considerable equalizing power: almost all of the grammars considered in Chapters 1 and 2 lead to the same family of languages under finite index restriction.

3.1. The Generative Power of Finite Index Grammars

Definition 3.1.1. Let G be a grammar of arbitrary type (from those discussed in Chapters 1 and 2), and let V_N, V_T, and S be its nonterminal alphabet, terminal alphabet, and axiom, respectively. For a derivation

$$D : S = w_1 \Rightarrow w_2 \Rightarrow \cdots \Rightarrow w_r = w \in V_T^*$$

according to G, we set

$$\text{Ind}\,(D, G) = \max\,\{|w_i|_{V_N} : 1 \leqq i \leqq r\},$$

and, for $w \in V_T^*$, we define

$$\text{Ind}\,(w, G) = \min\,\{\text{Ind}\,(D, G) : D \text{ is a derivation for } w \text{ in } G\}.$$

The *index of the grammar* G is defined as

$$\text{Ind}\,(G) = \sup\,\{\text{Ind}\,(w, G) : w \in L(G)\}.$$

For a language L in the family $\mathscr{L}(X)$ of languages generated by grammars of some type X, we define

$$\text{Ind}_X\,(L) = \inf\,\{\text{Ind}\,(G) : L(G) = L,\ G \text{ is of type } X\}.$$

When no danger of confusion exists, we shall write Ind (L) instead of $\text{Ind}_X\,(L)$.
For a family $\mathscr{L}(X)$, we set

$$\mathscr{L}_n(X) = \{L : L \in \mathscr{L}(X) \quad \text{and} \quad \text{Ind}_X\,(L) \leqq n\},\ n \geqq 1,$$

$$\mathscr{L}_{\text{fin}}(X) = \bigcup_{n \geqq 1} L_n(X).$$

The aim of this chapter is to investigate the families $\mathscr{L}_{\text{fin}}(X)$ for classes X of grammars with regulated rewriting; sometimes we shall also discuss the families $\mathscr{L}_n(X)$. Again, the matrix grammars (with context-free rules) will be the reference class of grammars.

Lemma 3.1.1. i) *For* $n \geqq 1$,

$$\mathscr{L}_n(\mathrm{M}, \mathrm{CF} - \lambda) \subseteq \mathscr{L}_n(\mathrm{M}, \mathrm{CF}) \quad \textit{and} \quad \mathscr{L}_n(\mathrm{M}, \mathrm{CF} - \lambda, \mathrm{ac}) \subseteq \mathscr{L}_n(\mathrm{M}, \mathrm{CF}, \mathrm{ac}).$$

ii) *For* $n \geqq 1$, $X \in \{\mathrm{CF}, \mathrm{CF} - \lambda\}$,

$$\mathscr{L}_n(\mathrm{M}, X) \subseteq \mathscr{L}_n(\mathrm{M}, X, \mathrm{ac}).$$

Proof. Obvious.

Lemma 3.1.2. *For* $n \geqq 1$,

$$\mathscr{L}_n(\mathrm{M}, \mathrm{CF}) = \mathscr{L}_n(\mathrm{M}, \mathrm{CF} - \lambda).$$

Proof. We shall prove the inclusion $\mathscr{L}_n(\mathrm{M}, \mathrm{CF}) \subseteq \mathscr{L}_n(\mathrm{M}, \mathrm{CF} - \lambda)$ in two steps.

Step 1. Let $G = (V_N, V_T, M, S)$ be a matrix grammar with $\mathrm{Ind}\,(G) = n$. We shall construct a matrix grammar $G' = (V'_N, V_T, M', S')$ equivalent to G and with

$$\mathrm{Ind}\,(G') \leqq n + 1,$$

$$V'_N = V_N^{(1)} \cup V_N^{(2)} \cup \{S'\},\ V_N^{(1)} \cap V_N^{(2)} = \emptyset,\ S' \notin V_N^{(1)} \cup V_N^{(2)},$$

and the matrices in M' have one of the following forms:

(i) $(S \to AB)$, $A \in V_N^{(1)}$, $B \in V_N^{(2)}$,

(ii) $(B \to \lambda)$, $B \in V_N^{(2)}$,

(iii) $(A_1 \to x_1, A_2 \to x_2, \ldots, A_m \to x_m, B \to C)$, $A_i \in V_N^{(1)}$,
$x_i \in (V_N^{(1)} \cup V_T)^+$, $1 \leqq i \leqq m$, $B, C \in V_N^{(2)}$,

(iv) $(S' \to x)$, $x \in V_T^*$.

Let us assume that $X_1, X_2, \ldots, X_r$ are the nonterminals in V_N for which we can obtain derivations $X_i \stackrel{*}{\Rightarrow} \lambda$ by using the rules in $P(M)$. We define the substitutions $s : V_G^* \to 2^{V_G^*}$ by

$$s(x) = \{x\},\ x \in V_G \setminus \{X_1, X_2, \ldots, X_r\},$$

$$s(X_i) = \{\lambda, X_i\},\ 1 \leqq i \leqq r.$$

Then we set

$$V_N^{(1)} = V_N,\ V_N^{(2)} = \{[i_1, i_2, \ldots, i_r] : 0 \leqq i_t \leqq n,\ 1 \leqq t \leqq r\},$$

further let S' be a new symbol, and let M' contain the following matrices:

(1) $(S' \to S[0, 0, \ldots, 0])$

(each derivation $D : S \Rightarrow w_1 \Rightarrow w_2 \Rightarrow \cdots \Rightarrow w_p$ in the grammar G will be simulated in G' by a derivation of the form

$$D' : S' \Rightarrow S[0, 0, \ldots, 0] \Rightarrow x_1[j_{1,1}, j_{1,2}, \ldots, j_{1,r}]$$
$$\Rightarrow x_2[j_{2,1}, j_{2,2}, \ldots, j_{2,r}] \Rightarrow \cdots \Rightarrow x_p[0, 0, \ldots, 0] \Rightarrow x_p$$

with $x_i \in s(w_i)$; the symbols $[j_{i,1}, j_{i,2}, \ldots, j_{i,r}]$ will memorize the number of symbols $X_1, X_2, \ldots, X_r$ which appear in w_i but not in x_i; they are erased in the derivation D at the subsequent steps),

(2) $([0, 0, \ldots, 0] \to \lambda)$,

(3) $(A_{k_1} \to x_{k_1}, A_{k_2} \to x_{k_2}, \ldots, A_{k_t} \to x_{k_t}, [i_1, i_2, \ldots, i_r] \to [j_1, j_2, \ldots, j_r])$

for a matrix $(A_1 \to w_1, A_2 \to w_2, \ldots, A_u \to w_u)$ in M and $[i_1, i_2, \ldots, i_r], [j_1, j_2, \ldots, j_r] \in V'_N$ such that

a) $k_1 < k_2 < \cdots < k_t$ and $\{k_1, k_2, \ldots, k_t\} \subseteq \{1, 2, \ldots, u\}$,

b) $x_{k_i} \in s(w_{k_i}) \setminus \{\lambda\}, 1 \leqq i \leqq t$,

c) $w_j \in \{X_1, X_2, \ldots, X_r\}^*$ for $j \in \{1, 2, \ldots, u\} \setminus \{k_1, k_2, \ldots, k_t\}$,

d) $j_v = i_v + |w_1 w_2 \ldots w_u|_{X_v} - |x_{k_1} x_{k_2} \ldots x_{k_t}|_{X_v} - |A_1 A_2 \ldots A_u|_{X_v} + |A_{k_1} A_{k_2} \ldots A_{k_t}|_{X_v}$, $1 \leqq v \leqq r$

(the symbols X_j, which will eventually be replaced by λ, are avoided and the use of rules which contain such symbols is simulated by modifying the vectors $[i_1, i_2, \ldots, i_r]$),

(4) $(S' \to \lambda)$ if $\lambda \in L(G)$.

From the above explanations one can see that $L(G) = L(G')$, Ind $(G') \leqq n + 1$, and the only λ-rule in G' is $[0, 0, \ldots, 0] \to \lambda$.

Step 2. We now consider the above grammar G' containing matrices of types (1) to (4). We shall transform the symbols in $V_N^{(2)}$ into "subscripts" of symbols in $V_N^{(1)}$, thus avoiding the final λ-rules $C \to \lambda$, $C \in V_N^{(2)}$, and decreasing the index by one.

We construct the matrix grammar $G'' = (V''_N, V_T, M'', S'')$ where

$$V''_N = V_N^{(1)} \cup \{S''\} \cup (V_N^{(1)} \cup \{S'\}) \times V_N^{(2)}$$

with a new symbol S'' and M'' contains the following matrices:

(1) $(S'' \to (A, B))$ for each matrix $(S' \to AB)$ in M', $A \in V_N^{(1)}, B \in V_N^{(2)}$

(at each moment there will be exactly one couple symbol),

(2) $(A \to (A, C), (B, C) \to B)$, $A, B \in V_N^{(1)}, C \in V_N^{(2)}$

(the symbol in $V_N^{(2)}$ can move freely),

(3) $(A_1 \to x_1, \ldots, A_p \to x_p, (B, C) \to (B, D))$ for each matrix $(A_1 \to x_1, \ldots, A_p \to x_p, C \to D) \in M'$, $C, D \in V_N^{(2)}$, $B \in V_N^{(1)}$

(we simulate in this way the rule $C \to D$; this supposes that the string contains a symbol (B, C) where B is not one of the symbols $A_1, A_2, \ldots, A_p$),

(4) $(A_1 \to x'_1, \ldots, A_{i-1} \to x'_{i-1}, (A_i, C) \to x'_i, A_{i+1} \to x'_{i+1}, \ldots, A_p \to x'_p)$
for each matrix $(A_1 \to x_1, \ldots, A_p \to x_p, C \to D) \in M'$, $C, D \in V_N^{(2)}$, $x'_j = x_j$ for $1 \leqq j \leqq p, j \neq k$, and x'_k being obtained from x_k by replacing some nonterminal $B \in V_N^{(1)}$ by (B, D) for some $k \in \{1, 2, \ldots, p\}$

(this simulates the rule $C \to D$ in the case when the current string contains at most the symbols $A_1, A_2, \ldots, A_p$; it supposes that at least one string x_k contains a nonterminal),

(5) $(A_1 \to x_1, \ldots, A_{i-1} \to x_{i-1}, (A_i, C) \to x_i, A_{i+1} \to x_{i+1}, \ldots, A_p \to x_p)$
for each matrix $(A_1 \to x_1, \ldots, A_p \to x_p, C \to D) \in M'$ with $x_1, x_2, \ldots, x_p \in V_T^+$, $C, D \in V_N^{(2)}$ such that there is a matrix $(D \to \lambda) \in M'$

(the use of the terminal matrix $(D \to \lambda)$ is simulated when the matrix $(A_1 \to x_1, A_2 \to x_2, \ldots, A_p \to x_p, C \to D)$ is simulated; thus the explicit application of the λ-rule $D \to \lambda$ is avoided).

The equality $L(G'') = L(G')$ can be easily checked. As G'' is λ-free and $\text{Ind}\,(G'') = \text{Ind}\,(G') - 1$, the proof is finished.

Corollary 1. $\mathscr{L}_{\text{fin}}(\text{M, CF}) = \mathscr{L}_{\text{fin}}(\text{M, CF} - \lambda)$.

Corollary 2. *All the families* $\mathscr{L}_n(\text{M, CF})$, $n \geqq 1$, *and* $\mathscr{L}_{\text{fin}}(\text{M, CF})$ *are closed under arbitrary homomorphisms.*

Proof. A standard construction replacing each terminal a by $h(a)$ in a given grammar proves the assertion.

Lemma 3.1.3. $\mathscr{L}_{\text{fin}}(\text{M, CF, ac}) = \mathscr{L}_{\text{fin}}(\text{M, CF})$.

Proof. Clearly, it is sufficient to prove the inclusion $\mathscr{L}_{\text{fin}}(\text{M, CF, ac}) \subseteq \mathscr{L}_{\text{fin}}(\text{M, CF})$. First let us note that for each matrix grammar $G = (V_N, V_T, M, S, F)$ of finite index we can find an equivalent matrix grammar $G' = (V'_N, V_T, M', S', F')$ also of finite index and in accurate normal form: we simply follow the proof of Lemma 1.3.7 observing that the involved constructions preserve the finiteness of the index. Therefore we can assume that

$$V'_N = V_N^{(1)} \cup V_N^{(2)} \cup \{S', Z\},\ V_N^{(1)} \cap V_N^{(2)} = \emptyset,\ S', Z \notin V_N^{(1)} \cup V_N^{(2)},$$

$V_N^{(1)} = \{A_1, A_2, \ldots, A_r\}$. We construct a matrix grammar $G'' = (V''_N, V_T, M'', S'')$ (without appearance checking) of finite index such that $L(G') = L(G'')$. We set

$$V''_N = V_N^{(1)} \cup \{S'\} \cup \{[i_1, i_2, \ldots, i_r; B] : 0 \leqq i_t \leqq \text{Ind}\,(G'),\ 1 \leqq t \leqq r,\ \ B \in V_N^{(2)}\},$$

$$\begin{aligned} M'' = {} & \{(S' \to A_t[i_1, \ldots, i_r; B]) : (S' \to A_tB) \in M',\ i_t = 1, \text{ and} \\ & \quad i_s = 0 \quad \text{for all} \quad s \neq t\} \\ & \cup \{(A_u \to w, [i_1, \ldots, i_r; B] \to [j_1, \ldots, j_r; C]) : (A_u \to w, B \to C) \in M', \\ & \quad i_u > 0,\ j_t = i_t - |A_u|_{A_t} + |w|_{A_t},\ 1 \leqq t \leqq r\} \\ & \cup \{([i_1, \ldots, i_r; B] \to [i_1, \ldots, i_r; C]) : (A_u \to Z, B \to C) \in M', \\ & \quad A_u \to Z \quad \text{appears in } F' \quad \text{and} \quad i_u = 0\} \\ & \cup \{(A_t \to w, [i_1, \ldots, i_r; B] \to \lambda) : (A_t \to w, B \to \lambda) \in M', \\ & \quad i_t = 1,\ i_s = 0 \quad \text{for all} \quad s \neq t,\ w \in V_T^*\} \\ & \cup \{(S' \to w) : (S' \to w) \in M',\ w \in V_T^*\}. \end{aligned}$$

The components $i_1, i_2, \ldots, i_r$ of the nonterminals $[i_1, \ldots, i_r; B]$ in V''_N count the number of occurrences of nonterminals $A_1, A_2, \ldots, A_r$ in the current string. In this way we can avoid the appearance checking use of rules in F': if $i_t = 0$ we can pass over rules $A_t \to Z$ in F'; if $i_t > 0$, then the derivation must be effective.

The equality $L(G'') = L(G')$ is easy to see and, clearly, $\text{Ind}(G'') \leqq \text{Ind}(G') + 1$.

Theorem 3.1.1.

$$\mathcal{L}_{\text{fin}}(\text{M, CF}) = \mathcal{L}_{\text{fin}}(\text{M, CF} - \lambda) = \mathcal{L}_{\text{fin}}(\text{M, CF, ac}) = \mathcal{L}_{\text{fin}}(\text{M, CF} - \lambda\text{, ac}).$$

Proof. These equalities were proved in the previous two lemmas or follow from them and Lemma 3.1.1.

Theorem 3.1.2. *All the following families of languages with* $X \in \{\text{CF, CF} - \lambda\}$ *are equal to the family* $\mathcal{L}_{\text{fin}}(\text{M, CF})$:

i) $\mathcal{L}_{\text{fin}}(\text{P}, X), \mathcal{L}_{\text{fin}}(\text{P}, X, \text{ac})$,

ii) $\mathcal{L}_{\text{fin}}(\text{RC}, X, \text{ac})$,

iii) $\mathcal{L}_{\text{fin}}(\text{TV}, X), \mathcal{L}_{\text{fin}}(\text{TV}, X, \text{ac})$,

iv) $\mathcal{L}_{\text{fin}}(\text{rC}, X), \mathcal{L}_{\text{fin}}(\text{rC}, X, \text{ac})$,

v) $\mathcal{L}_{\text{fin}}(\text{uM}, X), \mathcal{L}_{\text{fin}}(\text{uM}, X, \text{ac})$,

vi) $\mathcal{L}_{\text{fin}}(\text{V}, X), \mathcal{L}_{\text{fin}}(\text{V}, X, \text{ac})$,

vii) $\mathcal{L}_{\text{fin}}(\text{nP}, X), \mathcal{L}_{\text{fin}}(\text{nP}, X, \text{ac})$,

viii) $\mathcal{L}_{\text{fin}}(\text{B}, X)$,

ix) $\mathcal{L}_{\text{fin}}(\text{S}, X), \mathcal{L}_{\text{fin}}(\text{S}, X, \text{ac})$.

Proof. All these relations follow from the proofs in Chapters 1 or 2 for the corresponding equalities (those proofs involve constructions which preserve the index finiteness) with one exception: the proof of Lemma 2.1.3 (where $\mathcal{L}(\text{rC, CF}) \subseteq \mathcal{L}(\text{P, CF})$ is shown) must be modified in order to keep the index of G' finite. This can be done as follows (the data are those of the proof of Lemma 2.1.3): Take the initial rule $(x\colon S \to XS', \{[S^{(1)}, p] : p \in P\})$ for a new symbol X, do not introduce primed symbols, replace each label $[a]$, $a \in V_T$, by the unique label r_0 and introduce the terminating rule $(r_0 : X \to \lambda, \{r\}_0)$ which will ensure the correct termination of derivations. We obtain a programmed grammar G' such that $L(G') = L(G)$, $\text{Ind}(G') = \text{Ind}(G) + 1$. Therefore $\mathcal{L}_{\text{fin}}(\text{rC}, X) \subseteq \mathcal{L}_{\text{fin}}(\text{P, X})$.

The following lemma and also its proof present techniques which will be used sometimes in the sequel.

Lemma 3.1.4. *For each matrix grammar G of finite index one can construct a matrix grammar G' such that:*

1) $L(G) = L(G')$, $\text{Ind}(G) = \text{Ind}(G')$,

2) *all sentential forms derivable in G' contain distinct nonterminal occurrences,*

3) *if we apply some matrix $(A_1 \to x_1, A_2 \to x_2, \ldots, A_k \to x_k)$ to a string w, then all symbols $A_1, A_2, \ldots, A_k$ occur in w and each rule $A_i \to x_i$ replaces an occurrence of A_i in w.*

Proof. Let $G = (V_N, V_T, M, S)$ be a matrix grammar of finite index k. Let $z = A_1A_2 \ldots A_s$, $s \leqq k$, be a word of length s over V_N, and let $m \in M$. Further let $u_1, u_2,$

..., u_r be the different words with $z \underset{m}{\Longrightarrow} u_i$ in G, $1 \leqq i \leqq r$, which contain at most k nonterminals. Clearly, for each i, $1 \leqq i \leqq r$, there is a partition $u_i = u_{i1}u_{i2} \ldots u_{is}$ such that u_i is obtained from z by the substitution τ given by $\tau(A_j) = u_{ij}$, $1 \leqq j \leqq s$. If $u_i = v_1B_1v_2B_2 \ldots v_tB_tv_{t+1}$ with $v_j \in V_T^*$, $1 \leqq j \leqq t + 1$, and $B_j \in V_N$, $1 \leqq j \leqq t$, then we set

$$u_i' = v_1(B_1, 1, z')\, v_2(B_2, 2, z') \ldots v_t(B_t, t, z')\, v_{t+1},\ z' = B_1B_2 \ldots B_t,$$

$$u_i' = u_{i1}'u_{i2}' \ldots u_{is}' \quad \text{with} \quad |u_{ij}| = |u_{ij}'| \quad \text{for} \quad 1 \leqq j \leqq s.$$

Now we define the matrix grammar $G' = (V_N', V_T, M', S')$ by

$$V_N' = \{(A, i, z) : A \in V_N, 1 \leqq i \leqq |z| \leqq k, z \in V_N^+\},$$

$$S' = (S, 1, S),$$

and M' is the set of all matrices constructed as follows: with each $z = A_1A_2 \ldots A_s \in V_N^+$, $s \leqq k$, $m \in M$, and u_i given as above we associate the matrix

$$(m, z, u_i) : \big((A_1, 1, z) \to u_{i1}', (A_2, 2, z) \to u_{i2}', \ldots, (A_s, s, z) \to u_{is}'\big).$$

By this construction we obtain

$$S \overset{*}{\Rightarrow} \alpha_1A_1\alpha_2A_2 \ldots \alpha_sA_s\alpha_{s+1} \underset{m}{\Longrightarrow} \beta_1B_1\beta_2B_2 \ldots \beta_tB_t\beta_{t+1}$$

with α_m, $1 \leqq m \leqq s$, and β_m, $1 \leqq m \leqq t$, in V_T^* holds in G iff for some i

$$S' \Rightarrow \alpha_1(A_1, 1, z)\, \alpha_2(A_2, 2, z) \ldots \alpha_s(A_s, s, z)\, \alpha_{s+1}$$

$$\underset{(m,z,u_i)}{\Longrightarrow} \beta_1(B_1, 1, z')\, \beta_2(B_2, 2, z') \ldots \beta_t(B_t, t, z')\, \beta_{t+1}$$

with $z = A_1A_2 \ldots A_s$, $z' = B_1B_2 \ldots B_t$. Hence $L(G) = L(G')$ and G' satisfies all the desired conditions.

Now we can continue the list given in Theorem 3.1.2.

Theorem 3.1.3. *For* $X \in \{\text{CF}, \text{CF} - \lambda\}$,

$$\mathcal{L}_{\text{fin}}(\text{M}, X, \text{left-2}) = \mathcal{L}_{\text{fin}}(\text{M}, X).$$

Proof. Let G be a matrix grammar of finite index. Then we construct the matrix grammar G' as in Lemma 3.1.4. Since all derivations in G' are leftmost of type 2 we obtain $\mathcal{L}_{\text{fin}}(\text{M}, X) \subseteq \mathcal{L}_{\text{fin}}(\text{M}, X, \text{left-2})$.

Now let G be a matrix grammar which has finite index if we consider only leftmost derivations of type 2. Then we repeat the construction in the proof of Lemma 3.1.4 also taking into consideration only the leftmost derivations. The obtained grammar G' satisfies $L_{\text{left-2}}(G) = L_{\text{left-2}}(G') = L(G')$ and $\text{Ind}\,(G') = \text{Ind}\,(G)$.

Theorem 3.1.4. *The following inclusions are proper:*

$$\mathcal{L}_{\text{fin}}(\text{SM}, \text{CF} - \lambda) \subset \mathcal{L}_{\text{fin}}(\text{SM}, \text{CF}) \subset \mathcal{L}_{\text{fin}}(\text{M}, \text{CF}).$$

Proof. The language L of the beginning of the proof of Theorem 1.5.5 has $\text{Ind}_{\text{SM}}\,(L) \leqq 4$ because $\text{Ind}\,(G_0) = 4$ for the grammar G_0 constructed there. As this language is not in $\mathcal{L}(\text{SM}, \text{CF} - \lambda)$ the strictness of the first inclusion is shown. The second inclusion is proper because the language $\{a^nb^nc^n : n \geqq 1\}^*$ belongs to $\mathcal{L}_{\text{fin}}(\text{M}, \text{CF} - \lambda) \setminus \mathcal{L}(\text{SM}, \text{CF})$. It remains for us to prove the inclusion $\mathcal{L}_{\text{fin}}(\text{SM}, \text{CF}) \subseteq \mathcal{L}_{\text{fin}}(\text{M}, \text{CF})$.

Let $G = (V_1, V_2, \ldots, V_n, V_T, M, S)$ be a simple matrix grammar with Ind $(G) = nt$, i.e. with respect to each of the alphabets V_i we have the index t. We set $T = \{1, 2, \ldots, t\}$ and construct the grammar $G' = (V'_N, V_T, M', S)$ with

$$V'_N = \{S\} \cup V_N \times T \cup \{[\lambda, \lambda, \ldots, \lambda]\}$$
$$\cup \{[(A_{1,1}, j_1) \ldots (A_{1,r}, j_r), \ldots, (A_{n,1}, j_1) \ldots (A_{n,r}, j_r)] :$$
$$A_{i,p} \in V_i, 1 \leqq i \leqq n, 1 \leqq j_p \leqq t, 1 \leqq p \leqq r \leqq t, \quad \text{and}$$
$$j_u \neq j_v \quad \text{for all} \quad u \neq v\}$$

and the set M' consisting of all matrices of the following forms:

$\big(S \to (A_1, 1)(A_2, 1) \ldots (A_n, 1)[(A_1, 1), (A_2, 1), \ldots, (A_n, 1)]\big)$,

$A_i \in V_i, 1 \leqq i \leqq n$ for $(S \to A_1A_2 \ldots A_n) \in M$,

$\big((A_1, i) \to w'_1, \ldots, (A_n, i) \to w'_n, [x_1, \ldots, x_n] \to [y_1, \ldots, y_n]\big)$

for each matrix $(A_1 \to w_1, \ldots, A_n \to w_n) \in M$ where $x_i, y_i \in (V_i \cup T)^*$ and w'_i is obtained from w_i by replacing each symbol $X \in V_N$ by a symbol (X, s) such that:

a) if we rewrite the string $x_1x_2 \ldots x_n$ by the matrix $\big((A_1, i) \to w'_1, \ldots, (A_n, i) \to w'_n\big)$ as in a simple matrix grammar, (A_j, i) being the leftmost nonterminal in x_i, and then we erase the terminals, we obtain the string $y_1y_2 \ldots y_n$, each y_i being generated from x_i, $1 \leqq i \leqq n$,

b) the nonterminals introduced by strings w'_i are chosen in such a way that $[y_1, \ldots, y_n] \in V'_N$ (that is each y_i contains pairs with distinct second components).

$([\lambda, \lambda, \ldots, \lambda] \to \lambda)$.

It is easy to see that $L(G) = L(G')$ and that Ind (G') = Ind $(G) + 1$. Therefore $L(G) \in \mathscr{L}_{\text{fin}}(\text{M, CF})$ and the proof is complete.

Theorem 3.1.5. i) $\mathscr{L}_{\text{fin}}(\text{CF}) \subset \mathscr{L}_{\text{fin}}(\text{iCF})$,

i) $\mathscr{L}_{\text{fin}}(\text{CF} \subset \mathscr{L}_{\text{fin}}(\text{iCF})$,

ii) $\mathscr{L}_{\text{fin}}(\text{rCF}) \subset \mathscr{L}_{\text{fin}}(\text{M, CF})$,

iii) $\mathscr{L}_{\text{fin}}(\text{O, CF}) \subseteq \mathscr{L}_{\text{fin}}(\text{M, CF})$,

iv) $\mathscr{L}_{\text{fin}}(\text{SC, CF}) = \mathscr{L}_{\text{fin}}(\text{M, CF})$,

v) $\mathscr{L}_{\text{fin}}(\text{M, CF}) \subseteq \mathscr{L}_{\text{fin}}(\text{K, CF})$,

vi) $\mathscr{L}_{\text{fin}}(\text{RC, CF}) \subseteq \mathscr{L}_{\text{fin}}(\text{M, CF})$.

Proof. i) can be obtained by an idea used in some of the previous lemmas: replace each nonterminal A by (A, j) for some integer j; if only different nonterminals (A, j) are present in a sentential form (this can be arranged by choice of j), the parallel derivation is in fact a usual context-free one. Thus we obtain the inclusion $\mathscr{L}_{\text{fin}}(\text{CF}) \subseteq$

$\subseteq \mathcal{L}_{\text{fin}}(\text{iCF})$ which is proper because $\{a^nb^na^nb^n : n \geqq 1\}$ can be generated by an Indian parallel grammar of index 2.

Also the relations ii) to vi) are straightforward (use again the ideas of the proofs of the previous lemmas). The inclusion $\mathcal{L}_{\text{fin}}(\text{rCF}) \subset \mathcal{L}_{\text{fin}}(\text{M, CF})$ is proper because $\{a^nb^nc^n : n \geqq 1\}$ is in $\mathcal{L}_{\text{fin}}(\text{M, CF}) \setminus \mathcal{L}(\text{rCF})$ by Example 2.4.3.

So far we have compared only families of languages of finite index. A natural problem is also to compare $\mathcal{L}_{\text{fin}}(\text{M, CF})$ with $\mathcal{L}(\text{CF})$, $\mathcal{L}(\text{SM}, X)$, $X \in \{\text{REG, LIN, CF}\}$, and $\mathcal{L}(\text{M, CF} - \lambda)$.

Theorem 3.1.6. *$\mathcal{L}_{\text{fin}}(\text{M, CF})$ is incomparable with $\mathcal{L}(\text{CF})$, $\mathcal{L}(\text{SM, CF})$, $\mathcal{L}(\text{SM, CF} - \lambda)$, and it is strictly included in $\mathcal{L}(\text{M, CF} - \lambda)$. $\mathcal{L}(\text{SM, LIN})$ is strictly included in $\mathcal{L}_{\text{fin}}(\text{M, CF})$.*

Proof. As $\{a^nb^nc^n : n \geqq 1\}^*$ belongs to $\mathcal{L}_{\text{fin}}(\text{M, CF}) \setminus \mathcal{L}(\text{SM, CF})$ and the inclusions $\mathcal{L}(\text{SM, LIN}) \subseteq \mathcal{L}_{\text{fin}}(\text{M, CF}) \subseteq \mathcal{L}(\text{M, CF} - \lambda)$ are obvious, the proof would be finished by finding a language $L \in \mathcal{L}(\text{CF})$ which is not in $\mathcal{L}_{\text{fin}}(\text{M, CF})$.

Let $G = (V_N, V_T, M, S)$ be a matrix grammar of finite index. As in the proof of Lemma 3.1.4 we can construct an equivalent grammar G' which is also of finite index and which can generate only sentential forms with distinct nonterminal occurrences. Such a grammar G' can be easily modified into an EDTOL system: replace each matrix $(A_1 \to x_1, A_2 \to x_2, \ldots, A_r \to x_r)$ of G' by a table containing the productions $A_i \to x_i$ for $1 \leqq i \leqq r$ and $A \to A$ for $A \in V_G \setminus \{A_1, A_2, \ldots, A_r\}$. Consequently, $\mathcal{L}_{\text{fin}}(\text{M, CF}) \subseteq \mathcal{L}(\text{EDTOL})$.

In Ehrenfeucht and Rozenberg (1977) it is proved that there are context-free languages which are not in $\mathcal{L}(\text{EDTOL})$ (see also Theorem 0.2.11). This implies $\mathcal{L}(\text{CF}) \setminus \mathcal{L}_{\text{fin}}(\text{M, CF}) \neq \emptyset$ and finishes the proof.

Corollary 1. *For $X \in \{\text{CF, CF} - \lambda\}$, the inclusion*

$$\mathcal{L}_{\text{fin}}(\text{SM}, X) \subset \mathcal{L}(\text{SM}, X)$$

is strict.

Indeed, $\mathcal{L}(\text{CF}) \subseteq \mathcal{L}(\text{SM, CF} - \lambda)$, $\mathcal{L}_{\text{fin}}(\text{SM, CF}) \subseteq \mathcal{L}_{\text{fin}}(\text{M, CF})$, and $\mathcal{L}(\text{CF}) \setminus \mathcal{L}_{\text{fin}}(\text{M, CF}) \neq \emptyset$.

Corollary 2. *The inclusion $\mathcal{L}_{\text{fin}}(\text{M, CF}) \subset \mathcal{L}(\text{EDTOL})$ is strict.*

The inclusion is proper because $\mathcal{L}(\text{EDTOL})$ contains non-semilinear languages, whereas each language in $\mathcal{L}_{\text{fin}}(\text{M, CF})$ is semilinear according to the next lemma.

Lemma 3.1.5. *Each language in $\mathcal{L}_{\text{fin}}(\text{M, CF})$ is semilinear; moreover, it is letter equivalent to a regular language.*

Proof. Clearly, it is sufficient to prove the second statement.

Let $G = (V_N, V_T, M, S)$ be a finite index matrix grammar, $\text{Ind}(G) = k$. We set

$$V'_N = \{[\alpha] : \alpha \in V_N^*, 1 \leqq |\alpha| \leqq k\}$$

and consider the homomorphisms h_N and h_T given by

$$h_N(A) = A \quad \text{for} \quad A \in V_N, h_N(a) = \lambda \quad \text{for} \quad a \in V_T,$$

$$h_T(A) = \lambda \quad \text{for} \quad A \in V_N, h_T(a) = a \quad \text{for} \quad a \in V_T.$$

Further we define the regular grammar $G' = (V'_N, V_T, P, [S])$ by

$$P = \{[\alpha] \to [\beta]\, h_T(x_1x_2 \dots x_n) : [\alpha], [\beta] \in V'_N,$$

$$(A_1 \to x_1, A_2 \to x_2, \dots, A_n \to x_n) \in M, \text{ and } \beta = h_N(W) \text{ where } W \text{ is obtained from } \alpha \text{ by application of } (A_1 \to x_1, A_2 \to x_2, \dots, A_n \to x_n)\}$$

$$\cup \{[\alpha] \to w : [\alpha] \in V'_N, w \in V_T^*, \text{ there is a terminal matrix } (A_1 \to x_1, A_2 \to x_2, \dots, A_n \to x_n) \in M \text{ whose application to } \alpha \text{ yields } w\}.$$

Clearly, the languages $L(G)$ and $L(G')$ are letter equivalent.

Corollary. *Each one-letter language in* $\mathcal{L}_{\text{fin}}(\text{M, CF})$ *is regular.*

Let us now consider the families $\mathcal{L}_n(\text{M, CF})$, $n \geqq 1$. Their hierarchy is infinite. In order to prove this assertion we use the following generalization of the Bar-Hillel lemma to finite index matrix languages.

Lemma 3.1.6. *For each infinite language* $L \in \mathcal{L}_n(\text{M, CF})$, *there is a string* $z \in L$ *which can be written in the form*

$$z = u_1v_1w_1x_1u_2v_2w_2x_2 \dots u_kv_kw_kx_ku_{k+1}$$

with $k \leqq n$, $|v_1x_1v_2x_2 \dots v_kx_k| > 0$, *and*

$$u_1v_1^iw_1x_1^iu_2v_2^iw_2x_2^i \dots u_kv_k^iw_kx_k^iu_{k+1} \in L$$

for all $i \geqq 1$.

Proof. Let $G = (V_N, V_T, M, S)$ be a λ-free matrix grammar of index n such that the sentential forms contain only distinct nonterminals (by Lemma 3.1.4 this can be assumed). Then we set

$$Q = \{x : x \in V_N^*, 0 \leqq |x| \leqq n\} \quad \text{and} \quad N = \text{Card}\,(Q).$$

For a matrix m: $(A_1 \to x_1, A_2 \to x_2, \dots, A_r \to x_r) \in M$ let

$$c(m) = \sum_{i=1}^{r} |x_i| - r,\ C(M) = \max\,\{c(m) : m \in M\},\ p = N \cdot C(M).$$

Each string $z \in L(G)$ having $|z| > p$ has only derivations of length greater than $N + 1$. Therefore all derivations of z whose index is not greater than n have the form

$$D : S \overset{*}{\Rightarrow} z_1 \overset{+}{\Rightarrow} z_2 \overset{*}{\Rightarrow} z$$

with $h_N(z_1) = h_N(z_2)$ where h_N is the homomorphism defined in the proof of the previous lemma. As G is λ-free we obtain $z_1 = z_2$ if $|z_1| = |z_2|$, and we can remove the subderivation $z_1 \overset{+}{\Rightarrow} z_2$. Consequently, we can find a derivation D as above with $|z_1| < |z_2|$. Let us denote by d the sequence of matrices used in the subderivation $z_1 \overset{+}{\Rightarrow} z_2$; for an arbitrary string α, by $\alpha^{(t)}$ we denote the string obtained by applying t times the sequence d of matrices to α (the derivations are uniquely identified by the used matrices).

Let us assume that $z_1 = \alpha_1A_1\alpha_2A_2 \dots \alpha_kA_k\alpha_{k+1}$. Clearly, $k \leqq n$ holds. Let $j_1, j_2, \dots, j_s$, $1 \leqq j_1 < j_2 < \dots < j_s \leqq k$ be the subscripts for which the nonterminal A_{j_r} are recurrent in the derivation $z_1 \overset{+}{\Rightarrow} z_2$, that is, using the matrices in d each A_{j_r} produces a string $\beta_{j_r}A_{j_r}\gamma_{j_r}$. There is at least one such integer j_p. For all A_j with $j \notin \{j_1, j_2, \dots, j_s\}$, by the use of the matrices in d we get either a terminal string or a string which does not contain the symbol A_j. We write

$$z_1 = \alpha'_1 A_{j_1} \alpha'_2 A_{j_2} \ldots \alpha'_s A_{j_s} \alpha'_{s+1}$$

where α'_j are either terminal strings or contain only nonrecurrent nonterminals. There is a constant q_0 such that after applying the sequence d of matrices q_0 times all strings α'_j are replaced by some terminal strings $u_1, u_2, \ldots, u_{s+1}$ (otherwise the number of nonterminal occurrences is increased beyond n). Similarly, for each $r \in \{1, 2, \ldots, s\}$, there is an integer q_r such that after applying the sequence d of matrices q_r times each string $\beta_{j_r}, \gamma_{j_r}$ as above is replaced by a terminal string. Let q be the product of the integers $q_0, q_1, \ldots, q_s$. Then it follows that after using q times the matrices in d, starting from z_1, all strings $\alpha'_r, \beta_r, \gamma_r$ introduced in the derivation $z_1 \overset{*}{\Rightarrow} z_2$ are replaced by terminal strings. Let v_r, x_r be the strings obtained in this way from β_r, γ_r, respectively. After q applications of the sequence d we obtain a string

$$u_1 v_1 \delta_1 x_1 u_2 v_2 \delta_2 x_2 \ldots u_s v_s \delta_s x_s u_{s+1}$$

with $\delta_r = A_{j_r}^{(q-1)}$, $1 \leqq r \leqq s$. It follows that by applications of the matrices of d to δ_r we obtain a string $v_r \delta_r x_r$. Consequently, after $q \cdot t$ applications of the sequence d we obtain a string

$$\omega = u_1 v_1^{t+1} \delta_1 x_1^{t+1} u_2 v_2^{t+1} \delta_2 x_2^{t+1} \ldots u_s v_s^{t+1} \delta_s x_s^{t+1} u_{s+1}.$$

As $h_N(\omega) = h_N(z_2)$, it follows that we can apply to ω the matrices which were used in the subderivation $z_2 \overset{*}{\Rightarrow} z$ of D, and in this way we obtain a terminal string of the form

$$u_1 v_1^{t+1} w_1 x_1^{t+1} u_2 v_2^{t+1} w_2 x_2^{t+1} \ldots u_s v_s^{t+1} w_s x_s^{t+1} u_{s+1}.$$

For each t this string is in $L(G)$.

In conclusion, the string we look for is

$$u_1 v_1 w_1 x_1 u_2 v_2 w_2 x_2 \ldots u_s v_s w_s x_s u_{s+1}.$$

It satisfies $s \leqq n$ and $|v_1 x_1 v_2 x_2 \ldots v_s x_s| > 0$. This completes the proof.

Theorem 3.1.7. *The inclusions* $\mathcal{L}_n(\mathrm{M, CF}) \subset \mathcal{L}_{n+1}(\mathrm{M, CF})$ *are proper for all* $n \geqq 1$.

Proof. We consider the languages

$$L_n = \{b(a^i b)^{2n} : i \geqq 1\}$$

for $n \geqq 1$. The following grammar generates L_n:

$$G_n = (\{S, A_1, A_2, \ldots, A_n\}, \{a, b\}, M, S),$$

$$M = \{(S \to bA_1bA_2 \ldots bA_nb), (A_1 \to aA_1a, A_2 \to aA_2a, \ldots, A_n \to aA_na),$$

$$(A_1 \to aba, A_2 \to aba, \ldots, A_n \to aba)\}.$$

Since $\mathrm{Ind}(G_n) = n$, if follows that $L_n \in \mathcal{L}_n(\mathrm{M, CF})$, $n \geqq 1$.

Let us now assume that $L_n \in \mathcal{L}_{n-1}(\mathrm{M, CF})$, $n \geqq 2$. Let $z \in L_n$ be a string with the properties (see Lemma 3.1.6) $z = u_1 v_1 w_1 x_1 \ldots u_m v_m w_m x_m u_{m+1}$, $m \leqq n - 1$, $|v_1 x_1 \ldots v_m x_m| > 0$ and $z_i = u_1 v_1^i w_1 x_1^i \ldots u_m v_m^i w_m x_m^i u_{m+1} \in L_n$ for all $i \geqq 1$. There are $2m$ strings v_i, x_i. As $z \in L_n$, it contains $2n$ substrings of the form ba^pb. Each string in L_n contains exactly

$2n + 1$ symbols b, therefore no v_i or x_i can contain the symbol b. As $2m \leqq 2(n-1) < 2n$, it follows that there is at least one substring ba^pb in z which does not contain substrings v_i or x_i. In conclusion, each string z_j with $j \geqq 1$ contains at least two substrings ba^pb, ba^qb with $p \neq q$ (one as in z and one obtained by iterating some non-empty v_i or x_i). This means that z_i, $i \geqq 1$, are not in L_n which contradicts the previous lemma. Consequently, $L_n \notin \mathcal{L}_{n-1}(\mathrm{M, CF})$, and the proof is finished.

Open problems

3.1.1. Are there context-free languages such that $\mathrm{Ind}_{\mathrm{CF}}(L)$ is strictly greater than $\mathrm{Ind}_{\mathrm{M}}(L)$? In particular, are there context-free languages in $\mathcal{L}_{\mathrm{fin}}(\mathrm{M, CF})$ having infinite context-free index?

3.1.2. Which of these inclusions are proper (see Theorem 3.1.5): $\mathcal{L}_{\mathrm{fin}}(\mathrm{O, CF}) \subseteq \mathcal{L}_{\mathrm{fin}}(\mathrm{M, CF}) \subseteq \mathcal{L}_{\mathrm{fin}}(\mathrm{K, CF})$, $\mathcal{L}_{\mathrm{fin}}(\mathrm{RC, CF}) \subseteq \mathcal{L}_{\mathrm{fin}}(\mathrm{M, CF})$?

Exercises

3.1.1. Find matrix grammars of finite index generating regular one-letter languages.

3.1.2. For a finite index matrix grammar $G = (V_N, V_T, M, S)$ let Lab (M) be a set of labels of matrices in M, and let Sz (G) be the Szilard language associated to G (the set of strings in Lab $(M)^*$ corresponding to terminal derivations in G (see section 7.2)). Prove that Sz (G) $\in \mathcal{L}_{\mathrm{fin}}(\mathrm{M, CF})$ and that Sz (G) contains an infinite regular language when $L(G)$ is infinite.

3.1.3. An arbitrary language $L \subseteq V^*$ is completely prefixed if, for each $x, y \in L$, either $x \in \mathrm{Pref}(y)$ or $y \in \mathrm{Pref}(x)$. Prove that each completely prefixed language in $\mathcal{L}_{\mathrm{fin}}(\mathrm{M, CF})$ is regular. (*Hint:* use Lemma 3.1.6 as well as the fact that $\mathcal{L}_{\mathrm{fin}}(\mathrm{M, CF})$ is a full AFL.)

3.1.4. Prove an Ogden-like variant (with distinguished positions) of Lemma 3.1.6 (see Beauquier (1979)).

3.1.5. Prove that $\mathcal{L}_{\mathrm{fin}}(\mathrm{M, CF})$ equals the family of languages generated by tree-controlled grammars with finite control language (see Păun (1979-f)).

3.2. Properties of Grammars and Languages of Finite Index

By Theorems 3.1.1, 3.1.2, and 3.1.5 we shall restrict ourselves in this section to the consideration of $\mathcal{L}_{\mathrm{fin}}(\mathrm{M, CF})$ and $\mathcal{L}_n(\mathrm{M, CF})$, $n \geqq 1$. First we study the closure properties of these families.

Lemma 3.2.1. *Each family $\mathcal{L}_n(\mathrm{M, CF})$, $n \geqq 1$, is closed under union, arbitrary homomorphisms, and intersection with regular sets.*

Proof. The closure under union is obvious, the closure under homomorphisms was already pointed out after Lemma 3.1.2.

Let us consider the matrix grammar $G = (V_N, V_T, M, S)$ having finite index, and let

$A = (K, V_T, s_0, f, F)$ be a finite automaton. We construct the matrix grammar $G' = (V'_N, V_T, M', S')$ with

$$V'_N = \{S'\} \cup K \times V_N \times K,$$
$$M' = \{(S' \to (s_0, S, s_f)) : s_f \in F\} \cup A(M)$$

where $A(M)$ is the set of matrices obtained from M in the following way.

For a rule $r: X \to x_1X_1x_2X_2 \dots x_tX_tx_{t+1}$ of $P(M)$, $X_i \in V_N$, $1 \leqq i \leqq t$, $x_i \in V_T^*$, $1 \leqq i \leqq t + 1$, we consider the set of rules

$$A(r) = \{(s, X, s') \to x_1(s_1, X_1, s_1')\, x_2(s_2, X_2, s_2') \dots x_t(s_t, X_t, s_t')\, x_{t+1}:$$
$$s, s', s_i, s_i' \in K,\ 1 \leqq i \leqq t,\ s_1 \in f(s, x_1),$$
$$s_{i+1} \in f(s_i', x_{i+1}),\ 1 \leqq i \leqq t - 1,\ s' \in f(s_t', x_{t+1})\}.$$

Then

$$A(M) = \{(r_1', r_2', \dots, r_k') : (r_1, r_2, \dots, r_k) \in M,\ r_i' \in A(r_i),\ 1 \leqq i \leqq k\}.$$

The equality $L(G') = L(G) \cap L(A)$ is obvious since the required conditions for the first and third components of the nonterminals ensure that the word is accepted by A. Further, Ind (G') = Ind (G) holds.

Lemma 3.2.2. *Each family $\mathcal{L}_n$(M, CF), $n \geqq 1$, is closed under substitution by regular sets.*

Proof. Let $G = (V_N, V_T, M, S)$ be a λ-free matrix grammar of index n satisfying the conditions given in Lemma 3.1.4, and let $s: V_T^* \to 2^{U^*}$ be a substitution such that $s(a) \in \mathcal{L}(\text{REG})$ for all $a \in V_T$.

Assume $M = \{m_1, m_2, \dots, m_l\}$. We identify the kth terminal symbol appearing in the right hand member of the jth rule of the matrix m_i by a triple (i, j, k). For each such (i, j, k), let $G_{i,j,k}$ be a grammar for the language $s(a_{i,j,k})$. If the rule j is terminal, then all corresponding grammars $G_{i,j,k}$ are right-linear i. e. contain rules of the forms $A \to xB$, $A \to x$, A, B nonterminals, x a terminal string). If a rule j is non-terminal, $A \to xBy$, $B \in V_N$ and $y \in V_T^*$, then the grammars $G_{i,j,k}$ for the indeces (i, j, k) identifying symbols in y are left-linear i. e. contain rules of the forms $C \to Dz$, $C \to z$, C, D nonterminals, z a terminal string). Let

$$G_{i,j,k} = (V_N^{i,j,k}, V_T^{i,j,k}, P^{i,j,k}, S^{i,j,k}).$$

We assume that all alphabets $V_N^{i,j,k}$ are pairwise disjoint and disjoint to V_N. Now we construct the grammar $G' = (V'_N, U, M', S')$ in the following way:

a) We introduce in M' the matrix $(S' \to S)$ and all matrices of M which do not contain terminal symbols.

b.1) For each matrix $m_i : (A_1 \to x_1, A_2 \to x_2, \dots, A_r \to x_r)$ of M such that the string $x_1x_2 \dots x_r$ contains at least a terminal symbol, we introduce in M' the matrix

$$(A_1 \to (A_1, m_i), A_2 \to (A_2, m_i), \dots, A_r \to (A_r, m_i))$$

where (A_j, m_i) are new symbols, $1 \leqq j \leqq r$.

b.2) For each rule $A_j \to x_j$ as above with $x_j \in V_N^*$, we introduce in M' the matrix

$$((A_j, m_i) \to x_j).$$

b.3) If $A_j \to x_j$ as above and $x_j = a_1a_2 \ldots a_s \ldots a_p$, $a_s \in V_T$, for $i \leqq s \leqq p$; then we introduce in M' the matrices

$$\big((A_j, m_i) \to S^{i,j,1}\big),$$
$$(X_{i,j,k} \to wY_{i,j,k}) \text{ if this rule is in } P_i^{i,j,k},\ 1 \leqq k \leqq p,$$
$$(X_{i,j,k} \to wS^{i,j,k+1}) \text{ if } X_{i,j,k} \to w \in P^{i,j,k},\ w \in (V_T^{i,j,k})^*,\ 1 \leqq k \leqq p-1,$$
$$(X_{i,j,p} \to w) \text{ if this rule is in } P^{i,j,p},\ w \in (V_T^{i,j,p})^*.$$

b.4) If the rule $A_j \to x_j$ has the right-hand side

$$x_j = a_1 \ldots a_pB_1a_{p+1} \ldots a_{p+q}B_2a_{p+q+1} \ldots a_{u-1}B_sa_u \ldots a_{u+v}$$

with $a_k \in V_T$, $B_k \in V_N$ for all possible values of k, then we introduce in M' the following matrices:

$$\big((A_j, m_i) \to S^{i,j,1}\big),$$
$$(X_{i,j,k} \to wY_{i,j,k}) \text{ if this rule is in } P^{i,j,k},\ 1 \leqq k \leqq p,$$
$$(X_{i,j,k} \to wS^{i,j,k+1}) \text{ if } X_{i,j,k} \to w \text{ is a terminal rule in } P^{i,j,k},$$
$$1 \leqq k \leqq p-1,$$
$$(X_{i,j,p} \to wB_1S^{i,j,p+1}) \text{ if } X_{i,j,p} \to w \text{ is a terminal rule in } P^{i,j,p},$$
$$(X_{i,j,k} \to wY_{i,j,k}) \text{ if this rule is in } P^{i,j,k},\ p+1 \leqq k \leqq p+q,$$
$$\ldots$$
$$(X_{i,j,u-2} \to wS^{i,j,u-1}) \text{ if } X_{i,j,u-2} \to w \text{ is a terminal rule in } P^{i,j,u-2},$$
$$(X_{i,j,u-1} \to wY_{i,j,u-1}) \text{ if this rule is in } P^{i,j,u-1},$$
$$(X_{i,j,u-1} \to wS^{i,j,u+v}) \text{ if } X_{i,j,u-1} \to w \text{ is a terminal rule in } P^{i,j,u-1},$$
$$(X_{i,j,k} \to Y_{i,j,k}w) \text{ if this rule is in } P^{i,j,k},\ u \leqq k \leqq u+v,$$
$$(X_{i,j,k} \to S^{i,j,k-1}w) \text{ if } X_{i,j,k} \to w \text{ is a terminal rule in } P^{i,j,k},$$
$$u+1 \leqq k \leqq u+v,$$
$$(X_{i,j,u} \to B_sw) \text{ if } X_{i,j,u} \to w \text{ is a terminal rule in } P^{i,j,u}.$$

We introduce in V'_N all symbols of V_N and $V_N^{i,j,k}$ for all i, j, k as well as S' and all symbols (A_j, m_i), $A_j \in V_N$, $m_i \in M$.

The derivations in the grammar G' go as follows. Each matrix $m_i : (A_1 \to x_1, A_2 \to x_2, \ldots, A_r \to x_r)$ in M is simulated by replacing first each occurence of A_j (the symbols are distinct) by (A_j, m_i). Then each symbol (A_j, m_i) is rewritten by rules in the above groups b.2), b.3), b.4), performing in this way both the use of $A_j \to x_j$ and the substitution of the terminals in x_j according to s. It is easy to see that $L(G') = s\big(L(G)\big)$ and Ind (G') = Ind (G). Therefore $s\big(L(G)\big) \in \mathscr{L}_n(\mathrm{M, CF})$.

From the above Lemmas 3.2.1 and 3.2.2, and Theorem 0.1.2 we obtain

Theorem 3.2.1. *Each family* $\mathscr{L}_n(\mathrm{M, CF})$, $n \geqq 1$, *is a full semi-AFL (and is therefore also closed under gsm mappings, inverse gsm mappings, left and right quotients by regular sets).*

Theorem 3.2.2. *No family $\mathcal{L}_n(\mathrm{M, CF})$, $n \geqq 1$, is closed under concatenation, Kleene-closure, substitution, intersection, complementation, and permutation.*

Proof. We consider the language

$$L_n = \{b(a^ib)^{2n} : i \geqq 1\}$$

which belongs to $\mathcal{L}_n(\mathrm{M, CF}) \setminus \mathcal{L}_{n-1}(\mathrm{M, CF})$ (see the proof of Theorem 3.1.7) and the homomorphism $h : \{a, b\}^* \to \{c, d\}^*$ defined by $h(a) = c$, $h(b) = d$. Then the language $L_nh(L_n)$ does not belong to $\mathcal{L}_n(\mathrm{M, CF})$. Indeed, let $G = (V_N, V_T, M, S)$ be a (λ-free) matrix grammar of index at most n which generates this language. There is a finite number of derivations $S \stackrel{*}{\Rightarrow} w$ which do not contain two sentential forms w_1, w_2 with $h_N(w_1) = h_N(w_2)$ where h_N is again the homomorphism defined in the proof of Lemma 3.1.5. Let p be the maximal length of the strings generated in this way. For all other strings in $L_nh(L_n)$ we can follow the proof of Lemma 3.1.6 and identify in their derivations of index not greater than n recurrent nonterminals, $X \stackrel{*}{\Rightarrow} xXy$ with terminal strings x, y, appearing in subderivations of the form $w_1 \stackrel{*}{\Rightarrow} w_2$, $h_N(w_1) = h_N(w_2)$. At most n recurrent nonterminals can be simultaneously present. On the other hand, the strings in $L_nh(L_n)$ contain exactly $2n$ subwords ba^ib and exactly $2n$ subwords dc^jd, $i, j \geqq 1$. It follows that in each subderivation $w_1 \stackrel{*}{\Rightarrow} w_2$ as above at least n nonterminals must be recurrent in order to increase simultaneously $2n$ positions. Consequently, except for a finite set of strings, all strings in $L_nh(L_n)$ are generated by involving subderivations $w_1 \stackrel{*}{\Rightarrow} w_2$ in which n recurrent symbols appear, $X_i \stackrel{*}{\Rightarrow} x_iX_iy_i$, $1 \leqq i \leqq n$. The strings x_i, y_i in these derivations cannot contain occurrences of b and d. Moreover, if $x_i, y_i \in \{a\}^*$ for some i, then X_i cannot generate symbols c, and if $x_i, y_i \in \{c\}^*$, then X_i cannot generate symbols a. In conclusion, if $x_1x_2 \in L(G)$, $x_1 \in L_n$, $x_2 \in h(L_n)$, then either $|x_1| \leqq p$ or $|x_2| \leqq p$ (one half must be produced by a non-recurrent derivation). However, $L_nh(L_n)$ contains strings with arbitrarily many symbols a and arbitrarily many symbols c. This is the desired contradiction.

Now we consider the language $L_n\{e\} \in \mathcal{L}_n(\mathrm{M, CF})$ and suppose that $(L_n\{e\})^+ \in \mathcal{L}_n(\mathrm{M, CF})$. We define the substitution s and the homomorphism h' by

$$s: \{a, b, e\}^* \to 2^{\{a,b,c,d,e\}^*},\ s(a) = \{a, c\},\ s(b) = \{b, d\},\ s(e) = \{e\},$$

$$h': \{a, b, c, d, e\}^* \to \{a, b, c, d\}^+,\ h'(e) = \lambda,\ h'(x) = x \quad \text{for} \quad x \in \{a, b, c, d\}.$$

Then we obtain

$$h'\big(s((L_n\{e\})^*\big) \cap \{a\}\ \{b\}^*\ \{e\}\ \{c, d\}^*\ \{e\} = L_nh(L_n).$$

As $\mathcal{L}_n(\mathrm{M, CF})$ is a full semi-AFL and $L_nh(L_n) \notin \mathcal{L}_n(\mathrm{M, CF})$ it follows that this family is not closed under Kleene closure.

The nonclosure under substitution follows from the nonclosure under concatenation (or under Kleene-+).

Let

$$L_1 = \{a^nb^n : n \geqq 1\}^+,$$

$$L_2 = \{a^nb^{k_1}a^{k_1}b^{k_2}a^{k_2} \ldots b^{k_{n-1}}a^{k_{n-1}}b^m : n, m, k_i \geqq 1,\ 1 \leqq i \leqq n - 1\}.$$

These languages are generated by context-free grammars with the rules

$$S \to SA,\ S \to A,\ A \to aAb,\ A \to ab$$

and

$$S \to AB, B \to bB, B \to b, A \to aAC, C \to bCa, C \to ba, A \to a,$$

respectively. Therefore L_1 and L_2 are in $\mathscr{L}_2(\text{M, CF})$. Since

$$L_1 \cap L_2 = \{(a^n b^n)^n : n \geqq 1\}$$

and this language is not semilinear, we obtain the nonclosure under intersection for $\mathscr{L}_n(\text{M, CF}), n \geqq 2$. For $n = 1$, the result is known from the equality $\mathscr{L}_1(\text{M, CF}) = \mathscr{L}(\text{LIN})$.

The nonclosure under intersection (together with the closure under union) implies the nonclosure under complementation.

Finally, we consider the regular languages

$$L_n' = \{a_1 a_2 \dots a_{2(n+1)}\}^+ \quad \text{and} \quad R = \{a_1\}^* \{a_2\}^* \dots \{a_{2(n+1)}\}^*.$$

If Perm $(L_n') \in \mathscr{L}_n(\text{M, CF})$, then Perm $(L_n') \cap R \in \mathscr{L}_n(\text{M, CF})$. However,

$$\text{Perm } (L_n') \cap R = \{a_1^i a_2^i \dots a_{2(n+1)}^i : i \geqq 1\}$$

does not satisfy the generalization of the Bar-Hillel lemma to matrix languages of index n. This contradiction concludes the proof.

From the above results we see that the family $\mathscr{L}_{\text{fin}}(\text{M, CF})$ is also a full semi-AFL, (which is not closed under intersection and complementation, since the above language $L_1 \cap L_2$ is not in $\mathscr{L}_{\text{fin}}(\text{M, CF})$). In fact, we have

Theorem 3.2.3. *The family* $\mathscr{L}_{\text{fin}}(\text{M, CF})$ *is a substitution closed full AFL.*

Proof. It is sufficient to prove the closure under substitution. Let $G = (V_N, V_T, M, S)$ be a matrix grammar of finite index, and let s be a substitution such that $s(a) \in U^*$, $s(a) \in \mathscr{L}_{\text{fin}}(\text{M, CF})$ for each $a \in V_T$. Further, for $a \in V_T$, let $G^a = (V_N^a, V_T^a, M^a, S^a)$ be a grammar generating $s(a)$ and Ind $(G^a) = k_a$. Again, we assume that the alphabets V_N^a are pairwise disjoint and disjoint to V_N. Without loss of generality we can also assume that S and S^a, $a \in V_T$, appear only in the left-hand side of some rules. We construct the matrix grammar $G' = (V_N', U, M', S')$ with

$$V_N' = V_N \cup \bigcup_{a \in V_T} V_N^a \cup \{S', A\} \cup \{[a, i] : a \in V_T, 0 \leqq i \leqq k_a\} \cup \{a' : a \in V_T\},$$

$$M' = \{(S' \to AS)\}$$

$\cup \{(A \to A, X_1 \to x_1', X_2 \to x_2', \dots, X_t \to x_t') :$

$(X_1 \to x_1, X_2 \to x_2, \dots, X_t \to x_t) \in M$ and x_i' is obtained from x_i by replacing each $a \in V_T$ by $a'\}$

$\cup \{(A \to [a, 1], a' \to S^a) : a \in V_T\}$

$\cup \{([a, i] \to [a, j], X_1 \to x_1, X_2 \to x_2, X_t \to x_t) :$

$(X_1 \to x_1, X_2 \to x_2, \dots, X_t \to x_t) \in M^a$ and

$j = i - t + |x_1 x_2 \dots x_t|_{V_N^a}\}$

$\cup \{([a, 0] \to A) : a \in V_T\}$

$\cup \{(A \to \lambda)\}.$

In the presence of A we can simulate the matrices in M; the presence of some $[a, i]$ imposes the simulation of a matrix in M^a. At each moment at most one symbol a', $a \in V_T$, is replaced by S^a in order to perform a derivation in G^a and passing to another grammar G^b or to the simulation of a new matrix in M is possible only after finishing the derivation in G^a. In conclusion, $L(G') = s(L(G))$.

We set

$$q = \max \{|x_1 x_2 \dots x_t| : (X_1 \to x_1, X_2, \to x_2, \dots, X_t \to x_t) \in M\}.$$

Then

$$\text{Ind}(G') \leqq \text{Ind}(G) + q + \max \{k_a : a \in V_T\}.$$

Therefore $s(L(G)) \in \mathcal{L}_{\text{fin}}(\text{M, CF})$, and the proof is finished.

Let us consider now some decision problems for matrix grammars of finite index.

Theorem 3.2.4. *The membership, emptiness, and finiteness problems are decidable for finite index matrix grammars.*

Proof. Let G be a matrix grammar of finite index and let G' be the regular grammar constructed in the proof of Lemma 3.1.5. Obviously $L(G)$ is empty, finite, or infinite if and only if $L(G')$ is empty, finite, or infinite, respectively, which is decidable for regular grammars. The decidability of the membership problem follows from the decidability of this problem for (λ-free) matrix grammars of arbitrary index.

As the linear simple matrix grammars (and hence the regular ones) are matrix grammars of finite index, it follows that all the problems which are undecidable for regular simple matrix grammars are undecidable for finite index matrix grammars, too. Consequently, from Theorem 1.5.7 we obtain

Theorem 3.2.5. *The following decision problems are undecidable for arbitrary finite index matrix grammars G_1, G_2:*

i) *Is $L(G_1)$ regular or equal to V^*?*

ii) *Is $L(G_1) \cap L(G_2)$ empty, finite, or regular?*

iii) *Is $L(G_1) \subseteq L(G_2)$ or $L(G_1) = L(G_2)$?*

iv) *Is $L(G_1)$ context-free?*

v) *Is $L(G_1) \cap L(G_2)$ context-free or in $\mathcal{L}_{\text{fin}}(\text{M, CF})$?*

(Note that the latter two statements are not contained in Theorem 1.5.7, but they can be proved by analogous arguments.)

A specific question is the following.

Theorem 3.2.6. *It is undecidable whether an arbitrary matrix grammar generates a finite index matrix language.*

Proof. Let $L_1 \subseteq V_1^*, L_2 \subseteq V_2^*, V_1 \cap V_2 = \emptyset$, $L_1 \in \mathcal{L}_{\text{fin}}(\text{M, CF})$, $L_2 \in \mathcal{L}(\text{M, CF}) \setminus \mathcal{L}_{\text{fin}}(\text{M, CF})$. We consider the language $L_3 = L_1 V_2^* \cup V_1^* L_2$. We obtain $L_3 \in \mathcal{L}_{\text{fin}}(\text{M, CF})$ if and only if $L_1 = V_1^*$ (see the proof of Theorem 1.3.6), and this is undecidable. Therefore it is undecidable whether $L_3 \in \mathcal{L}_{\text{fin}}(\text{M, CF})$, too.

Remark. In GRUSKA (1969) it is proved that there is no algorithm for the calculation of Ind (G) for an arbitrary context-free grammar G. Since each context-free grammar can be interpreted as matrix grammar, this assertion is also true for matrix grammars.

As we already mentioned earlier, for each matrix language of finite index there is a matrix grammar of finite index in accurate normal form which generates this language. In fact — a context-free-like property — the matrices of the form $(A \to B, X \to Y)$ can also be eliminated. We omit the proof of this assertion and leave it to the reader (see Păun (1980-e)). Such a result is essentially involved in the proof of the next theorem.

Theorem 3.2.7. *The complement of a finite index matrix language is context-sensitive.*

Proof. Let us call a finite index matrix grammar in accurate normal form *reduced* if it generates only sentential forms with mutually different nonterminal occurrences and if it has no matrices of the form $(A \to B, X \to Y)$. According to the previous discussion and Lemma 3.1.4, for each language $L \in \mathcal{L}_{fin}(\mathrm{M, CF})$ there is a grammar G generating L which is reduced and of finite index. Let us note that in a reduced grammar each derivation is precisely identified only by the string of matrices. This holds because,

i) each matrix can be used in one position at most,

ii) if a derivation produces a string x then it has at most $2|x|$ steps,

iii) it uses at most $|x|$ matrices of the form $(A \to w, X \to Y)$ with $|w| \geqq 1$ and a nonterminal occurrence in w, including an S-matrix, and at most $|x|$ matrices of the form $(A \to w, X \to Y)$ or $(A \to w, X \to a)$ where w is a terminal string.

These remarks lead to the following construction.

Let $G = (V_N, V_T, M, S)$ be a reduced finite index matrix grammar, and let $R = \{m_1, m_2, \ldots, m_r\}$ be a set of labels for matrices in M. We consider the following procedure in order to produce the strings in the complement of $L(G)$:

(1) generate the string $x = \lambda \in V_T^*$;

(2) generate the string $y = m_1 \in R^*$;

(3) construct the derivation which corresponds to the string y (it is unique);

(4) if the above derivation is terminal and the generated string is x, then we pass to a string $x' \in V_T^*$ which follows x in the lexicographic order, and go to step (2) with $x = x'$;

(5) if the derivation is not possible at all, or if it is not terminating, or if it generates a string different from x, then we generate the next string $y' \in R^*$ in the lexicographic order, and we go to step (6);

(6) if $|y'| \leqq 2|x|$ then we go to step (3) with $y = y'$; if $|y'| > 2|x|$ then x belongs to the complement of $L(G)$; we write x, generate the next string $x' \in V_T^*$ in the lexicographic order and go to step (2) with $x = x'$.

It is a straightforward (but a tedious) task to encode the above procedure as a type-0 grammar with bounded workspace (remember that $|y| \leqq 2|x| + 1$ for all, x, y as above). Consequently, $V_T^* \setminus L(G) \in \mathcal{L}(\mathrm{CS})$.

This result is important in connection with the celebrated LBA problem and the open problem whether $\mathcal{L}(\mathrm{CS})$ is closed under complementation. Although it is not closed under complementation, the family $\mathcal{L}_{fin}(\mathrm{M, CF})$ leads by this operation to context-sensitive languages only.

Open problems

3.2.1. At the end of Section 2.1 (open problem 2.1.2) it is pointed out that a length-increasing grammar with a control in $\mathcal{L}$(SM, LIN) generates a context-sensitive language. *Conjecture*: a similar result holds also for control languages in $\mathcal{L}_{fin}$(M, CF).

3.2.2. In GRUSKA (1973) it is proved that the family of finite index context-free languages is the smallest full AFL closed under substitution and containing $\mathcal{L}$(LIN). Is there a similar result for $\mathcal{L}_{fin}$(M, CF)? For example, is $\mathcal{L}_{fin}$(M, CF) the smallest substitution closed full AFL containing $\mathcal{L}$(SM, LIN)?

Exercises

3.2.1. Prove that the family $\mathcal{L}_{fin}$(M, CF) is closed under doubling $\left(d(L) = \{xx : x \in L\}\right)$.

3.2.2. Prove that, for each language $L \in \mathcal{L}_{fin}$(M, CF), one can find a finite index matrix grammar G such that $L = L(G)$ and each matrix of G (different from $(S \to \lambda)$) introduces at least one terminal symbol.

3.2.3. Investigate the closure properties of the two families of finite index simple matrix languages $\mathcal{L}_{fin}$(SM, CF) and $\mathcal{L}_{fin}$(SM, CF $-\lambda$).

3.2.4. Let $s: V^* \to 2^{U^*}$ be a substitution and define the mapping $s^{-1}: 2^{U^*} \to 2^{V^*}$ by

$$s^{-1}(L) = \{x : x \in V^*, s(x) \subseteq L\} \quad \text{for} \quad L \subseteq U^*.$$

Prove that $\mathcal{L}_{fin}$(M, CF) is not closed under this operation. (*Hint*: the closure under this operation implies the closure under intersection.)

3.2.5. A language is called *Parikh-bounded* if it contains a letter-equivalent bounded sublanguage. Prove that each language in $\mathcal{L}_{fin}$(M, CF) is Parikh-bounded (see LATTEUX, TERTLUTTE (1985)), but there are matrix languages which do not have this property (PĂUN (1985-a)). (A language L is called *bounded* if $L \subseteq \{w_1\}^* \dots \{w_r\}^*$ for some words $w_1, \dots, w_r$.)

Bibliographical and historical remarks

The index was defined (for matrix grammars) by BRAINERD (1968), where it was proved that the length set of each finite index matrix language contains an infinite arithmetical progression. In MAYER (1972) this property was extended to many other classes of regulated grammars. The index was then investigated in a lot of papers for context-free grammars and languages. Theorem 3.1.1. and 3.1.3 are from PĂUN (1979-b). Many of the equalities in Theorem 3.1.2 appear in ROZENBERG and VERMEIR (1978-a), (1978-b) where the index is also defined for ETOL systems, and it has been proved that $\mathcal{L}_{fin}$(M, CF) equals the family of languages generated by ETOL(as well as EDTOL) systems of finite index and that the results of Theorem 3.1.1 and 3.1.2 hold for the families of languages of index n, too. Some of these results also appear in PĂUN (1979-e), (1981-c). Lemma 3.1.6 and Theorem 3.1.7 are from PĂUN (1980-c). The closure properties of the family of finite index matrix languages have been investigated in ROZENBERG and VERMEIR (1978-a), PĂUN (1977-b), (1979-b), (1983). Theorem 3.2.7

is from PĂUN (1980-e). The existence of context-free languages which have infinite matrix index has been proved in BEAUQUIER (1979) by a direct technical argument concerning the iterative pairs of finite index matrix languages. In that paper it is also proved that the full AFL $\mathscr{L}_{\text{fin}}(\text{M, CF})$ is not principal. (For a language L, by AFL (L) let us denote the smallest AFL containing L. A family $\mathscr{L}$ of languages is called *principal* if there is a language L such that $\mathscr{L} = \text{AFL}(L)$ and then L is called the generator of $\mathscr{L}$. Similar notions can be defined for semi-AFLs. For details on this area, see GINSBURG (1975).) LATTEUX (1979) is a related paper.

Recently, ROZOY (1985) proved that D_{ab}, the Dyck language over $\{a, b\}$, is also not a matrix language of finite index (from Theorem 3.1.6 here and from BEAUQUIER (1979) it only follows that any generator of $\mathscr{L}(\text{CF})$, therefore each Dyck language over at least two pairs of parantheses, is not in $\mathscr{L}_{\text{fin}}(\text{M, CF})$).

Another recent result in this area has been presented by FERMENT (1984-a), (1984-b): each semi-AFL $\mathscr{L}_n(\text{M, CF})$, $n \geqq 1$, is principal (compare this result to that of BEAUQUIER (1979): $\mathscr{L}_{\text{fin}}(\text{M, CF})$ is not principal).

Note added in proof: In 1987 N. IMMERMANN and R. SZELEPCZENYI proved that $\mathscr{L}(CS)$ is closed under complement. From this fact Theorem 3. 2. 7 follows easily.

Chapter 4. The Syntactic Complexity of Regulated Rewriting

Usually, the first step of the work of a computer is the compilation of a program written in a higher programming language (such (as FORTRAN, PASCAL, etc.) into a machine-oriented language. Thus a part of the working space of the computer (storage etc.) is blocked by the internal compiler, and, clearly, the size of the compiler depends on the size of the description of the grammar which underlies the higher programming language. Hence there is a practical need for economical descriptions of languages.

Simple measures for the complexity of a grammar $G = (V_N, V_T, P, S)$ are the cardinalities of V_N or P or the total number of occurrences of letters in P (note that for practical purposes one has to minimize mostly a combination of these parameters), and then the descriptional or syntactic complexity of a language is defined as the minimal complexity of grammars generating the considered language.

In the theory of context-free languages there are known some results about the relative succinctness of different types of grammars. Let us mention one of these (see Bucher et al. (1981)): For a finite language L, let $p_1(L)$ be the minimal number of productions which are necessary for the generation of L by linear grammars, and let p_2 be the minimal number of productions required in order to generate L by (arbitrary) context-free grammars. Obviously, $p_2(L) \leqq p_1(L)$ for all (finite) languages L. However, there is a sequence of finite languages L_n, $n \in \mathbb{N}$, such that $\lim\limits_{n \to \infty} \frac{p_2(L_n)}{p_1(L_n)} = 0$, i.e. with respect to the descriptional complexity measure "number of productions" the general context-free grammars can be much more economical representations of a language than the linear ones.

In Chapter 1 it is proved that matrix, programmed, and random context grammars are more powerful than context-free grammars. However, this concerns only the generative power. It is a natural question to ask what is the relative succinctness of the regulated grammars and the context-free grammars.

Further, it is shown that the three mentioned types of grammars with appearance checking generate the same family of languages. However, the constructions, which are given in the proofs for this fact and which simulate the derivation steps in a grammar of a certain type by the derivation in a grammar of another type, increase often the number of nonterminals and/or productions, i.e. usually the simulating grammar has a greater syntactic complexity. Therefore it is also a natural question whether or not the representation of languages by a certain type of grammar is more economical than the descriptions by grammars of a different type.

One of the aims of this chapter is to answer these and some related questions. Thus the results given below will also contribute to a comparative study of the regulation mechanisms.

This comparison will concern only context-free, matrix, programmed, and random context grammars, where the latter three have only context-free core productions.

4.1. Nonterminal Complexity. Comparison

Definition 4.1.1. Let X be a family of grammars, $G \in X$, $L \in \mathcal{L}(X)$. By $\mathrm{Var}(G)$ we denote the cardinality of the set of nonterminals of G, and we set

$$\mathrm{Var}_X(L) = \min\{\mathrm{Var}(G) : G \in X, L = L(G)\}.$$

Let us consider some examples.

Example 4.1.1. Let $T_n = \bigcup_{i=1}^{n} \{a_i^j : j \geqq 1\}$. Then

i) $\mathrm{Var}_{\mathrm{CF}\text{-}\lambda}(T_n) = n + 1$,

ii) $\mathrm{Var}_{(\mathrm{P},\mathrm{CF}\text{-}\lambda)}(T_n) = 1$,

iii) $\mathrm{Var}_{(\mathrm{RC},\mathrm{CF}\text{-}\lambda,\mathrm{ac})}(T_n) = n + 1$,

iv) there is an unbounded mapping $f : \mathbb{N} \to \mathbb{N}$ such that

$$f(n) \leqq \mathrm{Var}_{(\mathrm{RC},\mathrm{CF},\mathrm{ac})}(T_n) \leqq]\log_2 n[+ 2.$$

Proof. i) T_n is generated by the context-free grammar

$$G = (\{S, A_1, A_2, \ldots, A_n\}, \{a_1, a_2, \ldots, a_n\}, P, S)$$

with

$$P = \bigcup_{i=1}^{n} \{S \to A_i, A_i \to A_iA_i, A_i \to a_i\}.$$

This proves that $\mathrm{Var}_{\mathrm{CF}\text{-}\lambda}(T_n) \leqq n + 1$.

Now we show that the generation of T_n by context-free grammars (without λ-rules) requires at least $n + 1$ nonterminals. In order to do this, let $G' = (V_N, \{a_1, a_2, \ldots, a_n\}, P', S')$ be a context-free grammar generating T_n. For a sufficiently large number m, we consider a derivation of a_i^m in G', say

$$S' \Rightarrow w_{i,1} \Rightarrow w_{i,2} \Rightarrow w_{i,3} \Rightarrow \cdots \Rightarrow w_{i,u_i} \Rightarrow a_i^m.$$

Then $w_{i,u_i} = a_i^{j_i}A_ia_i^{j_i'}$ for some nonterminal A_i and some integers j_i, j_i', and the last rule which is applied in this derivation is $A_i \to a_i^{v_i}$ for some $v_i \geqq 1$. Now assume that there are two integers i, j, $1 \leqq i < j \leqq n$, such that $A_i = A_j$. Then there is a correct derivation

$$S' \Rightarrow w_{i,1} \Rightarrow \cdots \Rightarrow w_{i,u_i} = a_i^{j_i}A_ja_i^{j_i'} \Rightarrow a_i^{j_i}a_j^{v_j}a_i^{j_i'}$$

in G' which produces a word not contained in T_n. Hence for $1 \leqq i, j \leqq n$, $i \neq j$, $A_i \neq A_j$ holds.

Now assume that $S' = A_i$ for some i, $1 \leqq i \leqq n$. Then there is a derivation

$$S' \Rightarrow w_{i,1} \Rightarrow \cdots \Rightarrow w_{i,u_i} = a_i^{j_i}S'a_i^{j_i'} \Rightarrow a_i^{j_i}a_ja_i^{j_i'}$$

since $S' \stackrel{*}{\Rightarrow} a_j$ is a derivation in G'. Again, we obtain a contradiction.

Thus $V_N \supseteq \{S', A_1, A_2, \ldots, A_n\}$, and this implies $\mathrm{Var}_{\mathrm{CF}\text{-}\lambda}(T_n) \geqq n + 1$.

ii) T_n is generated by the programmed grammar

$$G'' = (\{S''\}, \{a_1, a_2, \ldots, a_n\}, P'', S'')$$

with

$$P'' = \{(0\colon S'' \to S''S'', \{0, 1, \ldots, n\}, \emptyset)\}$$
$$\cup \{(i\colon S'' \to a_i, \{i\}, \emptyset) : 1 \leqq i \leqq n\}.$$

Since $\mathrm{Var}(G'') = 1$, and obviously one nonterminal is necessary in each grammar, $\mathrm{Var}_{(\mathrm{P,CF}\text{-}\lambda)}(T_n) = 1$.

iii) Since the grammar given in the proof of i) is also a random context grammar, $\mathrm{Var}_{(\mathrm{RC,CF}\text{-}\lambda,\mathrm{ac})}(T_n) \leqq n + 1$.

Further, the proof for the lower estimation for the context-free grammars is valid for random context grammars, too, since the words w_{i,u_i}, $1 \leqq i \leqq n$, contain only one nonterminal and thus the conditions of random context are the same for all these words and also for the axiom. Hence $\mathrm{Var}_{(\mathrm{RC,CF}\text{-}\lambda,\mathrm{ac})}(T_n) \geqq n + 1$.

iv) First we prove the upper estimation by giving a random context grammar G which generates T_n. For the sake of simplicity we shall describe the construction for the case $n = 2^m$.

Let $U = \{A_1, A_2, \ldots, A_m\}$, and let $U_1, U_2, \ldots, U_{2^m}$ be an enumeration of the subsets of U. Further, let $U_i' = U \setminus U_i$ for $1 \leqq i \leqq 2^m$. Now we define G by

$$G = (U \cup \{S, A\}, \{a_1, a_2, \ldots, a_n\}, P, S)$$

where

$$P = \{(S \to A_iS, \emptyset, \emptyset) : 1 \leqq i \leqq m\}$$
$$\cup \{(S \to A, \emptyset, \emptyset), (A \to AA, \emptyset, \emptyset)\}$$
$$\cup \{(A \to a_i, U_i, \{S\} \cup U_i') : 1 \leqq i \leqq 2^m\}$$
$$\cup \{(A_j \to \lambda, \emptyset, \{S, A\}) : 1 \leqq j \leqq m\}.$$

Each derivation in G starts with

$$S \Rightarrow A_{i_1}S \Rightarrow A_{i_1}A_{i_2}S \Rightarrow \cdots \Rightarrow A_{i_1}A_{i_2} \ldots A_{i_k}S \Rightarrow A_{i_1}A_{i_2} \ldots A_{i_k}A$$
$$\Rightarrow A_{i_1} \ldots A_{i_k}AA \Rightarrow A_{i_1} \ldots A_{i_k}AAA \Rightarrow \cdots \Rightarrow A_{i_1}A_{i_2} \ldots A_{i_k}A^r,\ r \geqq 1.$$

If $\{A_{i_1}, A_{i_2}, \ldots, A_{i_k}\} = U_i$, then we can apply only the rules $A \to AA$ or $A \to a_i$ as long as A is present. Hence the only continuation is

$$A_{i_1}A_{i_2} \ldots A_{i_k}A^r \overset{*}{\Rightarrow} A_{i_1}A_{i_2} \ldots A_{i_k}a_i^s,\ s \geqq r,$$

and now we have to apply erasing rules $A_j \to \lambda$, $1 \leqq j \leqq m$, which shows that $L(G) = T_n$. Thus $\mathrm{Var}_{(\mathrm{RC,CF,ac})}(T_n) \leqq m + 2$.

We now prove the lower estimate. Assume the contrary, i.e. that there is a constant k such that, for each n, there is a random context grammar G_n with at most k nonterminals and with $L(G_n) = T_n$. Let $p\colon (A \to w, Q, R)$ be a production of G_n. With p we associate the following character: $(A, Q, R, \min(w) \cap V_N)$ where $\min(w)$ denotes the set of symbols occurring in w. It is easy to see that the number of rules in G with different characters is smaller than $q = k(2^k)^3$. Now let $n > q$ and let r be a sufficiently large number. We consider a derivation

$$S \Rightarrow w_{i,1} \Rightarrow w_{i,2} \Rightarrow \cdots \Rightarrow w_{i,s_i} \Rightarrow w_{i,s_i+1} \Rightarrow \cdots \Rightarrow w_{i,t_i} = a_i^r$$

where the core productions applied to $w_{i,j}$, $s_i + 1 \leqq j \leqq t_i - 1$, are of the form $A \to \lambda$ or $A \to B$, $A, B \in V_N$, and the production $p(i)$ applied to w_{i,s_i} is of the form $A_i \to v_i$ with $|v_i|_{a_i} \geqq 1$. Then $|w_{i,s_i}|_{a_i} \geqq 1$, $|w_{i,s_i}|_{a_j} = 0$ for $j \neq i$. Since $n > q$, there are two numbers k_1 and k_2 such that $p(k_1)$ and $p(k_2)$ have the same character. Hence there is a derivation

$$S \stackrel{*}{\Rightarrow} w_{k_1,1} \Rightarrow \cdots \Rightarrow w_{k_1,s_{k_1}} \xRightarrow[p(k_2)]{} u_1 \Rightarrow u_2 \Rightarrow \cdots \Rightarrow u_t$$

with $u_t \in V_T^*$, $|u_t|_{a_{k_1}} \geqq 1$, $|u_t|_{a_{k_2}} \geqq 1$. Thus $u_t \notin T_n$, and therefore the number of nonterminals is not bounded.

In the sequel we shall often use the following notation: if the production $A \to w$ occurs in a matrix i times in succession, then we write $[A \to w]^i$.

Example 4.1.2. Let $S_n = \bigcup_{i=1}^{n} \{a_i^i w a_i : w \in \{a_1, a_2, \ldots, a_i\}^*\}$. Then

i) $\mathrm{Var}_{(\mathrm{M,CF}\text{-}\lambda)}(S_n) \leqq 3$,

ii) $\mathrm{Var}_{(\mathrm{RC,CF}\text{-}\lambda,\mathrm{ac})}(S_n) = n + 1$.

Proof. i) S_n is generated by the matrix grammar

$$G = (\{S, A, B\}, \{a_1, a_2, \ldots, a_n\}, M, S, \emptyset)$$

where M consists of the matrices

$$r_i\colon (S \to A^i B),\ 1 \leqq i \leqq n,$$

$$s_i\colon ([A \to S]^i, [S \to A]^i, B \to a_i B),\ 1 \leqq i \leqq n,$$

$$t_i\colon ([A \to a_i]^i, B \to a_i),\ 1 \leqq i \leqq n.$$

This can be seen as follows. Let us consider a word of the form $z = A^i w B$ with $1 \leqq i \leqq n$. Clearly, to z we can apply only the matrices s_j and t_j with $j \leqq i$, and we obtain

$$z \Rightarrow A^i w a_j B \quad \text{if} \quad s_j \quad \text{is applied,}$$

$$z \Rightarrow a_i^i w a_i \quad \text{if} \quad t_i \quad \text{is applied,}$$

and without loss of generality

$$z \Rightarrow a_j^j A^{i-j} w a_j \quad \text{if} \quad t_j,\ j < i, \text{ is applied.}$$

In the latter case the derivation stops since no matrix is applicable (r_k requires S, s_k and t_k require a B). Thus the terminating derivations in G have the structure

$$S \Rightarrow A^i B \Rightarrow A^i a_{j_1} B \Rightarrow A^i a_{j_1} a_{j_2} B \Rightarrow \cdots \Rightarrow A^i a_{j_1} a_{j_2} \ldots a_{j_r} B$$

$$\Rightarrow a_i^i a_{j_1} a_{j_2} \ldots a_{j_r} a_i$$

where $j_u \leqq i$ for $1 \leqq u \leqq r$. Hence $L(G) = S_n$.

ii) Let $G' = (V_N, \{a_1, a_2, \ldots, a_n\}, P, S')$ be a random context grammar (without erasing rules) such that $L(G') = S_n$. For sufficiently large r, we consider the words $a_i^r \in S_n$ and their derivations

$$S' \Rightarrow w_{i,1} \Rightarrow \cdots \Rightarrow w_{i,u_i} \underset{p_i}{\Longrightarrow} a_i^r .$$

As in Example 4.1.1 iii) $w_{i,u_i} = a_i^{r_i} A_i a_i^{r_i'}$ and the production p_i is of the form $(A_i \to a_i^{k_i}, \emptyset, R)$ with $k_i \geqq 1$. Assume that $A_i = A_j$ for some $1 \leqq j < i \leqq n$. Then we have the correct derivation

$$S \Rightarrow w_{j,1} \Rightarrow \cdots \Rightarrow w_{j,u_j} = a_j^{r_j} A_i a_j^{r_j'} \Rightarrow a_j^{r_j} a_i^{k_i} a_j^{r_j'} = w .$$

Since r is sufficiently large and $j < i$, $w \notin S_n$. By analogous arguments, $S \neq A_i$ for $1 \leqq i \leqq n$. The assertion is proved.

Example 4.1.3. Let $R_n = \bigcup_{i=1}^{n-1} \{(a^i b)^m b : m \geqq 1\}$ for $n \geqq 3$. Then

i) $\mathrm{Var}_{\mathrm{CF}\text{-}\lambda}(R_n) = n$.

ii) $\mathrm{Var}_{(\mathrm{RC,CF}\text{-}\lambda,\mathrm{ac})}(R_n) \leqq 8$.

Proof. i) Let $G = (V_N, V_T, P, S)$ be a context-free grammar generating R_n. First let us note that, for each nonterminal $A \neq S$, there is a production $A \to uAv$, $uv \neq \lambda$, since otherwise we can replace A by w, if $A \to w \in P$, in all right-hand sides of productions in P. Thus by applying some rules in P to u and v we can get a derivation $A \overset{*}{\Rightarrow} u'Av'$, $u'v' \in V_T^*$ for $A \neq S$.

Now let us consider a derivation of $w_i = (a^i b)^m b$ for sufficiently large m, say

$$S \Rightarrow w_{i,1} \Rightarrow \cdots \Rightarrow z_{i,1} A_i z_{i,2} \Rightarrow z_{i,1} x_i z_{i,2} = w_i \in V_T^* .$$

Without loss of generality we may assume that $z_{i,1} = (a^i b)^t z_i$ for some $t > 0$. Obviously, $A_i \neq S$ since otherwise we have the derivation

$$S \overset{*}{\Rightarrow} z_{i,1} S z_{i,2} \overset{*}{\Rightarrow} (a^i b)^t z_{i,1} (a^j b)^s b z_{i,2} \notin R_n .$$

Let $A_i \overset{*}{\Rightarrow} u_i A_i v_i$ be the derivation with $u_i v_i \in V_T^+$ which exists for the letter A_i, and without loss of generality let $u_i \neq \lambda$. Then

$$S \overset{*}{\Rightarrow} z_{i,1} A_i z_{i,2} \overset{*}{\Rightarrow} z_{i,1} u_i A_i v_i z_{i,2} \Rightarrow \cdots \Rightarrow z_{i,1} u_i^n A_i v_i^n z_{i,2} \Rightarrow z_{i,1} u_i^n x_i v_i^n z_{i,2}$$

is a derivation in G. By the structure of the words in R_n and $z_{i,1} = (a^i b)^t z_i$ we obtain $u_i = y_i (a^i b)^r y_i'$. Now it is easy to prove that $A_i \neq A_j$ has to hold for $1 \leqq i < j \leqq n$. Thus we need at least $S, A_1, A_2, \ldots, A_{n-1}$.

On the other hand, it is easy to construct a context-free grammar which generates R_n and has n nonterminals.

ii) The following λ-free random context grammar generates R_n:

$$G = (\{S, A, B, C, D, E, X, Y\}, \{a, b\}, P, S)$$

where P consists of the following rules:

(1) $(S \to A^i b B, \emptyset, \emptyset)$, $1 \leqq i \leqq n$,

(2) $(B \to X, \emptyset, \emptyset)$,

(3) $(A \to C, \{X\}, \{C\})$,

(4) $(X \to ED, \{C\}, \emptyset)$,

(5) $(C \to a, \{D\}, \emptyset)$,

(6) $(D \to X, \emptyset, \{C\})$,

(7) $(X \to Y, \emptyset, \{A, C\})$,

(8) $(E \to A, \{Y\}, \emptyset)$,

(9) $(Y \to bB, \emptyset, \{E\})$,

(10) $(B \to b, \emptyset, \emptyset)$,

(11) $(A \to A, \emptyset, \{B, X, Y, D\})$.

A string $(a^ib)^m A^i bB$, $m \geqq 0$ (in the first step we have $m = 0$), can be rewritten only by rule (2) or by rule (10). After rule (10) only (11) can be used, and we obtain a terminal string $(a^ib)^{m+1} b$.

Using rule (2) we obtain the string $(a^ib)^m A^i bX$, which can be rewritten only by rule (3) and we get a string $(a^ib)^m A^k C A^j bX$, $k + j = i - 1$. Now, only rule (4) can be applied and then we have to use rule (5) passing to $(a^ib)^m A^k a A^j bED$. This word can be rewritten only by rule (6) which leads to $(a^ib)^m A^k a A^j bEX$. Now we have to use rule (3) again and so on until we obtain $(a^ib)^{m+1} E^i Y$, and in the presence of Y rule (8) can replace each E by A, and then rule (9) leads to $(a^ib)^{m+1} A^i bB$ which has the same form as the word at the beginning of the proof.

Consequently, $L(G) = R_n$ and $\mathrm{Var}_{(\mathrm{RC},\mathrm{CF}\text{-}\lambda,\mathrm{ac})}(R_n) \leqq 8$.

Example 4.1.4. Let $V = \{a_1, a_2, \ldots, a_k\}$, and let $p =]\log_2 k[+ 1$. We consider some auxiliary symbols $A_1, A_2, \ldots, A_p$, and with each $a_i \in V$ we associate a subset M_i of $\{A_1, A_2, \ldots, A_p\}$ such that $M_i \neq M_j$ for $i \neq j$ and $\mathrm{card}(M_i) \leqq p$ for $1 \leqq i \leqq k$ (the choice of p makes this possible). For $a_i, a_j \in V$, we write $a_i \prec a_j$ iff $M_i \subseteq M_j$. Now we regard the language

$$L_k = \{a_i a_1^p x : x \in \{a_{i_1}, a_{i_2}, \ldots, a_{i_t}\}^*, a_{i_j} \prec a_i \quad \text{for} \quad 1 \leqq j \leqq t\}.$$

Then the random context grammar with the nonterminals $S, B, C, A_1, A_2, \ldots, A_p$, the axiom S, and the rules

$$p_i\colon (S \to a_i A_{i_1} A_{i_2} \ldots A_{i_t} B, \emptyset, \emptyset),\ M_i = \{A_{i_1}, A_{i_2}, \ldots, A_{i_t}\},\ 1 \leqq i \leqq t,$$

$$q_i\colon (B \to Ba_i, M_i, \emptyset),\ 1 \leqq i \leqq k,$$

$$r_i\colon (B \to a_1^{p-t-1} C, M_i, \emptyset),\ 1 \leqq i \leqq k,$$

$$s_j\colon (A_j \to a_1, \{C\}, \emptyset),\ 1 \leqq j \leqq p,$$

$$f\colon (C \to a_1, \emptyset, \emptyset)$$

generate the language L_k since the terminating derivations have the following structure:

$$S \Rightarrow a_i A_{i_1} \ldots A_{i_t} B \Rightarrow a_i A_{i_1} \ldots A_{i_t} B a_{j_1} \overset{*}{\Rightarrow} a_i A_{i_1} \ldots A_{i_t} B a_{j_h} \ldots a_{j_1}$$

$$\Rightarrow a_i A_{i_1} \ldots A_{i_t} a_1^{p-t-1} C a_{j_h} \ldots a_{j_1} \overset{*}{\Rightarrow} a_i a_1^{p-1} C a_{j_h} \ldots a_{j_1} \Rightarrow a_i a_1^p a_{j_h} \ldots a_{j_1}$$

with $a_{j_s} < a_i$ for $1 \leqq s \leqq h$. Therefore

$$\mathrm{Var}_{(\mathrm{RC,CF}\text{-}\lambda)}(L_k) \leqq]\log_2 k[+ 4.$$

Now let G be a context-free grammar with $L(G) = L_k$. We consider the word $a_i a_1^p a_i^n$ for sufficiently large n. As in the preceding example we can show that in its derivation there has to be a subderivation $B_i \stackrel{*}{\Rightarrow} x_i B_i y_i$ with $x_i y_i \in \{a_i\}^+$. If for some $a_i < a_j$ we have $B_i = B_j$, then from a derivation

$$S \stackrel{*}{\Rightarrow} wB_iz \stackrel{*}{\Rightarrow} w'vz' = a_i a_1^p u$$

where $w \stackrel{*}{\Rightarrow} W'$, $z \stackrel{*}{\Rightarrow} z'$, $B_i \stackrel{*}{\Rightarrow} v$, $w' \neq \lambda$, we can obtain a derivation

$$S \stackrel{*}{\Rightarrow} wB_iz = wB_jz \stackrel{*}{\Rightarrow} wx_jB_jy_jz = wx_jB_iy_jz \stackrel{*}{\Rightarrow} w'x_jvy_jz'$$

which leads to a word beginning with a_i and containing a_j, $a_i < a_j$, and thus we derive a word which is not in L_k.

If $B_i = B_j$ for some incomparable a_i and a_j or for $a_j < a_i$, then we obtain a contradiction by analogous arguments.

Further, no B_i as above can be the axiom. Hence G has at least $k + 1$ nonterminals.

On the other hand, it is easy to construct a context-free grammar with $k + 1$ nonterminals which generates L_k. Thus $\mathrm{Var}_{\mathrm{CF}\text{-}\lambda}(L_k) = k + 1$.

These examples show that the non-terminal complexities with respect to different types of grammars can extremely differ, in some cases their difference cannot be bounded by an integer. However, the following theorems prove that for some couples of grammar classes, when going from one type to the other type, the difference is bounded.

Lemma 4.1.1. *Let* $\alpha \in \{\mathrm{CF}, \mathrm{CF} - \lambda\}$ and $\beta = \mathrm{ac}$ *or empty. Then, for all* $L \in \mathscr{L}(\mathrm{RC}, \alpha, \beta)$, *we have*

$$\mathrm{Var}_{(\mathrm{P},\alpha,\beta)}(L) \leqq \mathrm{Var}_{(\mathrm{RC},\alpha,\beta)}(L) + 2.$$

Proof. We give the proof only for $\beta = \mathrm{ac}$, $\alpha = \mathrm{CF} - \lambda$, because the construction is the same for $\beta = \mathrm{ac}$ and $\alpha = \mathrm{CF}$, and it has to be slightly modified for empty β.

Let $G = (V_N, V_T, P, S)$ be a random context grammar such that $L = L(G)$ and $\mathrm{Var}(G) = \mathrm{Var}_{(\mathrm{RC,CF}\text{-}\lambda,\mathrm{ac})}(L)$. Let

$$(A \to w, \{A_1, A_2, \ldots, A_s\}, \{B_1, B_2, \ldots, B_r\})$$

be the ith rule of P. With this rule we associate the following programmed productions:

$$([i, 1, 1]\colon A_1 \to A_1, \{[i, 1, 2]\}, \emptyset),$$
$$([i, 1, 2]\colon A_2 \to A_2, \{[i, 1, 3]\}, \emptyset),$$
$$\ldots$$
$$([i, 1, s]\colon A_s \to A_s, \{[i, 2, 1]\}, \emptyset),$$
$$([i, 2, 1]\colon B_1 \to B_1, \emptyset, \{[i, 2, 2]\}),$$
$$([i, 2, 2]\colon B_2 \to B_2, \emptyset, \{[i, 2, 3]\}),$$
$$\ldots$$
$$([i, 2, r]\colon B_r \to B_r, \emptyset, \{i\}),$$
$$(i\colon A \to w, \{[j, 1, 1]\colon 1 \leqq j \leqq \mathrm{card}(P)\}, \emptyset).$$

The rules with label $[i, 1, k]$, $1 \leqq k \leqq s$, check the appearance of $A_1, A_2, \ldots, A_s$; the rules with the labels $[i, 2, k]$, $1 \leqq k \leqq r$, check the absence of $B_1, B_2, \ldots, B_r$. (This construction has to be obviously modified if one or both of the sets $\{A_1, A_2, \ldots, A_s\}$ and $\{B_1, B_2, \ldots, B_r\}$ are empty. If $A \in \{A_1, A_2, \ldots, A_s\}$, say $A = A_j$, then we substitute

$$([i, 1, j]: A_j \to A_j, \{[i, 1, j + 1]\}, \emptyset)$$

using the following rules:

$$([i, 1, j]: A_j \to C, \{[i, 1, j]'\}, \emptyset),$$

$$([i, 1, j]': A_j \to A_j, \{[i, 1, j]''\}, \emptyset),$$

$$([i, 1, j]'': C \to A_j, \{[i, 1, j + 1]\}, \emptyset),$$

and an analogous modification is made if $A \in \{B_1, B_2, \ldots, B_r\}$.)

Let P' be the set of all productions constructed in this way. Then the grammar

$$G' = \left(V_N \cup \{C, C'\}, V_T, P' \cup \left\{(*, C' \to S, \{[j, 1, 1]: 1 \leqq j \leqq \text{card}(P)\}, \emptyset)\right\}, C'\right)$$

generates $L(G)$ and has two nonterminals which are not in V_N.

Lemma 4.1.2. *Let* $\alpha \in \{\mathrm{CF}, \mathrm{CF} - \lambda\}$, $\beta = \mathrm{ac}$ *or empty. Then, for all* $L \in \mathcal{L}(\mathrm{RC}, \alpha, \beta)$, *we have*

$$\mathrm{Var}_{(\mathrm{M},\alpha,\beta)}(L) \leqq \mathrm{Var}_{(\mathrm{RC},\alpha,\beta)}(L) + 1.$$

Proof. We use the notation of the proof of Lemma 4.1.1 and associate with $(A \to w, \{A_1, A_2, \ldots, A_s\}, \{B_1, B_2, \ldots, B_r\})$ the matrix

$$(A_1 \to A_1, A_2 \to A_2, \ldots, A_s \to A_s, B_1 \to C^2, B_2 \to C^2, \ldots, B_r \to C^2, A \to w)$$

or a matrix modified according to the modifications in the proof of Lemma 4.1.1. Clearly, before applying $A \to w$ one must check whether or not $A_1, A_2, \ldots, A_s$ are present and $B_1, B_2, \ldots, B_r$ are absent in the current string. Obviously

$$G' = (V_N \cup \{C\}, V_T, M, S, F)$$

where M is the set of all above introduced matrices and

$$F = \{B \to CC : B \in V_N\}$$

satisfies $L(G') = L(G)$. (We use $B \to CC$ for the test of absence since C also occurs in the modified matrices.)

Lemma 4.1.3. *Let* $\alpha = \mathrm{ac}$ *or empty. Then, for all languages* $L \in \mathcal{L}(\mathrm{M}, \mathrm{CF}, \alpha)$, *we have*

$$\mathrm{Var}_{(\mathrm{P},\mathrm{CF},\alpha)}(L) \leqq \mathrm{Var}_{(\mathrm{M},\mathrm{CF},\alpha)}(L) + 2.$$

Proof. Let $G = (V_N, V_T, M, S, F)$ be a matrix grammar with $L = L(G)$ and $\mathrm{Var}(G) = \mathrm{Var}_{(\mathrm{M},\mathrm{CF},\alpha)}(L)$. Let $M = \{m_1, m_2, \ldots, m_r\}$ with

$$m_i: (A_{i,1} \to w_{i,1}, A_{i,2} \to w_{i,2}, \ldots, A_{i,s_i} \to w_{i,s_i}), \; 1 \leqq i \leqq r.$$

We construct the programmed grammar

$$G' = (V_N \cup \{S', S''\}, V_T, P', S')$$

with the new symbols S', S'' and

$$P' = \{(1: S' \to S''S, U, \emptyset), (2: S'' \to \lambda, \emptyset, \emptyset)\}$$
$$\cup \{([i, j]: A_{i,j} \to w_{i,j}, E_{i,j}, F_{i,j}) : 1 \leqq i \leqq r, 1 \leqq j \leqq s_i\}$$

where

$$U = \{[i, 1] : 1 \leqq i \leqq r\},$$

$$E_{i,j} = \begin{cases} [i, j+1] & \text{if} \quad 1 \leqq j \leqq s_i - 1, \\ U & \text{if} \quad j = s_i, \end{cases}$$

$$F_{i,j} = \begin{cases} \emptyset & \text{if} \quad A_{i,j} \to w_{i,j} \notin F, \\ E_{i,j} & \text{otherwise.} \end{cases}$$

The symbols S' and S'' are introduced in order to ensure that we start with the first production of a matrix and that the derivation does not terminate inside a matrix. It is easy to see that $L(G') = L(G)$.

Lemma 4.1.4. *For all recursively enumerable languages L, we have*

$$\mathrm{Var}_{(M,CF,ac)}(L) \leqq \mathrm{Var}_{(P,CF,ac)}(L) + 1.$$

Proof. Let $G = (V_N, V_T, P, S)$ be a programmed grammar with $L = L(G)$ and $\mathrm{Var}(G) = \mathrm{Var}_{(P,CF,ac)}(L)$. Let C be a new symbol, and let $p = \mathrm{card}(P)$, $\mathrm{Lab}(P) = \{1, 2, \ldots, p\}$. With the rule $(b: A \to w, U, W)$ we associate the following matrices:

(1) $([C \to \lambda]^b, C \to C^{p+1}, A \to wC^i)$ for $i \in U$,

(2) $([C \to \lambda]^b, C \to C^{p+1}, A \to C^{p+1}, B \to BC^j)$, for $j \in W, B \in V_N$,

(3) $([C \to \lambda]^b, C \to C^{p+1}, A \to w)$.

Further we introduce the matrices

(4) $(C \to C^{p+1}, S \to C^r S)$ for $1 \leqq r \leqq p$.

Then we consider the matrix grammar

$$G' = (V_N \cup \{C\}, V_T, M, C, F)$$

where M is the union of all matrices of types (1) to (4) and

$$F = \{C \to C^{p+1}\} \cup \{A \to C^{p+1} : A \in V_N\}.$$

First we have to apply a matrix of type (4) and obtain a word C^rS. We can apply to C^rS only matrices of types (1) to (3) associated to the rule with label r. These matrices simulate the application of $(r: A \to w, U, W)$ in G (and those of type (3) terminate the derivation or block it). Otherwise a rule $C \to C^{p+1}$ or $A \to C^{p+1}$ is effectively used and then all matrices applied after that introduce the symbol C at least $p + 1$ times. Therefore the derivation only terminates if each application of a matrix simulates a derivation step in G. Hence $L(G') = L(G)$.

Without proof (which can be given by an analysis of the usual proof for the elimination of erasing rules) we mention

Lemma 4.1.5. *For all context-free languages L, we have*

$$\mathrm{Var}_{\mathrm{CF}}(L) = \mathrm{Var}_{\mathrm{CF}\text{-}\lambda}(L).$$

Therefore in the sequel we shall not distinguish between $\mathrm{Var}_{\mathrm{CF}}$ and $\mathrm{Var}_{\mathrm{CF}\text{-}\lambda}$.

We now introduce some notation which lead to a certain measure of the difference between classes of grammars with respect to complexity and also to a certain kind of complexity hierarchy.

Let X and Y be two distinct classes of grammars, and let $\mathcal{L} = \mathcal{L}(X) \cap \mathcal{L}(Y)$. Then we write

$X \leqq^V Y$ iff there is a constant k such that $|\mathrm{Var}_X(L) - \mathrm{Var}_Y(L)| \leqq k$ for all $L \in \mathcal{L}$;

$X \leqq_1^V Y$ iff there is a constant k such that $\mathrm{Var}_X(L) \leqq \mathrm{Var}_Y(L) + k$ for all $L \in \mathcal{L}$ and there is a sequence L_i of languages of $\mathcal{L}$, $i \in \mathbb{N}$, such that $\mathrm{Var}_Y(L_i) - \mathrm{Var}_X(L_i) \geqq i$;

$X \leqq_2^V Y$ iff there is a constant k such that $\mathrm{Var}_X(L) \leqq \mathrm{Var}_Y(L) + k$ for all $L \in \mathcal{L}$ and there is a sequence L_i of languages of $\mathcal{L}$, $i \in \mathbb{N}$, such that $\lim_{i\to\infty} \frac{\mathrm{Var}_X(L_i)}{\mathrm{Var}_Y(L_i)} = 0$;

$X \leqq_3^V Y$ iff there is a constant k such that $\mathrm{Var}_X(L) \leqq \mathrm{Var}_Y(L) + k$ for all $L \in \mathcal{L}$ and there is no function $f\colon \mathbb{N} \to \mathbb{N}$ such that $\mathrm{Var}_Y(L) \leqq f(\mathrm{Var}_X(L))$ for all $L \in \mathcal{L}$.

The intuitive meaning of these relations is: bounded difference, unbounded difference, unbounded quotient, bounded by no mapping.

Obviously $X \leqq_3^V Y \Rightarrow X \leqq_2^V Y \Rightarrow X \leqq_1^V Y$.

Clearly, $X \leqq_3^V Y$ holds if the first condition of its definition is satisfied and there is a sequence L_i of languages in $\mathcal{L}$, $i \in \mathbb{N}$, such that $\mathrm{Var}_X(L_i) \leqq k'$ for some constant k' and $\mathrm{Var}_Y(L_i) \geqq i$.

Theorem 4.1.1. *For* $X \in \{\mathrm{M}, \mathrm{P}\}$, $\alpha \in \{\mathrm{CF}, \mathrm{CF} - \lambda\}$, $\beta = \mathrm{ac}$ *or empty, we have*

$$(X, \alpha, \beta) \leqq_3^V \mathrm{CF}.$$

Proof. Obviously, it is sufficient to show that $(X, \mathrm{CF} - \lambda) \leqq_3^V \mathrm{CF}$. For $X = P$ this follows from the fact that each λ-free context-free grammar is also a λ-free programmed grammar with context-free productions and from Example 4.1.1. For $X = M$ the statement is proved by Example 4.1.2.

Theorem 4.1.2. *Let* $\alpha \in \{\mathrm{CF}, \mathrm{CF} - \lambda\}$. Then

$$(\mathrm{RC}, \alpha, \mathrm{ac}) \leqq_3^V \mathrm{CF} \quad \textit{and} \quad (\mathrm{RC}, \alpha) \leqq_2^V \mathrm{CF}.$$

Proof. Use Examples 4.1.3 and 4.1.4.

Theorem 4.1.3. *For* $X \in \{\mathrm{M}, \mathrm{P}\}$, $\alpha \in \{\mathrm{CF}, \mathrm{CF} - \lambda\}$, $\beta = \mathrm{ac}$ *or empty,*

$$(X, \alpha, \beta) \leqq_3^V (\mathrm{RC}, \alpha, \beta).$$

Proof. If $\alpha = \text{CF} - \lambda$, then the statement follows by Lemma 4.1.1, Lemma 4.1.2, and Examples 4.1.1 and 4.1.2. If $\alpha = \text{CF}$ and $X = \text{P}$, it can be derived from Lemma 4.1.1 and Example 4.1.1. If $\alpha = \text{CF}$ and $X = \text{M}$, it follows from the statement for $X = \text{P}$ and Lemma 4.1.4.

Theorem 4.1.4. $(\text{P}, \text{CF}, \text{ac}) =^V (\text{M}, \text{CF}, \text{ac})$.

Proof. Combine Lemmas 4.1.3 and 4.1.4.

The following theorem concerns the power of erasing rules with respect to nonterminal complexity.

Theorem 4.1.5. $(\text{RC}, \text{CF}, \text{ac}) \leqq_2^V (\text{RC}, \text{CF} - \lambda, \text{ac})$.

Proof. The statement follows from Example 4.1.1.

Open problems

4.1.1. What about CS with respect to the measure Var (possibly distinguishing between length-increasing and context-sensitive grammars)? Compare Var_{CS} and Var_X for X a class of regulated grammars.

4.1.2. Prove or disprove $(\text{RC}, \alpha) \leqq_3^V \text{CF}$, $\alpha \in \{\text{CF}, \text{CF} - \lambda\}$.

4.1.3. What is the relation between $(\text{M}, \text{CF} - \lambda, \text{ac})$ and $(\text{P}, \text{CF} - \lambda, \text{ac})$, (M, CF) and (P, CF), $(\text{M}, \text{CF} - \lambda)$ and $(\text{P}, \text{CF} - \lambda)$ with respect to the measure Var?

4.1.4. Prove or disprove $(\text{RC}, \text{CF}, \text{ac}) \leqq_3^V (\text{RC}, \text{CF} - \lambda, \text{ac})$. Study the relation between $(X, \text{CF} - \lambda, \text{ac})$ and $(X, \text{CF}, \text{ac})$, (Y, α, ac) and (Y, α) for $X \in \{\text{M}, \text{P}\}$, $Y \in \{\text{M}, \text{P}, \text{RC}\}$, $\alpha \in \{\text{CF}, \text{CF} - \lambda\}$.

4.1.5. What about the optimality of the relations in Lemmas 4.1.1, 4.1.2, and 4.1.3 (see also Exercise 4.1.1)?

Exercises

4.1.1. Let $L = \{ab^nc^nd : n \geqq 1\}$. Prove that $\text{Var}_{(\text{M,CF,ac})}(L) = 1$, $\text{Var}_{(\text{P,CF,ac})}(L) = 2$.

4.1.2. Prove that, for each $n \geqq 1$, there is a context-free language L_n such that $\text{Var}_{(\text{M,CF,ac})}(L_n) = 1$ and $\text{Var}_{\text{CF}}(L_n) \geqq n$ (see Dassow and Păun (1985-a)).

4.1.3. a) Let $Z_n = \{a^{m_1}b^{m_1}a^{m_2}b^{m_2} \dots a^{m_n}b^{m_n} : m_i \geqq 1, 1 \leqq i \leqq n\}$. Prove that $\text{Var}_{\text{CF}}(Z_n) \leqq 2$, $\text{Var}_{\text{iCF}}(Z_n) = n + 1$.

b) Let $U_n = \bigcup_{i=1}^{n} \{b_ia^mb_ia^mb_i : m \geqq 1\}$. Prove that $\text{Var}_{\text{iCF}}(U_n) \leqq 2$ and $\text{Var}_{\text{CF}}(U_n) = n + 1$.

This exercise points out the incomparability of CF and iCF — the Indian context-free parallel grammars — with respect to the nonterminal complexity and $\text{rCF} \leqq_3^V \text{CF}$ and $\text{rCF} \leqq_3^V \text{iCF}$ where rCF is the class of Russian parallel grammars (with context-free productions).

4.1.4. a) Prove that $\text{Var}_{(\text{P,CF-}\lambda\text{,ac})}(L) \leqq \text{Var}_X(L) + 1$ for $X \in \{\text{iCF}, \text{rCF}\}$.

b) Prove that $(\text{P}, \text{CF} - \lambda, \text{ac}) \leqq_3^V \text{rCF}$.

4.1.5. Prove that, for each language L over V,

$$\mathrm{Var}_{(\mathrm{P,CF}\text{-}\lambda,\mathrm{ac})}(L) \leqq \mathrm{Var}_{(\mathrm{M,CF}\text{-}\lambda,\mathrm{ac})}(L) + \mathrm{card}\,(V) + 1.$$

4.1.6. Let $V_i = \{a_i, b_i, c_i, d_i, e_i\}$ be n pairwise disjoint alphabets and

$$L'_i = \{e_i a_i^m b_i^m : m \geqq 1\} \cup \{e_i c_i^m d_i^m : m \geqq 1\},\ L_n = \bigcup_{i=1}^{n} L'_i.$$

Prove that $\mathrm{Var}_{\mathrm{rCF}}(L_n) = 2n + 1$, $\mathrm{Var}_{(\mathrm{RC,CF,ac})}(L_n) \leqq n + 3$, and $\mathrm{Var}_{(\mathrm{P,CF,ac})}(L_n) \leqq 2$.

4.2. Nonterminal Complexity. Families of Languages with Bounded Complexity

Already Example 4.1.1 shows that the complexity of regular languages with respect to a description by random context grammars is bounded by no constant. In this section we shall prove that the situation is completely different if we consider the complexity of languages generated by matrix or programmed grammars with appearance checking and erasing rules.

First we introduce some notation.

Definition 4.2.1. For a family X of grammars, we set

$$\mathcal{L}_k^V(X) = \{L : \mathrm{Var}_X(L) \leqq k\}.$$

Lemma 4.2.1. $\mathcal{L}(\mathrm{LIN}) \subseteq \mathcal{L}_2^V(\mathrm{M, CF, ac})$.

Proof. Let $G = (V_N, V_T, P, A_1)$ be a linear grammar with $V_N = \{A_1, A_2, \ldots, A_n\}$. We construct the matrix grammar $G' = (\{S, A\}, V_T, M, S, F)$ with

$$\begin{aligned} M = \{&(A \to A^{n+1}, S \to AS)\} \\ &\cup \{([A \to \lambda]^i, A \to A^{n+1}, S \to uSvA^j) : A_i \to uA_jv \in P\} \\ &\cup \{([A \to \lambda]^i, A \to A^{n+1}, S \to x) : A_i \to x \in P, x \in V_T^*\}, \end{aligned}$$

and F contains all rules $A \to A^{n+1}$.

Each nonterminal A_i is identified by a string of exactly i occurrences of A and i determines the set of applicable matrices since the application of $A \to A^{n+1}$ introduces $n + 1$ occurrences of A and then the derivation cannot terminate. Hence each derivation begins by using $(A \to A^{n+1}, S \to AS)$ (remember that A_1 is the axiom of G) which can then never be applied again, it continues with matrices which simulate the use of $A_i \to uA_jv$ and it ends with the use of the matrix $([A \to \lambda]^i, A \to A^{n+1}, S \to x)$. Therefore $L(G') = L(G)$.

The next lemma shows the optimality of Lemma 4.2.1, and also the optimality of Lemma 4.1.4.

Lemma 4.2.2. *Let*

$$L = \{a^n b^m c^p : n, m, p \geqq 1\} \cup \{b^m c^p : m, p \geqq 1\} \cup \{c^p : p \geqq 1\}.$$

Then

i) $\mathrm{Var}_{(\mathrm{M,CF,ac})}(L) = 2$,

ii) $\mathrm{Var}_{(\mathrm{P,CF,ac})}(L) = 1$.

Proof. i) Let us suppose that $L = L(G)$ for some matrix grammar $G = (\{S\}, \{a, b, c\}, M, S, F)$. We consider $w = a^n b^n c^n$ for a sufficiently large number n and a derivation of w, say

$$S \underset{m_{i_1}}{\Longrightarrow} w_1 \underset{m_{i_2}}{\Longrightarrow} w_2 \Rightarrow \cdots \underset{m_{i_r}}{\Longrightarrow} w_r = w.$$

Case 1. Assume that each sentential form w_j, $1 \leqq j \leqq r$, contains one nonterminal only. Then it has the form $w_j = v_j S v_j'$, $v_j, v_j' \in \{a, b, c\}^*$, and we can suppose that the application of m_{i_j} to $w_{j-1} = v_{j-1} S v_{j-1}'$ has the same effect as the application of the context-free production $S \to u_j S u_j'$ where $v_{j-1} u_j = v_j$, $u_j' v_{j-1}' = v_j'$. By the structure of w we can assume without loss of generality that there are integers j and j' such that u_j contains the symbol a and $u_{j'}$ contains the symbol b. Further, since each sentential form contains S we can change the order of the applied matrices, i.e. we have the correct derivation

$$S \Rightarrow w_1 \Rightarrow \cdots \Rightarrow w_{j-1} \underset{m_{i_{j'}}}{\Longrightarrow} w_j' \Rightarrow \cdots \Rightarrow w_{j'-1}' \underset{m_{i_j}}{\Longrightarrow} w_{j'}'' \Rightarrow \cdots \Rightarrow w_r''.$$

Then $w_r'' = z_1 b z_2 a z_3$ for some $z_1, z_2, z_3 \in \{a, b, c\}^*$, and moreover, $w_r'' \in L(G)$, $w_r'' \notin L$.

Case 2. Assume that there is a sentential form $w_j = v_1 S v_2 S \ldots v_t S v_{t+1}$ where $t \geqq 2$, $v_i \in \{a, b, c\}^*$, $1 \leqq i \leqq t + 1$. Further, $a^2b^2c^2 \in L$, and by our assumption $L = L(G)$, there are derivations $S \overset{*}{\Rightarrow} a^2b^2c^2$. We apply these derivations to each S in w_j and obtain

$$S \Rightarrow w_1 \Rightarrow \cdots \Rightarrow w_j \Rightarrow v_1 a^2b^2c^2 v_2 S v_3 S \ldots v_t S v_{t+1}$$

$$\overset{*}{\Rightarrow} v_1 a^2b^2c^2 v_2 a^2b^2c^2 v_3 S \ldots v_t S v_{t+1}$$

$$\overset{*}{\Rightarrow} v_1 a^2b^2c^2 v_2 a^2b^2c^2 v_3 a^2b^2c^2 \ldots v_t a^2b^2c^2 v_{t+1} = v.$$

Again, $v \in L(G)$, $v \notin L$.

Thus the generation of L by a matrix grammar requires at least two nonterminals, and by Lemma 4.2.1, two nonterminals are enough.

ii) L is generated by the programmed grammar $G = (\{S\}, \{a, b, c\}, P, S)$ with

$$P = \{(1\colon S \to aS, \{1, 2\}, \emptyset), (2\colon S \to bS, \{2, 3, 4\}, \emptyset),$$
$$(3\colon S \to cS, \{3, 4\}, \emptyset), (4\colon S \to c, \emptyset, \emptyset)\}.$$

Lemma 4.2.3. i) $L(\mathrm{MLIN}) \subseteq L_3^V(\mathrm{M}, \mathrm{CF}, \mathrm{ac})$.

ii) *There is a metalinear language L such that* $\mathrm{Var}_{(\mathrm{M},\mathrm{CF},\mathrm{ac})}(L) = 3$.

Proof. We prove only i), for ii) we refer to DASSOW and PĂUN (1985-a) where it is proved that $\mathrm{Var}_{(\mathrm{M},\mathrm{CF},\mathrm{ac})}(L) = 3$ for the language

$$L = \{a^n b^n c^m d^m e^p f^p : n, m, p \geqq 1\}.$$

Let $G = (V_N, V_T, P, S)$ be a metalinear grammar containing the non-linear rules $r_1, r_2, \ldots, r_p$ where

$$r_i\colon S \to w_{i,1} A_{i,1} w_{i,2} A_{i,2} \ldots w_{i,k_i} A_{i,k_i} w_{i,k_i+1},$$

$1 \leqq i \leqq p$, $w_{i,j} \in V_T^*$, $A_{i,j} \in V_N \setminus \{S\}$ for $1 \leqq j \leqq k_i$. We construct the matrix grammar

$$G' = (\{S, A, B\}, V_T, M, S, F)$$

in the following way.

For every triple (i,j,X), $1 \leq i \leq p$, $1 \leq j \leq k_i$, and $X \in V_N$, let $q(i,j,X)$ be a positive integer such that $q(i,j,X) \neq q(i',j',X')$ for $(i,j,X) \neq (i',j',X')$. Further, let

$$Q = 1 + \max\{q(i,j,X) : 1 \leq i \leq p,\ 1 \leq j \leq k_i,\ X \in V_N\}.$$

We set

$$F = \{A \to A^Q\}$$

and introduce in M the following matrices:

(1) $(S \to w)$ for $S \to w \in P$, $w \in V_T^*$,

(2) $(A \to A^Q, S \to w_{i,1}A^{q(i,1,A_{i,1})}BS)$, $1 \leq i \leq p$,

(3) $([A \to \lambda]^{q(i,j,X)}, A \to A^Q, B \to uA^{q(i,j,Y)}Bv)$, $1 \leq i \leq p$, $1 \leq j \leq k_i$,
$X \to uYv \in P$, $X, Y \in V_N$, $u, v \in V_T^*$,

(4) $([A \to \lambda]^{q(i,j,X)}, A \to A^Q, B \to z, S \to w_{i,j+1}A^{q(i,j+1,A_{i,j+1})}BS)$,
$1 \leq i \leq p$, $1 \leq j \leq k_i$, $X \to z \in P$, $X \in V_N$, $z \in V_T^*$,

(5) $([A \to \lambda]^{q(i,k_i,X)}, A \to A^Q, B \to z, S \to w_{i,k_i+1})$, $1 \leq i \leq p$,
$X \to z \in P$, $X \in V_N$, $z \in V_T^*$.

Each derivation in G starts with a rule r_i, $1 \leq i \leq p$, and then we can apply only linear rules in order to obtain the derivations $A_{i,j} \to z_{i,j}$. Therefore, without loss of generality, we have only the following terminating derivations in G:

$$\begin{aligned}
S &\Rightarrow w_{i,1}A_{i,1}w_{i,2}A_{i,2} \ldots w_{i,k_i}A_{i,k_i}w_{i,k_i+1}\\
&\Rightarrow w_{i,1}u_{i,1}B_{i,1}v_{i,1}w_{i,2}A_{i,2} \ldots w_{i,k_i}A_{i,k_i}w_{i,k_i+1}\\
&\overset{*}{\Rightarrow} w_{i,1}z_{i,1}w_{i,2}A_{i,2}w_{i,3}A_{i,3} \ldots w_{i,k_i}A_{i,k_i}w_{i,k_i+1}\\
&\overset{*}{\Rightarrow} w_{i,1}z_{i,1}w_{i,2}z_{i,2}w_{i,3}A_{i,3} \ldots w_{i,k_i}A_{i,k_i}w_{i,k_i+1}\\
&\ldots\\
&\overset{*}{\Rightarrow} w_{i,1}z_{i,1}w_{i,2}z_{i,2} \ldots w_{i,k_i}z_{i,k_i}w_{i,k_i+1}.
\end{aligned}$$

We now prove that the only possible derivations in G' are the same ones and thus $L(G) = L(G')$.

Since the rules $A \to \lambda$ have to be used effectively, a derivation in G' has to start with a matrix of type (1) or type (2). In the former case a derivation in G is simulated directly. In the latter case we obtain

$$S \Rightarrow w_{i,1}A^{q(i,1,A_{i,1})}BS = v_1.$$

We cannot apply a matrix of type (2) since it introduces at least Q occurrences of A, all matrices do not decrease the number of occurrences of A in sentential forms with at least Q occurrences of A and then no termination is possible.

Since the matrices of type (3) do not change the number of B and since the application of (4) and (5) requires the occurrence of S in the sentential form, (1) is also not applicable to v_1. Further the application of a matrix of type (3) or (4), or (5) is only possible if it starts with $[A \to \lambda]^{q(i,1,A_{i,1})}$, $A \to A^Q$, otherwise we cannot effectively use all productions $A \to \lambda$ or we can effectively use $A \to A^Q$. In consequence, we obtain

$$S \Rightarrow v_1 \Rightarrow w_{i,1}u_{i,1}A^{q(i,1,B_{i,1})}Bv_{i,1}S = v_2,$$

if we apply a rule of type (3). Now we can iterate this process and obtain

$$S \Rightarrow v_1 \Rightarrow v_2 \overset{*}{\Rightarrow} w_{i,1}z_{i,1}w_{i,2}A^{q(i,2,A_{i,2})}BS = v_3$$

by application of a matrix of type (4). Again we iterate and get

$$S \Rightarrow v_1 \Rightarrow v_2 \overset{*}{\Rightarrow} v_3 \overset{*}{\Rightarrow} w_{i,1}z_{i,1}w_{i,2}z_{i,2} \ldots w_{i,k_i}z_{i,k_i}w_{i,k_i+1}$$

terminating with a matrix of type (5). Thus we have simulated a derivation in G.

Since Var $(G') = 3$, we obtain $\mathrm{Var}_{(\mathrm{M,CF,ac})}\left(L(G)\right) \leqq 3$, and the lemma is proved.

Lemma 4.2.4. *The family* $\mathscr{L}_1^V(\mathrm{M, CF} - \lambda)$ *contains non-context-free languages.*

Proof. We consider the matrix grammar

$$G = (\{S\}, \{a, b, c, d\}, M, S, \emptyset)$$

with

$$M = \{(S \to SS), (S \to aSb, S \to cSd), (S \to ab, S \to cd)\}.$$

Clearly,

$$L(G) \cap a^*b^*c^*d^* = \{a^nb^nc^nd^n : n \geqq 1\}.$$

Since $\{a^nb^nc^nd^n : n \geqq 1\}$ is not context-free, $L(G)$ is also not context-free (by the closure properties of $\mathscr{L}(\mathrm{CF})$).

Combining Lemma 4.2.4 with Lemmas 4.2.1 and 4.2.3 we obtain

Theorem 4.2.1. $\mathscr{L}(\mathrm{LIN}) \subset \mathscr{L}_2^V(\mathrm{M, CF, ac})$,

$\mathscr{L}(\mathrm{MLIN}) \subset \mathscr{L}_3^V(\mathrm{M, CF, ac})$.

Without proof we mention the corresponding results for programmed grammars.

Theorem 4.2.2. $\mathscr{L}(\mathrm{LIN}) \subset \mathscr{L}_2^V(\mathrm{P, CF, ac})$,

$\mathscr{L}(\mathrm{MLIN}) \subset \mathscr{L}_3^V(\mathrm{P, CF, ac})$,

and there is a regular language L with $\mathrm{Var}_{(\mathrm{P,CF,ac})}(L) = 2$.

The preceding theorems show that languages generated by "simple" (e. g. linear, metalinear) grammars have also a low nonterminal complexity with respect to matrix and programmed grammars. The following theorem says that all languages have low complexity.

Theorem 4.2.3. i) $\mathscr{L}(\mathrm{RE}) = \mathscr{L}_6^V(\mathrm{M, CF, ac})$,

ii) $\mathscr{L}(\mathrm{RE}) = \mathscr{L}_8^V(\mathrm{P, CF, ac})$.

Proof. i) $\mathscr{L}_6^V(\mathrm{M, CF, ac}) \subseteq \mathscr{L}(\mathrm{RE})$ is obvious. For the (very long) proof of the opposite inclusion we refer to Păun (1984-b).

ii) This relation follows from i) by Lemma 4.1.3.

Finally, let us consider the semilinearity of languages as a function of their nonterminal complexity.

Theorem 4.2.4. i) *All languages in* $\mathcal{L}_1^V(\mathrm{M, CF, ac})$ *are semilinear.*

ii) *The family* $\mathcal{L}_3^V(\mathrm{M, CF, ac})$ *contains non-semilinear languages.*

Proof. i) Let $G = (V_N, V_T, M, S, F)$ be a matrix grammar with $V_N = \{S\}$. Since each sentential form containing a nonterminal contains an occurrence of S it follows that, possibly except for the last rules of the last matrix used in some derivations, all rules are effectively used.

For a matrix $m\colon (S \to x_1, S \to x_2, \ldots, S \to x_t) \in M$ we set

$$E(m) = |x_1 x_2 \ldots x_t|_S$$

and we define

$$E(M) = \max \{E(m) : m \in M\}.$$

Moreover, let

$$p = \max \{t : (S \to x_1, S \to x_2, \ldots, S \to x_t) \in M\},$$
$$q = 2p + E(M).$$

Clearly, any matrix of M can be applied to each string which contains at least p occurrences of S and each matrix of M replaces at most p occurrences of S by terminal strings. Therefore, given a derivation D with respect to G producing a string w, we can apply the matrices used in D in such an order that we obtain a derivation D' which produces a string w' letter-equivalent to w and all sentential forms occurring in the derivation D' have at most q occurrences of S. We take some initial steps of D and if we obtain more than $2p$ occurrences of S then we use one or more matrices of D which decrease the number of occurrences of S in order to obtain a sentential form with less than $2p$ occurrences of S, we continue by a matrix increasing the number of occurrences of S, etc., with the only restriction that the last matrix of D is also used as the last matrix in D'.

Consequently, a sublanguage $L \subseteq L(G)$ exists which is letter-equivalent to $L(G)$ and has only derivations with a bounded number of nonterminals in the sentential forms, i.e. is of finite index. Now we continue as in the proof of Lemma 3.1.5 in order to show that $L(G)$ is letter-equivalent to a regular language, and hence $L(G)$ is semilinear.

ii) We consider the matrix grammar

$$G = (\{S, A, B\}, \{a\}, M, S, F)$$

with

$$F = \{S \to S^4, A \to S^4, B \to S^4\},$$
$$M = \{(A \to S^4, B \to S^4, S \to SA),$$
$$(S \to \lambda, S \to S^4, A \to SBB),$$
$$(S \to \lambda, S \to S^4, A \to S^4, B \to SSA),$$
$$(S \to \lambda, S \to \lambda, S \to S^4, B \to SSA),$$
$$(S \to \lambda, S \to \lambda, S \to S^4, B \to S^4, A \to SBB),$$
$$(S \to \lambda, S \to \lambda, S \to S^4, B \to S^4, A \to SSSa),$$
$$(S \to \lambda, S \to \lambda, S \to \lambda, S \to S^4, A \to SSSa),$$
$$(S \to \lambda, S \to \lambda, S \to \lambda, S \to S^4, A \to a)\}.$$

If there is exactly one symbol S in the current string, then each occurrence of A is replaced by two occurrences of the symbol B; in the presence of exactly two symbols S each B is transformed into A (and these operations can be iterated); and if exactly three symbols S occur, then the derivation enters the final phase and terminates; if (at most) four occurrences of S are produced, then the derivation cannot terminate. Consequently,

$$L(G) = \{a^{2^n} : n \geqq 1\},$$

and this language is not semilinear.

Corollary. i) *If* $L \subseteq \{a\}^*$ *and* L *is not regular, then* $\mathrm{Var}_{(\mathrm{M,CF,ac})}(L) \geqq 2$.

ii) *If* $L \subseteq \{a\}^* \{b\}^*$ *and* L *is not context-free, then* $\mathrm{Var}_{(\mathrm{M,CF,ac})}(L) \geqq 2$.

Proof. The statements follow by Theorem 4.2.4 and the facts that $L \subseteq \{a\}^*$ ($L \subseteq \{a\}^* \{b\}^*$) is regular (context-free) iff it is semilinear.

Open problems

4.2.1. Improve $\mathrm{Var}_{(\mathrm{M,CF,ac})}(L) \leqq 6$ for all $L \in \mathcal{L}(\mathrm{RE})$ (Theorem 4.2.3) and/or find languages L with $\mathrm{Var}_{(\mathrm{M,CF,ac})}(L) = k$, $k \in \{4, 5, 6\}$. The related questions for (P, CF, ac) are open, too.

4.2.2. Does there exist an integer k such that $\mathcal{L}(X) \subseteq \mathcal{L}_k^V(X)$ for $X \in \{(\mathrm{M, CF}), (\mathrm{M, CF} - \lambda), (\mathrm{M, CF} - \lambda, \mathrm{ac})\}$?

4.2.3. Are there non-semilinear languages in $\mathcal{L}_2^V(\mathrm{M, CF, ac})$?

4.2.4. Investigate the closure properties of $\mathcal{L}_k^V(X)$ where X is a type of grammar with regulation (see Exercise 4.2.3).

Exercises

4.2.1. Prove the existence of a language in $\mathcal{L}_2^V(\mathrm{M, CF, ac})$ which is not a simple matrix grammar (see Dassow and Păun (1985-a)).

4.2.2. Prove Theorem 4.2.2.

4.2.3. Prove the closure of $\mathcal{L}_k^V(\mathrm{P}, \alpha, \beta)$ under union, $\alpha \in \{\mathrm{CF, CF} - \lambda\}$, $\beta = \mathrm{ac}$ or empty.

4.3. Further Complexity Measures

For a context-free grammar $G = (V_N, V_T, P, S)$, the number of productions, denoted by $\mathrm{Prod}(G)$ $\big(= \mathrm{card}(P)\big)$ is an interesting complexity measure, and it is studied in many papers (see Kelemenová (1982)). However, there are some difficulties in carrying over this complexity measure for grammars with regulated rewriting since a rule $A \to w$ can occur sometimes as a core production.

Definition 4.3.1. i) Let $G = (V_N, V_T, P, S)$ be a programmed (random context) grammar. Then we set

$$\mathrm{Prod}^1(G) = \mathrm{card}\,\{A \to w : (b: A \to w, \sigma(b), \varphi(b)) \in P\},$$

$$(\mathrm{Prod}^1(G) = \mathrm{card}\,\{A \to w : (A \to w, Q, R) \in P\}),$$

$$\mathrm{Prod}^2(G) = \mathrm{card}\,(P).$$

ii) Let $G = (V_N, V_T, M, S, F)$ be a matrix grammar with $M = \{m_1, m_2, \ldots, m_s\}$, $m_i: (A_{i,1} \to w_{i,1}, A_{i,2} \to w_{i,2}, \ldots, A_{i,k_i} \to w_{i,k_i})$, $1 \leqq i \leqq s$. Then we set

$$\mathrm{Prod}^1(G) = \mathrm{card}\,\{A \to w : A = A_{i,j}, w = w_{i,j} \quad \text{for some} \quad i, j\},$$

$$\mathrm{Prod}^2(G) = \sum_{i=1}^{s} k_i.$$

iii) For a family X of grammars and a language $L \in \mathcal{L}(X)$ we define

$$\mathrm{Prod}_X^i(L) = \min\,\{\mathrm{Prod}^i(G) : G \in X, L(G) = L\}, i \in \{1, 2\}.$$

Obviously, for a context-free language L and a context-free grammar G, we have

$$\mathrm{Prod}^1(G) = \mathrm{Prod}^2(G) = \mathrm{Prod}(G), \mathrm{Prod}_{\mathrm{CF}}^1(L) = \mathrm{Prod}_{\mathrm{CF}}^2(L) = \mathrm{Prod}_{\mathrm{CF}}(L).$$

First we give some properties of finite context-free languages with respect to the measure Prod.

Lemma 4.3.1. *For a finite language L, let $m = \max\,\{|v| : v \in L\}$. and let L' be the set of all words w of L with $|w| = m$. Then*

$$\mathrm{Prod}_{\mathrm{CF}}(L') \leqq \mathrm{Prod}_{\mathrm{CF}}(L).$$

Proof. Let $G = (V_N, V_T, P, S)$ be a context-free grammar generating L and satisfying $\mathrm{Prod}(G) = \mathrm{Prod}_{\mathrm{CF}}(L)$. Now we define

$$P' = \{A \to x : A \to x \in P \quad \text{and there are} \quad z \in L' \quad \text{and a derivation}$$
$$S \overset{*}{\Rightarrow} uAv \Rightarrow uxv \overset{*}{\Rightarrow} z\}$$

and V_N' as the set of all nonterminals involved in P'. Note that $S \in V_N'$. We consider the context-free grammar $G' = (V_N', V_T, P', S)$, and we prove $L(G') = L'$. By construction of G', $L' \subseteq L(G')$. Let us assume that there is a string $x \in L(G') \setminus L'$. Then there is a derivation

$$S \Rightarrow x_1 \Rightarrow x_2 \Rightarrow \cdots \Rightarrow x_n = x \notin L'$$

where only productions of P' are used. Clearly, $n \geqq 2$ since x is not directly generated from S. We prove that, for all i, $1 \leqq i \leqq n - 1$, there is a $z_i \in L'$ such that

$$S \Rightarrow x_1 \Rightarrow \cdots \Rightarrow x_i \overset{*}{\Rightarrow} z_i \in L'.$$

Assume the contrary, i.e. that there is an i, $1 \leqq i \leqq n - 1$, such that x_i does not generate a word of L'. Obviously, $i \geqq 2$ by $S \to x_1 \in P'$ and the definition of P'. Let

$$i_0 = \min\,\{i : \text{there is no } z_i \in L' \quad \text{with} \quad x_i \overset{*}{\Rightarrow} z_i\}.$$

Then there is a z_{i_0-1} in L' with $x_{i_0-1} \overset{*}{\Rightarrow} z_{i_0-1}$. Let $x_{i_0-1} = P_1AP_2$, $x_{i_0} = P_1wP_2$ where $P_1, P_2 \in V_G^*$, $A \in V_N$, $w \in V_G^*$, $A \to w \in P'$.

Then z_{i_0-1} can be written as $z_{i_0-1} = p_1w'p_2$ where $P_1 \overset{*}{\Rightarrow} p_1$, $w \overset{*}{\Rightarrow} w'$, $P_2 \overset{*}{\Rightarrow} p_2$. Since $A \to w \in P'$ there is a derivation

$$S \overset{*}{\Rightarrow} uAv \Rightarrow uwv \overset{*}{\Rightarrow} uw''v \quad \text{with} \quad uw''v \in L'.$$

By the definition of i_0, $p_1w''p_2 \notin L'$. Hence $|uv| > |p_1p_2|$. This implies $|uw'v| > |p_1w'p_2|$. Since $S \overset{*}{\Rightarrow} uAv \overset{*}{\Rightarrow} uw'v \in L$, we obtain $p_1w'p_2 \notin L'$ in contrast to $p_1w'p_2 = z_{i_0-1} \in L'$.

It follows that $x_{n-1} = y_1By_2$, $x_n = y_1wy_2$, $y_1, w, y_2 \in V_T^*$, $B \to w \in P'$. In the derivation

$$S \Rightarrow x_1 \Rightarrow x_2 \Rightarrow \cdots \Rightarrow x_{n-1} \Rightarrow z_{n-1} \in L'$$

we have $x_{n-1} = y_1By_2$, $z_{n-1} = y_1w'y_2$, $B \to w' \in P'$, $w' \in V_T^*$. As $z_{n-1} \in L'$, $x_n \in L'$, we have $|w'| > |w|$. As $B \to w \in P'$, there is a derivation

$$S \Rightarrow u_1 \Rightarrow \cdots \Rightarrow u_k \Rightarrow u \in L'$$

with $u_k = v_1Bv_2$, $u = v_1wv_2$, $u_1, u_2 \in V_T^*$. Further, $|v_1wv_2| = m$. The derivation

$$S \Rightarrow u_1 \Rightarrow \cdots \Rightarrow u_k \Rightarrow v_1w'v_2$$

is also correct. We obtain $v_1w'v_2 \in L(G') \subseteq L$ and $|v_1w'v_2| > |v_1wv_2|$, which is impossible.

Lemma 4.3.2. *Let L be a finite language, $n =$ card (L). Let G be a linear grammar which generates L. Then*

$$\text{Prod}(G) \geqq \log_2(n+1).$$

Proof. We prove the following statement: Let L be a finite language generated by a linear grammar G with n productions. Then card $(L) \leqq 2^{n-1}$. Clearly, it is equivalent to the lemma.

We prove this by induction on the number of productions.

$n = 1$. Then the only production is $S \to w$, $w \in V_T^*$, and then $L(G) = \{w\}$ and the statement holds.

Now assume that the statement holds for $i < n$. If there is a derivation $S \overset{*}{\Rightarrow} uSv$ with $uv \in V_T^+$, then G generates an infinite language, and this contradicts the supposition.

If there is a derivation $S \overset{*}{\Rightarrow} B \Rightarrow S$, then we construct G' from G by omitting the rule $B \to S$. It satisfies $L(G') = L(G)$ and by the induction assumption card $(L(G')) \leqq 2^{n-2}$. Hence card $(L(G)) \leqq 2^{n-1}$.

Assume now that S occurs in each derivation only once (as the axiom). Let $S \to \alpha_1$, $S \to \alpha_2$, ..., $S \to \alpha_r$ be all the rules with the left-hand side S, and let

$$L_i = \{w : \alpha_i \overset{*}{\Rightarrow} w, w \in V_T^*\}.$$

Then

$$L(G) = \bigcup_{i=1}^{r} L_i$$

and by the induction assumption card $(L_i) \leqq 2^{n-1-r}$. Therefore

$$\text{card}\,(L(G)) \leqq r \cdot 2^{n-1-r} \leqq 2^{n-1}.$$

Lemma 4.3.3. *Let* $L_n = \{a^kba^{k'} : k + k' \leqq n - 1\}$. *Then*

i) $\mathrm{Prod}_{\mathrm{CF}}(L_n) \geqq \log_2(n + 1)$,

ii) $\mathrm{Prod}^1_{(\mathrm{P,CF})}(L_n) \leqq 5$, $\mathrm{Prod}^2_{(\mathrm{P,CF})}(L_n) \leqq 5$,

iii) $\mathrm{Prod}^1_{(\mathrm{M,CF})}(L_n) \leqq 5$, $\mathrm{Prod}^2_{(\mathrm{M,CF})}(L_n) \leqq 7$,

iv) $\mathrm{Prod}^1_{(\mathrm{RC,CF,ac})}(L_n) \leqq 10$, $\mathrm{Prod}^2_{(\mathrm{RC,CF,ac})}(L_n) \leqq 10$.

Proof. i) By Lemma 4.3.1, it is sufficient to prove the statement for $L'_n = \{a^iba^j : i + j = n - 1\}$. Let $G = (V_N, V_T, P, S)$ be a context-free grammar with $L'_n = L(G)$ and $\mathrm{Prod}(G) = \mathrm{Prod}_{\mathrm{CF}}(L'_n)$. First we note that, for $A \in V_N$, there exist at least two different words $u, v \in V_T^*$ such that $A \overset{*}{\Rightarrow} u$, $A \overset{*}{\Rightarrow} v$. This follows from the fact that, for $A \neq S$, if there is a unique word w with $A \Rightarrow w$, then the substitution of all occurrences of A in the right-hand sides of productions by w and the omitting of rules with left-hand side A gives a grammar G' with $L(G') = L(G) = L'_n$ and $\mathrm{Prod}(G') \leqq \mathrm{Prod}(G)$, which contradicts the choice of G. For S this statement is trivial.

Next we prove that, for $A \in V_N$, $u \in V_T^*$, and $A \overset{*}{\Rightarrow} u$, b occurs in u. Assume that $u \in \{a\}^*$, and let v be the second word with $A \overset{*}{\Rightarrow} v$, $u \neq v$. Then there are derivations

$$S \overset{*}{\Rightarrow} xAy \overset{*}{\Rightarrow} xuy \in L'_n \quad \text{and} \quad S \overset{*}{\Rightarrow} xAy \overset{*}{\Rightarrow} xvy \in L'_n.$$

Clearly, $|xuy| = |xvy|$ and hence $|u| = |v|$. Further, since $u \in \{a\}^*$, xy contains a letter b, and because xvy contains exactly one letter b, we get $v \in \{a\}^*$. This implies $u = v$ in contrast to the choice of v.

Now let us suppose that there is a production $A \to z_1Bz_2Cz_3$ in P, $B, C \in V_N$. Then there is a derivation

$$S \overset{*}{\Rightarrow} u_1Au_2 \Rightarrow u_1z_1Bz_2Cz_3u_2 \overset{*}{\Rightarrow} u'_1z'_1w_1z'_2w_2z'_3u'_2 = z$$

with $|w_1|_b = |w_2|_b = 1$. Therefore $|z|_b \geqq 2$ which contradicts $z \in L'_n$.

Thus P contains only linear rules, and the statement now follows by Lemma 4.3.2.

ii) L_n is generated by the programmed grammar $G = (\{S, A, B\}, \{a, b\}, P, S)$ with

$$\begin{aligned} P = \{&(1\colon S \to A^{n-1}bB^{n-1}, \{2, 3\}, \emptyset),\\ &(2\colon A \to \lambda, \{4, 5\}, \emptyset),\\ &(3\colon A \to a, \{4\}, \emptyset),\\ &(4\colon B \to \lambda, \{2, 3\}, \emptyset),\\ &(5\colon B \to a, \{2, 3\}, \emptyset)\}. \end{aligned}$$

By the definition of the success fields it is easy to see that after applying $S \to A^{n-1}bB^{n-1}$ we iterate the application of the following pairs of core productions: $A \to \lambda$ and one of $B \to \lambda$, $B \to a$, or $B \to \lambda$ and one of $A \to \lambda$, $A \to a$. Hence we derive a word a^iba^j with $i + j \leqq n - 1$. This proves $L(G) = L_n$.

iii) L_n is also generated by the matrix grammar $G = (\{S, A, B\}, \{a, b\}, M, S, \emptyset)$ with

$$M = \{(S \to A^{n-1}bB^{n-1}), (A \to a, B \to \lambda), (A \to \lambda, B \to a), (A \to \lambda, B \to \lambda)\}.$$

iv) The random context grammar $G = (\{S, A_1, A_2, A, B, B_1, B_2\}, \{a, b\}, P, S)$ with

$$P = \{(S \to A^{n-1}bB^{n-1}, \emptyset, \emptyset), (A \to aA_1, \emptyset, \{A_1, A_2, B_1, B_2\}),$$
$$(A \to A_2, \emptyset, \{A_1, A_2, B_1, B_2\}), (B \to B_1, \{A_1\}, \{B_1, B_2\}),$$
$$(B \to B_2, \{A_2\}, \{B_1, B_2\}), (B \to B_2, \{A_2\}, \{B_1, B_2\}),$$
$$(A_1 \to \lambda, \{B_1\}, \emptyset), (A_2 \to \lambda, \{B_2\}, \emptyset),$$
$$(B_1 \to \lambda, \emptyset, \{A_1\}), (B_2 \to \lambda, \emptyset, \{A_2\})\}$$

generates L_n.

Using Prod^i, $i \in \{1, 2\}$, instead of Var we can define the relations $=^{P^i}$ and $\leqq_j^{P^i}$, $i \in \{1, 2\}, j \in \{1, 2, 3\}$. Then we can reformulate Lemma 4.3.3 as

Theorem 4.3.1. *Let* $X \in \{\mathrm{P}, \mathrm{M}\}$, $\beta = \mathrm{ac}$ *or empty,* $i \in \{1, 2\}$. *Then*

$$(X, \mathrm{CF}, \beta) \leqq_3^{P^i} \mathrm{CF},$$

and furthermore

$$(\mathrm{RC}, \mathrm{CF}, \mathrm{ac}) \leqq_3^{P^i} \mathrm{CF}.$$

Lemma 4.3.4. *Let* L *be a recursively enumerable language,* $i \in \{1, 2\}$, $\beta = \mathrm{ac}$ *or empty. Then*

i) $\mathrm{Prod}^i_{(\mathrm{P,CF},\beta)}(L) \leqq \mathrm{Prod}^i_{(\mathrm{M,CF},\beta)}(L) + 2$,

ii) $\mathrm{Prod}^1_{(\mathrm{M,CF,ac})}(L) \leqq \mathrm{Prod}^1_{(\mathrm{P,CF},\beta)}(L) + 5$.

Proof. i) follows directly from the construction in the proof of Lemma 4.1.3.

ii) Let $G = (V_N, V_T, P, S)$ be a programmed grammar, $\mathrm{card}(P) = p$, $\mathrm{Lab}(P) = \{1, 2, \ldots, p\}$. We introduce the new symbols S', N, C, B. With the programmed rule $(k\colon A \to w, U, V)$ we associate the following matrices:

(1) $([C \to \lambda]^k, C \to N, A \to wC, C \to \lambda, B \to CB^i), i \in U,$

(2) $([C \to \lambda]^k, C \to N, A \to wC, C \to N, B \to CB^j), j \in V,$

(3) $([C \to \lambda]^k, C \to N, A \to wC, C \to \lambda, B \to \lambda).$

Further we define the matrices

(4) $(S' - BS, B \to CB^r), 1 \leqq r \leqq p.$

Now we consider the matrix grammar

$$G' = (V_N \cup \{S', N, C, B\}, V_T, M, S', F)$$

where M is the set of all matrices of types (1), (2), (3), (4), and

$$F = \{C \to N\} \cup \{A \to wC : A \to w \in P\}.$$

By definition we can generate only words of the form C^kBw or w, $w \in V_G^*$, by application of matrices in M. To C^kBw we can apply only matrices of types (1), (2), (3) associated with the rule labelled by k, to a word w (obtained by an application of (3)) no matrix is applicable. Since the matrices of type (4) only choose the first value of k, it is easy to see that $L(G') = L(G)$. Now the statement follows.

This implies directly

Theorem 4.3.2. $(\mathrm{M}, \mathrm{CF}, \mathrm{ac}) =^{P^1} (\mathrm{P}, \mathrm{CF}, \mathrm{ac})$.

The following theorem relates the measures Var and Prod¹ to each other.

Lemma 4.3.5. *Let $X \in \{\mathrm{M}, \mathrm{P}\}$, $\beta =$ ac or empty. Then, for each $L \subseteq V^*$, $L \in \mathcal{L}(X, \mathrm{CF}, \beta)$, we have*

$$\mathrm{Prod}^1_{(X,\mathrm{CF},\beta)}(L) \leqq 2 \cdot \mathrm{Var}_{(X,\mathrm{CF},\beta)}(L) + \mathrm{card}(V) + 1 .$$

Proof. We give the proof only for (P, CF, ac). The necessary modifications for the other cases are left to the reader.

Let $G = (V_N, V_T, P, S)$ be a programmed grammar, and let $(b\colon A \to x_1x_2 \dots x_n, \sigma(b), \varphi(b))$, $x_i \in V_G$ for $1 \leqq i \leqq n$, be a production of P. With this rule we associate the following rules:

$$\big(b\colon A \to C, \{[b, 1]\}, \varphi(b)\big),$$
$$([b, i]\colon C \to x_iC, \{[b, i+1]\}, \emptyset),\ 1 \leqq i \leqq n,$$
$$\big([b, n+1]\colon C \to \lambda, \sigma(b), \emptyset\big).$$

Clearly, the succcessive applications of these rules simulate the application of $\big(b\colon A \to x_1x_2 \dots x_n, \sigma(b), \varphi(b)\big)$. Thus the grammar $G' = (V_N \cup \{C\}, V_T, P', S)$, where P' is the set of all productions introduced above satisfies $L(G') = L(G)$. The core productions of P' have the form

$$A \to C \quad \text{with} \quad A \in V_N, \quad \text{or} \quad C \to xC \quad \text{with} \quad x \in V_G, \quad \text{or} \quad C \to \lambda$$

and thus

$$\mathrm{Prod}^1(G') = \mathrm{card}(V_N) + \mathrm{card}(V_G) + 1 = 2 \cdot \mathrm{card}(V_N) + \mathrm{card}(V_T) + 1 .$$

Applying this to a grammar G which is minimal with respect to Var, we obtain the statement of the lemma.

Corollary. *For each recursively enumerable language $L \subseteq V^*$,*

i) $\mathrm{Prod}^1_{(\mathrm{M},\mathrm{CF},\mathrm{ac})}(L) \leqq \mathrm{card}(V) + 13$,

ii) $\mathrm{Prod}^1_{(\mathrm{P},\mathrm{CF},\mathrm{ac})}(L) \leqq \mathrm{card}(V) + 15$.

Proof. i) follows from Theorem 4.2.3 i) and Lemma 4.3.5, and ii) follows from i) and Lemma 4.3.4.

On the other hand, the following lemma can be easily proved.

Lemma 4.3.6. *Let $V = \{a_1, a_2, \dots, a_n\}$, $L = \bigcup_{i=1}^{n} \{a_i\}^*$. Then*

$$\mathrm{Prod}^1_{(\mathrm{M},\mathrm{CF},\mathrm{ac})}(L) \geqq \mathrm{card}(V),$$

$$\mathrm{Prod}^1_{(\mathrm{P},\mathrm{CF},\mathrm{ac})}(L) \geqq \mathrm{card}(V).$$

Hence there is no uniform upper bound for the complexities of all languages with respect to the number of productions.

For matrix grammars, the following measure is also of interest.

Definition 4.3.2. i) For a matrix grammar $G = (V_N, V_T, M, S, F)$ let

$$\text{Mat}(G) = \text{card}(M).$$

ii) For $X \in \{(\text{M, CF}), (\text{M, CF, ac}), (\text{M, CF} - \lambda), (\text{M, CF} - \lambda, \text{ac})\}$ and $L \in \mathcal{L}(X)$, we set

$$\text{Mat}_X(L) = \min\{\text{Mat}(G) : G \in X, L = L(G)\}.$$

Again, the language of Lemma 4.3.6 satisfies $\text{Mat}_X(L) \geqq n$. This proves that there are languages whose generation by matrix grammars requires an arbitrary large number of matrices.

Now we shall prove that the minimal grammars with respect to the measures Var and Prod^1 are not minimal ones with respect to Mat, in general. Let us formalize this concept of independence.

Definition 4.3.3. i) For syntactic complexity measures K, K' and a family X of grammars, let

$$K_X^{-1}(L) = \{G : G \in X, L = L(G), K(G) = K_X(L)\}.$$

ii) The measures K and K' are called *independent for* X if there is a language L such that

$$K_X^{-1}(L) \cap K_X'^{-1}(L) = \emptyset.$$

Theorem 4.3.3. *The complexity measures* Mat *and* Var *and* Mat *and* Prod^1 *are independent for* (M, CF, ac).

Proof. We give the proof only for the independence of Mat and Prod^1. Analogous arguments show the independence of Mat and Var.

We consider the language $L = \{\lambda, a, a^2, a^3\}$. Clearly, $\text{Prod}^1_{(\text{M,CF,ac})}(L) > 1$. On the other hand, $G = (\{S\}, \{a\}, M, S, \emptyset)$ with

$$M = \{(S \to \lambda), (S \to aS, S \to \lambda), (S \to aS, S \to aS, S \to \lambda),$$
$$(S \to aS, S \to aS, S \to aS, S \to \lambda)\}$$

generates L and therefore $\text{Prod}^1_{(\text{M,CF,ac})}(L) = 2$.

Now let G' be an arbitrary matrix grammar generating L and $\text{Prod}^1(G') = 2$. Let A be its axiom, and let $A \to w$, $B \to v$ be the two core productions of G'. Since $\lambda \in L$, there has to be a production with the right-hand side λ. If $B \to \lambda$ and $B \neq A$, then by substituting B by λ we obtain a grammar generating L with only one production, which is impossible. Hence $A \to \lambda$ is one core production.

The other production has to have the form $A \to A^i a A^j$ since we have to generate $a \in L$. If $i + j = 0$ then we do not generate L. If there is a matrix m with $A \underset{m}{\Longrightarrow} z$, $|z|_A > 0$, then $|z|_a > 0$ and hence by iterated application we generate an infinite language. Thus each matrix m satisfies $A \underset{m}{\Longrightarrow} z$ with $|z|_A = 0$, i.e. for each $p \in L$ we need a matrix. Thus $\text{Mat}(G') \geqq 4$.

Now the independence follows from the generation of L by the matrix grammar $G'' = (\{S, A\}, \{a\}, M, S, \emptyset)$ with

$$M = \{(S \to AAA), (A \to a), (A \to \lambda)\}.$$

Open problems

4.3.1. What about the production complexity with respect to context-sensitive (length-increasing) grammars?

4.3.2. What about the relations between (M, α, β) and (RC, α, β) and between (P, α, β) and (RC, α, β) with respect to Prod^1? What about the relations between regulated grammar families with respect to Prod^2?

4.3.3. It is known that Prod and Var are independent for CF. What about the independence of Prod^i and Var, $i \in \{1, 2\}$, or Prod^1 and Prod^2 for regulated grammar families?

Exercises

4.3.1. Let $L = \{a^{2^i} : 1 \leqq i \leqq n\}$. Prove that $\mathrm{Prod}_{\mathrm{CF}}(L) = n$, $\mathrm{Prod}^1_{(\mathrm{P,CF}\text{-}\lambda)}(L) = 2$.

4.3.2. Prove Lemma 4.3.6.

4.3.3. Prove Lemma 4.3.5 for matrix grammars.

4.3.4. Prove the independence of Mat and Var.

Bibliographical and historical remarks

Gruska (1967) and (1969) are basic papers on the syntactic complexity of context-free languages. A summary of the results in this field is given in Gruska (1973) and Kelemenova (1982). Further new results can be found in Blum (1983), Bucher (1981), Gabow (1984).

The first paper on the syntactic complexity of matrix and programmed grammars is Cremers et al. (1979). It contains very weak comparison results concerning Var and Prod^1 and the independence of these measures and Mat (Theorem 4.3.3).

A detailed study of the nonterminal complexity with respect to some regulated grammars is presented in Dassow (1984-b), Păun (1984-b), Dassow and Păun (1985-a) and (1986-b). The Sections 4.1 and 4.2. are based on these references.

In the paper by Bucher et al. (1981) the complexity of finite languages with respect to the number of productions and some classes of grammars is studied. Programmed grammars are also taken into consideration. Essentially, Lemma 4.3.3 is given there. Lemma 4.3.4 is contained in Dassow and Păun (1986).

Some material on the syntactic complexity can also be found in the monograph by Păun (1981-f). Dassow (1985-a) and Dassow and Păun (1984-b) give summaries of some results without proofs.

Chapter 5. Pure Regulated Grammars and Languages and Their Codings

Up to now we have considered grammars (with regulated rewriting) whose alphabet is divided into two parts, nonterminals and terminals, and whose languages consist only of words over the terminal alphabet. This is motivated by linguistic reasons. However, the intermediate steps of the derivation are not contained in the language, and therefore it often happens that the differences between the mechanisms disappear, e.g. they have the same generative power. Hence — in order to contribute to a comparison of the mechanisms — now we shall investigate languages which also contain the words of the intermediate steps, the languages of sentential forms or the so-called pure languages.

Let us mention that these languages are also of interest in themselves, which is illustrated by the following remarks:

— One of the main problems in formal language theory which is oriented to practical purposes (e.g. in the theory of programming languages) is the parsing of a given word, i.e. the construction of a (mostly leftmost) derivation of w in a given (context-free) grammar. It is known that, for general context-free grammars, there exists a parsing algorithm which needs $O(|w|^{2.73})$ time. In order to get faster algorithms one considers some special cases, e.g. unambiguous and $LL(k)$ grammars, whose time bounds are $O(|w|^2)$ and $O(|w|)$, respectively. Let us look at the definition of an $LL(k)$ grammar. A context-free grammar $G = (V_N, V_T, P, S)$ has the $LL(k)$ *property* (for a fixed integer k) if the following condition is satisfied: if there are two leftmost derivations

$$S \overset{*}{\Rightarrow} wA\alpha \Rightarrow w\beta\alpha \overset{*}{\Rightarrow} wx,\ S \overset{*}{\Rightarrow} wA\alpha \Rightarrow w\gamma\alpha \overset{*}{\Rightarrow} wy$$

with $A \in V_N$, $w, x, y \in V_T^*$, $\alpha, \beta, \gamma \in V_G^*$ and such that the first k symbols of x and y coincide, then $\beta = \gamma$. We see that the restriction required in this definition does not concern the generated language, it concerns the structure of derivations and implicitly the structure of the sentential forms too. Thus it is natural to study the properties of the set SF (G) of all sentential forms generated by a grammar G.

— L systems are a typical representative of language generating devices which work in parallel. In order to understand the differences between parallel and sequential rewriting, it is necessary to define a sequential counterpart of L systems. By their biological interpretation, L systems also differ from grammars (of the Chomsky hierarchy) in the following feature: there is no distinction between terminals and nonterminals, and all letters can be rewritten (perhaps only by productions $a \to a$). Thus it is clear that the set SF (G) can be considered as a sequential counterpart of L languages.

In this chapter we shall study the so-called pure grammars which use only one alphabet V and have rewriting rules for letters of a subset of V, and which differ from the grammars generating sets of sentential forms only in the choice of the axiom which is a finite set of words in pure grammars.

5.1. Hierarchy of Pure Regulated Languages

Now we give the formal definitions of pure versions of the context-free, context-sensitive, matrix, programmed, and random context grammars, and we give examples for the pure grammars with regulated rewriting.

In all the following definitions, let V be a finite alphabet and let S be a finite subset of V^+.

Definition 5.1.1. A *pure context-free grammar* is a triple $G = (V, P, S)$ where P is a finite set of productions of the form

$$a \to w, a \in V, w \in V^*.$$

We say that $x \in V^+$ *directly derives* $y \in V^*$, written as $x \Rightarrow y$, if

$$x = z_1 a z_2, \quad y = z_1 w z_2, \quad a \to w \in P \quad \text{for some} \quad z_1, z_2 \in V^*.$$

The language generated by G is defined as

$$L(G) = \{y : x \overset{*}{\Rightarrow} y \quad \text{for some} \quad x \in S\}$$

where $\overset{*}{\Rightarrow}$ is the reflexive and transitive closure of $\Rightarrow$.

Definition 5.1.2. A *pure context-sensitive grammar* is a triple $G = (V, P, S)$ where P is a finite set of productions of the form

$$x_1 a x_2 \to x_1 w x_2, a \in V, x_1, x_2 \in V^*, w \in V^*.$$

For $x \in V^+$, $y \in V^*$, the yield relation $x \Rightarrow y$ is defined by

$$x = z_1 x_1 a x_2 z_2, y = z_1 x_1 w x_2 z_2, x_1 a x_2 \to x_1 w x_2 \in P, z_1, z_2 \in V^*,$$

and the language $L(G)$ is defined as in Definition 5.1.1.

Definition 5.1.3. A *pure matrix grammar* is a quadruple $G = (V, M, S, F)$ where M is a finite set of finite sequences of productions, $M = \{m_1, m_2, \ldots, m_n\}$,

$$m_i: (a_{i,1} \to w_{i,1}, a_{i,2} \to w_{i,2}, \ldots, a_{i,r_i} \to w_{i,r_i}),$$

$a_{i,j} \in V, w_{i,j} \in V^*, 1 \leqq i \leqq n, 1 \leqq j \leqq r_i$, and F is a subset of occurrences of rules in the matrices of M. Then, for $1 \leqq i \leqq n$, we say that $x \underset{m_i}{\Longrightarrow} y$ iff

$$x = z_0 \Rightarrow z_1 \Rightarrow z_2 \Rightarrow \cdots \Rightarrow z_{r_i} = y$$

where

$$z_{j-1} = x_j a_{i,j} x_j', z_j = x_j w_{i,j} x_j', x_j, x_j' \in V^*,$$

or

$$a_{i,j} \text{ does not occur in } z_{j-1}, a_{i,j} \to w_{i,j} \in F, z_{j-1} = z_j.$$

The language $L(G)$ generated by G is defined as the set of all words y which are obtained by iterated applications of matrices to words of S and of all intermediate words of these applications (z_i in the above notation).

Example 5.1.1. We consider the pure matrix grammar

$$G_1 = \big(\{a, b, c\}, \{(a \to a^2, b \to b^2, c \to c^2)\}, \{abc\}, \emptyset\big).$$

As G_1 has only one axiom and also only one matrix we obtain the only possible derivation

$$abc \Rightarrow a^2bc \Rightarrow a^2b^2c \Rightarrow a^2b^2c^2 \Rightarrow a^3b^2c^2 \Rightarrow a^3b^3c^2 \Rightarrow a^3b^3c^3 \Rightarrow \cdots$$

and thus

$$L(G_1) = \{a^nb^nc^n : n \geqq 1\} \cup \{a^{n+1}b^nc^n : n \geqq 1\} \cup \{a^{n+1}b^{n+1}c^n : n \geqq 1\}.$$

Definition 5.1.4. A *pure programmed grammar* is a triple $G = (V, P, S)$ where P is a finite set of productions of the form

$$\big(r\colon a \to w,\ \sigma(r),\ \varphi(r)\big)$$

where r is the label of this production, $a \in V$, $w \in V^*$, $\sigma(r)$ and $\varphi(r)$ are subsets of the set of labels. Its language $L(G)$ consists of all words y such that there is a derivation

$$s = y_0 \underset{r_1}{\Longrightarrow} y_1 \underset{r_2}{\Longrightarrow} y_2 \underset{r_3}{\Longrightarrow} \cdots \underset{r_{n-1}}{\Longrightarrow} y_{n-1} \underset{r_n}{\Longrightarrow} y_n = y$$

where $s \in S$, $\big(r_i\colon a_i \to w_i, \sigma(r_i), \varphi(r_i)\big)$ are rules in P, $1 \leqq i \leqq n$, and

$$y_{i-1} = z_1a_iz_2,\ y_i = z_1w_iz_2,\ r_{i+1} \in \sigma(r_i)$$

or

$$a_i \quad \text{does not occur in} \quad y_{i-1},\ y_i = y_{i-1},\ r_{i+1} \in \varphi(r_i),$$

for $1 \leqq i \leqq n$.

Example 5.1.2. Let

$$L_2 = \{a, a^5\} \cup \{a^{7+10n} : n \geqq 0\} \cup \{a^{11+10n} : n \geqq 0\}.$$

This language is generated by the pure programmed grammar $G = (\{a\}, P, \{a\})$ with

$$P = \big\{(1\colon a \to a^5, \{2\}, \emptyset), (2\colon a \to a^7, \{3\}, \emptyset), (3\colon a \to a^{11}, \{3\}, \emptyset)\big\}.$$

This can be seen as follows. Each derivation has to start with the axiom a to which we can apply one of the three productions. Thus the following possibilities exist:

$$a \underset{1}{\Longrightarrow} a^5 \underset{2}{\Longrightarrow} a^{11} \underset{3}{\Longrightarrow} a^{21} = w_1 \Rightarrow \cdots,$$

$$a \underset{2}{\Longrightarrow} a^7 \underset{3}{\Longrightarrow} a^{17} = w_2 \Rightarrow \cdots,$$

$$a \underset{3}{\Longrightarrow} a^{11} \underset{3}{\Longrightarrow} a^{21} = w_1 \Rightarrow \cdots$$

where we specified the applied production by its label. By the definition, if we apply the production with label 3, then we have to continue with the production with label 3, again, i.e.: from w_1 and w_2 we get the following derivations

$$w_1 \underset{3}{\Longrightarrow} a^{31} \underset{3}{\Longrightarrow} a^{41} \underset{3}{\Longrightarrow} \cdots \underset{3}{\Longrightarrow} a^{11+10n} \underset{3}{\Longrightarrow} \cdots,$$

$$w_2 \underset{3}{\Longrightarrow} a^{27} \underset{3}{\Longrightarrow} a^{37} \underset{3}{\Longrightarrow} \cdots \underset{3}{\Longrightarrow} a^{7+10n} \underset{3}{\Longrightarrow} \cdots.$$

Thus $L(G_2) = L_2$.

Definition 5.1.5. A *pure random context grammar* is a triple $G = (V, P, S)$ where P is a finite set of rules of the form

$$(a \to w, Q, R),\ a \in V,\ w \in V^*,\ Q \subseteq V,\ R \subseteq V.$$

We say that $x \in V^+$ directly derives $y \in V^*$ (written as $x \Rightarrow y$) if

$$x = z_1 a z_2,\ y = z_1 w z_2,\ (a \to w, Q, R) \in P,$$

and $z_1 z_2$ contains all symbols of Q and no symbol of R.

The language $L(G)$ generated by G is defined as in Definition 5.1.1.

Example 5.1.3. The grammar

$$G_3 = \big(\{a, b\}, \big\{(b \to a^4, \{b\}, \emptyset), (a \to a^4, \{a\}, \emptyset)\big\}, \{bba\}\big)$$

generates

$$L_3 = \{bba\} \cup \{a^{4+3n} b a^{1+3m} : n \geqq 0, m \geqq 0\} \cup \{ba^{5+3k} : k \geqq 0\}.$$

This follows by the following facts. Only the letter b can be rewritten in the axiom bba since the application of $a \to a^4$ requires the permitting letter a. Hence we obtain ba^5 or a^4ba, and now we can only iterate the application of $a \to a^4$ because the generated words contain only one letter b. By $ba^{5+3n} \Rightarrow ba^{5+3(n+1)}$ and $a^{4+3n}ba^{1+3m} \Rightarrow a^{4+3(n+1)}ba^{1+3m}$ or $a^{4+3n}ba^{1+3m} \Rightarrow a^{4+3n}ba^{1+3(m+1)}$ we get $L(G_3) = L_3$.

Obviously, in all definitions we gave the most general type of pure versions, i.e. with erasing rules and with appearance checking.

The class of pure grammars of type X is denoted by pX. Thus we obtain the classes of grammars pCF, pCF $-\lambda$, pCS, pRE, (pM, CF), (pM, CF $-\lambda$), (pM, CF, ac), (pM, CF $-\lambda$, ac), and so on. (RE denotes here the class of context-sensitive grammars with erasing.) Accordingly, we have the families of languages $\mathscr{L}$(pCF), $\mathscr{L}$(pCS), $\mathscr{L}$(pM, CF, ac), etc.,

$$\mathscr{L}(X) = \{L : L = L(G) \quad \text{for some} \quad G \in X\}.$$

First we want to prove that each language generated by a pure grammar of type X can be generated by a (usual) grammar of type X too, i.e. $\mathscr{L}(\mathrm{p}X) \subseteq \mathscr{L}(X)$. More precisely, we show

Lemma 5.1.1. i) *Let* $X \in \{\mathrm{P, M, RC}\}$, $\alpha \in \{\mathrm{CF, CF} - \lambda\}$, $\beta =$ ac *or empty. Then* $\mathscr{L}(\mathrm{p}X, \alpha, \beta) \subset \mathscr{L}(X, \alpha, \beta)$.

ii) *If* $X \in \{\mathrm{CF, CF} - \lambda, \mathrm{CS, RE}\}$, *then* $\mathscr{L}(\mathrm{p}X) \subset \mathscr{L}(X)$.

Proof. We give the proof only for (RC, CF $-\lambda$) and (M, CF, ac).

$\mathscr{L}$(pRC, CF $-\lambda$) $\subseteq \mathscr{L}$(RC, CF $-\lambda$). Let L be a pure random context language, and let $L = L(G)$ for a pure random context grammar $G = (V, P, S)$ (without appearance checking and without λ-rules). We set

$$V' = \{a' : a \in V\},\ V'' = \{a'' : a \in V\}.$$

For a word $w = x_1x_2 \ldots x_n \in V^*$ and a set $Q \subseteq V$, we set $w' = x_1'x_2' \ldots x_n'$ and $Q' = \{a' : a \in Q\}$, and define w'' analogously. Now we construct a random context grammar $G' = (W, V, P', \bar{S})$ with

$$W = V' \cup V'' \cup \{\bar{S}\},$$

where $\bar{S}$ is a new symbol, and P' contains the following rules:

(0) $(\bar{S} \to x''w', \emptyset, \emptyset)$ for $xw \in S, x \in V, w \in V^*$,

(1) $(x' \to w', Q' \cup \{a''\}, \emptyset)$ for $(x \to w, Q, \emptyset) \in P, a \in V$,

(2) $(x' \to w', (Q' \setminus \{a'\}) \cup \{a''\}, \emptyset)$ for $(x \to w, Q, \emptyset) \in P, a \in Q$,

(3) $(x'' \to y''w', Q', \emptyset)$ for $(x \to yw, Q, \emptyset) \in P, y \in V, w \in V^*$,

(4) $(x'' \to x, \emptyset, \emptyset)$ for $x \in V$,

(5) $(x' \to x, \{a\}, \emptyset)$ for $x \in V, a \in V$.

Each derivation in G' has to start with $\bar{S}$. Only the productions of type (0) are applicable, and we obtain a word $x_1''w_1'$, $x_1 \in V$, $w_1 \in V^*$. Now the productions of type (5) are not applicable. The productions of type (1) to (3) again produce a word starting with a letter of V'' followed by a word over V', let us say $x_2''w_2'$ (if the rule is not of type (3) then $x_1 = x_2$). By the definition of P' it is easy to see that this derivation $x_1''w_1' \Rightarrow x_2''w_2'$ exists in G' if and only if $x_1w_1 \Rightarrow x_2w_2$ is a derivation in G. These arguments can be repeated. Thus

$$\bar{S} \Rightarrow x_1''w_1' \Rightarrow x_2''w_2' \Rightarrow \cdots \Rightarrow x_n''w_n'$$

holds in G' iff

$$x_1w_1 \Rightarrow x_2w_2 \Rightarrow \cdots \Rightarrow x_nw_n$$

holds in G. If we apply a rule of type (4) then $x_n''w_n' \Rightarrow x_nw_n'$, and now we can apply only rules of type (5) since the productions (1) to (4) require a letter of V'' in the word. These productions rename all letters of V' by the corresponding letter of V. Therefore we obtain the derivation $x_n''w_n' \Rightarrow x_nw_n$. Furthermore, this is the only possibility to terminate a derivation in G'. Hence $x_nw_n \in L(G')$ iff $x_nw_n \in L(G)$. Thus $L(G') = L(G)$.

(Note that it is necessary to introduce at least one copy of V since in the usual grammar any core production has to have a left-hand side which is not in the terminal alphabet; $\bar{S}$ is introduced in order to have a non-terminal symbol as the only axiom.)

$\mathcal{L}(\text{pM, CF, ac}) \subseteq \mathcal{L}(\text{M, CF, ac})$. We consider the language L generated by the pure matrix grammar $G = (V, M, S, F)$. Let V' be defined as above and let S', S'', S''' be different symbols which are not in $V \cup V'$. Then we consider the matrices

$$(S' \to S''w'),\ w \in S$$

(these matrices have to be applied to the axiom S'), and with each matrix m: $(x_1 \to v_1, x_2 \to v_2, \ldots, x_n \to v_n) \in M$ we associate the matrices

$$m' : (S'' \to S'', x_1' \to v_1', x_2' \to v_2', \ldots, x_n' \to v_n')$$

(the application of the matrix m' simulates the application of m) and

$$m_i : (S'' \to S'', x_1' \to v_1', x_2' \to v_2', \ldots, x_i' \to v_i', S'' \to S''')$$

where $1 \leqq i \leqq n$ (these matrices model the application of an initial part of the matrix m, and they introduce the letter S''' which marks the final terminating phase of a derivation), and we introduce the matrices

$$(S''' \to S''', x' \to x) \quad \text{for} \quad x \in V \quad \text{and} \quad (S''' \to \lambda)$$

(they form the termination which goes by renaming, again). Let

$$G' = (V' \cup \{S', S'', S'''\}, V, M', S', F')$$

where M' is the set of all matrices introduced above and

$$F' = \{x' \to w' : x \to w \in F\}.$$

It is easy to prove that $L(G') = L(G)$.

Properness of the inclusions. For a given pure grammar, let

$$k_1 = \max \{|z| : a \to z \quad \text{is a core production of the grammar}\},$$
$$k_2 = \max \{|s| : s \in S\},$$
$$k \ = \max \{k_1, k_2\} + 1.$$

Further, let $w \in L(G)$ and $|w| > k$. Then there is a derivation $S \overset{*}{\Rightarrow} w' \Rightarrow w$ of w and obviously $-k < |w| - |w'| < k$ and $w \neq w'$. Thus, for each pure language L there exists a constant k such that, for all words $w \in L$ with $|w| > k$, there is a word $w' \in L$ with $w' \neq w$ and $-k < |w| - |w'| < k$.

On the other hand, by Chapter 1, the non-pure regulated families contain languages L such that, for any n, there is a word $w \in L$ with $||w'| - |w|| > n$ for all $w' \in L, w' \neq w$. Hence these languages cannot be pure.

The same argument proves $\mathscr{L}(\text{pRE}) \subseteq \mathscr{L}(\text{RE})$ and $\mathscr{L}(\text{pCS}) \subset \mathscr{L}(\text{CS})$. $\mathscr{L}(\text{pCF}) \subset \mathscr{L}(\text{CF})$ also is proper; for instance, the context-free language $\{a^n b^n : n \geqq 1\}$ cannot be generated by a pure context-free grammar (as the reader may easily verify). In fact, one can see that $\{a^n b^n : n \geqq 1\}$ cannot be generated either by pure random context or pure programmed grammars: a rule $a \to a^i$, $i \geqq 2$, would lead to strings of the form $a^m b^n$, $m > n$ (and similarly for rules $b \to b^i$, $i \geqq 2$), whereas a rule $a \to w$ with w containing occurrences of a and b would lead to strings of the form $xbay$ which are not in our language (similarly for rules $b \to w$ with w containing occurrences of a and b).

The main purpose of this section is to determine the hierarchy of all the families of languages. introduced above This hierarchy is presented in the following theorem.

Theorem 5.1.1.

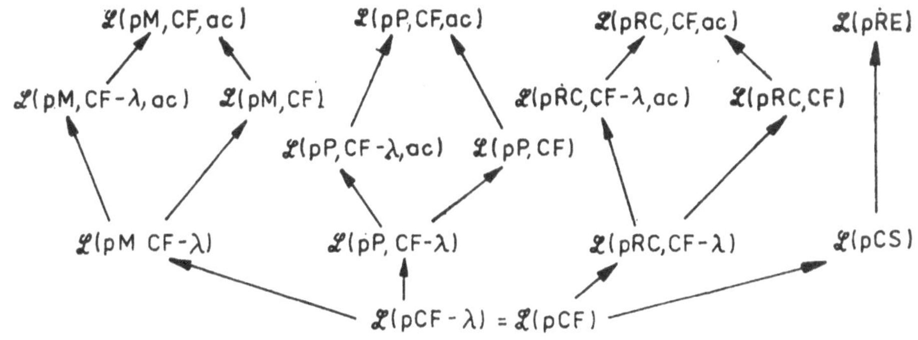

The proper containments are shown by an arrow, whereas the nonconnected families are incomparable.

Before giving the proof we note that Theorem 5.1.1 shows clearly that the pure languages can illustrate the differences between the different regulation mechanisms. In particular, we see that the simulation of one mechanism by another one needs — in general — auxiliary letters.

Instead of a proof of Theorem 5.1.1 we shall give some claims and prove them. The statement of the theorem follows by combination of these claims.

The first three claims will show the incomparability of two pure language families if they are generated by different regulating mechanisms.

Claim 5.1.1. *Let L_1 be the language of Example* 5.1.1. *Then*

$$L_1 \in \mathcal{L}(\mathrm{pM}, \mathrm{CF} - \lambda),\ L_1 \notin \mathcal{L}(\mathrm{pRC}, \mathrm{CF}, \mathrm{ac}),\ L_1 \notin \mathcal{L}(\mathrm{pP}, \mathrm{CF}, \mathrm{ac}).$$

Proof. i) The first statement follows from Example 5.1.1.

ii) Now let us assume that $L_1 = L(G)$ for some pure random context grammar $G = (V, P, S)$. Let n be sufficiently large such that $a^{n+1}b^nc^n \notin S$. Then there has to exist a derivation

$$S \overset{*}{\Rightarrow} z \underset{p}{\Longrightarrow} a^{n+1}b^nc^n$$

and, without loss of generality, we can assume that $z \neq a^{n+1}b^nc^n$. There are only two possibilities for z: $z = a^nb^nc^n$ or $z = a^{n+1}b^{n+1}c^n$ and the corresponding core production of p has to be $a \to a^2$ or $b \to \lambda$, respectively. However, $a^{n+1}b^nc^n$ has the same random context as z, and thus we can generate by application of p to $a^{n+1}b^nc^n$ either $a^{n+2}b^nc^n$ or $a^{n+1}b^{n-1}c^n$, respectively. Hence we can generate a word which is not in L_1, which contradicts our assumption.

iii) Let us assume that $L_1 = L(G)$ for some pure programmed grammar $G = (V, P, S)$ We consider a word $w = a^{n+1}b^{n+1}c^n$ for a sufficiently large number n and a derivation

$$s = w_0 \underset{p_1}{\Longrightarrow} w_1 \Rightarrow \cdots \Rightarrow w_{n-2} \underset{p_{n-1}}{\Longrightarrow} w_{n-1} \underset{p_n}{\Longrightarrow} w_n = w$$

such that $w_i \neq w$ for $0 \leqq i \leqq n - 1$. We consider the two possible cases for w_{n-1}.

Case 1. $w_{n-1} = a^{n+1}b^nc^n$. Then the last applied production p_n has the core production $b \to b^2$. This production is applicable to any axiom. If there is an axiom of the form $a^mb^mc^m$ or $a^{m+1}b^{m+1}c^m$, then its application derives $a^mb^{m+1}c^m$ or $a^{m+1}b^{m+2}c^m$, respectively. In both cases, the generated word is not in L_1. Therefore all axioms are of the form $a^{m+1}b^mc^m$, $m \geqq 1$. Further, $w_{n-2} = a^{n+1}b^{n+1}c^n$ or $w_{n-2} = a^nb^nc^n$, and the production p_{n-1} has the core production $b \to \lambda$ or $a \to a^2$. In the former case we get a contradiction to our assumption $w_{n-2} \neq w$, in the latter case we apply p_{n-1} to an axiom and obtain $a^{m+2}b^mc^m \notin L_1$. Thus Case 1 cannot appear.

Case 2. $w_{n-1} = a^{n+1}b^{n+1}c^{n+1}$. Then $w_{n-2} = a^{n+2}b^{n+1}c^{n+1}$ or $w_{n-2} = a^{n+1}b^{n+}{}_1c^n$. In the latter case $w_{n-2} = w$ in contrast to our assumption. Hence $w_{n-3} = a^{n+1}b^{n+1}c^{n+1}$ or $w_{n-3} = a^{n+2}b^{n+2}c^{n+1}$. In the former case we have $w_{n-3} = w_{n-1}$, in the latter case w_{n-3} has the same structure as $w_n = w$, and thus we can continue the process. In both cases we obtain $|w_{i+1}| < |w_i|$ for $0 \leqq i \leqq n$. Hence w cannot be generated from an axiom.

This proves $L_1 \notin \mathcal{L}(\mathrm{pP}, \mathrm{CF}, \mathrm{ac})$.

Claim 5.1.2. *Let L_2 be the language of Example* 5.1.2. *Then*

$$L_2 \in \mathcal{L}(\mathrm{pP}, \mathrm{CF} - \lambda),\ L_2 \notin \mathcal{L}(\mathrm{pM}, \mathrm{CF}, \mathrm{ac}),\ L_2 \notin \mathcal{L}(\mathrm{pRC}, \mathrm{CF}, \mathrm{ac}).$$

Proof. By Example 5.1.2 we have to prove only the noncontainments.

i) Assume that $L_2 = L(G)$ for some pure matrix grammar $G = (V, M, S, F)$. First we note that G is λ-free since $||w| - |w'|| \geqq 2$ for all $w, w' \in L_2$, $w \neq w'$. Further we can assume that $F = \emptyset$ because we can rewrite only a, and a is present in each element of L_2, and without loss of generality we can also assume that no core production has the form $a \to a$. Let n be sufficiently large, and let w be the word of minimal length satisfying $|w| > n$ and w is generated by iterated applications of matrices, i.e. $s \overset{*}{\Rightarrow} v \underset{m}{\Longrightarrow} w$ for some matrix $m \in M$. If $v = a^k$, $w = a^t$ and $k \not\equiv t \bmod 10$, then the application of m to w generates a word not belonging to L_2. Therefore there is a matrix which increases the number of a by a multiple of 10, say $10q$.

If a^5 is an axiom, then a^{5+10q} can be derived, and we obtain a contradiction. If a^5 is not an axiom, then there has to be a matrix m' starting with the production $a \to a^5$ in order to generate a^5 from a. Then the application of m to a and the application of the first production of m' to the generated word derives $a^{5+10q} \notin L_2$. Again, we get a contradiction.

ii) Assume that $L_2 = L(G)$ for some pure random context grammar $G = (V, P, S)$. As above G is λ-free. For a sufficiently large number n we can consider a derivation $s \overset{*}{\Rightarrow} a^k \underset{p}{\Longrightarrow} a^{7+10n}$. If $k \not\equiv 7 \bmod 10$, then the application of p to a^{7+10n} produces a word which is not in L_2. Therefore p has the core production $a \to a^{10q+1}$ for some $q > 0$. Since $a^5 \in L_2$ and it has the same random context as a^k we can apply p to a^5, and this gives a word which is not in L_2. Hence $L_2 \neq L(G)$.

Claim 5.1.3. *Let L_3 be the language of Example* 5.1.3. *Then*

$$L_3 \in \mathcal{L}(\mathrm{pRC}, \mathrm{CF} - \lambda),\ L_3 \notin \mathcal{L}(\mathrm{pP}, \mathrm{CF}, \mathrm{ac}),\ L_3 \notin \mathcal{L}(\mathrm{pM}, \mathrm{CF}, \mathrm{ac}).$$

Proof. We prove only the second statement; the third one can be proved analogously, and the first one follows from Example 5.1.3.

Let us assume that $L_3 = L(G)$ for some pure programmed grammar $G = (V, P, S)$. Again, G is λ-free, and hence bba is an axiom. Further, in order to generate ba^{5+3n} for sufficiently large n we need a production with the core rule $a \to a^{3m+1}$ for some $m \geqq 1$. Clearly, it can be applied to the axioms, and this gives $bba \Rightarrow bba^{3m+1} \in L(G)$. However, $bba^{3m+1} \notin L_3$.

As a direct consequence of the following claim we obtain that, for $X \in \{\mathrm{RC}, \mathrm{P}, \mathrm{M}\}$, $\mathcal{L}(\mathrm{pCS}) \setminus \mathcal{L}(\mathrm{pX}, \mathrm{CF}, \mathrm{ac}) \neq \emptyset$.

Claim 5.1.4. $L_2 \in \mathcal{L}(\mathrm{pCS})$, $L_3 \in \mathcal{L}(\mathrm{pCS})$.

Proof. We prove only the first statement, the second one can be proved by analogous arguments. Let

$$G = (\{a\}, \{a^7 \to a^{17}\}, \{a, a^5, a^7, a^{11}\}).$$

Since the production is only applicable to the axioms a^7 and a^{11}, and since the application of the rule to a^n produces a^{n+10}, it follows easily that $L_2 = L(G)$.

In order to derive the incomparability of the pure language families obtained by regulated rewriting and the pure context-sensitive language families we have to show that $\mathcal{L}(\text{pX}, \text{CF} - \lambda) \setminus \mathcal{L}(\text{pRE}) \neq \emptyset$ for $X \in \{\text{RC}, \text{P}, \text{M}\}$. This follows from

Claim 5.1.5. i) $L_1 \notin \mathcal{L}(\text{pRE})$.

ii) $L_1' = \{d\} \cup L_1 \in \mathcal{L}(\text{pP}, \text{CF} - \lambda)$, $L_1' \notin \mathcal{L}(\text{pRE})$,

iii) $L_4 = \{ea^ncb^n : n \geqq 1\} \cup \{fa^nc^mb^n : n, m \geqq 1\} \in \mathcal{L}(\text{pRC}, \text{CF} - \lambda)$,

$L_4 \notin \mathcal{L}(\text{pRE})$.

Proof. i) We use the same arguments as in the proof of i) in Claim 5.1.1.

ii) $L_1' \notin \mathcal{L}(\text{pRE})$ follows as i), and L_1' is generated by the pure programmed grammar

$$\big(\{a, b, c, d\}, \big\{(0: d \to abc, \{1\}, \emptyset), (1: a \to a^2, \{2\}, \emptyset), (2: b \to b^2, \{3\}, \emptyset),$$

$$(3: c \to c^2, \{1\}, \emptyset)\big\}, \{d\}\big).$$

iii) It is easy to see that the pure random context grammar

$$\big(\{e, f, a, b, c\}, \big\{(e \to f, \emptyset, \emptyset), (c \to acb, \{e\}, \emptyset), (c \to c^2, \{f\}, \emptyset)\big\}, \{eacb\}\big)$$

generates L_4.

Now let us assume that $L_4 = L(G)$ for some pure context-sensitive grammar G (with erasing rules). We consider the word $w = fa^nc^2b^n$ for a sufficiently large integer n. The string w can be generated only from fa^ncb^n by a rule $a^rcb^s \to a^rc^2b^s$, $r, s \geqq 0$. Obviously, this rule can be applied to $ea^ncb^n \in L_4$, too, and this produces $ea^nc^2b^n$ which is not in L_4.

Claim 5.1.6. *Let X, Y be two families of grammars (occurring in the formulation of Theorem* 5.1.1). *If $\mathcal{L}(\text{p}X) = \mathcal{L}(\text{p}Y)$, then $\mathcal{L}(X) = \mathcal{L}(Y)$.*

Proof. Let $L \in \mathcal{L}(X)$. Then $L = L(G)$ for some grammar G of type X. Let L' be the set of sentential forms generated by G. Clearly, $L = L' \cap V_T^*$ and L' is a pure X language. By supposition $L' \in \mathcal{L}(pY)$, and thus, by Lemma 5.1.1, $L' \in \mathcal{L}(Y)$. Since all the families of interest are closed under intersection with regular sets, we obtain $L \in \mathcal{L}(Y)$. This proves $\mathcal{L}(X) \subseteq \mathcal{L}(Y)$. Analogously we can prove the opposite inclusion.

By known relations between the usual language families and Claim 5.1.6 we get

$$\mathcal{L}(\text{pCF} - \lambda) \subset \mathcal{L}(\text{pCS}) \subset \mathcal{L}(\text{pRE}),$$

$$\mathcal{L}(\text{pCF}) \subset \mathcal{L}(\text{pX}, \text{CF} - \lambda),$$

$$\mathcal{L}(\text{pX}, \text{CF} - \lambda, \text{ac}) \subset \mathcal{L}(\text{pX}, \text{CF}, \text{ac}),$$

where $X \in \{\text{RC}, \text{M}, \text{P}\}$.

Claim 5.1.7. *For* $X \in \{\text{M}, \text{P}, \text{RC}\}$, $\mathcal{L}(\text{pX}, \text{CF}) \setminus \mathcal{L}(\text{pX}, \text{CF} - \lambda, \text{ac}) \neq \emptyset$.

Proof. $X = \text{M}$. Let

$$L_4' = \{ca^nb^n : n \geqq 2\} \cup \{ca^{n+1}b^n : n \geqq 2\} \cup \{a^nb^n : n \geqq 2\}.$$

Clearly, L_4' is generated by the pure matrix grammar

$$G_4' = \big(\{a, b, c\}, \{(c \to c, a \to a^2, b \to b^2), (c \to \lambda)\}, \{ca^2b^2\}, \emptyset\big).$$

Therefore $L_4' \in \mathcal{L}(\text{pM}, \text{CF})$.

Now assume that $L'_4 = L(G)$ for some pure matrix grammar G with appearance checking and without λ-rules. We consider the word $a^n b^n$ where n is chosen such that $a^n b^n$ is not an axiom. Then there is a word z with $z \Rightarrow a^n b^n$. If $z = a^r b^r$ for some $r < n$ ($r > n$ is impossible since G is λ-free and $r = n$ is not of interest: we can assume that $z \neq a^n b^n$), then we apply a rule of the form $a \to a^{s+1} b^s$ to the last a in z or $b \to a^s b^{s+1}$ to the first b, where $s \geqq 1$. Since $r \geqq 2$ we can apply this rule to the first a or to the last b, too, and we derive a word which is not in L'_4. Hence z is of the form $ca^r b^r$ or $ca^{r+1} b^r$, and we have to apply a rule of the form $c \to z'$ to z which gives $z' a^r b^r$ or $z' a^{r+1} b^r$. In the first case $z' = \lambda$ and $r = n$ have to hold and this contradicts the λ-free-ness of G; in the second case we do not obtain $a^n b^n$.

$X = P$. Let $L''_4 = \{d\} \cup L'_4$. It is easy to see that $L''_4 \in \mathcal{L}(\text{pP, CF})$, and $L''_4 \notin \mathcal{L}(\text{pP, CF} - \lambda, \text{ac})$ can be proved by the same arguments as above.

$X = \text{RC}$. We omit the proof which can be given analogously using the language

$$\{ca^n b^n d : n \geqq 2\} \cup \{c' a^{n+1} b^n d : n \geqq 2\} \cup \{c' a^n b^n d' : n \geqq 3\}$$
$$\cup \{ca^n b^n d' : n \geqq 3\} \cup \{a^n b^n d : n \geqq 2\}$$

(see also Exercise 5.1.1).

In order to finish the proof of Theorem 5.1.1 it is sufficient to prove that $\mathcal{L}(\text{p}X, \text{CF} - \lambda, \text{ac}) \setminus \mathcal{L}(\text{p}X, \text{CF}) \neq \emptyset$ for $x \in \{\text{M, P, RC}\}$. This is shown in the following three claims.

Let us consider the pure programmed grammar

$$G_5 = \big(\{a, b\}, \{(1 : a \to b^3, \{1\}, \{2\}), (2 : b \to a^3, \{2\}, \{1\})\}, \{a\}\big).$$

The language L_5 generated by G_5 contains only words w of $\{a, b\}^*$ which satisfy one of the following conditions:

$$|w|_a + \frac{|w|_b}{3} = 3^{2n}, \ |w|_b + \frac{|w|_a}{3} = 3^{2n+1}$$

for some $n \in \mathbb{N}$.

Claim 5.1.8. $L_5 \in \mathcal{L}(\text{pP, CF} - \lambda, \text{ac})$, $L_5 \notin \mathcal{L}(\text{pP, CF})$.

Proof. By the construction of L_5 we have to prove only the second statement. Let us assume the contrary, i.e. $L_5 = L(G)$ for some pure programmed grammar G without appearance checking. First we note that G is λ-free and that there is no rule whose core production is of the form $a \to b$ or $b \to a$. For a production $p = \big(b : x \to w, \sigma(b), \varphi(b)\big)$ we set $\lg(p) = |w| - 1$, and we define $\lg(G)$ as the maximum of $\lg(p)$ taken over all $p \in P$. Obviously, $\lg(G) \geqq 2$. Further, let t be the maximal length of a word in S, and let n be an integer such that $3^n > t \cdot \text{card}(P) \cdot \lg(G)$. We consider a derivation D of $a^{3^{2n}-1} b^3 \in L_5$, especially the last $q + 2$ steps of this derivation which increase the length, where $q = \text{card}(P)$, i.e.

$$D : S \stackrel{*}{\Rightarrow} y_0 \underset{b_0}{\Longrightarrow} y_1 \stackrel{*}{\Rightarrow} y_1 \underset{b_1}{\Longrightarrow} y_2 \stackrel{*}{\Rightarrow} y_2 \Rightarrow \cdots \underset{b_q}{\Longrightarrow} y_{q+1} \stackrel{*}{\Rightarrow} y_{q+1} \underset{b_{q+1}}{\Longrightarrow} a^{3^{2n}-1} b^3$$

where the derivation steps $y_i \Rightarrow y_{i+1}$ are obtained by application of the productions $\big(b_i : x_i \to w_i, \sigma(b_i), \emptyset\big)$ with $|w_i| \geqq 2$ and the phases $y_i \stackrel{*}{\Rightarrow} y_i$ contain only applications of rules with core productions $a \to a$ or $b \to b$. By definition of n and q the following facts are valid:

a) $|y_i|_b + \frac{|y_i|_a}{3} = 3^{2n-1}$ for $0 \leqq i \leqq q$,

b) there are two integers k, j with $0 \leqq k < j \leqq q$ such that $b_k = b_j$.

Let $|y_k|_a = 3^{2n} - 3r_1$, $|y_k|_b = r_1$,

$|y_j|_a = 3^{2n} - 3r_2$, $|y_j|_b = r_2$.

Then $3^n > r_i - r_2 > 0$. Thus the derivation

$$S \overset{*}{\Rightarrow} y_0 \underset{b_0}{\Longrightarrow} y_1 \overset{*}{\Rightarrow} \cdots \overset{*}{\Rightarrow} y_k \underset{b_j}{\Longrightarrow} z_j \overset{*}{\Rightarrow} z_j \underset{b_{j+1}}{\Longrightarrow} z_{j+1} \overset{*}{\Rightarrow} \cdots \underset{b_{q+1}}{\Longrightarrow} z_{q+1}$$

s als o correct and

$$|z_{q+1}|_a = 3^{2n} - 3(r_1 - r_2), |z_{q+1}|_b = 3 + (r_1 - r_2).$$

This contradicts the structure of words in L_5 and thus $z_{q+1} \notin L_5$. Since $z_{q+1} \in L(G)$ we obtain the desired contradiction to $L(G) = L_5$.

Now we consider the pure matrix grammar

$$G_6 = \Big(\{a, b, c, d\}, \big\{(a \to a^3, b \to b^3, c \to c^3), (a \to a^3, b \to d^3, c \to c^3)\big\}, \{abc\}, \{b \to b^3, b \to d^3\}\Big).$$

Then the words of the generated language L_6 satisfy the following conditions:

If $|w|_b = 0$, then $w = a^{2n+1}d^{3m}c^{2n-1}$ or $w = a^{2n+1}d^{3m}c^{2n+1}$ with $2n + 1 \geqq 3m$, $n, m \in \mathbb{N}$.

If $|w|_b \geqq 1$, then $w = a^{2n+1}w'c^{2n+1}$ or $w = a^{2n+1}w'c^{2n-1}$ where $w' \in \{b, d^3\}^*$, $|w'| = 2n + 1$ or $|w'| = 2n - 1$.

Claim 5.1.9. $L_6 \in \mathscr{L}(\mathrm{pM, CF} - \lambda, \mathrm{ac})$, $L_6 \notin \mathscr{L}(\mathrm{pM, CF})$.

Proof. Again we have to prove only the second statement. Let us assume that $L_6 = L(G)$ for some pure matrix grammar without appearance checking. As in the preceding proofs we can show that all core productions (besides $x \to x$) have the form $x \to w$ with $|w| \geqq 3$. Let n be a sufficiently large number. We consider a derivation D of $w = a^{2n+1}d^3c^{2n+1}$,

$$D: s \overset{*}{\Rightarrow} v_1 \Rightarrow v_2 \Rightarrow w.$$

Let us assume that $|v_1| < |v_2| < |w|$. By the structure of the words of L_6 it is easy to prove that $v_1 = a^{2n-1}d^3c^{2n-1}$, $v_2 = a^{2n+1}d^3c^{2n-1}$. Iterating this argument and taking into consideration the fact that we can omit length preserving matrices we obtain

$$D: s \overset{*}{\Rightarrow} u_1 \underset{m}{\Longrightarrow} u_2 \overset{*}{\Rightarrow} w$$

where the derivation $u_2 \overset{*}{\Rightarrow} w$ corresponds to the application of a proper initial part of a matrix or $u_2 = w$ and the application of m increases the number of a and/or of c only. If only the number of a^5 is measured, then by iterated application of m to u_2 we can generate a word y with $|y|_a - |y|_c > 2$ which contradicts the structure of the words in L_6. Analogously, the matrix m cannot only increase the number of c. Hence it has to increase both numbers. Now we consider a derivation D' of $w' = a^{2n+1}b^{2n+1}c^{2n+1}$. Again

$$D' : s' \overset{*}{\Rightarrow} z \Rightarrow w'$$

where $z \overset{*}{\Rightarrow} w'$ is the initial part of a matrix application or $z = w'$ and z is generated by iterated application of matrices. Clearly, $|z|_b > 1$. Then it is easy to show that the correct derivation

$$s' \overset{*}{\Rightarrow} z \underset{m}{\Longrightarrow} z_1 \underset{m}{\Longrightarrow} z_2 \underset{m}{\Longrightarrow} z_3$$

produces a word z_3 which is not contained in L_6.

Claim 5.1.10. *Let*

$$L_7 = \{a^2b^2c, ab^5c, b^3ab^2c, b^7c, b^{11}\} \cup \{a^{2n}b^5 : n \geqq 1\} \cup \{a^{2n+1}b^8 : n \geqq 0\} \cup \{b^3a^{2n+1}b^5, n \geqq 0\}.$$

Then $L_7 \in \mathscr{L}(\text{pRC}, \text{CF} - \lambda, \text{ac})$, $L_7 \notin \mathscr{L}(\text{pRC}, \text{CF})$.

Proof. The pure random context grammar

$$G_7 = \big(\{a, b, c\}, \{(c \to b^3, \emptyset, \emptyset), (a \to a^3, \emptyset, \{c\}), (a \to b^3, \{c\}, \emptyset)\}, \{a^2bc\}\big)$$

generates L_7.

Assume now that $L_7 = L(G)$ for some pure random context grammar G without appearance checking. We consider $a^{2n}b^5$ where n is sufficiently large. This word can be derived only from a word $a^{2m}b^5$ (without loss of generality we can assume that $m < n$) and thus we have a production $(a \to a^{2(n-m)+1}, Q, \emptyset)$ or $(b \to a^{2(n-m)}b, Q, \emptyset)$ with $Q \subseteq \{a, b, c\}$. This rule is applicable to a^2b^2c producing a word not in L_7.

We omit the proof of $\mathscr{L}(\text{pCF}) = \mathscr{L}(\text{pCF} - \lambda)$ which can be given by the standard arguments for the elimination of erasing rules.

The proof of Theorem 5.1.1 is complete.

Now we study the closure properties of pure language families.

Theorem 5.1.2. *For* $X \in \{\text{M, P, RC}\}$, $\alpha \in \{\text{CF}, \text{CF} - \lambda\}$, $\beta = \text{ac}$ *or empty, the family* $\mathscr{L}(\text{p}X, \alpha, \beta)$ *is closed under none of the AFL operations.*

Proof. We shall prove the statement only for pure programmed grammars. The cases of pure matrix and pure random context grammars are left to the reader.

i) *Union.* The languages $L_3' = \{ba\}$, $L_3'' = \{a^{5+3n} : n \geqq 0\}$, and $L_3''' = \{a^{4+3n}ba^{1+3m} : n \geqq 0, m \geqq 0\}$ are contained in $\mathscr{L}(\text{pP}, \text{CF} - \lambda)$ (in fact, they are also in $\mathscr{L}(\text{pCF})$). However, $L_3 = L_3' \cup L_3'' \cup L_3''' \notin \mathscr{L}(\text{pP}, \text{CF}, \text{ac})$ by Claim 5.1.3.

ii) *Concatenation.* The languages

$$L_8 = \{a^ncb^n : n \geqq 0\} \quad \text{and} \quad L_9 = \{a^ncb^{2n} : n \geqq 0\}$$

are generated by pure programmed grammars (without appearance checking and λ-rules). We show that $L_8L_9 \notin \mathscr{L}(\text{pP}, \text{CF}, \text{ac})$.

Assume the contrary, i.e. $L_8L_9 = L(G)$ for some pure programmed grammar G. Let m and n be sufficiently large numbers, and let $w_1 = a^ncb^n$, $w_2 = a^mcb^{2m}$, $w = w_1w_2 = a^ncb^n\, a^mcb^{2m}$. Assume that there is a rule with a core production different from $x \to x$ which is applicable to a letter x of w_1 in w. It is easy to see that $x = c$ has to hold and that its core production has to have the form $c \to a^kcb^k$ for some $k \geqq 1$. However, this rule is applicable to both occurrences of c in w. Applying it to c in w_2 we obtain

$$w \Rightarrow a^n cb^n a^{m+k} cb^{2m+n} \notin L_8 L_9 .$$

If there is a production applicable to a letter of w_2 in w, then we conclude analogously. Therefore we can generate only a finite number of words with the considered grammar G. Thus it does not generate the language $L_8 L_9$.

iii) *Kleene closure.* The language $L_{10} = L_8 \cup L_9$ is generated by the pure programmed grammar

$$\big(\{a, b, c\}, \{(1: c \to acb, \{1\}, \emptyset), (2: c \to acb^2, \{2\}, \emptyset)\}, \{c\}\big).$$

As in ii) we can prove that $L_{10}^+ \notin \mathcal{L}(\text{pP, CF, ac})$.

iv) *Homomorphisms.* Let $h(a) = h(c) = a$ and $h(b) = b$. Then

$$h(L_{10}) = \{a^{n+1}b^n : n \geqq 1\} \cup \{a^{n+1}b^{2n} : n \geqq 0\}.$$

Again, we can show that the productions of a grammar generating $h(L_{10})$ which are applicable to $a^{m+1}b^m$ or $a^{m+1}b^{2m}$ for sufficiently large m have the form $\big(r: a \to a, \sigma(r)$ $\varphi(r)\big)$ or $\big(r: b \to b, \sigma(r), \varphi(r)\big)$. Thus $h(L_{10}) \notin \mathcal{L}(\text{pP, CF, ac})$.

v) *Inverse homomorphisms.* Consider the language

$$L_{11} = \{a^n cb^n : n \geqq 0\} \cup \{a^{n+1}b^n : n \geqq 1\} \cup \{a^n db^{2n} : n \geqq 0\} \cup \{a^{n+1}b^{2n} : n \geqq 1\}.$$

It is easy to see that $L_{11} \in \mathcal{L}(\text{pCF}) \subseteq \mathcal{L}(\text{pP, CF} - \lambda)$. Let g be the homomorphism given by

$$g(a) = a, g(b) = b, g(c) = c^2, g(d) = d^2.$$

Then $g^{-1}(L_{11}) = h(L_{10})$ with h as in part iv) of the proof. Hence $g^{-1}(L_{11}) \notin \mathcal{L}(\text{pP, CF, ac})$.

vi) *Intersection by regular sets.* $L_{11} \cap \{a\}^* \{b\}^* = h(L_{10})$ which is not in $\mathcal{L}(\text{pP, CF, ac})$.

Without proof we mention that

- the families $\mathcal{L}(\text{pCF})$, $\mathcal{L}(\text{pCS})$, and $\mathcal{L}(\text{pRE})$ are closed under none of the AFL operations,
- the family of sets of sentential forms of grammars with regulated rewriting are closed with respect to no AFL operation, with one exception, the family of sets of sentential forms generated by programmed grammars which is closed under union.

Finally in this section we give a result on pure matrix languages which will be needed in the next section.

Lemma 5.1.2. *Let G be a pure matrix grammar without λ-rules. Then there are constants p and q (depending on G) such that, for each $w \in L(G)$ with $|w| > p$, each derivation D of w*

$$D: s = w_0 \underset{m_1}{\Longrightarrow} w_1 \underset{m_2}{\Longrightarrow} w_2 \Rightarrow \cdots \underset{m_r}{\Longrightarrow} w_r = w$$

has the property $p_V(w_i) < p_V(w_j)$ for some integers $i, j < q$.

Sketch of the proof. If $L(G)$ is finite the statement holds trivially. Therefore we assume that $L(G)$ is infinite. Let w be a word of sufficiently large length (the numbers p, q will be computed, and then $|w| > p$ is sufficient), and let

$$D: s = w_0 \underset{m_1}{\Longrightarrow} w_1 \underset{m_2}{\Longrightarrow} w_2 \underset{m_3}{\Longrightarrow} \cdots \underset{m_r}{\Longrightarrow} w_r = w$$

be a derivation of w where w_{i+1} is generated from w_i by application of a matrix m_{i+1}. Let $p_V(s) = (s_1, s_2, \ldots, s_n)$ be the Parikh vector of the string s. For t_i, $0 \leqq t_i \leqq s_i + 1$, $1 \leqq i \leqq n$, we define the following sets of vectors and sets of words:

$$M_{t_1, t_2, \ldots, t_n} = \{(x_1, x_2, \ldots, x_n) : x_i = t_i \quad \text{for} \quad t_i \leqq s_i \quad \text{and}$$
$$x_i > s_i \quad \text{for} \quad t_i = s_i + 1\},$$

$$M'_{t_1, t_2, \ldots, t_n} = \{v : p_V(v) \in M_{t_1, t_2, \ldots, t_n}\}.$$

Clearly, there exist exactly $N = \prod_{i=1}^{n} (s_i + 2)$ different sets $M'_{t_1, t_2, \ldots, t_n}$. Thus two of the words $w_0, w_1, \ldots, w_N$ are in the same set, say $w_i, w_j \in M'_{t_1, t_2, \ldots, t_n}$ and $i < j$.

Case 1. There is an integer k such that $t_k = s_{k+1}$, $t_{k'} \leqq s_{k'}$, $k' \neq k$, $1 \leqq k' \leqq n$, $1 \leqq k \leqq n$. Then

$$p_V(w_i) = (t_1, t_2, \ldots, t_{k-1}, r_k, t_{k+1}, \ldots, t_n),$$

$$p_V(w_j) = (t_1, t_2, \ldots, t_{k-1}, r'_k, t_{k+1}, \ldots, t_n).$$

Since $|w_i| < |w_j|$ we obtain $r'_k > r_k$ and hence $p_V(w_i) < p_V(w_j)$. The lemma is proved if we require $q = N$ and $p > N \cdot t \cdot \alpha$ with

$$t = \max \{|s| : s \in S\},$$
$$\alpha = \max \{\alpha(m) : m \in M\}, \ \alpha(a_1 \to v_1, \ldots, a_u \to v_u) = 1 + \sum_{i=1}^{u} (|v_i| - 1).$$

Case 2. There are at least two numbers k_1, k_2 such that $t_{k_1} = s_{k_1} + 1$, $t_{k_2} = s_{k_2} + 1$. For the sake of simplicity we assume that there are exactly two such numbers. Then

$$p_V(w_i) = (t_1, t_2, \ldots, t_{k_1-1}, r_{k_1}, t_{k_1+1}, \ldots, t_{k_2-1}, r_{k_2}, t_{k_2+1}, \ldots, t_n),$$

$$p_V(w_j) = (t_1, t_2, \ldots, t_{k_1-1}, r'_{k_1}, t_{k_1+1}, \ldots, t_{k_2-1}, r'_{k_2}, t_{k_2+1}, \ldots, t_n).$$

If $r_{k_1} < r'_{k_1}$ and $r_{k_2} < r'_{k_2}$ then $p_V(w_i) < p_V(w_j)$, and we are ready. Since $|w_i| < |w_j|$ let us consider (without loss of generality) that $r_{k_1} < r'_{k_1}$, $r_{k_2} > r'_{k_2}$. Then $p_V(w_i)$ and $p_V(w_j)$ are incomparable. Then we set

$$s'_i = s_i \quad \text{for} \quad 1 \leqq i \leqq n, \ i \notin \{k_1, k_2\},$$

$$s'_{k_1} = r'_{k_1}, \ s'_{k_2} = r_{k_2},$$

$$N' = \prod_{i=1}^{n} (s'_i + 2),$$

and we consider the corresponding sets $M'_{t_1, t_2, \ldots, t_n}$ (i.e. $0 \leqq t_i \leqq s'_i + 1$) and the words $w_1, w_2, \ldots, w_{N'}$. Then we can prove that $p_V(w_i) < p_V(w_j)$ for some $i < j \leqq N'$ or there are at least three integers k'_1, k'_2, k'_3 such that $t_{k'_i} = s_{k'_i} + 1$. This process can be continued. However, after n steps we obtain $p_V(w_i) < p_V(w_j)$ or there is a word w_u with $p_V(w_u) = (r_1, r_2, \ldots, r_n)$ and $r_i > s_i$ for $1 \leqq i \leqq n$, i.e. $p_V(s) < p_V(w_u)$. The integers p and q can be calculated since the numbers r_{k_1}, r_{k_2}, etc. are bounded in dependence on α. (In this discussion we assumed that $|w_i| < |w_{i+1}|$. If this is not the case, then only the calculation of p and q has to be modified.)

Exercises

5.1.1. Prove Claim 5.1.7 for $X = \mathrm{RC}$.

5.1.2. Denote by $\mathcal{L}(X)_1$ the family of languages in $L(X)$ over a single letter alphabet. Prove

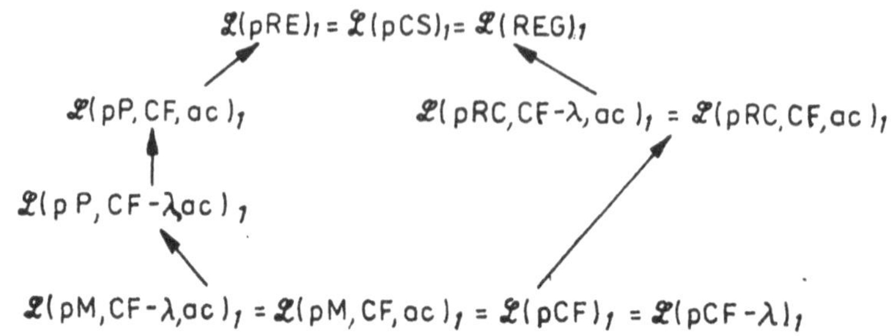

Further show that $L \in \mathcal{L}(\mathrm{pRC}, \mathrm{CF} - \lambda, \mathrm{ac})_1$ iff $L \in \mathcal{L}(\mathrm{pCF})_1$ or $L = L' \cup \{a\}$ for some $L' \in \mathcal{L}(\mathrm{pCF})_1$. Moreover, $L \in \mathcal{L}(\mathrm{pCF})_1$ iff there are integers p, $0 \leqq n_1 < n_2 < \cdots < n_s < m_1 < \cdots < m_r$, $m_r - m_1 < p$, and such that, for each i, $1 \leqq i \leqq s$, there is a j, $1 \leqq j \leqq r$, such that $n_i \equiv m_j \bmod p$ and

$$L = \{a^{n_1}, a^{n_2}, \ldots, a^{n_s}\} \cup \{a^{m_1}, a^{m_2}, \ldots, a^{m_r}\} \{a^p\}^*$$

(see Maurer et al. (1979), Dassow (1986)).

5.1.3. Define pure regularly controlled grammars and languages (with appearance checking, see Section 2.1.) and prove that the associated families $\mathcal{L}(\mathrm{prC}, \alpha, \mathrm{ac})$ of languages are incomparable with $\mathcal{L}(\mathrm{pP}, \alpha', \mathrm{ac})$ and $\mathcal{L}(\mathrm{pRC}, \alpha', \mathrm{ac})$ and that $\mathcal{L}(\mathrm{pM}, \alpha, \mathrm{ac}) \subset \mathcal{L}(\mathrm{prC}, \alpha, \mathrm{ac})$, $\alpha, \alpha' \in \{\mathrm{CF}, \mathrm{CF} - \lambda\}$ (see Dassow and Păun (1986-a).

5.1.4. Define pure conditional grammars and languages (see Chapter 2.3.) and show that the associated families $\mathcal{L}(\mathrm{pK}, \alpha)$ are incomparable with $\mathcal{L}(\mathrm{pP}, \alpha', \mathrm{ac})$, $\mathcal{L}(\mathrm{pM}, \alpha', \mathrm{ac})$, and $\mathcal{L}(\mathrm{prC}, \alpha', \mathrm{ac})$ and that $\mathcal{L}(\mathrm{pK}, \alpha) \supset \mathcal{L}(\mathrm{pRC}, \alpha, \mathrm{ac})$, $\alpha, \alpha' \in \{\mathrm{CF}, \mathrm{CF} - \lambda\}$ (see Dassow and Păun (1986-a)).

5.1.5. Define pure versions of Indian parallel, Russian parallel, and scattered context grammars and study the relation of their families of languages to the families introduced above (see Dassow (1986) and Dassow and Păun (1986-a)).

5.1.6. Prove the closure properties of the family of sets of sentential forms generated by programmed grammars or matrix grammars under the AFL operations.

5.1.7. Show the undecidability of the equivalence problem for pure context-free grammars (see Blattner (1973) and Salomaa (1973-b)). Note that this implies the undecidability of the equivalence problem for all pure grammars studied in this chapter.

5.1.8. For matrix grammars, the pure version can also be defined as follows. The language $L(G)$ of $G = (V, M, S, F)$ consists of all words w with $s \underset{m_{i_1}}{\Longrightarrow} w_1 \underset{m_{i_2}}{\Longrightarrow} w_2 \underset{m_{i_3}}{\Longrightarrow} \cdots \underset{m_{i_n}}{\Longrightarrow} w_n = w$ for some $s \in S$ and some matrices $m_{i_1}, m_{i_2}, \ldots, m_{i_n} \in M$, $n \in \mathbf{N}$. Prove that, for the corresponding pure matrix families, the same hierarchy as in Theorem 5.1.1 holds (see Păun (1986)).

5.2. Codings of Pure Languages

Let $G = (V_N, V_T, P, S)$ be a (context-free, random context, ...) grammar, and let us consider the pure grammar $G' = (V_N \cup V_T, P, \{S\})$. Then it is obvious that $L(G) = L(G') \cap V_T^*$, i.e. each (context-free, random context, ...) language can be obtained as the intersection of a pure (context-free, random context, ...) language and the Kleene closure of a subset of the alphabet of the underlying pure grammar. This corresponds to the definition of ETOL (EOL, ...) languages in the theory of L systems where the language generated by the system (V, V', P, w) is defined by $L(G) = \{x : w \overset{*}{\Rightarrow} x\} \cap (V')^*$, and $\{x : w \overset{*}{\Rightarrow} x\}$ is a TOL language by definition.

In the L system theory it is known that there is a second way to get ETOL languages from TOL languages. It has been shown that, for each ETOL language L, there are a letter-to-letter homomorphism h and a TOL language L' such that $L = h(L')$. If we set

$$\mathscr{C}(X) = \{L : L = h(L') \text{ for some coding } h \text{ and some } L' \in \mathscr{L}(X)\},$$

then this result can be reformulated as

$$\mathscr{L}(\mathrm{ETOL}) = \mathscr{C}(\mathrm{TOL}) \quad \big(\text{and } \mathscr{L}(\mathrm{EOL}) = \mathscr{C}(\mathrm{OL})\big)$$

(see Culik and Opatrny (1974), Ehrenfeucht and Rozenberg (1974-a) and (1974-b), Nielsen et al. (1974), Rozenberg and Salomaa (1980) for these and related results). One to the motivations for the study of pure languages was that they form a sequential counterpart of the (non-extended) L languages. Thus it is natural to ask whether or not the equality $\mathscr{L}(X) = \mathscr{C}(\mathrm{p}X)$ holds, too. Below we shall prove that $\mathscr{L}(\mathrm{p}X) \subset \mathscr{C}(\mathrm{p}X) \subset \mathscr{L}(X)$ for families X of sequential rewriting. Further, we shall study the hierarchy of the intermediate families $\mathscr{C}(\mathrm{p}X)$, and it will be seen that this hierarchy lies between that of pure language families and that of usual language families.

Theorem 5.2.1. i) *For* $X \in \{\mathrm{CF}, \mathrm{CF} - \lambda, \mathrm{CS}, \mathrm{RE}\}$,

$$\mathscr{L}(\mathrm{p}X) \subset \mathscr{C}(\mathrm{p}X) \subset \mathscr{L}(X).$$

ii) *For* $X \in \{\mathrm{RC}, \mathrm{M}, \mathrm{P}\}$, $\alpha \in \{\mathrm{CF}, \mathrm{CF} - \lambda\}$, *and* $\beta = \mathrm{ac}$ *or empty*,

$$\mathscr{L}(\mathrm{p}X, \alpha, \beta) \subset \mathscr{C}(\mathrm{p}X, \alpha, \beta) \subset \mathscr{L}(X, \alpha, \beta).$$

Proof. We give only the proof for ii); for the CF and CS cases we refer to Ehrenfeucht and Rozenberg (1974-b).

The first inclusion follows by definition and its properness follows by Claim 5.1.2, Claim 5.1.3 and $L_2, L_3 \in \mathscr{C}(\mathrm{pCF} - \lambda)$ (where L_2 and L_3 are the languages of Examples 5.1.2 and 5.1.3), which we prove now.

The pure context-free grammar

$$(\{a, b, c\}, \{a \to a^{11}\}, \{b, c^5, a^7, a^{11}\})$$

generates the language

$$L = \{b, c^5\} \cup \{a^{7+10n} : n \geqq 0\} \cup \{a^{11+10n} : n \geqq 0\}.$$

Clearly, $L_2 = h(L)$ for the coding h given by

$$h(a) = h(b) = h(c) = a.$$

$L_2 \in \mathscr{C}(\mathrm{pCF} - \lambda)$ can be proved analogously.

The second inclusion follows by Lemma 5.1.1 and the closure of the families $\mathcal{L}(X, \alpha, \beta)$ under codings and its properness can be shown as in Lemma 5.1.1.

Lemma 5.2.1. *Let X, Y be two classes of grammars of the previous theorem.*

i) *If* $\mathcal{L}(\mathrm{p}X) \subseteq \mathcal{C}(\mathrm{p}Y)$, then $\mathcal{C}(\mathrm{p}X) \subseteq \mathcal{C}(\mathrm{p}Y)$.

ii) *If* $\mathcal{C}(\mathrm{p}X) = \mathcal{C}(\mathrm{p}Y)$, then $\mathcal{L}(X) = \mathcal{L}(Y)$.

Proof. i) Let $L \in \mathcal{C}(\mathrm{p}X)$. Then $L = h(L')$ for some coding h and some $L' \in \mathcal{L}(\mathrm{p}X)$. By assumption, $L' \in \mathcal{C}(\mathrm{p}Y)$. Thus $L' = h'(L'')$ for some coding h' and some $L'' \in \mathcal{L}(\mathrm{p}Y)$. Hence $L = h(h'(L'')) = (h \circ h')(L'')$. Since $h \circ h'$ is a coding, we obtain $L \in \mathcal{C}(\mathrm{p}Y)$, and the proof is complete.

ii) can be proved analogously to Claim 5.1.6.

Lemma 5.2.2. $\mathcal{C}(\mathrm{pP}, \mathrm{CF} - \lambda) \subseteq \mathcal{C}(\mathrm{pM}, \mathrm{CF} - \lambda)$.

Proof. Let $G = (V, P, S)$ be a pure programmed grammar. We set

$$V' = \{(a, b) : a \in V, b \in \mathrm{Lab}\,(P)\}.$$

With the production $(b\colon a \to w, \sigma(b), \emptyset)$ we associate the matrices

$$((a, b) \to w, x \to (x, b')),\ b' \in \sigma(b),\ x \in V.$$

The set S' is defined as the set of all words $w_1(x, b)\, w_2$ where $w_1 x w_2 \in S$, $(x, b) \in V'$. We consider the pure matrix grammar $G' = (V \cup V', M, S', \emptyset)$ where M is the set of matrices of the above introduced type. Then the correct derivations in G' have the following form (in the second row we write the applied rule):

$$s = w_{1,1}(x_1, b_1)\, w_{2,1} \underset{(x_1,b_1)\to z_1}{\Longrightarrow} w_{1,1}z_1w_{2,1} \underset{x_2\to(x_2,b_2)}{\Longrightarrow} w_{1,2}(x_2, b_2)\, w_{2,2} \Rightarrow \cdots$$
$$\Rightarrow w_{1,n}(x_n, b_n)\, w_{2,n} \underset{(x_n,b_n)\to z_n}{\Longrightarrow} w_{1,n}z_nw_{2,n}$$
$$\underset{x_{n+1}\to(x_{n+1},b_{n+1})}{\Longrightarrow} w_{1,n+1}(x_{n+1}, b_{n+1})\, w_{2,n+1} \Rightarrow \cdots .$$

Further we consider the coding h given by

$$h(x) = x \quad \text{for} \quad x \in V \quad \text{and} \quad h((x, b)) = x \quad \text{for} \quad (x, b) \in V'.$$

Then the image of the above derivation is

$$w_{1,1}x_1w_{2,1} \underset{b_1}{\Longrightarrow} w_{1,1}z_1w_{2,1} = w_{1,2}x_2w_{2,2} \underset{b_2}{\Longrightarrow} \cdots \Rightarrow w_{1,n}x_nw_{2,n}$$
$$\underset{b_n}{\Longrightarrow} w_{1,n}z_nw_{2,n} = w_{1,n+1}x_{n+1}w_{2,n+1} \Rightarrow \cdots$$

where, by the definition of the matrices, b_{n+1} is in the success field $\sigma(b_n)$ of b_n. Thus we have proved that $L(G) = h(L(G'))$.

Therefore $\mathcal{L}(\mathrm{pP}, \mathrm{CF} - \lambda) \subseteq \mathcal{C}(\mathrm{pM}, \mathrm{CF} - \lambda)$, and the statement follows by Lemma 5.2.1.

Lemma 5.2.3. i) $\mathcal{C}(\mathrm{pM}, \mathrm{CF} - \lambda, \mathrm{ac}) \subseteq \mathcal{C}(\mathrm{pP}, \mathrm{CF} - \lambda, \mathrm{ac})$,

ii) $\mathcal{L}(\mathrm{pM}, \mathrm{CF} - \lambda) \subseteq \mathcal{C}(\mathrm{pP}, \mathrm{CF} - \lambda)$.

Proof. i) Let $G = (V, M, S, F)$ be a pure matrix grammar with

$$S = \{v_1, v_2, \ldots, v_t\},\ v_i = x_{i,1}x_{i,2} \ldots x_{i,t_i},\ x_{i,j} \in V,\ 1 \leqq i \leqq t,\ 1 \leqq j \leqq t_i,$$
$$M = \{m_1, m_2, \ldots, m_r\},\ m_i : (a_{i,1} \to w_{i,1}, a_{i,2} \to w_{i,2}, \ldots, a_{i,s_i} \to w_{i,s_i})\ 1 \leqq i \leqq r.$$

With a matrix m_i, $1 \leqq i \leqq r$, we associate the programmed rules

$$\big((i, j, 1): a_{i,j} \to w_{i,j}, U_{i,j}, V_{i,j}\big), \ 1 \leqq j \leqq s_i, \ 1 \leqq i \leqq r,$$

where

$$U_{i,j} = \begin{cases} \{(i, j+1, 1)\} & \text{for } j < s_i, \\ \{(k, 1, 1) : 1 \leqq k \leqq r\} & \text{for } j = s_i, \end{cases}$$

$$V_{i,j} = \begin{cases} \emptyset & \text{if } a_{i,j} \to w_{i,j} \notin F, j < s_i, \\ \{(i, j+1, 1)\} & \text{if } a_{i,j} \to w_{i,j} \in F, j < s_i, \\ \{(k, 1, 1) : 1 \leqq k \leqq r\} & \text{if } a_{i,j} \to w_{i,j} \in F, j = s_i. \end{cases}$$

It is clear that these productions simulate the application of m_i, since we have to apply the rules (given by their labels) in the order $(i, 1, 1)$, $(i, 2, 1)$, ..., $(i, s_i, 1)$ (the third coordinate of the label indicates that it is used for matrix simulation). In order to simulate derivations in G it is necessary to ensure that we apply a rule labelled by $(b, 1, 1)$, $1 \leqq b \leqq r$, to the axiom.

Let $x'_{i,j}$, $1 \leqq j \leqq t_i$, $1 \leqq i \leqq t$, be new pairwise different letters not contained in V. For $v_i = x_{i,1}x_{i,2} \dots x_{i,t_i}$, $1 \leqq i \leqq t$, let $v'_i = x'_{i,1}x'_{i,2} \dots x'_{i,t_i}$. Then we set

$$S' = \{v'_1, v'_2, \dots, v'_t\},$$

and for each i, $1 \leqq i \leqq t$, we define the productions

$$\big((i, j, 0): x'_{i,j} \to x_{i,j}, \{(i, j, 0)'\}, \emptyset\big), \ 1 \leqq j \leqq t_i,$$

$$\big((i, j, 0)': x_{i,1} \to x_{i,1}, \{(i, j+1, \emptyset)\}, \emptyset\big), \ 1 \leqq j < t_i,$$

$$\big((i, t_i, 0)': x_{i,1} \to x_{i,1}, \{(k, 1, 1) : 1 \leqq k \leqq r\}, \emptyset\big).$$

To a word $v'_i \in S'$ we can apply only rules with labels $(i, j, 0)$. However, we then have to apply a production with label $(i, j, 0)'$, and therefore the first letter of v'_i has to be rewritten already. Thus the only correct derivations in the grammar $G' = (V', P', S')$, where V' consists of all letters $x'_{i,j}$, $1 \leqq j \leqq t_i$, $1 \leqq i \leqq t$, and all letters of V and P' consists of all the productions introduced above, have the following form:

$$v'_i = x'_{i,1} \dots x'_{i,t_i} \underset{(i,1,0)}{\Longrightarrow} x_{i,1}x'_{i,2} \dots x'_{i,t_i} \underset{(i,1,0)'}{\Longrightarrow} x_{i,1}x'_{i,2}x'_{i,3} \dots x'_{i,t_i}$$

$$\underset{(i,2,0)}{\Longrightarrow} x_{i,1}x_{i,2}x'_{i,3} \dots x'_{i,t_i} \overset{*}{\Rightarrow} x_{i,1}x_{i,2} \dots x_{i,t_i} \underset{(k_1,1,1)}{\Longrightarrow} \dots \underset{(k_1,s_{k_1},1)}{\Longrightarrow} v_i^{(1)}$$

$$\underset{(k_2,1,1)}{\Longrightarrow} \dots \underset{(k_2,s_{k_2},1)}{\Longrightarrow} v_i^{(2)} \Rightarrow \dots$$

where

$$v_i \underset{m_{k_1}}{\Longrightarrow} v_i^{(1)} \underset{m_{k_2}}{\Longrightarrow} v_i^{(2)} \Rightarrow \dots$$

is a derivation in G. We define the coding h by

$$h(x'_{,j}) = x_{i,j} \quad \text{for} \quad 1 \leqq j \leqq t_i, 1 \leqq i \leqq t \quad \text{and} \quad h(x) = x \quad \text{for} \quad x \in V.$$

It is easy to see that $h\big(L(G')\big) = L(G)$. This proves $\mathscr{L}(\text{pM, CF} - \lambda, \text{ac}) \subseteq \mathscr{C}(\text{pP, CF} - \lambda, \text{ac})$, and the statement follows by Lemma 5.2.1.

ii) is proved by the same construction.

Lemma 5.2.4. i) $\mathscr{E}(\text{pRC}, \text{CF} - \lambda, \text{ac}) \subseteq \mathscr{E}(\text{pP}, \text{CF} - \lambda, \text{ac})$.

ii) $\mathscr{E}(\text{pRC}, \text{CF} - \lambda) \subseteq \mathscr{E}(\text{pP}, \text{CF} - \lambda)$.

Proof. i) Let $G = (V, P, S)$ be a pure random context grammar with $V = \{x_1, x_2, \ldots, x_n\}$, and let the ith rule of P be of the form

$$(c \to w, \{a_1, a_2, \ldots, a_s\}, \{b_1, b_2, \ldots, b_r\}).$$

We construct a pure programmed grammar G' in the following way. With the ith rule in P we associate the programmed rules

$$\big((i, j) : a_j \to a_j, \{(i, j + 1)\}, \emptyset\big), \ 1 \leqq j \leqq s,$$
$$\big((i, s + k) : b_k \to b_k, \emptyset, \{(i, s + k + 1)\}\big), \ 1 \leqq k < r,$$
$$\big((i, s + r) : b_r \to b_r, \emptyset, \{(i)\}\big),$$
$$\big((i) : c \to w, \{(j, 1) : 1 \leqq j \leqq \text{card}\,(P)\}, \emptyset\big).$$

(If $c \in \{a_1, a_2, \ldots, a_s\}$ or $c \in \{b_1, b_2, \ldots, b_r\}$, we modify the above rules as in the proof of Lemma 4.1.1.) It is easy to see that the above productions simulate the application of the ith rule of P. Again, by the method of the proof of Lemma 5.2.3 we can ensure that the simulations have to start with a production labelled by $(i, 1)$. Thus we can produce a pure programmed grammar G' and a coding h as in the proof of Lemma 5.2.3 such that $L(G) = h\big(L(G')\big)$.

ii) Use the same construction with the necessary modifications.

Lemma 5.2.5. $\mathscr{E}(\text{pP}, \text{CF} - \lambda, \text{ac}) \subseteq \mathscr{E}(\text{pRC}, \text{CF} - \lambda, \text{ac})$.

Proof. Let $G = (V, P, S)$ be a pure programmed grammar (without λ-rules). Let

$$V' = \{(a, b) : a \in V, b \in \text{Lab}\,(P)\} \cup \{(a, b)' : a \in V, b \in \text{Lab}\,(P)\}.$$

With each rule $\big(b : d \to w, \sigma(b), \varphi(b)\big)$ of P we associate the following random context rules:

(1) $\big((a, b) \to (a, g), \emptyset, \{d\}\big), g \in \varphi(b), a \neq d,$

(2) $\big(d \to (d, b)', \{(a, b)\}, \{(c, g)' : c \in V, g \in \text{Lab}\,(P)\}\big), a \in V,$

(3) $\big((a, b) \to a, \{(d, b)'\}, \emptyset\big),$

(4) $\big((d, b) \to (d, b)', \emptyset, \{(c, g)' : c \in V, g \in \text{Lab}\,(P)\}\big),$

(5) $\big((d, b)' \to w'(x, g), \emptyset, \{(a, b) : a \in V\}\big), w = w'x, x \in V, w' \in V^*, g \in \sigma(b).$

If $S = \{w_1, w_2, \ldots, w_t\}$, $w_i = x_i w_i'$, $x_i \in V$, $w_i' \in V^*$, $1 \leqq i \leqq t$, then we define

$$S' = \{(x_i, b)\, w_i' : 1 \leqq i \leqq t, b \in \text{Lab}\,(P)\},$$

and we consider the random context grammar $G' = (V \cup V', P', S')$ where P' is the set of all rules constructed previously.

Each string generated by G' contains a symbol (x, b) or $(x, b)'$ where $b \in \text{Lab}\,(P)$. To an axiom $z_i = (x_i, b)\, w_i'$ we can apply a rule of type (1), (2), or (4). After a rule (1) (which corresponds to passing over a rule in G) we can again apply a rule of type (2), (1), or (4). A rule of type (2) has to be followed by one of type (3) and one of type (5); this accomplishes the simulation of the application of a rule in P. After a rule (4), again, we have to apply a rule of type (5); this also simulates a derivation step in G. Thus each derivation in G' simulates a derivation in G. It is easy to see that any derivation in G can be simulated in G'.

Now we consider the coding h defined by

$$h(a) = a \quad \text{for} \quad a \in V,\ h\big((a, b)\big) = h\big((a, b)'\big) = a \quad \text{for} \quad a \in V,\ b \in \mathrm{Lab}\,(P).$$

Clearly, $L(G) = h\big(L(G')\big)$ and $\mathscr{E}(\mathrm{pP}, \mathrm{CF} - \lambda, \mathrm{ac}) \subseteq \mathscr{E}(\mathrm{pRC}, \mathrm{CF} - \lambda, \mathrm{ac})$ is proved.

Lemma 5.2.6. *Let* $K = \{a\}^+ \cup \{a^n b a^m : n + m = 2^p$ *for some* $p\}$. *Then* $K \in \mathscr{E}(\mathrm{pP}, \mathrm{CF} - \lambda, \mathrm{ac})$, $K \notin \mathscr{E}(\mathrm{pM}, \mathrm{CF} - \lambda, \mathrm{ac})$.

Proof. i) The pure programmed grammar $G = (\{a, b, c\}, P, \{a\})$ with

$$P = \big\{(1\colon a \to cc, \{1\}, \{2, 3\}),\ (2\colon c \to cb, \emptyset, \emptyset),\ (3\colon c \to a, \{3\}, \{1\})\big\}$$

and the coding h defined by $h(a) = h(c) = a$, $h(b) = b$ satisfy $K = h\big(L(G)\big)$. Hence $K \in \mathscr{E}(\mathrm{pP}, \mathrm{CF} - \lambda, \mathrm{ac})$.

ii) Let us suppose that $K = h\big(L(G)\big)$ for some pure matrix grammar $G = (V, M, S, F)$, $V = \{a_1, a_2, \ldots, a_t\}$, and a coding $h\colon V^* \to \{a, b\}^*$. Let p be a sufficiently large number and let w be a word in $L(G)$ with $h(w) = a^n b a^m$, $n + m = 2^p$. We consider a derivation D of w in G:

$$D\colon s = w_1 \underset{m_1}{\Longrightarrow} w_2 \underset{m_2}{\Longrightarrow} \cdots \underset{m_{u-1}}{\Longrightarrow} w_u \overset{*}{\Rightarrow} w.$$

If $p_V(v) < p_V(v')$, then v' is a shuffle of a permutation of v with a certain word $v'' \neq \lambda$. We use the notation $v' = v \circ v''$. By Lemma 5.1.4 we have

$$D\colon w_1 \underset{r}{\Longrightarrow} w_i \underset{s}{\Longrightarrow} w_j = w_i \circ w_i^{(1)} \underset{r'}{\Longrightarrow} w_u \overset{*}{\Rightarrow} w$$

where r, s, r' are sequences of matrices and the derivation $w_u \overset{*}{\Rightarrow} w$ is the initial part of the application of a matrix or $w_u = w$. Then there is also the following correct derivation:

$$D_1\colon w_1 \underset{r}{\Longrightarrow} w_i \underset{s}{\Longrightarrow} w_i \circ w_i^{(1)} \underset{s}{\Longrightarrow} w_i \circ w_i^{(1)} \circ w_i^{(2)} \underset{r'}{\Longrightarrow} w_u^{(1)} \overset{*}{\Rightarrow} w^{(1)}.$$

The word $w_i^{(2)}$ is generated from $w_1^{(1)}$ by the rules of the matrices in s which were not applicable (by the appearance checking) in $w_i \underset{s}{\Longrightarrow} w_i \circ w_i^{(1)}$ and are applicable in $w_i \circ w_i^{(1)} \underset{s}{\Longrightarrow} w_i \circ w_i^{(1)} \circ w_i^{(2)}$. Further, $w^{(1)} = w \circ v^{(1)}$ where $v^{(1)}$ is obtained from $w_i^{(2)}$. Note that $|h(w^{(1)})|_b \geqq 1$.

If we have a strict inequality, then we have a contradiction, because $w^{(1)} \in L(G)$. A contradiction is also obtained if $|w^{(1)}| \neq 2^q + 1$ for all q. Therefore $|w^{(1)}| = 2^{p_1} + 1$ and $p_1 > p$. If $w_i^{(1)} = w_i^{(2)} = v^{(1)}$, i.e. the appearance checking is not changed from one step to another, then we obtain a contradiction since p is sufficiently large, S is finite, and $j - i$ is bounded, and the length increase induced by the matrices of s and r' cannot be arbitrarily large (i.e. $2^{p_1} - 2^p > 2^p$). If one of the two equalities does not hold, then we continue the application of s until we obtain the derivations

$$w_1 \underset{r}{\Longrightarrow} w_i \underset{s}{\Longrightarrow} w_i \circ w_i^{(1)} \underset{s}{\Longrightarrow} w_i \circ w_i^{(1)} \circ w_i^{(2)} \underset{s}{\Longrightarrow} \cdots \underset{s}{\Longrightarrow} w_i \circ w_i^{(1)} \circ w_i^{(2)} \circ \cdots \circ w_i^{(k)}$$

$$\underset{s}{\Longrightarrow} w_i \circ w_i^{(1)} \circ w_i^{(2)} \circ \cdots \circ w_i^{(k-1)} \circ w_i^{(k)} \circ w_i^{(k)} \underset{s}{\Longrightarrow} \cdots$$

$$\underset{s}{\Longrightarrow} w_i \circ w_i^{(1)} \circ \cdots \circ w_i^{(k)} \circ (w_i^{(k)})^g \underset{r'}{\Longrightarrow} w_u^{(k+g)} \overset{*}{\Rightarrow} w^{(k+g)}$$

and

$$w_1 \underset{r}{\Longrightarrow} w_i \underset{s}{\Longrightarrow} w_i \circ w_i^{(1)} \underset{s}{\Longrightarrow} \cdots \underset{s}{\Longrightarrow} w_i \circ w_i^{(1)} \circ \cdots \circ w_i^{(k)} \circ (w_i^{(k)})^{g+1}$$

$$\underset{r'}{\Longrightarrow} w_u^{(k+g)} \circ w_i^{(k)} \overset{*}{\Rightarrow} w^{(k+g)} \circ w_i^{(k)}.$$

Such derivations are obtained if $w_i \circ w_i^{(1)} \circ \cdots \circ w_i^{(k)}$ contains all letters involved in the rules of the matrices of s and no further letters are introduced by the derivation s, i.e. if the appearance checking does not change the additional strings $w_i^{(k)}$ shuffled into the current string. As s and r' are given there is an integer t such that $|w_i^{(k)}| < 2^t$. Further we can choose g such that $|w^{(k+g)}| = 2^{t'} + 1$, $t' > t$. Therefore

$$2^{t'} + 1 < |w^{(k+g)} \circ w_i^{(k)}| \leqq 2^{t'} + 1 + 2^t < 2^{t'+1} + 1 .$$

Since $h(w^{(k+g)} \circ w_i^{(k)})$ contains the latter b we obtain a contradiction to $h\big(L(G)\big) = K$, and the proof is complete.

Lemma 5.2.7. $\mathscr{E}(\mathrm{pP}, \mathrm{CF} - \lambda, \mathrm{ac}) \subseteqq \mathscr{E}(\mathrm{pCS})$.

Sketch of the proof. Besides the letters of the alphabet V of a given pure programmed grammar G we use also the letters (x, b, d, z) with $x \in V$, b a label of G, $d \in \{r, l\}$ (it indicates the direction), $z \in \{0, 1\}$ (it indicates the occurrence of the letter which is rewritten by the rule with label b) and primed versions of them. With a programmed production $\big(b, a \to a_1a_2 \ldots a_t, \sigma(b), \varphi(b)\big)$ we associate the following rules:

$$\left.\begin{array}{l} x_1(x_2, b, l, z) \to (x_1, b, l, z)'\,(x_2, b, l, z) \\ (x_1, b, l, z)'\,(x_2, b, l, z) \to (x_1, b, l, z)'\,x_2 \\ (x_1, b, l, 1)'\,x_2 \to (x_1, b, l, 1)\,x_2 \\ (x_1, b, l, 0)'\,x_2 \to (x_1, b, l, 0)\,x_2, \quad \text{if} \quad x_1 \neq a, \\ (a, b, l, 0)'\,x_2 \to (a, b, l, 1)\,x_2 \end{array}\right\} \quad \text{for} \quad x_1, x_2 \in V$$

(these productions transport the indicator one letter to the left, and if a occurs it is noticed by the change from 0 to 1),

$$(a, b, l, z)'\,x_2 \to (a_1, b', l, 0)'\,a_2a_3 \ldots a_tx_2,\ b' \in \sigma(b),\ x_2 \in V$$

(this production simulates the application of the corresponding programmed rule). We give the further rules only informally: we can assume that the first and the last letter of each word are marked (use primed and twice primed versions of V). The above transport of the indicator produces the word $(x_1', b, l, z)'\,x_2x_3 \ldots x_{r-1}x_r''$. The rule

$$(x_1', b, l, z)'\,x_2 \to (x_1', b, r, z)\,x_2$$

changes the direction of the transport (the special case $x_1 = a$ requires some modifications as above). Now we add rules which cause a transport of the indicator from the left to the right. this it produces $v = x_1'x_2 \ldots x_{r-1}(x_r'', b, r, 1)$, $x_r \neq a$, then the derivation stops since we define no production applicable to v (i.e. a occurs in $x_1x_2 \ldots x_r$ and in order to continue the derivation it had to be rewritten already in an earlier step). If this produces $x_1'x_2 \ldots x_{r-1}(x_r'', b, r, 0)'$, $x_r \neq a$, then we apply

$$x_{r-1}(x_r'', b, r, 0)' \to x_{r-1}(x_r'', b'', l, 0),\ b'' \in \varphi(b)$$

(i.e. we continue with a rule of the failure field).

The coding is defined by

$$h(x) = h\big((x, b, b, z)\big) = h\big((x, b, d, z)'\big) = h\big((x', b, d, z)\big)$$
$$= h\big((x', b, d, z)'\big) = h\big((x'', b, d, z)\big) = h\big((x'', b, d, z)'\big) = x.$$

Theorem 5.2.2.

$$\mathscr{E}(\text{pCF} - \lambda) \subset \mathscr{E}(\text{pRC}, \text{CF} - \lambda)$$
$$\subseteq \mathscr{E}(\text{pP}, \text{CF} - \lambda) = \mathscr{E}(\text{pM}, \text{CF} - \lambda) \subseteq \mathscr{E}(\text{pM}, \text{CF} - \lambda, \text{ac})$$
$$\subset \mathscr{E}(\text{pP}, \text{CF} - \lambda, \text{ac}) = \mathscr{E}(\text{pRC}, \text{CF} - \lambda, \text{ac}) \subset \mathscr{E}(\text{pCS}).$$

Proof. The inclusions and equalities follow by definition and by Lemmas 5.2.3 to 5.2.5 and 5.2.7. The properness follows by Lemma 5.2.6, Lemma 5.2.1 ii), and the known relations for language families defined by the use of nonterminals (see Chapter 1).

Two facts seem to be of interest here:

1. The nice equality $\mathscr{E}(\text{p}X) = \mathscr{L}(X)$ known for some families of L systems does not hold for sequential rewriting. However, the application of codings gives an intermediate hierarchy in the following sense: the families of pure languages generated by random context, matrix, and programmed grammars (with appearance checking and without λ-rules) are pairwise incomparable. The codings applied to members of these families identify two of them $\big(\mathscr{E}(\text{pP}, \text{CF} - \lambda, \text{ac}) = \mathscr{E}(\text{pRC}, \text{CF} - \lambda, \text{ac})\big)$. The use of nonterminals leads to a collapse of the distinction, the three families coincide.

2. Surprisingly, the addition of appearance checking reverses the (possibly strict) inclusion between language families corresponding to random context and matrix grammars (without λ-rules).

3. In this context, the programmed grammars seem to have the best qualities since they are in the upper level in all cases.

Open problems

5.2.1. Investigate the closure properties of the families $\mathscr{E}(\text{p}X, \alpha, \beta)$, $X \in \{\text{P}, \text{M}, \text{RC}\}$, $\alpha \in \{\text{CF}, \text{CF} - \lambda\}$, $\beta = \text{ac}$ or empty.

5.2.2. Study the hierarchy of the families $\mathscr{E}(\text{p}X, \text{CF}, \beta)$ and compare these families with $\mathscr{E}(\text{p}Y, \text{CF} - \lambda, \beta')$, β, β' are equal to ac or empty.

5.2.3. Are the inclusions $\mathscr{E}(\text{pM}, \text{CF} - \lambda) \subseteq \mathscr{E}(\text{pM}, \text{CF} - \lambda, \text{ac})$ and $\mathscr{E}(\text{pRC}, \text{CF} - \lambda) \subseteq \mathscr{E}(\text{pM}, \text{CF} - \lambda)$ strict?

Exercises

5.2.1. Prove $\mathscr{E}(\text{prC}, \text{CF} - \lambda, \text{ac}) = \mathscr{E}(\text{pM}, \text{CF} - \lambda, \text{ac})$ (see Dassow and Păun (1984-a)).

5.2.2. Prove $\mathscr{E}(\text{pK}, \text{CF} - \lambda) = \mathscr{E}(\text{pCS})$ (see Dassow and Păun (1984-a)).

Bibliographical and historical remarks

The first paper on pure grammars and pure languages of the Chomsky hierarchy is Gabrielian (1970). Further basic papers on this subject are Buttelmann et al. (1974) and Maurer et al. (1979). Decidability results concerning pure grammars — sometimes restricted to special cases — are presented in SALOMAA (1973-b), BLATTNER (1973) and BUCHER and HAGAUER (1983). The deterministic case is studied in EHRENFEUCHT and ROZENBERG (1980).

In MAURER et al. (1979) some generalizations are suggested, the paper includes the sets of sentential forms of special random context grammars. The pure versions of grammars with regulation mechanisms are studied in DASSOW (1986) and (1985-a), DASSOW and PĂUN (1984-a). In addition to the results of Section 5.1., these papers contain contributions on pure regularly controlled, pure conditional, pure scattered context, pure Indian and Russian parallel grammars.

The effect of codings on L languages is studied in EHRENFEUCHT and ROZENBERG (1974-a) and (1974-b), NIELSEN et al. (1974), VITANYI (1976). First results for context-free and context-sensitive grammars are given in EHRENFEUCHT and ROZENBERG (1974-b). The case of regulated rewriting is studied in DASSOW and PĂUN (1984-a) and DASSOW (1988-a). The latter two papers are the basis of our presentation in Section 5.2., however, pure regularly controlled, and pure conditional grammars are also considered. The paper DASSOW (1985-a) contains a summary of basic results on pure languages and their codings with respect to regulated rewriting.

Chapter 6. Combined Regulations

In Chapters 1 and 2 we introduced a lot of regulating devices, and in all cases, if we equipped context-free grammars with such a mechanism we were able to generate non-context-free languages and (with exception of the Indian parallelism) the generative power was increased. Now let us start with a grammar which is already regulated and let us add to it a further mechanism which is compatible with the first one. Does this procedure enlarge the generative capacity again or do we obtain the same power as by the use of only one of the mechanisms? If the former is the case, can we construct an (infinite) hierarchy by iterating the construction? Questions of this type are the subject investigated in this Chapter. We shall see that in most cases the combination of two mechanisms does not increase the generative power.

As not all pair of regulations can (naturally) work together, we shall mainly consider here only three types of such pair: parallel (Indian and Russian) extensions of other regulated mechanisms, random context extensions and ordered extensions of other mechanisms. Generally, the parallel versions of matrix, programmed, etc. grammars lead to characterizations of $\mathcal{L}$(EDTOL), the order behaves like the appearance checking feature, whereas the random context extension does not increase the power of starting grammars (provided these grammars contain appearance checking features).

6.1. Indian and Russian Parallel Versions of Regulated Grammars

First let us impose the Indian and Russian parallelism on matrix, programmed, and random context grammars.

Definition 6.1.1. A *Russian parallel matrix grammar* is a construct $G = (V_N, V_T, M, S, F)$ whose components are defined as in a context-free matrix grammar (with appearance checking). The set $P(M)$ of all occurrences of rules in M is divided into two sets, $P(M) = P_1 \cup P_2$. For a matrix m: $(A_1 \to w_1, A_2 \to w_2, \ldots, A_r \to w_r)$, we say that $x \underset{m}{\Longrightarrow} y$ holds if there are words $x_1, x_2, \ldots, x_{r+1}$ in V_G^* such that $x = x_1$, $y = x_{r+1}$, and for $1 \leqq j \leqq r$, either

$$x_j = z_1 A_j z_2,\ x_{j+1} = z_1 w_j z_2,\ A_j \to w_j \in P_1,$$

or

$$x_j = z_1 A_j z_2 A_j \ldots z_s A_j z_{s+1},\ x_{j+1} = z_1 w_j z_2 w_j \ldots z_s w_j z_{s+1} \text{ for some }$$
$$z_k \in (V_G \setminus \{A_j\})^*,\ A_j \to w_j \in P_2,$$

or

$$x_j = x_{j+1},\ A_j \text{ does not occur in } x_j, \text{ and } A_j \to w_j \in F.$$

We set

$$L(G) = \{w : S \underset{m_{i_1}}{\Longrightarrow} w_1 \underset{m_{i_2}}{\Longrightarrow} w_2 \Rightarrow \cdots \underset{m_{i_t}}{\Longrightarrow} w_t = w \in V_T^* \text{ for some } m_{i_j} \in M,\ 1 \leqq j \leqq t\}.$$

Clearly, the only difference between context-free and Russian parallel matrix grammars consists in the application of the rules of the matrices. In the context-free case we have $x_j \Rightarrow x_{j+1}$ and in the Russian parallel case we get $x_j \overset{i}{\Longrightarrow} x_{j+1}$ if the applied rule is in P_2. Further, above we defined Russian parallel matrix grammars with appearance checking. If $F = \emptyset$ we say that the grammar is without appearance checking.

Definition 6.1.2. A *Russian parallel programmed grammar* is a construct $G = (V_N, V_T, P, S)$ whose components are defined as in a context-free programmed grammar and the set P is divided into two parts, $P = P_1 \cup P_2$. The generated language $L(G)$ is the set of all words $w \in V_T^*$ such that there is a derivation

$$S = w_0 \underset{b_1}{\Longrightarrow} w_1 \underset{b_2}{\Longrightarrow} w_2 \underset{b_3}{\Longrightarrow} \cdots \underset{b_k}{\Longrightarrow} w_k = w$$

such that, for $1 \leqq i \leqq k$,

$$w_{i-1} = x_1 A_i x_2,\ w_i = x_1 u_i x_2,\ (b_i : A_i \to u_i, \sigma(b_i), \varphi(b_i)) \in P_1,\ b_{i+1} \in \sigma(b_i),$$

or

$$w_{i-1} = x_1 A_i x_2 A_i \ldots x_s A_i x_{s+1},\ w_i = x_1 u_i x_2 u_i \ldots x_s u_i x_{s+1},$$
$$x_j \in (V_G \setminus \{A_i\})^* \text{ for } 1 \leqq j \leqq s+1,\ (b_i : A_i \to u_i, \sigma(b_i), \varphi(b_i)) \text{ is in } P_2, \text{ and } b_{i+1} \in \sigma(b_i),$$

or

$$w_{i-1} = w_i,\ A_i \text{ does not appear in } w_{i-1},$$
$$(b_i : A_i \to u_i, \sigma(b_i), \varphi(b_i)) \in P, \text{ and } b_{i+1} \in \varphi(b_i).$$

Definition 6.1.3. A *Russian parallel random context grammar* is a quadruple $G = (V_N, V_T, P, S)$ whose components are defined as in a (context-free) random context grammar and the set P is divided into two parts, $P = P_1 \cup P_2$. We say that $x \in V_G^*$ directly derives $y \in V_G^*$, written as $x \Rightarrow y$, if either

$$x = x_1 A x_2,\ y = x_1 w x_2,\ (A \to w, Q, R) \in P_1, \text{ and } x_1 x_2 \text{ contains all letters of } Q \text{ and no letter of } R$$

or

$$x = x_1 A x_2 A \ldots x_s A x_{s+1},\ y = x_1 w x_2 w \ldots x_s w x_{s+1},\ x_j \in (V_G \setminus \{A\})^* \text{ for } 1 \leqq j \leqq s+1,\ (A \to w, Q, R) \in P_2, \text{ and } x_1 x_2 \ldots x_{s+1} \text{ contains all symbols in } Q \text{ and no symbol of } R.$$

The language $L(G)$ generated by G is defined by

$$L(G) = \{z : z \in V_T^*,\ S \overset{*}{\Rightarrow} z\}$$

where $\overset{*}{\Rightarrow}$ denotes the reflexive and transitive closure of $\Rightarrow$.

The families of languages generated by Russian parallel matrix, programmed, and random context grammars are denoted by $\mathcal{L}(\mathrm{r}X, \alpha, \beta)$, $X \in \{\mathrm{M}, \mathrm{P}, \mathrm{RC}\}$, $\alpha \in \{\mathrm{CF}, \mathrm{CF} - \lambda\}$, $\beta = \mathrm{ac}$ or empty, with the usual meaning of the components. Moreover, we consider the family $\mathcal{L}(\mathrm{rfRC}, X)$, $X \in \{\mathrm{CF}, \mathrm{CF} - \lambda\}$, of languages generated by Russian parallel forbidding random context grammars (with $Q = \emptyset$ for all rules $(A \to w, Q, R)$).

Obviously, if P_2 is empty in all cases we obtain the families with context-free applications of the rules, i.e. the families studied in Chapters 1, 4 and 5. If the sets P_1 are empty, then all rules have to be applied in the Indian parallel manner. Then we also call the grammar an Indian parallel matrix (programmed, random context) grammar. In order to denote the corresponding families, we substitute the letter i for the letter r, e.g. the family $\mathcal{L}(\mathrm{iM}, \mathrm{CF})$ is the family of all Indian parallel matrix languages (generated with λ-rules but without appearance checking),

Lemma 6.1.1. $\mathcal{L}(\mathrm{EDTOL}) \subseteq \mathcal{L}(\mathrm{iM}, \mathrm{CF} - \lambda)$.

Proof. Let $L \in \mathcal{L}(\mathrm{EDTOL})$ be a language generated by the EDTOL system $G = (V, V_T, \{P_1, P_2, \dots, P_r\}, w)$ without erasing rules. Let $w_{x,P}$ be the right-hand side of the production with the left-hand side x in $P \in \{P_1, P_2, \dots, P_r\}$. We set

$$f(U, P) = \bigcup_{x \in U} \min(w_{x,P}) \quad \text{for} \quad U \subseteq V.$$

For a subset $U \subseteq V$ we introduce a new alphabet $V_U = \{x_U : x \in U\}$, and if $v = v_1 v_2 \dots v_s$ with $v_j \in U$ then we set $v_U = (v_1)_U (v_2)_U \dots (v_s)_U$. Now we define the following matrices for $U = \{x_{i_1}, x_{i_2}, \dots, x_{i_k}\} \subseteq V$ and $P \in \{P_1, P_2, \dots, P_r\}$:

$$P_U\colon \left((x_{i_1})_U \to (w_{x_{i_1},P})_{f(U,P)}, (x_{i_2})_U \to (w_{x_{i_2},P})_{f(U,P)}, \dots, (x_{i_k})_U \to (w_{x_{i_k},P})_{f(U,P)}\right),$$

$$Q_U\colon \left((x_{i_1})_U \to w_{i_1}, (x_{i_2})_U \to x_{i_2}, \dots, (x_{i_k})_U \to x_{i_k}\right),$$

and Q: $(\bar{S} \to w_{\min(w)})$, and we consider the Indian parallel matrix grammar

$$G' = \left((V \setminus V_T) \cup \bigcup_{U \subseteq V} V_U \cup \{\bar{S}\}, V_T, \bigcup_{i=1}^{r} \bigcup_{U \subseteq V} (P_i)_U \cup \bigcup_{U \subseteq V} Q_U \cup \{Q\}, \bar{S}\right).$$

et $z_U \in V_U^*$ with $\min(z) = U$. By the definition of $f(U, P)$ and since each letter $x_U \in V_U$ is rewritten by the application of P_U, we get $z_U \xRightarrow[P_U]{i} (z')_{U'}$ with $\min(z') = U' = f(U, P)$. Further $z_U \xRightarrow[P_U]{i} (z')_{U'}$ iff $z \xRightarrow[P]{} z'$ in G. Each derivation in G' starts with $\bar{S} \Rightarrow w_{\min(w)}$ and it terminates by application of a matrix Q_U which translates a word z_u in z. Hence

$$\bar{S} \Rightarrow (w_1)_{U_1} \xRightarrow[(P_{i_1})_{U_1}]{} (w_2)_{U_2} \xRightarrow[(P_{i_2})_{U_2}]{} \cdots \xRightarrow[(P_{i_r})_{U_r}]{} (w_{r+1})_{U_{r+1}} \xRightarrow[Q_{U_{r+1}}]{} w_{r+1} \in V_T^*$$

is a correct derivation in G' iff

$$w = w_1 \xRightarrow[P_{i_1}]{} w_2 \xRightarrow[P_{i_2}]{} \cdots \xRightarrow[P_{i_r}]{} w_{r+1}$$

is a correct derivation in G. Hence $L(G) = L(G') \in \mathcal{L}(\mathrm{iM}, \mathrm{CF} - \lambda)$.

The following statements follow from the definitions.

Lemma 6.1.2. i) $\mathcal{L}(\mathrm{iM}, \mathrm{CF} - \lambda) \subseteq \mathcal{L}(\mathrm{iM}, \mathrm{CF}) \subseteq \mathcal{L}(\mathrm{iM}, \mathrm{CF}, \mathrm{ac})$.

ii) $\mathcal{L}(\mathrm{iM}, \mathrm{CF} - \lambda) \subseteq \mathcal{L}(\mathrm{iM}, \mathrm{CF} - \lambda, \mathrm{ac}) \subseteq \mathcal{L}(\mathrm{iM}, \mathrm{CF}, \mathrm{ac})$.

Lemma 6.1.3. $\mathcal{L}(\text{iM, CF, ac}) \subseteq \mathcal{L}(\text{EDTOL})$.

Proof. Let $G = (V_N, V_T, M, S, F)$ be an Indian parallel matrix grammar, $M = \{m_1, m_2, \ldots, m_n\}$,

$$m_1\colon (A_{i,1} \to w_{i,1}, A_{i,2} \to w_{i,2}, \ldots, A_{i,r_i} \to w_{i,r_i}),\ 1 \leqq i \leqq n.$$

Let w be a word, and let $U = \min(w) \cap V_N$. Let $w \overset{i}{\Longrightarrow} w'$ be a derivation using the rule $A \to u$. Then

$$U' = \min(w') \cap V_N = (U \setminus \{A\}) \cup (\min(u) \cap V_N).$$

we set $U' = f(U, A \to u)$.

We introduce new letters $[i, j]$ for $1 \leqq i \leqq n$, $1 \leqq j \leqq r_i$, and $[U]$ for $U \subseteq V_N$, $U \neq \emptyset$, and we define the EDTOL system $G' = (V, V_T, P, \bar{S})$ with

$$V = V_T \cup V_N \cup \{[i, j] : 1 \leqq i \leqq n, 1 \leqq j \leqq r_i\} \cup \{[U] : U \subseteq V_N, U \neq \emptyset\}$$
$$\cup \{\bar{S}, N\}$$

$$P = \{Q_i : 1 \leqq i \leqq n\} \cup \{P_{i,j} : 1 \leqq i \leqq n, 1 \leqq j \leqq r_i\}$$
$$\cup \{P^F_{i,j} : 1 \leqq i \leqq n, 1 \leqq j \leqq r_i, A_{i,j} \to w_{i,j} \in F\}$$
$$\cup \{P^k_{i,r_i} : 1 \leqq i \leqq n, 1 \leqq k \leqq n\}$$
$$\cup \{P^{kF}_{i,r_i} : 1 \leqq i \leqq n, 1 \leqq k \leqq n, A_{i,r_i} \to w_{i,r_i} \in F\} \cup \{P\}$$

where

$$Q_i = \big\{\bar{S} \to S[i, 1]\,[\{S\}]\big\} \cup \big\{x \to x : x \in V \setminus \{\bar{S}\}\big\},$$

$$P_{i,j} = \{A_{i,j} \to w_{i,j}\} \cup \{[U] \to [f(U, A_{i,j} \to w_{i,j}]) : A_{i,j} \in U, U \subseteq V_N, U \neq \emptyset\}$$
$$\cup \{[U] \to N : A_{i,j} \notin U, U \subseteq V_N, U \neq \emptyset\} \cup \{[i, j] \to [i, j + 1]\}$$
$$\cup \{[i', j'] \to N : i \neq i' \text{ or } j \neq j'\}$$
$$\cup \big\{x \to x : x \in (V_G \setminus \{A_{i,j}\}) \cup \{\bar{S}, N\}\big\},$$

$$P^F_{i,j} = \{[i, j] \to [i, j + 1]\} \cup \{[i', j'] \to N : i \neq i' \text{ or } j \neq j'\}$$
$$\cup \{[U] \to N : A_{i,j} \in U, U \subseteq V_N, U \neq \emptyset\}$$
$$\cup \{[U] \to [U] : A_{i,j} \notin U, U \subseteq V_N, U \neq \emptyset\}$$
$$\cup \big\{x \to x : x \in V_G \cup \{\bar{S}, N\}\big\},$$

$$P^k_{i,r_i} = \{[i, r_i] \to [k, 1]\} \cup \{[i', j'] \to N : i \neq i' \text{ or } j' \neq r_i\}$$
$$\cup \{[U] \to N : A_{i,r_i} \notin U, U \subseteq V_N, U \neq \emptyset\}$$
$$\cup \{[U] \to [f(U, A_{i,r_i} \to w_{i,r_i})] : A_{i,r_i} \in U, U \subseteq V_N, U \neq \emptyset\}$$
$$\cup \{A_{i,r_i} \to w_{i,r_i}\} \cup \big\{x \to x : x \in (V_G \setminus \{A_{i,r_i}\}) \cup \{\bar{S}, N\}\big\},$$

$$P^{kF}_{i,r_i} = \{[i, r_i] \to [k, 1]\} \cup \{[i', j'] \to N : i \neq i' \text{ or } j' \neq r_i\}$$
$$\cup \{[U] \to N : A_{i,r_i} \in U, U \subseteq V_N, U \neq \emptyset\}$$
$$\cup \{[U] \to [U] : A_{i,r_i} \notin U, U \subseteq V_N, U \neq \emptyset\}$$
$$\cup \big\{x \to x : x \in V_G \cup \{\bar{S}, N\}\big\},$$

$$P = \{[i, 1] \to \lambda : 1 \leqq i \leqq n\} \cup \{[i, j] \to N : 2 \leqq j \leqq r_i, 1 \leqq i \leqq n\}$$
$$\cup \{[U] \to \lambda : U \subseteq V_N, U \neq \emptyset\} \cup \{A \to N : A \in V_N \cup \{\bar{S}, N\}$$
$$\cup \{x \to x : x \in V_T\}.$$

Now let us consider a word $z_1 = v_1[i, 1]\,[U]$ with $\min(v_1) \cap V_N = U$. Since the symbol N is a trap symbol which cannot be erased, its introduction in a terminating derivation is impossible. Therefore we can apply only the tables $P_{i,1}$ or $P^F_{i,1}$. Assume that $A_{i,1}$ occurs in z_1, i.e. it occurs in v_1. Then we can apply $P_{i,1}$ and we obtain

$$z_1 = v_1[i, 1]\,[U] \underset{P_{i,1}}{\Longrightarrow} v_2[i, 2]\,[f(U, A_{i,1} \to w_{i,1})] = z_2$$

and, obviously, $\min(v_2) \cap V_N = f(U, A_{i,1} \to w_{i,1})$ and $v_1 \overset{i}{\Longrightarrow} v_2$ by application of $A_{i,1} \to w_{i,1}$. If $A_{i,1}$ does not occur in z_1, then we can apply only $P^F_{i,1}$ and this table exists only if $A_{i,1} \to w_{i,1} \in F$. In this case we get

$$z_1 = v_1[i, 1]\,[U] \underset{P^F_{i,1}}{\Longrightarrow} v_1[i, 2]\,[U] = z_2,$$

and $v_1 \overset{i}{\Longrightarrow} v_1$ holds in G by application of $A_{i,1} \to w_{i,1}$ in appearance checking mode. This procedure can be iterated and we obtain that, if

$$z_1 = v_1[i, 1]\,[U_1] \Rightarrow v_2[i, 2]\,[U_2] \Rightarrow \cdots \Rightarrow v_{r_i}[i, r_i]\,[U_{r_i}] \Rightarrow v_1'[i', 1]\,[U_1']$$

holds in G' then $v_1 \underset{m_i}{\Longrightarrow} v_1'$ holds in G, i.e. the application of a matrix is simulated. It is easy to see that any matrix can be simulated.

By the initial tables Q_i we derive from $\bar{S}$ a word $S[i, 1]\,[\{S\}]$ of the above form, and the terminating table P is only applicable if an entire matrix is simulated and the current word contains no elements of V_N. Therefore

$$\bar{S} \overset{*}{\Rightarrow} S[i_1, 1]\,[U_1] \overset{*}{\Rightarrow} y_2[i_2, 1]\,[U_2] \overset{*}{\Rightarrow} \cdots \overset{*}{\Rightarrow} y_r[i_r, 1]\,[U_r] \overset{*}{\Rightarrow} y_r$$

is a correct terminating derivation in G' if and only if

$$S \underset{m_{i_1}}{\Longrightarrow} y_2 \underset{m_{i_2}}{\Longrightarrow} y_3 \underset{m_{i_3}}{\Longrightarrow} \cdots \underset{m_{i_{r-1}}}{\Longrightarrow} y_r$$

is a correct derivation in G. Therefore $L(G) = L(G') \in \mathcal{L}(\text{EDTOL})$.

Lemma 6.1.4. *Each* EDTOL *language L can be generated by a λ-free Indian parallel random context grammar with forbidding contexts only.*

Proof. Let $L \in \mathcal{L}(\text{EDTOL})$. Then $L = L(G)$ for some λ-free EDTOL system G. Now one can construct a λ-free Indian parallel random context grammar G' with empty permitting contexts such that $L = L(G')$ as in the proof of Theorem 1.5.11 (and by the Indian parallelism we obtain a deterministic L system).

Lemma 6.1.5. $\mathcal{L}(\text{iRC}, \text{CF} \dot{-} \lambda, \text{ac}) \subseteq \mathcal{L}(\text{EDTOL})$.

Proof. We introduce new letters $[U]$ for $U \subseteq V_N$, $U \neq \emptyset$, which can be used as in the proof of Lemma 6.1.3 in order to simulate the application of a random context rule. Using this method the statement can be proved easily.

Now we combine the relations obtained above and, without proof, we add corresponding relations for Indian programmed grammars.

Theorem 6.1.1.

$$\begin{aligned}\mathcal{L}(\mathrm{iRC, CF} - \lambda) &\subseteq \mathcal{L}(\mathrm{iRC, CF}) \subseteq \mathcal{L}(\mathrm{EDTOL}) = \mathcal{L}(\mathrm{ifRC, CF} - \lambda)\\ &= \mathcal{L}(\mathrm{ifRC, CF}) = \mathcal{L}(\mathrm{iRC, CF} - \lambda, \mathrm{ac}) = \mathcal{L}(\mathrm{iRC, CF, ac})\\ &= \mathcal{L}(\mathrm{iM, CF} - \lambda) = \mathcal{L}(\mathrm{iM, CF}) = \mathcal{L}(\mathrm{iM, CF} - \lambda, \mathrm{ac}) = \mathcal{L}(\mathrm{iM, CF, ac})\\ &= \mathcal{L}(\mathrm{iP, CF} - \lambda) = \mathcal{L}(\mathrm{iP, CF}) = \mathcal{L}(\mathrm{pP, CF} - \lambda, \mathrm{ac}) = \mathcal{L}(\mathrm{pP, CF, ac}).\end{aligned}$$

Note that we have obtained that appearance checking does not increase the generative power of Indian parallel matrix and programmed grammars. In the context-free case this is one of the most important open problems in the area of regulated rewriting.

Now we consider the Russian parallelism. It is easy to modify the proof of the corresponding statements for the context-free case in order to prove

Theorem 6.1.2. *For* $\alpha \in \{\mathrm{CF, CF} - \lambda\}$,

$$\mathcal{L}(\mathrm{rRC}, \alpha) \subseteq \mathcal{L}(\mathrm{rM}, \alpha) = \mathcal{L}(\mathrm{rP}, \alpha).$$

Theorem 6.1.3. *Let* $X \in \{\mathrm{M, P, RC}\}$. *Then,* for $\alpha \in \{\mathrm{CF, CF} - \lambda\}$,

$$\mathcal{L}(X, \alpha) \subseteq \mathcal{L}(\mathrm{r}X, \alpha) \quad \textit{and} \quad \mathcal{L}(\mathrm{i}X, \alpha) \subset \mathcal{L}(rX, \alpha).$$

Proof. The inclusions follow by definition. The existence of a context-free language which is not in $\mathcal{L}(\mathrm{EDTOL})$ (see EHRENFEUCHT and ROZENBERG (1977) and Theorem 0.2.11) implies the strictness of the second inclusion by Theorem 6.1.1.

Theorem 6.1.4. *For* $\alpha \in \{\mathrm{CF, CF} - \lambda\}$,

$$\mathcal{L}(\mathrm{rM}, \alpha, \mathrm{ac}) = \mathcal{L}(\mathrm{rP}, \alpha, \mathrm{ac}) = \mathcal{L}(\mathrm{rRC}, \alpha, \mathrm{ac}) = \mathcal{L}(\mathrm{P}, \alpha, \mathrm{ac}).$$

Proof. We prove only the equality $\mathcal{L}(\mathrm{P, CF} - \lambda, \mathrm{ac}) = \mathcal{L}(\mathrm{rP, CF} - \lambda, \mathrm{ac})$. The proofs for the other relations are analogous.

By definition, $\mathcal{L}(\mathrm{P, CF} - \lambda, \mathrm{ac}) \subseteq \mathcal{L}(\mathrm{rP, CF} - \lambda, \mathrm{ac})$ holds.

Let now $G = (V_N, V_T, P, S)$ be a Russian parallel programmed grammar with appearance checking, where $P = P_1 \cup P_2$. Then we consider the context-free programmed grammar $G' = (V'_N, V_T, P', S)$ with

$$V'_N = V_N \cup \{A' : A \in V_N\}$$

and $P' = P_1 \cup P'_2$ where P'_2 is constructed as follows. If $(r: A \to w, \sigma(r), \varphi(r)) \in P_2$, then let

$$\begin{aligned}&(r\ : A \to A, \{r'\}, \varphi(r)),\\ &(r'\ : A \to A', \{r'\}, \{r''\}),\\ &(r'': A' \to w, \{r''\}, \sigma(r))\end{aligned}$$

be in P'_2. It is obvious that these rules simulate the rule with label r in P_2 (the first checks for the presence of A, and if it is successful then, by the second and the third rules, all occurrences of A are replaced by w and we continue with a rule with label in $\sigma(r)$; if the first rule is not applicable, then the next rule has a label in $\varphi(r)$). This implies $L(G) = L(G')$ and therefore the statement.

Note that for unregulated grammars the families of context-free and Indian parallel languages are not comparable. In the regulated case with appearance checking, the family of languages generated by Indian parallelism is included in the family of languages generated by the sequential process and, moreover, the addition of Indian parallelism to context-freeness (i.e. Russian parallelism) does not increase the generative power in the regulated case.

Open problems

6.1.1. Prove or disprove $\mathcal{L}(X, \mathrm{CF}) = \mathcal{L}(\mathrm{r}X, \mathrm{CF})$ and/or $\mathcal{L}(X, \mathrm{CF} - \lambda) = \mathcal{L}(\mathrm{r}X, \mathrm{CF} - \alpha)$ for $X \in \{\mathrm{M}, \mathrm{P}, \mathrm{RC}\}$.

6.1.2. Prove or disprove $\mathcal{L}(\mathrm{rRC}, \mathrm{CF} - \lambda) = \mathcal{L}(\mathrm{rM}, \mathrm{CF} - \lambda)$ and/or $\mathcal{L}(\mathrm{rRC}, \mathrm{CF}) = \mathcal{L}(\mathrm{rM}, \mathrm{CF})$.

6.1.3. What is the relation between $\mathcal{L}(\mathrm{r}X, \mathrm{CF})$, $\mathcal{L}(\mathrm{r}X, \mathrm{CF} - \lambda)$ and $\mathcal{L}(Y, \mathrm{CF})$, $\mathcal{L}(Y, \mathrm{CF} - \lambda)$, $X \in \{\mathrm{M}, \mathrm{P}, \mathrm{RC}\}$, $Y \in \{\mathrm{M}, \mathrm{P}, \mathrm{RC}\}$?

Exercises

6.1.1. Construct a context-free programmed (matrix, random context) grammar G such that $L(G) \in \mathcal{L}(\mathrm{P}, \mathrm{CF} - \lambda, \mathrm{ac}) \setminus \mathcal{L}(\mathrm{iP}, \mathrm{CF} - \lambda, \mathrm{ac})$.

6.1.2. Give a formal complete proof of Lemma 6.1.5.

6.1.3. Prove $\mathcal{L}(\mathrm{rM}, \mathrm{CF}, \mathrm{ac}) = \mathcal{L}(\mathrm{M}, \mathrm{CF}, \mathrm{ac})$ (directly using the definitions).

6.1.4. Prove Theorem 6.1.2. i).

6.1.5. Investigate all these families and $\mathcal{L}(\mathrm{iCF})$ and $\mathcal{L}(\mathrm{rCF})$ with the finite index restriction (see Dassow (1984-a) and Rozenberg and Vermeir (1978-b)).

6.2. Ordered Versions of Regulated Rewriting

Again, we shall first consider ordered extensions of matrix, programmed, and random context grammars (with context-free rules) and then we shall briefly take into consideration other types of grammars.

Definition 6.2.1. An *ordered matrix grammar* is a construct $G = (V_N, V_T, M, S, F, <)$ where V_N, V_T, M, S, F are defined as in a usual matrix grammar and $<$ is a partial order relation on the set M. The language $L(G)$ is the set of all strings generated by the matrix grammar $G' = (V_N, V_T, M, S, F)$ in such a way that at each step of a derivation the used matrix is maximal among the matrices applicable to the current string.

Example 6.2.1. We consider the grammar

$$G = (\{S, A, A', B, B', B''\}, \{a\}, M, S, \emptyset, <)$$

with M containing the matrices

$$m_1\colon (S \to AB),$$
$$m_2\colon (A \to A'A', B \to B),$$

$m_3: (B \to B')$,

$m_4: (A' \to A, B' \to B')$,

$m_5: (B' \to B)$,

$m_6: (B' \to B'')$,

$m_7: (A \to a, B'' \to B'')$,

$m_8: (B'' \to a)$

and the relation $<$ being defined by

$$m_2 > m_3 > m_4 > m_5,\ m_4 > m_6.$$

Each derivation in G starts with m_1, thus producing the string AB. Given a string A^nB (initially we have $n = 1$), we have to apply the matrix m_2, which is the maximal applicable matrix, thus obtaining $A^iA'A'A^jB$, $i + j + 1 = n$. Now again m_2 is maximal and so on until all symbols A are replaced by $A'A'$; we obtain $(A'A')^n B$. In this moment the maximal applicable matrix is m_3 which leads to $(A'A')^n B'$, and now we have to use m_4 until each A' is replaced by A. The obtained string $A^{2n}B'$ can be rewritten either by m_5 or by m_6. In the former case we obtain $A^{2n}B$ and the derivation can be reiterated from m_2. In the latter case the derivation terminates by producing a^{2n+1}. In conclusion,

$$L(G) = \{a^{2^n+1} : n \geqq 1\}.$$

Definition 6.2.2. An *ordered programmed grammar* is a construct $G = (V_N, V_T, P, S, <)$ where V_N, V_T, P, S are as in a programmed grammar and $<$ is a partial order on the set P.

The derivation process according to G is defined as follows. Start with S and apply any maximal rule in P. After effectively using a rule $(b: A \to x, \sigma(b), \varphi(b))$ we pass to $\sigma(b)$ and choose the maximal applicable rule for the current string. If no rule with the label in $\sigma(b)$ is applicable, then we take an arbitrary rule $(b': A' \to x', \sigma(b'), \varphi(b'))$ with $b' \in \sigma(b)$, we "apply" it in the appearance checking mode (without being concerned about the relation $<$) and pass to $\varphi(b')$ for the next step: choose the maximal applicable rule in $\varphi(b')$ and proceed as with b (if no rule in $\varphi(b')$ is applicable, then take an arbitrary rule $(b'': A'' \to w'', \sigma(b''), \varphi(b''))$, $b'' \in \varphi(b')$, "apply" it in the appearance checking mode and pass to $\varphi(b'')$, etc.).

Example 6.2.2. We consider the grammar

$$G = (\{S, A, A', B\}, \{a\}, P, S, <)$$

with P consisting of the following rules:

$(b_1: S \to AB, \{b_2\}, \emptyset)$,

$(b_2: A \to A'A', \{b_2, b_3\}, \emptyset)$,

$(b_3: B \to B, \{b_4\}, \emptyset)$,

$(b_4: A' \to A, \{b_2, b_4, b_5\}, \emptyset)$,

$(b_5: B \to a, \{b_6\}, \emptyset)$,

$(b_6: A \to a, \{b_6\}, \emptyset)$

and the relation $<$ being defined by

$$b_2 > b_3,\ b_4 > b_2,\ b_4 > b_5$$

(we identify the rules by their labels). We obtain

$$L(G) = \{a^{2^n+1} : n \geqq 1\},$$

again. Indeed, after b_1 we have to use b_2 as long as b_2 is applicable by $b_2 > b_3$. Thus from A^nB (initially, $n = 1$) we have to produce $(A'A')^n B$. After b_3 we have to use b_4 whose success field contains b_2, b_4, b_5. b_4 is maximal, therefore we have to replace each A' by A, thus obtaining $A^{2n}B$ before using either b_2, again, or to finish the derivation via b_5 and b_6.

Definition 6.2.3. An *ordered random context grammar* is a system $G = (V_N, V_T, P, S, <)$ where V_N, V_T, P, S are defined as in a random context grammar and $<$ is a partial order on P. A rule $(A \to w, Q, R)$ is applicable to some string $x = x_1Ax_2$ in order to derive $y = x_1wx_2$ iff all symbols of Q and no symbol of R appear in x_1x_2 and there is no rule $(B \to v, Q', R') > (A \to w, Q, R)$ such that $x = x_1'Bx_2'$, and $x_1'x_2'$ contains all symbols of Q' and no symbol of R'.

Example 6.2.3. The previous language $\{a^{2^n+1} : n \geqq 1\}$ can be generated by the ordered random context grammar

$$G = (\{S, A, A', B, B'\}, \{a\}, P, S, <)$$

with P consisting of

$$r_1: (S \to AB, \emptyset, \emptyset),$$
$$r_2: (A \to A'A', \{B\}, \emptyset),$$
$$r_3: (B \to A'B', \emptyset, \emptyset),$$
$$r_4: (A' \to A, \{B'\}, \emptyset),$$
$$r_5: (B' \to B, \emptyset, \emptyset),$$
$$r_6: (B \to a^2, \emptyset, \emptyset),$$
$$r_7: (A \to a, \emptyset, \emptyset)$$

and the relation $<$ defined by

$$r_2 > r_3,\ r_4 > r_5,\ r_5 > r_7,\ r_6 > r_7.$$

A string A^nB (after using r_1 we have $n = 1$) can be rewritten only by r_2 and r_6. In the latter case we have to finish the derivation and obtain the string a^{n+2}. In the presence of B the rule r_2 must be used as many times as possible and only after that may we apply r_3 (otherwise we derive only words containing only the letters a and A by the use of r_6 and r_7 since r_4 is not applicable). Now r_4 and r_5 become applicable, but r_4 is maximal and has to be used for replacing each A' by A, thus returning to a string $A^{2n+1}B$. Note that r_7 cannot be used in the presence of B or B' and that A' cannot derive a terminal string after replacing B by a^2, therefore only strings of the form A^mB can lead to terminal strings via r_6, r_7.

We shall denote the families of languages generated by ordered versions of grammars of type (X, α, β), $X \in \{\mathrm{M, P, RC}\}$, $\alpha \in \{\mathrm{CF, CF} - \lambda\}$, $\beta =$ ac or empty, by $\mathcal{L}(\mathrm{O}X, \alpha, \beta)$.

As the above examples strongly suggest, the order extensions behave like an appearance checking. Thus the next theorem is not surprising.

Theorem 6.2.1. *For all* $X \in \{\mathrm{M}, \mathrm{P}, \mathrm{RC}\}$, $\alpha \in \{\mathrm{CF}, \mathrm{CF} - \lambda\}$,

$$\mathscr{L}(\mathrm{O}X, \alpha) = \mathscr{L}(\mathrm{O}X, \alpha, \mathrm{ac}) = \mathscr{L}(X, \alpha, \mathrm{ac}).$$

The theorem will result from the following three lemmas.

Lemma 6.2.1. *For* $\alpha \in \{\mathrm{CF}, \mathrm{CF} - \lambda\}$,

$$\mathscr{L}(\mathrm{M}, \alpha, \mathrm{ac}) = \mathscr{L}(\mathrm{OM}, \alpha, \mathrm{ac}) = \mathscr{L}(\mathrm{OM}, \alpha).$$

Proof. i) $\mathscr{L}(\mathrm{M}, \alpha, \mathrm{ac}) \subseteq \mathscr{L}(\mathrm{OM}, \alpha)$. Let $G = (V_N, V_T, M, S, F)$ be a matrix grammar in the accurate normal form. We construct the ordered matrix grammar $G' = (V_N, V_T, M', S, \emptyset, <)$ with

$$M' = M \cup \{(X \to Y) : (A \to Z, X \to Y) \in M\}$$

(Z is the distinguished trap symbol in Definition 1.3.7) and with $<$ defined by

$$(A \to Z, X \to Y) > (X \to Y)$$

for all $(A \to Z, X \to Y) \in M$. Therefore the matrix $(X \to Y)$ can be applied if and only if $(A \to Z, X \to Y)$ is not applicable, i.e. if and only if $A \to Z$ is not applicable. Note that the matrices without rules in F can be used without restrictions. The equality $L(G) = L(G')$ is now obvious.

ii) $\mathscr{L}(\mathrm{OM}, \alpha) \subseteq \mathscr{L}(\mathrm{OM}, \alpha, \mathrm{ac})$ is trivial.

iii) $\mathscr{L}(\mathrm{OM}, \alpha, \mathrm{ac}) \subseteq \mathscr{L}(\mathrm{M}, \alpha, \mathrm{ac})$. Let $G = (V_N, V_T, M, S, F, <)$ be an ordered matrix grammar and consider a matrix $m: (A_1 \to x_1, A_2 \to x_2, \ldots, A_k \to x_k) \in M$. We construct the matrices

$$m' : (A_1 \to x_1', A_2 \to x_2', \ldots, A_k \to x_k')$$

where $x_i' = x_i$ if $A_i \to x_i$ does not appear in F and $x_i' \in \{x_i, Z\}$ for $A_i \to x_i \in F$ (Z is a new symbol). Let M' be the set of all matrices m' obtained as above. We consider the grammar

$$G' = (V_N \cup \{Z\}, V_T, M', S, F', <)$$

where

$$F' = \{A \to Z : A \in V_N, A \to Z \text{ appears in } M'\}$$

and $<$ is naturally extended to M' ($m_1 > m_2$, $m_1' > m_2$, $m_1 > m_2'$, $m_1' > m_2'$ for $m_1 > m_2$ in G and m_1', m_2' obtained from m_1, m_2 as above). It is clear that the two ordered matrix grammars G and G' are equivalent.

Consider now a matrix m of M', and consider the matrix m_0 consisting of all rules in m different from $A \to Z$, $A \in V_N$. Assume that m_0: $(A_1 - x_1, A_2 \to x_2, \ldots, A_k \to x_k)$. Take the string $\gamma = A_1A_2 \ldots A_k$ and consider all the strings γ' obtained by erasing some symbols (possibly none) from γ. For each such string $\gamma' = A_{i_1}A_{i_2} \ldots A_{i_r}$ for which the matrix m_0 can be effectively (i.e. without appearance checking) applied to γ', we construct the matrices

$$(A_{i_1} \to A_{i_1}', A_{i_2} \to A_{i_2}', \ldots, A_{i_r} \to A_{i_r}')$$

where $A'_{i_j} \in \{A_{i_j}, Z\}$ and at least one rule has $A'_{i_j} = Z$. Denote by $M(m)$ the set of all such matrices associated to m_0, hence to m.

Clearly, if a matrix $m' \in M(m)$ can be applied to a given sentential form w, then m can also be applied to w and conversely.

Now, for $m \in M'$, let

$$\text{Sup}\,(m) = \{m' \in M' : m' > m\}.$$

We construct the grammar $G'' = (V'_N, V_T \cup \{c\}, M'', S', F'')$ with

$$V'_N = V_N \cup \{S', Z\} \cup \{[m, 0] : m \in M'\} \cup \{[m, 1] : m \in M'\}$$

and with M'' containing the following matrices:

(1) $(S' \to S[m, 0]),\ m \in M'$,

(2) $([m, 0] \to [m, 1]),\ m \in M'$ with $\text{Sup}\,(m) = \emptyset$,

(3) $([m, 0] \to [m, 1], m'_1, m'_2, \ldots, m'_s),\ \text{Sup}\,(m) = \{m_1, m_2, \ldots, m_s\}$,

$m'_j \in M(m_j),\ 1 \leqq j \leqq s$,

(4) $([m, 1] \to [m', 0], A_1 \to x_1, A_2 \to x_2, \ldots, A_k \to x_k)$,

$m: (A_1 \to x_1, A_2 \to x_2, \ldots, A_k \to x_k) \in M',\ m' \in M'$,

(5) $([m, 0] \to c)$,

and, moreover,

$$F' = \{A \to Z : A \in V_N, A \to Z \text{ appears in } M''\}.$$

The matrices in M'' can simulate only in the presence of the nonterminals $[m, 1]$ and such a nonterminal is introduced by a matrix of type (2) for maximal matrices in M' or by a matrix of type (3) if $\text{Sup}\,(m) \neq \emptyset$. However, if one of the matrices of $\text{Sup}\,(m)$ can be applied, that is, if all its rules not in F' can be effectively applied, then some of the matrices $m'_1, m'_2, \ldots, m'_s$ in $M(m)$ can be effectively applied. This introduces the trap symbol Z and the derivation is blocked. Therefore the correct termination supposes that no matrix greater than m is applicable if one uses m, and this is exactly the order restriction. In conclusion, $L(G'') = L(G')\ \{c\}$. As $\mathcal{L}(\text{M}, \alpha, \text{ac})$ is closed under right derivative, we obtain $L(G')\ \big(= L(G)\big) \in \mathcal{L}(\text{M}, \alpha, \text{ac})$, and the proof is finished.

Lemma 6.2.2. *For* $\alpha \in \{\text{CF}, \text{CF} - \lambda\}$,

$$\mathcal{L}(\text{P}, \alpha, \text{ac}) = \mathcal{L}(\text{OP}, \alpha) = \mathcal{L}(\text{OP}, \alpha, \text{ac}).$$

Proof. i) $\mathcal{L}(\text{P}, \alpha, \text{ac}) \subseteq \mathcal{L}(\text{OP}, \alpha)$. Let $G = (V_N, V_T, P, S)$ be a programmed grammar. For each rule $\big(b : A \to w, \sigma(b), \varphi(b)\big)$ of P we consider the set of labels

$$g(b) = \{b'\} \cup \big\{(B, b) : B \in V_N \setminus \{A\}\big\},$$

and for a set T of labels we set

$$g(T) = \bigcup_{b \in T} g(b).$$

We consider the following programmed rules:

$$(b' : A \to A, \{b\}, \emptyset),$$

$$\big(b : A \to w, g(\sigma(b)), \emptyset\big),$$

$$\big((B, b) : B \to B, g(\varphi(b)), \emptyset\big), B \in V_N \setminus \{A\},$$

associated to $(b, A \to w, \sigma(b), \varphi(b)) \in P$.

By P' we denote the set of all these rules, and we consider the ordered programmed grammar $G' = (V_N, V_T, P', S, <)$ with the relation $<$ defined by

$$b' > (B, b) \quad \text{for} \quad B \in V_N, b \in \text{Lab}(P).$$

Let us examine a derivation according to the grammar G'. First we have to use a rule with label b (the rules with labels b', (B, b) do not modify the initial string, hence we ignore such an initial step). This corresponds to producing the string w in the grammar G for a rule $(b: S \to w, \sigma(b), \varphi(b))$. We have to continue with a rule in $g(\sigma(b))$. This must be maximal according to $<$ Therefore, if $(h' : A \to A, \{h\}, \emptyset)$ can be applied, we cannot use $((B, h): B \to B, g(\varphi(h)), \emptyset)$ for any $B \in V_N$. Thus, if h' can be applied, we have to use then the rule with label h in P'; this again corresponds to using the rule with label h in P for rewriting the string w. If h' cannot be effectively applied (hence the corresponding rule $(h: C \to z, \sigma(h), \varphi(h))$ in P cannot be applied), we may apply a rule $((B, h) : B \to B, g(\varphi(h)), \emptyset)$ and we can apply such a rule if the current string is not terminal (otherwise the derivation is terminated). Such a rule does not modify the string, but determines the passing to a rule in the failure field, $\varphi(h)$, of h for the next step. This again simulates the work of G. Consequently, $L(G) = L(G')$, and we obtain $L(G) \in \mathcal{L}(\text{OP}, \alpha)$.

ii) $\mathcal{L}(\text{OP}, \alpha) \subseteq \mathcal{L}(\text{OP}, \alpha, \text{ac})$ is obvious.

ii) $\mathcal{L}(\text{OP}, \alpha, \text{ac}) \subseteq \mathcal{L}(P, \alpha, \text{ac})$. Let $G = (V_N, V_T, P, S, <)$ be an ordered programmed grammar (hence with rules in P of the form $(b: A \to w, \sigma(b), \varphi(b))$, where $\sigma(b)$ and $\varphi(b)$ are partially ordered sets). To such a rule we associate the following rules:

(1) $\big(b: A \to w, \{(g, b) : g \in \sigma(b)\}, \{(g', b) : g' \in \varphi(b)\}\big)$,

(2) $\big((g, b): B \to B, \{(g, k_1, b)\}, \{(b', g) : b \in \varphi(g)\}\big)$,

(3) $\big((g, k_i, b): C_i \to C_i, \emptyset, \{(g, k_{i+1}, b)\}\big)$, $1 \leq i < n(g)$,

(4) $\big((g, k_{n(g)}) : C_{n(g)} \to C_{n(g)}, \emptyset, \{g\}\big)$,

(5) $\big((g', b): D \to D, \{(g', k_1', b)\}, \{(b', g') : b \in \varphi(g')\}\big)$,

(6) $\big((g', k_i', b) : E_i \to E_i, \emptyset, \{(g', k_{i+1}', b)\}\big)$, $1 \leq u < n(g')$,

(7) $\big((g', k_{n(g')}', b) : E_{n(g')} \to E_{n(g')}, \emptyset, \{g'\}\big)$,

where $k_1, k_2, \ldots, k_{n(g)}$ are the elements of $\sigma(b)$ which are greater than g, $k_1', k_2', \ldots, k_{n(g')}'$ are the elements of $\varphi(b)$ which are greater than g', and B, C_i, D, E_i are the left-hand sides of the core productions of g, k_i, g', k_i', respectively. Let $G' = (V_N, V_T, P', S)$ be the programmed grammar with P' consisting of all rules constructed as above.

Let w be a sentential form obtained in a derivation in G and let the rule $(b: A \to x, \sigma(b), \varphi(b))$ be an applicable rule in G. We obtain $w \underset{b}{\Longrightarrow} v$ in G and the next applicable rule is a maximal element of $\sigma(b)$ which is applicable to v. In G' we then have the following situation. The rule of type (1) with label b is also applicable in G' and we have to continue with a rule labelled by (g, b). If this rule is not applicable, i.e. B does not occur in v, then $g \in \sigma(b)$ is not applicable to v in G', and therefore in G we continue in $\varphi(g)$; the same operation is determined by the definition of rules of type (2). If the rule of type (2) is applicable, we check by the rules of type (3) and (4) whether there is a rule greater than that labelled by g which is also applicable to v. If there is a greater rule, then the derivation stops and no terminal word is obtained in G'. If there is no greater rule, then we apply g by the definition of (4). However, the rule labelled by g is also applicable to v in G. Thus we have modelled the derivation in G in G'. The same holds if $A \to x$ is not applicable to w. This proves that $L(G) \subseteq L(G')$.

Analogous arguments show that in G' we can simulate only derivations in G, therefore $L(G) = L(G')$. This completes the proof.

Remark. For each language $L \in \mathcal{L}(\mathrm{RC}, \alpha, \mathrm{ac})$ $\big(L \in \mathcal{L}(\mathrm{ORC}, \alpha, \mathrm{ac})\big)$, $\alpha \in \{\mathrm{CF}, \mathrm{CF}-\lambda\}$, we can construct a random context grammar G (ordered random context grammar G) with $L = L(G)$ and G does not contain rules of the form $(A \to w, Q, R)$ with $A \in Q$ or $A \in R$. Indeed, assume that $A \in Q$ for some rule $p\colon (A \to w, Q, R)$. We replace this rule by the rules

$$\big(A \to A_p, (Q \setminus \{A\}), R \cup \{B_r : B \in V_N, r \in P\}\big),$$
$$(A_p \to w, Q, R),$$

where A_p is a new symbol associated to the rule $p \in P$. An analogous construction can be given for $A \in R$. Obviously, the new grammar generates the same language as the old one. The modifications for the ordered case are left to the reader.

Lemma 6.2.3. *For* $\alpha \in \{\mathrm{CF}, \mathrm{CF}-\lambda\}$,

$$\mathcal{L}(\mathrm{RC}, \alpha, \mathrm{ac}) = \mathcal{L}(\mathrm{ORC}, \alpha) = \mathcal{L}(\mathrm{ORC}, \alpha, \mathrm{ac}).$$

Proof. i) $\mathcal{L}(\mathrm{RC}, \alpha, \mathrm{ac}) \subseteq \mathcal{L}(\mathrm{ORC}, \alpha)$. Let $G = (V_N, V_T, P, S)$ be a random context grammar as in the preceding remark. We construct the grammar $G' = (V_N \cup \{Z\}, V_T, P', S, <)$ with P' containing all rules of the following forms:

$$r'\colon (A \to x, Q, \emptyset) \quad \text{for} \quad r\colon (A \to x, Q, R) \in P,$$
$$(A \to Z, \emptyset, \emptyset) \quad \text{for all} \quad A \in V_N,$$

and with the relation $<$ defined by

$$(B \to Z, \emptyset, \emptyset) > r' \quad \text{for} \quad r\colon (A \to x, \emptyset, R) \in P, B \in R.$$

Clearly, a rule of type r' is only applicable to a string w if no symbol of the forbidding context of r occurs in the string w. Consequently, $L(G) = L(G')$.

ii) $\mathcal{L}(\mathrm{ORC}, \alpha) \subseteq \mathcal{L}(\mathrm{ORC}, \alpha, \mathrm{ac})$ is obvious.

iii) $\mathcal{L}(\mathrm{ORC}, \alpha, \mathrm{ac}) \subseteq \mathcal{L}(\mathrm{RC}, \alpha, \mathrm{ac})$. Let $G = (V_N, V_T, P, S, <)$ be an ordered random context grammar in the form in the above remark. We construct the unordered random context grammar $G' = (V_N, V_T, P', S')$ in the following way. For $r \in P$, we define

$$\mathrm{Sup}\,(r) = \{r' : r' \in P, r' > r\}.$$

If $\mathrm{Sup}\,(r) = \emptyset$ for some $r \in P$, then we introduce r in P' without modifications.

Let Sup $(r) = \{r_1, r_2, \ldots, r_t\}$ with $t \geqq 1$, $r: (A \to x, Q, R)$ and $r_i: (A_i \to x_i, Q_i, R_i)$, $1 \leqq i \leqq t$. Then we introduce in P' the rules

$$(r, j): (A \to x, Q_{r,j}, R_{r,j})$$

(the second component of (r, j) enumerates all rules of this type associated to r) with

$$Q_{r,j} = Q \cup \bigcup_{i=1}^{t} R_i', \; R_{i,j} = R \cup \bigcup_{i=1}^{t} Q_i'$$

where $R_i' \subseteq R_i$, $Q_i' \subseteq Q_i \cup \{A_i\}$, both these sets contain at most one letter each and $R_i' \cup Q_i' \neq \emptyset$, $1 \leqq i \leqq t$.

By definition, (r, j) is applicable to a string if no rule r_i of Sup (r) is applicable to this string (either a permitting symbol of r_i does not appear or a forbidding symbol of r_i appears in the string). Thus this rule simulates the application of r according to the order restriction. Hence $L(G) = L(G')$. This completes the proof.

As the order extension of regulated grammars has the same power as the appearance checking extension, and as the appearance checking scattered context grammars characterize the family of context-sensitive languages (recursively enumerable languages if λ-rules are used), it can be expected that ordered scattered context grammars characterize the context-sensitive languages, again (recursively enumerable languages if λ-rules are allowed). The next theorem will show that this indeed holds.

Definition 6.2.4. An *ordered scattered context grammar* is a construct $G = (V_N, V_T, P, S, <)$ where V_N, V_T, P, S are defined as in a scattered context grammar and $<$ is a partial order relation on P. The derivation is defined as in a scattered context grammar (see Definition 2.4.4) including the order restriction: a rule $(A_1, A_2, \ldots, A_k) \to (x_1, x_2, \ldots, x_k)$ is applied to some string w only if no greater rule is applicable to w.

By $\mathscr{L}(\text{OSC})$ and $\mathscr{L}(\text{OSC} - \lambda)$ we denote the families of languages generated in this way.

Theorem 6.2.2. $\mathscr{L}(\text{OSC}) = \mathscr{L}(\text{RE})$, $\mathscr{L}(\text{OSC} - \lambda) = \mathscr{L}(\text{CS})$.

Proof. We shall prove only the equality for the λ-free case.

The inclusion $\mathscr{L}(\text{OSC} - \lambda) \subseteq \mathscr{L}(\text{CS})$ is straightforward and a "classical" (but long and tedious) construction will prove it (we have only to take care in checking that no greater rule is applicable if we apply some rule in the scattered context grammar).

Conversely, let $G = (V_N, V_T, P, S)$ be a length-increasing grammar in Kuroda normal form and construct the ordered scattered context grammar $G' = (V_N', V_P, P', S'', <)$ with

$$V_N' = V_N \cup \{X' : X \in V_N\} \cup \{A, B, C, T, S''\}$$

and P' consisting of the following rules:

$$(S'') \to (SA),$$

$$(X, A) \to (YZ, A) \quad \text{for} \quad X \to YZ \in P,$$

$$\left.\begin{array}{l}(X, A) \to (a, C)\\ (X, C) \to (a, C)\end{array}\right\} \quad \text{for} \quad X \to a \in P, a \in V_T,$$

$$\begin{aligned}
&(C) \to (c) \quad \text{where } c \text{ is a fixed terminal symbol,} \\
&\left.\begin{aligned}
&p_1(r)\colon (X, U, A) \to (X', U', B) \\
&p_2(r)\colon (X', U', B) \to (Y, Z, A) \\
&p(D, r)\colon (X', D, U', B) \to (T, T, T, T),\ D \in V_N
\end{aligned}\right\} \quad \text{for} \quad XU \to YZ \in P.
\end{aligned}$$

We define the order relation $<$ by

$$p(D, r) > p_2(r) \quad \text{for each} \quad r \in P, D \in V_N.$$

Therefore, after introducing the symbol B and the two primed symbols X' and U' we have to use the greatest rule in some set

$$p_2(r), p(D_1, r), p(D_2, r), \ldots, p(D_n, r)$$

where $V_N = \{D_1, D_2, \ldots, D_n\}$. If some matrix $p(D_i, r)$ is applicable, then the trap symbol T is introduced and the derivation is blocked. Thus a terminating derivation is only possible if there is no letter between X' and U' since the presence of A and B forbids terminals. It is easy to see that $L(G') = L(G)\,\{c\}$. Since $\mathcal{L}(\mathrm{CS})$ is closed under right derivative and $\mathcal{L}(\mathrm{OSC} - \lambda)$ is obviously closed under union, we can use the same trick as at the beginning of the proof of Lemma 1.5.12, for instance, and thus the inclusion $\mathcal{L}(\mathrm{CS}) \subseteq \mathcal{L}(\mathrm{OSC} - \lambda)$ is proved.

Combining this theorem with the results proved in Section 2.4. we obtain

$$\mathcal{L}(\mathrm{OSC}, \mathrm{CF}) = \mathcal{L}(\mathrm{OSC}, \mathrm{CF}, \mathrm{ac}) = \mathcal{L}(\mathrm{SC}, \mathrm{ac}),$$

$$\mathcal{L}(\mathrm{OSC}, \mathrm{CF} - \lambda) = \mathcal{L}(\mathrm{OSC}, \mathrm{CF} - \lambda, \mathrm{ac}) = \mathcal{L}(\mathrm{SC} - \lambda, \mathrm{ac}),$$

a statement similar to those in Theorem 6.2.1.

The last ordered regulated grammars which we consider here are the *ordered Indian parallel grammars* $G = (V_N, V_T, P, S, <)$ where (V_N, V_T, P, S) is an Indian parallel grammar and $<$ is a partial order relation on P. The generated language is defined in the natural way imposed by the two restrictions, and the obtained families of languages are denoted by $\mathcal{L}(\mathrm{iO}, \alpha)$, $\alpha \in \{\mathrm{CF}, \mathrm{CF} - \lambda\}$.

The following theorem is an interesting completion of the results in Section 6.1.

Theorem 6.2.3. $\mathcal{L}(\mathrm{iO}, \mathrm{CF}) = \mathcal{L}(\mathrm{iO}, \mathrm{CF} - \lambda) = \mathcal{L}(\mathrm{EDTOL})$.

Proof. Clearly, it is sufficient to prove the inclusions $\mathcal{L}(\mathrm{iO}, \mathrm{CF}) \subseteq \mathcal{L}(\mathrm{EDTOL})$ and $\mathcal{L}(\mathrm{EDTOL}) \subseteq \mathcal{L}(\mathrm{iO}, \mathrm{CF} - \lambda)$.

Let $G = (V_N, V_T, P, S, <)$ be an ordered Indian parallel grammar. If there are $A \in V_N$ and $A \to x, A \to y$ in P such that $A \to x > A \to y$, then the smaller rule can be removed as being never applicable. Therefore we can assume that each two rules $A \to x, A \to y$ are incomparable. Let Z be a new symbol. For each rule $A \to x$ in P we construct the table

$$\{A \to x\} \cup \{B_i \to Z : 1 \leqq i \leqq r, B_i \to w_i \in P, B_i \to w_i > A \to x\}$$
$$\cup \left\{C \to C : C \in (V_N \cup V_T \cup \{Z\}) \setminus \{A, B_1, B_2, \ldots, B_r\}\right\}.$$

Let P be the set of all such tables (they are deterministic) and $G' = (V_N \cup \{Z\}, V_T, V_T, P, S)$. The equality $L(G) = L(G')$ is obvious (the table definition ensures the use of only maximal rules applicable to the current string). Hence $\mathcal{L}(\mathrm{iO}, \mathrm{CF}) \subseteq \mathcal{L}(\mathrm{EDTOL})$.

Conversely, let $G = (V, V_T, P, x)$ be a λ-free EDTOL system and let

$$V = \{a_1, a_2, \ldots, a_n\},\ V_T = \{a_1, a_2, \ldots, a_m\},$$

$$P = \{P_1, P_2, \ldots, P_r\},\ P_i = \{a_1 \to w_{i,1}, a_2 \to w_{i,2}, \ldots, a_n \to w_{i,n}\},\ 1 \leqq i \leqq n.$$

We introduce the following pairwise disjoint alphabets:

$$V' = \{x' : x \in V\},\ V'' = \{x'' : x \in V\},$$

$$V^{(j,i)} = \{x^{(j,i)} : x \in V\} \quad \text{for} \quad 1 \leqq j \leqq r,\ i \in \{1, 2\}.$$

For $w = x_{i_1}x_{i_2} \ldots x_{i_s}$ we set $w' = x'_{i_1}x'_{i_2} \ldots x'_{i_s}$, $w'' = x''_{i_1}x''_{i_2} \ldots x''_{i_s}$, $w^{(j,i)} = x^{(j,i)}_{i_1}x^{(j,i)}_{i_2} \ldots x^{(j,i)}_{i_s}$. We define the ordered Indian parallel grammar $G' = (V_N, V_T, P, S, <)$ by

$$V_N = V' \cup V'' \cup \bigcup_{i=1}^{2} \bigcup_{j=1}^{r} V^{(j,i)} \cup \{S\},$$

$$P = \{S \to x'\}$$

$$\cup \bigcup_{j=1}^{r} \{a'_1 \to w^{(j,1)}_{j,1}, a'_2 \to w^{(j,1)}_{j,2}, \ldots, a'_n \to w^{(j,1)}_{j,n}\}$$

$$\cup \bigcup_{k=1}^{n} \{a'_k \to a'_k, a'_k \to a''_k\} \cup \bigcup_{k=1}^{m} \{a''_k \to a_k\}$$

$$\cup \bigcup_{j=1}^{n} \bigcup_{k=1}^{r} \{a^{(j,1)}_k \to a^{(j,2)}_k, a^{(j,2)}_k \to a'_k, a^{(j,1)}_k \to a^{(j,1)}_k, a^{(j,2)}_k \to a^{(j,2)}_k\}$$

and with the order relation $<$ defined by

$$a^{(k,1)} \to a^{(k,1)} > a'_1 \to w^{(j,1)}_{j,i},\ a, a_i \in V,\ 1 \leqq k, j \leqq r,\ k \neq j,$$

$$a' \to a > b^{(j,1)} \to b^{(j,2)},\ a, b \in V,\ 1 \leqq j \leqq r,$$

$$a^{(j,1)} \to a^{(j,1)} > b^{(j',2)} \to b',\ a, b \in V,\ 1 \leqq j, j' \leqq r,$$

$$a^{(j',2)} \to a^{(j',2)} > a'_i \to w^{(j,1)}_{j,i},\ a, a_i \in V,\ 1 \leqq j, j' \leqq r,$$

$$a^{(j,1)} \to a^{(j,1)} > b' \to b'',\ a, b \in V,\ 1 \leqq j \leqq r,$$

$$a^{(j,2)} \to a^{(j,2)} > b' \to b'',\ a, b \in V,\ 1 \leqq j \leqq r,$$

$$a' \to a' > b'' \to b,\ a \in V,\ b \in V_T,$$

$$a'' \to a'' > a'_i \to w^{(j,1)}_{j,i},\ a, a_i \in V,\ 1 \leqq j \leqq r.$$

Let us consider a string over V'. If we apply an active rule $a'_i \to w^{(j,1)}_{j,i}$, then, by the order relation, we have to apply all rules $a'_k \to w^{(j,1)}_{j,k}$. Then we have to replace each $a^{(j,1)}_k$ by $a^{(j,2)}_k$, and then we rewrite each $a^{(j,2)}_k$ by a'_k. This derivation simulates a derivation step in the EDTOL system G. Otherwise, we use the active rule $a'_i \to a''_i$, and then we have to translate the current string in its twice primed version, and we then replace it by its non-primed version (i.e. the obtained word is in V_T^*) or the derivation stops with a word containing at least one nonterminal (more precisely, we can apply only rules of the form $x \to x$ to the word). It follows that $L(G) = L(G')$ which proves the theorem.

Remember that $\mathcal{L}$(EDTOL) is strictly included in the family $\mathcal{L}$(O, CF), and $\mathcal{L}$(iCF) is strictly included in $\mathcal{L}$(EDTOL). The above Theorem 6.2.3 shows that by combining the parallelism and the order restriction we obtain a mixture with an "average" power.

Exercises

6.2.1. Prove that $\mathcal{L}(\mathrm{rO}, \alpha) = \mathcal{L}(\mathrm{O}, \alpha)$, $\alpha \in \{\mathrm{CF}, \mathrm{CF} - \lambda\}$, where rO denotes the ordered version of Russian parallel grammars.

6.2.2. Define ordered versions of EOL systems in the obvious way and of ETOL systems by introducing a partial order relation inside each table (an order on the rules in each table). Prove the following hierarchy results (see Dassow and Păun (1985-b)):

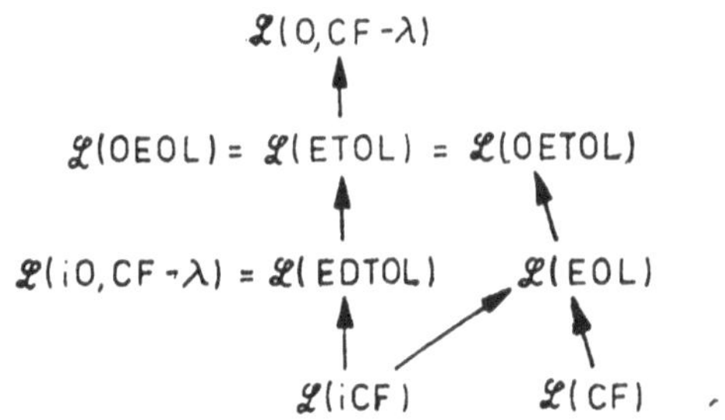

6.2.3. Define an *ordered string random context grammar of degree* (i, j) as a construct $G = (V_N, V_T, P, S, <)$ where (V_N, V_T, P, S) is a string random context grammar of degree (i, j) and $<$ is a partial order relation on P. A rule $r \in P$ is used for rewriting a string w only if no rule $r' \in P$, $r' > r$ can be applied to w.

Denote by $\mathcal{L}(\mathrm{OSRC}, \alpha, (i, j))$, $\alpha \in \{\mathrm{CF}, \mathrm{CF} - \lambda\}$, $i \geqq 0$, $j \geqq 0$, the family of languages generated in this way. Prove

$$\mathcal{L}(\mathrm{OSRC}, \mathrm{CF} - \lambda, (2, 0)) = \mathcal{L}(\mathrm{CS}) = \mathcal{L}(\mathrm{OSRC}, \mathrm{CF} - \lambda, (0, 2)),$$

$$\mathcal{L}(\mathrm{OSRC}, \mathrm{CF}, (2, 0)) = \mathcal{L}(\mathrm{RE}) = \mathcal{L}(\mathrm{OSRC}, \mathrm{CF}, (0, 2))$$

(see Păun (1985-c)).

6.3. Random Context Versions of Regulated Grammars

The ordered matrix grammars above contain an order relation on the set of matrices. Clearly, it makes no sense to consider an ordering inside matrices (as in ETOL systems, see Exercise 6.2.2) because the rules are already ordered. On the other hand, the Indian parallel matrix grammars contain the Indian parallelism at the level of rules, and it makes no sense to impose the parallelism to matrices.

In contrast, the random context restriction can be defined both inside matrices (matrices of random context rules) and over matrices (matrices with permitting and forbidding contexts and with usual context-free rules). Moreover, the random context restriction can suppose only permitting, only forbidding, or both kinds of contexts.

We consider random context matrix grammars first.

Definition 6.3.1. A *random context matrix grammar* is a construct $G = (V_N, V_T, M, S, F)$ where V_N, V_T, S, F are as in a usual matrix grammar and M is a finite set of triples

$$\big((A_1 \to x_1, A_2 \to x_2, \ldots, A_k \to x_k), Q, R\big)$$

where $A_i \to x_i$ are context-free rules over V_G, $1 \leqq i \leqq k$, $Q \subseteq V_N$, $R \subseteq V_N$, $Q \cap R = \emptyset$.

We call such a triple matrix, and a matrix as given above can be applied to a string $x = x_1X_1x_2X_2 \ldots x_tX_tx_{t+1}$ in order to rewrite effectively the symbols $X_1, X_2, \ldots, X_t$ only if $x_1x_2 \ldots x_{t+1}$ contains all symbols of Q and no symbol of R. (In other words, the application of the usual matrix $(A_1 \to x_1, A_2 \to x_2, \ldots, A_k \to x_k)$ is regulated by the random contexts Q, R in the usual way; the application of the matrix means the use of the rules $A_1 \to x_1, A_2 \to x_2, \ldots, A_k \to x_k$ in order, possibly in the appearance checking mode.)

By $\mathcal{L}(\mathrm{RC}_\alpha\mathrm{M}, \beta, \gamma)$ we denote the family of languages generated by random context grammars $G = (V_N, V_T, M, S, F)$ with rules of type β, $\beta \in \{\mathrm{CF}, \mathrm{CF} - \lambda\}$, with arbitrary F if $\gamma = \mathrm{ac}$ or with empty F if γ is empty, with arbitrary R in $\big((r_1, r_2, \ldots, r_k), Q, R\big) \in M$ if $\alpha = \mathrm{ac}$ and with empty α if no forbidding contexts are involved

For α, γ as above, we set $\max(\alpha, \gamma) = \mathrm{ac}$ iff at least one of α, γ is equal to ac.

Theorem 6.3.1. *For* $\alpha = \mathrm{ac}$ *or empty,* $\beta \in \{\mathrm{CF}, \mathrm{CF} - \lambda\}$, $\gamma = \mathrm{ac}$ *or empty,*

$$\mathcal{L}(\mathrm{RC}_\alpha\mathrm{M}, \beta, \gamma) = \mathcal{L}\big(\mathrm{M}, \beta, \max(\alpha, \gamma)\big).$$

Proof. Let us consider a grammar $G = (V_N, V_T, M, S, F)$ with matrices of the form $\big((r_1, r_2, \ldots, r_k), Q, R\big)$ in M. We construct the matrix grammar $G' = (V_N', V_T \cup \{c\}, M', S_0, F')$ where c is a new symbol,

$$V_N' = V_N \cup \{A' : A \in V_N\} \cup \{A'' : A \in V_N\} \cup \{C, D, S_0, Z\},$$

and M' contains the following matrices:

$(S_0 \to \mathrm{SC})$,

$(A_1 \to A_1', A_2 \to A_2', \ldots, A_k \to A_k', X_1 \to x_1'', Y_2 \to x_2'', \ldots, Y_t \to x_t'',$
$B_1 \to Z, B_2 \to Z, \ldots, B_s \to Z, C \to D)$

where $\big((X_1 \to x_1, \ldots, X_t \to x_t), \{A_1, \ldots, A_k\}, \{B_1, \ldots, B_s\}\big)$ is a matrix in M, x_i'' is obtained from x_i by replacing each symbol $E \in V_N$ by E'', $1 \leqq i \leqq t$, and Y_i, $2 \leqq i \leqq t$, is either X_i or X_i'',

$(E' \to E, D \to D)$, $E \in V_N$,

$(E'' \to E, D \to D)$, $E \in V_N$,

$(E_1' \to Z, E_2' \to Z, \ldots, E_u' \to Z, E_1'' \to Z, E_2'' \to Z, \ldots, E_u'' \to Z, D \to C)$,

$V_N = \{E_1, E_2, \ldots, E_u\}$,

$(D \to c)$,

and

$$F' = \bigcup_{X \to x \in F} \{X \to x'', X'' \to x''\} \cup \bigcup_{E \in V_N} \{E \to Z, E' \to Z, E'' \to Z\}.$$

Clearly, the matrices in M' (by the trap symbol Z and the primed symbols) simulate the matrices in M, including the random context restriction. Consequently, $L(G')$

$= L(G)\{c\}$. Using the closure of $\mathscr{L}(\mathrm{M}, \beta, \mathrm{ac})$ under right derivative, we obtain that $L(G) \in \mathscr{L}(M, \beta, \mathrm{ac})$. Hence we get $\mathscr{L}(\mathrm{RC}_\alpha\mathrm{M}, \beta, \gamma) \subseteq \mathscr{L}(\mathrm{M}, \beta, \mathrm{ac})$ if $\max(\alpha, \gamma) = \mathrm{ac}$.

If $\max(\alpha, \gamma)$ is empty, that is $F = \emptyset$ and all sets R in M are empty, then we take

$$M'' = \{(A_1 \to A_1', A_2 \to A_2', \ldots, A_k \to A_k', X_1 \to x_1, X_2 \to x_2, \ldots, X_s \to x_s, A_1' \to A_1, A_2' \to A_2, \ldots, A_k' \to A_k) : ((X_1 \to x_1, X_2 \to x_2, \ldots, X_s \to x_s), \{A_1, A_2, \ldots, A_k\}, \emptyset) \in M\}$$

and obtain $L(G) = L(G'')$ for

$$G'' = (V_N \cup \{A' : A \in V_N\}, V_T, M'', S, \emptyset).$$

Therefore $\mathscr{L}(\mathrm{RCM}, \beta) \subseteq \mathscr{L}(\mathrm{M}, \beta)$. Thus the inclusions in one direction are obtained.

Clearly, $\mathscr{L}(\mathrm{M}, \alpha, \beta) \subseteq \mathscr{L}(\mathrm{RC}_\gamma M, \alpha, \beta)$ for all possible α, β, γ (to the matrices of a usual matrix grammar add empty Q and R) and $\mathscr{L}(\mathrm{RC}, \alpha, \beta) \subseteq \mathscr{L}(\mathrm{RC}_\gamma\mathrm{M}, \alpha, \beta)$ for all possible α, β, γ (interpret the core rules of a random context grammar as one-rule matrices). Consequently, the only non-trivial relations, which remain to be proved, are the inclusions $\mathscr{L}(\mathrm{M}, \alpha, \mathrm{ac}) \subseteq \mathscr{L}(\mathrm{RC}_{\mathrm{ac}}\mathrm{M}, \alpha)$, but they follow from the equalities $\mathscr{L}(\mathrm{M}, \alpha, \mathrm{ac})$

$$= \mathscr{L}(\mathrm{RC}, \alpha, \mathrm{ac}).$$ Hence the proof is finished.

Let us now consider matrices of random context rules.

Definition 6.3.2. A *matrix random context grammar* is a construct $G = (V_N, V_T, M, S, F)$ where V_N, V_T, S, F are defined as usually and M is a finite set of matrices of the form

$$((A_1 \to x_1, Q_1, R_1), (A_2 \to x_2, Q_2, R_2), \ldots, (A_k \to x_k, Q_k, R_k)),$$

$k \geq 1$, $A_i \to x_i$ is a context-free rule over V_G and $Q_i \subseteq V_N$, $R_i \subseteq V_N$ for $1 \leq i \leq k$.

A rule $(A_i \to x_i, Q_i, R_i)$ is applied in the random context manner, hence such a rule in F can be passed over if A_i does not appear in the current string w or $w = w_1A_iw_2$ with w_1w_2 not containing all symbols in Q_i or containing one symbol of R_i at least.

By $\mathscr{L}(\mathrm{M}_\alpha\mathrm{RC}, \beta, \gamma)$, $\alpha = \mathrm{ac}$ or empty, $\beta \in \{\mathrm{CF}, \mathrm{CF} - \lambda\}$, $\gamma = \mathrm{ac}$ or empty, we denote the families of languages generated by such grammars ($\alpha = \mathrm{ac}$ for arbitrary set F and $\gamma = \mathrm{ac}$ for arbitrary sets R).

Theorem 6.3.2. *For* $\alpha = \mathrm{ac}$ *or empty,* $\beta \in \{\mathrm{CF}, \mathrm{CF} - \lambda\}$, $\gamma = \mathrm{ac}$ *or empty,*

$$\mathscr{L}(\mathrm{M}_\alpha\mathrm{RC}, \beta, \gamma) = \mathscr{L}(\mathrm{M}, \beta, \max(\alpha, \gamma)).$$

Proof. Let $G = (V_N, V_T, M, S, F)$ be a matrix random context grammar as above. We construct the grammar $G' = (V_N', V_T, M', S, F')$ with

$$V_N' = V_N \cup \{A' : A \in V_N\} \cup \{Z\}$$

and M' obtained from M by replacing each rule

$$r: (C \to x, \{A_1, A_2, \ldots, A_k\}, \{B_1, B_2, \ldots, B_t\})$$

by the sequence

a) $C \to C', A_1 \to A_1', A_2 \to A_2', \ldots, A_k \to A_k', A_1' \to A_1, A_2' \to A_2, \ldots, A_k' \to A_k,$
$B_1 \to Z, B_2 \to Z, \ldots, B_t \to Z, C' \to x$

if the rule r does not appear in F and by one of the sequences a), b), c), d) if r appears in F:

b) $C \to Z$ (the rule $C \to x$ cannot be applied),

c) $C \to C'$, $A_1 \to z_1$, $A_2 \to z_2$, ..., $A_k \to z_k$, $z_1 \to A_1$, $z_2 \to A_2$, ..., $z_k \to A_k$, $C' \to C$

where $z_i \in \{A_i', Z\}$, at least one z_i is equal to Z and the rules $z_i \to A_i$ appear only if $z_i = A_i'$ (at least one A_i does not occur in the current string),

d) $C \to C'$, $A_1 \to A_1'$, $A_2 \to A_2'$, ..., $A_k \to A_k'$, $A_1' \to A_1$, $A_2' \to A_2$, ..., $A_k' \to A_k$

$B_1 \to z_1$, $B_2 \to z_2$, ..., $B_t \to z_t$, $C' \to C$

where $z_i \in \{B_i, Z\}$ and at least one z_i is different from Z (at least one B_i appears in the current string)

(in all cases the rule $C \to x$ is passed over), and F' consists of all rules of the form $B \to Z$, $B \in V_N$. Clearly, $L(G) = L(G')$.

Conversely, the only non-trivial relations are $\mathcal{L}(\mathrm{M}, \beta, \mathrm{ac}) \subseteq \mathcal{L}(\mathrm{MRC}, \beta, \mathrm{ac})$, but they follow from the equalities $\mathcal{L}(\mathrm{M}, \beta, \mathrm{ac}) \doteq \mathcal{L}(\mathrm{RC}, \beta, \mathrm{ac})$, $\beta \in \{\mathrm{CF}, \mathrm{CF} - \lambda\}$.

Without proofs we shall mention here some further results similar to those above, concerning the following random context extensions of other types of regulated grammars (informal definitions):

i) *random context scattered context grammars* (scattered context rules with associated sets Q, R of nonterminals),

ii) *random context programmed grammars* (with rules of the form $(b: A \to x, \sigma(b), \varphi(b), Q, R)$; the core rules are applied to a string w only if the restrictions imposed by Q, R are observed: if the application is effective, $w = uAv$, $w \Rightarrow uxv$, uv contains all symbols of Q and no symbol of R; if the application is not effective, w does not contain A, contains all symbols of Q and no symbol of R; in the first case the next rule will be in $\sigma(b)$, in the second case the next rule will be in $\varphi(b)$),

iii) *programmed random context grammars* (with rules of the form $\big(b: (A \to x, Q, R), \sigma(b), \varphi(b)\big)$; if $(A \to x, Q, R)$ is applicable in the random context manner, then we apply it and pass to a rule in $\sigma(b)$; if $(A \to x, Q, R)$ is not applicable — either A does not appear in the current string or the restriction imposed by Q, R is not observed — then we pass to a rule in $\varphi(b)$),

iv) *regularly controlled random context grammars* (random context grammars with a regular control language associated to them).

The proof of the next theorem is left to the reader.

Theorem 6.3.3. *For all possible* $X \in \{\mathrm{M}, \mathrm{P}, \mathrm{SC}, \mathrm{rC}\}$, $\beta \in \{\mathrm{CF}, \mathrm{CF} - \lambda\}$, $\alpha = \mathrm{ac}$ *or empty*, $\gamma = \mathrm{ac}$ *or empty*,

$$\mathcal{L}(\mathrm{RC}_\alpha X, \beta, \gamma) = \mathcal{L}\big(X, \beta, \max(\alpha, \gamma)\big),$$
$$\mathcal{L}(X_\alpha \mathrm{RC}, \beta, \gamma) = \mathcal{L}\big(X, \beta, \max(\alpha, \gamma)\big).$$

The conclusion is that two (or more) simultaneous regulations behave as only one in what concerns the generative power. Maybe, from other points of view (descriptional complexity of languages, for example) such hybrids can be of interest.

Open problems

6.3.1. Consider other couples of regulated mechanisms not considered here (or in the subsequent exercises) and investigate their power. For instance, what about valence extensions of matrix, scattered context, random context, programmed, ordered, and of other grammars.?

Exercises

6.3.1. Consider programmed matrix grammars in the natural way (success and failure fields associated to matrices) and prove a result as in Theorem 6.3.3.

6.3.2. Solve the same problem for regularly controlled matrix grammars.

6.3.3. Solve the same problem for programmed and regularly controlled scattered context grammars.

6.3.4. Prove all relations of Theorem 6.3.3.

6.3.5. Consider matrix, programmed, and regularly controlled random string context grammars of degree (i, j) as well as string random context matrix grammars and prove that the grammars of each type and of degree (0,2) or (2,0) characterize $\mathscr{L}$(CS).

Bibliographical remarks

The material in Section 6.1 is based on DASSOW (1980) and (1984-a); Section 6.2 follows DASSOW and PĂUN (1985-b) and Section 6.3 contains the results reported in PĂUN (1984-c). All results concerning string random context grammars are taken from PĂUN (1985-c).

Chapter 7. Some Special Problems

In this chapter we shall present some results on regulated rewriting (mainly on matrix grammars and languages) qualified as "special" because either they have a reduced circulation (the automata characterization, for instance) or refer to very recent topics (the grammar forms, for instance).

7.1. Automata Characterizations

Although this is a very natural and important problem in formal language theory, the characterization of regulated rewriting languages by specific automata is only rarely investigated. Here we informally present some results in this area, starting with von Solms' (1975-a) characterization of matrix (and equivalent) languages by contraction automata. Roughly speaking, such an automaton is a linear bounded automaton with additional read/write restrictions.

Definition 7.1.1. A *contraction automaton of complexity* (n, k), where n, k are given natural numbers, is a system

$$A = (K, \Sigma, \Gamma, f, q_0, q_c, q_f, Z, *, ¢, \$)$$

where

1) K is the finite non-empty set of states,

2) Γ is the tape alphabet,

3) Σ is the input alphabet, $\Sigma \subseteq \Gamma$,

4) q_0, q_c, q_f of K are the initial state, the copy state, and the final state, respectively,

5) Z and $*$ are distinguished symbols in Γ (Z is the final symbol, and $*$ is the dummy symbol),

6) $¢$, $\$$ are distinguished symbols in Σ ($¢$ is the left marker, and $\$$ is the right marker),

7) f is the move mapping similar to that in a linear bounded automaton but ensuring the following behaviour of our conctraction automaton A.

Initially, the tape contains a string of the form $¢w\$$, where $w \in \Sigma^*$ does not contain occurrences of $¢$ and $\$$. The automaton starts in the state q_0 with the read-write head on the right marker $\$$. From here the head is moved to the left in the read only mode until the symbol $¢$ is scanned. In this phase the tape content remains unmodified, and the automaton state can be changed according to at most n different symbols in $\Gamma \setminus \Sigma$ (a subset $E \subseteq \Gamma \setminus \Sigma$ with card $(E) \leqq n$ can be checked). When the left marker ¢ is reached (in a state depending on q_0 and the occurrences of symbols in the mentioned set E), the automaton starts to move to the right. In the passing from ¢ to \$ it can perform at most k rewritings of the following types. We call two symbols of Γ *neighbouring* if they are separated by zero or more occurrences of *. The automaton can either replace a symbol in Γ by another symbol in Γ or replace two neighbouring symbols, the left one by the star symbol $*$ and the right one by another symbol of Γ. Depending on the state when the symbol ¢ is reached (and the moving to the right begins), the automaton has to perform p such replacements, where $p \leqq k$, and after completing these replacements it enters the copy state q_c, moves to the right without modifying the state, and passes again to state q_0 when it reaches the right marker \$.

The moving to the right can be characterized by a p-tuple, $p \leqq k$,

$$(x_1, x_2, \ldots, x_p),\ x_i \in \big(\Gamma \times (\Gamma \setminus \Sigma)\big) \cup \big(\Gamma \times \Gamma \times (\Gamma \setminus \Sigma)\big),\ 1 \leqq i \leqq p.$$

If $x_i = (A, B)$, $A \in \Gamma$, $B \in \Gamma \setminus \Sigma$, we have to replace A by B. If $x_i = (A, B, C)$, $A, B \in \Gamma$, $C \in \Gamma \setminus \Sigma$, we have to replace A by $*$ and the neighbouring B by C. The replacement defined by x_i must be performed after performing x_{i-1} and before performing x_{i+1}. If after more such cycles the tape contents is reduced to ¢ $*^s\, Z\, *^t$ \$, $s + t + 1 = |w|$, the automaton enters the state q_f and stops, one then says that the string w is recognized by A.

Interpreting the replacement of some symbol of Γ by $*$ as an erasing operation, we can consider that the tape string is contracted by one position (and the recognizing situation corresponds to the contraction to only one position which corresponds to the final Z).

Two kinds of contraction automaton can be defined, the *order-free* and the *order-sensitive* ones. An order-free automaton is one which, for each p-tuple $(x_1, x_2, \ldots, x_p)$ of replacements, can perform all permutations $(x_{i_1}, x_{i_2}, \ldots, x_{i_p})$ of this sequence. Otherwise, the automaton is called order-sensitive.

As we have seen in Chapter 1, each language $L \in \mathcal{L}(\mathrm{M}, \mathrm{CF} - \lambda)$ can be generated by a grammar in binary form with matrices consisting of at most two rules which have at most two symbols in their right-hand member. The derivation in such a grammar can be simulated by a contraction automaton of complexity (0, 2) which is order-free: no activity when passing to the left and at most two replacements when passing to the right. Conversely, the activity of such an automaton can be simulated by a λ-free matrix grammar in binary form. Thus we obtain

Theorem 7.1.1. *The family* $\mathcal{L}(\mathrm{M}, \mathrm{CF} - \lambda)$ *consists of all languages recognizable by order-free contraction automata of complexity* (0, 2).

Of course, this characterization holds true for all families equal to $\mathcal{L}(\mathrm{M}, \mathrm{CF} - \lambda)$; a similar theorem is true for scattered context languages, but involving order-sensitive contraction automata.

Remember now that in Exercise 1.3.1 we have noted that, for each language $L \in \mathcal{L}(\mathrm{RC}, \mathrm{CF} - \lambda, \mathrm{ac})$, there is a random context grammar $G = (V_N, V_T, P, S)$ with P containing only rules of the form $(A \to x, Q, R)$ with $|x| \leqq 2$ and card $(Q) \leqq 1$, card $(R) \leqq 1$. Therefore checking two symbols, those of $Q \cup R$, is enough to determine whether a rule $A \to x$ can be applied. In other words, an order-free contraction automaton of complexity (2, 1) can simulate such a grammar and conversely. Therefore

Theorem 7.1.2. *The family* $\mathcal{L}(\mathrm{RC}, \mathrm{CF}-\lambda, \mathrm{ac})$ *consists of all languages which can be recognized by order-free conctraction automata of complexity* (2, 1).

Again, this characterization holds true for all families equal to $\mathcal{L}(\mathrm{RC}, \mathrm{CF}-\lambda, \mathrm{ac})$.

The close similarity of a derivation in a matrix/random context grammar and the work of a contraction automaton gives the possibility for straightforward proofs of the previous theorems (however, the formalization is not too easy), but it diminishes the probability to obtain some results using contraction automata which cannot be similarly obtained using regulated grammars. Thus, in some sense, the above characterizations remain a goal per se.

A different conclusion can be inferred from an automata characterization of regular multiplicative valence languages (see Section 2.1.) by the multiplicative finite automata by IBARRA et al. (1976) ("one way non-deterministic finite automata with multiplication without equality"). Again, we prefer an informal presentation.

Definition 7.1.2. A *multiplicative finite automaton* is a system

$$A = (K, V, Q_{+}, f, q_0, ¢, \$, F)$$

where K is the finite non-empty set of states, V is the input alphabet, $\mathbb{Q}_{+}$ is the set of positive rational numbers, $F \subseteq K$ is the set of final states, q_0 is the initial state, ¢ and \$ are two symbols not in V marking the ends of the input string, and f is the move mapping, $f: K \times (V \cup \{¢, \$\}) \to 2^{K \times \{0,1\} \times \mathbb{Q}_{+}}$.

Such an automaton can be regarded as consisting of a finite automaton with an additional storage register which can contain any positive rational number. Initially, the register has the value 1. The relation $(q', d, r) \in f(q, a)$, $q, q' \in K$, $d \in \{0, 1\}$, $r \in \mathbb{Q}_{+}$, $a \in V \cup \{¢, \$\}$, means that from the state q the automaton reads the symbol a, passes to state q', moves the reading head d cells to the right ($d = 0$ means no move), and multiplies the register value by r. A string $x \in V^*$ is accepted if the automaton, starting in state q_0 with value 1 in its register, with ¢ x \$ on the tape and reading the symbol ¢, enters a final state with the head on the right marker \$ and with the register containing the value 1.

Theorem 7.1.3. *The family of languages generated by regular multiplicative valence grammars equals the family of languages accepted by multiplicative finite automata.*

The assertion can be proved by mutual simulation, appropriately modifying the constructions which prove that finite automata are equivalent to right-linear grammars. The only points to note in such constructions are the following:

a) Given a multiplicative valence grammar G with rules of the form $r: A \to xB$ or $r: A \to x$, $x = x_1x_2 \dots x_k$, $k \geqq 2$, $x_i \in V$, we replace these rules by

$$r_1: A \to x_1A_1,\ r_2: A_1 \to x_2A_2, \dots, r_{k-1}: A_{k-2} \to x_{k-1}A_{k-1},\ r_k: A_{k-1} \to x_kB$$

or

$$r_1: A \to x_1A_1,\ r_2: A_1 \to x_2A_2, \dots, r_k: A_{k-1} \to x_k$$

with

$$v(r_1) = v(r) \quad \text{and} \quad v(r_i) = 1 \quad \text{for} \quad 2 \leqq i \leqq k,$$

and we obtain an equivalent grammar with regular rules. The construction of an equivalent multiplicative finite automaton is now straightforward.

b) The moves $(q', d, r) \in f(q, a)$ with $d = 0$ in a multiplicative finite automaton (no move of the reading head) can be simulated by rules of the form $A \to B$ in the corresponding multiplicative valence grammar.

Of course, replacing everywhere "multiplicative" by "additive" and "1" by "0" we can obtain the additive finite automata and a similar characterization theorem for the regular additive valence languages.

Open problem

7.1.1. Characterize in a similar way the context-free valence languages by additive/multiplicative pushdown automata, thus obtaining automata characterizations for unordered vector languages also.

7.2. Szilard Language of Regulated Grammars

Definition 7.2.1. Let G be a grammar of arbitrary type and let each rule of G have an associated label. For a terminal derivation

$$D: S \underset{r_1}{\Longrightarrow} x_1 \underset{r_2}{\Longrightarrow} x_2 \underset{r_3}{\Longrightarrow} \cdots \underset{r_k}{\Longrightarrow} x_k \in L(G)$$

using the rules with labels $r_1, r_2, \ldots, r_k$, the string $c(D) = r_1 r_2 \ldots r_k$ is called the *control word* of the derivation D. Then we set

$$\mathrm{Sz}\,(G) = \{c(D) : D \text{ is a terminal derivation in } G\}$$

and call it the *Szilard language* associated to G. The language

$$\mathrm{ESz}\,(G) = \{xc(D) : x \in L(G), D \text{ is a derivation for } x\}$$

is called the *extended Szilard language* of G.

Similarly, we can define the Szilard and extended Szilard languages for matrix, simple matrix, scattered context grammars by considering labels associated to matrices of rules. For vector grammars, the Szilard languages can be naturally defined starting from labels assigned to rules not to matrices which, however, makes the definition rather uninteresting. Another possibility is to associate labels to matrices and to define the control word considering the labels in the order of the use of the first rule each matrix.

As one might expect, for many classes of regulated grammars (we shall consider here only the context-free case), the extended Szilard language $\mathrm{ESz}\,(G)$ is of the same type as $L(G)$.

Theorem 7.2.1. *For all grammars of type* (X, α, β), $X \in \{\mathrm{M}, \mathrm{P}, \mathrm{rC}, \mathrm{TV}, \mathrm{SC}, \mathrm{SM}\}$, $\alpha \in \{\mathrm{CF}, \mathrm{CF} - \lambda\}$, $\beta = \mathrm{ac}$ *or empty (for* $X = \mathrm{SM}$, β *is always empty), its extended Szilard language is in*

$$\mathcal{L}(X, \alpha, \beta).$$

Proof. We shall prove the assertion only for matrix and for programmed grammars.

Let $G = (V_N, V_T, M, S, F)$ be a matrix grammar, and let $\mathrm{Lab}\,(M)$ be a set of labels associated to the matrices of M. We construct the grammar $G' = (V'_N, V'_T, M', S', F)$ with

$$V'_N = V_N \cup \{S', X\},\ V'_T = V_T \cup \mathrm{Lab}\,(M),$$

and M' containing the matrices

$$(r_1, r_2, \ldots, r_k, X \to mX) \quad \text{and} \quad (r_1, r_2, \ldots, r_k, X \to m)$$

for each matrix $(r_1, r_2, \ldots, r_k)$ of M with label m, and the matrix

$$(S' \to SX).$$

The equality $L(G') = \text{ESz}(G)$ is obvious. (Please note that the same construction is also valid for scattered context grammars as well as for matrix grammars with leftmost or Russian or Indian parallel derivation.)

Take now a programmed grammar $G = (V_N, V_T, S, P)$, and let Lab (P) be the set of labels of rules in P. We construct the grammar

$$G' = (V_N \cup \{S', X\}, V_T \cup \text{Lab}(P) \cup \{c\}, P', S')$$

with P' containing the initial rule

$$\big(r_0 : S' \to SX, \text{Lab}(P), \emptyset\big),$$

the final rule

$$(r_f : X \to c, \emptyset, \emptyset)$$

as well as the next rules for each rule $\big(r : A \to x, \sigma(r), \varphi(r)\big) \in P$:

$$(\dot{r} : A \to x, \{r'\}, \{r''\}),$$
$$\big(r' : X \to rX, \sigma(r), \emptyset\big),$$
$$\big(r'' : X \to rX, \varphi(r), \emptyset\big).$$

Clearly, $L(G') = \text{ESz}(G)\{c\}$. By the closure properties of $\mathcal{L}(\text{P}, \alpha, \beta)$ (especially with respect to homomorphism and right derivatives), we get $\text{ESz}(G) \in \mathcal{L}(\text{P}, \alpha, \beta)$.

The same idea of intercalating new rules which introduce the labels of rules used in the "main" derivation also works for regularly controlled and for periodically time variant grammars.

The above theorem is also true for random context grammars with appearance checking. We construct a matrix for each random context rule as in the proof of Theorem 1.2.3, add a rule $X \to rX$ as in the first part of the previous proof and use the equality $\mathcal{L}(\text{M}, \alpha, \text{ac}) = \mathcal{L}(\text{RC}, \alpha, \text{ac})$, $\alpha \in \{\text{CF}, \text{CF} - \lambda\}$.

As Sz (G) is the homomorphic image of ESz (G) (by a homomorphism which erases the terminal symbols of G), the above theorem is also true for Szilard language of grammar with λ-rules. In fact, stronger results are true.

Theorem 7.2.2. *For each context-free matrix grammar* $G = (V_N, V_T, M, S, F)$, $\text{Sz}(G) \in \mathcal{L}(\text{M}, \text{CF} - \lambda, \text{ac})$, *and if* $F = \emptyset$, *then* $\text{Sz}(G) \in \mathcal{L}(\text{M}, \text{CF} - \lambda)$.

Proof. Let Lab $(M) = \{m_1, m_2, \ldots, m_n\}$ be the set of labels of the matrices of M, and let h be the homomorphism which erases the terminal symbols of G. We consider the set

$$h(M) = \big\{\big(A_1 \to h(x_1), A_2 \to h(x_2), \ldots, A_k \to h(x_k)\big) : (A_1 \to x_1, A_2 \to x_2, \ldots, A_k \to x_k) \in M\big\}$$

with the same set of labels as M. For a matrix m in $h(M)$, m: $(A_1 \to \alpha_1, A_2 \to \alpha_2, \ldots, A_k \to \alpha_k)$, let

$$\lg(m) = |\alpha_1\alpha_2 \ldots \alpha_k| \quad \text{and} \quad \lg(M) = \max\{\lg(m_i) : 1 \leqq i \leqq n\}.$$

We construct the matrix grammar

$$G' = (V'_N, \text{Lab}(M) \cup \{c\}, M', S', F)$$

with

$$V'_N = \{S', X, Z\}$$
$$\cup \{[m_i\, x\, \beta]: 1 \leqq i \leqq n, x \in V_N^*, 0 \leqq |x| \leqq \lg(M), \beta \in \{\lambda, R_1, \ldots, R_t\}\}$$
$$\cup \{(X, [m_i\, x\, \beta]): 1 \leqq i \leqq n, x \in V_N, 0 \leqq |x| \leqq \lg(M),$$
$$\beta \in \{\lambda, R_1, \ldots, R_t\}\}$$

where $R_1, R_2, \ldots, R_t$ are new symbols and

$$t = \max\{k : (r_1, r_2, \ldots, r_k) \in M\},$$

and the set M' is constructed as follows:

1) $(S' \to [m_i\alpha R_1]\, X)$ for m_i: $(S \to \alpha) \in h(M)$.

2) For each matrix m_i: $(A_1 \to \alpha_1, A_2 \to \alpha_2, \ldots, A_k \to \alpha_k)$, $k \geqq 2$, of $h(M)$ we introduce the matrices

$$([m_jx_1A_1y_1] \to [m_jx_1y_1], [m_rxR_1] \to [m_rx]\,[m_i\alpha_1R_2], X \to X) \quad \text{where}$$
$$x, x_1 \in V_N^*, y_1 \in V_N^*\{\lambda, R_1\}, 1 \leqq j, r \leqq n,$$
$$([m_jx_sA_sy_s] \to [m_jx_sy_s], [m_ixR_s] \to [m_ix\alpha_sR_{s+1}], X \to X) \quad \text{where}$$
$$x, x_s \in V_N^*, y_s \in V_N^*\{\lambda, R_s\}, 2 \leqq s \leqq k-1, 1 \leqq j \leqq n,$$
$$([m_jx_kA_ky_k] \to [m_jx_ky_k], [m_ixR_k] \to [m_ix\alpha_kR_1], X \to X) \quad \text{where}$$
$$x, x_k \in V_N^*, y_k \in V_N^*\{\lambda, R_k\}, 1 \leqq j \leqq n.$$

If a rule $A_s \to \alpha_s$ corresponds to a rule $A_s \to x_s$ which appears in F, then we consider the ordered set

$$q_1^{(i)}(A_s), q_2^{(i)}(A_s), \ldots, q_u^{(i)}(A_s)$$

of all symbols $[m_jx\beta]$ in V'_N, $1 \leqq j \leqq n$, $x \in V_N^*$, $0 \leqq |x| \leqq \lg(m)$, $\beta \in \{\lambda, R_1, R_2, \ldots, R_t\}$, such that x contains at least an occurrence of the symbol A_s, and we also introduce in M' the matrices

$$\left(q_1^{(i)}(A_s) \to Z, X \to \left(X, q_1^{(i)}(A_s)\right)\right),$$
$$\left(q_v^{(i)}(A_s) \to Z, \left(X, q_{v-1}^{(i)}(A_s)\right) \to \left(X, q_v^{(i)}(A_s)\right)\right), 2 \leqq v \leqq u,$$
$$\left([m_ixR_s] \to [m_ixR_{s+1}], \left(X, q_u^{(i)}(A_s)\right) \to X\right), 1 \leqq s \leqq k-1,$$
$$\left([m_ixR_k] \to [m_ixR_1], \left(X, q_u^{(i)}(A_k)\right) \to X\right).$$

If in the above matrix we have $A_1 = S$, then we also introduce the matrix

$$(S' \to [m_i \alpha_1 R_2]\, X).$$

3) For each matrix m_i: $(A \to \alpha) \in h(M)$, we consider the matrices

$$([m_j x A y] \to [m_j x y],\ [m_r w R_1] \to [m_r w]\,[m_i \alpha R_1],\ X \to X) \quad \text{where}$$

$$x, w \in V_N^*,\ y \in V_N^*\{\lambda, R_1\},\ 1 \leqq j, r \leqq n.$$

If this rule corresponds to a rule in F, then we also consider the matrices

$$\left(q_1^{(i)}(A) \to Z,\ X \to \left(X, q_1^{(i)}(A)\right)\right),$$

$$\left(q_v^{(i)}(A) \to Z,\ \left(X, q_{v-1}^{(i)}(A)\right) \to \left(X, q_v^{(i)}(A)\right)\right),\ 2 \leqq v \leqq u,$$

$$\left([m_r x R_1] \to [m_r x]\,[m_i R_1],\ \left(X, q_u^{(i)}(A)\right) \to X\right),\ x \in V_N^*,\ 1 \leqq r \leqq n.$$

In all these matrices, the strings x, x_s, y_s, w are of short enough lengths to obtain symbols $[m_i z]$ in V'_N.

4) $([m_i] \to m_i)$ and $([m_i R_1] \to m_i)$, $1 \leqq i \leqq n$.

5) $(X \to c)$.

The set F' consists of all occurrences of rules $q(A) \to Z$ in the above matrices.

Let us note that the symbols of V'_N associate to each label m_i of Lab (M) at most lg (M) nonterminals and that the symbols $[m_i x R_s]$ ensure the correct simulation of matrices of $h(M)$ (together with the symbols X, $(X, q(A))$ in the case of rules of F). The equality $L(G') = \mathrm{Sz}\,(G)\,\{c\}$ is easily checked. Therefore, using the closure properties of the families $\mathscr{L}(\mathrm{M}, \mathrm{CF} - \lambda, \mathrm{ac})$ and $\mathscr{L}(\mathrm{M}, \mathrm{CF} - \lambda)$, the theorem is proved. (Clearly, if $F = \emptyset$, then also $F' = \emptyset$.)

The above proof can easily be modified in order to obtain a similar theorem for scattered context grammars. Moreover, the same idea of "compound" nonterminals with the rightmost one distinguished in order to introduce on that position further labels can be used for proving this result also for programmed, regularly controlled, and periodically time-variant grammars. The details are left to the reader.

The conclusion of the above results and remarks is that, for many classes, the λ-free regulated rewriting grammars are powerful enough to generate also the Szilard languages associated to arbitrary context-free regulated grammar in that classes.

Open problems

7.2.1. Can the above theorems be extended to valence grammars or to permitting random context grammars?

7.2.2. By Igarashi (1977) it is proved that the Szilard language associated to an arbitrary type-0 Chomsky grammar is a deterministic context-sensitive one. Is such a language also in $\mathscr{L}(\mathrm{M}, \mathrm{CF} - \lambda, \mathrm{ac})$ or in other families of regulated languages strictly included in $\mathscr{L}(\mathrm{CS})$?

7.2.3. Consider the families Sz (X, Y, β) of Szilard languages associated to grammars of types (X, Y, β) with $X \in \{M, P, RC, \ldots\}$, $Y \in \{CS, CF - \lambda, REG, REG - \lambda\}$, $\beta = ac$ or empty, and investigate their size (mutual comparisons and relations with families of the Chomsky hierarchy and with families $\mathcal{L}(X, Y, \beta)$) and their closure properties.

Exercises

7.2.1. Prove that the Szilard language of a simple matrix grammar is context-free.

7.2.2. Prove that the extended Szilard language of a simple matrix grammar of degree n is in $\mathcal{L}(SM, CF, n + 1)$.

7.2.3. Find a matrix grammar G of finite index such that Sz (G) is not semilinear.

7.3. Grammar Forms

The grammar forms introduced by Cremers and Ginsburg (1975) are an attempt to formalize the idea of syntactic similarity of grammars and languages. Starting from a given grammar one can obtain a class of related "similar" grammars by means of a finite substitution (with some further properties) and hence also a family of "similar" languages.

Cremers and Ginsburg (1975) considered mainly context-free grammar forms. The notion was extended to L-forms by Maurer et al. (1977), and it was investigated by Maurer, Penttonen et al. (1979) for the non-context-free case. Greibach (1977) examined the effect of a control set on a context-free grammar form.

In the sequel we shall present some results about matrix grammar forms following the papers of Leipälä (1978), (1979-a), and (1979-b).

Definition 7.3.1. A *matrix grammar form* is a usual context-free matrix grammar $F = (N, T, M_0, S_0)$ (without appearance checking). Let $V_F = N \cup T$.

A matrix grammar $G = (V_N, V_T, M, S)$ is said to be an *interpretation* of the form F if there is a finite substitution $s\colon V_F^* \to 2^{V_G^*}$ such that

1) $s(a) \subseteq V_T$ for all $a \in T$,
2) $s(A) \subseteq V_N$ for all $A \in N$,
3) $s(x) \cap s(y) = \emptyset$ for all $x, y \in V_F, x \neq y$,
4) $S \in s(S_0)$,
5) M is a subset of

$$s(M_0) = \bigcup_{m \in M_0} s(m)$$

where, for $m\colon (A_1 \to x_1, A_2 \to x_2, \ldots, A_r \to x_r)$,

$$s(m) = \{(B_1 \to u_1, B_2 \to u_2, \ldots, B_r \to u_r) : B_i \in s(A_i),\ u_i \in s(x_i),\ 1 \leq i \leq r\}.$$

We set

$$\mathcal{G}(F) = \{G : G \text{ is an interpretation of } F\},$$

$$\mathcal{L}(F) = \{L : L = L(G) \text{ for some } G \in \mathcal{G}(F)\}.$$

A matrix grammar form F is called regular, linear, context-free, λ-free, etc., if F as a matrix grammar is of this type in the usual sense.

Two grammar forms F_1, F_2 are called *equivalent* if $\mathcal{L}(F_1) = \mathcal{L}(F_2)$ and *strongly equivalent* if $\mathcal{G}(F_1) = \mathcal{G}(F_2)$.

The main problem considered by LEIPÄLÄ (1978) is to find matrix grammar forms which can characterize the families $\mathcal{L}(\mathrm{M, CF})$, $\mathcal{L}(\mathrm{M, CF} - \lambda)$. Such forms are called *complete* and *complete modulo* λ, respectively. Some preliminary normal form results are useful for this aim (for some of them the proof is similar to that for the corresponding result for context-free grammar forms and it is omitted here).

Theorem 7.3.1. (i) *For an arbitrary matrix grammar G and a matrix grammar form F, it is decidable whether or not $G \in \mathcal{G}(F)$.*

(ii) *Let F_1 nad F_2 be two matrixgram mar forms. Then $F_2 \in \mathcal{G}(F_1)$ if and only if $\mathcal{G}(F_2) \subseteq \mathcal{G}(F_1)$. Consequently, the strong equivalence of two matrix grammar forms is decidable.*

Lemma 7.3.1. *If F is a matrix grammar form and $G \in \mathcal{G}(F)$ is an interpretation obtained by means of a finite substitution s, then for each derivation*

$$S \Rightarrow x_1 \Rightarrow x_2 \Rightarrow \cdots \Rightarrow x_k$$

with respect to G there is a derivation

$$S_0 \Rightarrow y_1 \Rightarrow y_2 \Rightarrow \cdots \Rightarrow y_k$$

with respect to F such that $x_i \in s(y_i)$ for $1 \leqq i \leqq k$.

Lemma 7.3.2. *For each matrix grammar form F there is an equivalent matrix grammar form $F' = (N', T', M_0', S_0')$ such that each matrix of F' containing terminal symbols is of the form $(A \to a)$ and each matrix of F' containing a λ-rule is of the form $(A \to \lambda)$, $A \in N'$, $a \in T'$.*

Proof. Take $F = (N, T, M_0, S_0)$, replace each terminal symbol $a \in T$ which appears in M_0 by a new symbol A_a and add to M_0 the matrices $(A_a \to a)$. The form F' obtained in this way is clearly equivalent to F.

For λ-rules an analogous construction can be performed.

Lemma 7.3.3. *Let $F = (N, T, M_0, S_0)$ be a matrix grammar form with*

$$M_0 = M_1 \cup \{(A_1 \to x_1, \ldots, A_{i-1} \to x_{i-1}, A_i \to uv, A_{i+1} \to x_{i+1}, \ldots, A_n \to x_n)\},$$

and let $F' = (N \cup \{X_1, X_2\}, T, M_0', S_0)$ be the form with

$$M_0' = M_1 \cup \{(A_1 \to x_1, \ldots, A_{i-1} \to x_{i-1}, A_i \to X_1X_2, X_1 \to u, X_2 \to v,$$
$$A_{i+1} \to x_{i+1}, \ldots, A_n \to x_n)\}.$$

Then the forms F, F' are equivalent.

Proof. The inclusion $\mathcal{L}(F) \subseteq \mathcal{L}(F')$ is obvious.

Consider now a language $L \in \mathcal{L}(F')$ generated by the grammar $G' = (V_N, V_T, M', S')$ of $\mathcal{G}(F')$ obtained by a finite substitution $s'\colon V_{F'}^* \to 2^{V_{G'}^*}$. We define the substitution $s\colon V_F^* \to 2^{V_{G'}^*}$ by $s(x) = s'(x)$ for $x \in V_F$.

Let m: $(A_1 \to x_1, \ldots, A_i \to X_1X_2, X_1 \to u, X_2 \to v, \ldots, A_n \to x_n)$. If $s'(m) \cap M' = \emptyset$, then we take the grammar

$$G = (V_N \setminus s'(\{X_1, X_2\}), V_T, M', S').$$

Clearly, $L = L(G)$ and $G \in \mathcal{G}(F)$. Therefore $L \in \mathcal{L}(F)$.

If

$$s'(m) \cap M' = \{(A_1^{(j)} \to x_1^{(j)}, \ldots, A_i^{(j)} \to X_1^{(j)}X_2^{(j)}, Y_1^{(j)} \to u^{(j)},$$
$$Y_2^{(j)} \to v^{(j)}, \ldots, A_n^{(j)} \to x_n^{(j)}) : 1 \leqq j \leqq t\},$$

then we assume, without loss of generality, that, for $j \in \{1, 2, \ldots, r\}$, $X_1^{(j)} = Y_1^{(j)}$ and $X_2^{(j)} = Y_2^{(j)}$ and, for $j \in \{r+1, r+2, \ldots, t\}$, $(X_1^{(j)}, X_2^{(j)}) \neq (Y_1^{(j)}, Y_2^{(j)})$. Then we consider the grammar

$$G = (V_N \setminus s'(\{X_1, X_2\}), V_T, M'', S')$$

with

$$M'' = \big(M' \setminus s'(m)\big) \cup \{(A_1^{(j)} \to x_1^{(j)}, \ldots, A_i^{(j)} \to u^{(j)}v^{(j)}, \ldots, A_u^{(j)} \to x_u^{(j)}) :$$
$$1 \leqq i \leqq r\}.$$

The equality $L = L(G)$ is obvious and, as $G \in \mathcal{G}(F)$, we obtain $L \in \mathcal{L}(F)$.

Lemma 7.3.4. *For each matrix grammar form $F = (N, T, M_0, S_0)$, there is an equivalent form $F' = (N', T, M_0', S_0)$ such that each rule $A \to x$ appearing in M_0' satisfies $|x| \leqq 2$.*

Proof. Let

$$r(F) = \max\{|x| : A \to x \text{ is a rule in } M_0\}$$

and assume $r(F) \geqq 3$. We construct a form $F'' = (N'', T, M_0'', S_0)$ equivalent to F and satisfying $r(F'') < r(F)$. By repeating this procedure a form F' as required can be obtained.

Assume $M = \{m_i : 1 \leqq i \leqq k\}$,

$$m_i: (p_1^{(i)}, p_2^{(i)}, \ldots, p_{n_i}^{(i)}),\ p_j^{(i)} : A_j^{(i)} \to x_j^{(i)},\ 1 \leqq i \leqq k,\ 1 \leqq j \leqq n_i.$$

For each rule $p_j^{(i)}$, we consider two new nonterminals $B_j^{(i)}$ and $C_j^{(i)}$ and define

$$N'' = N \cup \{B_j^{(i)} : 1 \leqq i \leqq k, 1 \leqq j \leqq n_i\} \cup \{C_j^{(i)} : 1 \leqq i \leqq k, 1 \leqq j \leqq n_i\}.$$

Further we set $M'' = \{m_i' : 1 \leqq i \leqq k\}$ where m_i' is obtained from m_i in the following way. If $p_j^{(i)}$ is a rule in m_i with $x_j^{(i} = \alpha_1\alpha_2 \ldots \alpha_{r(F)}$, $\alpha_i \in V_F$, $1 \leqq i \leqq r(F)$, then $p_j^{(i)}$ is replaced by

$$A_j^{(i)} \to B_j^{(i)}C_j^{(i)},\ B_j^{(i)} \to \alpha_1\alpha_2 \ldots \alpha_{r(F)-1},\ C_j^{(i)} \to \alpha_{r(F)}.$$

If $|x_j^{(i)}| < r(F)$, then the rule $p_j^{(i)}$ is introduced in m_i' without changes.

Using the previous lemma after each replacement of a rule $p_j^{(i)}$ we get $\mathcal{L}(F) = \mathcal{L}(F')$, and the proof is finished.

As one can see, the above proof is standard in its idea, but complicated in formalization. The previous lemmas are incorporated into the next theorem whose proof is omitted as being similarly straightforward but tedious.

Theorem 7.3.2. *For each matrix grammar form, there is an equivalent matrix grammar form with matrices consisting of at most two rules and with right-hand members of the rules of length at most 2.*

This result can be stressed in various ways.

Lemma 7.3.5. *For each matrix grammar form $F = (N, T, M_0, S_0)$, there is an equivalent matrix grammar form $F' = (N', T, M'_0, S_0)$ with matrices in M'_0 of one of the following forms: $(A \to BC)$, $(A \to a)$, $(A \to B, C \to D)$, $(A \to \lambda)$, $A, B, C, D \in N'$, $a \in T$.*

Proof. According to the preceding theorem, we may assume that M_0 contains only matrices of the forms $(A \to a)$, $(A \to \lambda)$, $(A \to BC)$, $(A \to B)$, $(A \to x_1, B \to x_2)$, $x_1, x_2 \in N^*$, $1 \leqq |x_i| \leqq 2$, $i \in \{1, 2\}$, $A, B, C \in N$, $a \in T$. Let $m: (A_1 \to x_1, B_1 \to x_2)$ be a matrix of M_0 which is not of the form $(A \to B, C \to D)$. We introduce the new nonterminals X_m, X'_m, Y_m, Z_m.

If $x_1 = C_1 \in N$, then $|x_2| = 2$. We replace the matrix m by the matrices $(A_1 \to C_1, B_1 \to Z_m)$, $(Z_m \to x_2)$.

If $x_1 = C_1D_1$, then $|x_2| \in \{1, 2\}$.

Case 1. Assume $|x_2| = 1$. We distinguish four possibilities:

(a) $C_1 \neq B_1$, $D_1 \neq B_1$. We replace the matrix $m: (A_1 \to C_1D_1, B_1 \to x_2)$ by the matrices $(A_1 \to X_m, B_1 \to x_2)$, $(X_m \to C_1D_1)$.

(b) $C_1 = B_1$, $D_1 \neq B_1$. Then we replace the matrix m by the matrices $(A_1 \to X_mY_m)$, $(X_m \to B_1, B_1 \to Z_m)$, $(Y_m \to D_1, Z_m \to x_2)$.

(c) $C_1 \neq B_1$, $D_1 = B_1$. We replace m by the matrices $(A_1 \to X_mY_m)$, $(Y_m \to B_1, B_1 \to Z_m)$, $(X_m \to C_1, Z_m \to x_2)$.

(d) $C_1 = D_1 = B_1$. We replace the matrix $m: (A_1 \to B_1B_1, B_1 \to x_2)$ by the matrices $(A_1 \to X_mX_m)$, $(X_m \to B_1, B_1 \to Z_m)$, $(X_m \to B_1, Z_m \to x_2)$.

Case 2. If $|x_2| = 2$, then again we distinguish the above four cases and introduce the same matrices to replace m with the only difference being that x_2 is replaced by X_m and the further matrix $(X'_m \to x_2)$ is added.

Applying this procedure to all matrices $m \in M_0$ of the form $(A \to x_1, B \to x_2)$ with $x_1 \notin N$ or $x_2 \notin N$ we obtain an equivalent form F'' containing only matrices of the forms $(A \to a)$, $(A \to \lambda)$, $(A \to BC)$, $(A \to B, C \to D)$, $(A \to B)$. In order to complete the proof we have also to remove the matrices $(A \to B)$. Each such matrix m is replaced by a matrix $(A \to Y'_m, Y'_m \to B)$ where Y'_m is a new symbol. Clearly, in this way we can obtain the matrix form F' looked for.

Lemma 7.3.6. *For each grammar form F, there is an equivalent matrix grammar form F containing only matrices of one of the following forms: $(A \to a)$, $(A \to \lambda)$, $(A \to B, C \to DE)$, $A, B, C, D, E \in V_N$, $a \in V_T$.*

Proof. In view of the previous lemma, we can assume that F contains only matrices of the forms $(A \to a)$, $(A \to \lambda)$, $(A \to BC)$, $(A \to B, C \to D)$. We replace each matrix $(A \to BC)$ by a matrix $(A \to X_m, X_m \to BC)$ where X_m is a new symbol. Moreover, we replace each matrix m: $(A \to B, C \to D)$ by matrices $(A \to B, C \to DZ_m)$, $(Z_m \to \lambda)$ with a new symbol Z_m. The form F' obtained in this way is equivalent to F.

Lemma 7.3.7. *For each matrix grammar form F there is an equivalent matrix grammar form $F' = (V_N, V_T, M, S)$ with matrices of one of the following forms: $(A \to a)$, $(A \to \lambda)$, $(A \to BC, D \to E)$, $A, B, C, D, E \in V_N$, $a \in V_T$.*

Proof. We start again from a matrix grammar form F as given by Lemma 7.3.5, that is with matrices of the forms $(A \to a)$, $(A \to \lambda)$, $(A \to BC)$, $(A \to B,\ C \to D)$. Each matrix m: $(A \to BC)$ is replaced by a matrix $(A \to BX_m,\ X_m \to C)$, and each matrix m: $(A \to B,\ C \to D)$ is replaced by matrices $(A \to BZ_m, C \to D)$, $(Z_m \to \lambda)$ where X_m, Z_m are new symbols. The form F' obtained in this way is obviously equivalent to F.

Theorem 7.3.3. *The following matrix grammar forms are complete:*

$$F_1 = \big(\{S_0\}, \{a\}, \{(S_0 \to S_0S_0), (S_0 \to S_0, S_0 \to S_0), (S_0 \to a), (S_0 \to \lambda)\}, S_0\big),$$

$$F_2 = \big(\{S_0\}, \{a\}, \{(S_0 \to S_0, S_0 \to S_0S_0), (S_0 \to a), (S_0 \to \lambda)\}, S_0\big),$$

$$F_3 = \big(\{S_0\}, \{a\}, \{(S_0 \to S_0S_0, S_0 \to S_0), (S_0 \to a), (S_0 \to \lambda)\}, S_0\big).$$

The next form is complete modulo λ

$$F_4 = \big(\{S_0\}, \{a\}, \{(S_0 \to S_0S_0), (S_0 \to S_0, S_0 \to S_0), (S_0 \to a)\}, S_0\big).$$

Proof. We shall discuss only the case of the form F_1, the other cases are similar.

Clearly, $\mathcal{L}(F_1) \subseteq \mathcal{L}(\mathrm{M, CF})$. Conversely, let $L \in \mathcal{L}(\mathrm{M, CF})$ be a matrix language generated by a matrix grammar $G = (V_N, V_T, M, S)$. This grammar can be viewed as being obtained by an interpretation of G considered as a grammar form. According to Lemma 7.3.5, there is a matrix grammar form $F' = (V_N', V_T, M', S)$ such that $\mathcal{L}(F') = \mathcal{L}(G)$ and with M' containing only matrices of the forms $(A \to BC)$, $(A \to B, C \to D)$, $(A \to a)$, $(A \to \lambda)$. Clearly, this form F' is an interpretation of the form F_1. As $\mathcal{L}(F') = \mathcal{L}(G)$, it follows that there is an interpretation G' of F' such that $L = L(G')$. According to Theorem 7.3.1, G' is also an interpretation of the form F_1. Therefore $L \in \mathcal{L}(F_1)$, and thus we obtain the inclusion $\mathcal{L}(\mathrm{M, CF}) \subseteq \mathcal{L}(F_1)$.

For F_4 the argument is similar with the change that the proof of Lemma 7.3.5 does not introduce λ-rules if no such rules exist in the starting grammar form.

Theorem 7.3.4. *There is no complete matrix grammar form containing exactly one matrix.*

Proof. If $F = (N, T, \{m\}, S_0)$ is a complete matrix grammar form then the matrix m must be terminal in the sense that it can perform a terminal derivation $S_0 \Rightarrow x$, $x \in T^*$. Therefore, each interpretation of F contains either terminal matrices or matrices which cannot be entirely applied to S_0. Consequently, each language of $\mathcal{L}(F)$ is finite. This contradicts the completeness.

It is still an open problem whether there exists a complete matrix grammar form with exactly two matrices. In particular, LEIPÄLÄ (1978) asked whether the following two forms are complete (modulo λ):

$$F_1 = \big(\{S_0\}, \{a\}, \{(S_0 \to S_0, S_0 \to S_0S_0), (S_0 \to a)\}, S_0\big),$$

$$F_2 = \big(\{S_0\}, \{a\}, \{(S_0 \to S_0S_0S_0, S_0 \to a), (S_0 \to \lambda)\}, S_0\big).$$

LEIPÄLÄ (1978) also investigated the closure properties of the families $\mathcal{L}(F)$ for a matrix grammar form F. It was proved that $\mathcal{L}(F)$ is closed under intersection with regular sets but it is not necessarily closed under union, homomorphisms, concatenation, Kleene-closure, or inverse homomorphisms. Sufficient conditions to have positive closure properties for these operations are given, too.

The papers LEIPÄLÄ (1979-a) and (1979-b) contain (among others) a study of the following natural problem: Find matrix grammar forms F such that $\mathcal{L}(F)$ is equal to important subfamilies of $\mathcal{L}(\mathrm{M}, \mathrm{CF})$ such as $\mathcal{L}(\mathrm{CF})$, $\mathcal{L}(\mathrm{LIN})$, $\mathcal{L}(\mathrm{REG})$, etc. We present here, without proof, only some results and some examples in this direction.

Theorem 7.3.5. *There is no matrix grammar form F such that $\mathcal{L}(F) = \mathcal{L}(\mathrm{FIN})$.*

Theorem 7.3.6. *Let $F = (\{S_0\}, T, M_0, S_0)$ be a matrix grammar form. Then $\mathcal{L}(F) = \mathcal{L}(\mathrm{REG})$ if and only if*

1) *there is an $a \in T$ such that $\{a\}^* \subseteq L(F)$,*
2) *there is no derivation of the form $S_0 \overset{*}{\Rightarrow} uS_0v$ with $u \neq \lambda$, $v \neq \lambda$ in F.*

Notation. For a matrix grammar form $F = (N, T, M_0, S_0)$ with

$$N = \{A_1, A_2, \ldots, A_r\},\ A_1 = S_0,$$

$$M = \{m_1, m_2, \ldots, m_t\},$$

$$m_i\colon (A_1^{(i)} \to x_1^{(i)}, A_2^{(i)} \to x_2^{(i)}, \ldots, A_{n_i}^{(i)} \to x_{n_i}^{(i)},)\ 1 \leqq i \leqq t,$$

let

$$k_{j,i} = |x_1^{(i)}x_2^{(i)} \ldots x_{n_i}^{(i)}|_{A_j} - |A_1^{(i)}A_2^{(i)} \ldots A_{n_i}^{(i)}|_{A_j}$$

for each i, j, $1 \leqq i \leqq t$, $1 \leqq j \leqq r$.

Theorem 7.3.7. *Let $F = (\{A_1, A_2, \ldots, A_r\}, T, \{m_1, m_2, \ldots, m_t\}, A_1)$ be a matrix grammar form with $k_{j,i} \leqq 0$ for all $1 \leqq i \leqq t$, $1 \leqq j \leqq r$.* Then *$\mathcal{L}(F) = \mathcal{L}(\mathrm{REG})$ if and only if*

1) *there is an $a \in T$ such that $\{a\}^* \subseteq L(F)$,*
2) *there is no derivation $A_1 \overset{*}{\Rightarrow} uA_1v$ with $u, v \in V_F^+$ in F.*

Here are some matrix grammar forms characterizing the family $\mathcal{L}(\mathrm{REG})$:

$$F_1 = \big(\{S_0\}, \{a\}, \{(S_0 \to S_0a), (S_0 \to \lambda)\}, S_0\big),$$

$$F_2 = \big(\{S_0\}, \{a\}, \{(S_0 \to S_0, S_0 \to S_0a, S_0 \to S_0), (S_0 \to S_0, S_0 \to \lambda)\}, S_0\big),$$

$$F_3 = \big(\{S_0, A, B\}, \{a\}, \{(S_0 \to S_0, S_0 \to AB, A \to \lambda, B \to \lambda), (S_0 \to aS_0)\}, S_0\big),$$

$$F_4 = \big(\{S_0\}, \{a\}, \{(S_0 \to a^kS_0)\} \cup \{(S_0 \to a^i) : 1 \leqq i \leqq k-1\}, S_0\big),\ k \geqq 1,$$

$$F_5 = \big(\{S_0, A\}, \{a\}, \{(S_0 \to a^iAa^j), (A \to Aa^k)\} \cup \{(A \to a^s) : 1 \leqq s \leqq k\}$$
$$\cup \{(S_0 \to a^t) : 0 \leqq t \leqq i + j\}, S_0\big),\ k \geqq 1,\ i, j \geqq 0,$$

$$F_6 = \big(\{S_0, A\}, \{a\}, \{(S_0 \to a^iAa^j), (A \to a^kA)\} \cup \{(A \to a^s) : 1 \leqq s \leqq k\}$$
$$\cup \{(S_0 \to a^t) : 0 \leqq t \leqq i + j\}, S_0\big),\ k \geqq 1,\ i, j \geqq 0.$$

Theorem 7.3.8. *Let $F = (\{S_0\}, \{a\}, M_0, S_0)$ be a matrix grammar form. Then $\mathcal{L}(F) = \mathcal{L}(\mathrm{LIN})$ if and only if:*

1) $\{a\}^* \subseteq L(F)$,
2) *there is no $m \in M_0$ which can produce derivations of the form $S_0 \Rightarrow x_1S_0x_2S_0x_3$ with $x_1, x_2, x_3 \in \{S_0, a\}^*$,*
3) *there are derivations of the form $S_0 \overset{*}{\Rightarrow} a^kS_0$, $S_0 \overset{*}{\Rightarrow} S_0\, a^t$ with $k > 0$, $t > 0$ in F.*

Theorem 7.3.9. *Let $F = (\{A_1, A_2, \ldots, A_r\}, T, \{m_1, m_2, \ldots, m_t\}, A_1)$ be a matrix grammar form with $k_{j,i} \leqq 0$ for all $i, j, 1 \leqq i \leqq t, 1 \leqq j \leqq r$. Then $\mathcal{L}(F) = \mathcal{L}(\mathrm{LIN})$ if and only if there is an $a \in T$ such that $\{a\}^* \subseteq L(F)$ and there are derivations $A_1 \overset{*}{\Rightarrow} a^k A_1$, $A_1 \overset{*}{\Rightarrow} A_1 a^t$ in F for some $k \geqq 0, t \geqq 0$.*

The following matrix grammar forms characterize the family $\mathcal{L}(\mathrm{LIN})$:

$$F_1 = \big(\{S_0\}, \{a\}, \{(S_0 \to S_0S_0, S_0 \to a, S_0 \to S_0),$$
$$(S_0 \to S_0S_0, S_0 \to \lambda, S_0 \to \lambda)\}, S_0\big),$$

$$F_2 = \big(\{S_0, A, B\}, \{a\}, \{(S_0 \to AB, A \to a, B \to S_0),$$
$$(S_0 \to S_0A, A \to B, B \to a),$$
$$(S_0 \to S_0A, A \to S_0, S_0 \to \lambda, S_0 \to \lambda)\}, S_0\big),$$

$$F_3 = \big(\{S_0\}, \{a\}, \{(S_0 \to a^kS_0), (S_0 \to S_0a^t)\}$$
$$\cup \{(S_0 \to a^i) : 0 \leqq i \leqq 2k + 2t - 4\}, S_0\big), k \geqq 1, t \geqq 1.$$

There are "simple" matrix grammar forms F for which $\mathcal{L}(F)$ contains non-context-free languages. For example, let us consider the form

$$F = \big(\{S_0\}, \{a\}, \{(S_0 \to S_0S_0), (S_0 \to a, S_0 \to \lambda)\}, S_0\big).$$

The inclusion $\mathcal{L}(\mathrm{CF}) \subseteq \mathcal{L}(F)$ can be easily proved (each context-free language can be generated by a grammar in Chomsky normal form). The inclusion is proper. Indeed, consider the grammar

$$G = (V_N, \{a, b, c\}, M, S) \quad \text{with}$$
$$V_N = \{S, S_1, S_2, S_3, S_4, S_a, S_b, S_c, S_A, S_B, S_C, A, B, C\},$$
$$M = \{(S \to S_1S_4), (S_4 \to S_2S_3), (S_1 \to S_aS_A), (S_A \to S_1A), (S_1 \to S_aA),$$
$$(S_2 \to S_bS_B), (S_B \to S_2B), (S_2 \to S_bB), (S_3 \to S_cS_C), (S_C - S_3C),$$
$$(S_3 \to S_cC), (S_a \to a, B \to \lambda), (S_b \to b, C \to \lambda),$$
$$(S_c \to c, A \to \lambda)\}.$$

Clearly, G can be obtained from F by an interpretation, and it generates the non-context-free language $L(G) = \{a^nb^nc^n : n \geqq 1\}$.

Similar conclusions hold for the following matrix grammar forms:

$$F_1 = \big(\{S_0\}, \{a\}, \{(S_0 \to S_0S_0S_0, S_0 \to a), (S_0 \to \lambda)\}, S_0\big),$$
$$F_2 = \big(\{S_0\}, \{a\}, \{(S_0 \to S_0, S_0 \to S_0S_0), (S_0 \to a)\}, S_0\big).$$

In fact, in Leipälä (1979-a) it has been proved the following theorem.

Theorem 7.3.10. *There is no matrix grammar form $F = (\{S_0\}, T, M_0, S_0)$ such that $\mathcal{L}(F) = \mathcal{L}(\mathrm{CF})$ and M_0 contains a matrix with at least two productions.*

Characterizations of matrix grammar forms F such that $\mathcal{L}(F) = \mathcal{L}(\mathrm{CF})$ are obtained by Leipälä (1979-b).

Theorem 7.3.11. *A matrix grammar form $F = (\{S_0\}, \{a\}, M_0, S_0)$ satisfies $\mathcal{L}(F) = \mathcal{L}(\mathrm{CF})$ if and only if*

1) $L(F) = \{a\}^+$,

2) *all matrices in* M_0 *consist of exactly one rule,*
3) *there is a derivation* $S_0 \overset{*}{\Rightarrow} a^r S_0 a^k S_0 a^s$ *in* F *for some* $r, k, s \geqq 0$.

The theorem can be extended to arbitrary terminal alphabets in the following way. For a given form $F = (N, T, M_0, S_0)$ and for some $b \in T$, let F_b be the form obtained by removing from M_0 all matrices in which terminal symbols different from b appear.

Theorem 7.3.12. *A matrix grammar form* $F = (\{S_0\}, T, M_0, S_0)$ *satisfies* $L(F) = \mathscr{L}(\mathrm{CF})$ *if and only if*

1) $\lambda \notin L(F)$,
2) *all matrices in* M_0 *consist of exactly one rule,*
3) *there is a* $b \in T$ *such that* $\mathscr{L}(F_b) = \mathscr{L}(\mathrm{CF})$.

As a corollary we obtain

Theorem 7.3.13. *The problem whether or not* $L(F) = \mathscr{L}(\mathrm{CF})$ *for some matrix grammar form* $F = (\{S_0\}, T, M_0, S_0)$ *is decidable.*

Open problems

7.3.1. Is the equivalence problem for matrix grammar forms decidable?

7.3.2. Are there complete matrix grammar forms with exactly two matrices?

7.3.3. Characterize matrix grammar forms $F = (N, T, M_0, S_0)$ with arbitrary N such that $\mathscr{L}(F) = \mathscr{L}(\mathrm{CF})$.

7.3.4. Consider matrix grammar forms with appearance checking and investigate their properties. More generally, consider and investigate grammar forms of other types of regulated rewriting.

Bibliographical remarks

As we have already referred for most notions and results to the papers where they appeared, only a few words are necessary.

For the non-appearance checking case, Theorem 7.2.2 has been proved in Păun (1979-a).

The contraction automata (of complexity $(0, \infty)$) have been used by von Solms (1975-b) in order to characterize the languages generated by propagating normal (with initial string consisting of only one letter) limited (each rule $a \to \alpha$ satisfies $|\alpha| \leqq 2$) ETOL systems.

For the theory of forms we refer to Wood (1980). Besides the work by Leipälä (1978), (1979-a), and (1979-b), and her dissertation and Greibach (1977) we know of no further paper dedicated to regulated grammar forms.

Chapter 8. Regulated L Systems

In this chapter we shall study the effect of regulating mechanisms applied to tabled L systems. We do this for the following reasons:

1) By their biological motivation, a derivation in an L system describes the development of an organism, and the different tables correspond to different environments (more precisely, to the different developmental rules which depend on the environment). In the definition of a tabled L system we allowed an arbitrary choice of the tables, however, this does not correspond to reality where e.g. the change of the seasons or the change in light (day) and darkness (night) is periodic. Thus we have to control the sequence of tables by some regulating mechanisms.

2) In Chapter 5 we mentioned that the pure grammars can be considered as a sequential counterpart of L systems. Thus we now study the parallel counterpart of the regulated pure grammars investigated in Chapter 5.

3) We want to demonstrate the effect of the mechanisms in another part of formal language theory especially, in order to continue the comparative study of these mechanisms.

Now we give the formal definitions of programmed, matrix, and random context TOL systems. In the following definitions, $\mathfrak{P}$ is a set of tables as in the TOL definition and the yield relation $\underset{P}{\Longrightarrow}$ is also defined as in the TOL definition, i.e., it is a parallel rewriting of all letters according to the productions of the table P, V is an alphabet and $w \in V^+$.

Definition 8.1. A *programmed TOL system* is a triple $G = (V, \mathfrak{P}, w)$ where with each table $P \in \mathfrak{P}$ a set $\sigma(P) \subseteq \mathfrak{P}$ is associated. The language $L(G)$ of a programmed TOL system G consists of all words x which have a derivation

$$w \underset{P_{i_1}}{\Longrightarrow} w_1 \underset{P_{i_2}}{\Longrightarrow} w_2 \underset{P_{i_3}}{\Longrightarrow} \cdots \underset{P_{i_{n-1}}}{\Longrightarrow} w_{n-1} \underset{P_{i_n}}{\Longrightarrow} w_n = x$$

such that $P_{i_{j+1}} \in \sigma(P_{i_j})$ for $1 \leqq j \leqq n$.

Definition 8.2. A *matrix TOL system* is a construct $G = (V, \mathfrak{P}, M, w)$, $\mathfrak{P} = \{P_1, P_2, \ldots, P_n\}$, where M is a finite set of finite sequences of elements of $\{1, 2, \ldots, n\}$,

$$M = \{m_1, m_2, \ldots, m_s\},\ m_i = (i_1, i_2, \ldots, i_{k_i}),\ 1 \leqq i \leqq s.$$

We write $x \underset{m_i}{\Longrightarrow} y$ iff there are words $x_1, x_2, \ldots, x_{k_i}$ such that

$$x = x_1 \underset{P_{i_1}}{\Longrightarrow} x_2 \underset{P_{i_2}}{\Longrightarrow} \cdots \underset{P_{i_{k_i-1}}}{\Longrightarrow} x_{k_i} \underset{P_{i_{k_i}}}{\Longrightarrow} y.$$

The language $L(G)$ of a matrix TOL system G consists of all words u with a derivation

$$w = w_0 \underset{m_{j_1}}{\Longrightarrow} w_1 \underset{m_{j_2}}{\Longrightarrow} w_2 \underset{m_{j_3}}{\Longrightarrow} \cdots \underset{m_{j_h}}{\Longrightarrow} w_h \underset{P_{i_1}}{\Longrightarrow} w_1' \underset{P_{i_2}}{\Longrightarrow} w_2' \underset{P_{i_3}}{\Longrightarrow} \cdots \underset{P_{i_t}}{\Longrightarrow} w_t' = u$$

where $m_{j_1}, m_{j_2}, \ldots, m_{j_h} \in M$ and $(i_1, i_2, \ldots, i_t)$ is the initial part of a matrix $m_i \in M$ (i.e., only the last matrix can be applied incompletely).

Definition 8.3. A *random context TOL system* is a construct $G = (V, \mathfrak{P}, w)$ where with each table $P \in \mathfrak{P}$ a subset Q of V is associated and the table P is applicable to a word x iff all letters of Q occur in x. The language $L(G)$ consists of all words y which have a derivation

$$w = w_0 \underset{P_{i_0}}{\Longrightarrow} w_1 \underset{P_{i_1}}{\Longrightarrow} w_2 \underset{P_{i_2}}{\Longrightarrow} \cdots \underset{P_{i_{n-1}}}{\Longrightarrow} w_n \underset{P_{i_n}}{\Longrightarrow} y$$

such that P_{i_j} is applicable to w_j for $1 \leq j \leq n$.

By (P) TOL, (M) TOL, (RC) TOL we denote the families of programmed, matrix, and random context TOL systems, respectively. Let $X \in \{(P), (M), (RC)\}$. We say that L is an X TOL *language* iff there is a $G \in X$ TOL such that $L = L(G)$. By $\mathcal{L}(X \text{ TOL})$ we denote the family of all X TOL languages.

The definition of deterministic and propagating X TOL systems is the same as for (usual unregulated) TOL systems, and they are denoted by adding the letters D and P, respectively, again. A language L is called an *extended* X TOL *language* iff there are an X TOL system G with the alphabet V and a subset V' of V such that $L = L(G) \cap (V')^*$. By $\mathcal{L}$ (EXTOL) we denote the family of extended X TOL languages.

We have only given the definitions without appearance checking. Since we required in the TOL definition that, for each $a \in V$ and each $P \in \mathfrak{P}$, there is a production $a \to w$ in P, it is obvious that in a programmed and matrix system each table is applicable to each word, and hence the appearance checking is not useful for these systems. Clearly, for random context TOL systems appearance checking can be introduced (see Definition 8.4 and Exercise 8.2).

In some cases, in the following theorems we state the result for all the families introduced above and we give the proof only for matrix TOL systems. The proofs for the other families can be given with slight modifications by the same arguments, and they are left to the reader.

First we study the effect of determinism and of the use of erasing rules.

Theorem 8.1. *Let* $X \in \{(P), (M), (RC)\}$. *Then*

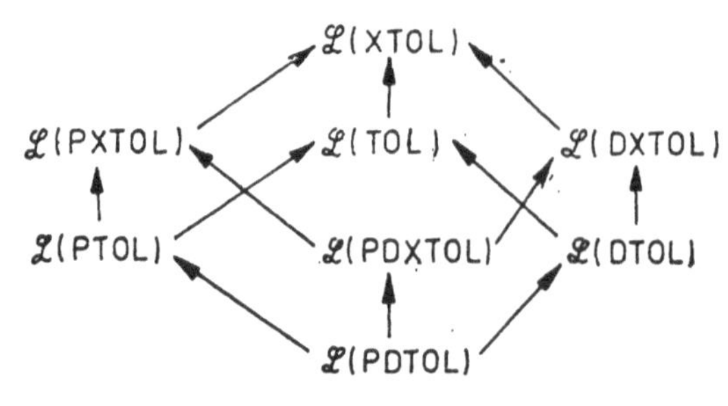

(Families which are not connected are incomparable.)

Proof. Since the inclusions follow by definition it is sufficient to prove the existence of languages $L_1 \in \mathcal{L}(\text{PD(M) TOL}) \setminus \mathcal{L}(\text{TOL})$, $L_2 \in \mathcal{L}(\text{PTOL}) \setminus \mathcal{L}(\text{D(M) TOL})$, $L_3 \in \mathcal{L}(\text{DTOL}) \setminus \mathcal{L}(\text{P(M) TOL})$.

i) Let $L_1 = \{a^2, a^4, b^4\}$. Then $L_1 \in \mathcal{L}(\text{PD(M) TOL})$ since it is generated by the matrix TOL system

$$G_1 = \left(\{a, b\}, \left\{\{a \to a^2, b \to b\}, \{a \to b, b \to b\}\right\}, \{(1, 2)\}, a^2\right).$$

$L_1 \notin \mathcal{L}(\text{TOL})$ can be seen as follows. Assume that $L_1 = L(G)$ for some TOL system $G = (V, \mathfrak{P}, w_0)$. If $w_0 = a^2$, then there is a derivation $a^2 \overset{*}{\Rightarrow} a^4$. Thus $a^4 \overset{*}{\Rightarrow} a^8$ also is a correct derivation using the same sequence of tables. Hence we obtain a contradiction.

Assume $b^4 \Rightarrow a^2$ for some $P \in \mathfrak{P}$. Then $\{b \to a, b \to \lambda\} \subseteq P$ or $\{b \to a^2, b \to \lambda\} \subseteq P$. In the former case we can also generate a^3, in the latter case a^6. Analogously, $a^4 \Rightarrow a^2$ is impossible. Therefore a^2 cannot be generated from $w_0 \neq a^2$.

ii) Let $L_2 = \{a^n : n \geqq 1\}$. The relation $L_2 \in \mathcal{L}(\text{PTOL})$ is obvious.

Assume $L_2 = L(G)$ for some deterministic matrix TOL system G. Without loss of generality, we can assume that no table contains the (only)rule $a \to a$. Now let $a \to a^{r_1}$, $a \to a^{r_2}, \ldots, a \to a^{r_p}$, $1 < r_1 < r_2 < \cdots < r_p$, be the rules which occur in the tables, and let a^r be the axiom. Then any word generated by G has the form

$$a^{r r_1^{n_1} r_2^{n_2} \cdots r_p^{n_p}}$$

for some integers $n_1, n_2, \ldots, n_p$. Thus $a^z \notin L(G)$ for some prime number $z > r_p, z > r$. Hence $L_2 \neq L(G)$ in contradiction to our assumption.

iii) $L_3 = \{ac^2\} \cup \{a^{2^n} : n \geqq 1\}$ is generated by the TOL system $G_3 = \left(\{a, c\}, \left\{\{a \to a^2, c \to \lambda\}\right\}, ac^2\right)$. Hence $L_3 \in \mathcal{L}(\text{DTOL})$.

Now assume that L_3 is generated by a propagating matrix TOL system G. Then a^2 has to be the axiom, and there has to be a table whose application to a^2 leads to ac^2. Obviously, then c^2a or cac can be also generated. Again, we have a contradiction.

Theorem 8.2. *For $X \in \{(\text{P}), (\text{M}), (\text{RC})\}$, $\mathcal{L}(X\,\text{TOL})$ is not closed under each of the AFL operations.*

Proof. i) *Union.* Clearly, $L_4 = \{a^{2^n}: n \geqq 1\}$ and $L_5 = \{b^{3^m}: m \geqq 1\}$ are PDTOL languages. We show that $L_4 \cup L_5 \neq L(G)$ for all (M) TOL systems G. Assume the contrary, and let $G = (V, \mathfrak{P}, M, w)$. If $w = a^{2^n}$ for some n, then there has to be a table containing a rule of the form $a \to b^k$, $k \geqq 1$. However, then $a^{2^i} \Rightarrow b^{2^i k}$ is a correct derivation for some i. Since $2^i k \neq 3^p$ for all i, k, p, we obtain a contradiction.

Similarly we can prove that $w = b^{3^m}$ for some m is impossible.

ii) *Product*: $L_6 = \{ab^{2^n} : n \geqq 1\}$ is also a PDTOL language. We prove that $L = L_4L_6 \notin \mathcal{L}(\text{(M) TOL})$. Assume that $L = L(G)$ for some (M) TOL system $G = (V, \mathfrak{P}, M, w)$. It is easy to prove that G has to be deterministic and that each table has the form $\{a \to a^i$, $b \to b^j\}$ with $i \geqq 1$, $j \geqq 1$ (or it is the table $\{a \to \lambda, b \to \lambda\}$ since we consider languages modulo λ). Further a^3b^2 has to be the axiom because — with exception of the table which possibly generates λ — all tables are propagating. Now we have

$$a^3b^{2^n} \underset{P}{\Longrightarrow} a^{3i}b^{2^n j}$$

for $P = \{a \to a^i, b \to b^j\}$, and since $3i = 3$ for $i = 1$ or $3i > 6$ for $i \geqq 2$, we cannot generate the word a^5b^2 which is in L.

iii) *Kleene closure.* We prove that $L_7 = \{a^{2^n}b^{2^n} : n \geqq 1\}^+$ is not an (M) TOL language. Assume that $L_7 = L(G)$ for some (M) TOL system $G = (V, \mathfrak{P}, M, w)$. It is easy to prove that

- each table $P \in \mathfrak{P}$ contains only productions of the form

$$a \to a^{2^{n_1}}b^{2^{n_1}}a^{2^{n_2}}b^{2^{n_2}} \dots a^{2^{n_k}}b^{2^{n_k}},\ b \to a^{2^{m_1}}b^{2^{m_1}}a^{2^{m_2}}b^{2^{m_2}} \dots a^{2^{m_r}}b^{2^{m_r}},$$

  or it contains only productions of the form $a \to a^{2^k}$, $b \to b^{2^m}$,
- there is a matrix $m \in M$ whose tables have only productions of the form $a \to a^{2^k}$, $b \to b^{2^m}$,
- all matrices which contain only tables with productions of the form $a \to a^{2^k}$, $b \to b^{2^m}$ are deterministic.

Hence there cannot be generated words of the form $a^{2^n}b^{2^n}a^{2^m}b^{2^m}$ with arbitrary numbers n, m. Since the words of L_7 can have arbitrary n, m, we have the desired contradiction.

iv) *Homomorphism.*

$$L_8 = \{c\} \cup \{a^{2^n} : n \geqq 1\} \cup \{b^{3^m} : m \geqq 1\}$$

is a PDTOL language. Obviously, for h defined by $h(a) = a$, $h(b) = b$, $h(c) = a^2$, we obtain $h(L_8) = L_4 \cup L_5 \notin \mathcal{L}\big((\text{M}) \text{ TOL}\big)$.

v) *Inverse homomorphisms.* Let $g(c) = c^2$, $g(a) = a$, $g(b) = b$. Then $h^{-1}(L_8) = L_4 \cup L_5$, again.

vi) *Intersection with regular sets.* $L_8 \cap \{a, b\}^* = L_4 \cup L_5$.

Theorem 8.3. $\mathcal{L}(\text{ETOL}) = \mathcal{L}\big(\text{E(M) TOL}\big) = \mathcal{L}\big(\text{E (P) TOL}\big) \subset \mathcal{L}\big(\text{E(RC) TOL}\big)$.

Proof. i) $\mathcal{L}(\text{ETOL}) \subseteq \mathcal{L}(\text{EXTOL})$ holds for $X \in \{(\text{P}), (\text{M}), (\text{RC})\}$ by definition.

ii) $\mathcal{L}\big(\text{E(P) TOL}\big) \subseteq \mathcal{L}(\text{ETOL})$. Let $G = (V, V', \mathfrak{P}, w_0)$ be an E(P) TOL system. For $P \in \mathfrak{P}$, we define an alphabet $V_P = \{a^{(P)} : a \in V\}$, and if $w = a_1a_2 \dots a_n \in V^*$, let $w^{(P)} = a_1^{(P)}a_2^{(P)} \dots a_n^{(P)}$. With a table $P \in \mathfrak{P}$ and $P' \in \sigma(P)$ we associate the table

$$T_{P,P'} = \{x \to x : x \in W \setminus V_P\} \cup \{x^{(P)} \to w^{(P')} : x \to w \in P\}$$

where $W = \{S\} \cup V \cup \bigcup_{P \in \mathfrak{P}} V_P$ and S is a new letter. Further we define the tables

$$T_i = \{S \to w_0^{(P)} : P \in \mathfrak{P}\} \cup \big\{x \to x : x \in W \setminus \{S\}\big\} \text{ (initial table)},$$

$$T_t = \{x^{(P)} \to x : P \in \mathfrak{P}, x \in V\} \cup \{S \to S\} \text{ (terminating table)}.$$

We consider the ETOL system $G' = (W, V', \mathfrak{P}', S)$ with

$$\mathfrak{P}' = \{T_i, T_t\} \cup \{T_{P,P'} : P \in \mathfrak{P}, P' \in \sigma(P)\}.$$

Then it is easy to see that a derivation in G' which produces a word over $(V')^*$ has the following structure:

$$S \underset{T_i}{\Longrightarrow} w_0^{(P)} \underset{T_{P,P_1}}{\Longrightarrow} w_1^{(P_1)} \underset{T_{P_1,P_2}}{\Longrightarrow} w_2^{(P_2)} \Rightarrow \dots \Rightarrow w_n^{(P_n)} \underset{T_t}{\Longrightarrow} w_n,$$

and it corresponds in a unique way to the derivation

$$w_0 \underset{P}{\Longrightarrow} w_1 \underset{P_1}{\Longrightarrow} w_2 \underset{P_2}{\Longrightarrow} \cdots \underset{P_{n-1}}{\Longrightarrow} w_n$$

in G. Therefore $L(G') = L(G)$.

iii) $\mathscr{L}(\text{E(M) TOL}) \subseteq \mathscr{L}(\text{ETOL})$ can be proved analogously.

iv) $\mathscr{L}(\text{ETOL}) \subset \mathscr{L}(\text{E(RC) TOL})$. First we prove that

$$K = \{g^m d(ab^n)^m : m \geqq n \geqq 1\}$$

is in $\mathscr{L}(E\text{(RC) TOL})$. It is generated by the system

$$G = (\{a, b, c, d, e, f, g\}, \{a, b, d, g\}, \mathfrak{P}, c)$$

where $\mathfrak{P}$ consists of the tables P_1 and P_2 with the corresponding random contexts Q_1 and Q_2, respectively, given as follows (we mention only the rules different from $x \to x$):

$$P_1 = \{c \to eca, c \to fda\}, Q_1 = \emptyset,$$

$$P_2 = \{e \to f, f \to g, a \to ab, e \to e\}, Q_2 = \{f\}.$$

Without loss of generality, each terminating derivation in G has the following form:

$$c \Rightarrow eca \Rightarrow e^2ca^2 \Rightarrow \cdots \Rightarrow e^{m-1}c^m a^{-1} \Rightarrow e^{m-1}fda^m$$

$$\Rightarrow e^{s_1}f^{m-1-s_1}gd(ab)^m \Rightarrow e^{s_2}f^{s_1-s_2}g^{m-s_1}d(ab^2)^m \Rightarrow \cdots$$

$$\Rightarrow e^{s_t}f^{s_{t-1}-s_t}g^{m-s_{t-1}}d(ab^t)^m \Rightarrow f^{s_t}g^{m-s_t}d(ab^{t+1})^m \Rightarrow g^m d(ab^{t+2})^m$$

with $m - 1 > s_1 > s_2 > \cdots > s_t > 0$. Hence $t + 2 \leqq m$ and $L(G) = K$.

If $K \in \mathscr{L}(\text{ETOL})$, then using the homomorphism h given by

$$h(a) = a, h(b) = b, h(d) = h(g) = \lambda$$

we obtain $h(K) = \{(ab^n)^m : m \geqq n \geqq 1\} \in \mathscr{L}(\text{ETOL})$ in contrast to Chapter 1.

Theorem 8.4.

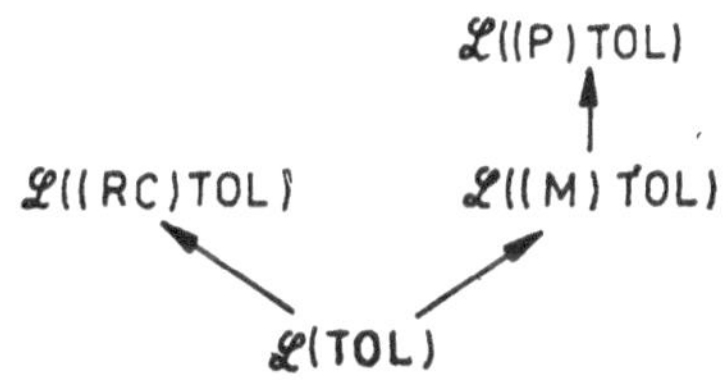

(Again, families which are nor connected are incomparable.)

Proof. i) $\mathscr{L}(\text{(RC) TOL}) \setminus \mathscr{L}(\text{(P) TOL}) \neq \emptyset$. Let K' be the language generated by the (RC) TOL system G defined in part iv) of the proof of the preceding theorem (we ignore the terminal set). If $K' \in \mathscr{L}(\text{(P) TOL})$, then $K' \cap \{a, b, d, g\}^* = K \notin \mathscr{L}(\text{E(P) TOL}) = \mathscr{L}(\text{ETOL})$ in contrast to the above proof.

ii) The language L_1 of the proof of Theorem 8.1 satisfies $L_1 \in \mathscr{L}(\text{(M) TOL}) \setminus \mathscr{L}(\text{(RC) TOL})$ since $L_1 \notin \mathscr{L}(\text{(RC) TOL})$ can be proved analogously to $L_1 \notin \mathscr{L}(\text{TOL})$.

iii) $\mathcal{L}((\mathrm{M})\ \mathrm{TOL}) \subseteq \mathcal{L}((\mathrm{P})\ \mathrm{TOL})$. Let $G = (V, \mathfrak{P}, M, w)$ be a matrix TOL system with $M = \{m_1, m_2, \ldots, m_s\}$, $m_i: (i_1, i_2, \ldots, i_{k_i})$, $1 \leqq i \leqq s$. With each pair (i, j), $1 \leqq i \leqq s$, $1 \leqq j \leqq k_i$, we associate the table

$$P(i, j) = \{a \to u : a \in V, u \in \tau_{i,j}(a)\}$$

where $\tau_{i,j}$ is the composition of the finite substitutions given by the tables $P_{i_1}, P_{i_2}, \ldots, P_{i_j}$. We define the programmed TOL system $G' = (V, P', w)$ by

$$\mathfrak{P}' = \{P(i, j) : 1 \leqq i \leqq s, 1 \leqq j \leqq k_i\}$$

and

$$\sigma(P(i, j)) = \begin{cases} \emptyset & \text{for } 1 \leqq j \leqq k_i - 1, \\ \mathfrak{P}' & \text{for } j = k_i. \end{cases}$$

It is easy to see that $L(G') = L(G)$.

iv) $\mathcal{L}((\mathrm{P})\ \mathrm{TOL}) \to \mathcal{L}((\mathrm{M})\ \mathrm{TOL}) \neq \emptyset$. Let us consider the language

$$L_{10} = \{a^{2^n} : n \geqq 0\} \cup \{a^{3^m} : m \geqq 0\}.$$

It is generated by the programmed TOL system $G = (\{a\}, \{P_1, P_2\}, a)$ with

$$P_1 = \{a \to a^2\},\ \sigma(P_1) = \{P_1\}$$

$$P_2 = \{a \to a^3\},\ \sigma(P_2) = \{P_2\}.$$

Assume that $L_{10} = L(G')$ for some matrix TOL system G'. Then G' has to be propagating and deterministic, since otherwise there is a fixed integer r such that, for each u, there exist three pairwise different words $w_i \in L_{10}$, $|w_i| > u$, $||w_i| - |w_j|| < r$ for $1 \leqq i, j \leqq 3$. Without loss of generality, there is a derivation $a \overset{*}{\Rightarrow} a^{2^n} \overset{*}{\Rightarrow} a^{3^m}$ where $n \geqq 1$ and the first phase is done by applications of (complete) matrices. Then $a \overset{*}{\Rightarrow} a^{2^n} \overset{*}{\Rightarrow} (a^{2^n})^{2^n} \overset{*}{\Rightarrow} (a^{3^m})^{2^n}$ also is a correct derivation. However, it produces a word not contained in L_{10}.

Note that Theorem 8.3 gives a situation where the random context is the most powerful mechanism; up to now, programs had at least the same power (if incomparability did not appear).

Finally in this chapter, we want to contribute to a decision problem in the area of L systems. First let us look at the decidability status of the equivalence problem, i.e. whether or not two systems (of the same type) generate the same language. The following results are known: the equivalence problem is decidable for deterministic L systems without interaction (DOL systems) (see Culik and Fris (1977)) and it undecidable for the following three generalizations (which are the weakest ones in the sense that they omit or add only one feature):

- non-deterministic systems without interaction (OL systems, see Blattner (1973) and Salomaa (1973-b)),
- deterministic interactionless tabled systems (DTOL systems, see Rozenberg (1972-b)),
- deterministic systems with interaction, i.e. context-sensitive productions (DIL systems, see Vitanyi (1974)).

We now introduce deterministic random context L systems (with appearance checking) and we shall prove that their equivalence problem is decidable.

Definition 8.4. A *deterministic random context L system* (DRCL system, for short) is a construct $G = (V, P, w_0)$ where V is a finite alphabet, $w_0 \in V^+$, and P is a set of productions of the form $(a \to w, Q)$, $a \in V$, $w \in V^*$, $Q \subseteq V$ such that, for each pair $a \in V$, $Q \subseteq V$, there is exactly one such rule.

We say that the production $(a \to w, Q)$ is applicable to a in the string uav iff uv contains all letters of Q and uv contains no letter of $V \setminus Q$.

A direct derivation $x \Rightarrow y$, $x \in V^+$, $y \in V^*$, in the DRCL system G is defined by the following conditions:

i) $x = x_1x_2 \dots x_n$, $x_i \in V$, $1 \leqq i \leqq n$,

ii) $y = y_1y_2 \dots y_n$, $y_i \in V^*$, $1 \leqq i \leqq n$,

iii) for $1 \leqq i \leqq n$, there is a Q_i such that $(x_i \to y_i, Q_i)$ is applicable to x_i in x.

Since we have chosen $V \setminus Q$ as forbidding context and have required a completeness condition with respect to Q, we have ensured the determinism in the application of a rule. Hence each DRCL system generates a unique sequence

$$w_0 \Rightarrow w_1 \Rightarrow w_2 \Rightarrow \cdots \Rightarrow w_n \Rightarrow \cdots.$$

We define

$$L(G) = \{w_n : n \geqq 0\}.$$

Note that a DOL system is a DRCL system satisfying the condition: if $(a \to w_1, Q_1) \in P$ and $(a \to w_2, Q_2) \in P$, then $w_1 = w_2$.

Theorem 8.5. *The (language) equivalence problem for DRCL systems is decidable.*

Proof. First we prove the existence of a decomposition of a DRCL language into finite and DOL languages. This gives a reduction of the equivalence problem for DRCL systems to that for DOL systems (which is decidable).

Let $G = (V, P, w_0)$ be a DRCL system, and let Q_1, Q_2 be two disjoint (possibly empty) subsets of V. Then we set

$$V(Q_1, Q_2) = \{w : w \in V^*, |w_a| = 0 \quad \text{for} \quad a \in Q_1, |w|_b = 1 \quad \text{for} \quad b \in Q_2,$$
$$|w|_c \geqq 2 \quad \text{for} \quad c \in V \setminus (Q_1 \cup Q_2)\}.$$

These sets form a decomposition of V^*, and thus they induce an equivalence relation ϱ on V^*. The following facts are obvious.

Fact 1. *The equivalence classes of ϱ are regular sets.*

Fact 2. *ϱ is a congruence relation with respect to the direct derivation in G.*

With each equivalence class $V(Q_1, Q_2) = K$ of ϱ we associate a homomorphism h_K such that $x \Rightarrow y$ in G iff $y = h_K(x)$, $x \in K$. We define h_K as follows:

if $a \in Q_1$, then $h_K(a)$ can be arbitrarily chosen,

if $a \in Q_2$, then $h_K(a) = w$ where $\big(a \to w, V \setminus (Q_1 \cup \{a\})\big) \in P$,

if $a \in V \setminus (Q_1 \cup Q_2)$, then $h_K(a) = v$ where $(a \to v, V \setminus Q_1) \in P$.

By construction, the desired property is satisfied.

Let $w_0 \Rightarrow w_1 \Rightarrow w_2 \Rightarrow \cdots$ be the unique derivation in G, and let K_i be the equivalence class of ϱ with $w_i \in K_i$. By Fact 2, the sequence $(K_0, K_1, \ldots, K_n, \ldots)$ is ultimately periodic, i.e. we can effectively find numbers i, r such that $K_m = K_{m+r}$ for $m \geqq i$ and $K_0, K_1, \ldots, K_{i+r-1}$ are pairwise different. Therefore the derivation in G can be described as follows:

$$w_0 \underset{h_{K_0}}{\Longrightarrow} w_1 \underset{h_{K_1}}{\Longrightarrow} \cdots \Rightarrow w_i \underset{h_{K_i}}{\Longrightarrow} w_{i+1} \underset{h_{K_{i+1}}}{\Longrightarrow} \cdots \underset{h_{K_{i+r-1}}}{\Longrightarrow} w_{i+r} \underset{h_{K_i}}{\Longrightarrow} w_{i+r+1} \underset{h_{K_{i+1}}}{\Longrightarrow} \cdots$$

Hence, for $0 \leqq m < r$, $j \geqq 1$,

$$w_{i+m+jr} = (h_{K_{i+m}} \circ h_{K_{i+m+1}} \circ \cdots \circ h_{K_{i+r-1}} \circ h_{K_i} \circ h_{K_{i+1}} \circ \cdots \circ h_{K_{i+m-1}}) (w_{i+m+(j-1)r}) .$$

We set

$$F = \{w_0, w_1, \ldots, w_{i-1}\},$$

$$G_m = (V, P_m, w_{i+m}),$$

$$P_m = \{a \to (h_{K_{i+m}} \ldots h_{K_{i+r-1}} h_{K_i} \ldots h_{K_{i+m-1}}) (a) : a \in V\}$$

for $0 \leqq m < r$. Then

$$L(G_m) = \{w_{i+m}, w_{i+m+r}, w_{i+m+2r}, \ldots\},$$

$$F \cap L(G_m) = \emptyset,\ L(G_m) \cap L(G_{m'}) = \emptyset \quad \text{for} \quad 0 \leqq m, m' \leqq r,\ m \neq m'.$$

Let K be an equivalence class of ϱ. Then by the above construction, $L(G) \cap K$ can be effectively determined and one of the following conditions holds:

$$L(G) \cap K = \emptyset,$$

or

$L(G) \cap K$ is contained in F and it contains exactly one element,

or

$$L(G) \cap K = L(G_m) \quad \text{for some} \quad m, 0 \leqq m < r.$$

Now let H_1 and H_2 be two DRCL systems. Let $F_i, G_{0i}, G_{1i}, \ldots, G_{r_i,i}$ be the components of the decomposition of H_i, $i \in \{1, 2\}$, derived above. Again, we consider an equivalence class K of ϱ. We construct the sets $U_{K,i} = L(H_i) \cap K$, $i = 1, 2$. By the above property, $U_{K,i}$ is finite or a DOL language (given by the DOL system G_m). Hence it is decidable whether or not $U_{K,1} = U_{K,2}$. Doing this for all equivalence classes we decide the (language) equivalence of H_1 and H_2.

Exercises

8.1. Define regularly controlled TOL systems (the sequence of tables has to be in a regular language over $\mathfrak{P}$) and prove that

i] $\mathcal{L}\big(E(\text{rC})\ \text{TOL}\big) = \mathcal{L}(\text{ETOL})$ (see GINSBURG and ROZENBERG (1974)),

ii) $\mathcal{L}\big((\text{P})\ \text{TOL}\big) \subset \mathcal{L}\big((\text{rC})\ \text{TOL}\big)$ (see DASSOW and FEST (1984)),

iii) $\mathcal{L}\big((\text{rC})\ \text{TOL}\big)$ is incomparable with $\mathcal{L}\big((\text{RC})\ \text{TOL}\big)$ (see DASSOW and FEST (1984)).

8.2. Introduce appearance checking for random context TOL systems as follows. Associate with $P \in \mathfrak{P}$ (besides Q) a second set $R \subseteq V$, and let P be applicable to w iff all letters of Q occur in w and no letter of R occurs in w. Prove that the corresponding family of languages is $\mathscr{L}$(P, CF $- \lambda$, ac) in the propagating case and $\mathscr{L}$(RE) if λ -rules are allowed, (see ROZENBERG and VON SOLMS (1978)).

8.3. Prove that it is decidable whether or not a deterministic random context L system generates a regular or context-free language (see DASSOW (1984-c). Hint: this problem is decidable for DOL systems, see SALOMAA (1975)).

8.4. One derivation step in a TOL system is performed by a parallel rewriting of all letters of the current word. RAJASETHUPATHY and SHYAMASUNDAR introduced the following alternative method: rewrite all letters of the current word sequentially (and this gives one step of the derivation). Prove that the corresponding families of extended programmed (matrix, random context) OL systems (with appearance checking) coincide with $\mathscr{L}$(P, CF $- \lambda$, ac) or with $\mathscr{L}$(RE) depending on the use of λ-rules (see RAJASETHUPATHY and SHYAMASUNDAR (1980), DASSOW (1983), and DASSOW and FEST (1984)).

Bibliographical remarks

Regulation mechanisms are defined for L systems in order

i) to obtain models which give an improved description of some biological phenomena,

ii) to obtain more general L systems with a decidable sequence and/or language equivalence problem (two system are sequence equivalent iff they generate the same sequence of words),

iii) to introduce the parallel counterpart for some existing type of sequential rewriting and to study formal language theoretical problems.

Mostly, two of these reasons appear simultaneously, e.g. periodically time-variant systems or matrix systems can model the change of seasons or random context can be used to describe the existence of ill cells in the organism, etc. We now give some typical representants of these directions.

i) Basic hierarchy properties and a fully biological motivation of periodically time variant, matrix and ordered systems have been given by REUSCH (1974). In DASSOW (1979-c) and JÜRGENSEN and WOOD (1982) L systems have been introduced where the unique derivation is obtained by a mechanism based on the subword structure of the current/preceding words.

ii) In CULIK and WOOD (1979) an infinite periodic word is used as a control set; hence there is a unique sequence of words and the sequence equivalence is shown to be decidable. A generalization of this result is given in DASSOW (1988-b) which seems to be the most general sequence equivalence result. With respect to language equivalence this seems to hold for DRCL systems (Theorem 8.5, DASSOW (1984-c)).

iii) Mostly here extended versions have been studied. At the first time regular control was used in GINSBURG and ROZENBERG (1974), and then it is intensively studied in connection with iteration grammars e.g. ASVELD (1978). Results on matrix L systems are contained in NIELSEN (1975). Programmed versions of L systems were introduced by VON SOLMS (1976). At the same time the study of random context L systems was initiated by ROZENBERG and VON SOLMS (1976) and (1978). All these papers e.g. contain the relation of the corresponding family of languages to $\mathscr{L}$(ETOL) (Theorem 8.3). The non-extended cases for these regulated systems were investigated by DASSOW and FEST (1984). The Indian parallel versions of OL systems were independently studied in SIROMONEY and SIROMONEY (1975), KUDLEK (1975), and DASSOW (1976).

The derivation process where one step is performed by a (regulated) sequential rewriting of all letters of the current word (see Exercise 8.4) was introduced by RAJASETHUPATHY and SHYAMASUNDAR (1980), and it is further considered by DASSOW (1983), DASSOW and FEST (1984).

Finally let us here mention some papers which concern regulated rewriting in other areas of formal language theory. Regulated contextual grammars (matrix, programmed, regular control) have been studied by PĂUN (1977-c), and some material on them can be found in the monograph by PĂUN (1982-b). Papers on regulated graph grammars are BUNKE (1979) and VON SOLMS (1984).

Chapter 9. Applications of Regulated Rewriting

In Section 0.4. we discussed various applications of formal language theory where context-free grammars are not enough, thus motivating the introduction of regulated (context-free) grammars. A natural problem now is to consider those applications again and to check whether the numerous grammars with restricted derivation investigated in this monograph are of some usefulness in approaching the corresponding questions. The problem is not simple. On the one hand, certain languages which appear in this framework are "complicated" enough to support the conjecture that they cannot be generated by many of these grammars. But, since in many cases in the theory of regulated rewriting there are no known necessary conditons for a language to be of a given type, and hence such a conjecture cannot be proved at this time. (This is the case, for instance, with programming languages versus regulated grammars without appearance checking.) On the other hand, regulated grammar are strong enough to generate certain languages in certain applications; however, in some circumstances the obtained grammars are too complicated (too "large") to be of practical interest and/or they correspond to a class of grammars with many unsolvable decision problems, which again diminishes the practical interest. Anyway, the problem of investigating the applicability of regulated grammars remains a rich topic for further research.

Below we discuss only some preliminary results in this area.

9.1. Relationships with Programming Languages

The example of Floyd (1962) that ALGOL 60 is not context-free mentioned in Section 0.4. is based on the requirement that each identifier has to be declared. Let us generalize this example slightly. We consider

$$L = \{\textsf{begin integer } x;\ x_1 = 1;\ x_2 = 1;\ \ldots x_n = 1;\ \textsf{end}:$$
$$n \geqq 1,\ x \in \{a, b\}^+,\ x_i = x,\ 1 \leqq i \leqq n\}.$$

We now show that L is in $\mathscr{L}(\mathsf{M}, \mathsf{CF} - \lambda, \mathsf{ac})$. Here is a grammar G generating L:

$$G = (V_N, \{a, b, ;, \textsf{begin}, \textsf{end}, \textsf{integer}, =, 1\}, M, S, F),$$

$$V_N = \{S, A, B, C, C', D, D_a, D_b, D'_a, D'_b, E, Z\},$$

$$M = \{(S \to \textsf{begin integer } C;\ A\ B),$$

$$(A \to C = 1;\ A, B \to B),$$

$$(A \to C = 1; B \to D),$$

$$(D \to D_a), (D \to D_b), (D \to D'_a), (D \to D'_b),$$

$$(C \to aC', D_a \to D_a), (C \to bC', D_b \to D_b),$$

$$(C \to Z, D_a \to E), (C \to Z, D_b \to E),$$

$$(C' \to C, E \to E), (C' \to Z, E \to D),$$

$$(C \to a, D'_a \to D'_a), (C \to b, D'_b \to D'_b),$$

$$(C \to Z, D'_a \to \mathsf{end}), \ (C \to Z, D'_b \to \mathsf{end})\},$$

and F contains all occurrences of rules $C \to Z$, $C' \to Z$.

Now let $ALGOL$ be the set of all syntactically and semantically (from the static point of view) correct ALGOL 60 programs, and let R be the regular language

$$R = \{\mathsf{begin\ integer}\ x_0; x_1 = 1; x_2 = 1; \ldots x_n = 1; \mathsf{end} :$$
$$n \geqq 1, x_i \in \{a, b\}^+, 0 \leqq i \leqq n\},$$

and let h be the homomorphism given by

$$h(a) = a, h(b) = b, h(;) = c, h(x) = \lambda \quad \text{for} \quad x \in V_T \setminus \{a, b, ;\}.$$

Then $L = ALGOL \cap R$ and

$$h(L) = \{(xc)^n : n \geqq 2, x \in \{a, b\}^+\}.$$

We shall prove that $h(L)$ is neither a finite index matrix language nor a simple matrix language. This shows that $ALGOL$ also is not contained in both these families. In order to prove that

$$h(L) \notin \mathscr{L}(\mathrm{SM}, \mathrm{CF}) \cup \mathscr{L}_{\mathrm{fin}}(\mathrm{M}, \mathrm{CF})$$

we can use the following common consequence of Corollary 4 of Lemma 1.5.2 and of the proof of Lemma 3.1.6:

Lemma 9.1.1. *Let $L \subseteq V^*$ be an infinite language in $\mathscr{L}(\mathrm{SM}, \mathrm{CF}) \cup \mathscr{L}_{\mathrm{fin}}(\mathrm{M}, \mathrm{CF})$. Then there exist the integers p, q such that, for each $x \in L$, $|x| > p$, there is a $y \in L$ such that*

1) $0 < |y| - |x| < q$,

2) $x = x_1x_2 \ldots x_r, y = y_1x_1y_2x_2 \ldots y_rx_ry_{r+1}, x_i, y_i \in V^*$ *for all i.*

The above language $h(L)$ does not satisfy this lemma. Indeed, let $z \in h(L)$ be a string, $z = (xc)^n$, $x \in \{a, b\}^+$, with $n > \max\{p, q\}$, $|x| > q$ for the possible p, q associated to $h(L)$. As $|z| > p$, there exists $y \in h(L)$ as in the lemma. Take $y = (wc)^m$, $w \in \{a, b\}^+$.

Clearly, we have $m \geqq n$. Suppose $|w| < |x|$. If we write $z = z_1z_2 \ldots z_r$, $y = y_1z_1y_2z_2 \ldots y_rz_ry_{r+1}$, it follows that each subword x of z is "intersected" by a pair z_iz_{i+1} such that y_i contains at least an occurrence of the symbol c. This means that at least n substrings $y_i \neq \lambda$ exist. This implies $|y| - |z| \geqq n > q$, and this is a contradiction.

Suppose now that $|w| > |x|$. Then

$$\begin{aligned}|y| &= m(|w| + 1) \geqq n(|w| + 1) = n(|x| + |w| - |x| + 1)\\ &= n(|x| + 1) + n(|w| - |x|) = |z| + n(|w| - |x|).\end{aligned}$$

As $n > q$ and $|w| - |x| \geqq 1$, we obtain $|y| - |z| > q$, again.

A similar contradiction appears for $|w| = |x|$, since we get

$$\begin{aligned}|y| &= m(|w| + 1) = m(|x| + 1) = (n + m - n)\,(|x| + 1)\\ &= n(|x| + 1) + (m - n)\,(|x| + 1) = |z| + (m - n)\,(|x| + 1).\end{aligned}$$

If $m = n$, then $y = z$, and this is a contradiction. If $m - n \geqq 1$, it follows that $|y| - |z| > q$ by $|x| > q$, and the proof is complete.

It is likely that the language $h(L)$ cannot be generated by a matrix grammar without appearance checking (or by equivalent grammars), therefore ALGOL 60 is probably not in $\mathscr{L}$(M, CF).

Of course, ALGOL 60 contains many other non-context-free features (besides the declaration of the identifiers). We do not know any systematic inventory of such features, although this is a meaningful problem; similarly the question of investigating such further features from the point of view of regulated rewriting is meaningful also taking grammars different from the above matrix grammars into account).

The previous considerations hold also for other programming languages, in particular for FORTRAN. In fact, FORTRAN has certain further properties which allow to prove also that it is not an ETOL language or an indexed language. This has been shown by Nicolescu (1985) using the pumping lemma for indexed languages (Hayashi (1973)) and the conditions for a language to be in $\mathscr{L}$(ETOL) given by Ehrenfeucht and Rozenberg (1976). The question is reduced to the language

$$L = \{(cw)^{|w|} : w \in \{a, b\}^+\}$$

which is neither in $\mathscr{L}$(ETOL) nor in $\mathscr{L}$(I) (the reader may verify, for comparison, that this language is in $\mathscr{L}$(M, CF $- \lambda$, ac)). For, we intersect the language Fortran of all correct FORTRAN programs with the regular language R given by all "programs"

$$J(\pi_1, \pi_2, \ldots, \pi_n) = 0$$

$$K = J\big(\varphi_1 J(\alpha_{1,1}, \alpha_{1,2}, \ldots, \alpha_{1,n_1})\, \gamma_1, \ldots, \varphi_m J(\alpha_{m,1}, \alpha_{m,2}, \ldots, \alpha_{m,n_m})\, \gamma_m\big)$$

```
  PRINT 3, K
  STOP
3 FORMAT (I4)
  END
```

where

1) $n, m, n_1, n_2, \ldots, n_m \geqq 1$,

2) $\pi_i = I^{s_i}$ or $\pi_i = U^{s_i}$ for some $s_i \geqq 1, 1 \leqq i \leqq n$,

3) $\varphi_i =$ FLOAT(or $\varphi_i = \lambda, \gamma_i =$) or $\gamma_i = \lambda$,
$1 \leqq i \leqq n$,

4) $\alpha_{i,j} \in \{1, 2.0\}, 1 \leqq i \leqq m.\ 1 \leqq j \leqq n_i$.

The result *Fortran* $\cap$ *R* consists of all programs

$$J(\pi_1, \pi_2, \ldots, \pi_n) = 0$$

$$K = J\big(\varphi_1 J(\alpha_1, \alpha_2, \ldots, \alpha_n)\, \gamma_1, \ldots, \varphi_n J(\alpha_1, \alpha_2, \ldots, \alpha_n)\, \gamma_n\big)$$

```
  PRINT 3, K
  STOP
3 FORMAT (I4)
  END
```

where

1) $n \geqq 1$, $\pi_i = I^{s_i}$ or $\pi_i = U^{s_i}$ for some $s_i \geqq 1$, $1 \leqq i \leqq n$, and $\pi_i \neq \pi_j$ for $i \neq j$,
2) for each i, $1 \leqq i \leqq n$, if $\pi_i = I^{s_i}$, then $\varphi_i = \lambda$, $\gamma_i = \lambda$, $\alpha_i = 1$, and if $\pi_i = U^{s_i}$, then $\varphi_i =$ FLOAT(, $\gamma_i =$), $\alpha_i = 2.0$.

Here the correspondence in number, order, and type between formaland actual parameters is involved when dealing with functions. (J is an integer function which is then evaluated for n internal evaluations of J itself.)

By a gsm g can we replace J by c, 1 by a, and 2 by b and erase all other symbols in the above language, including the first occurrence of J. We obtain

$$g(\mathit{Fortran} \cap R) = \left\{(c^{|w|}w\} : w \in \{a, b\}^+\right\}.$$

Similar constructions lead to the same result for other programming languages such as PASCAL and EDISON.

Moreover, as

$$\lg\big(g(\mathit{Fortran} \cap R)\big) = \{(n+1)\, n : n \geqq 1\}$$

where $\lg(L) = \{|x| : x \in L\}$

it follows that FORTRAN contains non-semilinear languages obtained by intersection with regular languages and gsm mappings. This is a stronger result than the above ones concerning ALGOL; in particular, this implies that FORTRAN (and other programming languages with similar properties) is not a simple matrix, a finite index matrix, or an unordered vector language (Lemma 2.1.11).

In fact, FORTRAN also has another, more visible non-semilinear feature, namely the Hollerith code in format statements: nHx^n where n is a decimal integer and x is a given symbol. As a "local" feature, specific to FORTRAN, this is not of such great interest (the above formal-actual parameter correspondence, for example, is, in some sense, a basic requirement for "all" programming languages).

9.2. Regulated Rewriting and Petri Nets

One of the most investigated models for the description of concurrent processes is Petri nets. For example, such nets can be used for the analysis and synthesis of concurrent systems. Often languages are associated with Petri nets. In this section we shall show that some of these languages can be described by grammars of regulated rewriting.

We give here only some basic definitions (and sometimes only informally). For the details we refer to PETERSON (1981) and STARKE (1982).

A *Petri net* is a construct $N = (P, T, I, O, \mu_0)$ where

- P and T are finite non-empty sets (the set P of places, the set T of transitions), $P \cap T = \emptyset$,
- the input function I is a function from $T \times P$ into $\mathbb{N}$,
- the output function O is a function from $T \times P$ into $\mathbb{N}$,
- μ_0 is a function from P into $\mathbb{N}$ (the initial marking of N).

Such a net will be presented by a labelled directed (bipartite) graph with the node set $P \cup T$, where, for all $p \in P$ and $t \in T$, there is an edge from p to t if $I(t, p) > 0$ and then $I(t, p)$ is the label of this edge, and there is an edge from t to p if $O(t, p) > 0$ and then $O(t, p)$ is the label of this edge. In order to simplify the figures, we omit the label if it is a 1. In the figures we shall use small circles for the nodes of P and strokes for the nodes of T. The value $\mu_0(p)$ will be written inside the circle, and it can be interpreted as the number of tokens at this place.

Example 9.2.1. Let $N_1 = (P_1, T_1, I_1, O_1, \mu_{01})$ and $N_2 = (P_2, T_2, I_2, O_2, \mu_{02})$ be the nets given in Figs. 9.2.1 and 9.2.2 $\big(P_1 = P_2 = \{p_1, p_2, p_3, p_4\}$, $T_1 = \{t_1, t_2\}$, $T_2 = \{t_1, t_2, t_3, t_4\}$, $\mu_{01} = (1, 0, 0, 0)$, $\mu_{02} = (1, 1, 0, 0)\big)$.

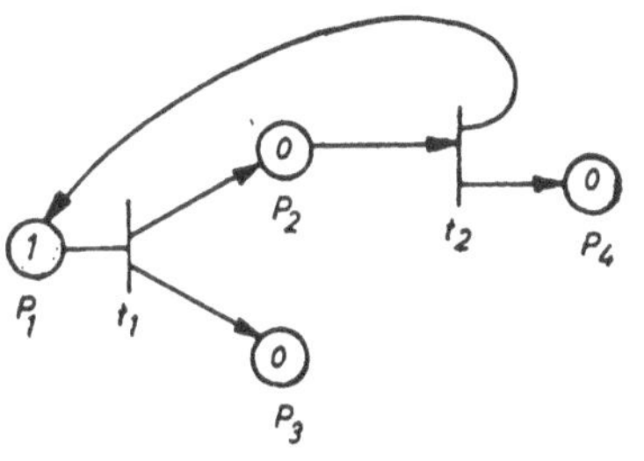

Fig. 9.2.1

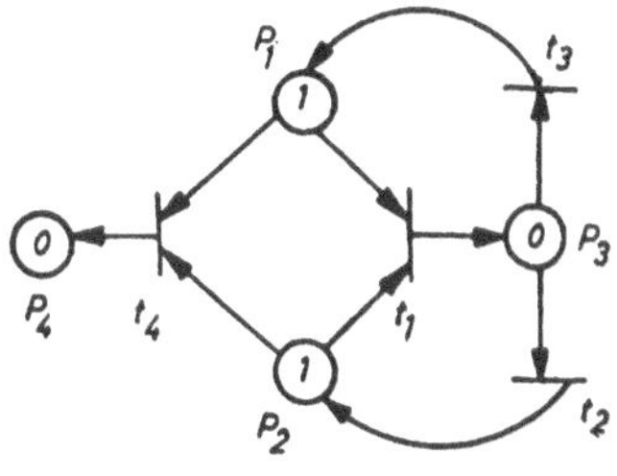

Fig. 9.2.2

Let N be a net, and let μ be a marking of N, i.e. a function from P into $\mathbb{N}$. We say that the transition $t \in T$ is *enabled* in μ if, for all $p \in P$, $\mu(p) \geqq I(t, p)$. If t is enabled in μ, then it can fire, that is it takes $I(t, p)$ tokens from the place p and puts $O(t, p)$ tokens at the place p; thus by the firing of a transition the marking is changed. Formally we define the transition function δ_N of the net N by

$$\delta_N(\mu, t) = \begin{cases} \mu' \quad \text{with} \quad \mu'(p) = \mu(p) - I(t, p) + O(t, p) \\ \qquad\qquad \text{for all } p \in P \text{ if } t \text{ is enabled in } \mu, \\ \text{undefined otherwise.} \end{cases}$$

This mapping can be extended from T to T^* in the usual way by setting

$$\delta_N(\mu, \lambda) = \mu \quad \text{for all markings } \mu,$$

$$\delta_N(\mu, wt) = \delta_N\big(\delta_N(\mu, w), t\big) \quad \text{for all markings } \mu, t \in T, w \in T^*.$$

In the theory of Petri nets the following three languages associated with N are of interest:

$$L_r(N) = \{\delta_N(\mu_0, w) : w \in T^*\},$$

$$L_f(N) = \{w : w \in T^* \text{ and } \delta_N(\mu_0, w) \text{ is defined}\},$$

$$L_t(N, F) = \{w : w \in T^*, \delta_N(\mu_0, w) \in F\} \text{ where } F \text{ is a given finite set of markings of } N.$$

$L_r(N)$ is the set of all markings which can be reached from the initial marking μ_0 by firing some (enabled) transitions. $L_f(N)$ — the so-called free Petri net language of N — consists of all possible firing sequences of the net, and $L_t(N, F)$ — the terminal Petri net language with respect to the set F of terminal markings — is the set of all firing sequences which transform the initial marking μ_0 into a terminal marking $\mu \in F$. (Note that the latter two languages associated with the net sequential firing sequences, i.e. parallelism and concurrency of firings are not considered although they are one of the motivations for Petri nets; but also these languages are important in Petri-net theory.)

Example 9.2.1. (continued). Let us consider the net N_1 of Fig. 9.2.1. and let $\mu = (1, 0, n_1, n_2)$ be a marking. Since $\mu(p_2) = 0$, only the transition t_1 is enabled in μ and its firing leads to $(0, 1, n_1 + 1, n_2)$. Now only t_2 is enabled and its firing derives $(1, 0, n_1 + 1, n_2 + 1)$. Thus it is easy to see that we obtain

$$L_r(N_1) = \{(1, 0, n, n) : n \geqq 0\} \cup \{(0, 1, n + 1, n) : n \geqq 0\},$$

$$L_f(N_1) = (t_1t_2)^* \cup (t_1t_2)^* t_1,$$

and, for $F_1 = \{(1, 0, 4, 4), (1, 0, 5, 3)\}$, we get

$$L_t(N_1, F_1) = \{(t_1t_2)^4\}$$

(since $(1, 0, 5, 3)$ is an unreachable marking).

In the net N_2 the transitions t_1 and t_4 are enabled in its initial marking μ_{02}. The firing of t_4 leads to $(0, 0, 0, 1)$, and then no transition is enabled. If t_1 fires, we get $(0, 0, 2, 0)$. Now t_2 and t_3 are enabled, and only if both fire again r_1 and t_4 are enabled. Thus we obtain

$$\delta_{N_2}((0, 0, 2, 0), t_2t_3) = \delta_{N_2}((0, 1, 1, 0), t_3) = (1, 1, 0, 0),$$

$$\delta_{N_2}((0, 0, 2, 0), t_3t_2) = \delta_{N_2}((1, 0, 1, 0), t_2) = (1, 1, 0, 0).$$

Further let $F_2 = \{(0, 0, 0, 1)\}$. Then

$$L_r(N_2) = \{(1, 1, 0, 0), (0, 0, 2, 0), (1, 0, 1, 0), (0, 1, 1, 0), (0, 0, 0, 1)\},$$

$$L_f(N_2) = [t_1\{t_2, t_3, t_3t_2\}]^* \{t_1, t_1t_2, t_1t_3, t_4, \lambda\},$$

$$L_t(N_2, F_2) = [t_1\{t_2t_3, t_3t_2\}]^* t_4.$$

We shall now demonstrate how the languages $L_r(N)$, $L_f(N)$, $L_t(N, F)$ can be described by means of grammars with regulated rewriting.

$L_f(N)$ and $L_t(N, F)$ are already languages over an alphabet T. In order to get this situation for $L_r(N)$, too, we use the following code: with a marking $\mu: P \to \mathbb{N}$ we associate the word

$$a_1^{\mu(p_1)}A_1a_2^{\mu(p_2)}A_2 \dots a_r^{\mu(p_r)}A_r$$

where $p_1, p_2, \dots, p_r$ is a fixed order of P. Clearly, this is a one-to-one correspondence, and it associates to N the language

$$L_r'(N) = \{a_1^{\mu(p_1)}A_1a_2^{\mu(p_2)}A_2 \dots a_r^{\mu(p_r)}A_r : \mu = \delta_N(\mu_0, w) \quad \text{for some} \quad w \in T^*\}$$

over the alphabet $\{a_1, a_2, \dots, a_r, A_1, A_2, \dots, A_r\}$.

In order to describe the languages by regulated rewriting we shall use pure matrix grammars (without appearance checking) in the sense of Exercise 5.1.7 and the associated Szilard languages. Let us briefly recall these notions. A pure matrix grammar is a triple $G = (V, M, w)$ where $w \in V^+$ and M is a set of matrices whose productions are of the form $a \to x$, $a \in V$, $x \in V^*$ (for our purpose here one axiom is sufficient). The language $L(G)$ consists of all words z such that

$$w = z_0 \underset{m_{i_1}}{\Longrightarrow} z_1 \underset{m_{i_2}}{\Longrightarrow} z_2 \underset{m_{i_3}}{\Longrightarrow} \cdots \underset{m_{i_n}}{\Longrightarrow} z_n = z$$

($n = 0$ is allowed), i.e. it consists of all words over V which can be obtained by iterated applications of entire matrices to the axiom (in contrast to pure languages of Chapter 5 we omit the intermediate steps of an application of a matrix). $m_{i_1}m_{i_2}\dots m_{i_n}$ is the control word of this derivation of z. The Szilard language Sz (G) of G is defined as the set of all control words of correct derivations in G. The extended Szilard language is defined by

$$\text{ESz}(G) = \{zm_{i_1}m_{i_2} \dots m_{i_n} : z \in L(G), m_{i_1}m_{i_2} \dots m_{i_n} \text{ is the control word of a derivation of } z\}.$$

Now let $N = (P, T, I, O, \mu_0)$ be a Petri net, $P = \{p_1, p_2, \dots, p_r\}$, $T = \{t_1, t_2, \dots, t_s\}$, $\mu_0 = (n_1, n_2, \dots, n_r)$. With N we associate the following pure (context-free) matrix grammar $G = (V, M, w)$, where

$$V = \{a_1, a_2, \dots, a_r, A_1, A_2, \dots, A_r\},$$

$$w = a_1^{n_1}A_1a_2^{n_2}A_2 \dots a_r^{n_r}A_r,$$

and the matrices m_i, $1 \leqq i \leqq s$, of M are constructed as follows: for $t_i \in T$, we define m_i by

$$m_i\colon ([a_1 \to \lambda]^{k_1}, [a_2 \to \lambda]^{k_2}, \dots, [a_r \to \lambda]^{k_r},$$
$$A_1 \to a_1^{u_1}A_1, A_2 \to a_2^{u_2}A_2, \dots, A_r \to a_r^{u_r}A_r)$$

where $k_j = I(t_i, p_j)$ and $u_j = O(t_i, p_j)$ for $1 \leqq k \leqq r$.

Clearly, m_i is applicable only to words $v = a_1^{v_1}A_1a_2^{v_2}A_2 \dots a_r^{v_r}A_r$ with $v_j \geqq k_j = I(t_i, p_j)$ for $1 \leqq j \leqq r$. Thus m_i is applicable to v if and only if the transition t_i is enabled in the corresponding marking $(v_1, v_2, \dots, v_r)$. Further

$$v \underset{m_i}{\Longrightarrow} z = a_1^{z_1}A_1a_2^{z_2}A_2 \dots a_r^{z_r}A_r$$

if and only if

$$\delta_N((v_1, v_2, \dots, v_r)\, t_i) = (z_1, z_2, \dots, z_r).$$

This proves

$$L'_r(N) = L(G).$$

Furthermore, $\delta_N(\mu_0, t_{i_1}t_{i_2} \dots t_{i_k})$ is defined if and only if $m_{i_1}m_{i_2}\dots m_{i_k}$ is a correct derivation in G. Therefore

$$\mathrm{Sz}\,(G) = \{m_{i_1}m_{i_2} \dots m_{i_k} : t_{i_1}t_{i_2} \dots t_{i_k} \in L_f(N)\},$$

$$\mathrm{ESz}\,(G) = \{a_1^{v_1}A_1a_2^{v_2}A_2 \dots a_r^{v_r}A_r m_{i_1}m_{i_2} \dots m_{i_k} : \delta_N(\mu_0, t_{i_1}t_{i_2} \dots t_{i_k}) = (v_1, v_2, \dots, v_r)\}.$$

Let h be the isomorphism (one-to-one homomorphism) defined by $h(m_i) = t_i$, $1 \leqq i \leqq s$. Then

$$L_f(N) = h(\mathrm{Sz}\,(G)).$$

Now let F be a finite set of markings. Then we consider the regular language

$$R_F = \bigcup_{(k_1,\dots,k_r)\in F} \{a_1^{k_1}A_1a_2^{k_2}A_2 \dots a_r^{k_r}A_r\}\,\{m_1, m_2, \dots, m_s\}^*.$$

Then

$$\mathrm{ESz}\,(G) \cap R_F$$

$$= \bigcup_{(k_1,\dots,k_r)\in F} \{a_1^{k_1}A_1a_2^{k_2}A_2 \dots a_r^{k_r}A_r m_{i_1}m_{i_2} \dots m_{i_k} : \delta_N(\mu_0, t_{i_1}t_{i_2} \dots t_{i_k}) = (k_1, k_2, \dots, k_r)\}.$$

We define the homomorphism g by

$$g(m_i) = t_i,\ 1 \leqq i \leqq s,\ g(a_j) = g(A_j) = \lambda,\ 1 \leqq j \leqq r.$$

Then

$$g(\mathrm{ESz}\,(G) \cap R_F) = L_t(N, F).$$

Using the known facts on pure matrix grammars and Szilard languages it is now easy to prove that, for each Petri net and each finite set F of markings,

$$L'_r(N) \in \mathscr{L}(\mathrm{M}, \mathrm{CF}),$$

$$L_f(N) \in \mathscr{L}(\mathrm{M}, \mathrm{CF} - \lambda),$$

$$L_t(N, F) \in \mathscr{L}(\mathrm{M}, \mathrm{CF}).$$

Example 9.2.1. (continued). The grammar associated with N_1 is

$$G_1 = (\{a_1, a_2, a_3, a_4, A_1, A_2, A_3, A_4\}, \{(a_1 \to \lambda, A_2 \to a_2A_2, A_3 \to a_3A_3),$$
$$(a_2 \to \lambda, A_1 \to a_1A_1, A_4 \to a_4A_4)\}, a_1A_1A_2A_3A_4),$$

and

$$G_2 = (\{a_1, a_2, a_3, a_4, A_1, A_2, A_3, A_4\},$$
$$\{(a_1 \to \lambda, a_2 \to \lambda, A_3 \to a_3^2), (a_3 \to \lambda, A_2 \to a_2A_2),$$
$$(a_3 \to \lambda, A_1 \to a_1A_1), (a_1 \to \lambda, a_2 \to \lambda, A_4 \to a_4A_4)\}, a_1A_1a_2A_2A_3A_4)$$

is associated with N_2.

Finally we note that vector addition systems (see Definition 1.3.3) can be considered as an interpretation of a Petri net, and therefore the proof of Theorem 1.3.4 also reflects a connection between regulated rewriting and Petri nets.

9.3. Modelling of Economic Processes

Let us consider again the processes discussed in Section 0.4. We start with the courier problem. Namely, we have a directed graph $\Gamma = (X, U)$ with $X = \{x_1, x_2, \ldots, x_n\}$, the alphabet $V = \{a_1, b_1, a_2, b_2, \ldots, a_n, b_n\}$ (a_i denotes the action of picking-up a letter from x_i, and b_i denotes the action of delivering a letter to point x_i), and a language $L_0 \subseteq \{a_i b_j : 1 \leqq i, j \leqq n, i \neq j\}$ which describes the pairs sender-receiver in some given circumstances. The courier activity is modelled by the language

$$LC = \mathrm{Shuf}^* (L_0)$$

which, for simple sets L_0, can be non-context-free. However, it is easy to see that this language can be generated by the vector grammar

$$G = (\{S\}, V, M, S)$$

with

$$M = \{(S \to a_i S, S \to b_j S), (S \to a_i S, S \to b_j) : a_i b_j \in L_0\}.$$

Therefore $LC \in \mathcal{L}(\mathrm{V}, \mathrm{REG})$.

Let us now consider the scheduling problem of Section 0.4. (with only two machines and two pieces to be manufactured). The process is described by all strings over the alphabet

$$V = \{(\alpha, \beta) : \alpha, \beta \in \{p_1, p_2, d\}\}$$

(a pair (α, β) corresponds to one time unit; α says what machine m_1 is doing and β what machine m_2 is doing — working on piece p_1, on piece p_2, or waiting) with the following property: each p_1 appearing in the first position is followed by a symbol p_1 appearing later in the second position of couples of V, and similarly for p_2.

We do not know whether this language can be generated by a vector or matrix grammar, but it can be easily generated by a scattered context grammar. Indeed, let us consider

$$G = \big(\{S, (p_1, X), (p_2, X), (X, p_1), (X, p_2)\}, V, M, S\big)$$

with

$$\begin{aligned} M = {} & \{(S) \to (SS), (S) \to ((d, d))\} \\ & \cup \{(S, S) \to ((\alpha, X), (X, \alpha)) : \alpha \in \{p_1, p_2\}\} \\ & \cup \{(S, (\beta, X)) \to ((\alpha, X), (\beta, \alpha)) : \alpha, \beta \in \{p_1, p_2\}\} \\ & \cup \{((X, \beta), S) \to ((\alpha, \beta), (X, \alpha)) : \alpha, \beta \in \{p_1, p_2\}\} \\ & \cup \{((X, \beta), (\gamma, X)) \to ((\alpha, \beta), (\gamma, \alpha)) : \alpha, \beta, \gamma \in \{p_1, p_2\}\} \\ & \cup \{((X, \alpha) \to (d, \alpha)) : \alpha \in \{p_1, p_2\}\} \\ & \cup \{((\alpha, X) \to (\alpha, d)) : \alpha \in \{p_1, p_2\}\}. \end{aligned}$$

Each production (together with the scattered context mode of the derivation) ensures the simulation of correct manufacturing of a given piece. Hence the whole process is simulated by this grammar.

The above construction can be easily generalized to processes with more machines and more pieces and with more complicated technological recipes. In conclusion, the scheduling problem can be solved at the level of scattered context grammar (which, remember, are very close, maybe equivalent, in generative capacity, to context-sensitive grammars).

PĂUN (1980-a) had investigated more variants of the above two processes as well as other economic questions, and in many cases the non-context-free languages which appear can be generated by various grammars with regulated rewriting. Here we briefly discuss another type of "economic" activity, namely the so-called "*inspector problem*": an "inspector" is moving on a graph, and he wants to plan his path in such a way that the arrivals in each point are "as unexpected as possible". More specifically, he wants to move in such a way that he does not repeat any portion of his route; in other words, his paths have to correspond to *Thue strings* over the alphabet describing the graph vertices, where Thue strings are such strings which do not contain substrings of the form xx for some string x.

Technically speaking, the problem is to place the Thue languages in the various hierarchies of regulated languages. As the DOL systems can generate infinite Thue languages and the DOL languages are also Indian parallel languages, it follows that $\mathscr{L}$(iCF) contains Thue languages. Clearly, each family for which a pumping lemma holds (for instance the simple matrix and finite index matrix families) does not contain infinite Thue languages. What about $\mathscr{L}$(M, CF)? The problem remains open. Another natural problem is the following. Let $T(k, j)$ be the set of all k-Thue strings (which cannot be written in the form xy^kz, $y \neq \lambda$) over a vocabulary with j symbols. What is the place of $T(k, j)$ (the language describes the "total inspector") with respect to families of regulated rewriting?

A possible answer is the following: for given k, j, $T(k, j)$ is the complement of a regular simple matrix language.

Indeed,

$$T(k, j) = V^* \setminus V^* L_{k,j} V^*$$

holds with

$$L_{k,j} = \{x^k : x \in V^+\}.$$

This language $L_{k,j}$ can be generated by the regular simple matrix grammar

$$G_{k,j} = (\{A_1\}, \{A_2\}, \ldots, \{A_k\}, V, M, S)$$

with

$$M = \{(S \to A_1A_2 \ldots A_k)\}$$
$$\cup \{(A_1 \to aA_1, A_2 \to aA_2, \ldots, A_k \to aA_k) : a \in V\}$$
$$\cup \{(A_1 \to a, A_2 \to a, \ldots, A_k \to a) : a \in V\}.$$

As the family $\mathscr{L}$(SM, REG) is closed under concatenation with regular sets, the assertion follows.

A more precise placement of $T(k, j)$ remains to be found.

9.4. Modelling Folklore Fairy-Tales, Dramatic, Musical and Visual Art Works

The procedure described in Section 0.4. for associating languages to fairly-tales was applied by S. Marcus and his collaborators to many Roumanian fairy-tales and a lot of non-context-free languages were obtained in this way. Here we only list some of them and discuss their type:

(a) "*Patru ţin pe opt*" ("Four catch eight")

$$L_{1,m} = \{(ab^{3n}c)^m : n \geqq 1\},\ m \geqq 1,$$

$$L_1 = \{(ab^{3n}c)^m : n, m \geqq 1\},$$

(b) "*Impăratul cu inelul furat*" ("The emperor with the stolen ring")

$$L_2 = \{a^{3n}b^{3n}c^{3n} : n \geqq 1\},$$

(c) "*Poveste din lume*" ("*World story*")

$$L_3 = \{a^n b^n a^n : n \geqq 1\},$$

(d) "*Petru Cenuşa*" ("Peter the Cinders")

$$L_4 = \{a^n b^{3n} a^{3n} b^n : n \geqq 1\},$$

(e) "*Fata unchiaşului*" ("The daughter of the old men")

$$L_5 = \{a^n b^{3n} c^{3n} d^n : n \geqq 1\},$$

(f) "*Roman Năzdrăvan*" ("Roman the Magician")

$$L_6 = \{a^n b^{2n} a^n c^{3n} d^{2n} : n \geqq 1\},$$

(g) "*Făt-Frumos cu părul de aur*" ("The prince Charming with the golden hair")

$$L_7 = \left\{a^{2n}\left((b^{2n})^3\, cd\right)^{2n} b^{2n} c^n : n \geqq 1\right\}.$$

The languages L_2 to L_6 can be obtained as homomorphic images of the "pattern language"

$$L_0 = \{a^n b^n c^n d^n e^n : n \geqq 1\}.$$

This language is a regular simple matrix language, and the family $\mathcal{L}(\mathrm{SM, REG})$ is closed under arbitrary homomorphisms. Hence also $L_2 - L_6$ are in $\mathcal{L}(\mathrm{SM, REG})$. Also the language $L_{1,m}$, for given m, is in $\mathcal{L}(\mathrm{SM, REG})$.

In opposition, the languages L_1 and L_7 are not simple matrix, finite index matrix, or unordered vector languages because they are not semilinear. (As a conclusion of this result we can infer that the fairy-tales (a) and (g) are more complex than the others; the reader interpreting them in this way is more "sophisticated" than the reader of other fairy-tales etc.)

Both languages L_1 and L_7 are in the family $\mathcal{L}(\mathrm{M, CF} - \lambda, \mathrm{ac})$. We prove this only for L_1 by consideration of the grammar

$$G_1 = (\{S, A, B, B', X, Y, Z, U, T\}, \{a, b, c\}, M_1, S, F_1)$$

with

$$M_1 = \{(S \to AX), (A \to aBcA, X \to X), (A \to aB, X \to Y),$$
$$(B \to b^3B', Y \to Y), (B \to T, Y \to Z), (B' \to B, Z \to Z),$$
$$(B' \to T, Z \to Y), (B' \to T, Z \to U), (B \to b^3, U \to U),$$
$$(B \to T, U \to c)\}$$

and F_1 containing all occurrences of rules $B \to T$, $B' \to T$ (T is a trap symbol).

More discussion on such languages and grammars (with interpretations from a literary semiotics point of view) can be found in MARCUS (1978).

Similar infinite readings, leading to languages of semantic marks, can be used to analyze dramatic and musical works. For instance, MOLIÈRE's play "Tartuffe" is read by GABRIELESCU in MARCUS (1977) in such a way that the regular simple matrix language

$$L_8 = \{ab^{2m}c^nb^mc^n : n \geqq m \geqq 1\}$$

is obtained. Analogously, SIMIONESCU (1976) read the menuets in the "Notenbüchlein für ANNA MAGDALENA" by BACH from 1725 and obtained languages of various complexities, like

$$L_9 = \{a^nb^n : n \geqq 1\},$$
$$L_{10} = \{a^nb^nc^nd^n : n \geqq 1\},$$
$$L_{11} = \{a^nb^na^nc^na^nb^na^nc^n : n \geqq 1\}.$$

Again, the second and and third of these languages are regular simple matrix languages and non-context-free.

Finally, let us briefly discuss a syntactical approach to two-dimensional structures, namely by means of the so-called head-tail pictural calculus. We consider the set of rectangles, first as surfaces and then as contours. (Combining rectangles we can obtain more complicated structures, architectural, artistic, etc.) We aim to "linearize" them by using the unit squares and the unit segments, respectively (see Fig. 9.4.1), as basic items. The arrows in that figure indicate the "heads" and the "tails" of each "picture". Three operations with these elementary pictures as well as with any compound can be defined in the following way.

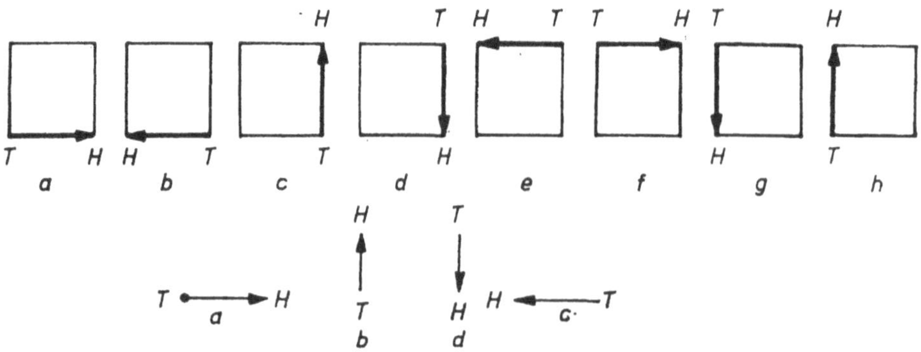

Fig. 9.4.1

Addition. Let p_1, p_2 be two pictures such that the head of p_1 (denoted by $H(p_1)$) can be superposed over the tail of p_2 (denoted by $T(p_2)$) without changing the orientation of any picture. The picture obtained in this way is denoted by $p_1 + p_2$ and it has $H(p_1 + p_2) = H(p_2)$, $T(p_1 + p_2) = T(p_1)$.

Subtraction. If p_1, p_2 are two pictures such that we can superpose their heads using only a translation, then we denote the obtained picture by $p_1 - p_2$ and let $H(p_1 - p_2) = H(p_1)$ and $T(p_1 - p_2) = T(p_1)$.

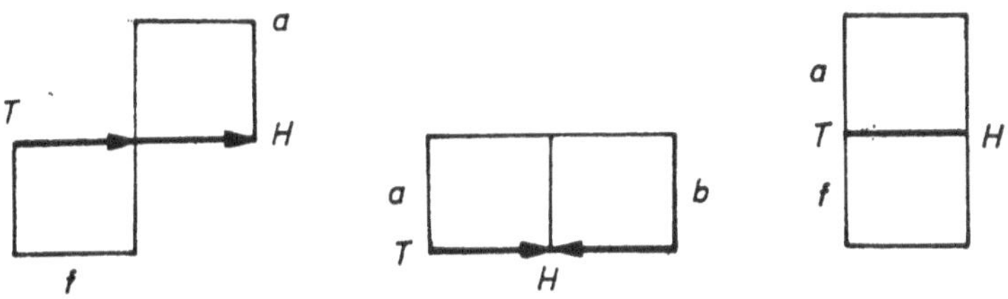

Fig. 9.4.2

Multiplication. If p_1, p_2 are two pictures whose heads and tails can be superposed, then we denote by $p_1 * p_2$ the obtained picture and set $H(p_1 * p_2) = H(p_1)$, $T(p_1 * p_2) = T(p_1)$.

In Fig. 9.4.2, the reader can find the pictures corresponding to $f + a$, $a - b$, $a * f$, where a, b, f are the elementary pictures of Figure 9.4.1.

Using these operations and the usual handling of parentheses, the set of all rectangles of dimensions $n \times m$, $n \geqq 2$, $m = 2k$, $k \geqq 1$, can be described by the following language

$$L = \{[[h +]^{n-1} a + a[+ d]^{n-1}]^{k-1} + ({}^{2(n-2)}a + h\,[+ h) - c)]^{n-2}$$
$$+ c + f : n \geqq 2, k \geqq 1\}$$

which is not context-free (not semilinear), but it can be generated by the Russian parallel matrix grammar

$$G = (\{S, A, B, C, D, E, H\}, V_T, M, S)$$

with

$$V_T = \{a, c, d, f, h, +, -, (,)\},$$
$$M = \{[S \to ABH], [S \to BC], [A \to Da + aEA], [A \to Da + aE, H \to C],$$
$$[D \to h + D, E \to + dE, B \to ((B, C \to + h) - cC],$$
$$[D \to h +, E \to + d +, B \to a + h, C \to +c + f]\}$$

and the rules in the set

$$P_2 = \{D \to h + D, E \to + dE, D \to h +, E \to + d +\}$$

are used in the parallel manner. (The parentheses [,] are used as metasymbols instead of (,) in writing the matrices and the iterated subwords of L.) A similar language (also with a similar Russian parallel matrix grammar) can be constructed for rectangles of dimension $n \times m$ with odd m.

If only contour rectangles are looked for, then the corresponding languages are much simpler. For instance,

$$([a+]^m\,[b+]^n\,[c+]^{m-1}\,c) * ([b+]^{n-1}\,b)$$

describes the rectangles with the head in the north-west corner and the tail in the south-west corner. The set of all such strings is a regular simple matrix language.

9.5. The Mappings Investigation

In Section 0.4. we presented some examples of (partial) mappings $f: \mathbb{N} \Rightarrow \mathbb{N}$ for which the languages

$$L_f = \{a_1^{n_1} a_2^{n_2} \ldots a_k^{n_k} a_{k+1}^{f(n_1, n_2, \ldots, n_k)} : n_i \in \mathbb{N},\ 1 \leqq i \leqq k,\ (n_1, n_2, \ldots, n_k) \in \mathrm{dom}\,(f)\}$$

are not context-free.

Let us denote by $\mathcal{F}_X(k)$ the set of all mappings $f: \mathbb{N}^k \to \mathbb{N}$, $k \geqq 1$, whose language L_f is in $\mathcal{L}(X)$. Further let $\mathcal{F}_X$ be the union of all sets $\mathcal{F}_X(k)$ taken over all $k \geqq 1$. In Păun and Tătarăm (1985) the sets $\mathcal{F}_X(k)$ and $\mathcal{F}_X$ are investigated for $X \in$ {REG, LIN, CF, (SM, REG), (SM, CF)}. Here are some results on $\mathcal{F}_{(\mathrm{SM,REG})}$ and $\mathcal{F}_{(\mathrm{SM,CF})}$.

Lemma 9.5.1. *If $f \in \mathcal{F}_{(\mathrm{SM,CF})}(k)$, then each language of the form*

$$L_i = \{a_i^n : \textit{there exist integers } n_1, \ldots, n_{i-1}, n_{i+1}, \ldots, n_k \text{ such that}$$
$$(n_1, \ldots, n_{i-1}, n, n_{i+1}, \ldots, n_k) \in \mathrm{dom}\,(f)\},$$

$1 \leqq i \leqq k$, and the language

$$L_{k+1} = \{a_{k+1}^n : n \in \mathrm{codom}\,(f)\}$$

are regular.

Proof. All languages L_i, $1 \leqq i \leqq k+1$, can be obtained as homomorphic images of L_f. As $\mathcal{L}$(SM, CF) is closed under arbitrary homomorphisms and each simple matrix language over a one-letter alphabet is regular, the assertion follows.

The converse of this lemma is not true. For, let us consider the mapping $f: \mathbb{N} \to \mathbb{N}$ defined by

$$f(n) = \begin{cases} 1 & \text{if } n = 2^k \text{ for some } k \geqq 1, \\ 0 & \text{otherwise.} \end{cases}$$

The associated languages L_1 and L_2 are regular, but L_f is not semilinear and hence not in $\mathcal{L}$(SM, CF).

Theorem 9.5.1. i) $\mathcal{F}_{\mathrm{CF}}(k) \subset \mathcal{F}_{(\mathrm{SM,CF})}(k)$ for $k \geqq 2$,

ii) $\mathcal{F}_{\mathrm{CF}}(1) = \mathcal{F}_{(\mathrm{SM,CF})}(1)$,

iii) $\mathcal{F}_{(\mathrm{SM,CF})}(k) \subset \mathcal{F}_{\mathrm{CS}}(k)$ for $k \geqq 1$,

iv) $\mathcal{F}_{(\mathrm{SM,CF})}(k) = \mathcal{F}_{(\mathrm{SM,REG})}(k)$ for $k \geqq 1$.

Proof. iii) The inclusion holds trivially. We prove its strictness. Let f be the above mapping. L_f is not semilinear. Now we consider the mapping $f^{(k)}: \mathbb{N}^k \to \mathbb{N}$ given by

$$f^{(k)}(n_1, n_2, \ldots, n_k) = \begin{cases} f(n_1) & \text{if } n_2 = n_3 = \cdots = n_k = 0, \\ \text{undefined} & \text{otherwise}. \end{cases}$$

Then

$$L_f(k) = \{a_1^{n_1} a_{k+1}^{f(n_1)} : n_1 \in \mathbb{N}\}$$

which is the "same" language as L_f up to the notation of the letters. Thus $L_{f^{(k)}}$ is not semilinear, and hence it is not in $\mathcal{L}$(SM, CF). Therefore we get $f^{(k)} \in \mathcal{F}_{\mathrm{CS}}(k) \setminus \mathcal{F}_{(\mathrm{SM,CF})}(k)$.

i) can be proved in the same way using the function f_1 from Section 0.4. since L_{f_1} is not context-free.

ii) The equality $\mathcal{F}_{\mathrm{CF}}(1) = \mathcal{F}_{(\mathrm{SM,CF})}(1)$ follows from the fact that L_f is semilinear for $f \in \mathcal{F}_{(\mathrm{SM,CF})}(1)$ and that each semilinear language included in $a_1^* a_2^*$ is linear (see Lemma 5.3.1 in Ginsburg (1966).

iv) These equalities follow from the following known assertions for simple matrix languages: each simple matrix language is semilinear, and each bounded (see Exercise 3.2.5) semilinear language is a regular simple matrix language. The languages L_f with $f \in \mathcal{F}_{(\mathrm{SM,CF})}$ are both bounded and semilinear.

In this grammatical approach to mappings certain natural problems appear which could be decided by reduction to formal language theoretical questions. For example, let $f, g: \mathbb{N}^k \to \mathbb{N}$ be two arbitrary mappings. Is dom (f) equal to $\mathbb{N}^k$? Is there a constant t such that $f(x) \leqq t$ for all $x \in$ dom (f)? Is the mapping f injective? Is the mapping f surjective? Does $f(x) = g(x)$ for all $x \in \mathbb{N}^k$? We call these problems the totality, the finiteness, the injectivity, the surjectivity, the equality problems, respectively. The following problem is a further problem (the mapping problem): given a language $L \subseteq a_1^* a_2^* \ldots a_{k+1}^*$, is there a mapping $f: \mathbb{N}^k \to \mathbb{N}$ such that $L = L_f$?

Clearly, for various classes $\mathcal{F}_X$, the above problems have different answers. In Păun and Tătarăm (1985), it is proved that all these problems are undecidable for $\mathcal{F}_{\mathrm{CS}}(k)$, $k \geqq 1$, however, we have

Theorem 9.5.2. *All the above problems are decidable for the family* $\mathcal{F}_{(\mathrm{SM,CF})}$.

Proof. For a mapping $f: \mathbb{N}^k \to \mathbb{N}$, $f \in \mathcal{F}_{(\mathrm{SM,CF})}(k)$, we consider the language L_{k+1} of Lemma 9.5.1. This language is regular. Hence it is decidable whether or not it is finite (the finiteness problem) and whether or not it is equal to $\{a_{k+1}\}^*$ (the surjectivity problem). As the equivalence problem is decidable for bounded simple matrix languages (since the equality of semilinear sets is decidable), it follows that the equality of semilinear sets is decidable), it follows that the equality problem is decidable for $\mathcal{F}_{(\mathrm{SM,CF})}$ as well. Using the same result, we obtain that the problem whether or not $\{a_1^{n_1} a_2^{n_2} \ldots a_k^{n_k} : (n_1, n_2, \ldots, n_k) \in \text{dom}(f)\}$ is equal to the language $a_1^* a_2^* \ldots a_k^*$ is decidable for $f \in \mathcal{F}_{(\mathrm{SM,CF})}$. Hence the totality problem is decidable.

For a mapping $f \in \mathcal{F}_{(\mathrm{SM,CF})}(k)$, $k \geqq 1$, we consider the language $L_1 = L_f\{c\}\,\mathrm{Mi}\,(L_f)$ which, obviously, is a bounded simple matrix language. Further we consider the context-free languages

$$L_2 = \{a_1, a_2, \ldots, a_k\}^* \{a_{k+1}^n c a_{k+1}^n : n \geqq 0\} \{a_1, a_2, \ldots, a_k\}^*,$$
$$L_3 = \{wcw' : w, w' \in \{a_1, a_2, \ldots, a_k\}^*, w' \neq \mathbf{Mi}\,(w)\},$$

and the homomorphism h which erases the symbol a_{k+1}. Then we obtain

$$h(L_1 \cap L_2) \cap L_3 = \{a_1^{n_1}a_2^{n_2} \dots a_k^{n_k}ca_k^{m_k}a_{k-1}^{m_{k-1}} \dots a_1^{m_1} : n_i, m_i \in \mathbf{N}, 1 \leqq i \leqq k, (n_1, \dots, n_k) \neq (m_1, \dots, m_k), f(n_1, \dots, n_k) = f(m_1, \dots, m_k)\}.$$

From the results presented in Section 1.5. it follows that this language is a simple matrix language and that it is empty if and only if the mapping f is injective. As the emptiness problem is decidable for simple matrix grammars, it follows that the injectivity problem is decidable for $\mathcal{F}_{(\mathrm{SM,CF})}$.

Now let $L \subseteq a_1^* a_2^* \dots a_{k+1}^*$ be a language of $\mathcal{L}(\mathrm{SM, CF})$. We construct the languages

$$L_1 = \{a_{k+1}\}^* \{c\} L,$$

$$L_2 = \{a_{k+1}^{n_{k+1}}ca_1^{n_1}a_2^{n_2} \dots a_k^{n_k} : a_1^{n_1}a_2^{n_2} \dots a_{k+1}^{n_{k+1}} \in L\} \{a_{k+1}\}^*.$$

Clearly, both these languages are in $\mathcal{L}(\mathrm{SM, CF})$. Let h be the homomorphism defined by

$$h(a_i) = \lambda, 1 \leqq i \leqq k, h(a_{k+1}) = a_{k+1}, h(c) = c.$$

Then the language

$$h(L_1 \cap L_2) \cap \{a_{k+1}^n c a_{k+1}^m : n, m \ \mathbf{N}, n \neq m\}$$

is a simple matrix language, and it is empty if and only if the language L defines a mapping. Therefore the mapping problem is also decidable for $\mathcal{F}_{(\mathrm{SM,FC})}$.

Of course, these investigations can be continued along various lines. One of them is the study of further classes $\mathcal{F}_X$ for different X (with regulated rewriting).

A general research topic is that of looking for further applications of regulated grammars, in other areas or in those considered above. The theory is mature enough to promise interesting results.

Chapter 10. A Common Generalization: Selective Substitution Grammars

In the preceding chapters we gave a lot of results concerning the comparison of mechanisms for regulated rewriting with respect to some parameters (e.g. generative power, descriptional complexity, etc.). Clearly, these results illustrate differences between the regulating devices. Another important area in the field of regulated rewriting concerns unifying approaches.

Here we shall discuss in some detail only one type of grammars, the so-called selective substitution grammars, which presents a unifying way to describe some of the grammars introduced in Chapters 1 and 2. These grammars are also of interest because some of their special cases give the possibility to define new types of regulated rewriting.

If V is an alphabet, then we set $\overline{V} = \{\overline{x} : x \in V\}$, and we define the homomorphism $h_V : (V \cup \overline{V})^* \to V^*$ by

$$h_V(a) = a \quad \text{for} \quad a \in V, h(\bar{a}) = a \quad \text{for} \quad \bar{a} \in \overline{V}.$$

Definition 10.1. A *selective substitution grammar* is a construct $G = (V, V', P, S, K)$ where

- V is a finite alphabet, $V' \subseteq V$,
- P is a finite subset of $V \times V^*$ (whose elements will be written in the form $x \to w$),
- $S \in V \setminus V'$,
- K is a language over $V \cup \overline{V}$ (the selector language of G).

We say that x directly derives y in G, written as $x \Rightarrow y$, if there exists a word $z \in K$ such that $h_V(z) = x$, and if $z = b_1 b_2 \ldots b_n$, $b_i \in V \cup \overline{V}$ for $1 \leqq i \leqq n$, then $y = \beta_1 \beta_2 \ldots \beta_n$ with $\beta_i = b_i$ for $b_i \in V$ and $a_i \to \beta_i \in P$ for $b_i = \bar{a}_i \in \overline{V}$. Further, we define

$$L(G) = \{y : S \overset{*}{\Rightarrow} y, y \in (V')^*\}.$$

(In other words, the rewriting of x yielding y requires the existence of a z in the selector language K which contains some barred letters and only the letters in x which correspond to these "activated" letters can be replaced according to the rules in P; thus the selector language K has two tasks: it selects which words can be rewritten — $z \in K$ with $h_V(z) = x$ has to exist — and it tells us which letters of x have to be replaced — the corresponding letters in z have to be barred.)

Example 10.1. We consider $G = (V, V', P, S, K)$ with

$$V = \{S, Z_1, Z_2, Z, *, a, b\},$$

$$V' = \{*, a, b\},$$

$$P = \{S \to Z_1Z_2, Z_1 \to **aZ_1, Z_1 \to bZ_1, Z_1 \to **, Z_2 \to aZ_2,$$

$$Z_2 \to **bZ_2, Z_2 \to **Z*, Z \to ***\},$$

$$K = \{\bar{S}\} \cup \bigcup_{\substack{m \geqq 1 \\ n+m \equiv 1 \bmod 4}} V^n\bar{Z}_1V^m \cup \bigcup_{\substack{n \equiv 0 \bmod 4 \\ \text{or } n \equiv 2 \bmod 4}} V^n\bar{Z}_2 \cup \bigcup_{n \equiv 0 \bmod 4} V^n\bar{Z}V.$$

Let $a_1 = **a$, $b_1 = b$, $a_2 = a$, $b_2 = **b$. Further we write $w_1 \equiv w_2$ for $w_i \in \{a_i, b_i\}^*$, $i \in \{1, 2\}$, if w_2 is obtained from w_1 by replacing each occurrence of a_1 by a_2 and each occurrence of b_1 by b_2. We prove

$$L(G) = \{w_1**w_2****** : w_1 \in \{a_1, b_1\}^*, w_2 \in \{a_2, b_2\}^*, w_1 \equiv w_2\}.$$

Let us consider a word of the form $w_1Z_1w_2Z_2$, $w_i \in \{a_i, b_i\}^*$, $i \in \{1, 2\}$, $w_1 \equiv w_2$. Then $|w_1Z_1w_2Z_2| \equiv 2 \bmod 4$. Hence we can rewrite only Z_1 by the definition of K.

Case 1. We use $Z_1 \to **aZ_1$. Then $w_1Z_1w_2Z_2 \Rightarrow w_1**aZ_1w_2Z_2 = v$ with $|v| \equiv 1 \bmod 4$. Therefore Z_2 has to be rewritten in v. If we apply $Z_2 \to **Z*$ or $Z_2 \to **bZ_2$, then we obtain a word of length $t \equiv 0 \bmod 4$ which cannot be rewritten. Hence we obtain $v \Rightarrow w_1**aZ_1w_2aZ_2$. This is again a word of the form $z_1Z_1z_2Z_2$ with $z_i \in \{a_i, b_i\}^*$, $i \in \{1, 2\}$, and $z_1 \equiv z_2$.

Case 2. We use $Z_1 \to bZ_1$. We obtain $w_1Z_1w_2Z_2 \Rightarrow w_1bZ_1w_2Z_2 = v'$ with $|v'| \equiv 3 \bmod 4$. We now have to replace Z_2 and as above it can be proved (however, we have to regard two derivation steps) that we have to use $Z_2 \to **bZ_2$ yielding $w_1bZ_1w_2**bZ_2$ which has the desired form, again.

Case 3. We use $Z_1 \to **$. Again, in the next step Z_2 has to be rewritten in the obtained word $w_1**w_2Z_2$, and if we apply $Z_2 \to aZ_2$ or $Z_2 \to **bZ_2$ no terminal string can be derived. Hence we replace Z_2 by $**Z*$, and then we can apply $Z \to ***$ yielding the terminal word $w_1**w_2******$.

Since each derivation starts with $S \Rightarrow Z_1Z_2$ and Z_1Z_2 has the above form, the statement concerning $L(G)$ is proved.

Note that the homomorphism g given by

$$g(x) = x \quad \text{for} \quad x \in \{a, b\},\ g(*) = \lambda$$

yields

$$g(L(G)) = \{ww : w \in \{a, b\}^*\}$$

which is not a context-free language. Hence also $L(G)$ is not context-free.

Next we shall show that we can get some of the grammars introduced in Chapters 1 and 2 by a special choice of the sets V, V', P, and K in the definition of the selective substitution grammar.

Example 10.2. Let $G = (V_N, V_T, P, S)$ be a context-free grammar. Then we consider the selective substitution grammar

$$G' = (V_G, V_T, P, S, V_G^*\bar{V}_NV_G^*).$$

Clearly, by the definition of the selector language we can apply the rules of P at any place and only one rule is applicable in one step. Hence $L(G) = L(G')$.

Example 10.3. Let $G = (V_N, V_T, P, S)$ be an Indian parallel grammar. Then we take the selective substitution grammar

$$G' = \left(V_G, V_T, P, S, \bigcup_{A \in V_N} \left((V_G \setminus \{A\})^* \bar{A}\right)^* (V_G \setminus \{A\})^*\right).$$

By the choice of the selector language it is obvious that in each derivation step in G' we have to replace all occurrences of some letter $A \in V_N$ in the current word. Therefore $L(G) = L(G')$.

Example 10.4. Let $G = (V, V', P, w)$ be an EOL system, i.e. an ETOL system with exactly one table P. Then we consider the selective substitution grammar

$$G' = (V \cup \{S\}, V', P \cup \{S \to w\}, S, \bar{V}^* \cup \{\bar{S}\}).$$

Clearly, each derivation in G' starts with $S \Rightarrow w$, and then we have to replace all letters in the current string according to P since — except S — the selector language contains only words which consist only of "activated" letters of V. Hence $L(G) = L(G')$.

Example 10.5. Let $G = (V, V', \mathfrak{P}, w)$ be an ETOL system and $\mathfrak{P} = \{P_1, P_2, \ldots, P_r\}$. Then we define the selective substitution grammar

$$G' = (\{S\} \cup V \cup \{[a, i] : a \in V, 1 \leqq i \leqq r\}, V', P', S, K)$$

with

$$P' = \left\{a \to [a, i] : a \in V, 1 \leqq i \leqq r\} \cup \{S \to w\} \cup \bigcup_{i=1}^{r} [a, i] \to x : a \to x \in P_i\right\}$$

and

$$K = \bar{V}^* \cup \bigcup_{i=1}^{r} \{\overline{[a, i]} : a \in V\}^* \cup \{\bar{S}\}.$$

All derivations in G' start with $S \Rightarrow w \in V^+$. By the definition of K, each $a \in V$ in w now is replaced by $[a, i]$, $1 \leqq i \leqq r$. If we obtain a word $w' = [a_1, i_1] [a_2, i_2] \ldots [a_k, i_k]$ with $i_j \neq i_t$ for some $j \neq t$, then the derivation is blocked by the choice of K. Therefore we get $w' = [a_1, i] [a_2, i] \ldots [a_k, i]$ for some i. The letters $[a, i]$ can be rewritten only according to rules in P_i by the definition of P, and K requires their parallel applications. Hence we get

$$w = a_1 a_2 \ldots a_k \Rightarrow w'' \Rightarrow \alpha_1 \alpha_2 \ldots \alpha_k$$

with $a_j \to \alpha_j \in P_i$ for $1 \leqq j \leqq k$. Thus the terminating derivations $S \stackrel{*}{\Rightarrow} z$ in G' correspond to terminating derivations $w \stackrel{*}{\Rightarrow} z$ in G. Since each derivation in G can be simulated by the above method, we obtain $L(G) = L(G')$. (The "nonterminals" $[a, i]$ are used in order to ensure that we apply only rules of one table in a derivation step.)

Example 10.6. Let $G = (V_N, V_T, P, S)$ be a random context grammar. With each rule $(A \to w, Q, R)$ we associate the new symbol (A, Q, R). Let W be the set of these new symbols. Then we define the selective substitution grammar

$$G' = (V_G \cup W, V_T, P', S, K)$$

with

$$P' = \{A \to (A, Q, R) : (A \to w, Q, R) \in P\}$$
$$\cup \{(A, Q, R) \to w : (A \to w, Q, R) \in P\},$$
$$K = V_G^* \overline{V}_N V_G^*$$
$$\cup [(V_G \setminus R)^* \overline{(A, Q, R)} (V_G \setminus R)^* \cap \bigcap_{X \in Q} (V_G \cup W \cup \overline{W})^* X (V_G \cup W \cup \overline{W})^*].$$

It is easy to see that each derivation in G' has the following form:

$$S \Rightarrow (S, Q_0, R_0) \Rightarrow w_1 = v_{1,1}A_1v_{1,2} \Rightarrow v_{1,1}(A_1, Q_1, R_1)\, v_{1,2}$$
$$\Rightarrow w_2 \Rightarrow \cdots \Rightarrow w_n = v_{n,1}A_nv_{n,2} \Rightarrow v_{n,1}(A_n, Q_n, R_n)\, v_{n,2} \Rightarrow w_{n+1}$$

and it consists of a context-free application of the rules $S \to (S, Q_0, R_0)$, $(S, Q_0, R_0) \to w_1$, $A_i \to (A_i, Q_i, R_i)$, $(A_i, Q_i, R_i) \to v_i$ with $w_{i+1} = v_{i,1}v_iv_{i,2}$, $1 \leqq i \leqq n$. By the definition of K only one nonterminal can be replaced by (A, Q, R) and $(A, Q, R) \to v$ is applicable to $x = x_1(A, Q, R)\, x_2$ iff $(A \to v, Q, R)$ is applicable to x_1Ax_2. Therefore in G there is a derivation

$$S \Rightarrow w_1 \Rightarrow w_2 \Rightarrow \cdots \Rightarrow w_n \Rightarrow w_{n+1}.$$

Obviously, in this way each derivation in G can be simulated by a derivation in G'. Therefore $L(G) = L(G')$.

Example 10.7. Let $G = (V_N, V_T, P, S)$ be a scattered context grammar. With each rule r: $(A_1, A_2, \ldots, A_{i_r}) \to (w_1, w_2, \ldots, w_{i_r})$ in P we associate the sets $V_r = \{[A_i, i, r]: 1 \leqq i \leqq i_r\}$. We define then the selective substitution grammar

$$G = (V_G \cup \bigcup_{r \in P} V_r, V_T, \bigcup_{r \in P} (P_r \cup \{A_i \to [A_i, i, r]: A \in V_N, 1 \leqq i \leqq i_r\})$$
$$\cup \{A \to A : A \in V_N,\} S, K)$$

by

$$P_r = \{[A_i, i, r] \to w_i : 1 \leqq i \leqq i_r\},$$
$$K = (\overline{V}_T^* V_N)^* V_T \cup \bigcup_{r \in P} V_G^* \overline{[A_1, 1, r]}\, V_G^* \overline{[A_2, 2, r]} \ldots V_G^* \overline{[A_{i_r}, i_r, r]}\, V_G^*.$$

Again, it is easy to see that, for $w \in V_G^*$, a non-blocked derivation in G' consisting of two steps has the form

$$w \Rightarrow \alpha_1[A_1, 1, r]\, \alpha_2[A_2, 2, r] \ldots \alpha_{i_r}[A_{i_r}, i_r, r]\, \alpha_{i_r+1} \Rightarrow \alpha_1w_1\alpha_2w_2 \ldots \alpha_{i_r}w_{i_r}\alpha_{i_r+1}$$

and that it exists if and only if

$$w = \alpha_1A_1\alpha_2A_2 \ldots \alpha_{i_r}A_{i_r}\alpha_{i_r+1} \Rightarrow \alpha_1w_1\alpha_2w_2 \ldots \alpha_{i_r}w_{i_r}\alpha_{i_r+1}$$

is a direct derivation in G (using r). Hence $L(G) = L(G')$.

Example 10.8. Since each matrix language can be generated by a matrix grammar in accurate normal form (Lemma 1.3.7) and since the application of its matrices has the same effect as its application as a scattered context rule, matrix grammars can be simulated by the method of Example 10.7.

It is clear that each grammar of the types considered in the above examples can be simulated also by a context-sensitive grammar (if we do not allow erasing rules); however, then the length of the derivation simulating one derivation step in the given grammar depends on the simulated rule and on the place where it is applied. In the above examples we used in all cases the same number of steps and at most two steps in order to simulate a direct derivation step (more precisely, one step is used in Examples 10.2 to 10.4, and two steps are used in Examples 10.5 to 10.8). Furthermore, if the number of simulation steps is 2, then the first step corresponds to a choice of the production (table, matrix) and the second one corresponds to a direct derivation step in the simulated grammar.

Our definition of a selective substitution grammar differs from that given in the paper Rozenberg (1977) where this concept has been introduced. Let us mention the main differences:

- Instead of one set of productions and one selector language Rozenberg considered sets of pairs consisting of a production set and a selector language. This allows the simulation of one direct derivation step by one direct derivation step.
- Rozenberg used, in addition, a control language (as in the sense of grammars with regular control — see Section 2.1.). This enables some further types of regulated grammars to be modelled.

However, by all these possibilities for modelling, the concept by Rozenberg (1977) can hardly be handled, and therefore in the most subsequent papers (e.g. Kleijn and Rozenberg (1981-a), (1981-b), Gonczarowski et al. (1983-a), (1983-b)) our definition is used.

As we have seen, different types of grammars can be described by selective substitution grammars with different selector languages. Thus it is a natural question to study the effect of the selector languages.

Let $\mathcal{K}$ be a family of languages. Then by $\mathcal{L}(\mathrm{s}\mathcal{K})$ we denote the family of all languages generated by selective substitution grammars $G = (V, V', P, S, K)$ with $K \in \mathcal{K}$.

First we mention a characterization result.

Lemma 10.1. *Let* $\mathcal{K} = \{K : V^*\overline{V}V^* \subseteq K \subseteq (V \cup \overline{V})^*\}$ *for some alphabet* V. *Then* $\mathcal{L}(\mathrm{s}\mathcal{K}) = \mathcal{L}(\mathrm{CF})$.

Proof. The easy proof is left to the reader (see Exercise 10.3).

Let X_1, X_2 be subsets of $V \cup \overline{V}$. A substitution $\varphi: X_1^* \to 2^{X_2^*}$ is called a *disjoint bar-preserving finite-letter substitution* from X_1 into X_2 if

$$\varphi(a) \subseteq X_2 \cap V \quad \text{for} \quad a \in X_1 \cap V,$$

$$\varphi(\bar{a}) \subseteq X_2 \cap \overline{V} \quad \text{for} \quad \bar{a} \in X_1 \cap \overline{V},$$

$$\varphi(a) \cap \varphi(b) = \emptyset \quad \text{for} \quad a \neq b,\ a, b \in X_1.$$

Lemma 10.2. *Let $\mathcal{K}$ be a family of languages which is closed under disjoint bar-preserving finite letter substitutions, union with activated (barred) monoids, and concatenation with non-activated monoids. Then $\mathcal{L}(s\mathcal{K})$ is closed under homomorphisms and Kleene closure.*

Proof. i) First we show that, for each $L \in \mathcal{L}(\mathrm{s}\mathcal{K})$, there is a selective substitution grammar $G = (V, V', P, S, K)$ such that S does not occur on the right-hand side of a production, no letter of V' occurs in words of K, and $K \in \mathcal{K}$.

Let $G' = (V_1, V_1', P_1, S_1, K_1)$ be a selective substitution grammar with $K_1 \in \mathcal{K}$. We define

$$V_1'' = \{a'' : a \in V_1'\},$$

$$V = V_1 \cup V_1'' \cup \{S\},\ V' = V_1'.$$

Let τ, τ' be the disjoint bar-preserving finite letter substitutions $\tau, \tau'\colon (V_1 \cup \overline{V}_1)^* \to 2^{(V \cup \overline{V})^*}$ given by

$$\tau(a) = \{a\} \quad \text{for} \quad a \in V_1 \setminus V_1',\ \tau(a) = \{a''\} \quad \text{for} \quad a \in V_1',$$

$$\tau(\bar{a}) = \overline{\tau(a)} \quad \text{for} \quad \bar{a} \in \overline{V}_1,$$

$$\tau'(a) = \tau(a) \quad \text{for} \quad a \in V_1 \setminus \{S_1\},\ \tau'(S_1) = \{S, S_1\},$$

$$\tau'(\bar{a}) = \overline{\tau(a)} \quad \text{for} \quad \bar{a} \in \overline{V}_1.$$

Let

$$P = \{x \to w : x \in \tau(x'), w \in \tau(w'), x' \to w' \in P_1\} \cup \{S \to S_1\},$$

$$K = \tau'(K_1) \cup \overline{V}_1''^*.$$

Now $G = (V, V', P, S, K)$ also generates $L(G')$. This can be seen as follows. There has to be $\bar{S}_1$ in K_1, otherwise no derivation in G' is possible. Hence $\bar{S}$ is in K and we obtain $S \Rightarrow S_1$ (the occurrences of S in other words of K are of no importance since apart from S no sentential form contains an occurrence of S). Now we can proceed as in G' but instead of x we use $\tau(x)$ in all cases. If a word over V_1'' $(= \tau'(V_1'))$ is obtained it can be rewritten, in addition, by replacing each letter a'' by a. If we use such a rule $a'' \to a$ and a rule $b \to w$, $w \in ((V_1 \cup V_1'') \setminus V_1')^*$ simultaneously, then the derivation is blocked since K contains no word with letters of V_1'. Therefore it is easily seen that

$$S \Rightarrow S_1 \Rightarrow \tau(w_1) \Rightarrow \tau(w_2) \Rightarrow \cdots \Rightarrow \tau(w_n) \Rightarrow w_n \in (V_1')^* = (V')^*$$

is a derivation in G if and only if

$$S_1 \Rightarrow w_1 \Rightarrow w_2 \Rightarrow \cdots \Rightarrow w_n$$

is a terminating derivation in G'. Hence $L(G) = L(G')$. Clearly, the constructed grammar G has the desired properties.

ii) *Homomorphisms.* The closure under homomorphisms, i.e. $h(L(G') \in \mathcal{L}(s\mathcal{K})$ for $L(G') \in \mathcal{L}(s\mathcal{K})$ and a homomorphism h, follows by the construction of i) if we substitute the rules $a'' \to h(a)$ for the rules $a'' \to a$.

iii) *Kleene closure.* Without loss of generality we can assume that L is generated by a selective substitution grammar $G = (V, V', P, S, K)$ of the form given in i). Then we construct

$$G' = (V \cup \{Z\}, V', P \cup \{Z \to SZ, Z \to S\}, Z, K')$$

with

$$K' = (V')^* (K\{Z\}^* \cup \{\bar{Z}\}) = (V')^* K\{Z\}^* \cup (V')^* \{\bar{Z}\}.$$

Let $w = vZ$ with $v \in (V')^*$. Then we apply $Z \to S$ or $Z \to SZ$ since the letters of V' do not occur in K and therefore, they cannot be replaced. In the former case, we get vS and now we have to rewrite S as in G and to continue also as in G. Therefore $vS \Rightarrow vv'$ with $v' \in L$. In the latter case vSZ is obtained and we have to rewrite S and its successors as in G until we obtain a word $vv'Z$, $v' \in L$, since Z can be rewritten only if no letter of $V \cup V'$ is present. Because the axiom is Z it is obvious that $L(G') = L^+$. Further, $K' \in \mathcal{K}$ and hence $L^+ \in \mathcal{L}(\mathrm{s}\mathcal{K})$.

Without proof we mention the following more general result.

Theorem 10.1. *Let $\mathcal{K}$ be a family of languages which is closed under disjoint bar-preserving finite letter substitutions, union, union with activated monoids, concatenation with non-activated monoids and such that $\mathcal{L}(\mathrm{s}\mathcal{K})$ contains a non-empty language. Then $\mathcal{L}(\mathrm{s}\mathcal{K})$ is a full AFL.*

Within the framework of selective substitution grammars we now want to study differences and similarities between sequential and parallel rewriting. A derivation process is purely sequential if in each step exactly one letter is replaced, and it is purely parallel if in each step all letters of the current word are rewritten. Therefore it is sequential or parallel if the words in the selector language are of the form $\alpha_1\bar{a}\alpha_2$ with $\alpha_1, \alpha_2 \in V^*$, $a \in V$, or they are contained in $\bar{V}^*$, respectively. This leads to the following definition.

We say that a selector language $K \subseteq (V \cup \bar{V})^*$ is *sequential* if K is of the form $K = \bigcup_{i=1}^{n} X_i^*\bar{Y}_iZ_i^*$ for some $n \geqq 1$ and some languages $X_i, Y_i, Z_i \subseteq V$ for $1 \leqq i \leqq n$. A selector language is called *parallel* if it has the form $K = \bigcup_{i=1}^{n} \bar{Y}_i^+$ for some $n \geqq 1$ and some languages $Y_i \subseteq V$ for $1 \leqq i \leqq n$. As an intermediate step we introduce *continuous* selector languages which are of the form $K = \bigcup_{i=1}^{n} X_i^*\bar{Y}_i^+Z_i^*$ for some $n \geqq 1$ and some languages $X_i, Y_i, Z_i \subseteq V$, $1 \leqq i \leqq n$. By $\mathcal{L}(\mathrm{seq})$, $\mathcal{L}(\mathrm{par})$, and $\mathcal{L}(\mathrm{cont})$ we denote the families of languages generated by selective substitution grammars whose selector languages are sequential, parallel, and continuous, respectively.

Theorem 10.2. $\mathcal{L}(\mathrm{par}) = \mathcal{L}(\mathrm{ETOL})$.

Proof. i) The construction of Example 10.5 shows that $\mathcal{L}(\mathrm{ETOL}) \subseteq \mathcal{L}(\mathrm{par})$.

ii) Let $L \in \mathcal{L}(\mathrm{par})$ be a language generated by some selective substitution grammar $G = (V, V', P, S, K)$ with $K = \bigcup_{i=1}^{n} \bar{Y}_i^+$, $Y_i \subseteq V$, $1 \leqq i \leqq n$. For $1 \leqq i \leqq n$, let $V^{(i)} = \{a^{(i)} : a \in V\}$, and we set

$$W = V \cup V^{(1)} \cup V^{(2)} \cup \cdots \cup V^{(n)} \cup \{F\}$$

where F is a new (trap-) symbol. Now we construct the following sets of productions:

$$P_i = \{a^{(i)} \to \alpha^{(i)} : a \to \alpha \in P, \alpha \in Y_i\} \cup \{b \to F : b \in W \setminus V^{(i)}\},\ 1 \leqq i \leqq n,$$

$$P' = \{a^{(i)} \to a^{(i+1 \bmod n)} : a \in V,\ 1 \leqq i \leqq n\} \cup \{a \to F : a \in V \cup \{F\}\},$$

$$P'' = \{a^{(i)} \to a : 1 \leqq i \leqq n,\ a \in V\} \cup \{a \to F : a \in V \cup \{F\}\},$$

and we consider the ETOL system

$$G' = (W, V', \{P_1, P_2, \ldots, P_n, P', P''\}, S^{(1)}).$$

We show $L(G') = L(G)$. This can be seen as follows. Let α be a word over $V^{(i)}$. We can apply to α only the tables P_i, P', or P'' (applications of the other tables introduce F). In the first case we simulate a derivation in G with respect to a word $y \in \overline{Y}_i^+$, and again we obtain a word β over $V^{(i)}$. In the second case, we increase all "indexes" by 1 (modulo n), i.e. we derive the version of α over $V^{(i+1)}$. In the third case, we obtain the non-indexed version of α and now the derivation is blocked (more precisely we introduce F in the next step). By this explanation it easily follows that $L(G) = L(G')$.

This proves $\mathcal{L}(\text{par}) \subseteq \mathcal{L}(\text{ETOL})$.

Lemma 10.3. $\mathcal{L}(\text{cont}) \subseteq \mathcal{L}(\text{seq})$.

Proof. We prove this inclusion in two steps. First we present a normal form for the selector language, and the second step proves that selective substitution grammars with such selector languages have an equivalent one with a sequential selector language.

Step 1. Let $G = (V, V', P, S, K)$ be a selective substitution grammar with the continuous selector language $K = \bigcup_{i=1}^{n} X_i^* \overline{Y}_i^+ Z_i^*$. We consider the sets

$$V^{(i)} = \{a^{(i)} : a \in V\}, \hat{V}^{(i)} = \{\hat{a}^{(i)} : a \in V\},$$

and

$$W = V \cup \bigcup_{i=1}^{n} V^{(i)} \cup \bigcup_{i=1}^{n} \hat{V}^{(i)}$$

(all the sets V, $V^{(i)}$, and $\hat{V}^{(i)}$ are pairwise disjoint), the set of productions

$$\begin{aligned} P' = {} & \{\hat{a}^{(i)} \to \alpha^{(i)} : a \to \alpha \in P, 1 \leqq i \leqq n\} \\ & \cup \{a^{(i)} \to a^{(i+1 \bmod n)} : a \in V, 1 \leqq i \leqq n\} \\ & \cup \{a^{(i)} \to \hat{a}^{(i+1 \bmod n)} : a \in V, 1 \leqq i \leqq n\} \\ & \cup \{a^{(i)} \to a : a \in V, 1 \leqq i \leqq n\}, \end{aligned}$$

and the selector language

$$K' = \overline{U} \cup X\overline{Y}^+Z$$

with

$$U = \bigcup_{i=1}^{n} V^{(i)}, X = \bigcup_{i=1}^{n} X_i^{(i)}, Y = \bigcup_{i=1}^{n} \overline{Y}_i^{(i)}, Z = \bigcup_{i=1}^{n} Z_i^{(i)},$$

and the selective substitution grammar

$$G' = (W, V', P', S^{(1)}, K').$$

By the definition of the selector language we cannot rewrite words which contain a letter of V. Now let $w^{(i)} = a_1^{(i)} a_2^{(i)} \dots a_k^{(i)}$, $a_j^{(i)} \in V^{(i)}$, $1 \leqq j \leqq k$, $1 \leqq i \leqq n$. Then we have to rewrite all letters of $w^{(i)}$. The only words which can be derived in one step without blocking the derivation are $w^{(i+1)} = a_1^{(i+1)} a_2^{(i+1)} \dots a_k^{(i+1)}$ and $w' = a_1^{(i+1)} \dots a_r^{(i+1)} \times \hat{a}_{r+1}^{(i+1)} \dots \hat{a}_{r+s}^{(i+1)} a_{r+s+1}^{(i+1)} \dots a_k^{(i+1)}$ where in the latter case $a_1 a_2 \dots a_r \in X_{i+1}$, $a_{r+1} a_{r+2} \dots a_{r+s} \in Y_{i+1}$, $a_{r+s+1} a_{r+s+2} \dots a_k \in Z_{i+1}$. In the former case we get a word over $V^{(i+1)}$, in the latter case we can continue in G' only as in G with respect to a word in $X_{i+1}^* \overline{Y}_{i+1}^+ Z_{i+1}^*$ and we obtain $a_1^{(i+1)} \ldots a_r^{(i+1)}\beta_{r+1}^{(i+1)} \ldots \beta_{r+s}^{(i+1)}a_{r+s+1}^{(i+1)} \ldots a_k^{(i+1)}$ which is in $(V^{(i+1)})^*$, too. Now we can repeat the process, i.e. we can change the "index" or we simulate a derivation step in G.

Now it is easy to see that $L(G) = L(G')$.

Step 2. Let $L \in \mathcal{L}(\text{cont})$. By Step 1 we can assume that $L = L(G')$ for some selective substitution grammar $G' = (V, V', P, S, K)$ with $K = \bar{U}^+ \cup X^*\bar{Y}^+Z^*$. Now we define the new alphabets

$$\hat{X} = \{\hat{a} : a \in X\},\ \check{Z} = \{\check{a} : a \in Z\},\ Y' = \{a' : a \in Y\},\ U'' = \{a'' : a \in U\},$$

$$W = V \cup \hat{X} \cup \check{Z} \cup Y' \cup U'',$$

the production set

$$P' = \{a \to \hat{a} : a \in X\} \cup \{a \to \check{a} : a \in Z\} \cup \{\hat{a} \to a : a \in X\}$$

$$\cup \{\check{a} \to a : a \in Z\} \cup \{a \to a' : a \in Y\} \cup \{a \to a'' : a \in U\}$$

$$\cup \{a' \to w : a \to w \in P, a \in Y\} \cup \{a'' \to w : a \to w \in P, a \in U\},$$

the selector language

$$K' = K_1 \cup K_2 \cup K_3 \cup K_4 \cup K_5$$

with

$$K_1 = (W \setminus V)^* \bar{V} V^*,\ K_2 = V^*\bar{\hat{X}}(\hat{X} \cup Y' \cup \check{Z})^*,$$

$$K_3 = V^*\bar{Y}'(Y' \cup \check{Z})^*,\ K_4 = X^*\bar{\check{Z}}\check{Z}^*,\ K_5 = V^*\bar{U}''U''^*,$$

and the selective substitution grammar

$$G'' = (W, V', P', S, K').$$

Clearly, K is a sequential selector language.

The equality $L(G') = L(G'')$ follows if the following facts are taken into consideration. A derivation starting from $w \in V^*$ begins with a rewriting of each letter of w by $\hat{a}$, $\check{a}$, a', or a'' in a non-deterministic way from left to right according to K_1. Let us obtain the word v. After that, we rewrite v, again from left to right. According to K_5 this is possible if $v \in (U'')^*$ or, according to K_2, K_3, and K_4, if $v \in XYZ$. In both cases we obtain a word over V, say z, and one can see that $w \overset{*}{\Rightarrow} z$ holds in G'' if and only if $w \Rightarrow z$ holds in G'.

Without proof we mention the opposite inclusion.

Lemma 10.4. $\mathcal{L}(\text{seq}) \subseteq \mathcal{L}(\text{cont})$.

Theorem 10.3. $\mathcal{L}(\text{par}) \subset \mathcal{L}(\text{seq}) = \mathcal{L}(\text{cont})$.

Proof. The equality $\mathcal{L}(\text{seq}) = \mathcal{L}(\text{cont})$ is a direct consequence of Lemmas 10.3 and 10.4. The inclusion $\mathcal{L}(\text{par}) \subseteq \mathcal{L}(\text{cont})$ follows by definition (take $X_i = Z_i = \emptyset$, $1 \leq i \leq n$). Example 10.6. proves that $\mathcal{L}(\text{seq})$ contains $\mathcal{L}(\text{fRC, CF} - \lambda)$. Since $\mathcal{L}(\text{fRC, CF} - \lambda) \supset \mathcal{L}(\text{ET0L})$ (by Theorem 1.5.11) and from Theorem 10.1, the strictness of the inclusion follows.

Theorem 10.3 tells that sequential rewriting is more powerful than purely parallel rewriting, however, partially parallel rewriting — precisely the rewriting of subwords — has the same generative capacity as sequential rewriting.

Open problems

10.1. Prove or disprove $\mathcal{L}(\text{seq}) = \mathcal{L}(\text{RE})$.

10.2. Prove or disprove $\mathcal{L}(\text{2-seq}) = \mathcal{L}(\text{seq})$, where $\mathcal{L}(\text{2-seq})$ is the family of all languages generated by selective substitution grammars whose selectors are of the form $K = X^*\overline{Y}Z^*$ or $K = X_1^*\overline{Y}_1Z_1^* \cup X_2^*\overline{Y}_2Z_2^*$.

10.3. Find a language in $\mathcal{L}(\text{ETOL}) \setminus \mathcal{L}(\text{1-cont})$, where $\mathcal{L}(\text{1-cont})$ is the family of languages generated by selective substitution grammars with a selector language of the form $X^*\overline{Y}^+Z^*$. (It is known that $\mathcal{L}(\text{1-cont}) \setminus \mathcal{L}(\text{ETOL}) \neq \emptyset$, see EHRENFEUCHT et al. (1980).)

Exercises

10.1. Construct selective substitution grammars for the languages $L_1 = \{a^nb^nc^n : n \geqq 1\}$ and $L_2 = \{a^{2^n} : n \geqq 1\}$.

10.2. Describe Russian parallel, context-sensitive grammars and context-free grammars with leftmost derivations by selective substitution grammars.

10.3. Prove Lemma 10.1.

10.4. Prove that each language $L \in \mathcal{L}(\text{seq})$ can be generated by a selective substitution grammar such that its selector language is of the form $X^*\overline{Y}Z^* \cup \overline{U}^+$ (see KLEIJN and ROZENBERG (1981-b)).

10.5. Prove Lemma 10.4 (see KLEIJN and ROZENBERG (1981-b), use Exercise 10.4).

10.6. Prove that $\mathcal{L}(s\mathcal{K})$ is closed under union if $\mathcal{K}$ is closed under union and disjoint bar-preserving finite letter substitutions.

10.7. Prove the closure of $\mathcal{L}(s\mathcal{K})$ under intersection with regular sets if $\mathcal{K}$ is closed under disjoint bar-preserving finite substitutions.

10.8. A regular pattern grammar is a construct $G = (V, V', P, S, K)$ where V, V', P, S are as in a selection substitution grammar and K is a regular language over $\{0, 1\}$. Then $x_1x_2 \ldots x_n \Rightarrow \beta_1\beta_2 \ldots \beta_n$, $x_i \in V$, $1 \leqq i \leqq n$, holds in G iff there is a word $\alpha = i_1i_2 \ldots i_n \in K$ such that $\beta_j = x_j$ if $i_j = 0$ and $x_j \to \beta_j \in P$ if $i_j = 1$ (i.e. all letters of x corresponding to an occurrence of 1 in α have to be rewritten). The associated language $L(G)$ is defined as usual. Let $\mathcal{L}(\text{rp})$ be the family of languages generated by regular pattern grammars.

a) Prove that the language of Example 10.1 is in $\mathcal{L}(\text{rp})$.
b) Prove that each $L \in \mathcal{L}(\text{rp})$ can be generated by a selective substitution grammar.
c) Prove $\mathcal{L}(\text{CF}) \subseteq \mathcal{L}(\text{rp})$.

10.9. Let $\mathcal{L}(n\text{-seq})$ be the family of all languages generated by selective substitution grammars with a sequential selector language of the form $K = \bigcup_{i=1}^{m} X_i^*\overline{Y}_iZ_i^*$ with $m \geqq n$. Let $\mathcal{L}(n\text{-par})$ and $\mathcal{L}(n\text{-cont})$ be defined analogously. Prove $\mathcal{L}(\text{par}) = \mathcal{L}(\text{2-par})$, $\mathcal{L}(\text{1-par}) = \mathcal{L}(\text{EOL})$, $\mathcal{L}(\text{cont}) = \mathcal{L}(\text{2-cont})$, $\mathcal{L}(\text{seq}) = \mathcal{L}(\text{3-seq})$,, $\mathcal{L}(\text{1-seq}) = \mathcal{L}(\text{CF})$ (see open problem 10.3).

Bibliographical remarks

Selective substitution grammars have been introduced by ROZENBERG (1977) in a more general fashion (see p. 283) but in all following papers the grammars are defined as in Definition 10.1 or slight modifications of it are used. GONCZAROWSKI et al. (1983-a) and (1983-b) discussed the effect of the selector language (family) to closure properties (e.g. Theorem 10.1) and on normal forms and related questions, respectively. Characterizations of $\mathscr{L}$(CF) and other families (as in Lemma 10.1) have been presented in KLEIJN and ROZENBERG (1981-a). The relationship between purely sequential, purely parallel, and partially parallel (continuous) rewriting are the subject of EHRENFEUCHT et al. (1980) and KLEIJN and ROZENBERG (1981-b). An analogous study comparing sequential and Indian parallel rewriting has been presented by KLEIJN and ROZENBERG (1980). Further papers on selective substitution grammars are ROZENBERG and WOOD (1980) and KLEIJN and ROZENBERG (1981-a). KLEIJN'S dissertation (1983) presents a summary of results in this area. The papers by GONCZAROWSKI and SHAMIR (1985) and GONCZAROWSKI and WARMUTH (1985) present some results on the complexity of parsing in special regular pattern grammars (see Exercise 10.8). ROZENBERG (1985) used an approach by selective substitution grammars for unifying formal languages to obtain a analogous framework for the automata oriented to formal languages.

Finally we mention that other attempts at unifying approaches of rewriting have been made by DIETERICH (1978), WOOD (1976), and ROVAN (1981). The latter two use gsm-mappings for simulating rules/tables/matrices. They have discussed e.g. the effect of the number of gsm mappings and the number of states in the gsms.

Bibliography

Besides the papers and monographs quoted in the text the following list also contains some further papers on regulated rewriting which present some material which is not reflected in the text. Thus we hope that it contains most of the papers of interest, but we are sure that it is not an exhaustive bibliography on regulated rewriting.

ABRAHAM, S. (1965), Some questions of phrase-structure grammars. Comput. Linguistics 4, 61–70.

ABRAHAM, S. (1972), Compound and serial grammars. Inform. Control **20**, 432–438.

AGASANDJAN, G. A. (1967), Automata with a variable structure. Dokl. Akad. Nauk SSSR **174**, 529–530 (*in Russian*).

AHO, A. V. (1968), Indexed grammars. An extension of context-free grammars. Journal of the ACM **15**, 647–671.

AHO, A. V., and J. D. ULLMAN (1972), The Theory of Parsing, Translation, and Compiling. Prentice Hall Inc., Englewood Cliffs.

ALBERT, J. (1973), M-indizierte Grammatiken. Techn. Report Nr. 11, Univ. Karlsruhe.

ALBERT, J. (1982), A note on the undecidability of context-free-ness. RAIRO **16**, 3–11.

ASVELD, P. R. J. (1976), Controlled iteration grammars and full Hyper-AFL's. Inform. Control **34**, 248–269.

ASVELD, P. R. J. (1978), Iterated context-independent rewriting. Dissertation, Techn. Hogeschool Twente.

ASVELD, P. R. J. (1981), Time and space complexity of inside-out macro languages. Intern. J. Comp. Math. **10**, 3–14.

BACHMANN, P. (1979), Theoretical investigations on functional grammars. EIK **15**, 497–506.

BAER, R. M., and E. H. SPANIER (1969), Referenced automata and metaregular families. J. Comp. Syst. Sci. **3**, 423–446.

BAKER, B. S. (1974), Non-context-free grammars generating context-free languages. Inform. Control **24**, 231–246.

BAR-HILLEL, Y., M. PERLES, and E. SHAMIR (1961), On formal properties of simple phrase structure grammars. Zeitschrift für Phonetik, Sprachwiss. u. Kommunikation **14**, 143–172.

BAR-HILLEL, Y. and E. SHAMIR (1960), Finite-state languages. Formal representation and adequacy problems. Bull. Res. Council of Israel **8F**, 155–166.

BARTH, G. (1977), Protokollgrammatiken. Ein Konzept zur zeitvarianten Kontrolle bei kontextfreien Ersetzungen. Dissertation, Univ. Kaiserslautern.

BARTH, G. (1978-a), Grammars with dynamic control. *In:* AUSIELLO, G., and C. BÖHM (eds.), Proc. 5th ICALP, LNCS 62

BARTH, G. (1978-b), Mastering context-sensitivity in programming languages. *In:* WINKOWSKI, J. (ed.), Proc. 7th MFCS, LNCS **64**, 124–133

BEAUQUIER, J. (1979), Deux familles de langages incomparables. Inform. Control **43**, 101–122.

BLATTNER, M. (1973), The unsolvability of the equality problem for the sentential forms of context-free grammars. J. Comput. Syst. Sci. **7**, 463–468.

BLATTNER, M., and M. LATTEUX (1981), Parikh bounded languages. *In:* NIELSEN, M. (ed.), Proc. 8th ICALP, LNCS **115**, 316–323

BLUM, N. (1983), More on the power of chain rules in context-free grammars. Theor. Comp. Sc. **27**, 287–295.

BOOK, R. V. (1973), On the structure of context-sensitive grammars. Int. J. Comput. Inf. Sci. 2, 129–139.
BRAINERD, B. (1968), An analog of a theorem about context-free languages. Inform. Control **11**, 561–568.
BRAUNSTEINEROVA, E., and J. HROMKOVIC (1984), Graphic controlled table Lindenmayer systems. *In:* DEMETROVICS, J., and J. KELEMEN (eds.), Proc. 3rd IMYCS, 53–59.
BUCHER, W. (1981), A note on a problem in the theory of grammatical complexity. Theor. Comp. Sc. **14**, 337–344.
BUCHER, W., K. CULIK II, H. A. MAURER, and D. WOTSCHKE (1981), Concise description of finite languages. Theor. Comp. Sc. **14**, 227–246.
BUCHER, W., and J. HAGAUER (1983), It is decidable whether a regular language is pure context-free. Theor. Comp. Sc. **26**, 233–241.
BUNKE, H. (1979), Programmed graph grammars. *In:* CLAUS, V., H. EHRIG and G. ROZENBERG (eds.), Proc. Graph Grammars and Their Application to Computer Science and Biology, LNCS **73**, 155–166
BUTTELMANN, H. W., A. PYSTER, and L. H. REEKER (1974), Grammars without syntactic variables. Univ. of Oregon, Dept. Comp. Science, Techn. rep. 74-1.
CIOBUTARU, S., and Gh. Păun (1975), On the generative capacity of strict global grammars. *In:* SIEFKES, D. (ed.), GI — 4. Jahrestagung, LNCS 26.
CREMERS, A. B., and S. GINSBURG (1975), Context-free grammar forms. J. Comp. Syst. Sci. **11**, 86–117.
CREMERS, A. B., H. A. MAURER, and O. MAYER (1973), A note on leftmost restricted random context grammars. Inform. Proc. Letters **2**, 31–33.
CREMERS, A. B., and O. MAYER (1973), On matrix languages. Inform. Control **23**, 86–96.
CREMERS, A. B., and O. MAYER (1974), On vector languages. J. Comp. Syst. Sci. **8**, 158–166.
CREMERS, A. B., O. MAYER, and K. WEISS (1974), On the complexity of regulated rewriting. Inform. Control **25**, 10–19.
CRESPI-REGHIZZI, S., and D. MANDRIOLI (1977), Petri-nets and Szilard languages. Inform. Control **33**, 177–192.
CULIK II, K., and I. FRIS (1977), The decidability of the equivalence problem for DOL systems. Inform. Control **35**, 20–39.
CULIK II, K., and T. HEAD (1983), Transductions and the parallel generation of languages. Intern. J. Comp. Math **13**, 3–15.
CULIK II, K., and H. A. MAURER (1977), Tree controlled grammars. Computing **19**, 129–139.
CULIK II, K., and J. OPATRNY (1974), Literal homomorphisms of OL languages. Intern. J. Comp. Math. **4**, 247–267.
CULIK II, K., and D. WOOD (1979), Doubly deterministic tabled OL systems. Int. J. Comp. Inf. Sci. **8**, 335–347.
DASSOW, J. (1976), Über quasideterministische Sprachen. Rostock. Math. Kolloq. **1**, 51–60.
DASSOW, J. (1979-a), ETOL systems and compound grammars. Rostock. Math. Kolloq. **11**, 41 to 46.
DASSOW, J. (1979-b), On the circular closure of languages. EIK **15**, 87–94.
DASSOW, J. (1979-c), Concentration dependent OL systems. Intern. J. Comp. Math. **7**, 187–206.
DASSOW, J. (1980), Some extensions of Indian parallel context-free grammars. Acta Cybern. **4**, 303–310.
DASSOW, J. (1982), Grammars with valuations — a discrete model for self-organization of biopolymers. Discr. Applied Math. **4**, 161–174.
DASSOW, J. (1983), A note on programmed OL systems. Inform. Sci. **30**, 1–4.
DASSOW, J. (1984-a), On some extensions of Russian parallel context-free grammars. Acta Cybern. **6**, 355–360.
DASSOW, J. (1984-b), Remarks on the complexity of regulated rewriting. Fundamenta Informaticae **7**, 83–103.
DASSOW, J. (1984-c), On deterministic random context *L* systems. *In:* WECHSUNG, G. (ed.), Proc. 2nd Frege Conf., Math. Research 20, Akademie-Verlag Berlin, 309–313.
DASSOW, J. (1985-a), Comparison of some types of regulated rewriting. *In:* DEMETROVICS, J., and A. SALOMAA (eds.), Proc. Colloq. Algebra, Logic and Combinatorics in Comp. Sc., Colloq. Math. Soc. J. Bolyai 42, North-Holland Publ. Co., 301–313.

DASSOW, J. (1985-b), On compound Lindenmayer systems. *In:* ROZENBERG, G., and A. SALOMAA (eds.), The Book of L, Springer-Verlag, Berlin, 75–86.
DASSOW, J. (1986), Pure grammars with regulated rewriting. Rev. Roum. Math. Pures Appl. **31**, 657–666.
DASSOW, J. (1988-a), Pure languages of regulated rewriting and their codings. Acta Cybernetica 8, 227–235.
DASSOW, J. (1988-b), On the sequence equivalence problem for OL systems with controlled derivations. Computers and Artificial Intelligence **7**, 97–105.
DASSOW, J., and U. FEST (1984), On regulated *L* systems. Rostock. Math. Kolloq. **25**, 99–118.
DASSOW, J., and GH. PĂUN (1984-a), Codings of pure languages obtained by regulated rewriting. Found. Control Engineering **9**, 3–14.
DASSOW, J., and GH. PĂUN (1984-b), On the description of languages by regulated rewriting. *In:* DEMETROVICS, J., and J. KELEMEN (eds.), Proc. 3rd IMYCS, 15–21.
DASSOW, J., and GH. PĂUN (1985-a), Further remarks on the complexity of regulated rewriting. Kybernetika **21**, 213–227.
DASSOW, J., and GH. PĂUN (1985-b), On ordered variants of some regulated grammars. EIK **21**, 491–504.
DASSOW, J., and GH. PĂUN (1986-a), Further remarks on pure grammars with regulated rewriting. Rev. Roum. Math. Pures Appl. **31**, 855–864.
DASSOW, J., and GH. PĂUN (1986-b), Some notes on the complexity of regulated rewriting. Bull. Math. Soc. Sci. Math. R. S. Roumanie **30**.
DEMBIŃSKI, P., and J. MAŁUSZYNSKI (1978), Attribute grammars and two-level grammars: a unifying approach. *In:* WINKOWSKI, J. (ed.), Proc. 7th MFCS, LNCS 64, 143–154.
DIETERICH, E. W. (1978), Context-pattern grammars: a unifying approach to generalized phrase structure grammars. TUM-INFO-7827, Techn. Univ. München.
DUSKE, J., and R. PARCHMANN (1984), Linear indexed languages. Theor. Comput. Sci. **32**, 47–60.
DUSKE, J., R. PARCHMANN, and H. SCHUHMACHER (1976), A pattern representation of indexed languages. Inform. Proc. Letters **5**, 152–154.
DUSKE, J., R. PARCHMANN, and J. SPECHT (1979-a), A homomorphic characterization of indexed languages. EIK **15**, 187–195.
DUSKE, J., R. PARCHMANN, and J. SPECHT (1979-b), Szilard languages of IO grammars. Inform. Control **40**, 319–331.
EHRENFEUCHT, A., H. C. M. KLEIJN, and G. ROZENBERG (1985), Adding global forbidding context to context-free grammars. Theor. Comput. Sci. **37**, 337–360.
EHRENFEUCHT, A., H. A. MAURER, and G. ROZENBERG (1980), Continuous grammars. Inform. Control **46**, 71–91.
EHRENFEUCHT, A., and G. ROZENBERG (1974-a), The equality of EOL languages and codings of OL languages. Intern. J. Comput. Math. **4**, 95–104.
EHRENFEUCHT, A., and G. ROZENBERG (1974-b), Nonterminals versus homomorphisms in defining languages for some classes of rewriting systems. Acta Inform. **3**, 265–283.
EHRENFEUCHT, A., and G. ROZENBERG (1976), On proving that certain languages are not ETOL. Acta Inform. **6**, 407–415.
EHRENFEUCHT, A., and G. ROZENBERG (1977), On some context-free languages that are not deterministic ETOL languages. RAIRO **11**, 273–291.
EHRENFEUCHT, A., and G. ROZENBERG (1980), DOS systems and languages. *In:* DE BAKKER, J., and J. VAN LEEUWEN (eds.), Proc. 7th ICALP, LNCS 85, 134–141.
ENGELFRIET J., and E. M. SCHMIDT (1977/78), IO and OI, I and II. J. Comput. Syst. Sci. **15**, 328 to 353, and **16**, 67–99.
ENGELFRIET, J. (1985), Hierarchies of hyper-AFL's. J. Comput. Syst. Sci. **30**, 86–115.
FERMENT, D. (1984-a), Langages matriciels et principalité. Dissertation, Univ. Paris VII.
FERMENT, D. (1984-b), Principality results about some matrix language families. *In:* PARADAENS, J. (ed.), Proc. 11th ICALP, LNCS 172, 151–161.
FILE, L. G. (1977), The characterization of some families of languages by classes of indexed grammars. Dissertation, Pennsylvania State Univ., Dept. Comp. Science.
FISCHER, M. J. (1968), Grammars with MACRO-like productions. Dissertation. Harvard Univ.
FLOYD, R. W. (1962), On the non-existence of a phrase-structure grammar for ALGOL 60. Comm. of the ACM **5**, 483–484.

FRIANT, J. (1968), Grammaires ordonnées — grammaires matricielles. Univ. Montréal, MA — 101.
FRIANT, J. (1971), Grammaires de Chomsky, matrices de règles, fonctions de poids. Dissertation, Univ. Paris.
FRIS, I. (1968), Grammars with partial ordering of the rules. Inform. Control **12**, 415—425.
GABOW, H. M. (1984), Priming the pump for lower bounds on Chomsky normal form grammars. Bull. EATCS **20**, 54—67.
GABRIELIAN, S. A. (1970), Pure grammars and pure languages. Techn. rep. CSRR 2027, Univ. of Waterloo, Dept. Comp. Science.
GALJUKSHOV, B. S. (1978), Compound grammars. Math. Linguistics and Theory of Algorithms, Univ. Kalinin, 15—34 (*in Russian*).
GAREY, M. R., and D. S. JOHNSON (1979), Computers and Intractability. A Guide to the Theory of *NP*-Completeness. W. H. Freeman and Co., San Francisco.
GHEORGHE, M., and GH. PĂUN (1986), Two (infinite?) hierarchies of vector languages. Bull. EATCS **29**, 27—31.
GINSBURG, S. (1966), The Mathematical Theory of Context-Free Languages. McGraw Hill Book Comp., New York.
GINSBURG, S. (1975), Algebraic and Automata-Theoretic Properties of Formal Languages. North-Holland Publ. Co., Amsterdam.
GINSBURG, S., and H. G. RICE (1962), Two families of languages related to ALGOL. Journal of the ACM **9**, 350—371.
GINSBURG, S., and G. ROZENBERG (1974), TOL schemes and control sets. Inform. Control **27**, 109—125.
GINSBURG, S., and E. H. SPANIER (1968), Control sets on grammars. Math. Syst. Th. **2**, 159—177.
GONCZAROWSKI, J., H. C. M. KLEIJN, and G. ROZENBERG (1983-a), Grammatical constructions in selective substitution grammars. Acta Cybern. **6**, 239—269.
GONCZAROWSKI, J., H. C. M. KLEIJN, and G. ROZENBERG (1983-b), Closure properties of selective substitution grammars I and II. Intern. J. Comp. Math. **14**, 19—42, and 109—135.
GONCZAROWSKI, J., and E. SHAMIR (1985), Pattern selector grammars and several parsing algorithms in the context-free style. J. Comput. Syst. Sci. **30**, 249—273.
GONCZAROWSKI, J., and M. K. WARMUTH (1985), Application of scheduling theory to formal language theory. Theor. Comput. Sci. **37**, 217—243.
GREIBACH, S. A. (1977), Control sets of context-free grammar forms. J. Comput. Syst. Sci. **15**, 35—98.
GREIBACH, S. A., and J. E. HOPCROFT (1969), Scattered context grammars. J. Comput. Syst. Sci. **3**, 232—247.
GRUSKA, J. (1967), On a classification of context-free languages. Kybernetica **13**, 22—29.
GRUSKA, J., (1969), Some classifications of context-free languages. Inform. Control **14**, 152—179.
GRUSKA, J. (1973), Descriptional complexity of context-free languages. Proc. 2nd MFCS, 71—83.
HAYASHI, T. (1973), On the derivation trees of indexed grammars. An extension of the *uvwxy* theorem. Publ. RIMS, Kyoto Univ. **9**, 61—92.
HERMAN, G. T., and G. ROZENBERG (1975), Developmental Systems and Languages. North-Holland Publ. Co., Amsterdam.
HERMES, H. (1961), Aufzählbarkeit, Entscheidbarkeit, Berechenbarkeit. Springer-Verlag, Berlin, Heidelberg, New York (*engl. Translation* 1965).
HOPCROFT, J. E., and J. D. ULLMAN (1969), Formal Languages and Their Relation to Automata. Addison-Wesley, Reading.
HÖPNER, M. (1974), Über den Zusammenhang von Szilard-Sprachen und Matrixgrammatiken. Bericht Nr. 12, Univ. Hamburg.
IBARRA, O. H. (1970), Simple matrix grammars. Inform. Control **17**, 359—394.
IBARRA, O. H., S. K. SAHNI, and C. E. KIM (1976), Finite automata with multiplication. Theor. Comput. Sci. **2**, 271—294.
IGARASHI, Y. (1977), The tape complexity of some classes of Szilard languages. SIAM J. Comput. 460—466.
JANTZEN, M. (1979), A note on vector grammars. Inform. Proc. Letters **8**, 32—33.
JÜRGENSEN, H., and D. WOOD (1982), Self-regulating L systems. EIK **18**, 375—387.
KASAI, T. (1970), An hierarchy between context-free and context-sensitive languages. J. Comput. Syst. Sci. **4**, 492—508.

KELEMEN, J. (1984-a), Conditional grammars: motivations, definitions, and some properties. *In:* PEAK, I., and J. SZEP (eds.), Proc. Conf. Autom., Lang., Math. Sci., Salgotarjan, 110–123.

KELEMEN, J. (1984-b), Conditional grammars and their use for the investigation of properties of production systems. Dissertation. Comput. Centre of the Acad. of Sci. Moscow (*in Russian*).

KELEMEN, J. (1985), On measuring complexity of rule-based systems. *In:* VAN BEMMEL, J. H., et al. (eds.), Proc. Int. Conf. Comp. Aided Medical Decision Making, North-Holland Publ. Comp.

KELEMENOVA, A. (1982), Grammatical complexity of context-free languages and normal forms of context-free grammars. *In:* MIKULECKY, P. (ed.), Proc. 2nd IMYCS.

KELEMENOVA, A., and J. KELEMEN (1985), On hierarchy and closure properties of languages generated by *c*-grammars. *In:* IVANYI, A. (ed.), Proc. First Conf. of Program Designers, Budapest, 83–88.

KHABBAZ, N. A. (1974-a), A geometric hierarchy of languages. J. Comp. Syst. Sci. **8**, 142–157.

KHABBAZ, N. A. (1974-b), Control sets on linear grammars. Inform. Control **25**, 206–221.

KLEENE, C. C. (1967), Introduction to Metamathematics. North-Holland Publ. Co., Amsterdam.

KLEIJN, H. C. M. (1983), Selective substitution grammars based on context-free productions. Dissertation, Univ. Leiden.

KLEIJN, H. C. M., and G. ROZENBERG (1980), A study in parallel rewriting systems. Inform. Control **44**, 134–163.

KLEIJN, H. C. M., and G. ROZENBERG (1981-a), Context-free-like restrictions on selective rewriting, Theor. Comput. Sci. **16**, 237–269.

KLEIJN, H. C. M., and G. ROZENBERG (1981-b), Sequential, continuous, and parallel grammars. Inform. Control **48**, 221–260.

KLEIJN, H. C. M., and G. ROZENBERG (1983-a), On the generative power of regular pattern grammars. Acta Inform. **20**, 391–411.

KLEIJN, H. C. M., and G. ROZENBERG (1983-b), Multi grammars. Intern. J. Comput. Math. **12**, 177–201.

KNUTH, D. (1968), Semantics of context-free languages. Math. Syst. Th. **2**, 127–145.

KOSARAJU, S. R. (1982), Decidability of reachability in vector addition systems. Proc. 14th Symp. Theory of Comput. 267–281.

KOSTER, C. H. A. (1972), Affix grammars. Proc. IFIP Conf. Algol 68 Implementation, 95–109.

KRAL, J. (1969), On multiple grammars. Kybernetika **1**, 60–85.

KRAL, J. (1973), A note on grammars with regular restrictions. Kybernetika **9**, 159–161.

KUDLEK, M. (1975), Comparing several ways of context-independent parallel rewriting. *In:* SIEFKES, D. (ed.), GI – 4. Jahrestagung, LNCS 26, 122–130.

KUICH, W. (1971), The complexity of skewlinear tuple languages and 0-regular languages. Inform. Control **19**, 353–367.

KUICH, W. (1976), The structure generating function of some families of languages. Inform Control **32**, 85–92.

KUICH, W., and H. A. MAURER (1970), Tuple languages. Proc. Intern. Comp. Symp., Bonn, 881 to 891.

KUICH, W., and H. A. MAURER (1971-a), The structure generating function and entropy of tuple languages. Inform. Control **19**, 195–203.

KUICH, W., and H. A. MAURER (1971-b), On the inherent ambiguity of simple tuple languages. Computing **7**, 194–203.

KURODA, S. Y. (1964), Classes of languages and linear bounded automata. Inform. Control **7**, 207–223.

LATTEUX, M. (1979), Substitutions dans les EDTOL systèmes ultralinéaires. Inform. Control **42**, 194–206.

LATTEUX, M., and A. TERLUTTE (1985), The Parikh-boundedness of ETOL languages of finite index. *In:* ROZENBERG, G., and A. SALOMAA (eds.), The Book of L, Springer-Verlag, Berlin, 253–258.

VAN LEEUWEN, J. (1972), Rule-labelled programs: a study of a generalization of context-free grammars and some classes of formal languages. Dissertation, Univ. of Utrecht.

VAN LEEUWEN, J. (1975), The membership question for ETOL languages is polynomial complete. Inform. Proc. Letters **3**, 138–143.

van Leeuwen, J. (1979), A useful lemma for context-free programmed grammars. Acta Inform. **11**, 373–386.
Leipälä, R. (1978), On context-free matrix forms. Inform. Control **39**, 158–176.
Leipälä, R. (1979-a), On the generative capacity of context-free matrix forms. Intern. J. Comput. Math. **7**, 251–269.
Leipälä, R. (1979-b), Generation of context-free languages by matrix forms. Ann. Univ. Turku, Ser. A1, **179**.
Leipälä, R. (1979-c), On matrix forms. Dissertation, Univ. of Turku.
Lepistö, T. (1973), On ordered context-free grammars. Inform. Control **22**, 56–68.
Levitina, M. K. (1972), On some grammars with global productions, NTI, Ser. 2, No. 3, 32–36 (*in Russian*).
Lindenmayer, A. (1968), Mathematical models for cellular interaction in development, I and II. J. Theor. Biology **18**, 280–315.
Liu, L. Y., and P. Weiner (1973), An infinite hierarchy of intersections of context-free languages. Math. Syst. Th. **7**, 187–192.
Lomkovskaja, M. V. (1972-a), Conditional grammars and intermediate classes of languages. Soviet Math. Dokl. **207**, 781–784 (*in Russian*).
Lomkovskaja, M. V. (1972-b), On some properties of c-conditional grammars. NTI, Ser. **2**, No. 1, 16–21 (*in Russian*).
Lomkovskaja, M. V. (1972-c), On c-conditional and other commutative grammars. NTI, Ser. 2, No. 2, 28–31 (*in Russian*).
Luker, M. (1980), Control sets on grammars using depth-first derivations. Math. Syst. Th. **13**, 349–359.
Marcus, S. (1964), Finite grammars and automata. Publ. House of the Romanian Acad. of Sciences, Bucharest (*in Romanian*).
Marcus, S. (ed.) (1977), The formal study of drama. Poetics **6**, No. 3–4.
Marcus, S. (ed.) (1978), La sémiotique formelle du folklore. Klincksieck, Paris; Publ. House of the Romanian Acad. of Science, Bucharest.
Marcus, S. (ed.) (1982), The mathematical semiotics of visual arts. Scientific and Encyclopadic Publ. House, Bucharest (*in Romanian*).
Marcus, M., and Gh. Păun (1987), Valence gsm mappings. Bull. Math. Soc. Sci. Math. R. S. Romania **31**.
Masalagiu, C. (1981), On the regularity of time-variant languages. Analele Univ. Al. I. Cuza, Iasi **27**, 417–420.
Matthews, G. H. (1964), A note on asymmetry in phrase structure grammars. Inform. Control **7**, 360–365.
Maurer, H. A. (1969), Theoretische Grundlagen der Programmiersprachen. Bibliograph. Institut, Mannheim.
Maurer, H. A. (1973), Simple matrix language with a leftmost restriction. Inform. Control **23**, 128–139.
Maurer, H. A., M. Penttonen, A. Salomaa, and D. Wood (1979), On non-context-free grammar forms. Math. Syst. Th. **12**, 297–324.
Maurer, H. A., A. Salomaa, and D. Wood (1977), EOL forms. Acta Inform. 8, 75–96.
Maurer, H. A., A. Salomaa, and D. Wood (1979), Pure grammars. Inform. Control **42**, 103–141.
Mayer, O. (1972), Some restrictive devices for context-free grammars. Inform. Control **20**, 69 to 92.
Meersman, R., and G. Rozenberg (1978), Cooperating grammar systems. *In:* Winkowski, J. (ed.), Proc. 7th MFCS, LNCS 64, 364–373.
Meersman, R., G. Rozenberg, and D. Vermeir (1978), Cooperating grammar systems. Techn. rep. 78–12, Univ. Antwerpen.
Mehlhorn, K. (1979), Parsing macro grammars top down. Inform. Control **40**, 123–143.
Milgram, D., and A. Rosenfeld (1971), A note on scattered context grammars. Inform. Proc. Letters **1**, 47–50.
Moriya, E. (1973-a), Associate languages and derivational complexity of formal grammars and languages. Inform. Control **22**, 139–162.
Moriya, E. (1973-b), Some remarks on state grammars and matrix grammars. Inform. Control **23**, 48–57.

Mückstein-Wotschke, E., D. Wotschke, and P. J. Downey (1977), Size, index and context-sensitivity of partition controlled grammars. Math. Syst. Th. **11**, 47–60.

Naur, P. (ed.) (1960), Report on the algorithmic language ALGOL 60. Comm. of the ACM **3**, 299–314.

Navratil, E. (1970), Context-free grammars with regular conditions. Kybernetika **2**, 118–126.

Nicolescu, R. (1985), Formal languages and programming languages. Dissertation, Univ. of Bucharest (*in Romanian*).

Nielsen, M. (1975), EOL systems with control devices. Acta Inform. **4**, 373–386.

Nielsen, M., G. Rozenberg, A. Salomaa, and S. Skyum (1974), Nonterminals, homomorphisms, and codings in different variations of OL systems, I and II. Acta Inform. **4**, 87–106, and **3**, 357–364.

Ogden, W. (1967), A helpful result for proving inherent ambiguity. Math. Syst. Th. **2**, 191–194.

Parchmann, R. (1984), Balanced context-free languages and indexed languages. EIK **20**, 543 to 556.

Parchmann, R., J. Duske, and J. Specht (1980-a), On deterministic indexed languages. Inform. Control **45**, 48–67.

Parchmann, R., J. Duske, and J. Specht (1980-b), Closure properties of deterministic indexed languages. Inform. Control **46**, 200–218.

Parchmann, R., J. Duske, and J. Specht (1983), Indexed $LL(k)$ grammars. Acta Cybern. **7**, 33–53.

Parikh, R. J. (1966), On context-free languages. Journal of the ACM **13**, 570–581.

Pascu, A., and Gh. Păun (1976), On simple matrix grammars. Bull. Math. Soc. Sci. Math. R. S. Roumanie **20** (68), 333–340.

Pascu, A., and Gh. Păun (1977), A homomorphic representation of simple matrix languages. Inform. Control **35**, 267–275.

Pascu, A., and Gh. Păun (1979), On the planarity of bicolored digraph grammar systems. Discr. Math. **25**, 195–197.

Păun, Gh. (1976), A note on grammars with restricted use of rules. Bull. Math. Soc. Sci. Math. R. S. Roumanie **20** (68), 353–357.

Păun, Gh. (1977-a), The generative capacity of compound grammars. Inform. Control **34**, 50 to 54.

Păun, Gh. (1977-b), On the index of grammars and languages. Inform. Control **35**, 259–266.

Păun, Gh. (1977-c), Contextual grammars with restrictions in derivation. Rev. Roum. Math. Pures Appl. **22**, 1147–1154.

Păun, Gh. (1978-a), On the generative capacity of simple matrix grammars of finite index. Inform. Proc. Letters **7**, 100–102.

Păun, Gh. (1978-b), Linear simple matrix languages. EIK **14**, 377–384.

Păun, Gh. (1979-a), On Szilard languages associated to a matrix grammar. Inform. Proc. Letters **8**, 104–105.

Păun, Gh. (1979-b), On the family of finite index matrix languages. J. Comput. Syst. Sci. **18**, 267 to 280.

Păun, Gh. (1979-c), On the generative capacity of conditional grammars. Inform. Control **43**, 178–186.

Păun, Gh. (1979-d), Normal forms for bicolored digraph grammar systems. Intern. J. Comput. Math. **7**, 109–118.

Păun, Gh. (1979-e), Some further remarks on the family of finite index matrix languages. RAIRO **13**, 289–297.

Păun, Gh. (1979-f), On the generative capacity of tree controlled grammars. Computing **21**, 213 to 220.

Păun, Gh. (1979-g), On the generative capacity of parallel matrix grammars. Bull. Math. Soc. Sci. Math. R. S. Roumanie **23** (71), 367–371.

Păun, Gh. (1979-h), A note on the intersection of context-free languages. Fundamenta Informaticae **2**, 135–139.

Păun, Gh. (1980-a), The Generative Mechanisms of Some Economic Processes. Techn. Publ. House, Bucharest (*in Romanian*).

Păun, Gh. (1980-b), A new generative device: valence grammars. Rev. Roum. Math. Pures Appl. **25**, 911–924.

PĂUN, GH. (1980-c), An infinite hierarchy of matrix languages. Stud. Cerc. Mat. **32**, 697–707 (*in Romanian*).

PĂUN, GH. (1980-d), Some consequences of a result of EHRENFEUCHT and ROZENBERG. RAIRO **14**, 119–122.

PĂUN, GH. (1980-e), The complement of a finite index matrix language is context sensitive. Inform. Control **47**, 166–274 (*with a Corrigendum in*: Inform. Control **51** (1981), 188–192).

PĂUN, GH. (1981-a), The propositional calculus languages versus the Chomsky hierarchy. Stud. Cerc. Mat. **33**, 299–310 (*in Romanian*).

PĂUN, GH. (1981-b), Thue languages and matrix grammars. Found. Control Engineering **6**, 273 to 278.

PĂUN, GH. (1981-c), On some classes of grammars with restrictions in derivation. Mathematica **23** (46), 55–60.

PĂUN, GH. (1981-d), On the place of programming languages in the Chomsky hierarchy. Stud. Cerc. Mat. **33**, 455–466 (*in Romanian*).

PĂUN, GH. (1981-e), On eliminating the λ-rules from simple matrix grammars. Fundamenta Informaticae **4**, 185–195.

PĂUN, GH. (1981-f), Matrix grammars. Scientific and Encyclopadic Publ. House, Bucharest (*in Romanian*).

PĂUN, GH. (1982-a), On simple matrix languages versus scattered context languages. RAIRO **16**, 245–253.

PĂUN, GH. (1982-b), Contextual grammars. Scientific and Encyclopadic Publ. House, Bucharest (*in Romanian*).

PĂUN, GH. (1983), Some context-free-like properties of finite index matrix languages. Bull. Math. Soc. Sci. Math. R. S. Roumanie **27** (75), 83–87.

PĂUN, GH. (1984-a), An elementary proof of a theorem by D. J. ROSENKRANTZ. Stud. Cerc. Mat. **30**, 143–146 (*in Romanian*).

PĂUN, GH. (1984-b), Six nonterminals are enough for generating each r.e. language by a matrix grammar. Intern. J. Comp. Math. **15**, 23–37.

PĂUN, GH. (1984-c), On grammars with double restrictions in derivations. *In:* DEMETROVICS, J., and J. KELEMEN (eds.), Proc. 3rd IMYCS, 126–131.

PĂUN, GH. (1985-a), On the Parikh-boundedness of matrix languages. Bull. EATCS **25**, 34–37.

PĂUN, GH. (1985-b), On leftmost derivation restriction in regulated rewriting. Rev. Roum. Math. Pures Appl. **30**, 751–758.

PĂUN, GH. (1985-c), A variant of random context grammars: semi-conditional grammars. Theor. Comput. Sci. **41**, 1–17.

PĂUN, GH. (1986), Some recent restrictions in the derivation of context-free grammars. *In:* KELEMENOVA, A., and J. KELEMEN (eds.), Proc. 4th IMYCS, LNCS 281, 96–108.

PĂUN, GH., and M. TĂTARĂM (1985), Classes of mappings having context sensitive graphs. Rev. Roum. Math. Pures Appl. **30**, 273–288.

PENTTONEN, M. (1975), ETOL-grammars and N-grammars. Inform. Proc. Letters **4**, 11–13.

PETERS, S. (1966), A note on ordered phrase-structure grammars. Report No. NSF-17, Harvard Univ., Math. Ling. Aut. Trans. Comp. Lab.

PETERSON, J. L. (1981), Petri-net theory and the modelling of systems. Prentice-Hall, Englewood Cliffs.

PETRI, C. A. (1973), Concepts of net theory. Proc. 2nd MFCS, 137–146.

RAJASETHUPATHY, K. S., and R. K. SHYAMASUNDAR (1980), Programmed OL-systems. Inform. Sci. **20**, 137–150.

RAJLICH, V. (1972), Absolutely parallel grammars and two-way finite state transducers. J. Comput. Syst. Sci. **6**, 324-342.

REUSCH, P. J. A. (1974), Regulierte TOL Systeme I. Techn. rep. No. 81, Gesellsch. f. Math. u. Datenverarbeitung, Bonn.

RIEDEWALD, G. (1975), Die Grammatik syntaktischer Funktionen, eine andere Form der van-Wijngaarden Grammatik. EIK **11**, 479–487.

RIEDEWALD, G. (1978), Attribute grammars. Rostock. Math. Kolloq. **9**, 105–125.

ROSEBRUGH, R. D., and D. WOOD (1973), A characterization theorem for n-parallel right linear languages. J. Comput. Syst. Sci. **7**, 579–582.

ROSEBRUGH, R. D., and D. WOOD (1974), Image theorems for simple matrix languages and n-parallel languages. Math. Syst. Th. **8**, 150–155.
ROSEBRUGH, R. D., and D. WOOD (1975), Restricted parallelism and right linear grammars. Utilitas Math. **7**, 151–186.
ROSENFELD, A. (1971), Isotonic grammars, parallel grammars, and picture grammars. Machine Intell. **6**, 281–294.
ROSENKRANTZ, D. J. (1969), Programmed grammars and classes of formal languages. Journal of the ACM **16**, 107–131.
ROVAN, B. (1981), A framework for studying grammars. Proc. 10th MFCS, LNCS **118**, 473–482.
ROZENBERG, G. (1972-a), Direction controlled programmed grammars. Acta Inform. **1**, 242–252.
ROZENBERG, G. (1972-b), The equivalence problem for deterministic TOL systems is undecidable. Inform. Proc. Letters **1**, 201–204 (*Errata* p. 252).
ROZENBERG, G. (1976), More on ETOL systems versus random context grammars. Inform. Proc. Letters **5**, 102–106.
ROZENBERG, G. (1977), Selective substitution grammars (toward a framework for rewriting systems). Part I: Definitions and examples. EIK **13**, 455–463.
ROZENBERG, G. (1985), On coordinated selective substitutions: Toward a unified theory of grammars and machines. Theor. Comput. Sci. **37**, 31–50.
ROZENBERG, G., and A. SALOMAA (1980), The Mathematical Theory of L Systems. Academic Press, New York.
ROZENBERG, G., and S. H. VON SOLMS (1976), Some aspects of random context grammars. Informatik-Fachberichte **5**, 63–75.
ROZENBERG, G., and S. H. VON SOLMS (1977), Rewriting systems with a clocking mechanism. Techn. rep. 57/1977, Univ. of Utrecht, Dept. Math.
ROZENBERG, G., and S. H. VON SOLMS (1978), Priorities on context conditions in rewriting systems. Inform. Sci. **14**, 15–51.
ROZENBERG, G., and D. VERMEIR (1978-a), On ETOL systems of finite index. Inform. Control **38**, 103–133.
ROZENBERG, G., and D. VERMEIR (1978-b), On the effect of the finite index restriction on several families of grammars I and II, Inform. Control **39**, 284–302 and Found. Control Engineering **3**, 125–142.
ROZENBERG, G., and D. VERMEIR (1978-c), On the relationships between context-free programmed grammars and ETOL systems. Fundamenta Informaticae **1**, 325–345.
ROZENBERG, G., and D. WOOD (1980), Context-free grammars with selective rewriting. Acta Inform. **13**, 257–268.
ROZOY, B. (1985), About two-way transducers. *In:* BUDACH, L. (ed.), Proc. 5th FCT, LNCS **199**, 371–379.
SALOMAA, A. (1968), On finite automate with a time-variant structure. Inform. Control **13**, 85–98.
SALOMAA, A. (1969-a), On grammars with restricted use of productions. Ann. Acad. Sci. Fenn., Ser. A, **454**.
SALOMAA, A. (1969-b), Probabilistic and weighted grammars. Inform. Control **15**, 529–544.
SALOMAA, A. (1970-a), Periodically time-variant context-free grammars. Inform. Control **17**, 294 to 311.
SALOMAA, A. (1970-b), On some families of formal languages obtained by regulated derivations. Ann. Acad. Sci. Fenn., Ser. A, **479**.
SALOMAA, A. (1972), Matrix grammars with a leftmost restriction. Inform. Control **20**, 143–149.
SALOMAA, A. (1973-a), Formal Languages. Academic Press, New York.
SALOMAA, A. (1973-b), On sentential forms of context-free grammars. Acta Inform. **2**, 40–49.
SALOMAA, A. (1974), Parallelism in rewriting systems. *In:* LOECKS, J. (ed.), Proc. 2nd ICALP, LNCS 14, 523–533.
SALOMAA, A. (1975), Comparative decision problems between sequential and parallel rewriting. Proc. Int. Symp. Uniformly Structured Automata and Logic, Tokyo, 62–66.
SHAMIR, E., and C. BEERI (1974), Checking stacks and context-free programmed grammars accept P-complete languages. LNCS **14**, 27–33.
SIMIONESCU, F. (1976), The grammars of the menuets, Stud. Cerc. Mat. **28**, 243–248 (*in Romanian*).
SIROMONEY, R. (1969-a), On equal matrix languages. Inform. Control **14**, 135–151.
SIROMONEY, R. (1969-b), A characterization of semilinear sets. Proc. Amer. Math. Soc. **21**, 689–694.

SIROMONEY, R., and K. KRITHIVASAN (1974), Parallel context-free languages. Inform. Control **24**, 155–162.
SIROMONEY, R., and G. SIROMONEY (1975), Parallel OL languages. Intern. J. Comput. Math. **5**, 109–123.
SIROMONEY, R., and G. SIROMONEY (1977), Extended controlled table L-arrays. Inform. Control. **35**, 119–138.
SIROMONEY, R., K. G. SUBRAMANIAN, and K. RANGARJAN (1976), Control on kolam arrays. Inform. Control **32**, 272–275.
SKYUM, S. (1974), Parallel context-free languages. Inform. Control **26**, 280–285.
SKYUM, S. (1976), Decomposition theorems for various kinds of languages parallel in nature. SIAM J. Comput. **5**, 284–296.
VON SOLMS, S. H. (1975-a), The characterization by automata of certain classes of languages in the context sensitive area. Inform. Control **27**, 262–271.
VON SOLMS, S. H. (1975-b), On the characterization of certain classes of developmental languages by automata. Intern. J. Comp. Math. **5**, 125–132.
VON SOLMS, S. H. (1975-c), On TOL languages over terminals. Inform. Proc. Letters **3**, 69–70.
VON SOLMS, S. H. (1976), Some notes on ETOL languages. Intern J. Comput. Math. **5**, 285–296.
VON SOLMS, S. H. (1979), Rewriting sytems with limited distance permitting context. Intern. J. Comput. Math. **8**, 223–231.
VON SOLMS, S. H. (1982), Rewriting systems with limited distance forbidding context. Intern. J. Comput. Math. **11**, 227–239.
VON SOLMS, S. H. (1984), Node label controlled graph grammars with context conditions. Intern. J. Comput. Math. **15**, 39–49.
STARKE, P. H. (1982), Petri-Netze. VEB Deutscher Verlag der Wissenschaften, Berlin.
STOTSKIJ, E. D. (1968), Generative grammars with regulated derivations. NTI, Ser. 2, No. 1, 28–31 (*in Russian*).
STOTSKIJ, E. D. (1971-a), On grammars with rules of a special form. NTI, Ser. **2**, No. 1, 34–37 (*in Russian*).
STOTSKIJ, E. D. (1971-b), Formal grammars and limitations for derivations. Probl. Pered. Inform. **7**, 1, 87–101 (*in Russian*).
STOTSKIJ, E. D. (1971-c), Control of derivations in formal grammars. Probl. Pered. Inform. **7**, 3, 86–102.
STOTSKIJ, E. D. (1972-a), On strict hierarchies of languages. NTI, Ser. 2, No. 4, 40–45.
STOTSKIJ, E. D. (1972-b), Remarks on the paper by M. K. LEVITINA. NTI, Ser. 2, No. **4**, 40–45.
SUBRAMANIAN, K. G., and R. SIROMONEY (1982), On the generative capacity of compound string and array grammars. Inform. Sci. **26**, 231–241.
SUDBOROUGH, I. H. (1977), The complexity of the membership problem for some extensions of context-free languages. Intern J. Comp. Math. **6**, 191–215.
TEGZE, M. (1979), Dyck language D_2 is not absolutely parallel. Proc. 8th MFCS, LNCS 74, 434 to 442.
TEIXEIRA, S. P. R. (1974), Time-varying languages. Techn. rep., Cath. Univ. Rio de Janeiro, Dept. Comp. Science.
TRACHTENBROT, B. A. (1977), Algorithmen und Rechenautomaten. VEB Deutscher Verlag der Wissenschaften, Berlin.
URBANEK, F. J. (1983), A note on conditional grammars. Rev. Roum. Math. Pures Appl. **28**, 341 to 342.
VIRKKUNEN, V. (1973), On scattered context grammars. Acta Univ. Oulu, Ser. A, Math., **6**.
VITANYI, P. M. B. (1974), Growth of strings in context-dependent Lindenmayer systems. *In:* SALOMAA, A., and G. ROZENBERG (eds.), *L* Systems, LNCS 15, 104–123.
VITANYI, P. M. B. (1976), Deterministic Lindenmayer languages, nonterminals and homomorphisms. Theor. Comput. Sc. **2**, 49–71.
VOGLER, H. (1986), Tree transducers and push-down machines. Dissertation, Techn. Hogeschol Twente.
VAN DER WALT, A. P. J. (1970), Random context grammars. Proc. Symp. on Formal Languages, Oberwolfach.
VAN DER WALT, A. P. J. (1971), Random context grammars. Proc. IFIP Congress, North-Holland Publ. Co., 66–68.

WECHSUNG, G. (1984), Grammars based on graphs. Manuscript, Friedrich-Schiller-Univ. Jena.
VAN WIJNGAARDEN A. (ed.) (1969), Report on the algorithmic language ALGOL 68. Numer. Math. **14**, 79–218.
WOOD, D. (1973-a), Bicolored digraph grammar systems. RAIRO, Rech. Oper., **R-1**, 45–50.
WOOD, D. (1973-b), A note on bicolored digraph grammar systems. Intern. J. Comput. Math. **3**, 301–308.
WOOD, D. (1975), M-parallel, n-right linear simple matrix languages. Utilitas Math. **8**, 3–28.
WOOD, D. (1976), Iterated a-NGSM maps and Γ systems. Inform. Control **32**, 1–26.
WOOD, D. (1977), N-linear simple matrix languages and n-parallel linear languages. Rev. Roum. Math. Pures Appl. **22**, 403–412.
WOOD, D. (1980), Grammars and L Forms. An Introduction. LNCS 91.

References added in proof

BALANESCU, T., M. GHEORGHE and GH. PĂUN (1988-a), Three variants of apical growth filamentous systems. *Submitted.*
BALANESCU, T., M. GHEORGHE and GH. PĂUN (1988-b), On fully initial grammars with regulated rewriting. *Submitted.*
BORDIHN, H. (1987), On deterministic grammars with valuations. Wiss. Zeitschrift Techn. Univ. Magdeburg **31**, 1–3.
BORDIHN, H. (1988), On some deterministic grammars with regulation. *To appear in* Proc. 5th IMYCS.
CSUHAJ-VARJU, E., and J. DASSOW (1989), On distributed grammars. *Submitted.*
CSUHAJ-VARJU, E. (1986), Cooperating rewriting systems — regulated rewriting revisited. Techn. Rep. Hungarian Acad. Sciences, Comp. Automation Institute.
DASSOW, J. (1988-c), A remark on limited OL systems. EIK **24**, 287–291.
DASSOW, J. (1988-d) Subregularly controlled derivations: context-free case. Rostock. Math. Kolloq. **34**, 61–70.
EHRENFEUCHT, A., H. J. HOOGEBOOM and G. ROZENBERG (1988), Recording the use of memory in right-booundary grammars and push-down automata. Acta Inform. **25**, 203–231.
ENGELFRIET, J. (1986), Context-free grammars with storage. Dept. Comp. Sc. Univ. Leiden, July 1986.
FILE, G. (1987), Classical and incremental attribute evaluation by means of recursive procedures. Theor. Comp. Sci. **53**, 25–65.
FRINGS, M. (1985), Systeme mit eingeschränkter paralleler Ersetzung. Diplomarbeit, Techn. Univ. Braunschweig.
GHEORGHE, M. (1988), Compound pure grammars. Manuscript.
HOOGEBOOM, H. J. (1987), Coordinated pair systems. Dissertation, Univ. Leiden.
IKEKAWA, M., and T. KASAI (1986), Modified one-way alternating pushdown automata and indexed languages. Transact. IECE Japan **69**, 1213–1216.
IMMERMANN, N. (1987), Nondeterministic space is closed under complement. Techn. Rep. Yale Univ., Dept. Comp. Science 552.
KELEMEN, J. (1986), A grammatical model of learning and fallibility. *In:* Proc. 2nd Internat. Conf. Artificial intelligence: Methodology, Systems, Applications.
KLEIJN, H. C. M. (1987), Basic ideas of selective substitution grammars. *In:* KELEMENOVA, A., and J. KELEMEN (eds.), Proc. 4th IMYCS, LNCS 281, 75–95.
MEDUNA, A. (1987-a), Evaluated grammars. Acta Cybern. **8**, 169–176.
MEDUNA, A. (1987-b), Characterization of the Chomsky hierarchy through sequential-parallel grammars. Rostock. Math. Kolloq. **32**, 4–14.
MEDUNA, A., and GY. HORVATH (1988), On state grammars. Acta Cybern. **8**, 237–245.
NIRMAL, N., and K. KRITHIVASAN (1983), Filamentous systems with apical growth. Internat. J. Comp. Math. **12**, 203–215.
PARCHMANN, R., and J. DUSKE (1986), Self-embedding indexed languages. Theoret. Comp. Sci. **47**, 219–223.
PARCHMANN, R., and J. DUSKE (1987), Grammars, derivation modes and properties of indexed type-0 languages. Theoret. Comp. Sci. **49**, 23–42.

PĂUN, GH. (1988), Some further remarks on regular controlled apical growth filamentous systems. *Submitted.*

REICHEL, B. (1988), A remark on some classifications of Indian parallel languages. *To appear in* Proc. 5th IMYCS.

ROVAN, B. (1986), Complexity classes of g-systems are AFL. Acta Math. Univ. Comeniana, 283 −297.

ROZOY, B. (1986), Outils et resultats pour les transducteurs houstrophedons, RAIRO Theor. Inf. et Appl. **20**, 221−249.

ROZOY, B. (1987), The Dyck language $D_1'^*$ is not generated by any matrix grammar of finite index. Inform. Comput. **74**, 64−89.

STOTZKIJ, E. D. (1969), The index concept in generalized grammars. Naučno-techn. Inform. **2**, 5, 16−17 (*in Russian*).

STOTZKIJ, E. D. (1972), Conditional grammars with scattered context. Dokl. Akad. Nauk **207**, 796−799 (*in Russian*).

SUBRAMANIAN, K. G., and R. SIROMONEY (1982), On the generative capacity of compound string and arrays grammars. Inform. Sci. **26**, 331−241.

SUBRAMANIAN, K. G., and R. SIROMONEY (1987), On array grammars and languages. Cybernetics and Systems **18**, 77−98.

SZELEPCSENYI, R. (1987), The method of forcing for nondeterministic automata. Bull. EATCS **33**, 96−99.

WÄTJEN, D. (1988), k-limited OL systems and languages. EIK **24**, 267−285.

Notation Index

$\cup$ — union
$\cap$ — intersection
$\setminus$ — set difference
$\subseteq$ — inclusion
$\subset$ — strict inclusion
$\in$ — "is a member of"
2^A — the power set of the set A
card (A) — the cardinality of the set A
$\{x : P(x)\}$ — the set of subjects x having the property P
$\times$ — Cartesian product
$\emptyset$ — empty set
$\mathbb{N}$ — set of natural numbers
$\mathbb{Q}$ — set of rational numbers
$\mathbb{R}$ — set of real numbers
V^* — free monoid generated by V
λ — empty word (empty string, null element of V^*)
V^+ — free semigroup generated by V
$|x|$ — length of the string x
$|x|_U$ — number of occurrences of the symbols of the set U in x
$|x|_a$ — number of occurrences of the symbol a in the string x
min (x) — set of symbols occurring in the string x
min (L) — minimal alphabet V such that $L \subseteq V^*$
$p_V(x)$ — Parikh vector of the string x with respect to the alphabet V
Mi (x) — mirror image of the string x
Pref (x) — set of all prefixes of the string x
Sub (x) — set of all subwords of the string x
Suf (x) — set of all suffixes of the string x
x^n — string $xx \ldots x$ consisting of n copies of the string x
Shuf — the shuffle operation
Shuf* — iterated shuffle operation
Perm — permutation operation
Qi — quasiintersection
$d_L^r(d_L^l)$ — right (left) quotient with respect to the language L
V_N — nonterminal alphabet
V_T — terminal alphabet

V_G — set of terminals and nonterminals of the grammar G
P — set of rewriting rules
$\mathfrak{P}$ — finite set of tables
S — axiom
$G = (V_N, V_T, P, S)$ — (Chomsky) grammar
M — set of matrices
$G = (V_N, V_T, M, S, F)$ — matrix grammar with appearance checking with respect to the rules in F
$\alpha \to \beta$ — rule in a Chomsky grammar
$(\alpha_1 \to \beta_1, \ldots, \alpha_k \to \beta_k)$ — matrix of rules
$(b: \alpha \to \beta, \sigma(b), \varphi(b))$ — rule in a programmed grammar (b is a label, $\alpha \to \beta$ the core production, $\sigma(b)$ the success field, $\varphi(b)$ the failure field)
Lab (R) — set of labels associated to rules in R
$(\alpha \to \beta, Q, R)$ — rule in a random context grammar ($\alpha \to \beta$ is the core production, Q the permitting context, R the forbidding context)
$(\alpha \to \beta, R)$ — rule in a conditional grammar ($\alpha \to \beta$ is a core production, R the condition language)
$(A_1, \ldots, A_k) \to (x_1, \ldots, x_k)$ — scattered context rule
ac — appearance checking
left — leftmost derivation
Var, Prod, Ind, Mat — measures of complexity
$\mathcal{G}(X)$ — family of grammars
$\mathcal{L}(X)$ — family of languages generated by grammars of type X
$\mathcal{L}_{\text{fin}}(X)$ — family of languages with finite index
$\mathcal{C}(X)$ — family of languages obtained by codings from languages in $L(X)$

Types of languages and grammars:

FIN — finite
REG — regular
CF — context-free
CS — context-sensitive
RE — recursively enumerable
LIN — linear
MLIN — metalinear
M — matrix
P — programmed
RC — random context
SRC — string random context
fRC — forbidding random context
SM — simple matrix
TV — time-variant (periodically)
rC — with regular control (regularly controlled)
B, B_c — controlled by a bicolored digraph
V — vector

aV (mV) – additive (multiplicative) valence
S – state
nP – nonterminal-programmed
Z – iterated
K – conditional
TC – tree controlled
O – ordered
I – indexed
iCF – Indian parallel
rCF – Russian parallel
SC – scattered context
RW – regular walk
uX – unordered of type X
pX – pure of type X
iX – Indian parallel of type X
rX – Russian parallel of type X
OX – ordered of type X
$X - \lambda$ – λ-free of type X
s$\mathcal{K}$ – selective substitution with selector language in the family $\mathcal{K}$
seq – selective substitution with sequential selector language
par – selective substitution with parallel selector language
cont – selective substitution with continuous selector language
$L(G)$ – lauguage generated by G
Sz (G) – Szilard language of G
$\mathcal{F}_k(Xm)$ – class of natural mappings of k'arguments with graphs in the family $\mathcal{L}(X)$
ESz (G) – extended Szilard language of G
$\mathrm{Space}_M(X)$ – number of cells entered by the head of M working on the input word x

Subject Index

Author Index

MIX
Papier | Fördert gute Waldnutzung
FSC® C083411

Kolibri 360 GmbH
Ferdinand-Jühlke-Straße 7
99095 Erfurt, Deutschland
produktsicherheit@kolibri360.de